Toyota Corolla Owners Workshop Manual

by J H Haynes
Associate Member of the Guild of Motoring Writers
and B L Chalmers-Hunt
TEng (CEI), AMIMI, AMIRTE, AMVBRA

Models covered

UK: Corolla 1100 Saloon. 1077cc
            Corolla 1200 Saloon, Coupe and Estate. 1166cc
USA: Corolla 1100 Sedan. 65.7 cu in
            Corolla 1200 Sedan, Coupe and Wagon. 71.1 cu in
            Corolla 1600 Sedan (2 and 4 door), Coupe and Wagon

---

ISBN 0 85696 201 5

© J H Haynes and Company Limited 1975

All rights reserved. No part of this book may be reproduced or transmitted in any form or by any means, electronic or mechanical, including photocopying, recording or by any information storage or retrieval system, without permission in writing from the copyright holder.

Printed in England

ABCDE 201
FGHIJ
KLM

Haynes

HAYNES PUBLISHING GROUP
SPARKFORD YEOVIL SOMERSET ENGLAND
distributed in the USA by
HAYNES PUBLICATIONS INC
861 LAWRENCE DRIVE
NEWBURY PARK
CALIFORNIA 91320
USA

Acknowledgements

Our thanks are due to the Toyota Motor Sales Company Limited (USA) and Toyota (GB) Limited for their assistance with technical information and the supply of certain illustrations. Castrol Limited supplied lubrication details.

Special thanks are due to all of those people at Sparkford who have helped with the production of this manual; particularly Brian Horsfall and Les Brazier who carried out the mechanical work and took the photographs, respectively; Rod Grainger who edited the text and Stanley Randolph who planned the layout of each page.

About this manual

Its aims

This is a manual by a practical owner/maintainer for practical owner/maintainers. The author, and those assisting him, learned about this range of models the only thorough way, by studying all available information and then going ahead and doing the work, under typical domestic conditions and with a typical range of tools, backed only by their experience as keen car men over a number of years.

Unlike other books of this nature, therefore, the hands in most of the photographs are those of the author, and the instructions cover every step in full detail, assuming no special knowledge on the part of the reader except how to use tools and equipment in a proper manner, firmly and positively but with due respect for precise control where this is required.

Its arrangement

The manual is divided into twelve Chapters, each covering a logical sub-division of the vehicle. The Chapters are each divided into Sections, numbered with single figures, eg; 5; and the Sections into paragraphs (or sub-sections), with decimal numbers following on from the Section they are in, eg; 5.1, 5.2, 5.3, etc.

It is freely illustrated, especially in those parts where there is a detailed sequence of operations to be carried out. There are two forms of illustration: figures and photographs. The figures are numbered in sequence with decimal numbers, according to their position in the Chapter: eg; Fig. 6.4 is the 4th drawing/illustration in Chapter 6. Photographs are numbered (either individually or in related groups) the same as the Section or sub-section of the text where the operation they show is described.

There is an alphabetical index at the back of the manual as well as a contents list at the front.

References to the 'left' or 'right' of the vehicle are in the sense of a person in a seat facing forwards towards the engine.

Points for the reader

The accumulation of good tools normally must take place over a period of time and this is the one expense which the do-it-yourself owner must face. Cheap tools are never worth having, as they are not cheap in the long run. They rarely last, often make the work more difficult, and may even cause accidental damage which could cost more to put right than the cost of a good tool in the first place.

Certain jobs require special tools and where these are essential the manual points this out, otherwise, alternative methods are given.

Be discreet about borrowing tools; even with great care, accidents still happen, and the replacement of a lost or damaged tool can be costly. Do not be offended, if refused; he may have had an unhappy experience already!

Where appropriate, fault finding instructions are given at the end of Chapters. Accurate diagnosis of troubles depends on a careful, and above all, systematic approach, so avoid the attitude "if all else fails, read the handbook". It is better, and almost always quicker, to say: "This could be one of several things, so let's have a look at the *Haynes* manual before trying anything".

The policy of the manufacturer of these vehicles is one of continuous development, and designs and specification are frequently being changed as a result. It follows naturally that spares may sometimes be purchased which differ both from the original part removed and from the part referred to in this manual. However, supplies of genuine Toyota spare parts can usually settle queries about interchangeability by reference to the latest information issued by the manufacturer. (Read the Section 'Buying Spare Parts').

Every care has been taken to ensure the accuracy of this manual but no liabilty can be accepted by the authors and publishers for any loss, damage or injury caused by any errors in or omissions from the information given.

Contents

Chapter	Section	Page	Section	Page
Introductory Sections	Use of English	4	Buying spare parts	9
	Metric conversion tables	6	Routine maintenance	10
1 Engine	**KE models**		**TE models**	
	Removal	19	Removal	52
	Dismantling	23	Dismantling	52
	Renovation	30	Renovation	52
	Reassembly	35	Reassembly	59
	Replacement	43	Refitting	66
	Fault diagnosis	44	Fault diagnosis	66
2 Cooling system	Draining	69	Thermostat	70
	Flushing	69	Water pump	71
	Filling	69	Antifreeze solution	71
	Radiator	69	Fault diagnosis	72
3 Fuel system and carburation	Air cleaner	76	Fuel tank	86
	Fuel pump	76	Exhaust emission control	89
	Carburettor	78	Fault diagnosis	96
4 Ignition system	Contact breaker points	101	Spark plugs	107
	Distributor	102	Fault diagnosis	107
	Timing	106		
5 Clutch	Adjustment	113	Slave cylinder	117
	Bleeding	113	Removal and replacement	117
	Master cylinder	115	Fault diagnosis	120
6 Manual gearbox and automatic transmission	**Manual gearbox - KE models**		**Manual gearbox - TE models**	
	Removal and replacement	129	Removal and replacement	141
	Dismantling	130	Dismantling	141
	Reassembly	137	Reassembly	148
	Automatic transmission (all models)			
	Removal and replacement	153	Neutral safety switch	156
	Selector lever	153	Fault diagnosis	157
7 Propeller shaft and universal joints	Propeller shaft removal and replacement	158	Universal joints	158
			Fault diagnosis	160
8 Rear axle	Removal and replacement	163	Differential assembly	165
	Halfshaft	163	Fault diagnosis	168
9 Braking system	Bleeding	170	Handbrake	181
	Front disc brakes	173	Brake pedal	183
	Front drum brakes	174	Master cylinder	184
	Rear drum brakes	177	Fault diagnosis	190
10 Electrical system	Battery	196	Horn	207
	Alternator	197	Windscreen wiper	209
	Starter motor	199	Heater	217
	Lights	203	Wiring diagrams	221
11 Suspension and steering	Front wheel hub	232	Rear spring	239
	Front suspension unit strut	234	Steering linkage	243
	Front suspension arm	236	Steering gearbox	245
	Rear shock absorbers	239	Fault diagnosis	248
12 Bodywork and fittings	2 door Saloon/Sedan (1968-70)	255	4 door Saloon/Sedan (1971 on)	276
	Estate/Wagon (1968-70)	263	Estate/Wagon (1971 on)	278
	2 door Saloon/Sedan (1971 on)	269		
List of illustrations				281
Index				288

Use of English

As this book has been written in England, it uses the appropriate English component names, phrases, and spelling. Some of these differ from those used in America. Normally, these cause no difficulty, but to make sure, a glossary is printed below. In ordering spare parts remember the parts list will probably use these words:

Glossary

English	American
Allen screw	Hexagon socket screw
Anti-roll bar	Stabiliser or Sway bar
Bonnet (engine cover)	Hood
Boot (luggage compartment)	Trunk
Bottom gear	1st gear
Bulk head	Firewall
Clearance	Lash
Crown wheel	Ring gear (of differential)
Catch	Latch
Camfollower (or tappet)	Valve lifter
Drop arm (steering box)	Pitman arm
Drop arm shaft	Pitman shaft
Dynamo	Generator (DC)
Damper	Shock absorber
Earth (electrical)	Ground
Free play	Lash
Free wheel	Coast
Gudgeon Pin	Piston pin or wrist pin
Gearchange	Shift
Gearbox	Transmission
Hood	Soft top
Hard top	Hard top
Leading shoe (of brake)	Primary shoe
Lay shaft (in gearbox)	Counter shaft
Mudguard or wing	Fender
Motorway	Freeway
Petrol	Gas
Reverse	Back-up
Split cotter (as in valve spring cap)	Lock (for valve spring retainer)
Split pin	Cotter pin
Sump	Oil pan
Silencer	Muffler
Self-locking nut	Pawl nut
Steering arm	Spindle arm
Saloon	Sedan
Side light	Parking light
Tappet	Valve lifter
Tab washer	Tang; lock
Top gear	High
Transmission	Whole drive line from clutch to axle shaft
Trailing shoe (of brake)	Secondary shoe
Track rod (of steering)	Tie rod (or connecting rod)
Warning light	Tell Tale
Windscreen	Windshield

Miscellaneous points

An "Oil seal" is fitted to components lubricated by grease!

A "Damper" is a "Shock absorber": it damps out bouncing, and absorbs shocks of bump impact. Both names are correct, and both are used haphazardly.

Note that British drum brakes are different from the Bendix type that is common in America, so different descriptive names result. The shoe end furthest from the hydraulic wheel cylinder is on a pivot; interconnection between the shoes as on Bendix brakes is most uncommon. Therefore the phrase "Primary" or "Secondary" shoe does not apply. A shoe is said to be Leading or Trailing. A "Leading" shoe is one on which a point on the drum, as it rotates forward, reaches the shoe at the end worked by the hydraulic cylinder before the anchor end. The opposite is a trailing shoe, and this one has no self servo from the wrapping effect of the rotating drum.

Toyota Corolla 1200 Coupe - UK specification

Toyota Corolla 1200 Estate - UK specification

Metric conversion tables

Inches	Decimals	Millimetres	Millimetres to Inches		Inches to Millimetres	
			mm	Inches	Inches	mm
1/64	0.015625	0.3969	0.01	0.00039	0.001	0.0254
1/32	0.03125	0.7937	0.02	0.00079	0.002	0.0508
3/64	0.046875	1.1906	0.03	0.00118	0.003	0.0762
1/16	0.0625	1.5875	0.04	0.00157	0.004	0.1016
5/64	0.078125	1.9844	0.05	0.00197	0.005	0.1270
3/32	0.09375	2.3812	0.06	0.00236	0.006	0.1524
7/64	0.109375	2.7781	0.07	0.00276	0.007	0.1778
1/8	0.125	3.1750	0.08	0.00315	0.008	0.2032
9/64	0.140625	3.5719	0.09	0.00354	0.009	0.2286
5/32	0.15625	3.9687	0.1	0.00394	0.01	0.254
11/64	0.171875	4.3656	0.2	0.00787	0.02	0.508
3/16	0.1875	4.7625	0.3	0.01181	0.03	0.762
13/64	0.203125	5.1594	0.4	0.01575	0.04	1.016
7/32	0.21875	5.5562	0.5	0.01969	0.05	1.270
15/64	0.234375	5.9531	0.6	0.02362	0.06	1.524
1/4	0.25	6.3500	0.7	0.02756	0.07	1.778
17/64	0.265625	6.7469	0.8	0.03150	0.08	2.032
9/32	0.28125	7.1437	0.9	0.03543	0.09	2.286
19/64	0.296875	7.5406	1	0.03937	0.1	2.54
5, 16	0.3125	7.9375	2	0.07874	0.2	5.08
21/64	0.328125	8.3344	3	0.11811	0.3	7.62
11/32	0.34375	8.7312	4	0.15748	0.4	10.16
23/64	0.359375	9.1281	5	0.19685	0.5	12.70
3/8	0.375	9.5250	6	0.23622	0.6	15.24
25/64	0.390625	9.9219	7	0.27559	0.7	17.78
13/32	0.40625	10.3187	8	0.31496	0.8	20.32
27/64	0.421875	10.7156	9	0.35433	0.9	22.86
7/16	0.4375	11.1125	10	0.39370	1	25.4
29/64	0.453125	11.5094	11	0.43307	2	50.8
15/32	0.46875	11.9062	12	0.47244	3	76.2
31/64	0.484375	12.3031	13	0.51181	4	101.6
1/2	0.5	12.7000	14	0.55118	5	127.0
33/64	0.515625	13.0969	15	0.59055	6	152.4
17/32	0.53125	13.4937	16	0.62992	7	177.8
35/64	0.546875	13.8906	17	0.66929	8	203.2
9/16	0.5625	14.2875	18	0.70866	9	228.6
37/64	0.578125	14.6844	19	0.74803	10	254.0
19/32	0.59375	15.0812	20	0.78740	11	279.4
39/64	0.609375	15.4781	21	0.82677	12	304.8
5/8	0.625	15.8750	22	0.86614	13	330.2
41/64	0.640625	16.2719	23	0.90551	14	355.6
21/32	0.65625	16.6687	24	0.94488	15	381.0
43/64	0.671875	17.0656	25	0.98425	16	406.4
11/16	0.6875	17.4625	26	1.02362	17	431.8
45/64	0.703125	17.8594	27	1.06299	18	457.2
23/32	0.71875	18.2562	28	1.10236	19	482.6
47/64	0.734375	18.6531	29	1.14173	20	508.0
3/4	0.75	19.0500	30	1.18110	21	533.4
49/64	0.765625	19.4469	31	1.22047	22	558.8
25/32	0.78125	19.8437	32	1.25984	23	584.2
51/64	0.796875	20.2406	33	1.29921	24	609.6
13/16	0.8125	20.6375	34	1.33858	25	635.0
53/64	0.828125	21.0344	35	1.37795	26	660.4
27/32	0.84375	21.4312	36	1.41732	27	685.8
55/64	0.859375	21.8281	37	1.4567	28	711.2
7/8	0.875	22.2250	38	1.4961	29	736.6
57/64	0.890625	22.6219	39	1.5354	30	762.0
29/32	0.90625	23.0187	40	1.5748	31	787.4
59/64	0.921875	23.4156	41	1.6142	32	812.8
15/16	0.9375	23.8125	42	1.6535	33	838.2
61/64	0.953125	24.2094	43	1.6929	34	863.6
31/32	0.96875	24.6062	44	1.7323	35	889.0
63/64	0.984375	25.0031	45	1.7717	36	914.4

Metric Conversion Tables

Spanner size equivalents

AF		Whit	Fits	Metric Equivalent	Metric size A/F*	Inch Equivalent A/F*
4BA	0.248		9/64	6.3	7	0.276
2BA	0.32		3/16	8.1	8	0.315
					9	0.35
					10	0.39
7/16	0.44		1/4 UNF	11.2	11	0.413
	0.45	3/16	1/4 BSF	11.4	12	0.47
1/2	0.50		5/16 UNF	12.7	13	0.51
	0.53	1/4	5/16 BSF	13.5		
9/16	0.56		3/8 UNF	14.2	14	0.55
	0.604	5/16	3/8 BSF	15.3	15	0.59
5/8	0.63		7/16 Bolt	16	16	0.63
					17	0.67
11/16	0.69		7/16 Some nuts	17.5		
	0.72	3/8	7/16 BSF	18.3	18	0.71
3/4	0.76		1/2 UNF	19.3	19	0.75
					20	0.79
13/16	0.82			20.8		
	0.83	7/16	1/2 BSF	21.1	21	0.83
7/8	0.88		9/16 Some nuts	22.4	22	0.87
	0.93	1/2	9/16 BSF	23.6	23	0.91
15/16	0.94		5/8 UNF	23.8	24	0.945
					25	0.985
1"	1.01			25.6		
	1.02	9/16	5/8 BSF	25.9	26	1.02
1.1/16	1.07		5/8 Heavy UNF	27.2	27	1.06
	1.11	5/8	11/16 BSF	28.2	28	1.10
1.1/8	1.13		3/4 UNF	28.7	29	1.14
					30	1.18
	1.21	11/16	3/4 BSF	30.7	31	1.22
1.1/4	1.26		3/4 Heavy UNF	32.0	32	1.26
	1.31	3/4	7/8 BSF	33.3	33	1.3
1.5/16	1.32		7/8 UNF	33.5	34	1.34
					35	1.38
	1.49	7/8	1" BSF	37.8	36	1.42
					37	1.46

Underbonnet view of the UK Corolla 1200 SL Coupe

Toyota Corolla 1200 (71.1 cu in) Sedan - North American Specification

Toyota Corolla 1600 (96.9 cu in) Sedan - North American Specification

Buying spare parts and vehicle identification numbers

Buying spare parts

Spare parts are available from many sources, for example: Toyota garages, other garages and accessory shops, and motor factors. Our advice regarding spare part sources is as follows:

Officially appointed Toyota garages - This is the best source of parts which are peculiar to your car and are otherwise not generally available (eg; complete cylinder heads, internal gearbox components, badges, interior trim, etc). It is also the only place at which you should buy parts if your car is still under warranty - non-Toyota components may invalidate the warranty. To be sure of obtaining the correct parts it will always be necessary to give the storeman your car's engine and chassis number, and if possible, to take the 'old' part along for positive identification. Remember that many parts are available on a factory exchange scheme - any parts returned should always be clean! It obviously makes good sense to go straight to the specialist on you car for this type of part for they are best equipped to supply you.

Other garages and accessory shops - These are often very good places to buy materials and components needed for the maintenance of your car (eg; oil filters, spark plugs, bulbs, fan belts, oils and greases, touch-up paint, filler paste etc). They also sell general accessories, usually have convenient opening hours, charge lower prices and can often be found not far from home.

Motor factors (mainly UK) - Good factors will stock all of the more important components which wear out relatively quickly (eg; clutch components, pistons, valves, exhaust sytems, brake cylinders/pipes/hoses/seals/shoes and pads etc). Motor factors will often provide new or reconditioned components on a part exchange basis - this can save a considerable amount of money.

Vehicle identification numbers

Always have details of the car, its serial and engine numbers available when ordering parts. If you can take along the part to be renewed, it is helpful. Modifications were and are being continually made and often are not generally publicised. A storeman in a parts department is quite justified in saying that he cannot guarantee the correctness of a part unless these relevant numbers are available.

The vehicle identification plate is located on the bulkhead firewall top panel in the engine compartment.

The engine number is stamped on the right-hand side of the cylinder block.

The frame number is stamped in the bulkhead/firewall top panel.

Car identification plate

Routine maintenance

Introduction

1 In the maintenance schedule that follows this introduction is tabulated the routine servicing that the car requires. This work has two important functions: First, adjustment and lubrication to ensure the least wear and greatest efficiency. Second, thorough inspection of the car, this is very important as by looking your car over, thoroughly, you have the opportunity to check that all is in order.

2 Every component should be inspected; working systematically over the whole car. Dirt cracking near a nut or a flange can indicate something loose. Leaks will be evident. Electric cables chafing, rust appearing through the paint underneath, will also be found before they cause a failure on the road, or a more expensive repair.

3 The tasks to be done on the car are in general those recommended by the manufacturer. The author has also put in some additional ones. For someone having his servicing done at a garage it may be more cost effective to accept component replacement after a somewhat short life in order to avoid maintenance costs. For the home mechanic this is not so. The manufacturers' must detail the work to be done as a careful balance of such factors. Leaving it too long gives risk of defects occurring between the service checks. Making intervals too frequent, tempts owners' into disrespect of their advice, to leave work undone - disastrously long.

4 When you are checking the car, if something looks wrong, look it up in the appropriate Chapter. If something seems to be working badly look in the relevant fault finding Section.

5 Always road test after a repair, and inspect the work after it, and check nuts etc., for tightness. Check again after about 150 miles (250 Km).

Tools

1 The most useful type of spanner is a 'combination spanner'. This has one end open jaw, the other a ring of the same size. Alternatively, a set of open ended and ring spanners will be required. Whenever possible use a ring spanner as it will not slip off the bolt or nut especially when very tight. Remember metric size tools are required.

2 You will need a set of feeler gauges. Preferably these should be in metric sizes although imperial equivalents are quoted in the manual.

3 You will see throughout the manual that tightening torques for nuts and bolts are quoted. To achieve the correct torque a torque wrench is needed. Many people get on well without them. Contrariwise many others are plagued by things falling off or leaking through being too loose; whilst others, suffer from broken bolts, stripped threads, or warped cylinder heads, through overtightening. Torque wrenches use the socket of normal socket spanner sets.

4 Sockets, with extensions and ratchet handles are a boon. In the meantime you will need box spanners for such things as cylinder head attachments, and the spark plugs. They are thinner than sockets in small sizes, and will often go where the latter cannot, so will always be useful even if later you plan to buy sockets.

5 Screwdrivers should have large handles for a good grip. You need a large ordinary one, a small electrical one, and a medium crossheaded one. Do not purchase one handle with interchangeable shafts. The large screwdriver must have a tough handle that will take hitting with a hammer when you misuse it as a chisel.

6 You can use an adjustable spanner and a self grip or pipe wrench of the Mole or Stillsons type but it is not to be recommended.

7 With these tools you will get by. Do not purchase cheap ones but be prepared to spend a little extra. Good tools will last far longer.

8 If you undertake major dismantling of the engine or transmission you will need a drift. This is a steel or soft metal rod about 3/8 inch (9.525 mm) in diameter. Where possible use the steel drift which will withstand hammering. Do not use brass as little chips can fly off, unknowingly get into the component and ruin it. You will need a ball pein hammer, fairly heavy too, because it is easier to use gently, than a light one hard.

9 Files are soon needed. Four types make a good selection.
  6 inch half round smooth
  8 inch flat second cut
  8 inch round second cut
  10 inch half round bastard

10 You will need a good, firm, hydraulic jack. A trolley jack is of major value when removing any of the major units. If you do obtain one, it must be in addition to, and cannot replace the simple jack which is needed for the smaller jobs.

11 The manufacturer's base their own servicing operations on a 3,000 mile (5,000 Km) or 3 month basis.

12 The maintenance information given is not detailed in this Section as information will be found in the appropriate Chapters of this book, if not obvious.

13 Because of the Federal Regulations to limit exhaust emissions, several modifications have been made to the engine and ancilliary equipment. This equipment must not be tampered with unless absolutely necessary. The car must then be taken to the local Toyota garage so that any adjustments necessary, as indicated by electronic test equipment, may be made.

Daily

1 Check and adjust fan belt tension.
2 Check and clean spark plugs.
3 Check battery electrolyte level.
4 Check tyre pressures, examine tread depth and also for signs of tyre damage.
5 Check operation of all lights.
6 Check master cylinder reservoir hydraulic fluid level.
7 Check windscreen washer fluid level.

First 1000 miles (1600 Km) only

Carry out daily service as applicable plus:
1 Check and adjust fan belt tension.
2 Check and clean spark plugs.
3 Generally check tightness of all bolts on engine.
4 Check and adjust valve clearances.
5 Check and if necessary adjust engine idle speed.

6 Check and adjust ignition timing
7 Renew engine oil filter.
8 Check brake pedal free-play and adjust if necessary.
9 Check and adjust clutch pedal free-play.
10 Check steering free-play and linkage.
11 Generally check all fluid lines and hoses for leaks. Check tightness and security of all unions.
12 Generally check all chassis and body attachments.
13 Change engine oil.
14 Check gearbox oil level and top-up if necessary.
Models with exhaust emission control equipment
15 Check and adjust air pump drive belt tension.
16 Check air injection system.
17 Generally check tightness of air injection system nuts and bolts.

3,000 miles (5,000 Km) service

Carry out daily service as applicable plus:
1 Clean or renew air cleaner element.
2 Check brake pedal free-play and adjust if necessary.
3 Generally check all fluid lines and hoses for leaks. Check tightness and security of all unions.
4 Change engine oil.
5 Check gearbox oil level and top-up if necessary.

Models fitted with exhaust emission control equipment
6 Check and adjust air pump drive belt tension.

6,000 Miles (10,000 Km) service

Carry out first 100 mile service except items 3 and 17, plus
1 Check and adjust distributor contact breaker points; renew if necessary.
2 Rotate the tyres in a diagonal manner.
3 Check rear axle oil level and top-up if necessary.

9,000 mile (15,000 Km) service

Carry out the service items in the 3,000 mile service

12,000 mile (20,000 Km) service

Carry out the service items in the 6,000 mile service with the exception of item 2, plus:
1 Renew spark plugs.
2 Renew engine coolant (unless antifreeze is being used, see Chapter 2).
3 Check brake linings, pads, discs and drums for wear. Renew as necessary.
4 Generally check all chassis and body attachments.
5 Check steering gearbox oil level and top-up if necessary.

Models fitted with exhaust emission control equipment
Carry out the service items in the first 1,000 mile service plus:
6 Replace positive crankcase ventilation valve. Clean and check all connections.
7 Clean air filter of case storage system.

18,000 mile (30,000 Km) service

Carry out 6,000 mile service but note the following:
1 Renew air cleaner element.
2 Renew gearbox oil.
3 Renew rear axle oil.

24,000 mile (40,000 Km) service

Carry out 12,000 mile service, plus:
1 Renew hydraulic fluid, seals and hoses. Discuss this with the local Toyota garage.

2 Check resistive cord resistance.
3 Lubricate balljoints and wheel bearings.

Every 4 years

1 Renew all fuel hoses

Other aspects of routine maintenance

1 Jacking-up

Always chock a wheel on the opposite side in front and behind. The car's own jack has to be supplemented with blocks for safety reasons.

2 Wheel nuts

These should be cleaned and lightly smeared with grease as necessary during work, to keep them moving easily. If the nuts are stubborn to undo due to dirt and overtightening it may be necessary to hold them by lowering the jack till the wheel rests on the ground. Normally if the wheel brace is used across the hub centre a foot or knee held against the tyre will prevent the wheel from turning, and so save the wheel studs and nuts from wear if the nuts are slackened with weight on the wheel. After replacing a wheel make a point of re-checking the nuts again for tightness.

3 Safety

Whenever working, even partially under the car, put an extra strong box or piece of timber underneath onto which the car will fall rather than onto you if the jack should slip.

4 Cleanliness

Whenever you do any work allow time for cleaning. When something is in pieces or components removed to improve access to other areas it gives an opportunity for a thorough clean. This cleanliness will allow you to cope with a crisis on the road without getting yourself too dirty. During bigger jobs when you expect a bit of dirt it is less extreme and can be tolerated at least whilst removing a component. When an item is being taken to pieces there is less risk of ruinous grit finding its way inside. The art of cleaning focuses your attention onto parts and you are more likely to spot trouble. Dirt on ignition parts is a common cause for poor starting. Large areas such as the engine compartment inner wings or bulkhead should be brushed thoroughly with a solvent like 'Gunk' allowed to soak and then very carefully hosed down. Water in the wrong places, particularly the carburettor, or electrical components will do more harm than the dirt. Use petrol or paraffin and a small paintbrush to clean the more inaccessible places.

5 Waste disposal

Old oil and cleaning paraffin must be destroyed. Although it makes a good base for a bonfire, this practice is dangerous. It is also illegal to dispose of oil and paraffin down domestic drains. By purchasing your new engine oil in one gallon cans you can refill with old oil and take back to the local garage who will have facilities for its disposal.

6 Long journeys

Before taking the car on long journeys, particularly such trips as holidays, make sure that the car is given a thorough check in the form of the next service due, plus a full visual inspection well in advance so that any faults found can be rectified in time.

Lubrication chart

1. Engine — Castrol GTX
2. Gearbox: (Manual) — Castrol Hypoy Light
   (Automatic) — Castrol TQF
3. Rear axle — Castrol Hypoy B

   Chassis lubrication — Castrol LM Grease

Note: The above recommendations are general; lubrication requirements vary depending on vehicle specification, operating territory and usage. Consult the operators handbook supplied with your car

Chapter 1 Part A: Engine KE models

For TE models see Chapter 1/Part B (page 47)

Contents

Camshaft and camshaft bearings - examination and renovation ... 32	Final assembly ... 58
Camshaft - removal ... 14	Flywheel and engine backplate - removal ... 17
Camshaft, timing gears and chain, tensioner and timing chain cover - reassembly ... 47	General description ... 1
Connecting rods and gudgeon pins - examination and renovation ... 31	Gudgeon pins - removal ... 19
Connecting rod to crankshaft - reassembly ... 45	Lubrication system - description ... 22
Crankshaft and main bearings - removal ... 21	Major operations requiring engine removal ... 3
Crankshaft bearings (main) and big-end (connecting rod) bearings - examination and renovation ... 28	Methods of engine removal ... 4
Crankshaft - examination and renovation ... 27	Oil filter - removal and replacement ... 23
Crankshaft front oil seal - removal ... 15	Oil pressure relief valve - removal and replacement ... 24
Crankshaft rear oil seal - removal ... 16	Oil pump - overhaul ... 38
Crankshaft rear oil seal - replacement ... 48	Oil pump - removal and dismantling ... 25
Crankshaft - replacement ... 41	Oil pump - replacement ... 49
Cylinder bores - examination and renovation ... 29	Operations possible with engine in place ... 2
Cylinder head - decarbonisation ... 39	Piston rings - removal ... 20
Cylinder head removal - engine in car ... 9	Piston rings - replacement ... 43
Cylinder head removal - engine on bench ... 10	Pistons and connecting rods - reassembly ... 42
Cylinder head - replacement ... 54	Pistons and piston rings - examination and renovation ... 30
Dismantling the engine - general ... 7	Pistons - replacement ... 44
Distributor and drive - replacement ... 57	Rocker arm/valve - adjustment ... 56
Engine ancillaries - removal ... 8	Rockers and rocker shaft - examination and renovation ... 36
Engine backplate, flywheel and clutch replacement ... 51	Rocker shaft - reassembly ... 53
Engine components - examination for wear ... 26	Sump, pistons, connecting rods and big-end - removal ... 18
Engine front plate - replacement ... 46	Sump - replacement ... 50
Engine - initial start up after overhaul or major repair ... 60	Tappets - examination and renovation ... 33
Engine reassembly - general ... 40	Tappets, pushrods and rocker shaft - replacement ... 55
Engine - removal less gearbox ... 6	Timing cover, tensioner, gears and chain - removal ... 13
Engine - removal with gearbox ... 5	Timing gears and chain - examination and renovation ... 37
Engine - replacement ... 59	Valve and spring - reassembly ... 52
Fault diagnosis - engine ... 61	Valve guide - examination and renovation ... 35
	Valve guide - removal ... 12
	Valve - removal ... 11
	Valves and valve seats - examination and renovation ... 34

Specifications

General:

Engine type ...	4 cylinder, in line overhead valve
Engine designation:	
1077 cc (65.7 cu in.) ...	K., K - B, K - C
1166 cc (71.1 cu in.) ...	3K, 3K - D, 3K - B
Firing order ...	1 3 4 2
Displacement ...	See engine designation
Bore ...	2.95 in. (75 mm)
Stroke:	
1077 cc (65.7 cu in.) ...	2.40 in. (61 mm)
1166 cc (71.1 cu in.) ...	2.598 in. (66 mm)
Compression ratio:	
1077 cc (65.7 cu in.) K	9 : 1
1077 cc (65.7 cu in.) K - B	10 : 1
1077 cc (65.7 cu in.) K - C	9 : 1
1166 cc (71.1 cu in.) 3K	9 : 1
1166 cc (71.1 cu in.) 3K - D	10 : 1
1166 cc (71.1 cu in.) 3K - B	10 : 1

Chapter 1/Part A: Engine KE models

Compression pressure:
- 1077 cc (65.7 cu in.) K ... 170 lb/in² (12.0 kg/cm²)
- 1077 cc (65.7 cu in.) K - B ... 185 lb/in² (13.0 kg/cm²)
- 1077 cc (65.7 cu in.) K - C ... 171 lb/in² (12.0 kg/cm²)
- 1166 cc (71.1 cu in.) 3K ... 171 lb/in² (12.0 kg/cm²)
- 1166 cc (71.1 cu in.) 3K - D ... 185 lb/in² (13.0 kg/cm²)
- 1166 cc (71.1 cu in.) 3K - B ... 185 lb/in² (13.0 kg/cm²)

Gross horsepower (SAE):
- 1077 cc (65.7 cu in.) K ... 60 at 6,000 rpm
- 1077 cc (65.7 cu in.) K - B ... 73 at 6,600 rpm
- 1077 cc (65.7 cu in.) K - C ... 60 at 6,000 rpm
- 1166 cc (71.1 cu in.) 3K ... 73 at 6,000 rpm
- 1166 cc (71.1 cu in.) 3K - D ... 79 at 6,600 rpm
- 1166 cc (71.1 cu in.) 3K - B ... 83 at 6,600 rpm

Gross torque (maximum - SAE):
- 1077 cc (65.7 cu in.) K ... 8.5 k gm at 3,800 rpm
- 1077 cc (65.7 cu in.) K - B ... 9.0 k gm at 4,600 rpm
- 1077 cc (65.7 cu in.) K - C ... 8.5 k gm at 3,800 rpm
- 1166 cc (71.1 cu in.) 3K ... 9.5 k gm at 3,800 rpm
- 1166 cc (71.1 cu in.) 3K - D ... 9.6 k gm at 4,200 rpm
- 1166 cc (71.1 cu in.) 3K - B ... 10.4 k gm at 4,600 rpm

Sump capacity ... 4.8 pints (2.7 litres, 5.8 US pints)

Cylinder head:

Maximum warpage - head/block face:
- 1100 (65.7 cu in.) engine ... 0.001 in. (0.04 mm)
- 1200 (71.1 cu in.) engine ... 0.004 in. (0.1 mm)

Maximum warpage - manifold face:
- 1100 and 1200 (65.7 and 71.1 cu in.) engines ... 0.004 in. (0.1 mm)

Valve seat contact face:
- Inlet valve ... 0.056 in. (1.4 mm)
- Exhaust valve ... 0.059 in. (1.5 mm)

Valve seat angle ... 45°
Valve seat correction angles (inlet and exhaust) ... 30°, 45°, 65°

Cylinder block:

- Bore standard diameter ... 2.952 - 2.955 in. (75.00 - 75.05 mm)
- Bore wear limit ... 0.008 in. (0.2 mm)
- Bore maximum taper ... 0.0008 in. (0.02 mm)
- Bore maximum ovality ... 0.0008 in. (0.02 mm)
- Crankshaft bearing diameter ... 2.126 - 2.127 in. (54.004 - 54.028 mm)

Camshaft bearing bore diameter:
- No. 1 (front) ... 1.890 - 1.891 in. (48.00 - 48.025 mm)
- No. 2 ... 1.870 - 1.871 in. (47.500 - 47.525 mm)
- No. 3 ... 1.850 - 1.851 in. (47.00 - 47.025 mm)
- No. 4 ... 1.831 - 1.832 in. (46.500 - 46.525 mm)

Valve tappet bore diameter:
- Standard ... 0.787 - 0.788 in. (20.00 - 20.021 mm)
- Oversize (0.05) ... 0.789 - 0.790 in. (20.050 - 20.071 mm)

Cylinder liners:
- Outer diameter ... 3.114 - 3.115 in. (79.091 - 79.126 mm)
- Inner diameter ... 2.930 - 2.936 in. (74.430 - 74.570 mm)
- Cylinder block bore ... 3.111 - 3.114 in. (79.031 - 79.086 mm)
- Interference fit ... 0.0015 - 0.0024 in. (0.04 - 0.06 mm)
- Fitting pressure ... 4420 - 6620 lb f (2000 - 3000 kg f)

Pistons:

Outer diameter:
- Standard ... 2.951 - 2.953 in. (74.96 - 75.01 mm)
- 0.25 oversize ... 2.961 - 2.963 in. (75.21 - 75.26 mm)
- 0.50 oversize ... 2.971 - 2.973 in. (75.46 - 75.51 mm)
- 0.75 oversize ... 2.981 - 2.983 in. (75.71 - 75.76 mm)
- 1.00 oversize ... 2.991 - 2.993 in. (75.96 - 76.01 mm)

Running clearance (20° C) ... 0.001 - 0.002 in. (0.03 - 0.05 mm)
Gudgeon pin diameter ... 0.7086 - 0.7091 in. (17.999 - 18.011 mm)

Chapter 1/Part A: Engine KE models

Gudgeon pin bore diameter	0.7085 - 0.7089 in. (17.995 - 18.007 mm)
Gudgeon pin fitting temperature	70 - 80º C (158 - 176º F)
Piston ring to groove clearance:	
No. 1 (compression)	0.0011 - 0.0027 in. (0.03 - 0.07 mm)
No. 2 (compression)	0.0007 - 0.0023 in. (0.02 - 0.06 mm)
No. 3 (oil control)	0.0006 - 0.0023 in. (0.015 - 0.060 mm)
Piston ring end-gap	0.0006 - 0.014 in. (0.015 - 0.035 mm)

Connecting rod:

Twist limit	0.006 in. (0.15 mm)
Bend limit	0.002 in. (0.05 mm)
Gudgeon pin to small end bush clearance:	
Standard	0.0002 - 0.0003 in. (0.004 - 0.008 mm)
Wear limit	0.002 in. (0.05 mm)
Big-end side play:	
Standard	0.004 - 0.008 in. (0.110 - 0.214 mm)
Wear limit	0.012 in. (0.3 mm)
Big-end running clearance:	
Standard	0.0006 - 0.015 in. (0.016 - 0.040 mm)
Wear limit	0.004 in. (0.1 mm)
Small-end bush:	
Inner diameter	0.7895 - 0.7903 in. (20.054 - 20.075 mm)
Outer diameter	0.7088 - 0.7093 in. (18.005 - 18.017 mm)

Crankshaft:

Maximum run-out	0.001 in. (0.03 mm)
Endfloat:	
Standard	0.002 - 0.009 in. (0.04 - 0.22 mm)
Wear limit	0.011 in. (0.3 mm)
Thrust washer thickness:	
Standard	0.096 - 0.098 in. (2.43 - 2.48 mm)
0.125 oversize	0.098 - 0.100 in. (2.49 - 2.54 mm)
0.250 oversize	0.100 - 0.102 in. (2.55 - 2.60 mm)
Journals (main bearing):	
Running clearance	0.0005 - 0.0015 in. (0.016 - 0.040 mm)
Wear limit	0.004 in. (0.1 mm)
Maximum taper	0.0003 in. (0.008 mm)
Maximum ovality	0.0003 in. (0.008 mm)
Journal diameter (main bearing):	
Standard	1.9675 - 1.9685 in. (49.976 - 50.000 mm)
0.25 oversize	1.9580 - 1.9584 in. (49.733 - 49.743 mm)
0.50 undersize	1.9481 - 1.9485 in. (49.483 - 49.493 mm)
0.75 undersize	1.9383 - 1.9387 in. (49.233 - 49.243 mm)
Crankpin diameter (big-end):	
Standard	1.6525 - 1.6535 in. (41.976 - 42.000 mm)
0.25 undersize	1.6426 - 1.6430 in. (41.723 - 41.733 mm)
0.50 undersize	1.6328 - 1.6331 in. (41.473 - 41.483 mm)
0.75 undersize	1.6230 - 1.6233 in. (41.223 - 41.233 mm)
Bearing available undersizes:	
a)	0.002 in. (0.05 mm)
b)	0.01 in. (0.25 mm)
c)	0.02 in. (0.50 mm)
d)	0.03 in. (0.75 mm)

Timing chain, gears and tensioner:

Chain deflection	0.531 in. (13.5 mm) at 22 lb f (5 kg f)
Stretch limit	10.736 in. (272.7 mm)
Gear wear limit:	
(Outer diameter of timing gears when the chain is wrapped around the gear)	
Camshaft gear	4.48 in. (113.8 mm)
Crankshaft gear	2.34 in. (59.4 mm)
Tensioner thickness	0.47 in. (12 mm)
Vibration damper pad thickness	0.28 in. (7 mm)

Camshaft:

Maximum run-out	0.001 in. (0.03 mm)

End-float:
- Standard ... 0.0028 - 0.0054 in. (0.070 - 0.138 mm)
- Wear limit ... 0.012 in. (0.3 mm)

Bearing running clearance:
- Standard ... 0.001 - 0.0026 in. (0.025 - 0.066 mm)
- Wear limit ... 0.004 in. (0.1 mm)

Journal:
- Taper - maximum ... 0.001 in. (0.02 mm)
- Ovality - maximum ... 0.001 in. (0.02 mm)

Cam lobe height:
- Inlet ... 1.436 - 1.439 in. (36.469 - 36.569 mm)
- Exhaust ... 1.432 - 1.436 in. (36.369 - 36.469 mm)

Cam lobe height wear limit:
- Inlet ... 1.424 in. (36.17 mm)
- Exhaust ... 1.420 in. (36.07 mm)

Camlift:
- Inlet ... 0.225 in. (5.72 mm)
- Exhaust ... 0.237 in. (6.02 mm)

Journal diameters:
- Standard:
  - No. 1 ... 1.701 - 1.702 in. (43.209 - 43.225 mm)
  - No. 2 ... 1.691 - 1.692 in. (42.959 - 42.975 mm)
  - No. 3 ... 1.681 - 1.682 in. (42.709 - 42.725 mm)
  - No. 4 ... 1.671 - 1.672 in. (42.459 - 42.475 mm)
- Undersize:
  - No. 1 ... 1.6963 - 1.697 in. (43.087 - 43.097 mm)
  - No. 2 ... 1.686 - 1.687 in. (42.837 - 42.847 mm)
  - No. 3 ... 1.677 - 1.678 in. (42.587 - 42.597 mm)
  - No. 4 ... 1.667 - 1.668 in. (42.337 - 42.347 mm)

Thrust plate thickness ... 0.1961 - 0.1968 in. (4.982 - 5.000 mm)
Thrust clearance ... 0.0028 - 0.0054 in. (0.070 - 0.138 mm)
Clearance limit ... 0.012 in. (0.3 mm)

Valves:

Head diameter:
- Inlet ... 1.417 in. (36 mm)
- Exhaust ... 1.141 in. (29 mm)

Stem diameter:
- Inlet ... 0.3139 - 0.3143 in. (7.975 - 7.986 mm)
- Exhaust ... 0.3134 - 0.3145 in. (7.960 - 7.975 mm)

Length:
- Overall ... 3.940 in. (100.1 mm)
- Wear ... 0.02 in. (0.5 mm)

Head thickness limit:
- Inlet ... 0.031 in. (0.8 mm)
- Exhaust ... 0.035 in. (0.9 mm)

Seat width:
- Inlet ... 0.055 in. (1.4 mm)
- Exhaust ... 0.059 in. (1.5 mm)

Seat angle ... 45°

Valve guides:

Overall length:
- Inlet ... 1.811 in. (46 mm)
- Exhaust ... 1.969 in. (50 mm)

Fitting temperature ... 80° C (176° F)
Protrusion from top of head ... 0.708 in. (18 mm)
Inner diameter ... 0.315 - 0.316 in. (8.01 - 8.03 mm)

Valve springs:

Free-length ... 1.830 in. (46.5 mm)
Minimum ... 1.760 in. (45.1 mm)
Fitted length ... 1.512 in. (38.4 mm)

Fitted load:
- 1077 cc (65.7 cu in.) engine:
  - K, K - B, K - C ... 55.1 lb f (25.0 kg f)
- 1166 cc (71.1 cu in.) engine:
  - 3K ... 55.2 lb f (25.05 kg f)
  - 3K - B ... 62.5 lb f (28.3 kg f)
  - 3K - D ... 62.5 lb f (28.3 kg f)

Fitted load limit:
    1077 cc (65.7 cu in.) engine:
        K, K - B, K - C ... ... 70.1 lb f (31.8 kg f)
    1166 cc (71.1 cu in.) engine:
        3K ... ... 70.2 lb f (31.8 kg f)
        3K - B ... ... 77.0 lb f (35.0 kg f)
        3K - D ... ... 77.0 lb f (35.0 kg f)

Valve rocker shaft:
    Outer diameter ... ... 0.629 - 0.630 in. (15.976 - 15.994 mm)
    Bush inner diameter (support) ... ... 0.630 - 0.631 in. (16.000 - 16.018 mm)

Rocker arm:
    Running clearance:
        Standard ... ... 0.0002 - 0.0017 in. (0.006 - 0.042 mm)
        Wear limit ... ... 0.003 in. (0.08 mm)

Tappets:
    Outer diameter:
        Standard ... ... 0.7864 - 0.7872 in. (19.974 - 19.995 mm)
        Oversize (0.25) ... ... 0.7883 - 0.7899 in. (20.024 - 20.065 mm)
    Running clearance:
        Standard ... ... 0.0007 - 0.0013 in. (0.019 - 0.033 mm)
        Wear limit ... ... 0.004 in. (0.1 mm)

Valve clearance:
    Inlet (cold) ... ... 0.003 in. (0.08 mm)
    Exhaust (cold) ... ... 0.007 in. (0.18 mm)
    Inlet (hot) ... ... 0.008 in. (0.2 mm)
    Exhaust (hot) ... ... 0.012 in. (0.3 mm)

Oil pump:
    Type ... ... Trochoid
    Tip clearance ... ... 0.002 - 0.006 in. (0.04 - 0.165 mm)
    Clearance limit ... ... 0.008 in. (0.2 mm)
    Side clearance ... ... 0.001 - 0.003 in. (0.03 - 0.09 mm)
    Clearance limit ... ... 0.006 in. (0.15 mm)
    Body clearance ... ... 0.004 - 0.006 in. (0.10 - 0.16 mm)
    Clearance limit ... ... 0.008 in. (0.20 mm)

Oil pressure relief valve:
    Free length ... ... 1.85 in. (47 mm)
    Fitted length ... ... 1.45 in. (36.8 mm)
    Fitted tension ... ... 13.2 - 14.5 lb f (5.99 - 6.59 kg f)
    Operating pressure ... ... 51.2 - 62.6 psi (3.6 - 4.4 kg/cm^2)

Oil filter:
    Type ... ... Replaceable canister
    Filtration ... ... Full flow
    Bypass of valve operating pressure ... ... 11.4 - 17.0 psi (0.8 - 1.2 kg/cm^2)

Flywheel:
    Maximum run-out ... ... 0.008 in. (0.2 mm)

Torque wrench settings:

	lb f ft	kg fm
Crankshaft journal bearing bolts	39 - 47	5.398 - 6.47
Big-end cap bolts	29 - 37	4.0 - 5.1
Oil pump to crankcase	7 - 11	1.0 - 1.53
Camshaft thrustplate	4 - 6	0.55 - 0.83
Camshaft gear retaining bolt	16 - 22	2.21 - 3.04
Timing chain tensioner bolts	4 - 6	0.55 - 0.83
Timing chain damper bolts	4 - 6	0.55 - 0.83
Timing chain cover	4 - 6	0.55 - 0.83
Crankshaft rear oil seal retainer	4 - 6	0.55 - 0.83

Sump to crankcase	...	...	...	...	...	...	2 - 3	0.3 - 0.41
Crankshaft pulley	...	...	...	...	...	...	29 - 43	4.0 - 5.91
Cylinder head bolts	...	...	...	...	...	...	36 - 48	4.8 - 6.6
Rocker pedestal bolts	...	...	...	...	...	...	13 - 16	1.8 - 2.21
Fuel pump nuts	...	...	...	...	...	...	7 - 11	1.0 - 1.53
Engine mounting brackets	...	...	...	...	...	...	14 - 22	1.94 - 3.04
Oil filter bracket	...	...	...	...	...	...	7 - 11	1.0 - 1.53
Alternator bracket	...	...	...	...	...	...	7 - 11	1.0 - 1.53
Manifold bolts	...	...	...	...	...	...	14 - 22	1.94 - 3.04
Fan and pulley bolts	...	...	...	...	...	...	4 - 6	0.55 - 0.83
Engine backplate	...	...	...	...	...	...	4 - 6	0.55 - 0.83
Flywheel securing bolts	...	...	...	...	...	...	39 - 48	5.398 - 6.6
Clutch cover bolts	...	...	...	...	...	...	7 - 11	1.0 - 1.53
Gearbox to bellhousing bolts	...	...	...	...	...	...	36 - 51	4.8 - 7.0

1 General description

The engine covered by part 'A' of this Chapter is that fitted to Toyota Corolla KE models and is of the four cylinder overlead valve type.

The cylinder head is of aluminium alloy with a wedge shaped combustion chamber. Independent inlet and exhaust parts are used to provide a smooth performance at all engine speeds.

The cylinder block and crankcase are cast together which results in a rigid unit. Coolant passages run through the entire length of the cylinder block. Located within the cylinder block are the crankshaft, camshaft, pistons and all associated equipment.

The counterbalanced crankshaft is supported by five main bearings which are of the steel backed Babbit lined type with lead plated bearing surfaces. Crankshaft endfloat is controlled by thrust washers at No 3 main journal and these are separate from the main bearing shells. Large main bearing caps ensure that the crankshaft remains adequately supported at all engine speeds.

The pistons are made of a special light alloy with an eccentric finish slightly larger at right angles to the gudgeon pin (piston pin). Two compression rings and one oil control ring are used on each piston. The gudgeon pin is offset towards the camshaft side of the engine by about 0.04 inch (1.0 mm) to assist in smooth running. The gudgeon pin is retained with snap rings (circlips) at both ends.

The connecting rods are of 'I' beam cross section forged steel with bronze gudgeon pin bushes for the small end and precision type sintered alloy bearing inserts for the big-ends.

The camshaft is of cast iron with the cam lobe surfaces chill treated. It is supported in four bearings and is driven from the crankshaft by gear sprockets and a chain.

The lubrication system is of the force feed, full flow filter type. The oil pump located at the bottom of the crankcase is driven by the camshaft through the distributor shaft. Oil under pressure passes along various oil passages within the cylinder block to lubricate the internal components of the engine and also the valve rocker gear.

2 Operations possible with engine in place

The following major operations can be carried out with the engine in place in the car.
1 Removal and replacement of camshaft.

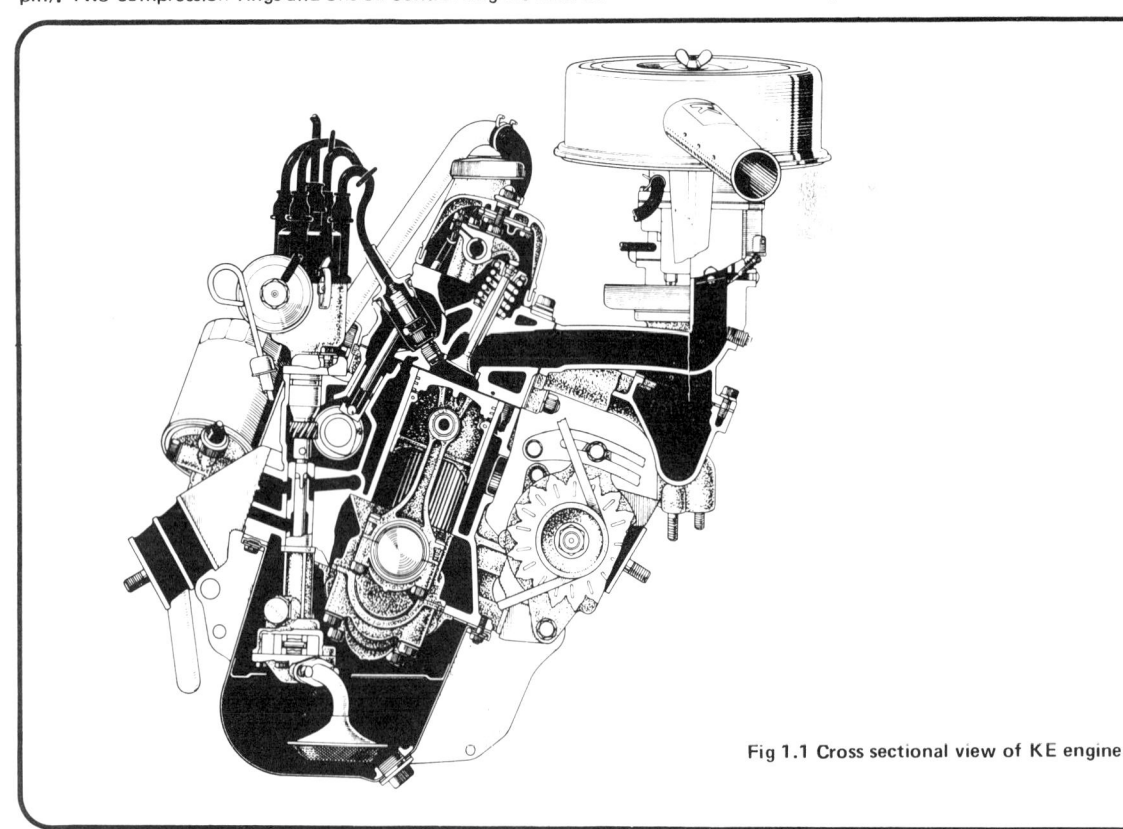

Fig 1.1 Cross sectional view of KE engine

2 Removal and replacement of the cylinder head.
3 Removal and replacement of the engine mountings.
4 Removal of sump and pistons.
5 Removal of flywheel.

3 Major operations requiring engine removal

The following major operations can only be carried out with the engine out of the car.
1 Removal and replacement of the main bearings.
2 Removal and replacement of the crankshaft.

4 Methods of engine removal

There are two methods of engine removal: complete with clutch and gearbox and without the gearbox. Both methods are described.

It is easier if a hydraulic trolley jack is used in conjunction with two axle stands, so that the car can be raised sufficiently to allow easy access underneath. Overhead lifting tackle will be necessary in all cases.

Note: Cars fitted with automatic transmission necessitating engine and transmission removal, should have the transmission removed *first* as described in Chapter 6. The transmission even on its own is very heavy.

5 Engine - removal with gearbox

1 The complete unit can be removed easily in abour four hours. It is essential to have a good hoist, and two strong axle stands if an inspection pit is not available. Removal will be much easier if there is someone to assist, especially during the later stages.
2 With few exceptions, it is simplest to lift out the engine with all ancillaries still attached, (alternator, distributor, carburettor etc.) but some may find it easier to remove these first.
3 Before starting work it is worthwhile to get all dirt cleaned off the engine at a garage which is equipped with steam or high pressure air and water cleaning equipment. This makes the job quicker, easier and, of course, much cleaner.
4 Using a pencil or scriber mark the outline of the bonnet hinges on either side to act as a datum for refitting. An assistant should now take the weight of the bonnet.
5 Undo and remove the two bolts and washers that secure the bonnet to the hinge and also the stay to bonnet. Detach the washer hose and carefully lift the bonnet up and then over the front of the car. Store in a safe place where it will not be scratched. Push down the hinges to prevent any accidents. (photos).
6 Undo the positive, and then the negative, battery terminal clamp bolts and detach from the terminal posts. (photo)
7 Place a container under the drain plug and unscrew the plug. Allow all the coolant to drain out and then refit the plug. (photo)
8 Place a container under the engine sump drain plug. Unscrew the drain plug and allow all the oil to drain out. Refit the drain plug.
9 Place a container under the gearbox drain plug. Unscrew the drain plug and allow all the oil to drain out. Refit the drain plug.
10 Undo and remove the radiator cowl to radiator securing bolts. (photo)
11 Slacken the radiator top hose clips and remove the top hose completely. (photo)
12 Slacken the radiator bottom hose clip at the water pump and detach the hose. (photo)
13 Undo and remove the four bolts, spring and plain washers securing the radiator to the front panel. (photo).
14 Carefully lift away the radiator. Note the cowl is positioned over the fan. (photo)
15 Lift away the radiator cowl (photo)
16 Refer to Chapter 3 and remove the air cleaner assembly. (photos)
17 Suitably mark the HT leads and detach from the spark plugs

Fig 1.2 Longitudinal cross sectional view of KE engine

5.5a Bonnet hinge securing bolt removal

5.5b Bonnet stay assembly

5.6 Disconnecting battery positive terminal cables

5.7 Cylinder block drain plug

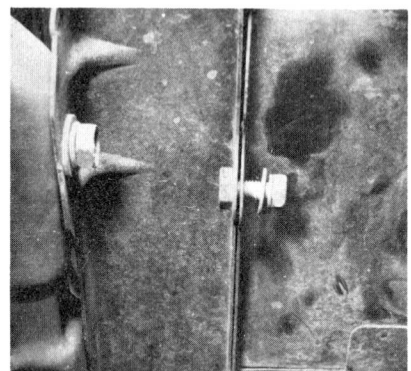

5.10 Fan cowl securing bolt

5.11 Detaching top hose from elbow

5.12 Detaching bottom hose from water pump

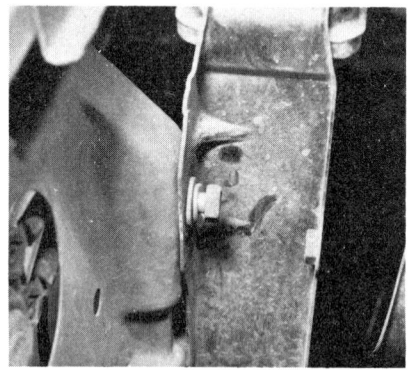

5.13 Radiator securing bolt

5.14 Lifting away radiator

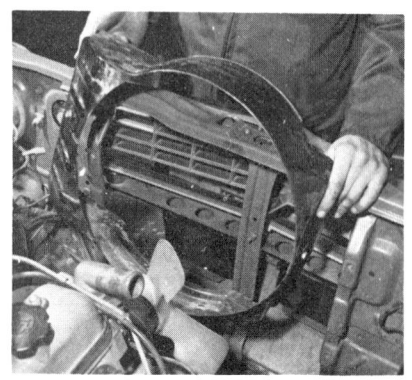

5.15 Removal of cowl

5.16a Air cleaner support on manifold

5.16b Lifting away air cleaner

Chapter 1/Part A: Engine KE models

and ignition coil.
18 Release the distributor cap retaining clips and lift away the distributor cap and HT leads. (photo)
19 Detach the heater hose from the rocker cover. (photo)
20 Remove the hose supporting clip securing bolt from the rocker cover. (photo)
21 Undo and remove the two bolts securing the cable clamp bracket to the rocker cover. (photo)
22 Detach the throttle control cable from the side of the carburettor assembly. (photo)
23 Slacken the clamp screw and detach the choke control inner cable from the carburettor linkage. (photo)
24 Detach the fuel inlet hose from the fuel pump. (photo)
25 Slacken the hose clip and detach the small diameter hoses from the water pump and angled union located just above the water pump. (photo)
26 Undo and remove the four bolts securing the fan blades and pulley to the water pump spindle. Lift away the fan blades. (photo)
27 The water pump pulley may next be lifted away. (photo)
28 Detach the cable from the thermal transmitter which is located at the base of the thermostat housing. (photo)
29 Detach the earth cable from the rear of the cylinder block. (photo)
30 Detach the earth cable from the front right-hand side of the cylinder block. (photo)
31 Detach the multi-pin terminal connector from the rear of the alternator. (photo)
32 Undo and remove the nuts and washers securing the exhaust downpipe to manifold clamp. Detach the downpipe. (photo)
33 Working under the car detach the clutch cable from the clutch actuating arm. (photo)

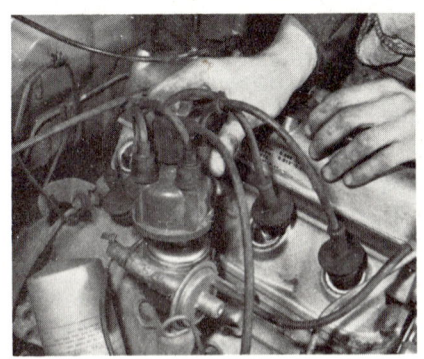

5.18 Removal of distributor cap and HT leads

5.19 Breather hose detached from top cover

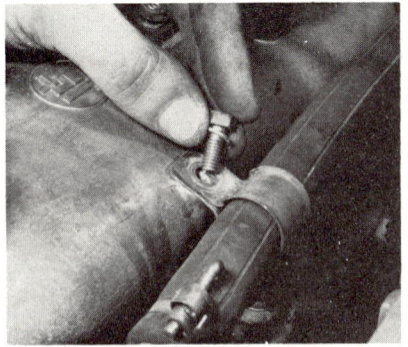

5.20 Removal of hose supporting clip from top cover

5.21 Cable clamp securing bolts on top cover

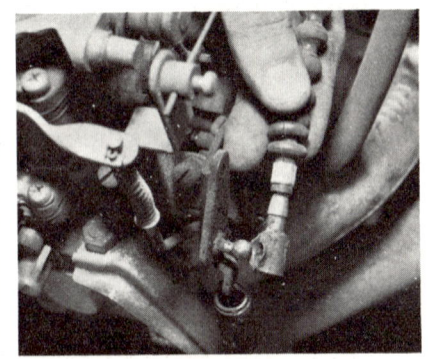

5.22 Detaching throttle cable from carburettor

5.23 Detaching choke cable from carburettor

5.24 Removal of fuel inlet hose from pump

5.25 Detaching hoses from pump and union pipe

5.26 Fan securing bolts removal

5.27 Lifting away water pump pulley

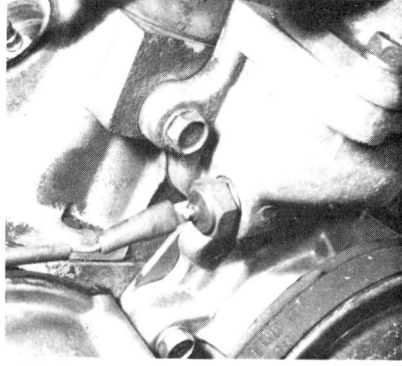

5.28 Cable attached to temperature sender unit

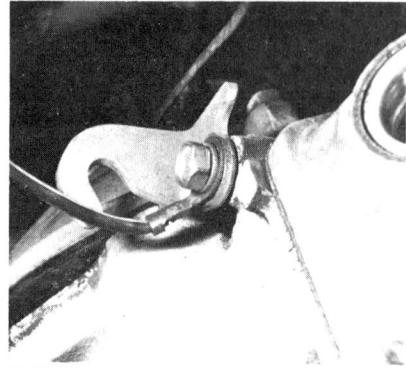

5.29 Engine earth cable at rear of cylinder block

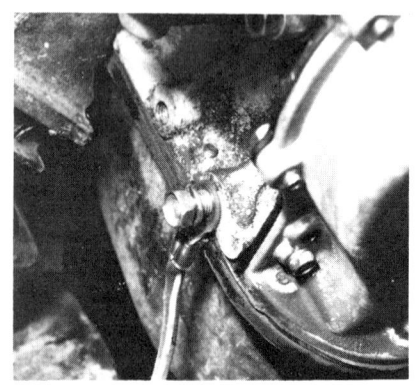

5.30 Second earth cable at base of crankcase

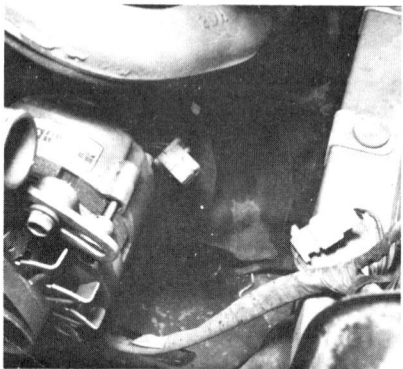

5.31 Terminal block detached from alternator

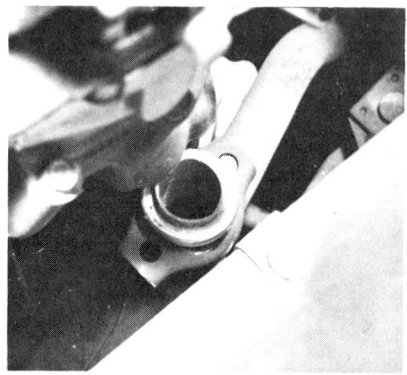

5.32 Exhaust downpipe detached from manifold

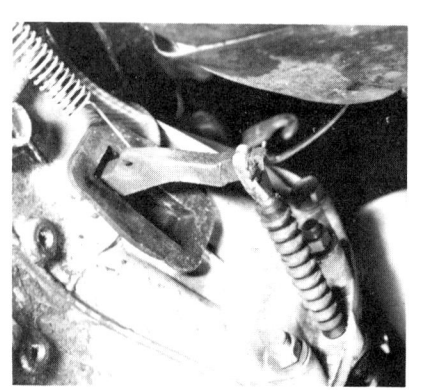

5.33 Clutch control cable attached to actuating arm

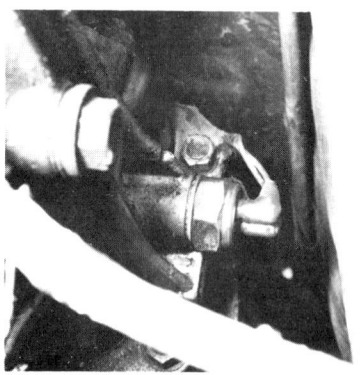

5.34 Reverse light switch on side of gearbox

5.37 Detaching fuel inlet hose from carburettor

5.38 Manifold assembly removed from cylinder head

5.40 Removal of radiator grille and front crossmember

5.42 Engine mounting detached from bracket

Chapter 1/Part A: Engine KE models

34 Detach the two cable terminal connectors from the reverse light switch located on the side of the gearbox. (photo)
35 Refer to Chapter 7, and remove the propeller shaft.
36 Refer to Chapter 6 and remove the gearchange lever. Also detach the gearbox mounting and crossmember. Don't forget the weight of the gearbox must be supported on a small jack.
37 Disconnect the fuel pipe from the carburettor at the union. (photo)
38 Undo and remove the nuts and washers securing the inlet and exhaust manifolds to the side of the cylinder head. Lift away the two manifolds and carburettor assembly. (photo)
39 Make a note of and then disconnect the electric cables from the rear of the starter motor solenoid.
40 Undo and remove the radiator grille and front crossmember securing bolts and lift away this assembly. By removing these it is far easier to remove the engine and gearbox assembly. (photo)
41 Fit a chain bracelet to the centre manifold stud of the cylinder head and then support the weight of the engine. The second chain can be wrapped around the engine mounting or filter head.
42 Undo and remove the mounting lower securing nuts and washers. (photo)
43 Check that all electrical cables, control cables, hoses and pipes have been detached and that all mountings are free. This is particularly important where engines have been modified for exhaust emission control.
44 Slowly raise the engine and lowering the jack under the gearbox ease the complete unit up until the sump is just clear of the body member located behind the front bumper. (photos)
45 When the sump is clear of the body member the complete power unit may be drawn forwards between the front panels. (photo)
46 Lower the unit to the ground away from the car.
47 Check that the engine compartment and floor area around the car are clear of loose nuts and bolts as well as tools.

6 Engine - removal less gearbox

1 If it is necessary to remove only the engine, leaving the gearbox in position, the engine can be detached from the gearbox and then lifted away.
2 Follow the instructions given in Section 5 paragraphs 1-8, 10-32, 37-39. Support the weight of the gearbox with a jack.
3 Undo and remove the two nuts and bolts securing the starter motor to the engine backplate. Lift away the starter motor.
4 Refer to Section 5 paragraphs 40-43 inclusive.
5 Undo and remove the remaining nuts and bolts that secure the engine to the gearbox bellhousing.
6 Raise the engine slightly to enable the engine mountings to clear. Move it forwards until the clutch is clear of the input shaft. Continue lifting the unit taking care not to damage the front body member. Then push the car rearwards or the hoist forwards until the engine is clear of the engine compartment. Lower the unit to the ground away from the car. (photo)

7 To complete, clear out any loose nuts and bolts and tools from the engine compartment and floor area.

7 Dismantling the engine - general

Keen D.I.Y. mechanics who dismantle a lot of engines will probably have a stand on which to put them, but most will make do with a work bench which should be large enough to spread around the inevitable bits and pieces and tools, and strong enough to support the engine weight. If the floor is the only place, try and ensure that the engine rests on a hard wood platform or similar rather than on concrete.
2 Spend sometime on cleaning the unit. If you have been wise this will have been done before the engine was removed at a service bay. Good solvents such as 'Gunk' will help to 'float' off caked dirt/grease under a water jet. Once the exterior is clean dismantling may begin. As parts are removed clean them in petrol/paraffin (do not immerse parts with oilways in paraffin - clean them with a petrol soaked cloth and clean oilways with nylon pipe cleaners). If an air line is available use it for final cleaning off. Paraffin, which could possibly remain in oilways and would dilute the oil for initial lubrication after reassembly, must be blown out.
3 Always fit new gaskets and seals - but do **not** throw the old ones away until you have the new one to hand. A pattern is then available if they have to be made specially. Hang them up on a nail.
4 In general it is best to work from the top of the engine

5.44a Commencement of engine removal RH view

5.44b Commencement of engine removal LH view

5.45 Engine and gearbox assembly removal through front of car

6.6 Engine removal - less the gearbox

downwards. In all cases support the engine firmly so that it does not topple over when you are undoing stubborn nuts and bolts.
5 Always place nuts and bolts back with their components or place of attachment, if possible - its saves much confusion later. Otherwise put them in small, separate pots or jars so that their groups are easily identified.
6 If you have an area where parts can be laid out on sheets of paper, do so - putting the nuts and bolts with them. If you are able to look at all the components in this way it helps to avoid missing something on reassembly.
7 Even though you may be dismatling the engine only partly - possible with it still in the car - the priniciples still apply. It is appreciated that most people prefer to do engine repairs, if possible with the engine in position. Consequently an indication will be given as to what is necessary to lead up to carrying out repairs on a particular component. Generally speaking the engine is easy enough to get at as far as repairs and renewals of the ancillaries are concerned. When it comes to repair of the major engine components, however, it is only fair to say that repairs with the engine in position are more difficult than with it out.

8 Engine ancillaries - removal

1 If you are stripping the engine completely or preparing to install a reconditioned unit, all the ancillaries must be removed first. If you are going to obtain a reconditioned 'short' motor (block, crankshaft, pistons and connecting rods) then obviously the cylinder head and associated parts will need retention for fitting to the new engine. It is advisable to check just what you will get with a reconditioned unit as changes are made from time to time.
2 The removal of all those items connected with fuel, ignition and charging systems are detailed in the respective Chapters but for clarity they are merely listed here:
  Distributor
  Carburettor (can be removed together with inlet manifold)
  Alternator
  Fuel pump
  Water pump
  Starter motor
  Thermostat

9 Cylinder head removal - engine in car

1 Refer to Chapter 2, and drain the cooling system.
2 Refer to Chapter 3, and remove the air cleaner.
3 Detach the accelerator cable from the support bracket on the cylinder head cover and then disconnect the throttle control arm.
4 Detach the choke control cable from the carburettor.
5 If a water hose retainer is attached to the cylinder head cover this should next be removed.
6 Slacken the hose clips and then disconnect the water hoses from the water pump and water valve to the heater.
7 Disconnect the control cable from the heater water valve.
8 Disconnect the ventilation tube from the cylinder head cover and then detach the fuel line from the carburettor.
9 Undo and remove the nuts securing the cylinder head cover and carefully lift away the cylinder head cover and gasket. (photo)
10 Undo and remove the nuts and bolts securing the valve rocker assembly to top of the cylinder head. Lift away the complete valve rocker assembly. (photo)
11 Remove the valve push rods and place in order so that they may be refitted in their original positions. (photo)
12 Slacken the clip and disconnect the radiator upper hose from the water outlet.
13 Suitably mark the high tension cables and detach from the spark plugs.
14 Remove the windscreen washer reservoir.
15 Disconnect the exhaust downpipe from the exhaust manifold.
16 Undo and remove the cylinder head securing bolts, in a progressive and diagonal manner. Check that no cables, controls or services have been left connected and then lift off the cylinder head. If it is stuck to the cylinder head gasket try to rock it to break the seal. There are special slots into which a screwdriver blade may be inserted to assist in breaking the seal. (photos)
17 Recover the old cylinder head gasket.

10 Cylinder head removal - engine on bench

The sequence for removal of the cylinder head with the engine on the bench is basically identical to the latter operations for removal with the engine in the car. Refer to Section 9 and follow the instructions given in paragraphs 9, 10, 11, 13, 16 and 17.

11 Valve removal

1 The valves are easily removed from the cylinder head by the following method. First remove the 'O' ring seals and then compress each spring in turn with a universal valve spring compressor until the two halves of the collets can be removed. Release the compressor and lift away the spring retainer collets, retainer, seal, spring, plate washer and finally the valve.
2 If, when the valve spring compressor is screwed down, the valve spring retainer refuses to free and expose the split collets, do not continue to screw down on the compressor as there is a liklihood of damaging it.
3 Gently tap the top of the tool directly over the retainer with a light hammer. This should free the retainer. To avoid the compressor jumping off the valve retainer when it is tapped, hold the compressor firmly in position with one hand.
4 It is essential that the valves are kept in their correct sequence unless they are so badly worn that they are to be renewed. If they are going to be re-used place them in a sheet of card having eight holes numbered 1 to 8 corresponding with the relative positions the valves were in when fitted. Also keep the valve springs, retainers etc in this same correct order.

12 Valve guide - removal

Valve guides removal is a simple task but it is not recommended that you should do this because their replacement is difficult to do accurately. It is far better to leave their removal and insertion to a Toyota garage. (see also Section 35).

13 Timing cover, tensioner, gears and chain - removal

The timing cover, gears and chain can be removed with the engine in the car provided that the radiator and fan belt are removed first (see Chapter 2). The procedure for removing the timing cover, tensioner gears and chain is otherwise the same irrespective of whether the engine is in the car or on the bench.
1 Remove the crankshaft pulley retaining bolt and then remove the crankshaft pulley. (photo)
2 Remove the engine under cover (engine in car)
3 Remove the stiffener plate (engine in car)
4 Undo and remove the timing chain cover securing bolts and nuts. Note that one bolt also holds a spring clip. (photo)
5 If the engine is in the car drain the oil from the sump.
6 Undo and remove the bolts and washers securing the sump to the underside of the crankcase. Lift away the sump and recover the old gasket.
7 The timing chain cover may now be lifted away. (photo)
8 Suitably mark the spark plug HT leads and detach them from the spark plugs. Remove the spark plugs.
9 Rotate the engine and check that the bright links on the

9.9 Removal of top cover

9.10 Lifting away valve rocker assembly

9.11 Removal of push rods

9.16a Screwdriver being used to release cylinder head

9.16b Lifting cylinder head from cylinder block

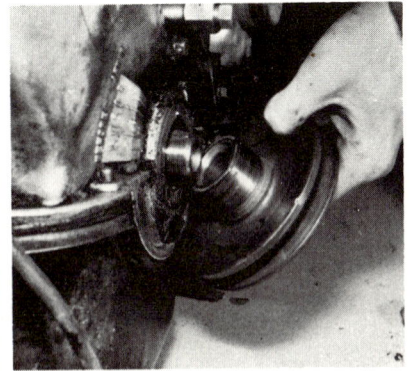

13.1 Removal of crankshaft pulley

13.4 Note that one timing chain cover securing bolts also holds on a clip

13.7 Timing chain cover removed

13.9 Timing chain bright links (Sometimes 'O' marks are used)

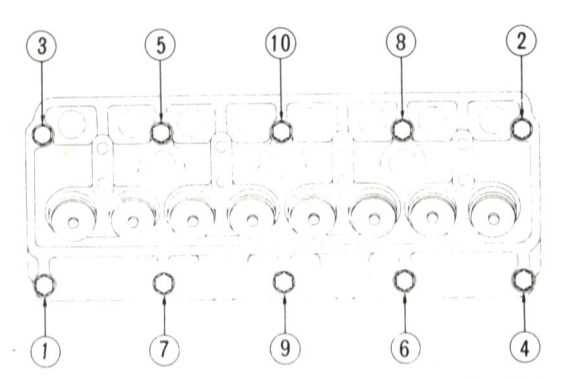

Fig 1.3 Correct sequence for slackening cylinder head bolts

Fig 1.4 Valve components

timing chain line up with the marks on the timing gears. (photo)
10 Undo and remove the timing chain tensioner securing bolts and lift away the tensioner. (photo)
11 Lock the camshaft gear with a screwdriver through one of the web holes and then undo and remove the securing bolt and washer. (photo)
12 Lift the gear from the end of the camshaft and detach the timing chain from the crankshaft gear. (photo)
13 The crankshaft gear can now be eased off the nose of the crankshaft.

14 Camshaft - removal

The camshaft can be removed with the engine either in or out of the car. Follow the instructions given in Section 13 and then proceed as follows:
1 Remove the bonnet lock supporting crossmember and centre vertical member.
2 Disconnect the accelerator flexible cable and the choke cable from the carburettor. Remove the cable support from the top of the cylinder head cover. (photo)
3 Disconnect the ventilation tube from the cylinder head cover.
4 Undo and remove the cylinder head cover securing cap nuts and lift away the cylinder head cover. Recover the gasket.
5 Slacken off the valve adjuster screws and remove the pushrods. Keep these in order by pushing through a piece of stiff paper or card (If the cylinder head or rocker gear has already been removed this sequence is obviously not applicable).
6 Using a piece of hooked wire recover the pushrod tappets and place in order so that they can be refitted in their original position. (photo)
7 The distributor must next be removed. Disconnect the LT cable from the side and the vacuum hose from the unit. Release the clamp and lift away the distributor. (photo)
8 Disconnect the fuel hoses from the fuel pump. Undo and remove the two securing nuts and washers and lift away the fuel pump. (photo).
9 Undo and remove the two camshaft thrust plate securing bolts and washers and lift away the thrust plate. (photo)
10 Remove the engine mounting nuts and washers.
11 Disconnect the exhaust downpipe from the manifold.
12 Raise the engine slightly using a suitable hoist or crane. (photo)
13 The camshaft may now be lifted away through the front of the engine. Take great care not to allow the cam peaks to damage the bearings as the shaft is drawn forwards. (photo)

15 Crankshaft front oil seal - removal

It is possible to renew the crankshaft front oil seal with the engine still in position. To gain access to the front of the engine the following items should be removed.
1 Refer to Chapter 2, and drain the cooling system.
2 Drain the oil from the sump.
3 Refer to Chapter 3, and remove the air cleaner assembly.
4 Remove the bonnet lock supporting crossmember and centre vertical member.
5 Refer to Chapter 2, and remove the radiator.
6 Remove the fan belt.
7 Remove the crankshaft pulley retaining bolt and washer and remove the pulley.
8 Remove the engine under cover.
9 Undo and remove the engine mounting nuts and washers.
10 Disconnect the exhaust downpipe from the exhaust manifold.
11 Raise the engine slightly using an overhead hoist or crane.
12 The crankshaft front oil seal can now be removed from the timing chain cover by carefully dismantling or using a special oil seal puller.
13 Refitting the oil seal is the reverse sequence to removal. Carefully tap into position using a suitable diameter tubular drift.

16 Crankshaft rear oil seal - removal

It is possible to renew the crankshaft rear oil seal with the engine still in position.
1 Refer to Chapter 6 and remove the gearbox.
2 Refer to Section 17 and remove the flywheel
3 Undo and remove the bolts securing the oil seal retainer to the rear of the crankcase and carefully draw rearwards from the end of the crankshaft.
4 Tap the old oil seal from the retainer.
5 Fit a new oil seal to the retainer using a suitable diameter tubular drift. Thereafter reassembly is the reverse sequence to removal.

17 Flywheel and engine backplate - removal

It is possible to remove the flywheel with the engine still in position.
1 Refer to Chapter 6 and remove the gearbox.
2 Refer to Chapter 5 and remove the clutch from the rear of the flywheel.
3 Tap back the flywheel retaining bolts lockplate tabs. (photo)
4 Undo and remove the six flywheel securing bolts and lockplate. The flywheel may now be lifted away from the end of the crankshaft. (photos)
5 To remove the engine backplate undo and remove the three securing bolts and washers and lift away the backplate. (photo)

18 Sump, piston, connecting rod and big-end bearing - removal

The sump, pistons and connecting rods can be removed with the engine still in the car or with the engine on the bench. Proceed with the appropriate method in either case for removing

13.10 Lifting away timing chain tensioner

13.11 Removal of camshaft gear securing bolt and washer

13.12 Lifting away camshaft gear and chain

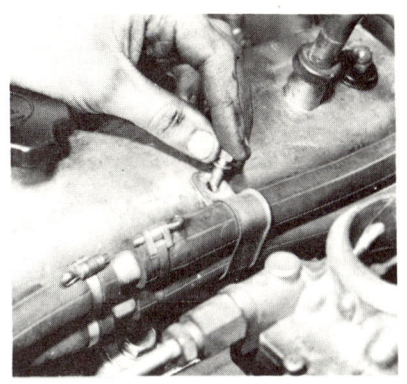

14.2 Removal of support clip from top cover

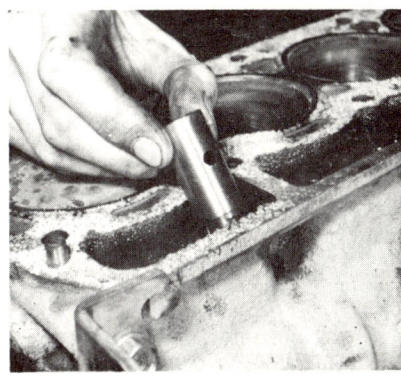

14.6 Lifting out tappet from crankcase

14.7 Removal of distributor

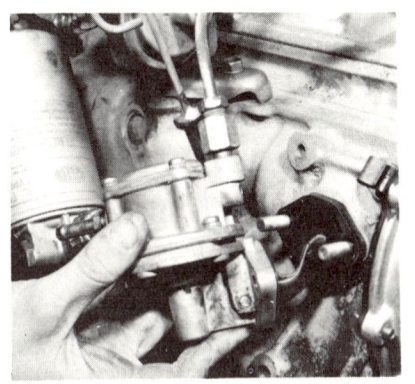

14.8 Fuel pump removal

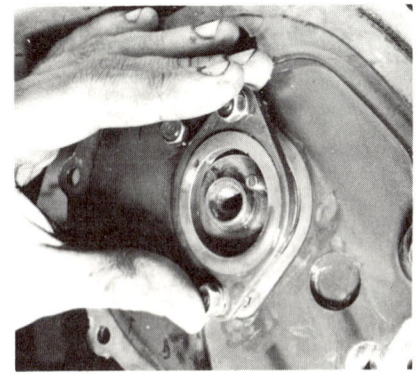

14.9 Camshaft thrust plate removal

14.12 Engine and mounting raised

14.13 Withdrawing camshaft from front of engine

17.3 Tapping back flywheel bolt lockplate tabs

17.4a Flywheel bolts

17.4b Removal of flywheel

17.5 Engine backplate removal

18.1 Removal of sump

the cylinder head. The pistons and connecting rods are drawn up out of the top of the cylinder bores.

1 Undo and remove the nuts, bolts and washers securing the sump in position. Lift away the sump and gasket. (photo)
2 To gain better access to the crankshaft undo and remove the bolt and washer securing the oil pump to the underside of the crankcase. Withdraw the oil pump. (photo)
3 Note that on reassembly it will be necessary to reset the ignition timing.
4 Undo and remove the big-end cap retaining nuts using a socket and remove the big-end caps one at a time, taking care to keep them in the right order and the correct way round. (photo)
5 Ensure that the shell bearings are also kept with their correct connecting rods and caps unless they are to be renewed. Normally the numbers 1 to 4 are stamped on adjacent sides of the big-end caps and connecting rods, indicating which cap fits on which rod and which way round the cap fits. If no numbers or lines can be found then scratch mating marks across the joint from the rod to the cap with a sharp screwdriver. One line for connecting rod number 1, two for connecting rod number 2 and so on. This will ensure there is no confusion later as it is most important that the caps go back in the position on the connecting rods from which they were removed.
6 If the big-end caps are difficult to remove they may be gently tapped with a soft hammer.
7 To remove the shell bearings press the bearing opposite the groove in both connecting rod and the connecting rod cap, and the bearing shell will slide out easily.
8 Withdraw the pistons and connecting rods upwards and ensure they are kept in the correct order for replacement in the same bore. Refit the connecting rod caps and bearings to the rods if the bearings do not require renewal to minimise the risk of getting the caps and rods muddled. (photo)

19 Gudgeon pin - removal

1 To detach a connecting rod from a piston, use a pair of circlip pliers and remove one of the two circlips located at the outer end of the gudgeon pin bore in the piston.
2 Make sure that identification marks are visible on the piston crown and connecting rod so that they can be reassembled the correct way round.
3 Carefully push out the gudgeon pin and separate the two parts.

20 Piston ring - removal

1 To remove the piston rings, slide them carefully over the top of the piston taking care not to scratch the aluminium alloy of the piston. Never slide them off the bottom of the piston skirt. It is very easy to break piston rings if they are pulled off roughly so this operation should be done with extreme caution. It is helpful to use an old 0.020 inch feeler gauge to facilitate their removal.
2 Lift one end of the piston ring to be removed out of its groove and insert the end of the feeler gauge under it.
3 Turn the feeler gauge slowly round the piston and as the ring comes out of its groove it rests on the land above. It can then be eased off the piston with the feeler gauge stopping it from slipping into any empty grooves if it is any but the top piston ring that is being removed.

21 Crankshaft and main bearing - removal

Drain the engine oil, and remove the timing gears and then the sump, oil pump, big-end bearings, flywheel and engine backplate, crankshaft rear oil seal as already described. Removal can only be attempted with the engine on the bench.

1 Undo and remove the ten bolts securing the main bearing caps to the cylinder block.
2 Make sure that the main bearing caps are numbered 1 to 5 on the front faces and also an arrow towards the front of the engine.
3 Remove the main bearing caps and the bottom half of each bearing shell, taking care to keep the bearing shells in the right caps. (photo)
4 When removing the centre bearing cap, note the bottom semi- circular halves of the thrust washers, one half lying on either side of the main bearing. Lay them with the centre bearing along the correct side.
5 Slightly rotate the crankshaft to free the upper halves of the bearing shells and thrust washers which can be lifted away and placed over the correct bearing cap when the crankshaft has been lifted out.
6 Remove the crankshaft by lifting it away from the crankcase. (photo)
7 Lift away the bearing shells. (photo)

22 Lubrication system - description

A force feed system of lubrication is fitted, with oil circulated around the engine from the sump below the cylinder block. The level of oil in the engine sump is indicated by the dipstick which is fitted to the right-hand side of the engine. The optimum level is indicated by the maximum mark. The level of oil in the sump, ideally, should neither be above or below this line. Oil is replenished, via the filler cap, towards the front of the top cover.

The eccentric rotor type oil pump is bolted within the right-hand side of the crankcase and is driven by a short shaft from the skew gear on the camshaft which also drives the distributor shaft.

The pump is of the non-draining variety to allow rapid pressure build up when starting from cold. Oil is drawn from the sump through a gauze screen in the oil strainer, this being shown in Fig 1.6 and is sucked up the pickup and drawn into the oil pump. From the oil pump it is forced under pressure along a gallery on the right-hand side of the engine, and through drillings to the big-end, main and camshaft bearings. A small hole in each connecting rod allows a jet of oil to lubricate the cylinder wall with each revolution.

From the second camshaft bearing oil is fed through drilled passages in the cylinder block and lead to the second rocker pedestal where it enters the hollow rocker shaft. Holes drilled in the shaft allow for lubrication of the rocker arm bushes and a small hole in each rocker arm directs a small oil jet to the valve stem and pushrod end. This oil is at a reduced pressure to the oil delivered to the crankshaft bearings. A little oil from the drilling to the front main bearing is directed to the timing gears and chain via the chain tensioner. Oil returns to the sump by various passages, the tappets being lubricated by oil returning via the pushrod drillings in the block.

A full flow cartridge type filter is fitted and oil passes through this filter before it reaches the main oil gallery. The oil is passed directly from the oil pump to the filter.

23 Oil filter - removal and replacement

1 The external oil filter is of the disposable cartridge type and is located on the right-hand side of the engine.
2 Before removing the cartridge place an absorbent cloth around the base to catch the oil released from the cartridge when it has been unscrewed.
3 To renew the oil filter unscrew the old cartridge from the filter head and discard it. Smear the seal on the new filter with a little oil and position it on the filter head. Screw it on and tighten with the hands only. Do not attempt to tighten with a spanner or strap wrench. (photo)

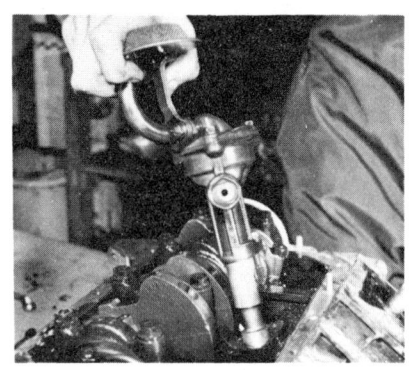

18.2 Lifting away oil pump assembly

18.4 Big end cap removal

18.8 Withdrawing piston through the top of the cylinder block

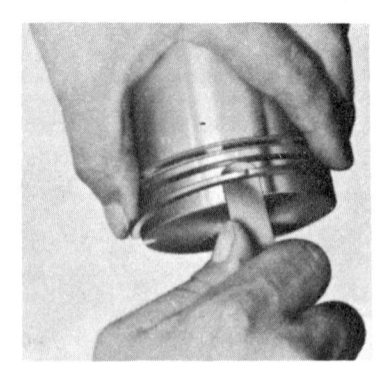

Fig 1.5 Removal of piston rings with feeler gauge

21.3 Main bearing cap removal

21.6 Lifting crankshaft from underside of crankcase

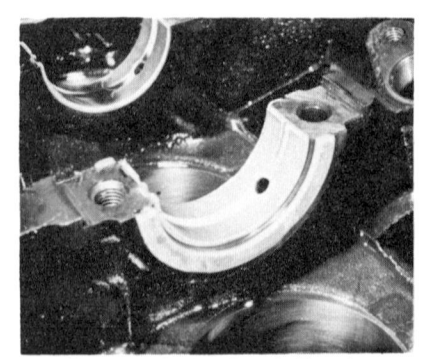

21.7 Centre main bearing shell and thrust washers

23.3 Oil filter canister removal

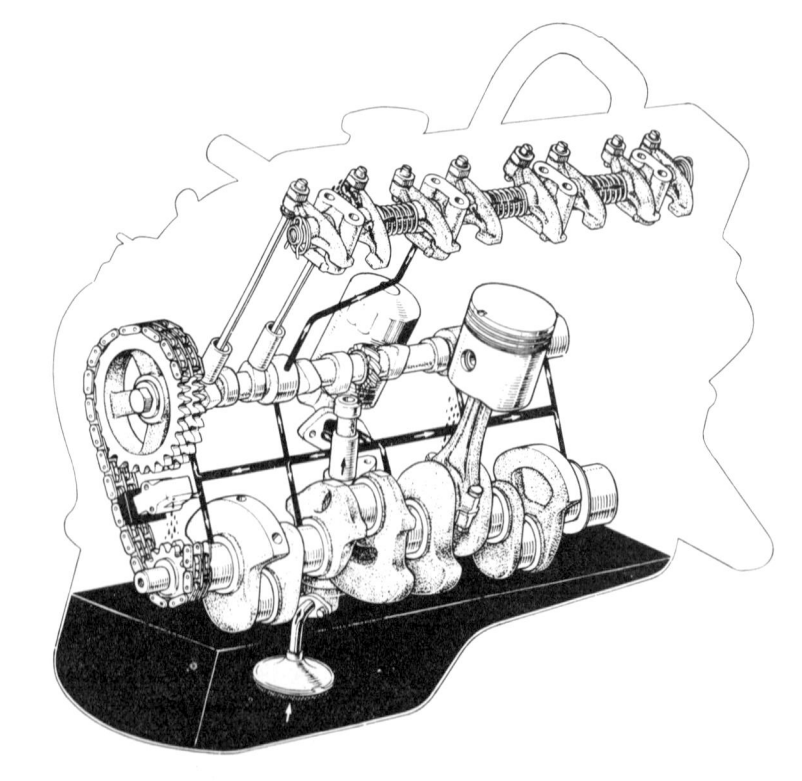

Fig 1.6 Engine lubrication system

24 Oil pressure relief valve - removal and replacement

To prevent excessive oil pressure - which might result when the engine oil is thick and cold - an oil pressure relief valve is built into the side of the oil pump body.

1 To gain access to the valve it is advisable to remove the oil pump (Section 25).
2 Unscrew the relief valve plug and remove it complete with sealing washer. The relief spring and valve can then be easily extracted. (photos)
3 In position the valve fits over the opposite end of the relief valve spring resting in the dome of the hexagon plug and bears against a machined seating in the oil pump body.
4 When the oil pressure exceeds approximately 70 lb/in^2 (4.92 Kg/cm^2) the valve is forced off its seat and the oil bypasses and returns, via a drilling, directly into the sump.
5 Check the tension of the spring by comparing its length with a new spring. If it is a different length it should be replaced with a new spring.
6 Examine the valve for signs of pitting and, if evident, it should be carefully lapped using cutting paste. Remove all traces of paste when a good seating has been obtained.
7 Reassembly of the relief valve is the reverse sequence to removal.

25 Oil pump - removal and dismantling

1 With the sump removed undo and remove the bolt and spring washer securing the pump to the underside of the crankcase.
2 The oil pump may now be drawn downwards and away from the underside of the crankcase.
3 Undo and remove the two bolts and washers securing the oil strainer to the oil pump cover (lower body). Lift away the oil strainer. (photo)
4 Undo and remove the three bolts and spring washers securing the oil pump cover to the body. Lift away the cover. (photo)
5 Pull out the pump body, the outer rotor and the inner rotor together with pump shaft. (photo)

26 Engine components - examination for wear

When the engine has been stripped down and all parts properly cleaned decisions have to be made as to what needs renewal and the following Sections tell the examiner what to look for. In any border line case it is always best to decide in favour of a new part. Even if a part may still be serviceable its life will have been reduced by wear and the degree of trouble needed to replace it in future must be taken into consideration. However these things are relative and it depends on whether a quick 'survival' job is being done or whether the car as a whole is being regarded as having many thousands of miles of useful and economical life remaining.

27 Crankshaft - examination and renovation

1 Look at the main bearing journals and the crankpins and if there are any scratches or score marks then the shaft will need regrinding. Such conditions will nearly always be accompanied by similar deterioration in the matching bearing shells.
2 Each bearing journal should also be round and can be checked with a micrometer or caliper gauge around the periphery at several points. If there is more than 0.0004 in (0.01 mm) of ovality or taper regrinding is necessary.
3 The main Toyota dealer or motor engineering specialist will be able to decide to what extent regrinding is necessary and also supply the special under-size shell bearings to match whatever may need grinding off the journals.
4 Before taking the crankshaft for regrinding check also the cylinder bores and pistons as it may be more convenient to have the engineering operations performed at the same time by the same engineer.

28 Crankshaft (main) bearings and big-end (connecting rod) bearings - examination and renovation

1 With careful servicing and regular oil and filter changes bearings will last for a very long time but they can still fail for unforeseen reasons. With big-end bearings the indications are regular rhythmic loud knocking from the crankcase, the frequency depending on engine speed. It is particularly noticeable when the engine is under load. This symptom is accompanied by a fall in oil pressure although this is not normally noticeable unless an oil pressure gauge is fitted. Main bearing failure is usually indicated by serious vibration, particularly at higher engine revolutions, accompanied by a more significant drop in oil pressure and a rumbling noise.
2 Bearing shells in good condition have bearing surfaces with a smooth, even, matt silver/grey colour all over. Worn bearings will show patches of a different colour where the bearing metal has worn away and exposed the underlay. Damaged bearings will be pitted or scored. It is nearly always well worthwhile fitting new shells as their cost is relatively low. If the crankshaft is in good condition it is merely a question of obtaining another set of standard size. A reground crankshaft will need new bearing shells as a matter of course.

29 Cylinder bores - examination and renovation

1 A new cylinder bore is perfectly round and the walls parallel throughout its length. The action of the piston tends to wear the walls at right angles to the gudgeon pin due to side thrust. This wear takes place principally on that section of the cylinder swept by the piston rings.
2 It is possible to get an indication of bore wear by removing the cylinder head with the engine still in the car. With the piston down in the bore first signs of wear can be seen and felt just below the top of the bore where the piston ring reaches, and there will be a noticeable lip. If there is no lip it is fairly reasonable to expect that bore wear is low and any lack of compression or excessive oil consumption is due to worn or broken piston rings or pistons. (see next Section).
3 If it is possible to obtain a bore measuring micrometer measure the bore in the thrust plane below the lip and again at the bottom of the cylinder in the same plane. If the difference is more than 0.008 in (0.2 mm) then a rebore is necessary. Similarly a difference of 0.008 in (0.2 mm) or more across the bore diameter is a sign of ovality calling for a rebore.
4 Any bore which is significantly scratched or scored will need reboring. This symptom usually indicates that the piston or rings are damaged in that cylinder. In the event of only one cylinder being in need of reboring it will still be necessary for all four to be bored and fitted with new oversize pistons and rings.

Your Toyota dealer or local engineering specialist will be able to rebore and obtain the necessary matched pistons. If the crankshaft is undergoing regrinding it is a good idea to let the same firm renovate and reassemble the crankshaft and pistons to the block. A reputable firm normally gives a guarantee for such work. In cases where engines have been rebored already to their maximum, new cylinder liners are available which may be fitted. In such cases the same reboring processes have to be followed and the services of a specialist engineering firm are required.

30 Pistons and piston rings - examination and renovation

1 Worn pistons and rings can usually be diagnosed when the symptoms of excessive oil comsumption and low compression occur and are sometimes, though not always, associated with worn cylinder bores. Compression testers that fit into the spark

Chapter 1/Part A: Engine KE models

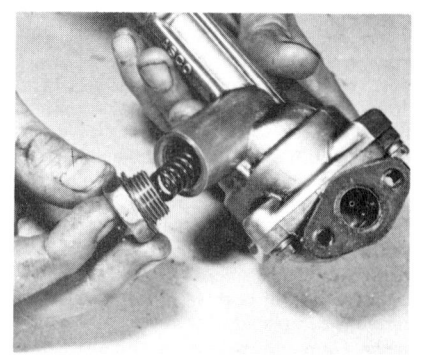

24.2a Relief valve plug removal

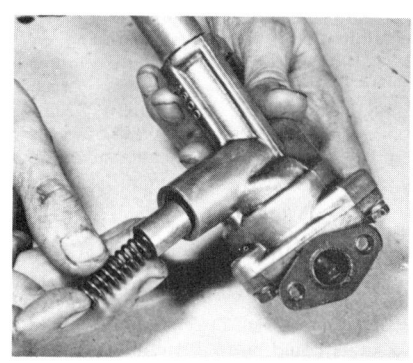

24.2b Lifting away relief valve spring and valve

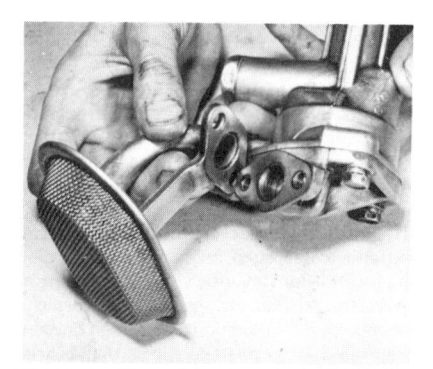

25.3 Detaching oil strainer assembly from pump body

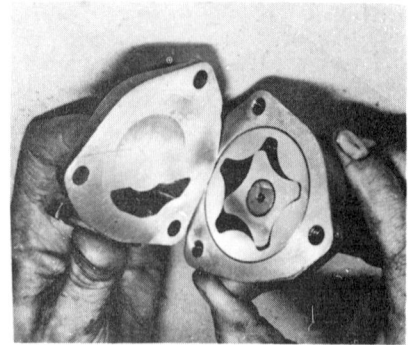

25.4 Removal of oil pump cover from body

25.5 Oil pump component parts

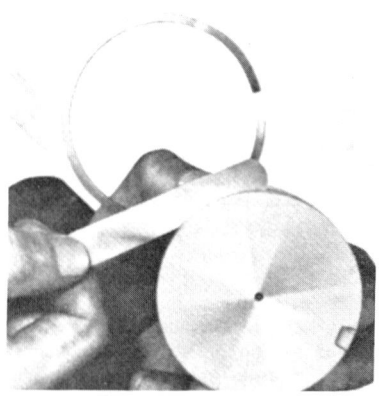

Fig 1.7 Measurement of piston ring groove clearance

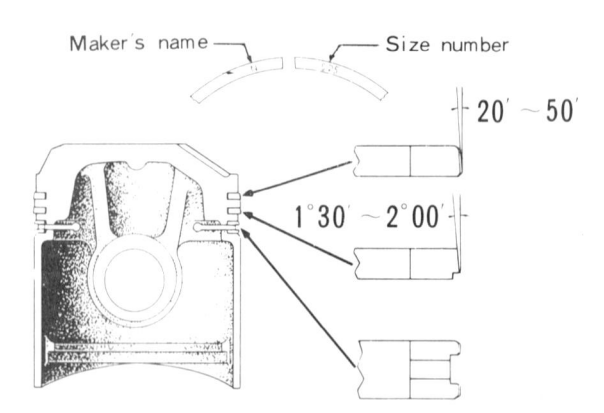

Fig 1.8 Piston ring identification

Fig 1.9 Measurement of piston ring end gap

plug holes are available and these can indicate where low compression is occurring. Wear usually accelerates the more it is left so when the symptoms occur early action can possibly save the expense of a rebore.

2 Another symptom of piston wear is piston slap - a knocking noise from the crankcase not to be confused with big-end bearing failure. It can be heard clearly at low engine speed when there is no load (idling for example) and the engine is cold, and is much less audible when the engine speed increases. Piston wear usually occurs in the skirt or lower end of the piston and is indicated by vertical streaks in the worn area which is always on the thrust side. It can be seen when the skirt thickness is different.

3 Piston ring wear can be checked by first removing the rings from the pistons as described in Section 20. Then place the rings in the cylinder bores from the top, pushing them down about 1.5 inches (38.1 mm) with the head of a piston (from which the rings have been removed) so that they rest square in the cylinder. Then measure the gap at the ends of the ring with a feeler gauge. If it exceeds the limits specified at the beginning of this Chapter then they will need renewal.

4 The grooves in which the rings locate in the piston can also become enlarged in use. The clearance between ring and piston, in the groove should not exceed the limits specified at the beginning of this Chapter.

5 However, it is rare that a piston is only worn in the ring grooves and the need to replace them for this fault alone is hardly ever encountered. Whenever the pistons are renewed the weight of the four piston/connecting rod assemblies should be kept within the limit variation of 8 gms to maintain engine balance.

31 Connecting rods and gudgeon pins - examination and renovation

1   Gudgeon pins are secured with snaprings (circlips) at both ends. Neither the connecting rod or gudgeon pin normally need replacement unless the pistons are being charged in which case the new pistons would automatically be supplied with new gudgeon pins.
2   Connecting rods are not normally subject to wear but in extreme cases such as engine seizure they could be distorted. Such conditions may be visually apparent but where doubt exists they should be changed. The bearing caps should also be examined for indications of filing down which may have been attempted in a mistaken idea that bearing slackness could be remedied in this way. If there are such signs then the connecting rods should be renewed.

32 Camshaft and camshaft bearings - examination and renovation

1   The camshaft bearing bushes should be examined for signs of scoring or pitting. If they need renewal they will have to be dealt with professionally as although it may be relatively easy to remove the old bushes, the correct fitting of new ones requires special tools. If they are not fitted evenly and square from the very start they can be distorted thus causing localised wear in a very short time. See your Toyota dealer or local engineering specialist for this work.
2   The camshaft itself may show signs of wear on the bearing journals, cam lobes or the skew gear. The main decision to take is what degree of wear justifies replacement, which is costly. Any signs of scoring or damage to the bearing journals must be rectified and as undersize bearing bushes are available the journals may be reground. If there is excessive wear on the skew gear which can be seen by close inspection of the contact pattern the whole camshaft will have to be renewed.
3   The cam lobes themselves may show signs of ridging or pitting at the high points. If the ridging is light then it may be possible to smooth it out with fine emery. The cam lobes, however, are surface hardened and once this is penetrated wear will be very rapid thereafter. The cams are also offset and tapered to cause the tappets to rotate - thus ensuring that wear is even - so do not mistake this condition for wear.

33 Tappets - examination and renovation

The faces of the tappets which bear on the camshaft should show no signs of pitting, scoring or other form of wear. They should also not be a loose fit in their housing. Wear is only normally encountered at very high mileage or in cases of neglected engine lubrication - renew if necessary.

34 Valves and valve seats - examination and renovation

1   With the valves removed from the cylinder head examine the head for signs of cracking, burning away and pitting of the edge where it seats in the port. The seats of the valves in the cylinder head should also be examined for the same signs. Usually it is the valve that deteriorates first but if a bad valve is not rectified the seat will suffer and this is more difficult to repair.
2   If pitting on the valve and seat is very slight the marks can be removed by grinding the seats and valves together with coarse and then fine valve grinding paste.
3   Where bad pitting has occurred to the valve seats it will be necessary to fit new valve seat inserts. These latter two jobs should be entrusted to the local Toyota dealer or engineering works. In practice it is very seldom that the seats are so badly worn that they require renewal. Normally it is the valve that is too badly worn for replacement, and the owner can easily purchase a new set of valves and match them to the seats by valve grinding.
4   Valve grinding is carried out as follows:
   Smear a trace of coarse carborundum paste on the seat face and apply a suction grinder tool to the valve head. With a semi-rotary motion, grind the valve head to its seat, lifting the valve occasionally to redistribute the drinding paste. When a dull matt even surface finish is produced on both the valve seat and the valve, wipe off the paste and repeat the process with fine carborundum paste, lifting and turning the valve to redistribute the paste as before. A light spring placed under the valve head will greatly ease this operation. When a smooth unbroken ring of light grey matt finish is produced, on both valve and valve seat faces, the grinding operation is completed.
5   Scrape away all carbon from the valve head and the valve stem. Carefully clean away every trace of grinding compound, taking care to leave none in the ports or in the valve guides. Clean the valves and valve seats with a paraffin soaked rag, with a clean rag and finally, if an air line is available blow the valves, valve guides and valve ports clean.

35 Valve guides - examination and renovation

1   Test each valve in its guide for wear. After a considerable mileage the valve guide bore may wear elliptically and can be tested by rocking the valve in the guide.
2   The remedy for wear is to ream the valve guide bores by the minimum amount to accommodate the smallest oversize valve which may be available at the time. Alternatively a new set of guides will have to be fitted and reamed to a standard size. In both cases this is a job for the local Toyota dealer or engineering works.

36 Rockers and rocker shaft - examination and renovation

1   Thoroughly clean the rocker shaft and then check the shaft for straightness by rolling it on a flat surface. It is most unlikely that it will deviate from normal, but, if it does, then a judicious attempt may be made to straighten it. If this is not successful purchase a new shaft. The surface of the shaft must be free from any worn ridges caused by the rocker arms. If any wear is present renew the shaft.
2   Check the rocker arms for wear of the bushes, for wear at the rocker arm face which bears on the valve stem, and for wear of the adjusting ball ended screws. Wear in the rocker arm bush can be checked by gripping the rocker arm tip and holding the rocker arm in place on the shaft, noting if there is any lateral rocker arm shake. If the shake is present, and the arm is very loose on the shaft a new rocker arm must be fitted.
3   Check the pushrods for straightness by rolling them on the bench. Renew any that are bent.

37 Timing gears and chain - examination and renovation

1   Examine the teeth on both the crankshaft gear wheel and the camshaft gear wheel for wear. Each tooth forms an inverted 'V' with the gearwheel periphery, and if worn the side of each tooth under tension will be slightly concave in shape when compared with the other side of the tooth ie; one side of the inverted 'V' will be concave when compared with the other. If any sign of wear is present the gearwheels must be renewed.
2   Examine the links of the chain for side slackness and renew the chain if any slackness is noticeable when compared with a new chain. It is a sensible precaution to renew the chain at about 30,000 miles (48000 Km) and at a lesser mileage if the engine is stripped down for major overhaul. The actual rollers on a very badly worn chain may be slightly grooved.

Limit
In. 0.031 in. (0.8 mm)
Ex. 0.035 in. (0.9 mm)

45

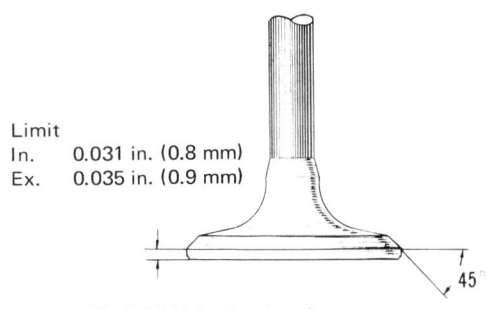

Fig 1.10 Valve head angles

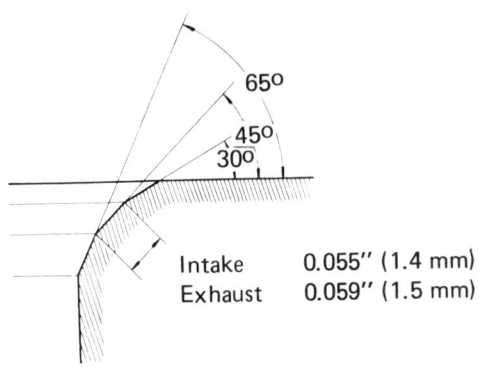

65°
45°
30°

Intake 0.055" (1.4 mm)
Exhaust 0.059" (1.5 mm)

Fig 1.11 Valve seat angles

Front

Fig 1.12 Valve rocker assembly

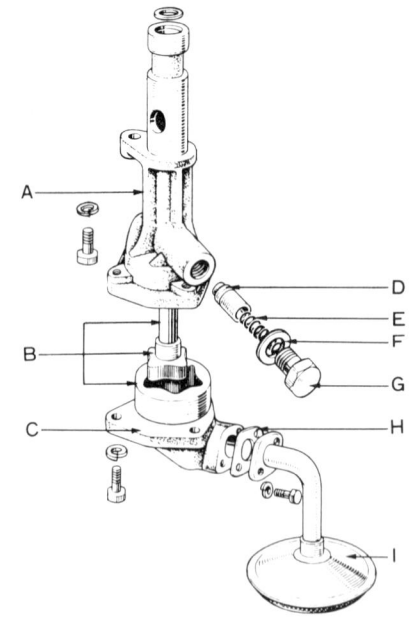

Fig 1.13 Oil pump and strainer components

A Oil pump body
B Oil pump rotor set
C Oil pump cover
D Relief valve
E Relief valve spring
F Gasket
G Relief valve plug
H Gasket
I Oil strainer

Fig 1.14 Relief valve located in filter bracket (Check this whenever overhauling lubrication system)

38 Oil pump - overhaul

1 If the oil pump is worn it is best to purchase an exchange reconditioned unit as a good oil pump is at the very heart of long engine life. Generally speaking an exchange or overhauled pump should be fitted at a major engine reconditioning.
2 If it is wished to check the oil pump for wear undo and remove the three bolts securing the oil pump body to the lower body and pick-up assembly. Separate the two parts.
3 Undo and remove the relief valve plug and withdraw the washer, spring and valve plunger.
4 Check the clearance between the lobes of the inner and outer rotors using feeler gauges. The clearance should not exceed 0.008 inch (0.2 mm) - (photo)
5 Replacement rotors are supplied only as a matched pair so that, if the clearance is excessive, a new rotor assembly must be fitted.
6 Lay a straight edge across the face of the pump in order to check the clearance between the faces of the rotors and the bottom of the straight edge. This clearance should not exceed

0.008 inch (0.2 mm). If the clearance is excessive the face of the pump body can be carefully lapped on a flat surface.
7 Using feeler gauges measure the clearance between the rotor and the body and this should not exceed 0.008 inch (0.2 mm). If wear is evident a new pump will be required. (photo)
8 Inspect the relief valve for pitting and the oil passages and sliding surfaces for damage in the form of score marks. Check that the spring is not damaged and finally the pick-up gauze for blockage or tearing.
9 Reassembly of the pump is the reverse sequence to dismantling. Both the drive and driven rotors are provided with punch marks and these must be aligned during reassembly. (Fig 15).

39 Cylinder head - decarbonisation

1 When the cylinder head is removed either in the course of an overhaul or inspection of the bores or valve condition when the engine is in the car, it is normal to remove all carbon deposits from the piston crowns and head.

38.4 Checking lobe tip clearance

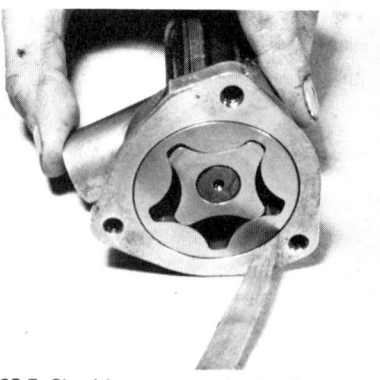

38.7 Checking rotor to body clearance

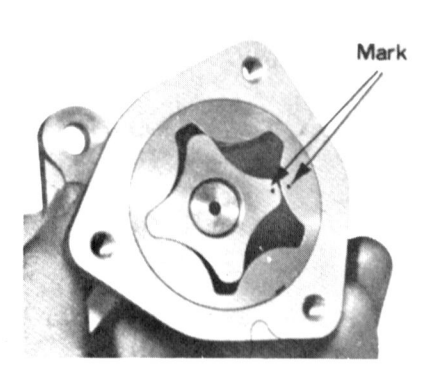

Fig 1.15 Correct reassembly of oil pump rotors

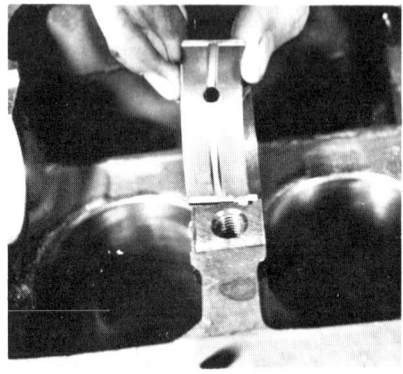

41.1 Main bearing shell replaced in crankcase

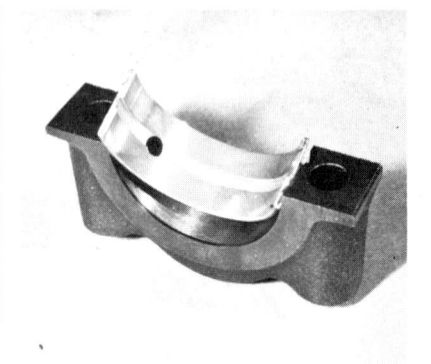

41.4 Main bearing shell fitted to cap

41.6 Positioning thrust washers to centre main bearing

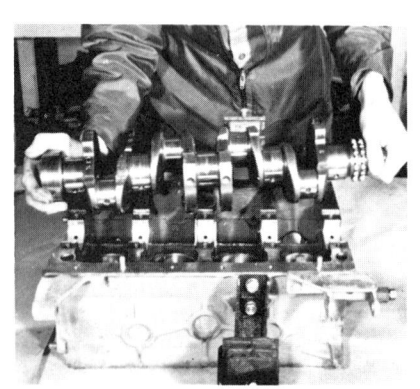

41.7 Lowering crankshaft into position

41.8 Refitting main bearing cap

41.9a Centre main bearing cap with thrust washer fitted

41.9b Replacing centre main bearing cap

41.12 Tightening cap securing bolts

41.13 Checking crankshaft endfloat

2 This is best done with a cup shaped wire brush and an electric drill and is fairly straightforward when the engine is dismantled and the pistons removed. Sometimes hard spots of carbon are not easily removed except by a scraper. When cleaning the pistons with a scaper take care not to damage the surface of the piston in any way.
3 When the engine is in the car certain precautions must be taken when decarbonising the piston crowns in order to prevent dislodged pieces of carbon falling into the interior of the engine which could cause damage to the cylinder bores, piston and rings - or if allowed into the water passages - damage to the water pump. Turn the engine, therefore so that the piston being worked on is at the top of its stroke and then mask off the adjacent cylinder bore and all surrounding water jacket orifices with paper and adhesive tape. Press grease into the gap all round the piston to keep particles out and then scrape all carbon away by hand, carefully. Do not use a power drill and wire brush when the engine is in the car as it will be virtually impossible to keep all the carbon dust clear of the engine. When completed carefully clean out the grease round the rim of the piston with a matchstick or something similar - bringing any carbon particles with it. Repeat the process on the other three piston crowns. It is not recommended that a ring of carbon is left round the edge of the piston on the theory that it will aid oil comsumption control. This was valid in the earlier days of long stroke low revving engines but modern engines, fuels and lubricants cause less carbon deposits anyway and any left behind tends merely to cause hot spots.

40 Engine reassembly - general

1 All components of the engine must be cleaned of oil sludge and old gaskets and the working area should also be clear and clean. In addition to the normal range of good quality socket spanners and general tools which are essential, the following must be available before reassembly begins:
1 Complete set of new gaskets.
2 Supply of clean rags.
3 Oil can full of clean engine oil.
4 Torque wrench.
5 All new spare parts as necessary.

41 Crankshaft - replacement

Ensure that the crankcase is thoroughly clean and that the oilways are clear. A thin twist drill is useful for cleaning them out. If possible blow them out with compressed air. Treat the crankshaft in the same fashion and then inject engine oil into the crankshaft oilways.

Commence work on rebuilding the engine by replacing the crankshaft and main bearings.
1 Fit the five upper halves of the main bearing shells to their location in the crankcase, after wiping the location clean. (photo)
2 Note that on the back of each bearing is a tab which engages in the locating grooves in either the crankcase or the main bearing cap housings.
3 If new bearings are being fitted, carefully clean away all traces of the protective grease with which they are coated.
4 With the five upper bearings shells securely in place, wipe the lower bearing cap housings and fit the five lower bearing shells to their caps ensuring that the right shell goes into the right cap if the old bearings are being refitted. (photo)
5 Wipe the recesses either side of the centre main bearing which locate the upper halves of the thrust washers.
6 Smear a little grease onto the thrust washers and slip into position. (photo)
7 Generously lubricate the crankshaft journals and the upper and lower main bearing shells and carefully lower the crankshaft into position. Make sure it is the right way round. (photo)
8 Fit the main bearing caps in position ensuring that they locate properly. The mating surfaces must be spotlessly clean or the caps will not seat correctly. (photo)
9 When replacing the centre main bearing cap ensure that the thrust washers, generously lubricated, are fitted with their oil grooves facing outwards and the locating tab of each washer is in the slot in the bearing cap. (photos)
10 Replace the main bearing cap bolts and screw them up finger tight.
11 Test the crankshaft for freedom of rotation. Should it be very stiff to turn or possess high spots a most careful inspection must be made, preferably by a skilled mechanic with a micrometer to trace the cause of the trouble. It is very seldom that any trouble of this nature will be experienced when fitting the crankshaft.
12 Tighten the main bearing cap bolts to a torque wrench setting of 39-47 lb f ft (5.4-6.6 Kg fm). (photo)
13 Using a screwdriver between one crankshaft web and main bearing cap, lever the crankshaft forwards and check the endfloat using feeler gauges. This should be 0.002-0.009 in (0.04-0.22 mm). If excessive new thrust washers or slightly oversize ones must be fitted. (photo)
14 During removal of the crankshaft gear it may have been noted that there were some shims behind the gearwheel. Replace the shims and then the inner Woodruff key.

42 Piston and connecting rod - reassembly

If the same pistons are being used, then they must be mated to the same connecting rod with the same gudgeon pin. If new pistons are being fitted it does not matter which connecting rod is used, but the gudgeon pins are not to be interchanged.
1 Note the location of the notch on the piston crown which is the front facing position and the mark on the connecting rod web just above the bid-end bearing. (photo)
2 Warm the piston in hot water to a temperature of approximately 70-80° C (158-176° F) and with one circlip removed push out the gudgeon pin.
3 Position the connecting rod in the piston and return the gudgeon pin. (photo) Note the cutaway in the crown of the piston and the oil jet hole in the connecting rod.
4 Refit the circlip and make double sure that the circlip is well seated in its groove. (photo)

43 Piston ring - replacement

1 Check that the piston ring grooves and oilways are thoroughly clean and not blocked. Piston rings must always be fitted over the crown of the piston and never from the bottom.
2 Refitment is the exact opposite procedure to removal, see Section 20.
3 Set all ring gaps at 120° to each other.
4 An alternative method is to fit the rings by holding them slightly open with the thumbs and both index fingers. This

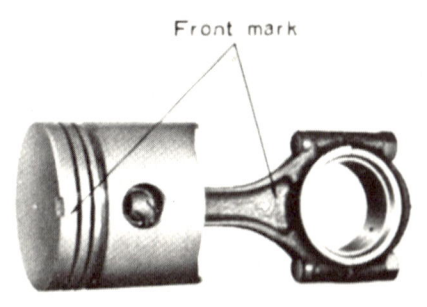

Fig 1.16 Piston and connecting rod reassembly marks

42.1 Piston marking

42.3 Refitting gudgeon pin

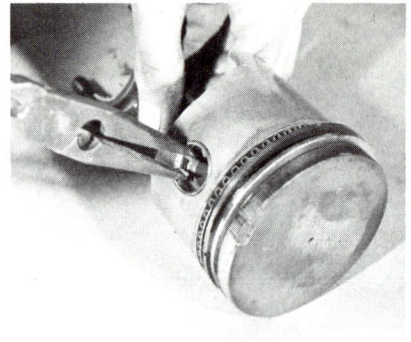

42.4 Refitting gudgeon pin retaining circlip

44.4 Fitting piston ring clamp

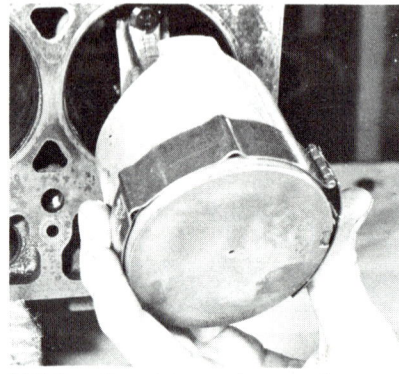

44.5 Inserting piston and connecting rod assembly into bore

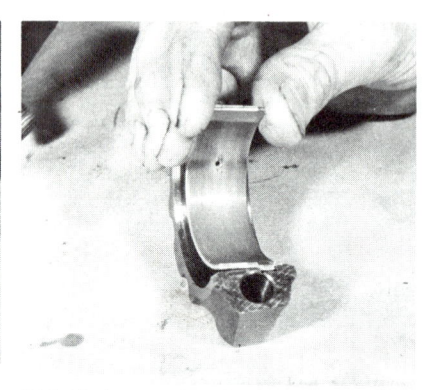

45.3 Fitting bearing shell to connecting rod end cap

45.4 Fitting end cap to connecting rod

45.5 Tightening the connecting rod retaining nuts

46.1 New gasket fitted to front end of crankcase

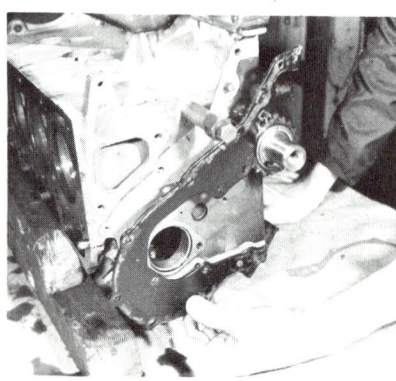

46.2 Fitting engine front plate

47.1 Chain vibration damper fitted to front plate

47.2 Replacement of camshaft

Chapter 1/Part A: Engine KE models

method requires a steady hand and great care for it is easy to open the ring too much and break it.
5 The special oil control ring requires a special fitting procedure. First fit the bottom rail of the oil control ring to the piston and position it below the bottom groove. Refit the oil control expander into the bottom groove and move the bottom oil control ring rail up into the bottom groove. Fit the top oil control rail into the bottom groove.

44 Piston - replacement

Fit pistons complete with connecting rods to the cylinder bores as follows:
1 Wipe the cylinder bores clean with clean non-fluffy rag.
2 The pistons, complete with connecting rods, must be fitted to their bores from above. As each piston is inserted into the bore ensure that it is the correct piston/connecting rod assembly for that particular bore and that the front of the piston is towards the front of the bore assuming that the connecting rod is fitted correctly ie; towards the front of the engine. Lubricate the piston well with clean engine oil.
3 Check that the piston ring gaps are 120° to each other.
4 Fit a piston ring clamp to compress the rings so that the piston may completely enter the bore. (photo)
5 Insert the connecting rod and assembly the correct way round into the bore until the compressor reaches the end of the bore. Gently tap the piston into the cylinder bore with a wooden or plastic hammer. (photo)

45 Connecting rod to crankshaft - reassembly

1 Wipe the connecting rod half of the big-end bearing location and the underside of the shell bearing clean, (as for the main bearing shells) and fit the shell bearing in position with its locating tongue engaged with the corresponding groove in the connecting rod. Always fit new shells.
2 Generously lubricate the crankpin journals with engine oil and turn the crankshaft so that the crankpin is in the most advantageous position for the connecting rod to be drawn onto it.
3 Fit the bearing shell to the connecting rod cap in the same way as with the connecting rod itself. (photo)
4 Generously lubricate the shell bearing and offer up the connecting rod bearing cap to the connecting rod. Fit the connecting rod retaining nuts. (photo)
5 Tighten the retaining nuts to a torque wrench setting of 29-37 lb f ft (4.0-5.2 Kg fm). (photo)
6 Using feeler gauges measure the thrust clearance between the connecting rod and crankshaft journal. The clearance should be 0.004-0.008 in (0.11-0.214 mm).

46 Engine front plate - replacement

1 Wipe the front end of the crankcase and fit a new gasket over the two dowels. (photo)
2 Fit the engine front plate over the locating dowels and secure in position with the two bolts adjacent to the camshaft front bearing. (photo)
3 Tighten these bolts to a torque wrench setting of 4-6 lb f ft (0.6-0.9 Kg fm). (photo)

47 Camshaft, timing gears and chain, tensioner and timing chain cover - reassembly

1 Fit the chain vibration damper (not to be confused with the tensioner) and secure in position with the two bolts which should be tightened to a torque wrench setting of 4-6 lb f ft (0.6-0.9 Kg fm).
2 Well lubricate the camshaft bearings and journals and carefully insert the camshaft into the cylinder block. The cam lobes must not touch the bearing surfaces. (photo)
3 Refit the camshaft thrust plate and secure with the two bolts which should be tightened to a torque wrench setting of 4-6 lb f ft (0.6-0.9 Kg fm). (photo)
4 The crankshaft timing gear is provided with an 'O' mark and this must be aligned with the camshaft pin as shown in Fig 1.17
5 Fit the timing chain onto the crankshaft timing gear lining up the bright link or 'O' mark on the chain link with the 'O' mark on the crankshaft gear.
6 Line up the camshaft 'O' mark with the second bright link or 'O' mark on the chain and position on the end of the camshaft. (Fig 1.18)
7 Refit the camshaft gear retaining bolt and washer and tighten to a torque wrench setting of 16-22 lb f ft (2.3-3.1 Kg fm).
8 Refit the chain tensioner assembly and secure with the two bolts which should be tightened to a torque wrench setting of 4-6 lb f ft (0.6-0.9 Kg fm). (photo)
9 Fit a new gasket to the front plate, locating over the two dowels. (photo)
10 It is desirable to always fit a new oil seal to the timing cover as it does not cost much to purchase bearing in mind the work involved in replacing it later. The old seal is simply eased out with a screwdriver and the new one fitted using a suitable diameter tubular drift.
11 Fit the timing cover and secure with the bolts and washers. These should be tightened to a torque wrench setting of 4-6 lb f ft (0.6-0.9 Kg fm). Do not forget one of these bolts also retains a clip - see photo 13:4. (photo)

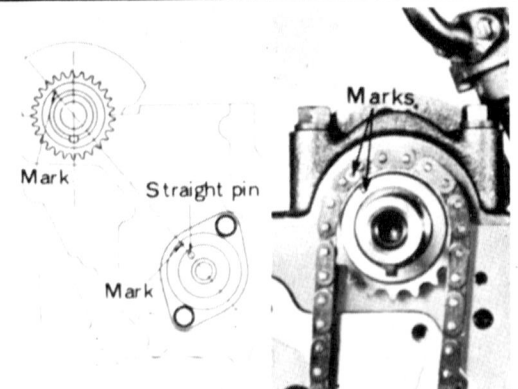

Fig 1.17 Timing chain identification and alignment (crankshaft gearwheel)

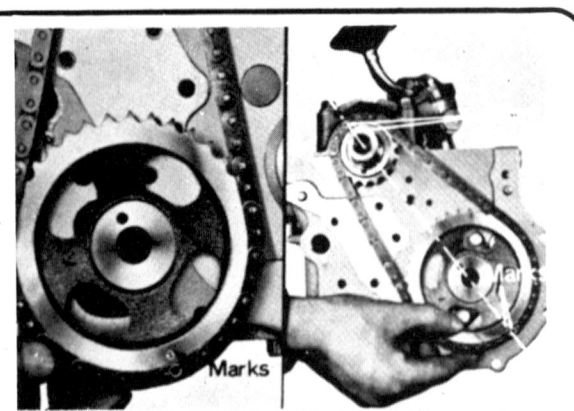

Fig 1.18 Timing chain identification and alignment (camshaft gearwheel)

47.3 Camshaft thrust plate fitted

47.8 Timing gears, chain and tensioner fitted

47.9 New gasket fitted to front of cylinder block

47.11 Timing chain cover ready for refitting to engine

48.2 Refitting crankshaft rear oil seal

49.2 Refitting oil pump and strainer

50.1 This part must be particularly well cleaned of old gasket and sealing compounds

50.2 New sump gasket fitted

50.3 Refitting sump to underside of crankcase

50.5 Crankshaft pulley replacement

51.1 Replacement of engine backplate

51.2 Refitting flywheel

Chapter 1/Part A: Engine KE models

48 Crankshaft rear oil seal - replacement

1 Fit a new gasket onto the dowels.
2 With a new seal fitted to the oil seal retainer carefully fit to the two dowels at the rear of the crankcase. (photo)
3 Fit the retainer securing bolts and tighten to a torque wrench setting of 4-6 lb f ft (0.6-0.9 Kg fm).

49 Oil pump - replacement

1 With the pump assembled and the oil strainer refitted, carefully insert into its location in the underside of the crankcase.
2 Secure the oil pump with the bolt and washer and tighten to a torque wrench setting of 7-11 lb f ft (1.0-1.5 Kg fm). (photo)

50 Sump - replacement

1 After the sump has been thoroughly cleaned, scrape all traces of the old sump gasket from the sump flange, and fit a new rear main bearing cap seal into the seal housing. (photo)
2 Thoroughly clean and scrape the crankcase to sump flange. Apply grease, or better still some jointing compound, to the mating faces and fit a new gasket to the underside of the crankcase. (photo)
3 Carefully fit the sump to the underside of the crankcase. (photo)
4 Refit the sump retaining bolts, nuts and washers, and tighten to a torque wrench setting of 2-3 lb f ft (0.25-0.35 Kg fm).
5 Now is a good time to replace the crankshaft pulley. Lubricate the oil seal location on the pulley hub and carefully fit to the crankshaft - ensure the woodruff key is still in position. (photo)
6 Refit the crankshaft pulley bolt and washer and tighten to a torque wrench setting of 29-43 lb f ft (4.0-6.0 Kg fm).

51 Engine backplate, flywheel and clutch - replacement

1 With the mating faces clean refit the engine backplate and secure with the three bolts and washers which should be tightened to a torque wrench setting of 4-6 lb f ft (0.6-0.9 Kg fm). (photo)
2 Refit the flywheel taking care to correctly seat the flywheel on the end the crankshaft. (photo)
3 Replace the flywheel securing bolts and lockplate and tighten the six bolts to a torque wrench setting of 39-48 lb f ft (5.4-6.6 Kg fm). (photo)
4 Using a chisel carefully bend up the lockplate tabs.
5 Refit the clutch disc and pressure plate assembly and lightly secure the position with the six bolts and spring washers. (photo)

6 If a first motion shaft is available use this to link up the clutch disc with the crankshaft spigot bearing. As an alternative use a suitable piece of wood such as a dowel rod.
7 Firmly tighten the clutch securing bolts in a diagonal manner.

52 Valve and spring - reassembly

To refit the valves and the valve springs to the cylinder head proceed as follows:
1 Rest the cylinder on its side.
2 Fit each valve and valve spring in turn, wiping down and lubricating each valve stem as it is inserted into the same valve guide from which it was removed. (photo)
3 Refit the plate washer over the valve stem and guide and position at the base of the guide. (photo)
4 Next replace the valve spring. (photo)
5 Fit the seal and retainer to the top of the valve spring. (photo)
6 Compress the valve spring and refit the retainer collets and 'O' ring seal. (photo)
7 Release the compressor and check that the collets and 'O' ring seal are correctly located.

53 Rocker shaft - reassembly

If the valve rocker shaft has been dismantled, which is a straightforward enough operation, a little care must be taken for reassembly. The following points should be noted:
a) The rockers are handed so make sure they are fitted to the rocker shaft with the offset at the valve stem end to the correct side.
b) The rocker supports (pedestals) must only be fitted the right way round. The 'F' mark must face towards the front of the engine.
c) Well lubricate the various parts during assembly to provide initial lubrication on starting.

54 Cylinder head - replacement

1 After checking that both the cylinder block and head mating faces are perfectly clean, generously lubricate each cylinder bore with engine oil.
2 Always use a new cylinder head gasket. The old gasket will be compressed and incapable of giving a good seal as well as probably being damaged during removal.
3 Never smear grease or gasket cement either side of the gasket for pressure leaks may blow through it.
4 The cylinder head gasket is usually marked 'Front' and should be fitted in position according to the markings. Ensure that all holes line up. (photo)

51.3 Tightening flywheel securing bolts

51.5 Clutch disc and pressure plate assembly refitted

52.2 Inserting valve into guide

52.3 Positioning plate washer

52.4 Fitting spring over valve stem and guide

52.5 Placing seal and retainer on top of spring

52.6 Compressing valve spring

54.4 Cylinder head gasket placed on cylinder block

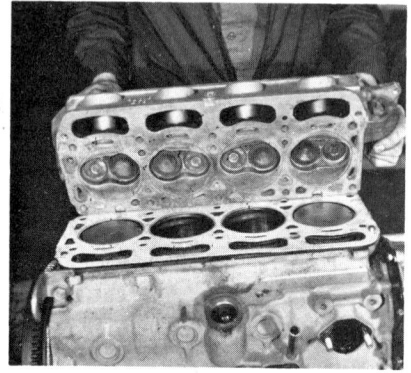

54.5 Lowering cylinder head onto gasket

54.7 Tightening cylinder head bolts

55.2 Fitting tappet into bore in cylinder block

55.3 Inserting push rod and engaging with tappet

55.5 Refitting rocker assembly to top of cylinder head

56.3 Top cover securing nut and sealing washer

56.5 Checking valve/rocker arm clearance

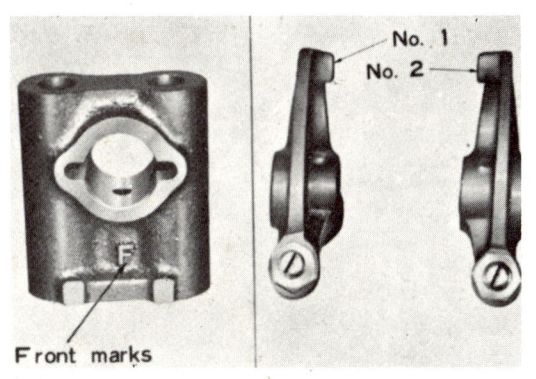

Fig 1.19 rocker assembly pedestal and rocker arm identification

No 1 Inlet   No 2 Exhaust

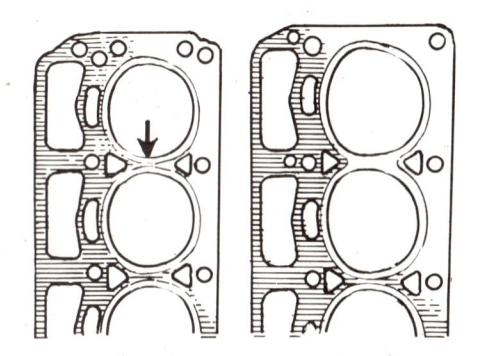

Fig 1.20 cylinder head gasket top side identification

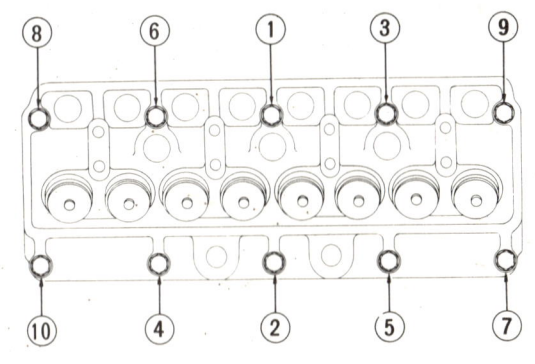

Fig 1.21 Correct sequence for tightening cylinder head bolts

56 Rocker arm/valve - adjustment

1 The valve adjustments should be made with the engine cold. The importance of correct rocker/valve stem clearances cannot be overstressed as they vitally affect the performance.
2 If the clearances are set too wide, the efficiency of the engine is reduced as the valves open late and close earlier than was intended. If the clearances are set too close there is a danger that the stem and pushrods upon expansion when hot will not allow the valves to close properly which will cause burning of the valve head and possible warping.
3 If the engine is in the car, to get at the rockers, it is merely necessary to remove the top cover. Once the cable support bracket and hose bracket have been detached undo and remove the two securing nuts and sealing washers then lift off the top cover and gasket. (photo)
4 It is important that the clearance is set when the tappet of the valve being adjusted is on the heel of the cam (ie; opposite the peak). This can be done by carrying out the adjustments in the following order, which also avoids turning the crankshaft more than necessary:

Valve fully open	Check and adjust
Valve number 8	Valve number 1
Valve number 6	Valve number 3
Valve number 4	Valve number 5
Valve number 7	Valve number 2
Valve number 1	Valve number 8
Valve number 3	Valve number 6
Valve number 5	Valve number 4
Valve number 2	Valve number 7

5 The correct valve clearances are given in the 'Specifications' Section at the beginning of this Chapter. Clearance is obtained by slackening the hexagonal locknut with a spanner while holding the ball pin against rotation with a screwdriver. Then, still pressing down with the screwdriver, insert a feeler gauge of the required thickness between the valve stem and head of the rocker arm and adjust the ball pin until the feeler gauge will just move in and out without nipping. Then still holding the ball pin in the correct position, tighten the locknut. (photo)

6 Refit the top cover and gasket and secure with the nuts and washers. (photo)

57 Distributor and drive - replacement

1 Rotate the crankshaft in its normal direction of rotation until No 1 piston is at its tdc position of the compression stroke.
2 Align the 'V' groove on the crankshaft pulley with the btdc 8° graduation on the timing chain cover. (photo)
3 Align the oil pump shaft slot with the mating point on the oil pump body. A torch and screwdriver will be required for this.
4 Set the octane selector on the distributor to its normal position.
5 Move the distributor rotor to the position shown in Fig 1.23 and then fit the distributor to the cylinder block.
6 When in the fitted position the distributor rotor should be in

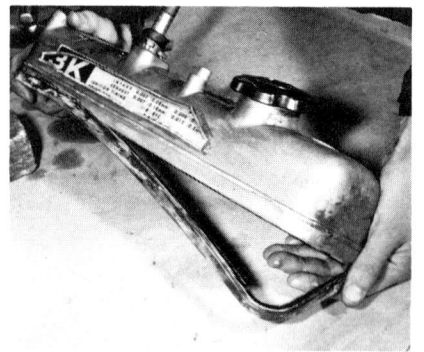

56.6 Top cover and gasket

57.2 Crankshaft pulley notch lined up to graduations on timing chain cover

57.7 Distributor with contact breaker points just opening

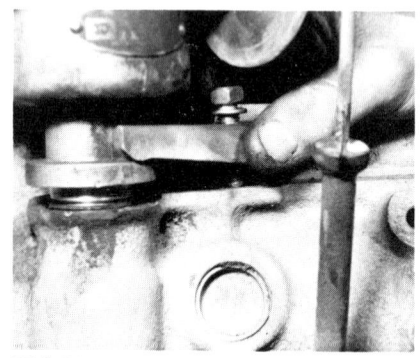

57.8 Distributor clamp and securing bolt

58b Refitting fuel pump

58c Refitting oil filter backset

58f Water outlet housing and thermostat
position shown in Fig 1.24

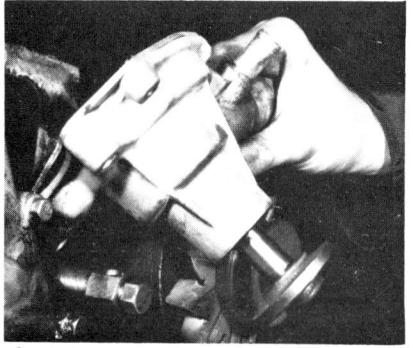

58g Refitting water pump

58h Positioning alternator on support bracket

7 Rotate the distributor housing slightly until the contact breaker points just start to open. (photo)
8 Fit the distributor clamp and tighten the securing bolt. (photo)

58 Final assembly

The ancillary equipment must now be refitted and this will depend on what was removed during dismantling. In the main these will be as follows but it is desirable to fit as much as possible before the engine is fitted into the car.
a) Spark plug tubes and washers. Spark plugs, distributor cap and HT leads.
b) Fuel pump. Note two gaskets and one insulator are used. Tighten nuts to torque wrench setting of 7-11 lb f ft (1.0-1.5 Kg fm). (photo)
c) Oil filter bracket and gasket. Tighten bolts to torque wrench setting of 7-11 lb f ft (1.0-1.5 Kg fm). Fit a new oil filter. (photo)
d) Dipstick.
e) Alternator bracket. Tighten bolts to torque wrench setting of 7-11 lb f ft (1.0-1.5 Kg fm).
f) Water outlet housing, gasket and thermostat. Tighten bolts to torque wrench setting of 7-11 lb f ft (1.0-1.5 Kg fm). (photo)
g) Water pump assembly. Tighten bolts to a torque wrench setting of 7-11 lb f ft (1.0-1.5 Kg fm). (photo)
h) Fit alternator to bracket. Tighten pivot bolt to torque wrench setting of 11-14 lb f ft (1.5-2.0 Kg fm). (photo)
i) Fan pulley and fan. Tighten bolts to torque wrench setting of 4-6 lb f ft (0.6-0.9 Kg fm).
j) Refit fan belt. Deflection to be 0.31-0.51 in (8-13 mm) on longest. (Fig 1.25)
k) Coat threads of water drain plug with sealer and fit to

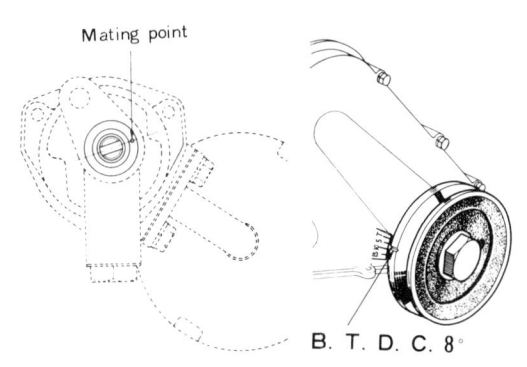

Fig 1.22 Oil pump shaft alignment

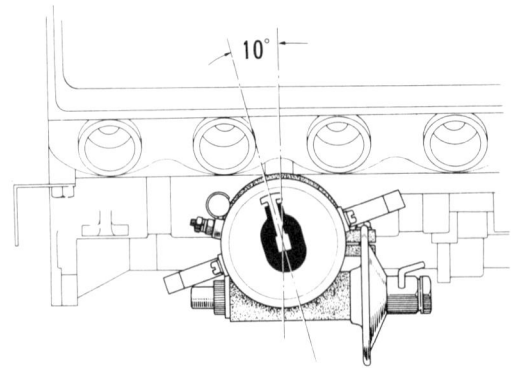

Fig 1.23 Position of rotor arm before refitting distributor

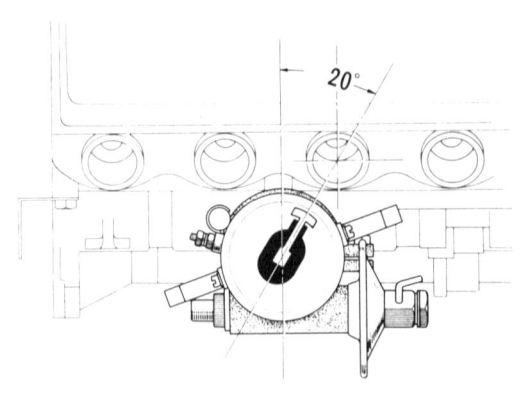

Fig. 1.24 Position of rotor arm after refitting distributor

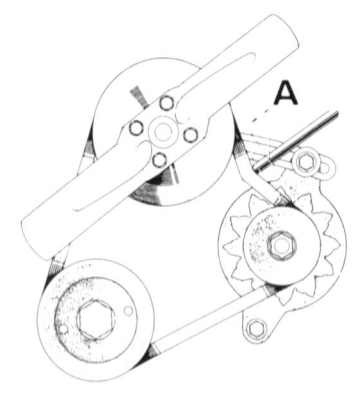

Fig 1.25 Correct fan belt tension

cylinder block.

59 Engine - replacement

Although the engine or engine and gearbox can be replaced by one man using a suitable hoist it is easier if two are present. Generally replacement is the reverse sequence to removal. In addition however:
1 Ensure all the loose leads, cables, etc are tucked out of the way. It is easy to trap one and cause much additional work after the engine is refitted.
2 Refit the following:
a) Mounting nuts, bolts and washers.
b) Propeller shaft coupling.
c) Clutch control assembly.
d) Speedometer cable.
e) Gearchange lever and surround.
f) Carpets.
g) Oil pressure switch cable.
h) Water temperature indicator sender unit cable.
i) Wires to coil, distributor and alternator.
j) Manifolds, carburettor, controls and air cleaner.
k) Exhaust manifold to downpipe.
l) Earth cables.
m) Starter motor and cables.
n) Radiator and hoses.
o) Heater hoses.
p) Vacuum advance and retard pipe.
q) Engine closed circuit breather hoses.
r) Battery (if removed).
s) Fuel lines to carburettor and pump.
t) Exhaust emission control units - if fitted.
u) Bonnet.
3 Finally check that the drain plugs are closed and refill the cooling system, engine and gearbox.

60 Engine - initial start up after overhaul or major repair

Make sure that the battery is fully charged and that all lubricants, coolant and fuel are replenished.

If the fuel system has been dismantled, it will require several revolutions of the engine on the starter motor to pump petrol to the carburettor. An initial 'prime' of about 1/3 cup full of petrol down the air intake of the carburettor will help the engine to fire quickly, thus relieving the load on the battery. Do not overdo this however, as flooding may result.

As soon as the engine fires and runs, keep it going at a fast tickover only (no faster) and bring it up to normal working temperature.

As the engine warms up, there will be odd smells and some smoke from parts getting hot and burning off oil deposits. Look for water or oil leaks which will be obvious if serious. Check also the clamp connection of the exhaust pipe to the manifold as these do not always 'find' their exact gas tight position until the warmth and vibration have acted on them, and it is almost certain that they will need tightening **further**. This should be done of course with the engine stationary.

When the engine running temperature has been reached, adjust the idling speed as described in Chapter 3.

Stop the engine and wait a few minutes to see if any lubricant or coolant leaks.

Road test the car to check that the timing is correct and giving the necessary smoothness and power. Do not race the engine. If new bearings and or pistons and rings have been fitted, it should be treated as a new engine and run in at reduced revolutions for 500 miles (800 Km).

61 Fault diagnosis - engine

Symptom	Reason/s	Remedy
Engine fails to turn over when starter operated	Discharged or defective battery	Charge or replace battery, push-start car (manual gearbox only)
	Dirty or loose battery leads	Clean and tighten both terminals and earth ends of earth lead
	Defective starter solenoid or switch	Run a heavy duty wire direct from the battery to the starter motor or by-pass the solenoid
	Engine earth strap disconnected	Check and retighten strap
	Jammed starter motor drive pinion	Place car in gear and rock from side to side. Alternatively, free exposed square end of shaft with spanner.
	Defective starter motor	Remove and recondition.
Engine turns over but will not start	Ignition damp or wet	Wipe dry the distributor cap and ignition leads.
	Ignition leads to spark plugs loose	Check and tighten at both spark plug and distributor cap ends.
	Shorted or disconnected low tension leads	Check the wiring on the CB and SW terminals of the coil and to the distributor.
	Dirty, incorrectly set or pitted contact breaker points	Clean, file smooth and adjust.
	Faulty condenser	Check contact breaker points for arcing, remove and fit new condenser.
	Defective ignition switch	By-pass switch with wire.
	Ignition LT leads connected wrong way round	Remove and replace leads to coil in correct order.
	Faulty coil	Remove and fit new coil.
	Contact breaker point spring earthed or broken	Check spring is not touching metal part of distributor, Check insulator washers are correctly placed. Renew points if the spring is broken.
	No petrol in petrol tank	Refill tank!
	Vapour lock in fuel line (in hot conditions or at high altitude)	Blow into petrol tank, allow engine to cool, or apply a cold wet rag to the fuel line in engine compartment.
	Blocked float chamber needle valve	Remove, clean and replace.
	Fuel pump filter blocked	Remove, clean and replace.
	Choked or blocked carburettor jets	Dismantle and clean.
	Faulty fuel pump	Remove, overhaul and replace.
	Too much choke allowing too rich a mixture to wet plugs	Remove and dry spark plugs or with wide open throttle, push-start the car (manual gearbox only)
	Float damaged or leaking or needle not seating	Remove, examine, clean and replace float and needle valve as necessary.
	Float lever incorrectly adjusted	Remove and adjust correctly.
Engine stalls and will not start	Ignition failure - sudden	Check over low and high tension circuits for breaks in wiring.
	Ignition failure - misfiring precludes total stoppage	Check contact breaker points, clean and adjust. Renew condenser if faulty.
	Ignition failure - in severe rain or after traversing water splash	Dry out ignition leads and distributor cap.
	No petrol in petrol tank	Refill tank.
	Petrol tank breather choked	Remove petrol cap and clean out breather hole or pipe.
	Sudden obstruction in carburettor	Check jets, filter, and needle valve in float chamber for blockage.
	Water in fuel system	Drain tank and blow out fuel lines.
Engine misfires or idles unevenly	Ignition leads loose	Check and tighten as necessary at spark plug and distributor cap ends.
	Battery leads loose on terminals	Check and tighten terminal leads.
	Battery earth strap loose on body attachment point	Check and tighten earth lead to body attachment point.
	Engine earth lead loose	Tighten lead.
	Low tension leads to SW and CB terminals on coil loose	Check and tighten leads if found loose.

Chapter 1/Part A: Engine KE models

Symptom	Reason/s	Remedy
	Low tension lead from CB terminal side to distributor loose	Check and tighten if found loose.
	Dirty, or incorrectly gapped spark plugs	Remove, clean and regap.
	Dirty, incorrectly set or pitted contact breaker points	Clean, file smooth and adjust.
	Tracking across distributor cap	Remove and fit new cap.
	Ignition too retarded	Check and adjust ignition timing.
	Faulty coil	Remove and fit new coil.
	Mixture too weak	Check jets, float chamber needle valve and filters for obstruction. Clean as necessary Carburettor incorrectly adjusted.
	Air leak in carburettor	Remove and overhaul carburettor.
	Air leak at inlet manifold to cylinder head, or inlet manifold to carburettor	Test by pouring oil along joints. Bubbles indicate leak. Renew manifold gasket as appropriate.
	Incorrect valve clearances	Adjust rocker arm clearances.
	Burnt out exhaust valves	Remove cylinder head and renew defective valves.
	Sticking or leaking valves	Remove cylinder head, clean, check and renew valves as necessary.
	Worn or broken valve springs	Check and renew as necessary.
	Worn valve guides or stems	Renew valves.
	Worn pistons and piston rings	Dismantle engine, renew pistons and rings.
Lack of power and poor compression	Burnt out exhaust valves	Remove cylinder head, renew defective valves
	Sticking or leaking valves	Remove cylinder head, clean, check and renew valves as necessary.
	Worn valve guides and stems	Remove cylinder head and renew valves.
	Weak or broken valve springs	Remove cylinder head, renew defective springs.
	Blown cylinder head gasket (accompanied by increase in noise)	Remove cylinder head and fit new gasket.
	Worn pistons and piston rings	Dismantle engine, renew pistons and rings.
	Worn or scored cylinder bores	Dismantle engine, rebore, renew pistons and rings.
	Ignition timing wrongly set. Too advanced or retarded	Check and reset ignition timing.
	Contact breaker points incorrectly gapped	Check and reset contact breaker points.
	Incorrect valve clearances	Adjust rocker arm clearances.
	Incorrectly set spark plugs	Remove, clean and regap.
	Carburettor too rich or too weak	Tune carburettor for optimum performance.
	Dirty contact breaker points	Remove, clean and replace.
	Fuel filters blocked causing top end fuel starvation	Dismantle, inspect, clean, and replace all fuel filters.
	Distributor automatic balance weights or vacuum advance and retard mechanisms not functioning correctly	Overhaul distributor.
	Faulty fuel pump giving top end fuel starvation	Remove, overhaul, or fit exchange reconditioned fuel pump.
Excessive oil consumption	Badly worn, perished or missing valve stem oil seals	Remove, fit new oil seals to valve stems.
	Excessively worn valve stems and valve guides	Remove cylinder head and fit new valves.
	Worn piston rings	Fit oil control rings to existing pistons or purchase new pistons.
	Worn pistons and cylinder bores	Fit new pistons and rings, rebore cylinders.
	Excessive piston ring gap allowing blow-by	Fit new piston rings and set gap correctly.
	Piston oil return holes choked	Decarbonise engine and pistons.
Oil being lost due to leaks	Leaking oil filter gasket	Inspect and fit new gasket as necessary.
	Leaking rocker cover gasket	Inspect and fit new gasket as necessary.
	Leaking timing case gasket	Inspect and fit new gasket as necessary.
	Leaking sump gasket	Inspect and fit new gasket as necessary.
	Loose sump plug	Tighten, fit new gasket as necessary.
Unusual noises from engine	Worn valve gear (noisy tapping from rocker box)	Inspect and renew rocker shaft, rocker arms and ball pins as necessary.

Worn big-end bearings (regular heavy knocking)	Drop sump, if bearings broken up clean out oil pump and oilways, fit new bearings. If bearings not broken but worn fit bearing shells.
Worn timing gears (rattling from front of engine)	Remove timing cover, fit new timing gears.
Worn main bearings (rumbling and vibration)	Drop sump, remove crankshaft; if bearings worn but not broken up, renew. If broken up strip oil pump and clean out.
Worn crankshaft (knocking, rumbling and vibration)	Regrind crankshaft, fit new main and big-end bearings.

Fig 1.1 Cross sectional view of TE engine

Chapter 1 Part B: Engine TE models

Contents

Camshaft - removal ... 19	Flywheel - removal, inspection and renovation ... 11
Camshaft, timing chain and gears and front cover - replacement ... 38	General description ... 1
Connecting rod to crankshaft - refitting ... 35	Gudgeon pins - removal ... 23
Crankshaft pulley - replacement ... 45	Lubrication and crankcase ventilation system - description ... 27
Crankshaft rear oil seal - removal ... 25	Major operations requiring engine removal ... 3
Crankshaft rear oil seal and retainer - replacement ... 37	Main bearings and crankshaft - removal ... 26
Crankshaft - replacement ... 31	Methods of engine removal ... 4
Cylinder head removal - engine in car ... 12	Oil filter - removal and replacement ... 10
Cylinder head removal - engine on bench ... 13	Oil pump and sump - replacement ... 39
Cylinder head - replacement ... 42	Oil pump - removal ... 18
Dismantling the engine - general ... 7	Operations possible with engine in place ... 2
Dismantling the rocker assembly ... 15	Piston rings - removal ... 24
Engine ancillaries - removal ... 8	Piston rings - replacement ... 33
Engine (and transmission) - refitting ... 47	Pistons and connecting rods - reassembly ... 32
Engine backplate - replacement ... 40	Pistons, connecting rods and big-end bearings - removal ... 22
Engine components - examination for wear and renovation ... 29	Pistons - replacement ... 34
Engine - final assembly ... 46	Rocker arms and shafts - reassembly ... 41
Engine - initial start up after overhaul or major repair ... 48	Sump - removal ... 17
Engine mountings - removal and replacement ... 9	Tappets - removal ... 20
Engine reassembly - general ... 30	Timing chain tensioner - removal ... 21
Engine - removal less gearbox ... 6	Timing cover, gearwheels and chain - removal ... 16
Engine - removal with gearbox ... 5	Valve clearance - adjustment ... 43
Fault diagnosis - engine ... 49	Valve removal ... 14
Flywheel - refitting ... 44	Valves and valve springs - reassembly ... 36
	Ventilation valve - inspection ... 28

Specifications

General:

Engine type	4 cylinder, in line overhead valve
Engine designation	2T - C
Firing order	1 3 4 2
Displacement	1588 cc (96.9 cu in.)
Bore	3.35 in. (85 mm)
Stroke	2.75 in. (70 mm)
Engine idle speed:	
Manual	650 rpm
Automatic	750 rpm
Compression ratio	8.5 : 1
Maximum horsepower	SAE 88 at 6,000 rpm
Compression pressure:	
Average	170.6 lb/in^2 (11.994 kg/cm^2)
Minimum	127.9 lb/in^2 (9.0 kg/cm^2)
Ignition timing	5° btdc
Manifold vacuum (idle speed)	17.0 in. hg (430 mm hg)
Sump capacity (with filter)	7.8 pints (4.5 litres, 9.6 US pints)

Cylinder head:

Maximum warpage	0.002 in. (0.05 mm)
Gasket thickness	0.06 in. (1.5 mm)
Valve seat:	
Contact surface angle	45°
Contact width	0.055 in. (1.4 mm)
Refacing angles:	
Inlet	30°, 45°, 60°, 75°
Exhaust	30°, 45°, 65°

Cylinder block:
- Maximum warpage … 0.002 in. (0.05 mm)
- Tappet bore diameter:
  - Standard … 0.874 - 0.8748 in. (22.2 - 22.221 mm)
  - Oversize … 0.876 - 0.8768 in. (22.25 - 22.271 mm)

Cylinder bore:
- Standard diameter … 3.346 - 3.348 in. (85 - 85.05 mm)
- Wear limit … 0.008 in. (0.2 mm)
- Honing limit … Less than 0.0008 in. (0.02 mm)
- Maximum ovality and taper … 0.0004 in. (0.01 mm)
- Bore deviation between cylinders … 0.0004 in. (0.01 mm)

Pistons:
- External diameter:
  - Standard … 3.344 - 3.346 in. (84.93 - 84.98 mm)
  - Oversize … 0.25, 0.50, 0.75 and 1.00
- Piston/cylinder clearance … 0.0024 - 0.0031 in. (0.06 - 0.08 mm)
- Gudgeon pin fitting temperature … 20º C (68º F)
- Piston ring end-gap:
  - No. 1 … 0.008 - 0.016 in. (0.2 - 0.4 mm)
  - No. 2 … 0.004 - 0.012 in. (0.1 - 0.3 mm)
  - Oil control … 0.004 - 0.012 in. (0.1 - 0.3 mm)
- Piston ring to groove clearance:
  - No. 1 … 0.0008 - 0.0024 in. (0.02 - 0.06 mm)
  - No. 2 … 0.0008 - 0.0024 in. (0.02 - 0.06 mm)
  - Oil control … 0.0008 - 0.0024 in. (0.02 - 0.06 mm)
- Gudgeon pin diameter … 0.8661 - 0.8665 in. (22.0 - 22.01 mm)

Connecting rods:
- Thrust clearance (big-end):
  - Standard … 0.0063 - 0.0102 in. (0.16 - 0.26 mm)
  - Maximum … 0.0118 in. (0.3 mm)
- Gudgeon pin/bush clearance … 0.0004 - 0.0016 in. (0.01 - 0.04 mm)
- Bearing oil clearance … 0.0008 - 0.0020 in. (0.02 - 0.005 mm)
- Bearing undersize … 0.05, 0.25, 0.50 and 0.75

Crankshaft:
- Maximum bend … 0.0012 in. (0.03 mm)
- Thrust clearance:
  - Standard … 0.003 - 0.007 in. (0.07 - 0.18 mm)
  - Maximum … 0.012 in. (0.3 mm)
- Taper and ovality limit … 0.0004 in. (0.01 mm)
- Journal diameter:
  - Standard … 2.2827 - 2.2834 in. (57.98 - 58.00 mm)
  - Undersize - 0.05 … 2.2800 - 2.2815 in. (57.90 - 57.95 mm)
  - Undersize - 0.25 … 2.2732 - 2.2736 in. (57.74 - 57.75 mm)
  - Undersize - 0.50 … 2.2634 - 2.2640 in. (57.49 - 57.50 mm)
- Bearing oil clearance … 0.0012 - 0.0024 in. (0.03 - 0.06 mm)
- Crankpin diameter:
  - Standard … 1.8890 - 1.8900 in. (47.98 - 48.00 mm)
  - Undersize - 0.05 … 1.8858 - 1.8878 in. (47.90 - 47.95 mm)
  - Undersize - 0.25 … 1.8795 - 1.8800 in. (47.74 - 47.75 mm)
  - Undersize - 0.50 … 1.8700 - 1.8701 in. (47.49 - 47.50 mm)
- Bearing oil clearance … 0.0008 - 0.0020 in. (0.02 - 0.05 mm)

Tappets:
- Outside diameter:
  - Standard … 0.8732 - 0.8740 in. (22.179 - 22.199 mm)
  - Oversize … 0.05
- Oil clearance … 0.0006 - 0.0011 in. (0.015 - 0.029 mm)

Valves:
- Valve head diameter:
  - Inlet … 1.6083 - 1.6201 in. (40.85 - 41.15 mm)
  - Exhaust … 1.4114 - 1.4232 in. (35.85 - 36.15 mm)
- Valve overall length … 4.29 in. (109 mm)

Valve head face angle		45°
Valve stem diameter:		
Inlet and exhaust		0.3138 - 0.3146 in. (7.97 - 7.99 mm)
Guide bush to stem oil clearance:		
Inlet		0.0012 - 0.0024 in. (0.03 - 0.06 mm)
Exhaust		0.0012 - 0.0028 in. (0.03 - 0.07 mm)
Guide bush to stem clearance limit:		
Inlet		0.0031 in. (0.08 mm)
Exhaust		0.0039 in. (0.10 mm)
Valve head thickness limit:		
Inlet		0.0197 in. (0.5 mm)
Exhaust		0.0236 in. (0.6 mm)

Valve seats:

Contact face angle		45°
Valve seat contact width		0.055 in. (1.4 mm)
Correction angles:		
Inlet		30°, 45°, 60°, and 75°
Exhaust		30°, 45°, and 65°

Valve guides:

Diameter		0.3154 - 0.3161 in. (8.01 - 8.03 mm)
Outside diameter:		
Standard		0.5134 - 0.5125 in. (13.04 - 13.05 mm)
Oversize		0.002 in. (0.05 mm)
Valve guide protrusion from cylinder head		0.6693 in. (17 mm)
Valve guide installation temperature		176° F (80° C)

Valve springs:

Free-length		1.658 in. (42.1 mm)
Fitted length		1.484 in. (37.7 mm)
Fitted tension		58.4 lb f (26.3 kg f)
Tension limit		58.4 lb f (26.3 kg f)
Squareness limit		53.9 lb f (24.3 kg f)

Valve rocker shaft and rocker arm:

Rocker shaft outer diameter		0.6287 - 0.6295 in. (15.97 - 15.99 mm)
Valve rocker arm bush inner diameter		0.6300 - 0.6307 in. (16.00 - 16.02 mm)
Valve rocker bush to shaft clearance		0.0008 - 0.0016 in. (0.02 - 0.04 mm)

Valve clearances:	Cold (20° C/68° F)	Hot (80° C/176° F)
Inlet	0.007 in. (0.18 mm)	0.008 in. (0.20 mm)
Exhaust	0.012 in. (0.30 mm)	0.013 in. (0.33 mm)

Inlet and exhaust manifolds:

Maximum face warpage		0.006 in. (0.15 mm)

Oil pump:

Type		Trochoid
Tip clearance		0.0016 - 0.0063 in. (0.04 - 0.16 mm)
Tip clearance limit		0.010 in. (0.25 mm)
Side clearance		0.0012 - 0.0035 in. (0.03 - 0.09 mm)
Side clearance limit		0.006 in. (0.15 mm)
Body clearance		0.0034 - 0.0063 in. (0.10 - 0.16 mm)
Body clearance limit		0.010 in. (0.25 mm)
Relief valve operating pressure (at 2,000 rpm)		51.2 - 67.6 psi (3.6 - 4.4 kg/cm^2)
Relief valve operating pressure limit (at 2,000 rpm)		35.6 psi (3.5 kg/cm^2)
Relief valve spring fitted length		1.449 in. (36.8 mm)
Relief valve spring fitted tension		13.9 lb f (6.3 kg f)

Oil filter:

Relief valve operating pressure		11.4 - 17.1 psi (0.8 - 1.2 kg/cm^2)

Chapter 1/Part B: Engine TE models

Torque wrench settings:

	lb f ft	kg f m
Crankshaft bearing cap to cylinder block	52.0 - 63.5	7.2 - 8.8
Connecting rod cap to connecting rod	28.9 - 36.1	4.0 - 5.0
Camshaft thrust plate to cylinder block	7.2 - 11.6	1.0 - 1.6
Timing chain cover to cylinder block	7.2 - 11.6	1.0 - 1.6
Oil pump to cylinder block	12.3 - 18.8	1.7 - 2.6
Chain tensioner bolt to cylinder block	7.2 - 11.6	1.0 - 1.6
Crankshaft pulley to crankshaft	28.9 - 43.3	4.0 - 6.0
Cylinder head to cylinder block	52.0 - 63.5	7.2 - 8.8
Camshaft timing gear to camshaft	50.6 - 79.6	7.0 - 11.0
Valve rocker support to cylinder head	52.0 - 63.5	7.2 - 8.8
Manifold to cylinder head	7.2 - 11.6	1.0 - 1.6
Cylinder head cover to cylinder head	2.9 - 5.1	0.4 - 0.7
Oil sump to cylinder block	3.6 - 5.8	0.5 - 0.8
Oil sump drain plug	21.7 - 28.9	3.0 - 4.0
Spark plug	10.8 - 15.2	1.5 - 2.1
Flywheel to crankshaft	41.9 - 47.7	5.8 - 6.6
Clutch cover to flywheel	10.8 - 14.4	1.5 - 2.0
Clutch housing to cylinder block	34.7 - 49.1	4.8 - 6.8

1 General description

The engine fitted to Toyota Corolla TE models covered by this manual is of the four cylinder overhead valve type.

The cast cylinder block contains the four bores and acts as a rigid support for the five bearing crankshaft. The machined cylinder bores are surrounded by water jackets to dissipate heat and control the operating temperature.

A disposable type oil filter is located on the right-hand side of the cylinder block and supplies clean oil to the main gallery and various oilways. The main bearings are lubricated from oil holes drilled in the webs. The steel crankshaft is suitably drilled for directing lubricating oil from the main bearing journals to the big-end journals so ensuring full bearing lubrication.

To lubricate the connecting rod small-end, drillings are located in the big-ends of the connecting rods so that the oil is directed upwards.

Crankshaft endfloat is controlled by the centre main bearing which has thrust faces on the sides of the half shell inserts.

The camshaft is driven by a twin track timing chain from the forward end of the crankshaft. An automatic tensioner is fitted

The 'Y' design cylinder head is rigidly bolted to the cylinder block and is of the crossflow type with the inlet manifold on the right-hand side and exhaust manifold on the left-hand side. The cooling water outlet and thermostat are located at the top front face of the cylinder head.

Any references in the text to the left-hand side or right-hand side of the engine are applicable when sitting in the driver's seat.

2 Operations possible with engine in place

The following major operations can be carried out with the engine in place in the car.
1 Removal and replacement of camshaft.
2 Removal and replacement of cylinder head.
3 Removal and replacement of the engine mountings.
4 Removal of sump and pistons.
5 Removal of flywheel.

Fig 1.2 Longitudinal cross sectional view of TE engine

Chapter 1/Part B: Engine TE models

3 Major operations requiring engine removal

The following major operations must be carried out with the engine out of the car and on a bench or floor.
1 Removal and replacement of the main bearings.
2 Removal and replacement of the crankshaft.

4 Methods of engine removal

There are two methods of engine removal: complete with clutch and gearbox and without the gearbox. Both methods are described.

It is easier if a hydraulic trolley jack is used in conjunction with two axle stands, so that the car can be raised sufficiently to allow easy access underneath. Overhead lifting tackle will be necessary in both cases.

Note: Cars fitted with automatic transmission necessitating engine and transmission removal should have the transmission removed *first* as described in Chapter 6. The transmission even on its own is very heavy.

5 Engine - removal with gearbox

The sequence for removal of the TE engine and gearbox assembly is basically identical to that as described in Part A of this Chapter, Section 5. One or two minor differences may be found but provided the sequence described is followed and these differences noted no problems should arise.

6 Engine - removal less gearbox

See the previous Section (Section 5) and Part A of this Chapter, Section 6.

7 Dismantling the engine - general

1 Keen DIY mechanics who dismantle a lot of engines will probably have a stand on which to put them, but most will make do with a workbench, which should be large enough to spread around the inevitable bits and pieces and tools, and strong enough to support the engine weight. If the floor is the only work place available, try and ensure that the engine rests on a hardwood platform or similar rather than on concrete or beaten earth.
2 Spend sometime on cleaning the unit. If you have been wise this will have been done before the engine was removed, at a service bay. Good solvents such as 'Gunk' will help to float off caked dirt /grease under a water jet. Once the exterior is clean dismantling may begin. As parts are removed clean them in petrol/paraffin - clean them with a petrol soaked cloth and clean oilways with nylon pipe cleaners. If an air line is available use it for final cleaning off. Paraffin, which could possibly remain in oilways and would dilute the oil for initial lubrication after reassembly, must be blown out.
3 Always fit new gaskets and seals - but do not throw the old ones away until you have the new one to hand. A pattern is then available if they have to be made specially. Hang them up on a nail.
4 In general it is best to work from the top of the engine downwards. In all cases support the engine firmly so that it does not topple over when you are undoing stubborn nuts and bolts.
5 Always place nuts and bolts back with their components or place of attachment, if possible - it saves much confusion later. Otherwise put them in small, separate pots or jars so that their groups are easily identified.
6 If you have an area where parts can be laid out on sheets of paper, do so - putting the nuts and bolts with them. If you are able to look at all the components in this way it helps to avoid missing something on reassembly.
7 Even though you may be dismantling the engine only partly possibly with it still in the car - the priniciples still apply. It is appreciated that most people prefer to do engine repairs, if possible with the engine in position. Consequently an indication will be given as to what is necessary to lead up to carrying out repairs on a particular component. Generally speaking the engine is easy enough to get at as far as repairs and renewals of the ancillaries are concerned. When it comes to repair of the major engine components, however, it is only fair to say that repairs with the engine in position are more difficult than with it out.

8 Engine ancillaries - removal

1 If you are stripping the engine completely or preparing to install a reconditioned unit, all the ancillaries must be removed first. If you are going to obtain a reconditioned 'short' motor (block, crankshaft, pistons and connecting rods) then obviously the cylinder head and associated parts will need retention for fitting to the new engine. It is advisable to check just what you will get with a reconditioned unit as changes are made from time-to-time.
2 The removal of all those items connected with fuel, ignition and charging systems are detailed in the respective Chapters: for clarity they are listed here:
Distributor.
Carburettor (can be removed together with inlet manifold).
Alternator.
Fuel pump.
Water pump.
Starter motor.
Thermostat.

9 Engine mountings - removal and replacement

If the rubber insulator has softened because of oil contamination or failure of attachment, it will be necessary to fit a new mounting. Always cure the cause of the leak before fitting a new mounting.

Chock the rear wheels, apply the handbrake, jack up the front of the car and support on firmly based axle stands.

Front mountings
1 Undo and remove the two nuts, plain and spring washers at the top and bottom of the mounting.
2 Position a piece of wood on the saddle of a jack and locate under the engine sump.
3 Carefully jack-up the engine until the mounting can be withdrawn.
4 Refitting of the front mountings is the reverse sequence to removal. The securing nuts should only be tightened when the weight of the engine is on the mountings.

Rear mounting
1 Position a piece of wood on the saddle of a jack and locate under the gearbox assembly.
2 Carefully raise the jack until the weight of the gearbox assembly is supported by the jack.
3 Undo and remove the bolts and spring washers that secure the rear crossmember to the underside of the body.
4 Undo and remove the two bolts and spring washers that secure the rear mounting to the crossmember. Lift away the crossmember.
5 Undo and remove the bolts and spring washers that secure the rear mounting to the extension housing. Lift away the rear mounting.
6 Refitting is the reverse sequence to removal. The following additional points should be noted:
a) Make sure that the mounting is correctly positioned before securing.

b) The securing nuts and bolts should only be tightened when the weight of the gearbox is on the mountings.

10 Oil filter - removal and replacement

1 The oil filter is a throw away cartridge type which is changed regularly under service procedures.
2 To remove the filter grasp and turn in an anti-clockwise direction.
3 Smear the filter element seating ring with engine oil before refitting to prevent binding and removal difficulty later.
4 Screw on the filter and tighten hand tight only otherwise an oil leakage may occur. (photo)

11 Flywheel - removal, inspection and renovation

1 The flywheel is held to the rear of the crankshaft by six bolts. It can be removed with the engine in the car once the gearbox and clutch have been removed but is not recommended.
2 Bend back the lockwasher tabs and then using a socket undo and remove the bolts. (photo)
3 Pull the flywheel off squarely. It is important not to damage the mating surfaces. (photo)

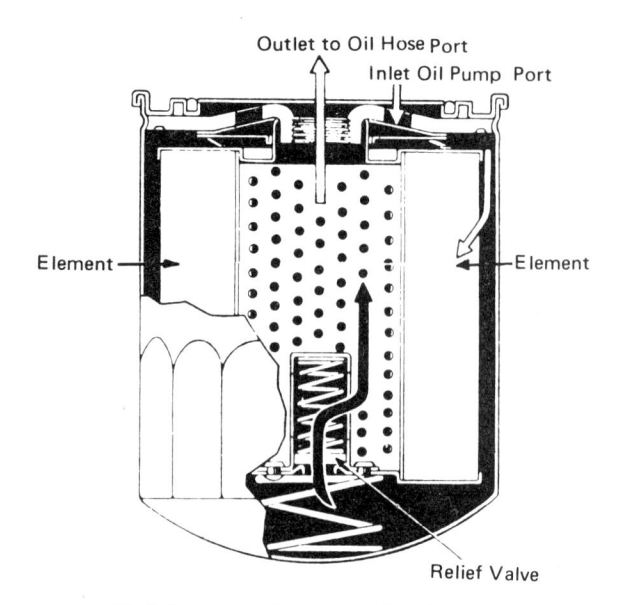

Fig 1.3 Cross sectional view of oil filter

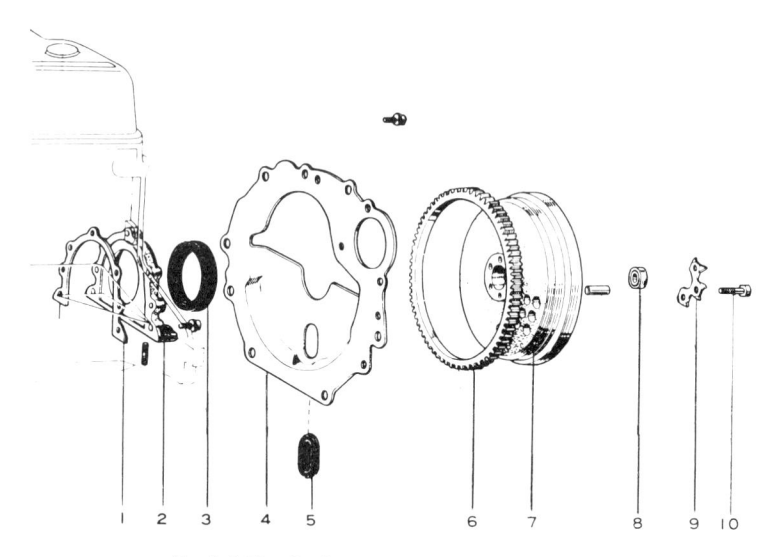

Fig. 1.4 Flywheel and backplate assembly

1 Gasket, oil seal retainer
2 Oil seal retainer
3 'T' type oil seal
4 Rear end plate
5 Hole plug (automatic transmission only)
6 Flywheel ring gear
7 Flywheel
8 Bearing
9 Lock plate
10 Bolt

10.4 Oil filter removal

11.2 Flywheel securing bolts removal

11.3 Flywheel ready for removal

Chapter 1/Part B: Engine TE models

4 The flywheel/clutch friction surface should be shiny and un-scored. Minor blemishes and scratches can be overlooked but deep grooves will probably cause clutch problems in time. Renewal may be advisable.

If the starter ring gear teeth are badly worn the ring can be removed by splitting it between two teeth with a chisel. Do not try to drive it off. If you have never fitted a new ring gear yourself it is best to have it done for you. It needs heating to a temperature of 200° C evenly in order to shrink - fit it on the flywheel. The champers on the ring gear teeth must face the same way in which the original ring gear was fitted otherwise the starter motor will not engage correctly.

12 Cylinder head removal - engine in car

1 Open the bonnet and using a soft pencil mark the outline of both the hinges at the bonnet to act as a datum for refitting.
2 With the help of a second person to take the weight of the bonnet undo and remove the hinge to bonnet securing bolts with plain and spring washers. There are two bolts to each hinge.
3 Lift away the bonnet and put in a safe place where it will not be scratched.
4 Refer to Chapter 10, and remove the battery.
5 Place a container of suitable capacity and drain the cooling system as described in Chapter 2.
6 Refer to Chapter 3, and remove the air cleaner assembly from the top of the carburettor.
7 Mark the HT leads so that they may be refitted in their original positions and detach from the spark plugs.
8 Spring back the clips securing the distributor cap to the distributor body. Lift off the distributor cap.
9 Detach the HT lead from the centre of the ignition coil. Remove the distributor cap from the engine compartment.
10 Refer to Chapter 3, and remove the carburettor and torque rod. Recover the gasket.
11 Disconnect the hoses from the inlet manifold and then undo and remove the securing nuts and washers.
12 Lift away the inlet manifold and recover the manifold gasket.
13 Disconnect the exhaust downpipe from the exhaust manifold.
14 Undo and remove the nuts and bolts securing the exhaust manifold to the cylinder head. Lift away the exhaust manifold and recover the manifold gasket.
15 Detach the thermal transmitter electric cable from the side of the thermostat housing.
16 Detach the radiator top hose from the water outlet elbow

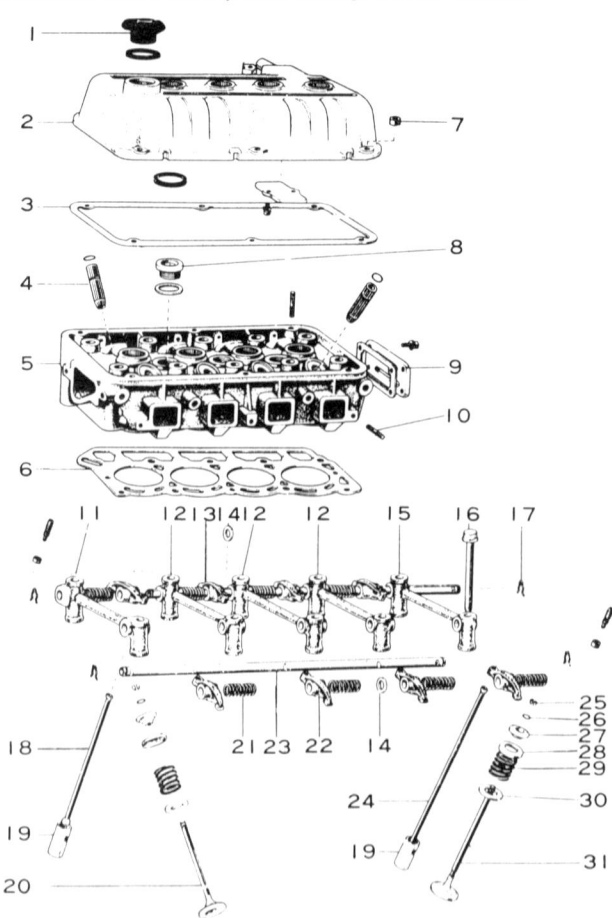

Fig 1.5 Cylinder head removal - engine in car

Fig 1.6 Cylinder head component parts

1 Cap, oil filter
2 Cover, cylinder head
3 Gasket
4 Bush
5 Cylinder head
6 Cylinder head gasket
7 Nut
8 Plug
9 Plate
10 Stud/bolt
11 Valve rocker support no 1
12 Valve rocker support no 3
13 Valve rocker arm no 1
14 Washer
15 Valve rocker support no 2
16 Bolt
17 Spring, retainer
18 Pushrod no 1
19 Valve lifter
20 Inlet valve
21 Spring
22 Valve rocker arm no 2
23 Valve rocker shaft
24 Pushrod no 2
25 Lock
26 'O' ring
27 Spring retainer
28 Shield
29 Spring
30 Plate washer
31 Exhaust valve

and radiator top tank.
17 Disconnect the two heater hoses and also the hose between the water pump and water outlet elbow.
18 Detach the clutch flexible hose bracket at the cylinder head.
19 Undo and remove the six nuts and washers securing the cylinder head cover. Lift away the cover.
20 Undo and remove the bolts securing the rocker shaft assembly. This must be done in a progressive and diagonal manner so as not to strain the rocker shaft assembly or cylinder head.
21 Withdraw the pushrods and place in a piece of card so that they may be refitted in their original positions.
22 Check that all cylinder head attachments have been released and then lift away the cylinder head. If the head is stuck, try to rock it to brake the seal. Under no circumstances try to prise it apart from the cylinder block with a screwdriver or cold chisel. as damage may be done to the faces of the cylinder head and block. If the head will not readily free, turn the engine over by the flywheel using the starter motor, as the compression in the cylinders will often break the cylinder headjoint. If this fails to work, strike the head sharply with a plastic headed or wooden hammer, or with a metal hammer with an interposed piece of wood to cushion the blow.
Under no circumstances hit the head directly with a metal hammer as this may cause the casting to fracture. Several sharp taps with the hammer, at the same time pulling upwards, should free the head. Lift the head off and place to one side.
23 Remove the cylinder head gasket. This must not be reused when refitting the cylinder head.

Fig 1.8 Valve and spring assembly

13 Cylinder head removal - engine on bench

The procedure for removing the cylinder head with the engine on the bench is similar to that for removal when the engine is in the car, with the exception of disconnecting the controls and services. For full information refer to Section 12.

14 Valve - removal

1 The valves can be removed from the cylinder head by the

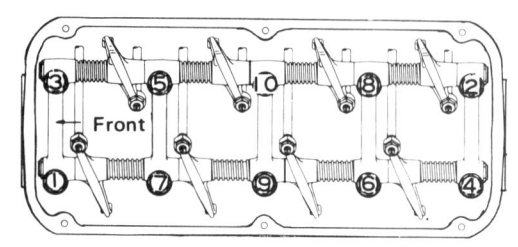

Fig 1.7 Cylinder head securing bolt removal sequence

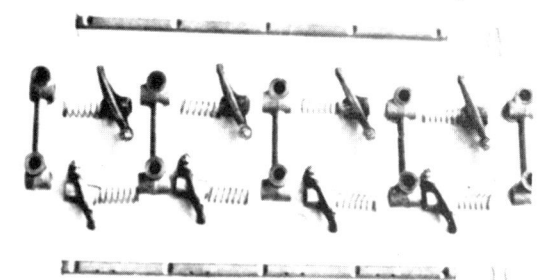

Fig 1.9 Rocker and rocker shaft components

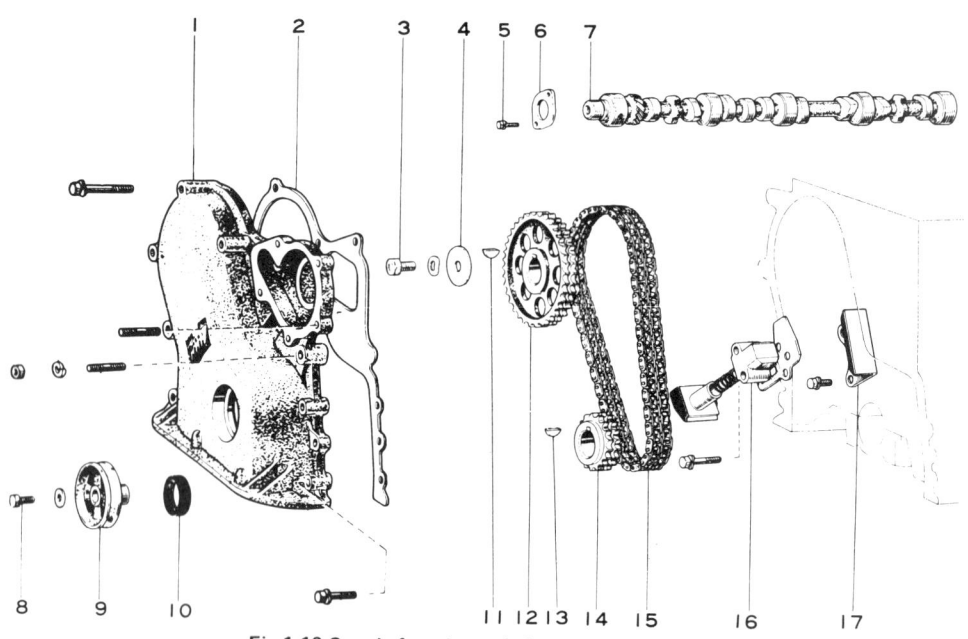

Fig 1.10 Camshaft and camshaft drive assembly

1	Timing chain cover	5	Bolt	10	'T' type oil seal	14	Gear - crankshaft
2	Gasket	6	Plate	11	Woodruff key	15	Chain sub-assembly
3	Bolt	7	Camshaft	12	Gear - camshaft	16	Tensioner
4	Plate washer	8	Bolt	13	Woodruff key	17	Damper
		9	Crankshaft pulley				

Chapter 1/Part B: Engine TE models

following method. Compress each spring in turn with a valve spring compressor until the two halves of the collets can be removed.
2 Release the compressor and remove the collets, 'O' ring, retainer, shield, spring, plate washer and valve.
3 If, when the valve spring compressor is screwed down, the valve spring retainer refuses to free to expose the split collet, do not continue to screw down on the compressor as there is a likelihood of damaging it.
4 Gently tap the top of the tool directly over the cap with a light hammer. This will free the cap. To avoid the compressor jumping off the valve spring retaining cap when it is tapped, hold the compressor firmly in position with one hand.
5 It is essential that the valves are kept in their correct sequence unless they are so badly worn that they are to be renewed. If they are going to be kept and used again, place them in a sheet of card having eight holes numbered 1 to 8 corresponding with the relative position the valves were in when fitted. Also keep the valve components in the correct order.

15 Dismantling the rocker assembly

1 Pull out the spring retainers from the ends of the shaft and slide off the supports, rockers, springs and washers noting in order they are fitted.
2 If necessary unscrew the plug screws from the ends of the rocker shafts.

16 Timing cover, gearwheels and chain - removal

1 Open the bonnet and referring to Chapter 12 remove the radiator grille.
2 Undo and remove the bolts securing the front crossmember to the body.
3 Move the crossmember to one side.
4 Undo and remove the bolt securing the lower half of the centre crossmember support. Lift away the support.
5 Refer to Chapter 2, and remove the radiator and water pump.
6 Using a large socket undo and remove the crankshaft pulley securing bolt and washer.
7 The crankshaft pulley must next be removed. If it is an easy fit on the crankshaft it may be prised off using two screwdrivers. If tight however, a universal puller must be used. Take care not to damage the pulley.
8 Undo and remove the bolts and washers securing the sump to the underside of the cylinder block.
9 It may be necessary to remove the engine undercover and right-hand stiffener plate before the sump can be completely removed.
10 Undo and remove the bolts, nuts and washers securing the timing chain cover. Lift away the cover.
11 Check the chain for wear by measuring how much the tensioner head has extended. If more than 0.532 in (13.5 mm) the chain must be renewed.
12 Undo and remove the two bolts and spring washers securing the tensioner to the front face of the cylinder block. Lift away the tensioner. Also remove No 1 chain vibration damper.
13 To remove the camshaft and crankshaft timing wheels complete with chain first undo and remove the bolt and washers securing the gear to the camshaft.
14 Ease each wheel forward a little at a time levering behind each gear wheel in turn with two large screwdriver at 180° to each other. If the gear wheels are locked solid it will then be necessary to use a proper gearwheel and pulley extractor, and if one is available this should be used anyway in preference to screwdrivers.
15 With both gearwheels safely off remove the woodruff key from the crankshaft with a pair of pliers and place it in a jam jar for safe keeping.

17 Sump - removal

The sump can be removed with the engine in or out of the car. If out of the car it is only necessary to follow the instructions in paragraph 4. If the engine is in the car the following additional instructions apply.
1 Place a suitable container under the sump drain plug. Remove the drain plug and allow the oil to drain out. Refit the drain plug.
2 Undo and remove the screws securing the engine undercover. Lift away the undercover. This is only applicable when an undercover is fitted.
3 Remove the right-hand stiffener plate.
4 Undo and remove the sump bolts and remove the sump from under the car. Recover the old gasket.

18 Oil pump - removal

1 Refer to Section 17 and remove the sump.
2 Undo and remove the bolt and washer securing the pump to the underside of the cylinder block.
3 Carefully draw the oil pump assembly from the underside of the cylinder block. If it is very tight remove the distributor (Chapter 4) and tap it out from the distributor side.

19 Camshaft - removal

1 The camshaft may be removed with the engine either in or out of the car.
2 Refer to Section 16 and remove the timing cover, gearwheels

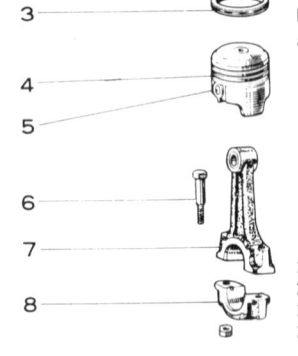

Fig 1.11 Piston, connecting rod and crankshaft assemblies

1 No 1 compression ring
2 No 2 compression ring
3 Oil ring
4 Piston
5 Piston gudgeon pin
6 Bolt
7 Connecting rod
8 End cap
9 Bearing
10 Gasket
11 Sump
12 Plug
13 Bolt

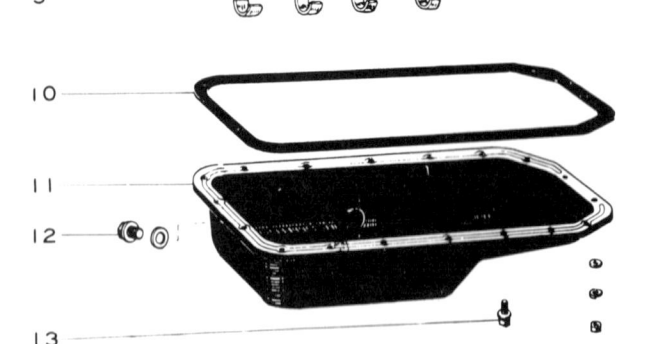

and chain.
3 Refer to Chapter 3 and remove the fuel pump.
4 Refer to Chapter 4 and remove the distributor.
5 Refer to Section 12 or 13 and remove the cylinder head.
6 Place a jack under the gearbox and remove the crossmember. Lower the jack slightly so as to raise the front of the engine.
7 Undo and remove the two bolts and spring washers securing the camshaft thrust plate to the front of the cylinder block.
8 Carefully remove the cam followers (tappets) and keep in the sequence as removed for correct replacement.
9 The camshaft may now be withdrawn from the cylinder block. Take great care that the cam lobe peaks do not damage the camshaft bearings as the shaft is pulled forward.

20 Tappets - removal

1 Remove the cylinder head as described in Section 12 or 13.
2 Using a piece of tapered wood draw out the tappets. Keep in the sequence as removed for correct replacement.

21 Timing chain tensioner - removal

1 Refer to Section 16 and remove the timing cover as described in paragraphs 1 to 7 and 10.
2 Undo and remove the two bolts and spring washers securing the tensioner to the front face of the cylinder block. Lift away the tensioner.

22 Piston, connecting rod and big-end bearing - removal

1 The pistons and connecting rods can be removed with the engine still in the car or with the engine on the bench.
2 With the cylinder head and sump removed undo the big-end securing nuts.
3 The connecting rods and pistons are lifted out from the top of the cylinder block, after the carbon or 'wear' ring at the top of the bore has been scraped away.
4 Remove the big-end caps one at a time, taking care to keep them in the right order and the correct way round. Also ensure that the shell bearings are kept with their correct connecting rods and caps unless they are to be renewed. Normally the numbers 1 to 4 are stamped on adjacent sides of the big-end caps and connecting rods, indicating which cap fits on which rod and which way round the cap fits. If no numbers or lines can be found then with a sharp screwdriver or file, scratch mating marks across the joint from the rod to the cap. One line for connecting rod No 1, two for connecting rod No 2 and so on. This will ensure there is no confusion later as it is most important that the caps go back in the correct position on the connecting rods from which they were removed.
5 If the big-end caps are difficult to remove they may be tapped gently with a soft hammer.
6 To remove the shell bearings, press the bearing opposite the groove in both the connecting rod, and the connecting rod caps and the bearings will slide out easily.
7 Withdraw the pistons and connecting rods upwards and ensure they are kept in the correct order for replacement in the same bore. Refit the connecting rod caps and bearings to the rods if the bearings do not require renewal, to minimise the risk of getting the caps and rods muddled.

23 Gudgeon pin - removal

The gudgeon pins need removal if the pistons are being renewed. New pistons are supplied with new pins for fitting to the existing connecting rods. The gudgeon pin is semi floating - that is it is a tight shrink fit with the connecting rod and a moving fit in the piston. To press it out requires considerable force and under usual circumstances a proper press and special tools are essential. Otherwise piston damage will occur.

If damage to the pistons does not matter, then the pins may be pressed out using suitable diameter pieces of rod and tube between the jaws of a vice. However, this is not recommended as the connecting rod might be damaged also. It is recommended that gudgeon pins and pistons are removed from, and refitted to, connecting rods, by Toyota dealers with the necessary facilities.

24 Piston rings - removal

1 Remove the pistons from the engine.
2 The rings come off over the top of the piston. Starting with the top one, lift one end of the ring out of the groove and gradually ease it out all the way round. With the second and third rings an old feeler blade is useful for sliding them over the other grooves. However, as rings are only normally removed if they are going to be renewed it should not matter if breakages occur.

25 Crankshaft rear oil seal - removal

It is possible to remove the crankshaft rear oil seal with the engine in or out of the car.
1 Refer to Chapter 6, and remove the gearbox.
2 Refer to Chapter 5, and remove the clutch assembly.
3 Refer to Section 11, and remove the flywheel.
4 Undo and remove the bolts that locate the rear endplate on the end of the cylinder block. Lift away the endplate.
5 Undo and remove the bolts and spring washers that secure the oil seal retainer to the end of the cylinder block. Lift away the oil seal retainer;
6 The oil seal may now be drifted out using a tube of suitable diameter or a tapered soft metal drift. Take great care not to damage the casting.

26 Main bearings and crankshaft - removal

1 The engine should be taken from the car and the sump, cylinder head, timing gears and piston assemblies removed.
2 With a good quality socket undo and remove the ten bolts holding the five main bearing caps in position.
3 Make sure that caps are marked for identification and lift out the caps. If they should be tight, tap the sides gently with a piece of wood or soft mallet to dislodge them.
4 Lift out the crankshaft.
5 Slide out the bearing shells from the caps and from the crankshaft seats. Note the centre main bearing also incorporates the thrust washers.

27 Lubrication and crankcase ventilation system - description

1 A general description of the oil system is given in Section 1 of this Chapter.
2 The oil pump is of the eccentric bi-rotor type.
3 The oil is drawn through a gauze screen and tube which is below the oil level in the well of the sump. It is then pumped via the full flow filter to the system of oil galleries in the block. The oil filter is mounted externally on the right-hand side of the block.
4 The crankcase is positively ventilated. The amount of blow-by gas produced in an engine is usually greatest when the engine load is high and the inlet manifold vacuum is low. When the load is lighter a correspondingly smaller amount of blow-by gas is created.
5 At engine idle speed a ventilation valve is drawn towards the inlet manifold so that the gas passage area in the valve becomes smaller and less blow-by gas is led into the inlet manifold.
6 When the car is at cruising speed and under light load the inlet manifold blow-by gas will be higher than that given in

Chapter 1/Part B: Engine TE models

paragraph 5 and the valve will be in the same position as that for idling. When the load increases and the amount of blow-by gas increases the gas passage area in the valve is increased allowing more blow-by gas to be passed to the inlet manifold.

7 Under accelerating and heavy load conditions when there are greatest blow-by gas conditions a certain amount is drawn into the inlet manifold and if needs be the remainder is passed into the air cleaner. Because the crankcase internal pressure is lower than atmospheric pressure at all times no blow-by gases will be released direct to the atmosphere.

28 Ventilation valve - inspection

1 The ventilation valve is located on the side of the inlet manifold below the carburettor. Check that the hoses are in good order and the clips are tight. Renew the hoses and/or clips as necessary. (photo)

2 Start the engine and whilst idling pinch the hose several times. If the valve can be heard to strike against its seat the valve is operating correctly.

3 Should engine performance be poor especially at idle speed, check the operation of the ventilation valve before commencing a complete engine tune exercise.

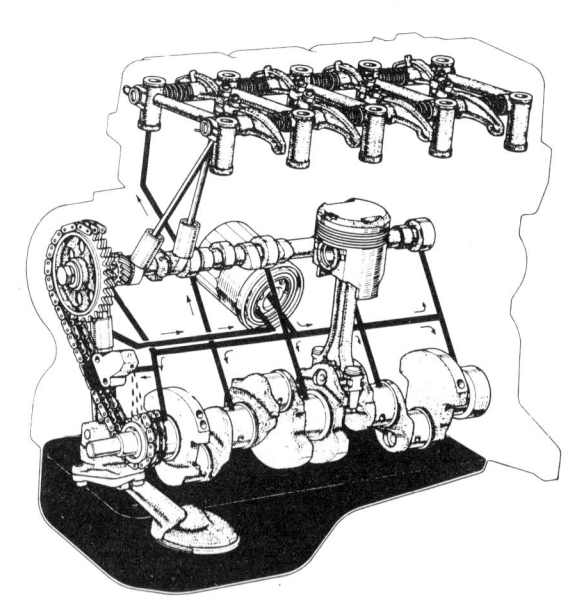

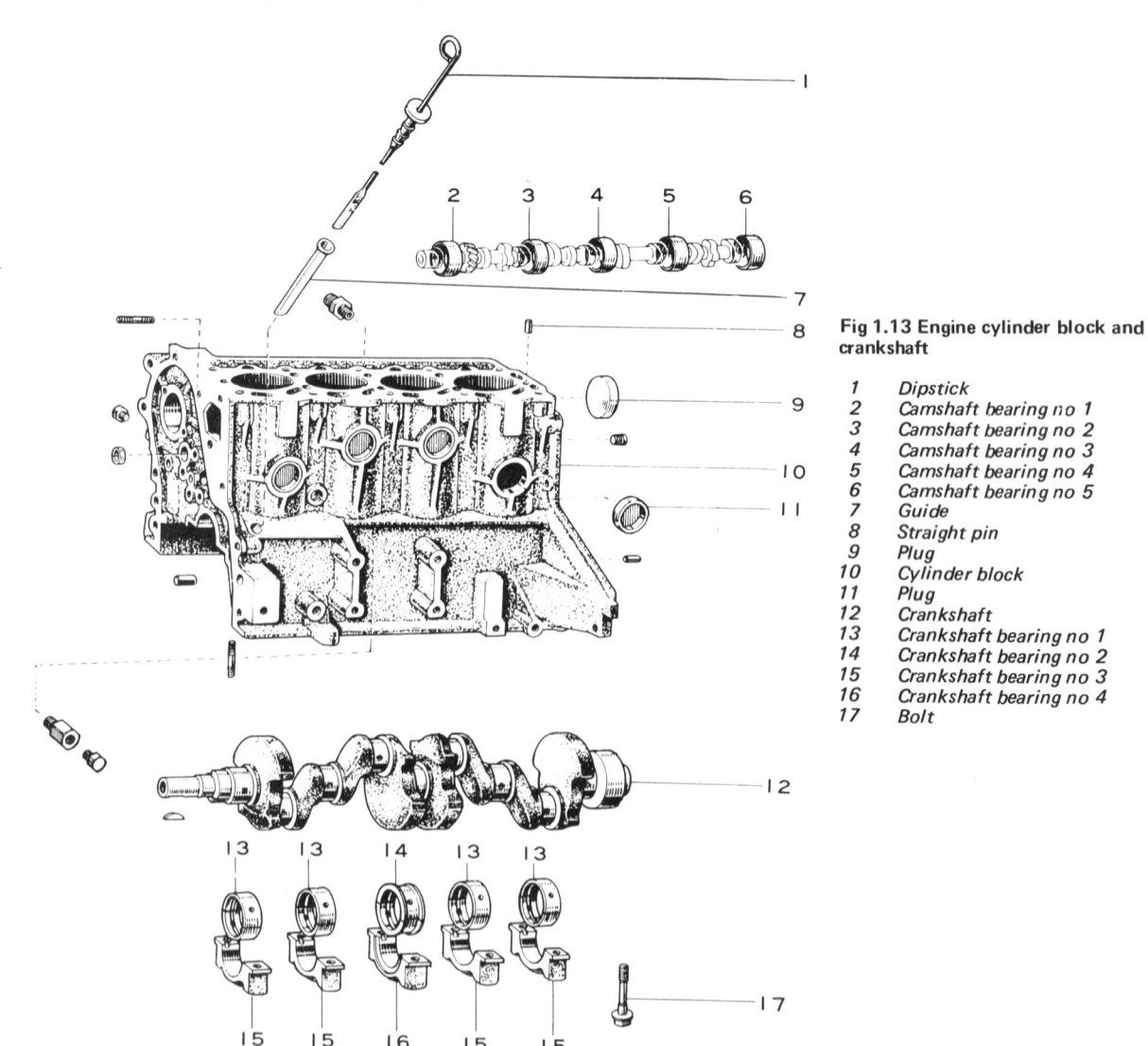

Fig 1.12 Engine lubrication system

Fig 1.13 Engine cylinder block and crankshaft

1 Dipstick
2 Camshaft bearing no 1
3 Camshaft bearing no 2
4 Camshaft bearing no 3
5 Camshaft bearing no 4
6 Camshaft bearing no 5
7 Guide
8 Straight pin
9 Plug
10 Cylinder block
11 Plug
12 Crankshaft
13 Crankshaft bearing no 1
14 Crankshaft bearing no 2
15 Crankshaft bearing no 3
16 Crankshaft bearing no 4
17 Bolt

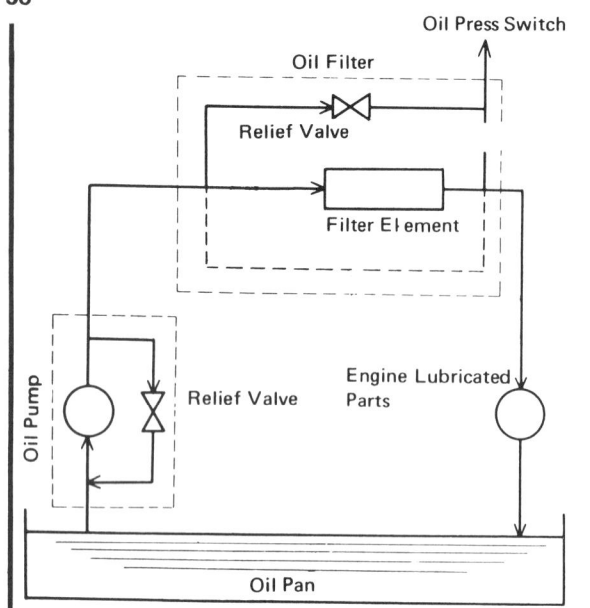

Fig 1.14 Oil filter circuit

28.1 Ventilation valve

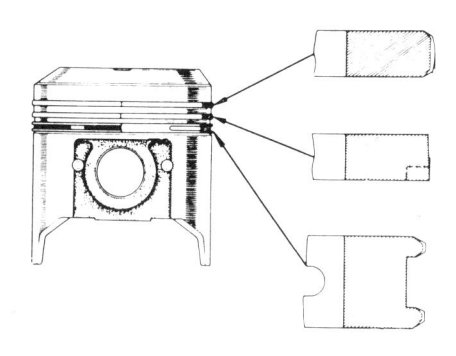

Fig 1.15 Oil pump component parts

1 Oil pump body
2 Rotor set
3 Cover assembly
4 Relief valve
5 Spring
6 Gasket
7 Plug

Fig 1.17 Standard piston rings

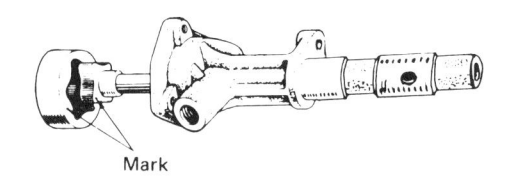

Fig 1.18 Oil pump rotor mating marks

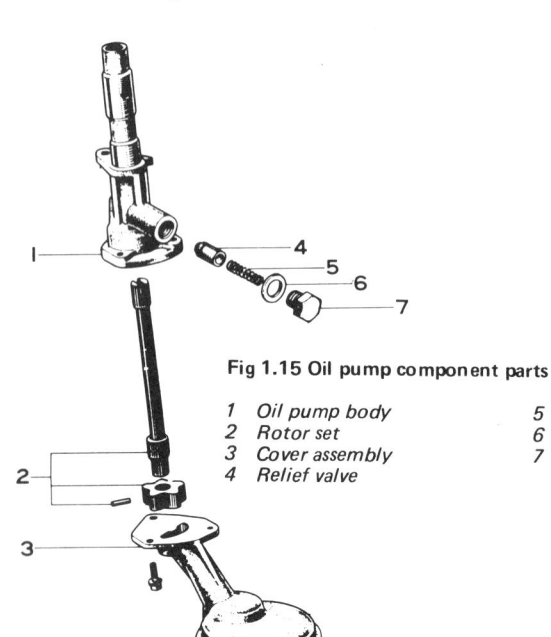

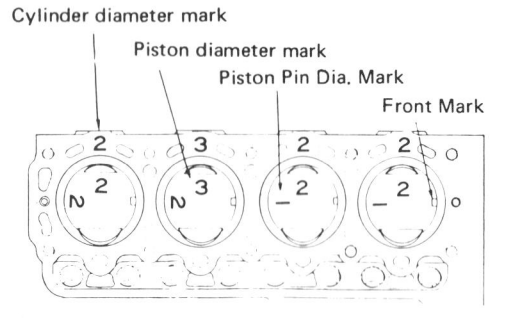

Fig 1.16 Piston and cylinder identification marks

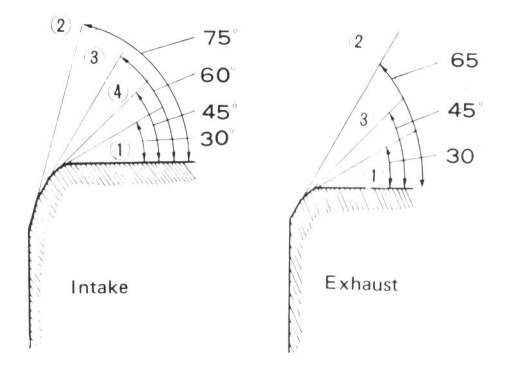

Fig 1.19 Valve seat correction angles

Chapter 1/Part B: Engine TE models

29 Engine components - examination for wear and renovation

The sequence for inspection of all internal engine components is basically identical for all types of engine. Full information will be found in Part 1 of this Chapter, Sections 26 to 39 inclusive.

30 Engine reassembly - general

1 All components of the engine must be cleaned of oil sludge and old gaskets and the working area should also be clear and clean. In addition to the normal range of good quality socket spanners and general tools which are essential, the following must be available before reassembly begins:
1 Complete set of new gaskets.
2 Supply of clean rags.
3 Oil can full of clean engine oil.
4 Torque wrench.
5 All spare parts as necessary.

31 Crankshaft - replacement

Ensure the crankcase is thoroughly clean and that all the oilways are clear. A thin drill is useful for cleaning them out. If possible, blow them out with compressed air. Treat the crankshaft in the same fashion and then inject engine oil into the crankshaft oilways.
Commence work on rebuilding the engine by replacing the crankshaft and main bearings.
1 Place the main bearing shells by fitting the five upper halves of the main bearing shells to their location in the crankcase, after wiping the location clean. The centre bearing is the location for the thrust washers.
2 Note that on the back of each bearing is a tab which engages in locating grooves in either the crankcase or the main bearing cap housing. (photo)
3 New bearings are coated with protective grease; carefully clean away all traces of this with paraffin.
4 With the five upper bearing shells securely in place, wipe the lower bearing cap housings and fit the five lower shell bearings to their caps.
5 Smear a little grease onto the sides of the centre main bearing location and fit the two half thrust washers. The grooves must face outwards. (photo)
6 Smear a little grease onto the sides of the centre main bearing cap and fit the second pair of half thrust washers. The grooves must face outwards and the tags be located in the slots in the cap. (photo)
7 Generously lubricate the crankshaft journals and the upper and lower main bearing shells and carefully lower the crankshaft into position. Make sure it is the right way round. (photo)
8 Fit the main bearing caps in position making sure they are correctly located as indicated by the identification marks noted or made during dismantling. The arrows must also face forwards. (photo)
9 Replace the bearing cap bolts and tighten in the order 3 2 4 1 and 5 in a progressive manner to a final torque wrench setting of 52.1 - 63.7 lb f ft (7.20 - 8.80 Kg fm). (photo)
10 Test the crankshaft to ensure that it rotates freely. Should it be very stiff to turn, or passes high spots, a most careful inspection must be made, preferably by a skilled mechanic with a micrometer to trace the cause of the trouble. It is seldom that any trouble of this nature will be experienced when fitting the crankshaft.
11 The endfloat of the crankshaft may next be checked. Using a screwdriver as a lever at one of the crankshaft webs and main bearing caps. Move the crankshaft longitudually as far as possible in one direction. Measure the gap between the side of the journal and the centre bearing thrustwasher. The thrust clearance should be 0.0028 - 0.0071 in. (0.07 - 0.18 mm). (Fig 1.20)

31.2 Refitting main bearing shell

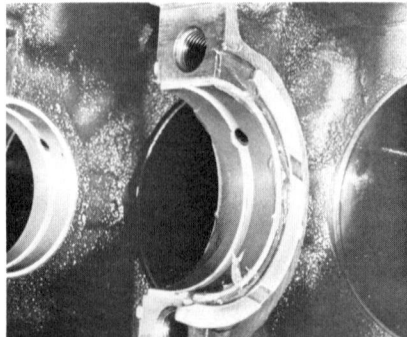

31.5 Centre main bearing with thrust washers retained with grease

31.6 Centre main bearing cap

31.7 Refitting crankshaft

31.8 Refitting crankshaft main bearing cap

31.9 Tightening main bearing cap securing bolts

Fig 1.20 Measurement of crankshaft endfloat

Fig 1.21 Piston and connecting rod mating marks

32.2a Piston identification notch

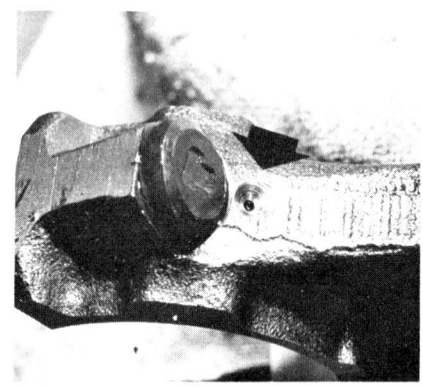

32.2b Connecting rod 'jet' hole

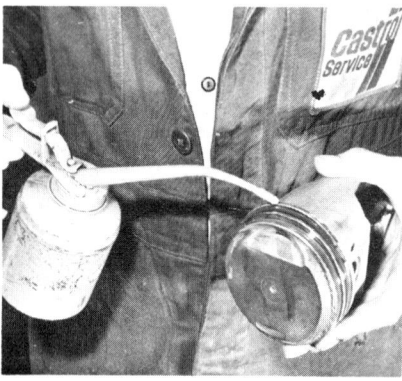

34.4 Lubricating piston rings

34.6 Refitting piston into bore

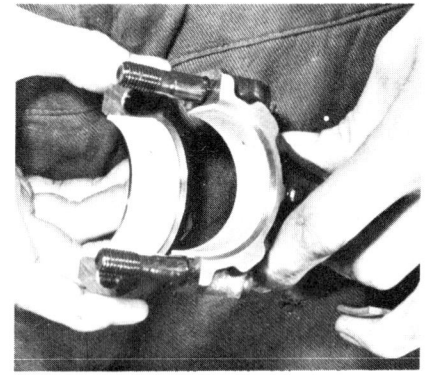

35.1 Big end bearing shells correctly fitted

35.4 Fitting big end cap to connecting rod

35.5 Tightening big end bolts

36.1 Inserting valve into guide

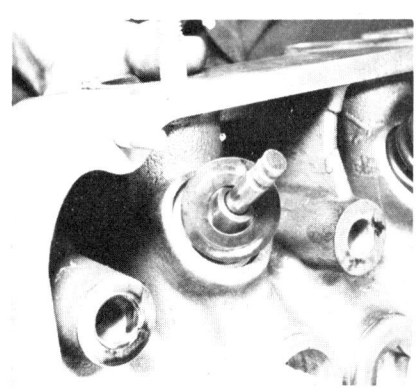

36.2 Plate washer fitted over valve stem

32 Piston and connecting rods - reassembly

1 If the same pistons are being used, then they must be mated to the same connecting rod with the same gudgeon pin. If new pistons are being fitted it does not matter with which connecting rods they are used, but the gudgeon pin must be kept matched to its piston.
2 Upon reference to Section 23 it will be seen that special equipment, including a large press is required to fit the piston to the connecting rod. This is a job for the local Toyota dealer. The notch in the piston crown must face forwards to the engine when fitted and the jet hole in the connecting rod must face to the right-hand side of the engine. (photos)
3 Make sure that the piston pivots freely on the gudgeon pin and it is free to slide sideways. Should stiffness exist, wash the assembly in paraffin, lubricate the gudgeon pin with Achesons Colloid 'Oildag' and recheck. Again, if stiffness exists, the assembly must be dismantled and rechecked for signs of ingrained dirt and possible damage.

33 Piston ring - replacement

1 Check the piston ring grooves and oilways are thoroughly clean and not blocked. Piston rings must always be fitted over the head of the piston and never from the bottom.
2 The easiest method to use when fitting rings is to wrap a long 0.020 inch feeler gauge round the top of the piston and place the rings, one at a time, starting with the bottom oil control ring.
3 Where a three-part oil control ring is to be fitted, fit the bottom rail of the oil control ring to the piston and position it below the bottom groove. Refit the oil control expander into the bottom groove and move the bottom oil control ring rail up into the bottom groove. Fit the top oil control rail into the bottom groove.
4 Ensure that the ends of the expander are butting, but not overlapping. Set the gaps of the rails and expander at 120° to each other.
5 Where a one-piece oil control ring is used fit this to the bottom groove. It can be fitted either way up.
6 Replace the lower and upper compression rings making sure that they are fitted the correct way up as marked on the top face.
7 Measure the ring to groove gap and the end gap to ensure they are within specification.

34 Piston - replacement

The pistons complete with connecting rods, can be fitted to the cylinder bores in the following sequence.

1 With a wad of clean non-fluffy rag wipe the cylinder bores clean.
2 The pistons, complete with connecting rods, are fitted to their bores from above.
3 Set the piston ring gaps so that the gaps are equidistant around the circumference of the piston.
4 Well lubricate the top of the piston and fit a ring compressor or a jubilee clip of suitable diameter and shim steel. (photo)
5 As each piston is inserted into its bore ensure that it is the correct piston/connecting rod assembly for that particular bore; that the connecting rod is the right way round, and that the front of the piston is towards the front of the bore. Lubricate the bore and piston well with engine oil.
6 The piston will slide into the bore only as far as the ring compressor. Gently tap the piston into the bore with a wooden or plastic hammer. (photo)

35 Connecting rod to crankshaft - refitting

1 Wipe clean the connecting rod and big-end bearing cap and underside of the shell bearing and fit the shell bearing in position with the locating tongue engaged with the corresponding groove in the connecting rod or end cap. (photo)
2 Never re-use old bearing shells.
3 Generously lubricate the crankpin journals with engine oil and turn the crankshaft so that the crankpin is in the most advantageous position for the connecting rod to be drawn onto it.
4 Generously lubricate the shell bearing and offer up the connecting rod cap to the connecting rod. (photo)
5 Check that the big-end bolts are correctly located and then refit the cap retaining nuts. These should be tightened to a torque wrench setting of 28.9-36.2 lb f ft (4.0-5.0 Kg fm) - (photo)
6 Repeat the above described procedure for the three remaining piston/connecting rod assemblies.

36 Valve and valve spring - reassembly

To refit the valves and valve springs to the cylinder head, proceed as follows:
1 Rest the cylinder head on its side and insert each valve into its own guide. (photo)
2 Fit the plate washer over the valve stem. (photo)
3 Next fit the valve spring and valve spring shield over the valve stem. (photo)
4 Place the valve spring retainer over the shield then compress the valve spring. (photo)
5 Slip the two split collets into position and release the spring compressor. Refit the 'O' ring oil seal. (photo)

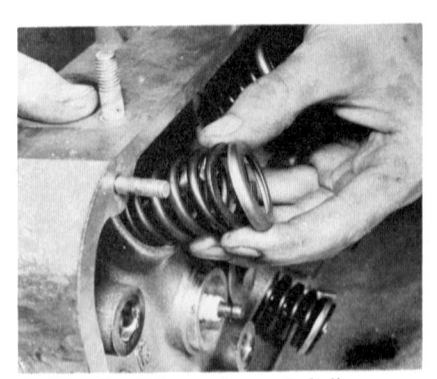

36.3 Fitting valve spring and shell

36.4 Valve spring compressed

36.5 Split collets and 'O' ring in position

Fig 1.22 Valve and attachments removed from cylinder head

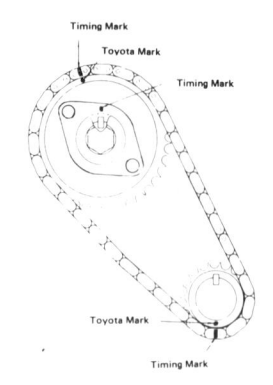

Fig 1.23 Timing chain and sprocket alignment marks

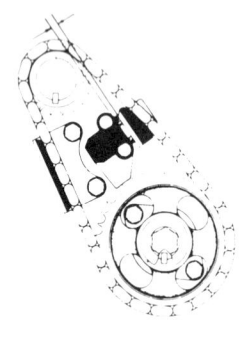

Fig 1.24 Measurement of timing chain deflection

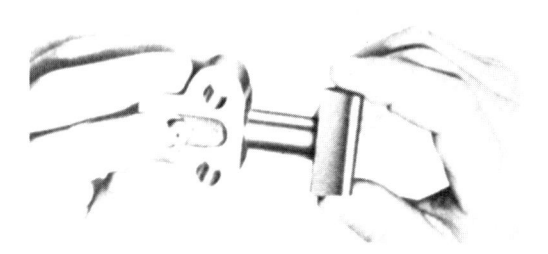

Fig 1.25 Assembling timing chain tensioner

37.2 Refitting oil seal retainer

38.2 Fitting camshaft onto bearings

38.3 Refitting camshaft thrust plate

38.7 Timing chain and sprockets correctly fitted

38.9 Timing chain tensioner fitted

38.10 Timing chain damper fitted

37 Crankshaft rear oil seal and retainer - replacement

1 With a new seal fitted to the retainer (Section 25) wipe the mating faces of the retainer and cylinder block.
2 Fit a new gasket over the dowels on the cylinder block and carefully refit the retainer. Lubricate the crankshaft boss to provide lubrication when the engine is initially started after overhaul. (photo)
3 Secure the retainer with the bolts and spring washers, tightening in a progressive and diagonal manner.

38 Camshaft, timing chain and gears, and front cover replacement

1 Wipe the camshaft journals and bearings with a clean non-fluffy rag and then lubricate with engine oil.
2 Carefully insert the camshaft into the camshaft bearings making sure the sharp lobes do not damage the bearing surfaces. (photo)
3 Refit the camshaft thrustplate and secure with the two bolts and spring washers. (photo)
4 Fit the woodruff key to the crankshaft nose and then with a tubular drift of suitable diameter partially drive the crankshaft sprocket onto the crankshaft until the sprocket is over the first keyway in the crankshaft. Make sure that the timing mark on the sprocket is facing outwards.
5 Line up the keyways as shown in Fig 1.23 and place the timing chain onto the crankshaft sprockets lining up the bright link in the chain with the sprocket timing mark.
6 Fit the camshaft sprocket onto the chain lining up the timing mark with the second bright link in the chain.
7 Carefully fit the camshaft sprocket onto the camshaft and then drift the two sprockets into their final position. (photo)
8 Refit the camshaft sprocket securing bolts and washer and fully tighten to a torque wrench setting of 28.9-36.2 lb f ft (4.00-5.00 Kg fm).
9 Fill the timing chain tensioner with engine oil and refit the timing chain tensioner. Secure in position with the two bolts and spring washers. Make sure the slipper head is the correct way round. (photo)
10 Refit the timing chain damper and secure with the two bolts and spring washers. (photo)
11 It is always advisable to renew the timing cover oil seal during engine overhaul. The old seal may be tapped out using s screwdriver or chisel and hammer. Make a note which way round the seal is fitted.
12 Fit a new seal, tapping into position with a suitable diameter tube. Lubricate the seal lip.
13 Wipe the mating faces of the timing cover and cylinder block and fit a new gasket.
14 Fit the timing cover over the dowels and tap fully home. (photo)
15 Secure the timing cover with the bolts and spring washers which should be tightened in a progressive and diagonal manner.

39 Oil pump and sump - replacement

1 Wipe the mating faces of the oil pump and underside of the cylinder block. Fit a new gasket (if originally fitted).
2 Carefully insert the oil pump shaft and body and secure in position with the bolt and spring washer. (photo)
3 Wipe the mating faces of the sump and underside of the cylinder block and fit a new gasket. Apply a liquid sealer to the points shown in Fig 1.26
4 Position the sump on the studs and refit the securing nuts, bolts and spring washers. Tighten the bolts and nuts to a torque wrench setting of 3.6 - 5.8 lb f ft (0.5 - 0.8 Kg fm) - (photo)
5 Refit the stabiliser brackets and tighten the securing bolts and washers to a torque wrench setting of 21.7-32.6 lb f ft (3.0 - 4.5 Kg fm) - (photo)

38.14 Refitting front cover

39.2 Refitting oil pump

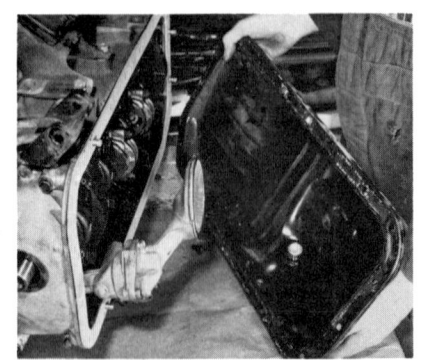

39.4 Refitting oil sump

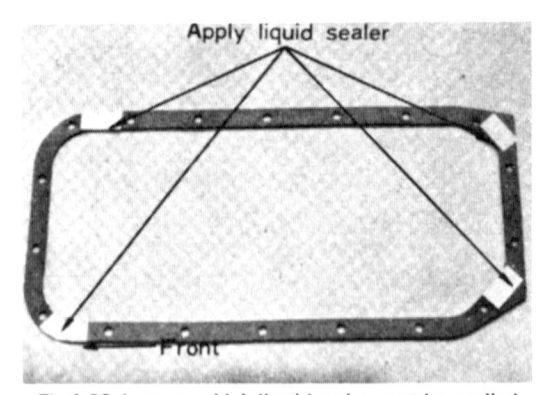

Fig 1.26 Areas to which liquid sealer must be applied

39.5 Refitting stabiliser bracket

40 Engine backplate - replacement

1 Wipe the mating faces of the engine backplate and carefully fit into position over the dowels. (photo)
2 Secure the backplate in position with the one bolt and spring washer. (photo)

41 Rocker arms and shafts - reassembly

Reassembly of the rocker arm assemblies is the reverse sequence to dismantling. The location of the various parts is shown in Fig 1.9. Lubricate the rocker bushes before sliding onto the shafts with clean engine oil.

42 Cylinder head - replacement

1 After checking that both the cylinder block and cylinder head mating faces are perfectly clean generously lubricate each cylinder bore with engine oil.
2 Insert the tappets into their respective positions as was noted during removal. (photo)
3 Always use a new cylinder head gasket as the old one will be compressed and not capable of giving a good seal.
4 Never smear grease on either side of a gasket, for, when the engine heats up, the grease will melt and could allow pressure leaks to develop.
5 Carefully lower the new cylinder head gasket into position. It is not possible to fit it the wrong way round. (photo) It is accurately located by dowels.
6 With the gasket in position carefully lower the cylinder head onto the cylinder block. (photo)
7 Insert the pushrods into the cylinder head and locate the ends in the tappets. The pushrods should be refitted in their original positions. (photo)
8 Carefully lower the rocker arm and shaft assembly into position on the cylinder head. (photo)
9 Locate the adjustment screw ball end into the pushrod cup.
10 Refit the cylinder head and rocker arm and shaft assembly securing bolts and tighten finger tight.
11 When all are in position tighten in a progressive manner to a final torque wrench setting of 52.1-63.7 lb f ft (7.20-8.80 Kg fm) - (photo)

43 Valve clearance - adjustment

The valve clearances may be checked and adjusted with the engine either in or out of the car. Remove the cylinder head cover and then proceed as follows:
1 With the engine either hot or cold rotate the crankshaft until No 1 cylinder is on the compression stroke tdc position.
2 Using a feeler gauge check the clearance between the rocker arm and valve stem. (photo) The gap should be within the limits specified at the beginning of this Chapter for rockers.
   Inlet side   1 and 2
   Exhaust side   1 and 3
3 If the clearances are outside the specified limits slacken the locknut and turn the adjuster screw until the correct clearance is obtained. Tighten the locknut and recheck the clearance. (photo)
4 Turn the crankshaft one revolution clockwise and repeat the sequence for the following valve rockers.
   Exhaust side   3 and 4
   Exhaust side   2 and 4
5 Refit the cylinder head cover and gasket and tighten the securing bolts to a torque wrench setting of 2.89-5.06 lb f ft (0.4 - 0.7 Kg fm) - (photo)

44 Flywheel - refitting

1 This Section is also applicable where an adaptor plate is fitted, instead of a flywheel, when automatic transmission is fitted.
2 Inspect the bearing in the end of the crankshaft and if it is not worn it must be removed.
   Withdraw the old one using a small internal puller. If one is not available it is possible to remove it by filling with grease and inserting a drift the same diameter as the internal diameter of the bearing. As a last resort the local garage should be able to help.
3 Fit a new bearing using a tubular drift on the outer track.
4 Wipe the mating faces of the crankshaft and flywheel (or adaptor plate).
5 Offer up the flywheel (or adaptor plate) to the crankshaft and secure with the two shaped tab washers and six bolts. (photo)
6 Tighten the bolts to a torque wrench setting of 41.9-47.7 lb f ft (5.8-6.6 Kg fm) and lock by bending up the tabs.

45 Crankshaft pulley - replacement

1 Lubricate the hub with a little engine oil. Make sure the key is in position and refit the pulley. (photo)
2 Secure the pulley with the bolts and washers and tighten to a torque wrench setting of 28.9-43.4 lb f ft (4.0-6.0 Kg fm).

46 Engine - final assembly

With the basic engine completely assembled the ancillary equipment may now be refitted. The actual items will depend on whether the unit was stripped to the last nut and bolt. In all cases refitting of these parts is the reverse sequence to removal. Additional information will be found in the relevant Chapter or Section should this be found necessary.

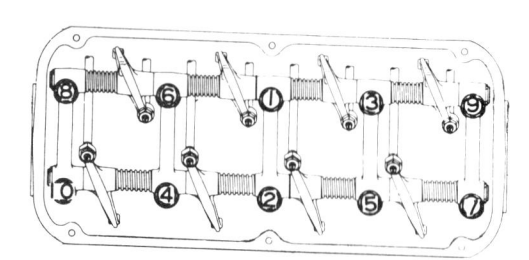

Fig 1.27 Cylinder head bolt tightening sequence

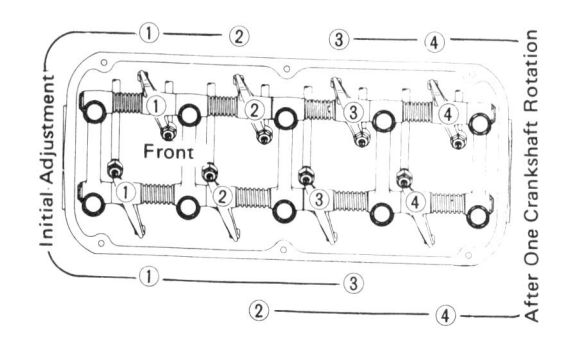

Fig 1.28 Valve adjustment sequence

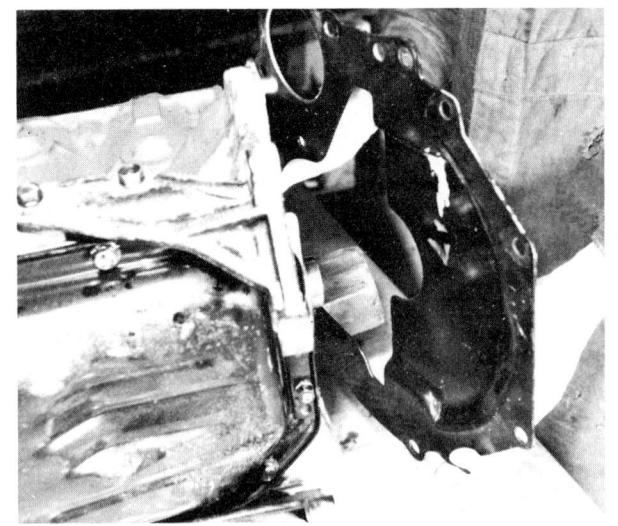

40.1 Refitting engine backplate

40.2 Backplate retained in position with bolt

42.2 Inserting tappet into bore

42.5 Fitting new cylinder head gasket

42.6 Lowering cylinder head into position

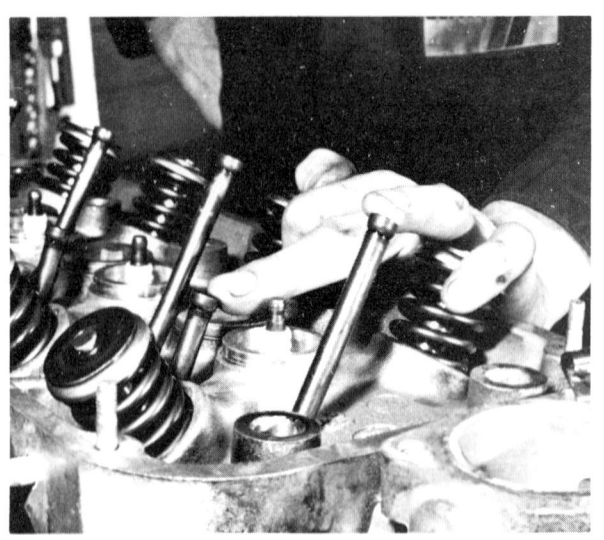

42.7 Refitting pushrods

42.8 Rocker arm assembly being placed on cylinder head

42.11 Tightening cylinder head securing bolts

43.2 Checking valve clearance

43.3 Adjustment of valve clearance

43.5 Refitting engine top cover

44.5 Flywheel securing bolts replacement

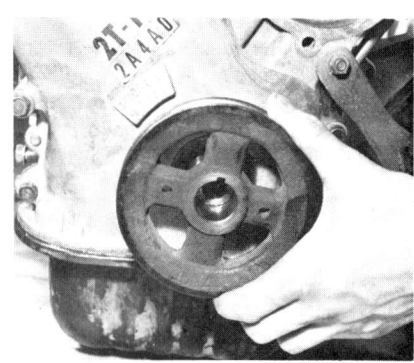

45.1 Refitting the crankshaft pulley

47 Engine (and transmission) - refitting

This is basically the reverse sequence to removal. Refer to Part A of this Chapter, Section 59 for additional information.

48 Engine - initial start up after overhaul or major repair

Refer to Part A of this Chapter, Section 60 for full information.

49 Fault diagnosis - engine

Refer to Part A of this Chapter, Section 61.

Chapter 2 Cooling system

Contents

Antifreeze coolant solution ... 9	General description ... 1
Cooling system - draining ... 2	Radiator - removal, inspection, cleaning and replacement ... 5
Cooling system - filling ... 4	Thermostat - removal, testing and replacement ... 6
Cooling system - flushing ... 3	Water pump - dismantling, overhaul and reassembly ... 8
Fan belt - removal, replacement and adjustment ... 10	Water pump - removal and replacement ... 7
Fault diagnosis - cooling system ... 11	

Specifications

Type of system: ... Pressurised, pump assisted circulation with thermostat temperature control

Radiator:
- Type ... Pressurized, corrugated fin and tube
- Leak test pressure ... 20 lb/sq in. (1.41 kg/sq cm)
- Filter cap valve opening pressure:
  - 1100 (65.7 cu in.) ... 7.0 lb/sq in. (0.5 kg/sq cm)
  - 1200 (71.1 cu in.) ... 7.1 lb/sq in.
  - 1600 (96.9 cu in.) ... 12.8 lb/sq in.

Water pump:
- Type ... Centrifugal with impeller and six blade fan
- Impeller to body clearance ... 0.020 in. (0.508 mm)
- Bearing removal/refitting temperature ... 75 - 85º C (167 - 185º F)

Thermostat:
- Type ... Wax
- Opening temperature ... 82º C (180º F)
- Fully open ... 95º C (203º F)
- Valve opening travel ... Over 0.3 in. (8 mm)

Fan belt:
- Type ... V pulley drive
- Tension ... Set to 0.5 in. (13 mm) of movement midway between pump and alternator pulleys at finger pressure

Capacity (coolant):
- With heater ... 8.25 pints (4.7 litres, 9.908 US pints)

Note: Models fitted with automatic transmission have an oil cooler incorporated in the bottom of the radiator.

1 General description

The engine cooling water is circulated by a thermo syphon, water pump assisted system, and the coolant is pressurised. This is both to prevent the loss of water down the overflow pipe with the radiator cap in position and to prevent premature boiling in adverse conditions.

The radiator cap is, in effect, a safety valve designed to open at a pressure slightly above atmospheric pressure, which means that the coolant can reach a temperature above 100°C (212°F) before the pressure generated opens the valve. It then boils: steam escaping down the overflow pipe. When the temperature (therefore the pressure), decreases, the valve reseats until the temperature builds up again.

This means that the engine can operate at its most efficient temperature, which is around the normal boiling point of water, without the water boiling away.

In addition there is a vacuum valve in the cap which permits air to enter the system as it cools down thereby preventing collapse of the radiator or hoses.

It is, therefore, important to check that the radiator cap fitted is of the correct specification (the release pressure is stamped on the top) and in good condition, and that the spring behind the sealing washer has not weakened. Some garages have a device in which radiator caps can be tested. Check that the rubber sealing washer is in good condition, without signs of distortion or perishing.

The system functions in the following manner: Cold water in the bottom of the radiator circulates up the lower radiator hose to the water pump where it is pushed around the water passages in the cylinder block, helping to keep the cylinder bores and pistons cool.

The water then travels up the cylinder head and circulates round the combustion space and valve seats absorbing more heat, and then when the engine is at its correct operating temperature water flows past the open thermostat into the upper radiator hose and so into the radiator header tank.

The water travels down through the radiator where it is cooled by the passage of cold air through the radiator core,

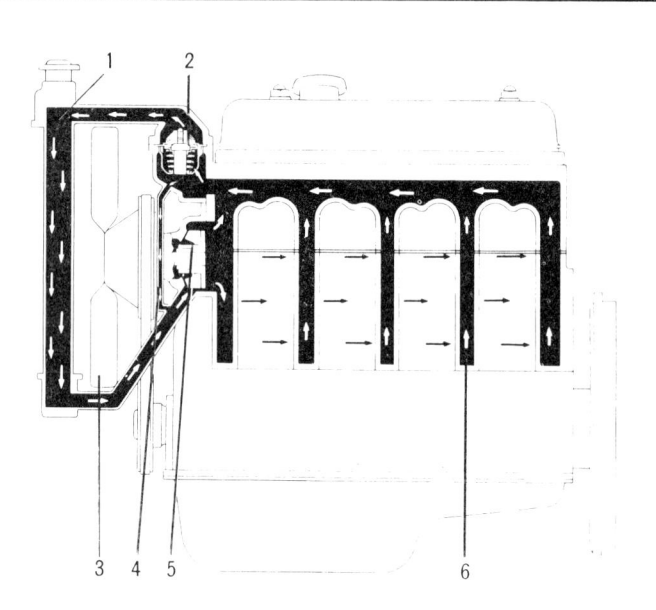

Fig 2.1 Cross sectional view of cooling system

1 Radiator
2 Thermostat
3 Fan blade
4 By-pass tube
5 Water pump
6 Water jacket

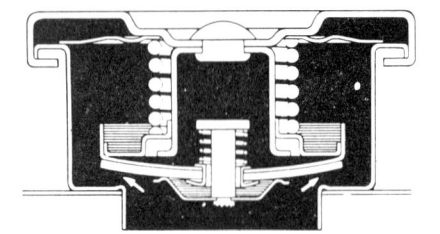

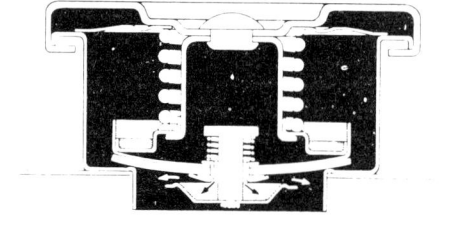

Fig 2.2 Operation of radiator cap
Press regulating valve   Vacuum valve operation

Chapter 2/Cooling system

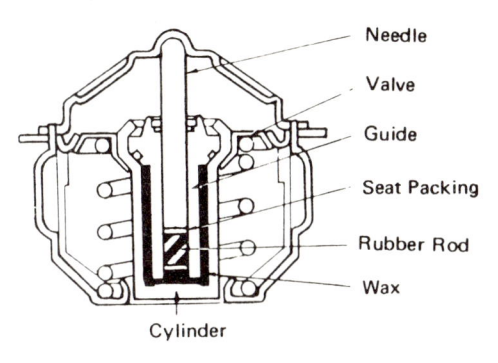

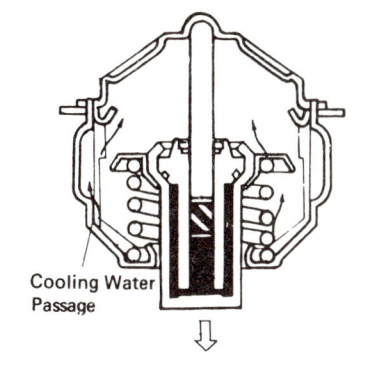

Fig 2.3 Operation of thermostat

Closed — Open

Labels: Needle, Valve, Guide, Seat Packing, Rubber Rod, Wax, Cylinder, Cooling Water Passage

which is created by both the fan and the motion of the car. The water, now much cooler, reaches the bottom of the radiator, whereupon the cycle is repeated.

When the engine is cold the thermostat (a valve which opens and closes according to the temperature of the water) maintains the circulation of the same water in the engine excluding that in the radiator.

Only when the correct minimum operating temperature has been reached does the thermostat begin to open, allowing water to return to the radiator.

The cooling system comprises the radiator, top and bottom hoses, heater hoses, the impeller water pump mounted on the front of the engine (it carries the fan blades and is driven by the fan belt), the thermostat and the drain plugs.

2 Cooling system - draining

With the car on level ground drain the system as follows:
1   If the engine is cold, remove the filler cap from the radiator by turning it anticlockwise. If the engine is hot, then turn the filler cap very slightly until the pressure in the system has had time to disperse. Use a rag over the cap to protect your hand from escaping steam. If, with the engine very hot, the cap is released suddenly the drop in pressure can cause the water to boil. With the pressure released the cap can be removed.
2   If antifreeze is in the cooling system drain it into a clean bowl for re-use. A wide bowl will be necessary to catch all the coolant.
3   Open the radiator and cylinder block drain plugs/taps. When the water has finished running probe the plug holes or taps with a piece of short wire to dislodge any particles of rust or sediment which may be causing a blockage and preventing all the coolant draining out. (photo)

3 Cooling system - flushing

1   With time the cooling system will gradually lose its efficiency as the radiator becomes choked with rust scale, deposits from the water and other sediment. To clean the system out, first drain it - leaving the drains open. Then remove the radiator cap and leave a hose running in the radiator cap orifice for ten to fifteen minutes.
2   In very bad cases the radiator should be reverse flushed. This can be done with the radiator in position. A hose must be arranged to feed water into the lower radiator outlet pipe. Water, under pressure, is then forced up through the radiator and out of the header tank filler orifice.
3   The hose is removed and placed in the filler orifice and the radiator washed out in the usual manner.

4 Cooling system - filling

1   Refit the drain plugs/close the drain taps as applicable.
2   Move the heater control to the "hot" position and fill the system slowly to ensure that air locks are minimised.
3   Do not fill the system higher than within 0.5 in. (12.7 mm) of the filler cap orifice. Overfilling will merely result in wastage, which is especially to be avoided when antifreeze is in use.
4   Only use antifreeze mixture with an ethylene glycol base. See Section 9 for further information.
5   Replace the radiator cap and run the engine at a fast idle speed for approximately half a minute and remove the filler cap slowly. Top-up as necessary, and finally replace the filler cap, turning it clockwise firmly to lock it in position.

5 Radiator - removal, inspection, cleaning and replacement

1   Refer to Section 2 and drain the cooling system.
2   Slacken the clip which holds the top water hose to the radiator and carefully pull off the hose.
3   Slacken the clip which holds the bottom water hose to the radiator bottom tank and carefully pull off the hose.
4   On models fitted with the Toyoglide automatic transmission wipe the area around the oil cooler pipe unions and then detach these pipes from the radiator. Plug the ends to prevent dirt

2.3 Cylinder block drain plug

ingress.

5 If a fan shroud is fitted this should be detached from the radiator and placed over the fan.
6 Undo and remove the radiator securing bolts and lift the radiator upwards and away from the front of the car. The shroud (if fitted) may next be lifted away. (photo)
7 Clean out the inside of the radiator by flushing as described in Section 3. When the radiator is out of the car it is well worthwhile to invert it for reverse flushing. Clean the exterior of the radiator by hosing down the matrix with a strong water jet to clean away embedded dirt and debris, which will impede the air flow. When an oil cooler is fitted (automatic transmission) make sure no water is allowed to enter.
8 If it is thought that the radiator is partially blocked, a good proprietary chemical product such as 'Radflush' should be used to clean it.
9 With the radiator away from the car it can be soldered or repaired with a filler paste such as 'Cataloy'. Full information and instructions for use will be found on the pack.
10 Inspect the radiator hoses for cracks, internal or external perishing and damage caused by the securing clips. Replace the hoses as necessary. Examine the radiator hose securing clips and renew them if they are rusted or distorted.
11 Refitting the radiator is the reverse sequence to removal. If automatic transmission is fitted check and top-up its fluid level.

6 Thermostat - removal, testing and replacement

1 To remove the thermostat, partially drain the cooling system as described in Section 2. The removal of 4 pints (2.27 litres) is usually enough.
2 Slacken the radiator top hose at the thermostat housing elbow and carefully draw if off the elbow. (photo)
3 Unscrew the two bolts and spring washers securing the thermostat housing elbow, (photo) and lift the housing and gasket away. If it has stuck because a sealing compound has been previously used, tap with a soft faced hammer to break the seal.
4 Lift out the thermostat and observe if it is stuck open. If this is the case discard it.
5 Suspend it by a piece of string together with a thermometer in a saucepan of cold water. Neither the thermostat nor the thermometer should touch the sides or bottom of the saucepan or a false reading could be obtained.
6 Heat the water, stirring it gently with the thermometer to ensure temperature uniformity, and note when the thermostat begins to open. Note the temperature and this should be comparable with the figure given in the 'Specifications' Section at the beginning of this Chapter.
7 Continue heating the water until the thermostat is fully open. Now let it cool down naturally and check that it closes fully. If

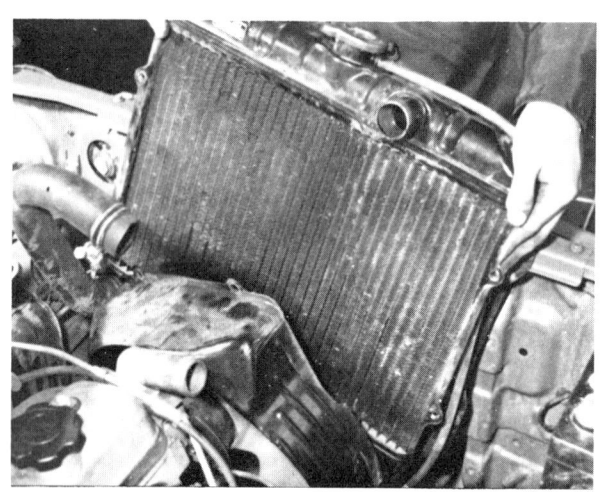

5.6a Lifting away radiator

5.6b Removal of radiator shroud

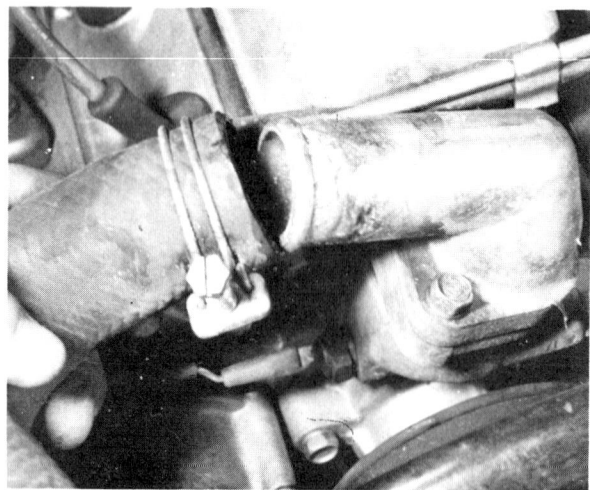

6.2 Removal of top hose from thermostat housing elbow

6.3 Removal of thermostat housing elbow set bolts

Fig 2.4 Thermostat removal

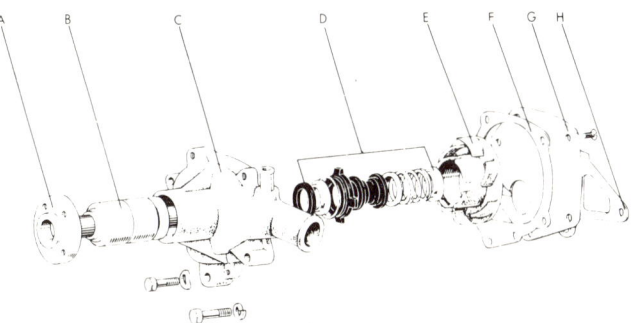

Fig 2.5 Exploded view of water pump

A Pulley seat
B Water pump bearing
C Water pump body
D Water pump seal
E Water pump rotor
F Gasket
G Water pump plate
H Gasket

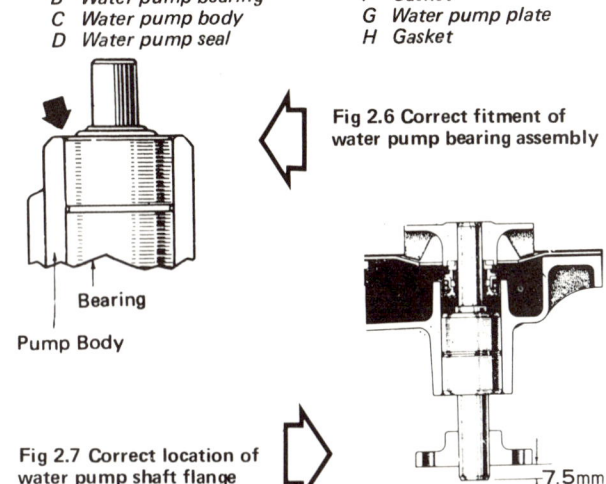

Fig 2.6 Correct fitment of water pump bearing assembly

Fig 2.7 Correct location of water pump shaft flange

the thermostat does not fully open or close then it must be discarded and a new one obtained.

8 Replacement of the thermostat is the reverse of the removal procedure. Always clean the mating faces thoroughly and use a new paper gasket.

7 Water pump - removal and replacement

1 Refer to Section 2 and drain the cooling system.
2 Refer to Section 5 and remove the radiator.
3 Refer to Section 10 and remove the fan belt.
4 Slacken the bottom hose clip and carefully detach the hose from the water pump.
5 Slacken the water bypass hose clip and carefully detach the bypass hose from the water pump.
6 Undo and remove the four bolts securing the fan and hub assembly from the water pump spindle flange and lift away the fan assembly.
7 Undo and remove the bolts securing the water pump body to the cylinder block. Lift away the water pump and recover the old gasket.
8 Refitting the water pump is the reverse sequence to removal, but the following additional points should be noted:
a) Make sure the mating faces of the pump body and cylinder block are clean. Always use a new gasket.
b) Refer to Section 10 and adjust the fan belt tension. If the belt is too tight undue strain will be placed on the water pump and alternator bearings. If the belt is too loose, it will slip and wear rapidly as well as giving rise to possible engine overheating and low alternator output.

8 Water pump - dismantling, overhaul and reassembly

1 Before dismantling the water pump check the economics of overhaul compared with the cost of a guaranteed new unit. Then make quite sure all the spare parts required are to hand.
2 Using a universal puller carefully draw the shaft flange from the end of the spindle.
3 On KE models and later TE models remove the pump plate securing bolts and lift off the plate and gasket.
4 Using a universal puller carefully draw the impeller from the end of the spindle.
5 Remove the seal set from the spindle.
6 Immerse the water pump body in hot water for about ten minutes and using a large bench vice or press carefully remove the bearing assembly from the front of the pump. It is possible to use a suitable size soft metal drift if a large vice or press are not available.
7 With all parts clean, inspect the bearing assembly for wear; there should be no signs of end-play or roughness in movement.
8 Examine the seal seat on the impeller for signs of pitting or score marks. Obtain a new impeller if either are evident.
9 Generally inspect the impeller and water pump body for signs of damage or wear. Obtain new parts as necessary.
10 On KE models commence reassembly by fitting new seals to the impeller and water pump body.
11 Immerse the water pump body in hot water for about ten minutes and press the bearing assembly into the body until the outer track is flush with the water pump body. (Fig 2.6)
12 On TE models fit new seals into the pump body seal cover and then assemble the gasket and floating seat to the impeller.
13 On KE models carefully press the shaft flange onto the end of the spindle.
14 Press the impeller onto the shaft until it is flush with the end of the shaft. There should be an impeller to body clearance of approximately 0.020 in (0.508 mm).
15 On TE models press the shaft flange onto the end of the spindle so that the shaft end protrudes through the flange by 0.3 in (7.5 mm). (Fig 2.7)
16 Where applicable fit a new gasket and replace the water pump plate. Tighten the securing bolts in a diagonal and progressive manner.

9 Antifreeze coolant solution

1 Where temperatures are likely to drop below freezing point (0° C, 32° F) the cooling system must be adequately protected by the addition of antifreeze. It is still possible for water to freeze in the radiator with the engine running in very cold conditions - particularly if the engine cooling is being adequately dealt with by the heater radiator. The thermostat will remain closed and the coolant in the radiator will not circulate.
2 Before refilling the cooling system with antifreeze solution it is best to drain and flush the system as described in Sections 2 and 3 of this Chapter.

3 Because antifreeze has a greater searching effect than water make sure that all hoses and joints are in good condition.
4 The table below gives the details of the antifreeze percentage to be used:

%	complete protection	
25	−11°C	12.2°F
30	−14°C	6.8°F
35	−19°C	−2.2°F
40	−23°C	−9.4°F
45	−29°C	−20.2°F
50	−35°C	−31.0°F

5 Mix the equal quantity of antifreeze with 4 pints (2.27 litres) of water and pour into the cooling system. Top-up with water and check the level as described in Section 4.

10 Fan belt - removal, replacement and adjustment

1 If the fan belt is worn or has stretched unduly it should be replaced. A common reason for replacement is breakage in use-so always carry a spare.
2 Even though the belt may have broken and fallen off, go through the removal routine. Firstly loosen the alternator securing bolts and push the alternator towards the engine and lift off the old belt.
3 Position the new belt over the pulleys.
4 The alternator must now be used as a tensioner in effect by pulling it away from the engine and locking in the required position. This can call for some sustained effort unless the pivot bolts are slackened only a little so that the alternator is quite stiff to move. A lever between the alternator and cylinder block will help. However, avoid applying pressure to the rear end-cover or it may break. Always tighten the front end-cover securing bolts first.
5 The movement of the belt under finger pressure of the belt, midway between the water pump and alternator pulleys, should be set to 0.5 in (13 mm). If in doubt it is better for it to be a little too slack rather than too tight. Only slipping will occur if it is too slack. If too tight, damage can be caused by excessive strain on the pulley bearings.
6 When the adjustment is correct tighten the alternator mountings fully.
7 With a new belt check the tension 250 miles (400 Km) after fitting.
8 Periodic checking of the belt tension is necessary and there is no hard and fast rule as to the most suitable interval, because a fan belt does not necessarily stretch or wear at a predetermined rate. Assuming most owners check their own oil and water levels regularly it is suggested as a good habit to check the fan belt tension every time the bonnet is opened.

11 Fault diagnosis - cooling system

Symptom	Reason/s	Remedy
Heat generated in cylinder not being successfully disposed of by radiator	Insufficient water in cooling system	Top-up radiator.
	Fan belt slipping (accompanied by a shrieking noise on rapid engine acceleration)	Tighten fan belt to recommended tension or replace if worn.
	Radiator core blocked or radiator grille restricted	Reverse flush radiator, remove obstructions.
	Bottom water hose collapsed, impeding flow	Remove and fit new hose.
	Thermostat not opening properly	Remove and fit new thermostat.
	Ignition advance and retard incorrectly set (accompanied by loss of power and perhaps, misfiring)	Check and reset ignition timing.
	Carburettor incorrectly adjusted (mixture too weak)	Tune carburettor.
	Exhaust system partially blocked	Check exhaust pipe for constrictive dents and blockages.
	Oil level in sump too low	Top-up sump to full mark on dipstick.
	Blown cylinder head gasket (Water/steam being forced down the radiator overflow pipe under pressure)	Remove cylinder head, fit new gasket.
	Engine not yet run-in	Run-in slowly and carefully.
	Brakes binding	Check and adjust brakes if necessary.
Too much heat being dispersed by radiator	Thermostat jammed open	Remove and renew thermostat.
	Incorrect grade of thermostat fitted allowing premature opening of valve	Remove and replace with new thermostat which opens at a higher temperature.
	Thermostat missing	Check and fit correct thermostat.
Leaks in system	Loose clips on water hoses	Check and tighten clips if necessary.
	Top or bottom water hoses perished and leaking	Check and replace any faulty hoses.
	Radiator core leaking	Remove radiator and repair.
	Thermostat gasket leaking	Inspect and renew gasket.
	Pressure cap spring worn or seal ineffective	Renew pressure cap.
	Blown cylinder head gasket (Pressure in system forcing water/steam down overflow pipe)	Remove cylinder head and fit new gasket.
	Cylinder wall or head cracked	Dismantle engine, dispatch to engineering works for repair.

Chapter 3 Fuel system and carburation

Contents

Air cleaner and element - removal and replacement ... 3	Fuel pipes and lines - general inspection 19
Automatic choke - adjustment 13	Fuel pump - dismantling, inspection and reassembly ... 7
Carburettor - adjustment 15	Fuel pump - general description 4
Carburettor - dismantling and reassembly 10	Fuel pump - removal and replacement 5
Carburettor float level - adjustment 11	Fuel pump - testing 6
Carburettor - general description 8	Fuel tank - cleaning and repair 18
Carburettor - removal and replacement 9	Fuel tank - removal and replacement 17
Charcoal canister storage system (exhaust emission control system) 25	General description 1
	Idle speed - adjustment 14
Exhaust emission control - general description 21	Mixture control system (exhaust emission control system) 22
Fault diagnosis - exhaust emission control system ... 27	Throttle positioner system (exhaust emission control system) 24
Fault diagnosis - fuel system and carburation 26	
Federal Regulations (USA only) - servicing 2	Throttle valve opening - adjustment 12
Fuel filter - removal and replacement 16	Transmission controlled spark system (exhaust emission control system) 23
Fuel gauge sender unit - fault finding 20	

Specifications

Fuel pump:
- Type ... Mechanical driven from eccentric on camshaft
- Delivery capacity ... More than 900 cc/min. at 3,000 rpm
- Delivery pressure ... 2.3 - 2.8 lb/in^2 (0.2 - 0.3 kg/cm^2)

Fuel tank:
- Location ... Rear of car
- Capacity:
  - Saloon/Sedan and Coupe ... 10 gallons, 12 US gallons, 45 litres
  - Estate/Wagon ... 9 gallons, 10.5 US gallons, 40 litres
- Fuel grade ... 90 octane (minimum)

Carburettor:
- Type ... Downdraught, twin barrel

1100 models
- Air horn diameter ... 2.480 in. (63.0 mm)
- Large venturi diameter (first) ... 0.827 in. (21 mm)
- Large venturi diameter (second) ... 0.945 in. (24 mm)
- Small venturi diameter (first) ... 0.276 in. (7 mm)
- Small venturi diameter (second) ... 0.315 in. (8 mm)
- Throttle bore diameter (first) ... 1.102 in. (28 mm)
- Throttle bore diameter (second) ... 1.102 in. (28 mm)
- Main jet diameter (first) ... 0.0425 in. (1.08 mm)
- Main jet diameter (second) ... 0.0689 in. (1.75 mm)
- Slow jet diameter (first) ... 0.0185 in. (0.381 mm)
- Slow jet diameter (second) ... 0.0276 in. (0.70 mm)
- Power jet diameter ... 0.0276 in. (0.70 mm)
- Pump jet diameter ... 0.0197 in. (0.50 mm)
- Economiser jet diameter ... 0.0402 in. (1.02 mm)
- Main air bleed diameter (first) ... 0.0197 in. (0.5 mm)
- Main air bleed diameter (second) ... 0.0197 in. (0.5 mm)
- Slow air bleed diameter (first) ... 0.0433 in. (1.10 mm)
- Slow air bleed diameter (second) ... 0.0482 in. (1.225 mm)
- Power piston operation (in Hg) ... 3.15 - 3.94
- Accelerator pump stroke:
  - Normal ... 0.118 - **0.138** in. (3.0 - 3.5 mm)
  - Cold ... 0.157 - 0.177 in. (4.0 - 4.5 mm)

Chapter 3/Fuel system and carburation

Accelerator pump diameter	0.551 in. (139.95 mm)
Idle mixture screw	2.5 turns
Float level	0.256 in. (65 mm)
Float drop	1.89 in. (48 mm)
Fast idle (choke closed), first throttle valve opening	0.04 in. (1.016 mm) (valve to bore)
Stop lever to high speed valve arm clearance	0.020 in. (0.508 mm) (secondary throttle valve just starting to open)

1200 models

Air horn diameter	2.480 in. (63.0 mm)
Large venturi diameter (first)	0.827 in. (21 mm)
Large venturi diameter (second)	0.945 in. (24 mm)
Small venturi diameter (first)	0.276 in. (7 mm)
Small venturi diameter (second)	0.315 in. (8 mm)
Throttle bore diameter (first)	1.102 in. (28 mm)
Throttle bore diameter (second)	1.102 in. (28 mm)
Main jet diameter (first)	0.039 in. (0.991 mm)
Main jet diameter (second)	0.069 in. (1.75 mm)
Slow jet diameter (first)	0.019 in. (0.50 mm)
Slow jet diameter (second)	0.0276 in. (0.70 mm)
Power jet diameter	0.030 in. (0.762 mm)
Pump jet diameter	0.016 in. (0.406 mm)
Economiser jet diameter	0.040 in. (1.02 mm)
Main air bleed diameter (first)	0.02 in. (0.54 mm)
Main air bleed diameter (second)	0.02 in. (0.54 mm)
Slow air bleed diameter (first)	0.032 in. (0.825 mm)
Slow air bleed diameter (second)	0.048 in. (1.225 mm)
Power piston operation (in Hg)	3.1 - 3.9
Accelerator pump stroke:	
Normal	0.138 in. (3.5 mm)
Cold	0.177 in. (4.5 mm)
Accelerator pump diameter	0.551 in. (139.95 mm)
Idle mixture screw	2 turns
Float level	0.26 in. (6.5 mm)
Float drop	1.90 in. (48 mm)
Fuel level	0.866 in. (21.996 mm)
Fast idle (choke closed), first throttle valve opening	17º
Stop lever to high speed valve arm clearance	0.020 in. (0.508 mm) (secondary throttle valve just starting to open)

1600 models

Air horn diameter	2.480 in. (63.0 mm)
Large venturi diameter (first)	0.91 in. (23.11 mm)
Large venturi diameter (second)	1.06 in. (26.924 mm)
Small venturi diameter (first)	0.31 in. (8 mm)
Small venturi diameter (second)	0.35 in. (8.89 mm)
Throttle bore diameter (first)	1.18 in. (29.97 mm)
Throttle bore diameter (second)	1.33 in. (23.78 mm)
Main jet diameter (first):	
2T	0.0421 in. (1.0668 mm)
2T-C	0.0425 in. (1.0795 mm)
Main jet diameter (second)	0.0638 in. (1.6605 mm)
Slow jet diameter (first)	0.0197 in. (0.5 mm)
Slow jet diameter (second)	0.0276 in. (0.70 mm)
Power jet diameter	0.236 in. (5.99 mm)
Pump jet diameter	0.0197 in. (0.5 mm)
Economiser jet diameter	0.0354 in. (0.899 mm)
Main air bleed diameter (first)	0.024 in. (0.6096 mm)
Main air bleed diameter (second)	0.020 in. (0.508 mm)
Slow air bleed diameter (first)	0.0344 in. (0.874 mm)
Slow air bleed diameter (second)	0.0433 in. (1.10 mm)
Power piston operation (in Hg)	4.31 - 5.12
Idle mixture screw:	
2T	2 5/8 turns
2T-C	lean best idle
Float level	0.138 in. (3.505 mm)
Float drop	0.047 in. (1.194 mm) (float tang to float needle)
Fuel level	0.787 in. (19.99 mm)
Fast idle (choke closed) first throttle valve opening	13º
Stop lever to high speed valve air clearance	0.020 in. (secondary throttle valve just starting to open)
First throttle valve angle (from fully closed angle of 7º) when second throttle valve begins to open	50º

Chapter 3/Fuel system and carburation

Choke valve angle (from fully closed angle of 20°) when first throttle valve is fully open ... 27°
Kick-up, first throttle valve (55° from fully closed angle, second throttle valve to bore clearance) ... 0.008 in. (0.2032 mm)

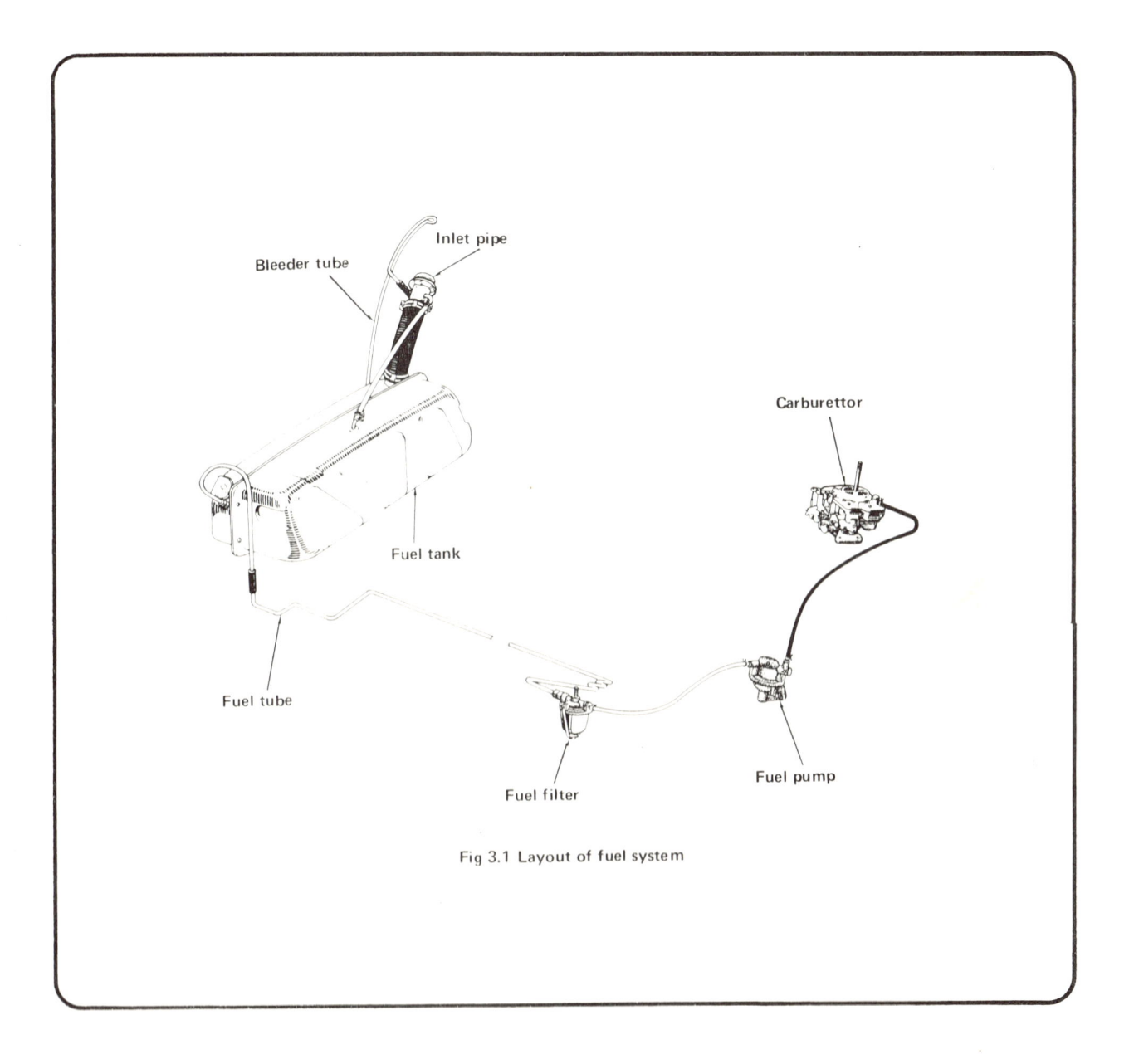

Fig 3.1 Layout of fuel system

Chapter 3/Fuel system and carburation

1 General description

The fuel system comprises a fuel tank at the rear of the vehicle, a mechanical fuel pump mounted on the engine and a twin barrel downdraft carburettor. A renewable paper element air cleaner is fitted as standard.

The fuel pump draws petrol from the fuel tank and delivers it to the carburettor installation. The level of petrol in the carburettor is controlled by a float operated needle valve. Petrol flows past the needle until the float rises sufficiently to close the valve. The pump will then free-wheel until the petrol level drops. The needle valve will then open and petrol continue to flow until the level rises again.

2 Federal regulations - (USA only) - servicing

It is important to appreciate that any adjustments made to the fuel system as well as the ignition system (see Chapter 4) will probably result in the car failing to meet the legal requirements in respect of air pollution unless special test equipment is used during the adjustments.

Information given in this Chapter is aimed specifically at the owner who is able to have the various settings and adjustments checked at the earliest possible opportunity. Full information on the exhaust emission control systems will be found at the end of this Chapter.

3 Air cleaner and element - removal and replacement

Standard Fitment

1 To remove the air cleaner element unscrew the wing nut located at the centre of the air cleaner body. (Fig 3.2)
2 On some models three clamps are fitted. These should next be released so allowing the air cleaner body cover to be removed.
3 Lift away the air cleaner body cover. (photo)
4 The element may now be lifted out.
5 Should it be necessary to remove the air cleaner body from the carburettor undo and remove the support bracket securing bolt.
6 Lift the air cleaner body up from the carburettor body and detach the hose from the underside.
7 Refitting the air cleaner and element is the reverse sequence to removal. Make sure that the gaskets are seating correctly. Finally line up the arrow on the air cleaner element with that on the cover.

Optional fitment

8 In some export areas the air cleaner is fitted with a valve which is capable of changing the air inlet port position depending on the time of year.

To move the valve slacken the wing nut and slide to the desired position. Retighten the wing nut. (photo)

4 Fuel pump - general description

The mechanically operated fuel pump is actuated through a spring loaded rocker arm. One end of the split rocker arm bears against an eccentric on the camshaft and the other end operates the diaphragm pullrod.

As the engine camshaft rotates the eccentric moves the pivoted rocker arm outwards which in turn pulls the diaphragm pullrod and diaphragm drum against the pressure of the diaphragm spring.

This creates sufficient vacuum in the pump chamber to draw in fuel from the tank through the sediment chamber and non-return inlet valve.

The rocker arm is held in constant contact with the eccentric by an anti-rattle spring, and as the engine camshaft continues to rotate, the eccentric allows the rocker arm to move inwards. The

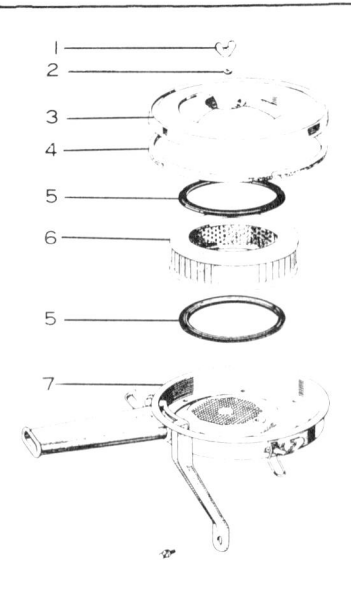

Fig 3.2 Air cleaner component parts

1 Wing nut
2 Seal washer
3 Cover
4 Gasket
5 Gasket
6 Element
7 Main body

diaphragm spring is thus free to push the diaphragm upwards forcing the fuel in the pump chamber out to the carburettor through the non-return outlet valve.

When the float chamber in the carburettor is full the float chamber needle valve will close so preventing further flow from the fuel pump.

The pressure in the delivery line will hold the diaphragm downwards against the pressure of the diaphragm spring, and it will remain in this position until the needle in the float chamber opens to admit more petrol.

5 Fuel pump - removal and replacement

1 Disconnect the flexible inlet hose and outlet pipe from the fuel pump. Tape over the ends to stop dirt ingress.
2 Undo and remove the nuts and spring washers or bolts securing the fuel pump to the engine. Lift away the fuel pump. Recover the gasket. (photo)
3 Refitting the fuel pump is the reverse sequence to removal. Always fit a new gasket. Start the engine and check for fuel and oil leaks.

6 Fuel pump - testing

If operation of the fuel pump is suspect, or it has been overhauled it may be quickly dry tested by holding a finger over the inlet pipe connector and operating the rocker arm through three complete strokes. When the finger is released a suction noise should be heard. Next hold a finger over the outlet nozzle and press the rocker arm fully. The pressure generated should hold for a minimum of fifteen seconds.

7 Fuel pump - dismantling, inspection and reassembly

1 Before dismantling, clean the interior of the pump and wipe dry with a clean non-fluffy rag.
2 Undo and remove the screws securing the top cover to the upper body. Lift away the screws, spring washer, top cover and gasket.
3 Make a mark across the upper and lower bodies so that they

3.3 Lifting away air cleaner body cover

3.8a Air cleaner intake adjustment valve

3.8b Always abide by the manufacturer's recommendations

5.2 Removal of fuel pump

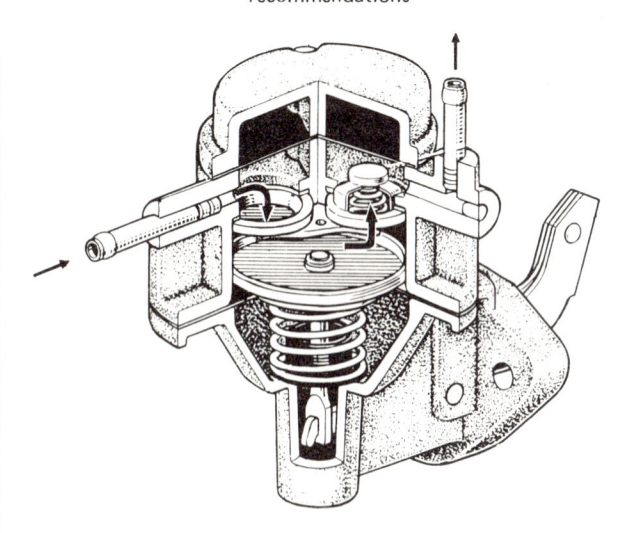

Fig 3.4 Cross sectional view of fuel pump

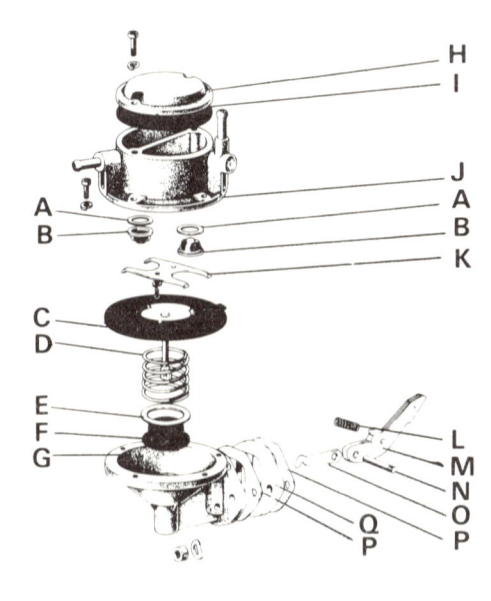

Fig 3.3 Fuel pump component parts (Type 1)

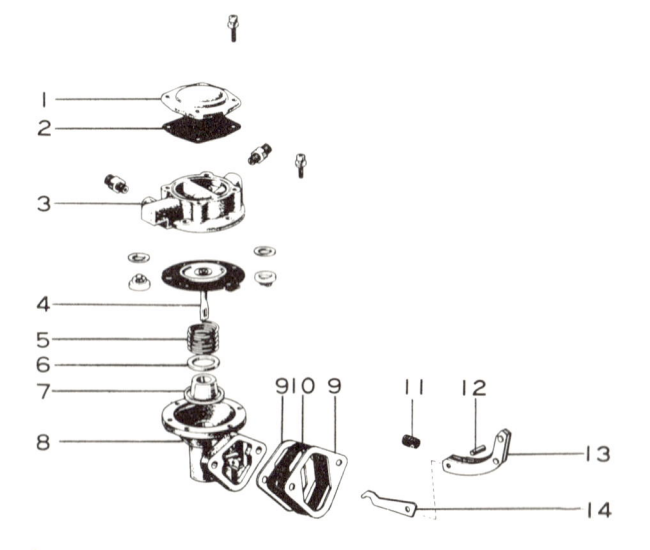

- A Seal
- B Valve
- C Diaphragm
- D Spring
- E Seal retainer
- F Oil seal
- G Lower body
- H Cover
- I Gasket
- J Upper body
- K Valve retainer
- L Spring
- M Rocker arm
- N Pin
- O Rocker arm link
- P Gasket
- Q Insulator

Fig 3.5 Fuel pump component parts (Type 2)

1. Cover
2. Gasket
3. Upper body
4. Diaphragm
5. Spring
6. Seal retainer
7. Oil seal
8. Lower body
9. Gasket
10. Insulator
11. Rocker arm spring
12. Pin
13. Rocker arm
14. Rocker arm link

may be refitted in their original positions.

4 On some pump models undo and remove the screws and spring washers securing the two body halves together. With other models the top cover securing screws also hold the upper body in position.

5 Carefully lift off the upper body. It is possible for the diaphragm to stick to the mating flanges. If this is the case free with a sharp knife. (Fig. 3.6).

6 Using a parallel pin punch carefully tap out the rocker arm pin (Fig. 3.7).

7 Lift out the rocker arm and recover the spring.

8 Depress the centre of the diaphragm and detach the rocker arm link. Lift away the rocker arm link. (Fig. 3.8).

9 Carefully lift the diaphragm and spring up and away from the lower body.

10 The valve should not normally require renewal but in extreme cases this may be done. On some models the valves are retained with an 'H' shaped retainer which is secured with two screws. These should be removed. On other models carefully remove the peening and lift out the valves. Note which way round they are fitted. (Fig. 3.9).

11 To remove the oil seal from the lower body, note which way round it is fitted and then prise out the seal and retainer using a screwdriver.

12 Carefully examine the diaphragm for signs of splitting, cracking or deterioration. Obtain a new one if suspect.

13 Obtain a new oil seal ready for reassembly.

14 Inspect the pump bodies for signs of cracks or stripped threads. Also inspect the rocker arm, link and pin for wear. Obtain new parts as necessary.

15 Clean the recesses for the two valves and refit the valves making sure they are the correct way round. Use a sharp centre panel to peen the edges of the casting or retain them with the 'H' shaped retainer and two screws as applicable.

16 Carefully refit the oil seal and retainer.

17 Replace the diaphragm spring and insert the diaphragm pull rod through the oil seal.

18 Insert and hook the end of the rocker arm link onto the end of the pullrod.

19 Replace the rocker arm into the lower body and locate the spring.

20 Insert the rocker arm pin, lining up the hole with a small screwdriver. Peen over the pin hole edges with a sharp centre punch to retain the pin in position.

21 Fit the upper body to the lower body and line up the previously made marks. Where retaining screws are used these should next be refitted.

22 Refit the cover and gasket to the upper body and secure with the screws and spring washers.

23 The fuel pump is now ready for refitting to the engine.

8 Carburettor - general description

The carburettor fitted to models covered by this manual is of the two barrel design although there are slight modifications depending on the year of production and the engine application. Some KE models and all TE models are fitted with an automatic choke.

The carburettor design gives correct and efficient performance under all operating conditions so giving a good engine performance whilst maintaining an acceptable fuel economy. It is similar to two single barrel carburettors but built into one body.

The primary system incorporates a double type venturi whilst the secondary system is provided with a triple type venturi. Each system comprises an air horn, main nozzle and throttle valve. One set forms the primary circuit whilst the other set forms the secondary circuit. The primary circuit comprises the low speed, high speed, power valve, accelerating and choke systems and is able to supply the correct air/fuel ratio for normal operation.

When the throttle valve is fully open as for fast motoring or acceleration, or a fully laden car, the secondary system also operates to supply an additional air/fuel mixture together with the primary circuit. The throttle valves of both the primary and secondary circuits are operated by a linkage which is interlocked so enabling both the throttle valves to open fully simultaneously. The high speed valve is located in the secondary circuit together with the power valve and enables the performance range to be extremely smooth.

The automatic choke fitted to some carburettors is brought into action by depressing the accelerator pedal.

Upon inspection of Figs. 3.14 and 3.15 which is the carburettor for TE models it will be noticed that it differs slightly from that fitted to the KE models in the throttle and linkage design. The high speed throttle is controlled by a combination of linkage, counterweight and vacuum diaphragm. The auxiliary slave system has been replaced by the throttle positioner vacuum diaphragm. Also a thermostatic valve has been added to the body for pollution control. A float level glass has also been added to the body.

9 Carburettor - removal and replacement

2 Remove the choke inlet hose and outlet pipe (automatic choke).

3 Disconnect the fuel pipe(s) from the carburettor union. Tape over the end to prevent dirt ingress.

4 Disconnect the choke (manual control when fitted) and throttle linkage from the side of the carburettor.

5 Disconnect the vacuum lines from the carburettor.

6 Undo and remove the four nuts and spring washers securing the carburettor to the inlet manifold. Lift away the carburettor and insulator.

7 Place a wedge of rag into the inlet manifold aperture to stop any foreign matter falling in.

8 Refitting the carburettor is the reverse sequence to removal. It will be necessary to check the various adjustments as described later in this Chapter. Also refer to Section 2.

10 Carburettor - dismantling and reassembly

1 Wash the exterior of the carburettor and wipe dry with a clean non-fluffy rag. As the unit is dismantled note the location of each part and place in order on clean newspaper. Also be prepared for slight constructional differences.

2 For the location of the various parts refer to Figs. 3.10 to 3.15 inclusive.

3 Undo and remove the screw on the side of the air horn and lift away the pump lever and connecting rod.

4 Detach and remove the linkage below the automatic choke and then remove the six screws securing the air horn to the main body. Lift away the air horn and its gasket (Fig 3.xx).

5 Drain the float chamber. Withdraw the float lever pin and lift away the float (Fig. 3.16).

6 Remove the needle seat, spring, push pin and seating. (Fig. 3.17).

7 Lift out the power piston, spring and pump plunger.

8 Unscrew and remove the plug, gasket and fuel filter.

9 Undo and remove the three screws securing the automatic choke coil housing to the choke body. Lift away the coil housing, gasket and housing plate. (Fig. 3.18).

10 Remove the cam float and sliding rod from the choke body.

11 The following operation should only be carried out if necessary. File off the peened part of the valve set screw and remove the choke valve. Undo and remove the connector set screw and lift out the choke shaft and vacuum piston. (Fig. 3.19).

12 Undo and remove the screws securing the thermostat body to the main body. Lift away the thermostat body.

13 Remove the gasket, stopper, discharge weight and ball bearing.

14 Detach the back spring and diaphragm from the diaphragm lever.

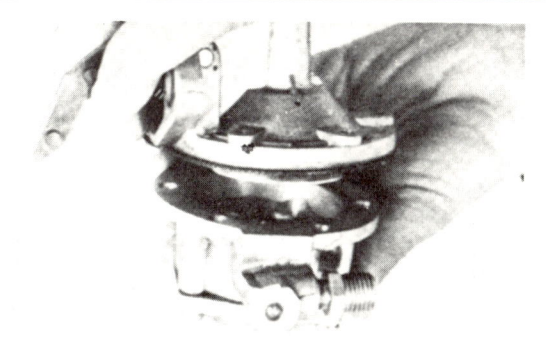

Fig 3.6 Separating upper and lower bodies of fuel pump

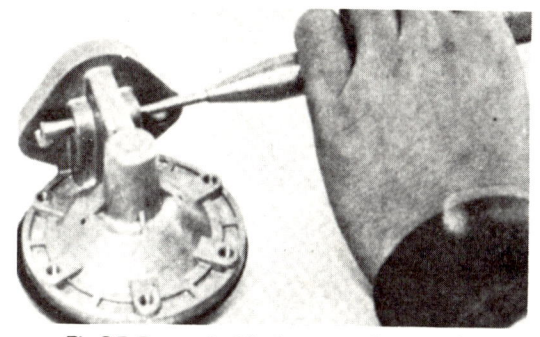

Fig 3.7 Removal of fuel pump rocker arm pin

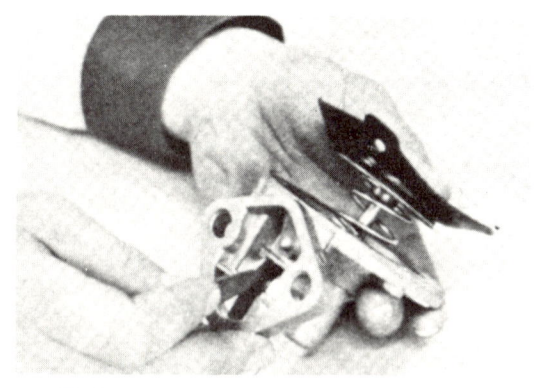

Fig 3.8 Removal of fuel pump rocker arm link

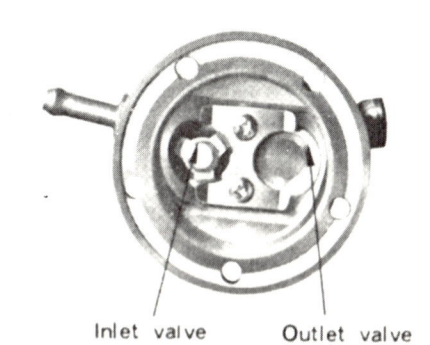

Fig 3.9 Fuel pump valves

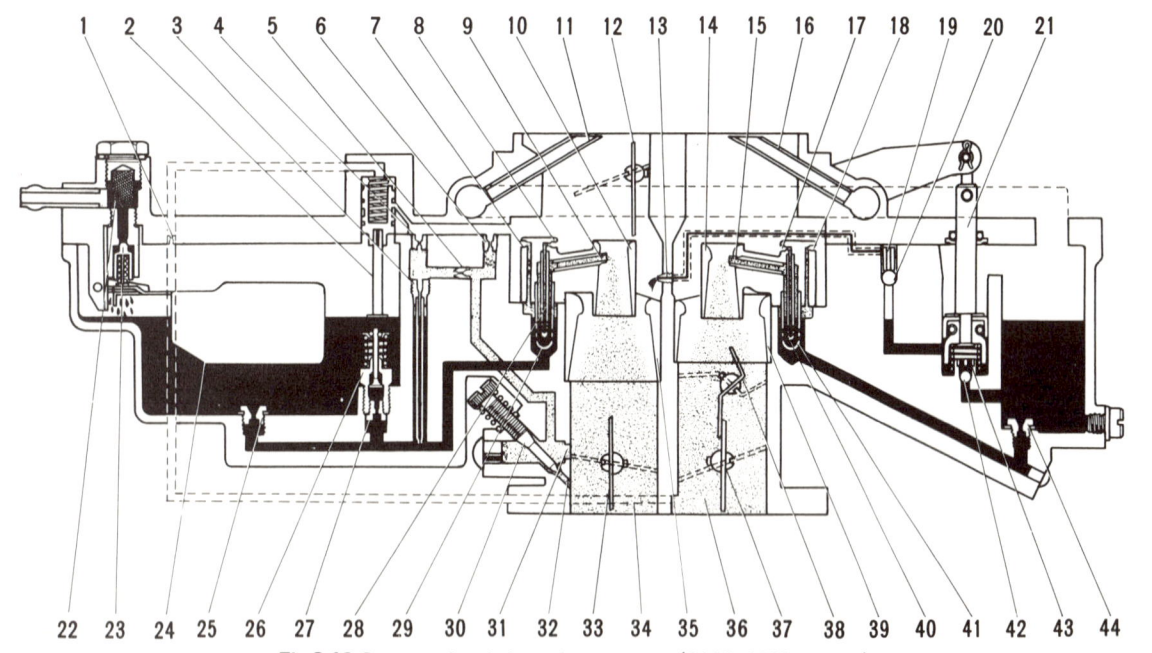

Inlet valve   Outlet valve

Fig 3.10 Cross sectional view of carburettor (1100, 1200 models)

1 Cushion jet
2 Power piston
3 Slow jet
4 Primary air bleeder No.1
5 Economizer jet
6 Primary air bleeder No.2
7 Primary vapour bleeder
8 Primary main air bleeder
9 Primary main nozzle
10 Primary small venturi
11 Primary air vent tube
12 Choke valve
13 Pump jet
14 Secondary small venturi
15 Secondary main nozzle
16 Secondary air vent tube
17 Secondary main air bleeder
18 Secondary vapour bleeder
19 Discharge weight
20 Check ball
21 Pump plunger
22 Strainer
23 Needle valve
24 Float
25 Primary main jet
26 Power valve
27 Power jet
28 Primary main air bleeder tube
29 Tube
30 Idle adjusting screw
31 Slow port
32 Idle port
33 Primary throttle valve
34 Primary bore
35 Primary main venturi
36 Secondary bore
37 Secondary throttle valve
38 High speed valve
39 Secondary main venturi
40 Secondary main air bleeder tube
41 Tube
42 Check ball
43 Check ball retainer
44 Secondary main jet

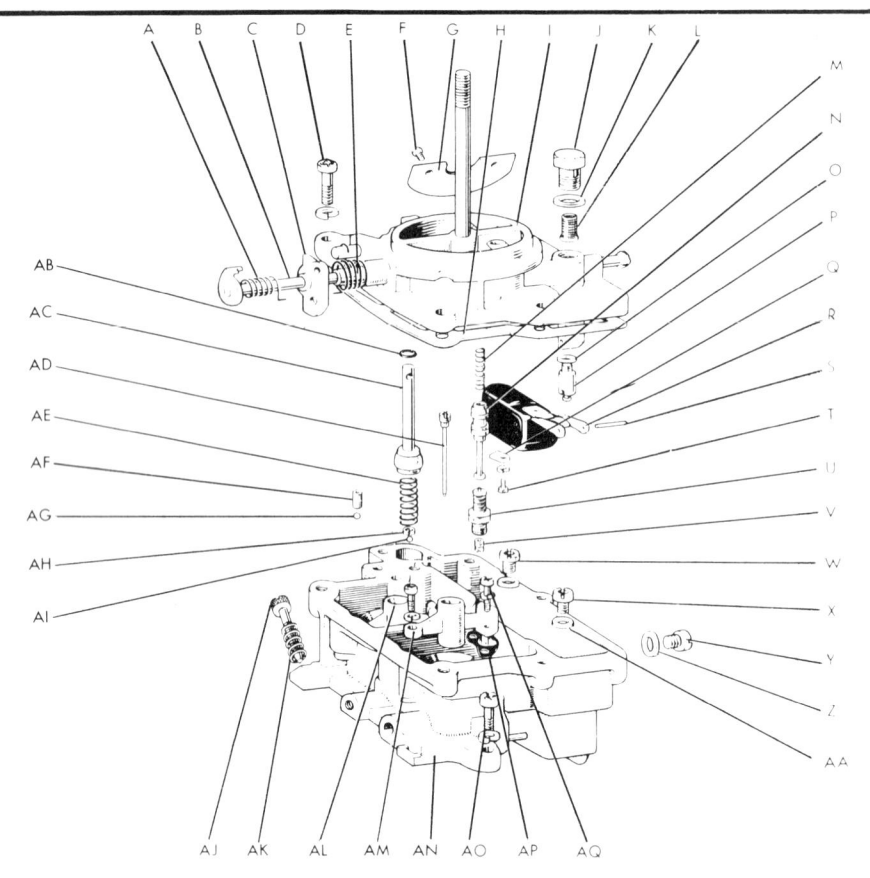

Fig 3.11 Carburettor air horn and main body components (1100, 1200 models)

- A Choke valve relief spring
- B Choke shaft
- C Choke lever
- D Screw
- E Choke return spring
- F Screw
- G Choke valve
- H Air horn gasket
- I Air horn
- J Main passage plug
- K Inlet strainer gasket
- L Strainer
- M Power piston spring
- N Power piston
- O Needle valve seat gasket
- P Needle valve
- Q Power piston stopper
- R Float
- S Float lever pin
- T Screw
- U Power valve
- V Power jet
- W Primary main jet
- X Secondary main jet
- Y Drain plug
- Z Gasket
- AA Main jet gasket
- AB "O" ring
- AC Pump plunger
- AD Slow jet
- AE Pump damping spring
- AF Pump discharge weight
- AG Check ball
- AH Check ball retainer
- AI Check ball
- AJ Throttle adjusting screw
- AK Spring
- AL Primary small venturi
- AM Secondary small venturi
- AN Main body
- AO Screw
- AP Venturi No.1 gasket
- AQ Screw

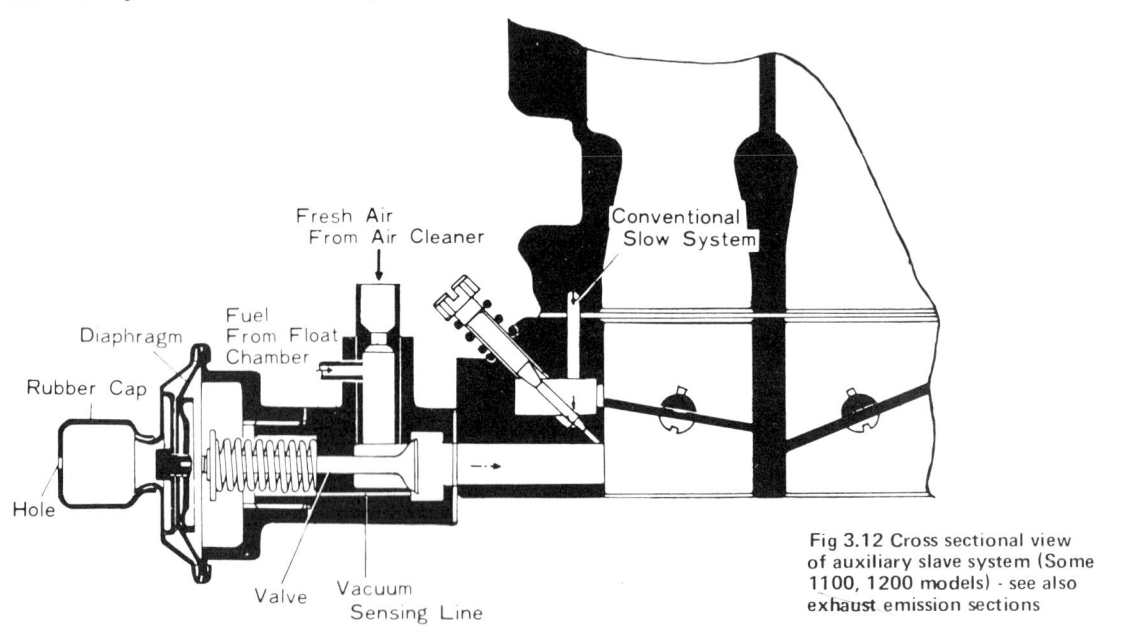

Fig 3.12 Cross sectional view of auxiliary slave system (Some 1100, 1200 models) - see also exhaust emission sections

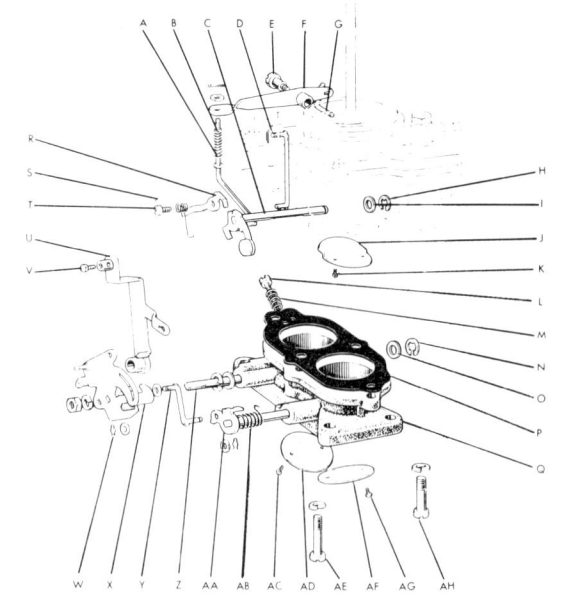

Fig. 3.13. Auxiliary slow system components

A	Pump arm spring		lever
B	Connecting link	S	Spring
C	High speed valve shaft	T	Screw
D	Fast idle connector	U	Fast idle lever
E	Pump lever retaining screw	V	Screw
F	Pump lever	W	Snap ring
G	Pump connecting link	X	Fast throttle arm
H	Retaining ring	Y	Throttle shaft link
I	Shim	Z	Primary throttle shaft
J	High speed valve	AA	Secondary throttle shaft
K	Screw	AB	Secondary throttle return
L	Idle adjusting screw	AC	Screw
M	Spring	AD	Primary throttle valve
N	Retaining ring	AE	Screw
O	Shim	AF	Secondary throttle valve
P	Body flange gasket	AG	Screw
Q	Flange	AH	Screw

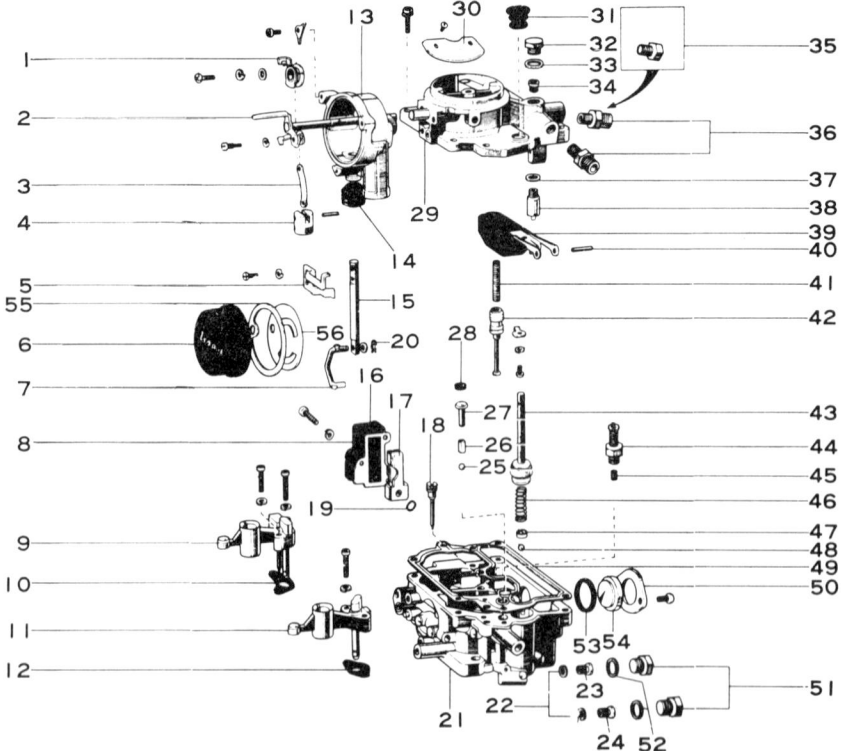

Fig 3.14 Carburettor main body components (1600 models)

1. Cam, fast, idle
2. Shaft, choke valve
3. Connector, piston
4. Piston, vacuum
5. Follower, fast idle cam
6. Housing, coil
7. Link, connecting
8. Cover
9. Venturi, second small
10. Gasket, second venturi
11. Venturi, first small
12. Gasket, venturi
13. Case, thermostat
14. Boot
15. Rod, sliding
16. Gasket
17. Valve, thermostatic
18. Jet, slow,
19. Ring, "O"
20. Snap, connecting link
21. Body
22. Gasket, main jet
23. Jet, first main
25. Ball, steel
26. Weight, pump discharge
27. Stopper
28. Gasket
29. Horn, air
30. Valve, choke
31. Boot
32. Plug, main passage
33. Gasket inlet strainer
34. Strainer
35. Plug
36. Fitting
37. Gasket, needle valve seat
38. Valve, needle
39. Float
40. Pin, float lever
41. Spring, power piston
42. Piston, power
43. Plunger, pump
44. Valve subassembly, power
45. Jet, power
46. Spring, pump damping
47. Retainer, check ball
48. Ball, steel
49. Gasket, air horn
50. Clamp, lever gauge
51. Plug main passage
52. Gasket, main passage
53. Gasket
54. Glass, lever gauge
55. Gasket, coil housing
56. Plate, coil housing

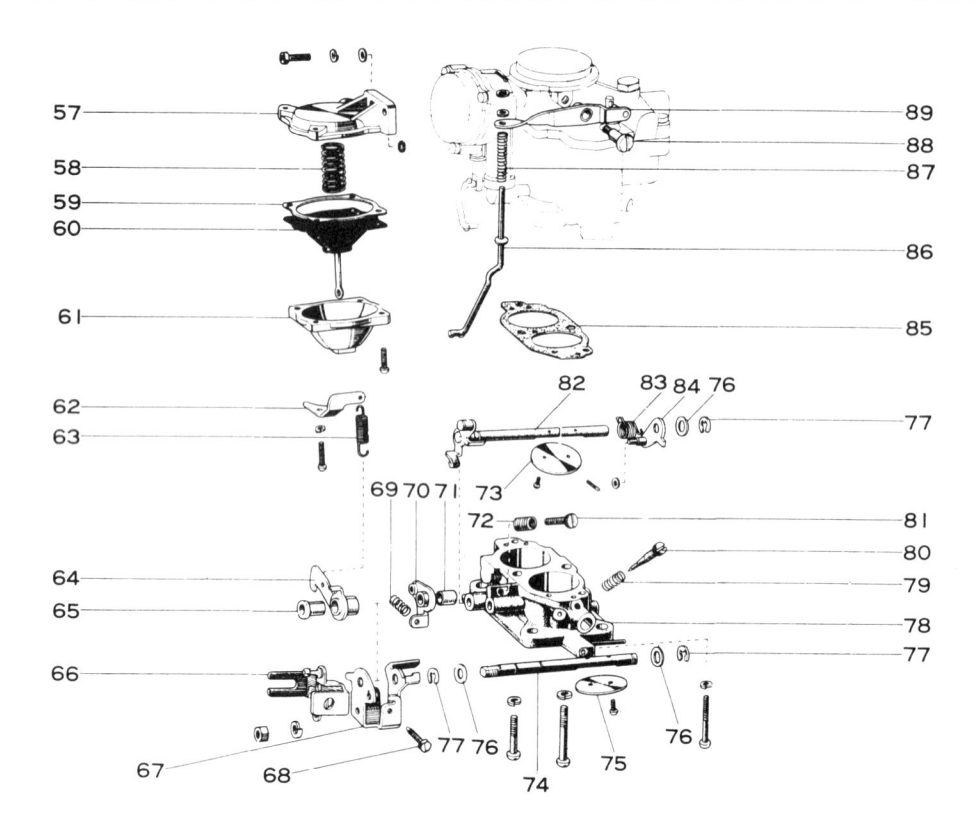

Fig 3.15 Carburettor air horn components (1600 models)

57 Cap, diaphragm housing
58 Spring, diaphragm
59 Gasket, diaphragm
60 Diaphragm
61 Housing diaphragm
62 Support, back spring
63 Spring, back
64 Lever, second kick
65 Collar
66 Lever, first throttle
67 Arm, first throttle shaft
68 Bolt
69 Spring
70 Lever, first idle adjusting
71 Collar
72 Spring
73 Shaft, first throttle
74 Shaft, first throttle
75 Valve, first throttle
76 Shim, throttle shaft
77 Ring, retainer
78 Flange
79 Spring
80 Screw, idle adjusting
81 Screw, throttle adjusting
82 Shaft, second throttle
83 Spring, diaphragm relief
84 Lever, diaphragm
85 Gasket, body flange
86 Link, pump connecting
87 Spring, pump
88 Screw, pump arm set
89 Lever, pump

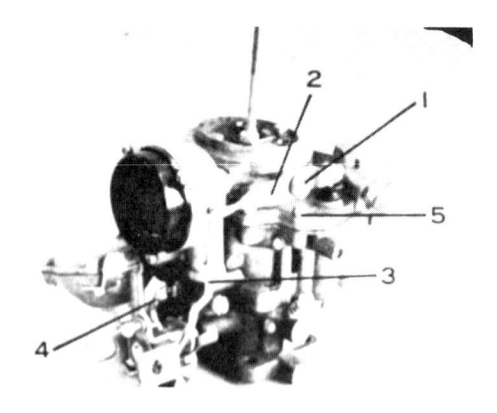

Fig 3.16 Carburettor Air horn removal

1 Pump lever screw
2 Pump lever
3 Connecting rod
4 Linkage
5 Securing screws

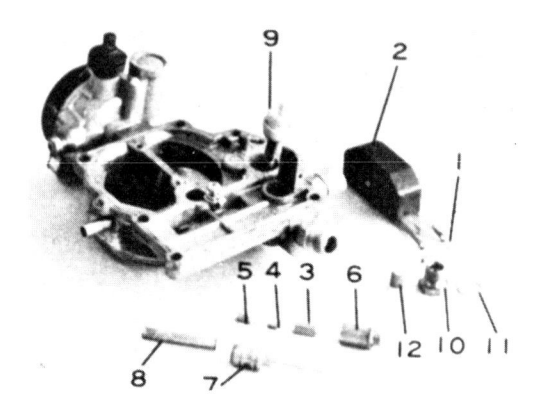

Fig 3.17 Removal of carburettor float from air horn

1 Float lever pin
2 Float
3 Needle valve
4 Spring
5 Push pin
6 Needle valve seat
7 Power piston
8 Spring
9 Plunger
10 Plug
11 Gasket
12 Strainer

Chapter 3/Fuel system and carburation

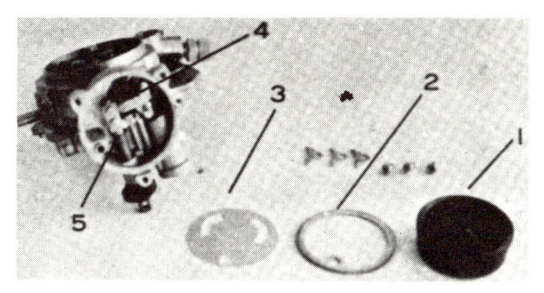

Fig 3.18 Automatic choke removal

1. Coil housing
2. Gasket
3. Housing plate
4. Cam float
5. Sliding rod

Fig 3.19 Choke shaft removal

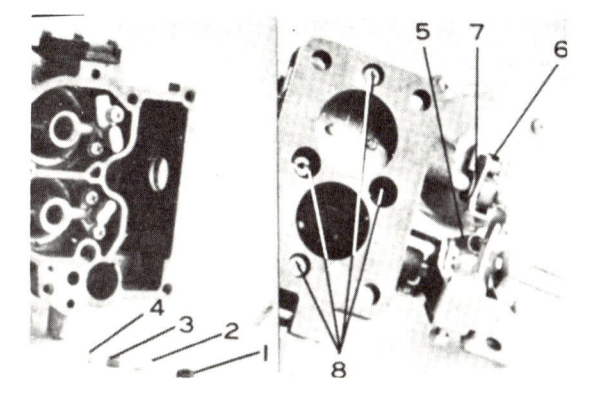

1. Set Screw
2. Choke shaft
3. Vacuum piston
4. Thermostat body

Fig 3.20 Ball and flange removal

1. Gasket
2. Stopper
3. Discharge weight
4. Ball
5. Spring
6. Diaphragm
7. Diaphragm lever
8. Flange set screws

Fig 3.21 Jet and venturi removal

1. Ball
2. Slow jet
3. Screws
4. Second small venturi
5. First small venturi
6. Power valve
7. 'T' bar wrench
8. Plugs
9. Second main jet
10. First main jet

Fig 3.22 Valve and petrol lever gauge removal

1. Cover
2. Gasket
3. Thermostatic valve
4. Level gauge clamp
5. Glass
6. Gasket

Fig 3.23 Diaphragm removal

1. Diaphragm housing
2. Housing
3. Diaphragm
4. Spring
5. Gasket

5 Undo and remove the four flange set screws and separate the flange from the main body. (Fig. 3.20).
6 Remove the check ball retainer and steel ball.
7 Remove the slow running jet and then remove the four screws and remove the second small venturi and first small venturi. (Fig. 3.21).
8 Using a suitable key remove the power valve.
9 Undo and remove the plug and lift away the second main jet and first main jet.
10 The following operation should only be carried out when necessary. Undo and remove the three screws securing cover. Lift away the cover, gasket and thermostatic valve. Undo and remove the two screws and lift away the level gauge glass and its gasket. (Fig. 3.22).
21 Undo and remove the four screws and lift away the diaphragm housing. Lift away the housing, diaphragm, spring and gasket. To ensure correct reassembly mark the relative positions of the housing, spring bracket and diaphragm. (Fig 3.23).
22 Undo and remove the idle adjustment screw.

23 The remaining dismantling instructions should only be carried out when necessary.
24 File off the peened point of the valve set screws and lift away the first and second throttle valves.
25 Withdraw the second throttle shaft and throttle lever. (Fig 3.24).
26 Remove the idle adjustment lever complete with throttle shaft arm.
27 Finally remove the retainer ring and withdraw the first throttle shaft. Dismantling is now complete and after cleaning the components they will be ready for inspection.
28 If a compressed air line is available carefully blow through all drillings. Do not use a wire probe to clean jets as it will only upset the calibration.
29 Lay a straight edge across all mating faces to ensure that no part is warped causing either air or fuel leaks.
30 Inspect all castings for signs of cracking and gasket surfaces for unevenness.
31 Check the seating surface and the thread of the idle adjustment screw for damage.
32 Place the shafts back into the castings and check for an excessive clearance. If excessive, obtain new parts.
33 Reassembly of the carburettor is the reverse sequence to removal and provided that the location of each part was noted during dismantling no problems will arise. It will be necessary to check and adjust the float lever, first throttle valve opening, second throttle valve opening, automatic choke and idle adjustment screw. Information on all these checks will be found later in this Chapter.

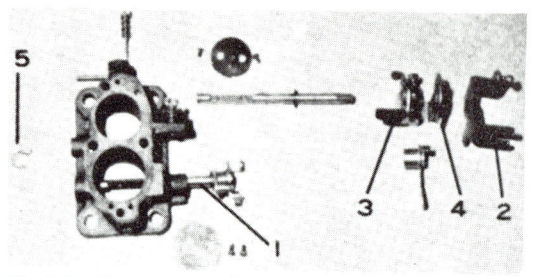

Fig 3.24 Throttle valve shaft removal

1 Second throttle shaft
2 Throttle lever
3 Idle adjustment lever
4 Throttle shaft arm
5 Retainer ring

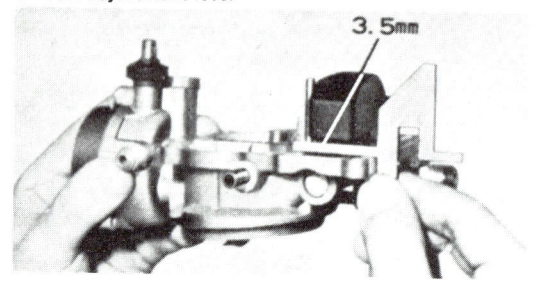

Fig 3.25 Float top level adjustment

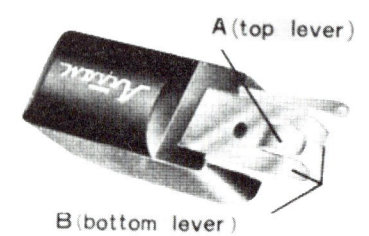

Fig 3.26 Float adjustment parts

A (top lever)
B (bottom lever)

11 Carburettor float level - adjustment

1 Adjustment of the fuel level in the float chamber is made by bending the float lever lips. When the top and level positions are correctly adjusted the float will maintain the correct level as indicated on the glass level mark when the engine is running.
2 With the air horn removed, hold it upside down and allow the float to hang down by its own weight. Measure the gap between the float tip and air horn. When correct the gap should be 0.138 in (3.5 mm).
3 If necessary adjust the gap by bending the float lip 'A' located as shown in Fig. 3.26.
4 Insert the air horn and measure the gap between the needle valve bush pin and float lip. When correct the gap should be 0.047 in (1.2 mm) (Fig. 3.27).
5 If necessary adjust the gap by bending the float lip 'B' located as shown in Fig. 3.26.

12 Throttle valve opening - adjustment

1 With the carburettor removed from the engine fully open the first and second valve throttle valves separately and ensure each throttle valve is vertical to the flange face.
2 If necessary adjust the first valve and second throttle valve by bending the throttle levers.
3 When this adjustment has been carried out ensure that the linkage is free and not binding.
4 The first throttle valve lever must contact the second valve lever when the first throttle valve opens 57° from the fully closed position. Any adjustment necessary is made by bending the valve lever.
5 The 'kick-up' position is achieved by bending the second throttle lever to obtain a clearance of 0.008 in (0.2 mm) between the second throttle valve and body when the first throttle valve opening is between 62° and the fully open position.
6 Fully open the choke valve and check and adjust the clearance between the bore and throttle valve. This measurement should be between 0.032 - 0.036 in (0.8 - 0.9 mm).
7 To check the unloader adjustment measure the angle of the choke valve when the first throttle valve is fully open. The angle should be 27°. Any necessary adjustment may be made by bending the fast idle cam follower or the choke shaft lip.

13 Automatic choke - adjustment

1 With the choke valve fully open, turn the coil housing anticlockwise and see if the choke valve closes.
2 Reset the coil housing scale to the centre line of the thermostat casing.
3 Now turn the coil housing slightly and adjust the engine starting mixture to suit the engine and operating conditions.
4 If the mixture is too rich turn the coil housing clockwise or if it is too weak turn anticlockwise.
5 The choke valve closes fully at an atmspheric temperature of 77°F (25°C) and one graduation of the scale on the thermostat case is equal to a 9°F (5°C) change.

14 Idle speed - adjustment

1 With the engine at normal operating temperature screw the idle adjustment screw in as far as possible without forcing. (Fig 3.34).
2 Unscrew it three turns from the fully closed position.

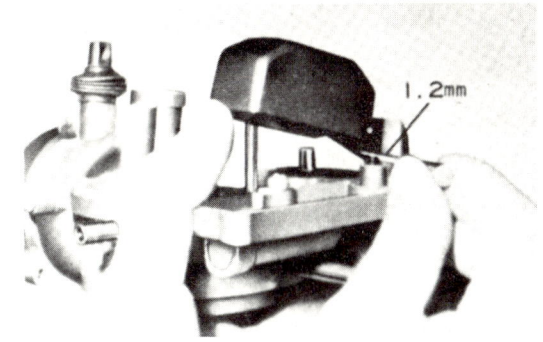

Fig 3.27 Float bottom level adjustment

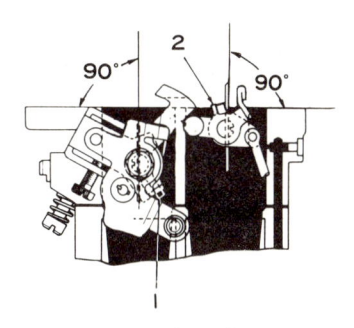

Fig 3.28 Throttle valve opening adjustment

1 First throttle valve 2 Second throttle valve

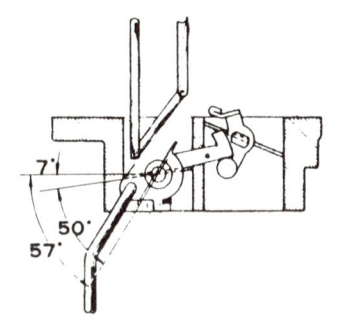

Fig. 3.29. Second throttle lever contact adjustment

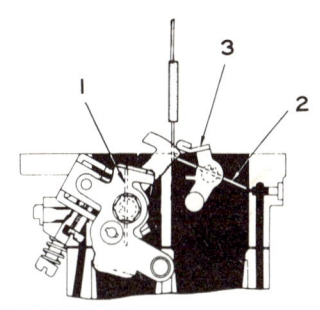

Fig 3.30 Kick-up adjustment

1 Fisrt throttle valve 3 Throttle lever
2 Second throttle valve

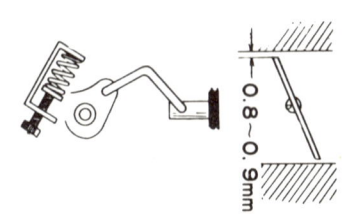

Fig 3.31 Fast idle adjustment

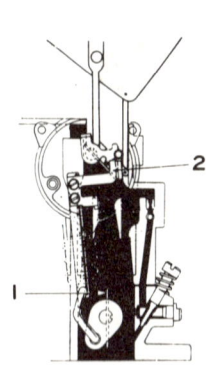

Fig 3.32 Unloader adjustment

1 First throttle valve 2 Choke valve

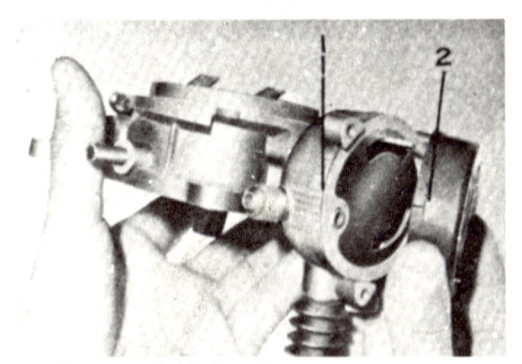

Fig 3.33 Automatic choke adjustment

1 Housing 2 Thermostat casing

Fig 3.34 Idle adjustment screw

15 Carburettor - adjustment

To enable the carburettor to be correctly set a vacuum gauge, adaptor and electric tachometer is necessary.
1 Start the engine and allow to reach normal operating temperature.
2 Connect the tachometer and vacuum gauge.
3 Adjust the engine idle speed as described in Section 14.
4 Turn the throttle adjustment and idle adjustment screw slowly until maximum vacuum is obtained at the specified idling speed (see Specifications).
5 Slowly screw the idle adjustment screw in until the point is reached whereby the speed or vacuum just begins to drop.
6 For engines operating in areas under control of the US Federal exhaust emission regulations refer to Section 2.

16 Fuel filter - removal and replacement

Two types of fuel filter have been used depending on the engine application. On 1100 and 1200 models the filter may be dismantled and cleaned but on 1600 models a disposable cartridge type is fitted into the fuel line.

Type 1 (1100/1200)
1 Disconnect the fuel inlet pipe and outlet hose from the fuel filter assembly.
2 Undo and remove the filter securing nut and spring washer. Lift away the filter assembly.
3 Slacken the filter bowl stirrup nut and ease back the stirrup. Remove the filter bowl, element and gasket.
4 Wash all parts in petrol. If sediment sticks to the element gauge use an old toothbrush to dislodge it.
5 Reassembly and refitting is the reverse sequence to removal.

Type 2 (1600)
1 Disconnect the fuel inlet and outlet hoses. Remove the filter from the mounting bracket by unscrewing the bolt and lockwasher. Note which way round it is fitted (photo).
2 Because this type of filter cannot be cleaned it should be discarded and a new one obtained.
3 Refitting the fuel filter is the reverse sequence to removal.

17 Fuel tank - removal and replacement

In all cases drain the petrol into a suitable sized container. Disconnect the battery for safety reasons and then proceed as follows. (Figs. 3.37/3.38).

Saloon/Sedan and Coupe models
1 Release the hose clamps and carefully detach the filler hose and bleed hose from the fuel tank.
2 Remove the filler hose from the luggage compartment.
3 Disconnect the fuel tank sender unit terminal connector and then unscrew the outlet pipe flared nut.
4 Undo and remove the four nuts and washers securing the tank and carefully lift away.
5 Refitting the fuel tank is the reverse sequence to removal.

Estate car models
1 Remove the spare wheel and release the hose clamps. Carefully detach the filler hose and bleed hose from the fuel tank.
2 Disconnect the fuel tank sender unit terminal connector and then unscrew the outlet pipe flared nut.
3 Undo and remove the nuts and washers securing the tank and spare wheel carrier and carefully lift away.
4 Should it be necessary to remove the filler hose access is gained once the right-hand side rear quarter trim panel is removed.
5 Refitting the fuel tank is the reverse sequence to removal.

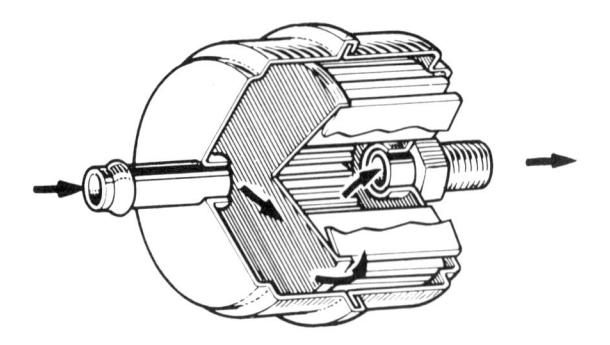

Fig 3.35 Cross sectional view of fuel filter (disposable type)

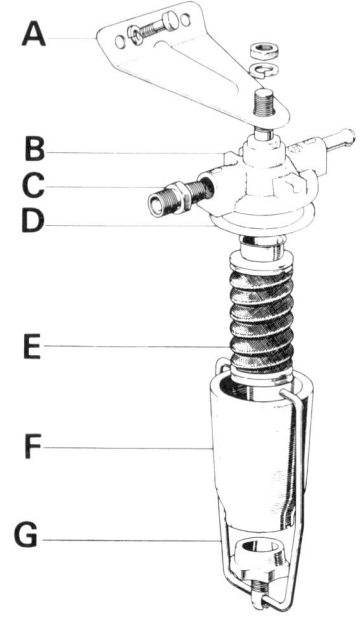

Fig 3.36 Exploded view of fuel filter

A Fuel filter support
B Fuel filter body
C Union
D Filter bowl gasket
E Fuel filter element
F Filter bowl
G Filter bowel stirrup

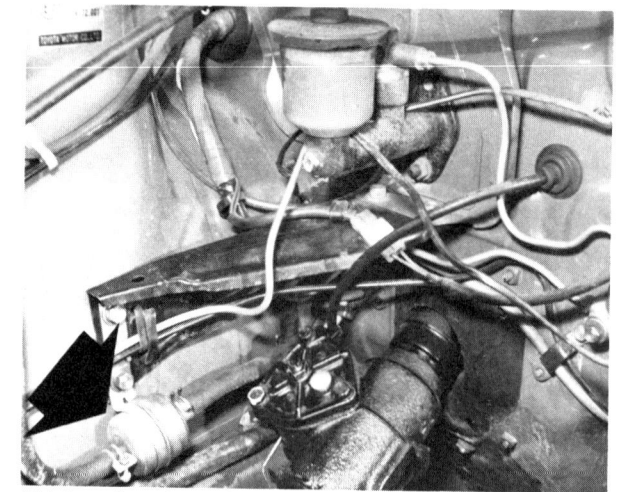

16A Location of type 2 fuel filter

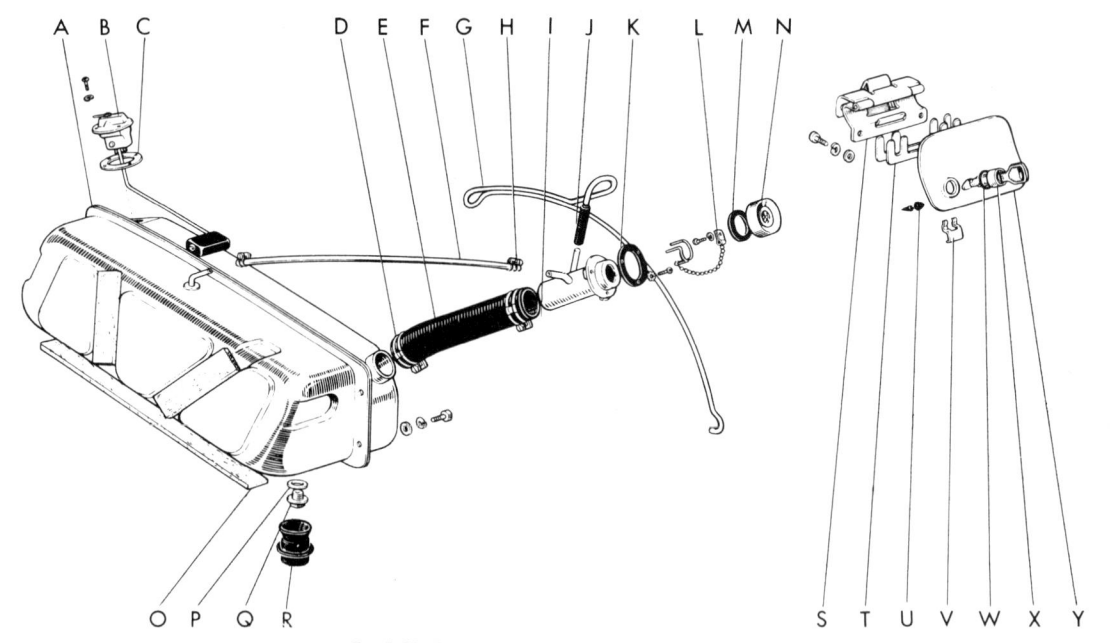

Fig 3.37 Fuel tank and attachments (Saloon models)

A Fuel tank
B Fuel sender gauge
C Fuel sender gauge gasket
D Hose clamp
E Fuel tank sub-inlet pipe
F Bleeder hose
G Bleeder long tube
H Hose clamp
I Fuel tank inlet pipe
J Hose
K Fuel tank inlet pipe shield
L Chain
M Fuel tank cap gasket
N Fuel tank cap
O Fuel tank bottom cushion
P Gasket
Q Drain plug
R Fuel tank drain plug shield
S Fuel inlet box cover hinge
T Fuel inlet box cover spacer
U Cushion
V Lock cylinder retainer
W Lock cylinder pad
X Cylinder and key set
Y Fuel inlet box cover

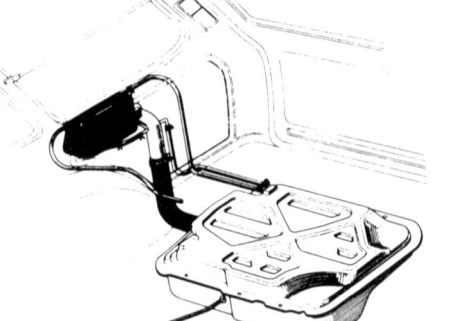

Fig 3.38 Later type fuel tank installation fitted to estate cars

18 Fuel tank - cleaning and repair

1 With time it is likely that sediment will collect in the bottom of the fuel tank. Condensation, resulting in rust and other impurities is sometimes found in the fuel tank.
2 With the tank removed it should be vigorously flushed out and turned upside down, and if facilities are available, steam cleaned.
3 Repairs to the fuel tank to stop leaks are best carried out using resin adhesive and hardeners as supplied by most accessory shops. In cases of repairs being done to large areas, glass fibre mats or perforated zinc sheet may be required to give the area support. If any soldering, welding or brazing is contemplated, the tank must be steamed out to remove any traces of petroleum vapour. It is dangerous to use naked flames on a fuel tank without this, even though it may have been lying empty for a considerable time.

19 Fuel pipes and lines - general inspection

1 Check all flexible hoses for signs of perishing, cracking or damage and replace if necessary.
2 Carefully inspect all metal fuel pipes for signs of corrosion, cracking, kinking or distortion and replace any pipe that is suspect. These pipes are clipped to the underbody.

20 Fuel gauge sender unit - fault finding

1 The sender unit is mounted on the fuel tank and access is straightforward.
2 If the fuel gauge does not work correctly then the fault is either in the sender unit, the gauge in the instrument cluster, the wiring or the voltage regulator.
3 First test for operation: switch on the ignition and observe if the fuel and temperature gauges operate. If only one operates it can be assumed that the voltage regulator is satisfactory. However, if neither operates then check the regulator.
4 To check the sender unit first disconnect the wire from the unit at the connector. Switch on the ignition and the gauge should read 'Empty'. Now connect the lead to earth and the gauge should read 'Full'. Allow 30 seconds for each reading.
5 If both the situations are correct then the fault lies in the sender unit.
6 If the gauge does not read 'Empty' with the wire disconnected from the sender unit, the wire should then also be disconnected from the gauge to the sender unit.
7 If not, the gauge is faulty and should be replaced. (For details see Chapter 10).
8 With the wire disconnected from the sender unit and earthed,

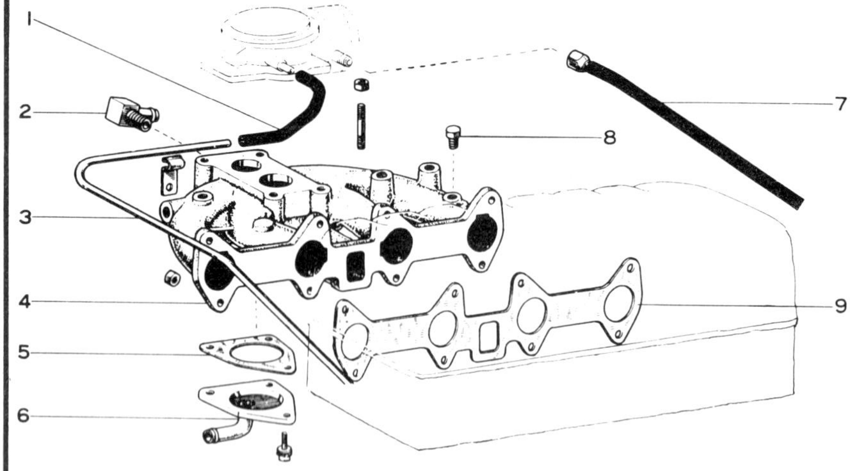

Fig 3.39 Inlet manifold components (1100,1200 models)

1. Hose, stove inlet
2. Elbow
3. Pipe, automatic stove inlet
4. Manifold, intake
5. Gasket, water by-pass
6. Outlet subassembly, water by-pass
7. Outlet subassembly, automatic stove
8. Plug, with head, tapered screw
9. Gasket, intake manifold to head

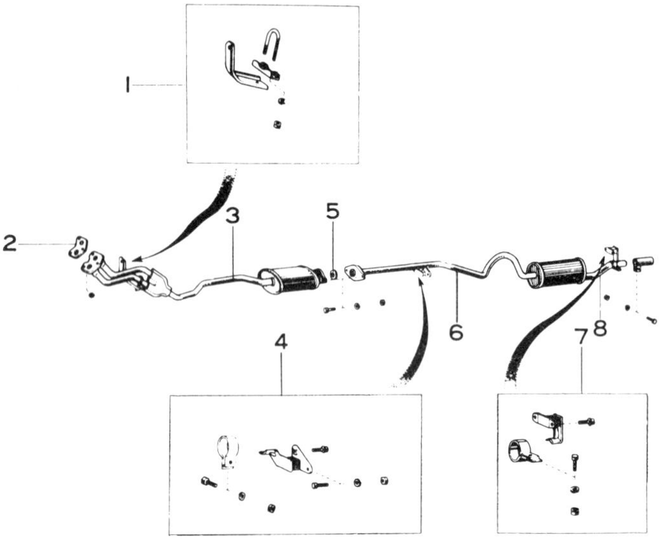

Fig 3.40 Exhaust system components (1600 models)

1. Bracket, exhaust pipe support
2. Gasket, exhaust pipe
3. Pipe assembly, exhaust, front
4. Support, exhaust pipe, No. 1
5. Gasket, exhaust pipe
6. Pipe subasembly, exhaust centre
7. Support, exhaust pipe, No. 2
8. Pipe assembly, tail

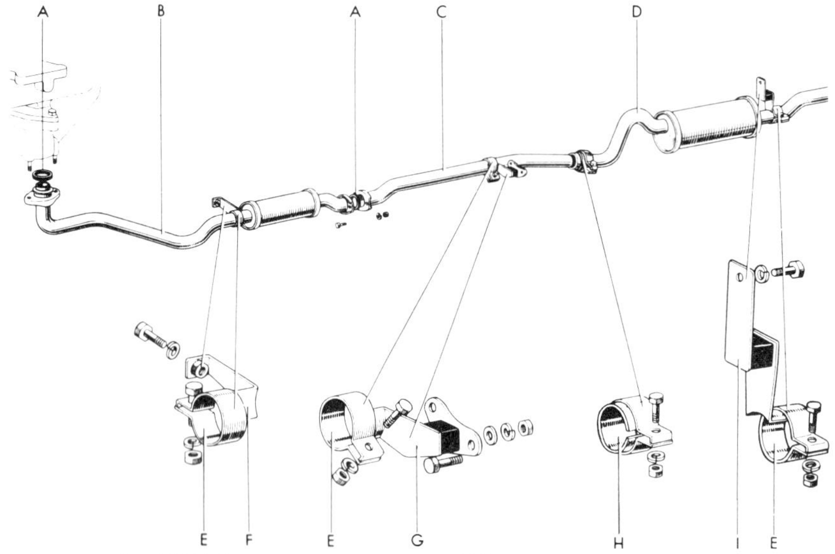

Fig 3.41 Exhaust system components (1100, 1200 models)

A Exhaust pipe gasket
B Exhaust front pipe
C Exhaust centre pipe
D Exhaust tail pipe
(muffler)
E Clamp
F Exhaust pipe support
bracket
G Exhaust pipe No. 1 support
H Exhaust pipe clamp
I Exhaust pipe No. 2 support

Chapter 3/Fuel system and carburation   89

if the gauge reads anything other than 'Full' check the rest of the circuit (see Chapter 10 for the wiring diagram).
9 To remove the unit first remove the tank as described in Section 17.
10 Undo and remove the screws and spring washers securing the unit to the tank. Lift away the unit taking care not the bend the wire arm. Recover the gasket.
11 Refitting the sender unit is the reverse sequence to removal. Always use a new gasket.

21 Exhaust emission control - general description

Vehicles being operated in areas controlled by the US Federal regulations on air pollution must have their ancilliary equipment modified and accurately tuned so that carbon monoxide, hydrocarbons and nitrogen produced by the engine are within finely controlled limits.

To achieve this there are several systems used. Depending on

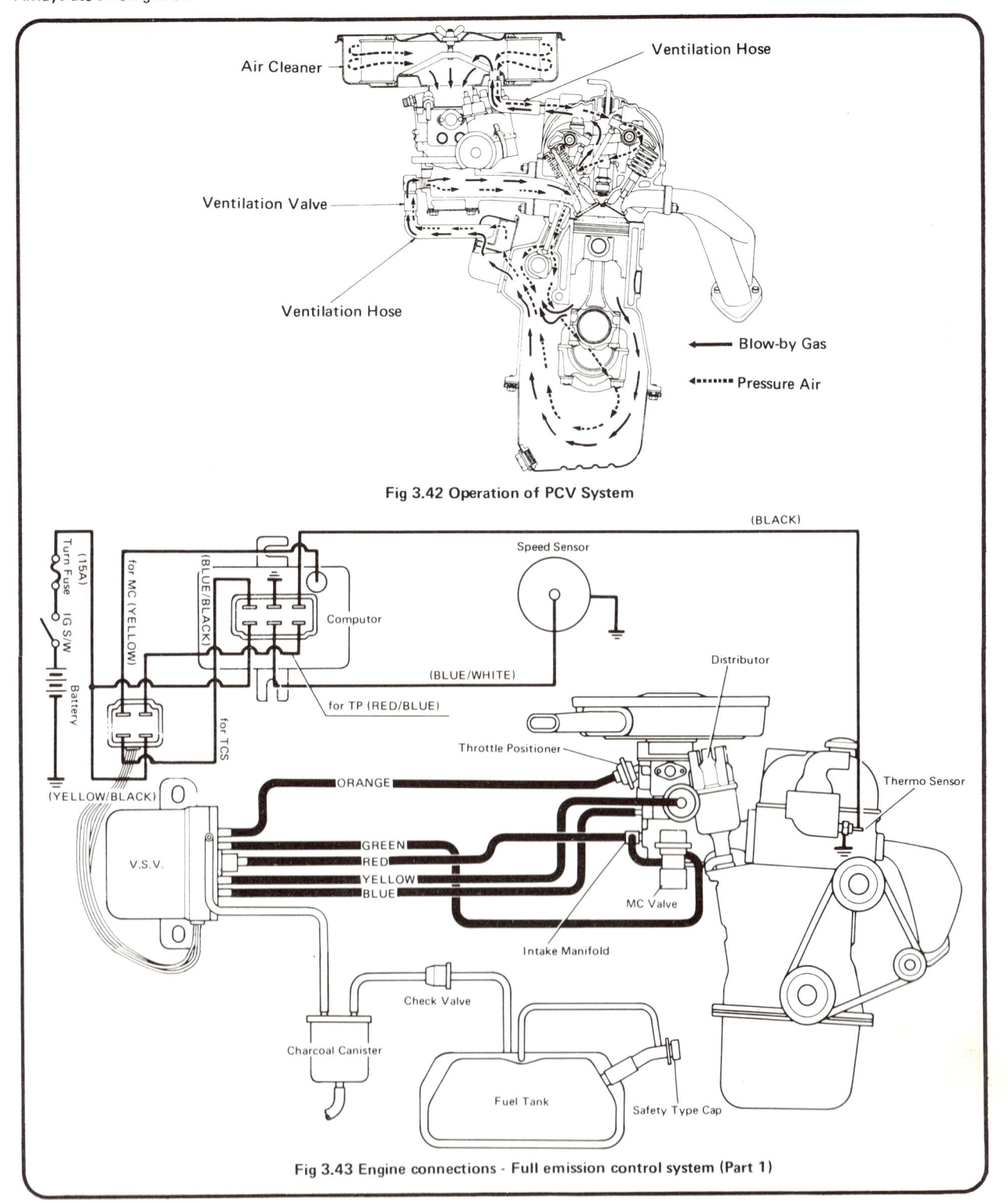

Fig 3.42 Operation of PCV System

Fig 3.43 Engine connections - Full emission control system (Part 1)

Remarks:

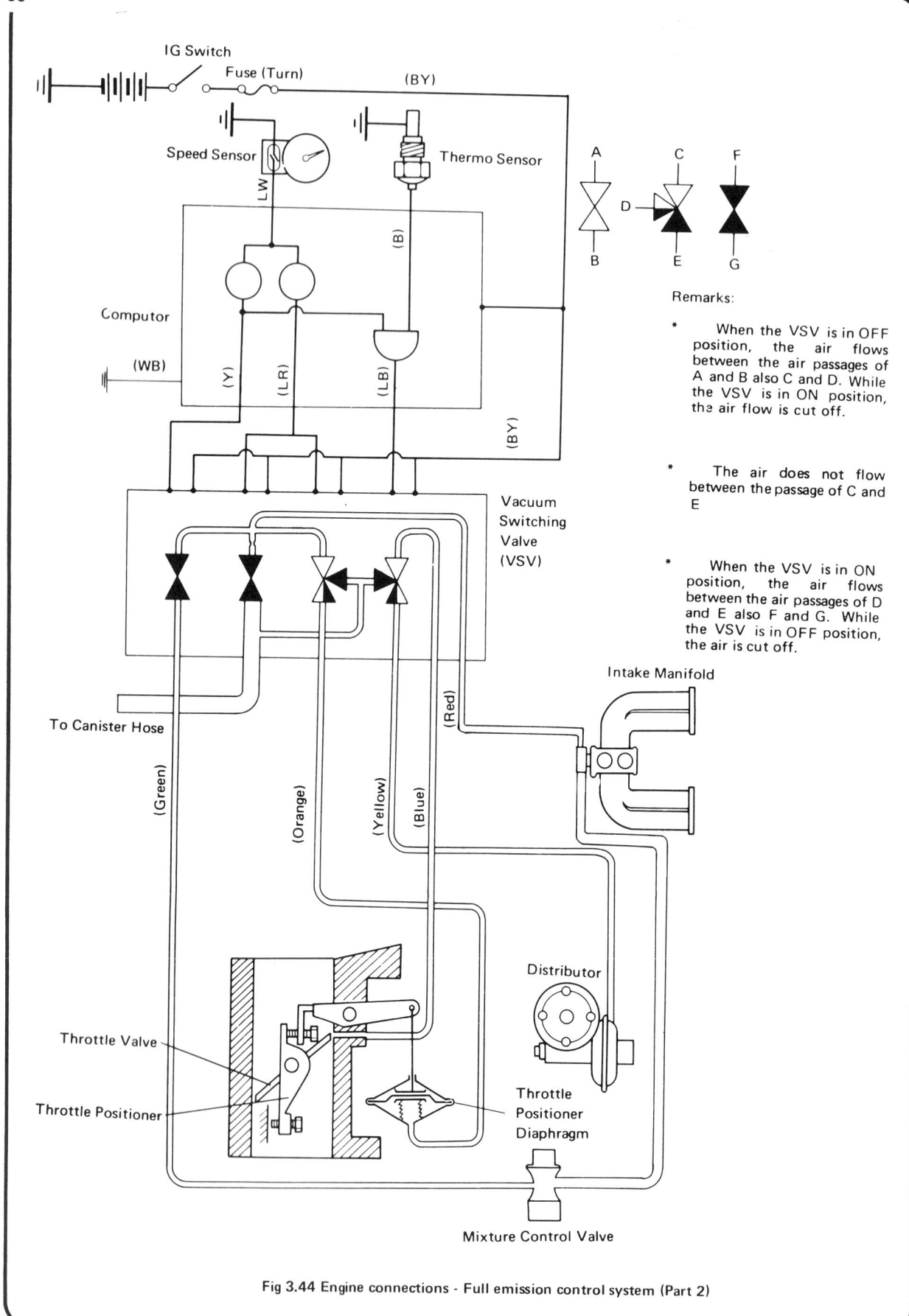

* When the VSV is in OFF position, the air flows between the air passages of A and B also C and D. While the VSV is in ON position, the air flow is cut off.

* The air does not flow between the passage of C and E

* When the VSV is in ON position, the air flows between the air passages of D and E also F and G. While the VSV is in OFF position, the air is cut off.

Fig 3.44 Engine connections - Full emission control system (Part 2)

Chapter 3/Fuel system and carburation

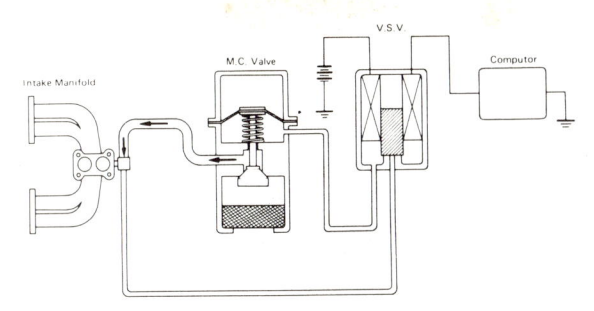

Fig 3.45 Mixture control system - Idling or low speed operation

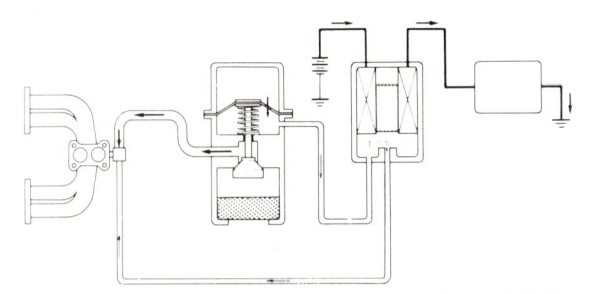

Fig 3.46 Mixture control system - Intermediate and high speed operation

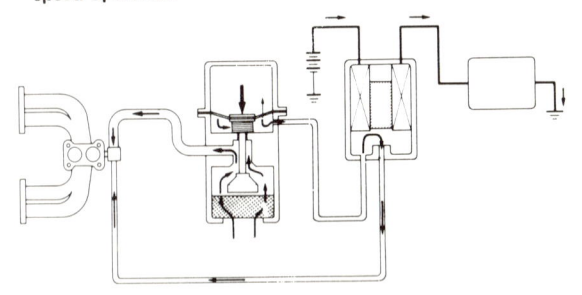

Fig 3.47 Mixture control system - sudden deceleration

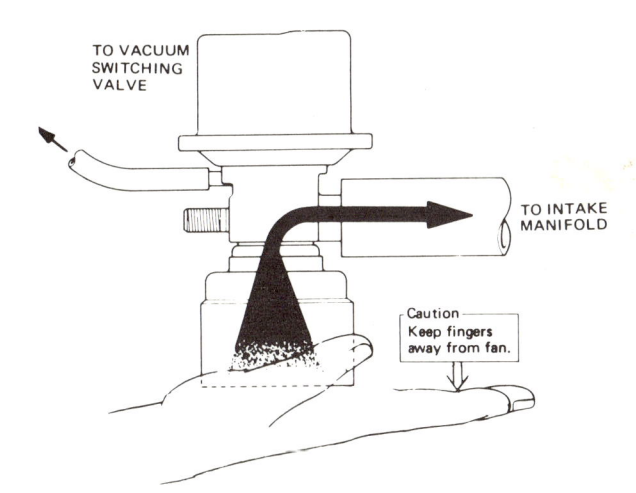

Fig 3.48 Testing operation of mixture control system

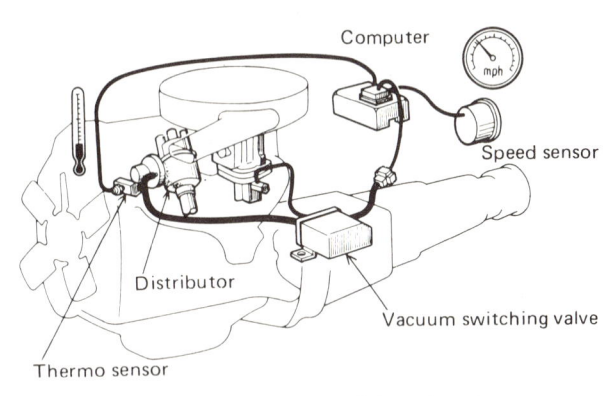

Fig 3.49 Transmission controlled spark system

the standard required, the systems may be fitted either singly or as a combination of several types. The solution to the problem is achieved by modifying various parts of the engine and fuel supply system as will be seen in subsequent Sections. It must be pointed out that the information is of a more general nature as this is a vast subject which requires specialist knowledge as well as expensive test equipment. Whenever possible always leave emission problems to the local Toyota garage.

22 Mixture control system (Exhaust emission control system)

With the engine under sudden deceleration conditions the air intake will become insufficient and cause incomplete combustion of the fuel. This will give a greater emission of carbon monoxide and hydrocarbons to the atmosphere. A mixture control valve is fitted and designed to open momentarily and allow fresh air to enter the inlet manifold under these conditions thereby ensuring complete combustion.

When the engine is idling or running at a low speed a speed sensor will emit a signal and the current from a computor will stop, switching off the vacuum valve. The vacuum valve will remain closed and render the mixture control valve inoperative. inoperative.

Under normal running, at medium and high speeds, signals from a speed sensor will allow current to flow from the computor to the vacuum switching valve, opening the valve and allowing a free passage from the mixture control valve sensing hose to the inlet manifold. This condition will remain as long as there is no sudden change in the inlet manifold depression level.

The pressure at both sides of the valve diaphragm will remain equal because of the regulating port connecting the upper and lower diaphragm chambers.

If the car is suddenly decelerated from a high speed when the vacuum switching valve is open, the mixture control valve will open momentarily and allow fresh air to enter into the manifold. The pressures on both sides of the diaphragm become equal quickly through the regulating port. The diaphragm is then returned by a return spring so that the mixture control valve remains open momentarily when the car is suddenly decelerated.

To check the operation of the system requires the use of special equipment but a rough check can be made by starting the engine and seeing if there is a momentary vacuum at the inlet when the engine is decelerated. This will show if the mixture control system is in operation. Use the hand for this but take care as the fingers will be near the fan. To achieve best results the rear of the car should be jacked-up and the rear wheels driven.

Alternatively detach the vacuum sensing hose at the vacuum switch valve and suck the vacuum sensing hose with the mouth. If air can be drawn into the mixture valve for a second or so the valve is satisfactory. If this cannot be done the valve should be renewed.

23 Transmission controlled spark system (Exhaust emission control system)

The objective of this system is to control the release of nitrogen oxides contained in the exhaust gases to a minimal level. It comprises a computor and other components which regulate the ignition vacuum advance by monitoring the speed of the car and engine coolant temperature. No regular maintenance is called for but in the event of a suspected malfunction, test the components in the following manner:-

A Distributor diaphragm unit and TCS on/off test

1 To test that the distributor vacuum diaphragm is in good order run the engine to normal operating temperature. Raise the rear wheels and support the rear axle on stands. Securely chock the front wheels.
2 Accelerate the engine and have an assistant note the movement of the vernier adjuster on the distributor body. The TCS alters the distributor advance characteristics when the car road speed is between 16 - 62 mph (26 - 100 kph) and so the distributor should appear as diagram 'A' (Fig. 3.50) between these speeds and as diagram 'B' when below or above this speed range and the distributor advance mechanism is working normally. This testing procedure also proves the on/off positions of the system as a whole.
3 An alternative method which is also less dangerous as it does not require the jacking-up of the rear wheels for speed testing is to remove the hoses from the nozzles 'F' and 'G' of the vacuum switching valve and in their place connect two vacuum gauges which can be seen by the driver.
4 Road test the car and when the engine is at its normal operating temperture note the operation of the vacuum gauges.
5 The main disadvantage of this last method is that it does not indicate the condition of the distributor diaphragm unit.

B Vacuum switching valve

1 Check the vacuum switching valve for leaks by blowing air or smoke (pipe or cigarette smoke) through the nozzles.
2 Check the vacuum switching valve electrically by unplugging the connector and then using a circuit tester check for shorting between each of the connector plug terminals in turn and the vacuum switching valve casing.
3 Test for open circuit by checking the resistance between the connector plug (+) terminal and each of the other terminals in turn; the resistance should be 28.0 ohms.

C Thermo Sensor test

The thermo sensor is screwed into the base of the cooling system thermostat housing and it should only be moved if essential. Test by connecting a circuit tester when a resistance of between 15 and 30 kilo-ohms should be registered when the engine is cold or approximately 2 kilo-ohms with the engine at operating temperature.

D Computor and speed sensor

1 It will be appreciated that if the test described in part A of this Section have proved positive then there cannot be a fault in either the computor or speed sensor units. Where however the distributor, the vacuum switching valve and the thermo sensor have been individually tested as described but the TCS system still operates incorrectly then the fault must lie in the computor or speed sensor.
2 The computor unit can only be tested by the local Toyota garage or by substitution of another unit.
3 The speed sensor operates by the action of the speedometer head. Correct functioning can be checked by pulling out the speed marker relay connector and connecting a circuit tester. Disconnect the speedometer drive at the transmission housing and turn the cable by hand, observing that there are six on/off cycles for each revolution of the cable. If this is not the case, renew the speedometer head.
4 Having carried out all the preceding checks and tests any component which fails must be renewed as a unit, no repair being possible.

24 Throttle positioner system (Exhaust emission control system)

When the engine is decelerated the air/fuel mixture supply becomes insufficient, causing incomplete combustion in the engine and allowing a greater discharge of carbon monoxide and hydrocarbons to the atmosphere. To cope with this condition, a throttle positioner is fitted to open the throttle valve slightly more than at idling speed when the engine is being decelerated. By slightly increasing the air/fuel supply at this time, complete combustion will take place to minimise carbon monoxide and hydrocarbons to the atmospnere.

During medium and high speed motoring the speed sensor signal allows the vacuum switching valve to be energised by the computor which causes the valve to open, enabling fresh air to be led into the positioner diaphragm. The positioner is then set by the tension of the return spring. When the accelerator pedal is released the throttle valve strikes against the positioner and being unable to return to the full idling position remains slightly open.

When the car is driven at a low speed a signal from the speed sensor causes the vacuum switching valve to be closed and the valve shuts off. This allows the inlet manifold vacuum to act on the positioner diaphragm and release the positioner from the throttle valve. The throttle valve then returns to its idling speed position.

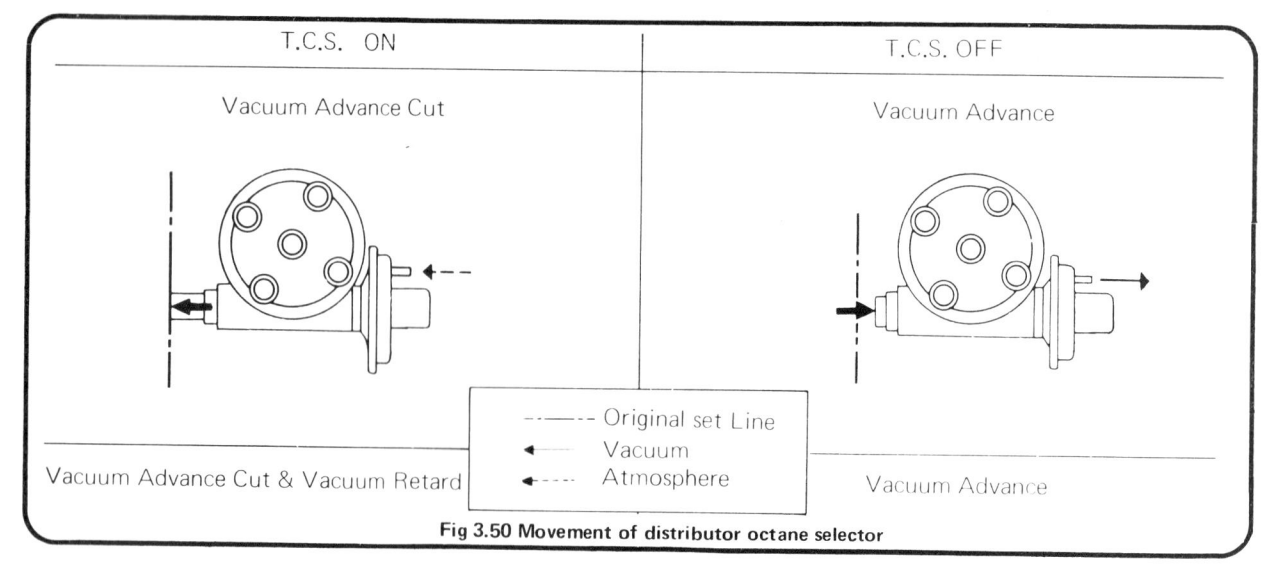

Fig 3.50 Movement of distributor octane selector

Chapter 3/Fuel system and carburation

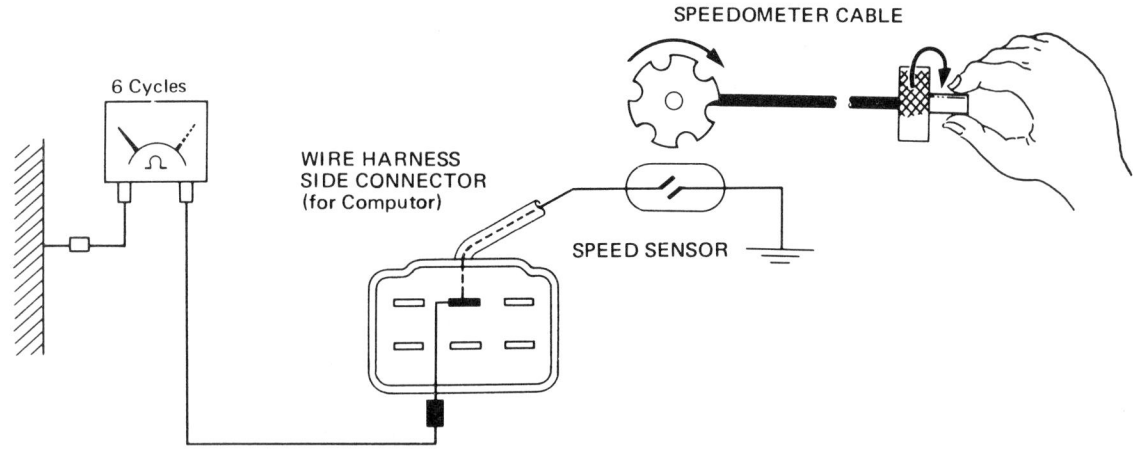

Fig 3.51 Checking speed sensor

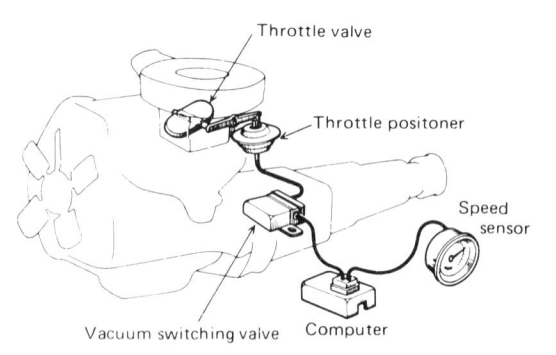

Fig 3.52 Throttle positioner system

Checking the operation of the system should be left to the local Toyota garage. However a quick check may be made by the owner. When the positioner diaphragm is held in the returned position by the spring the system is 'on' whereas the system is 'off' when the positioner is released from the throttle link due to vacuum acting on the positioner diaphragm.

If a vacuum gauge and long hose is available disconnect the positioner diaphragm hose from the vacuum switching valve and connect the vacuum gauge hose in its place. Connect the other end of the hose to the gauge. Drive the car throughout its operating range and check that during operation when a vacuum is indicated on the gauge, the throttle positioner is off. When there is no vacuum the system is 'on'.

25 Charcoal canister storage system (Exhaust emission control system)

The charcoal canister storage system is designed to lead the

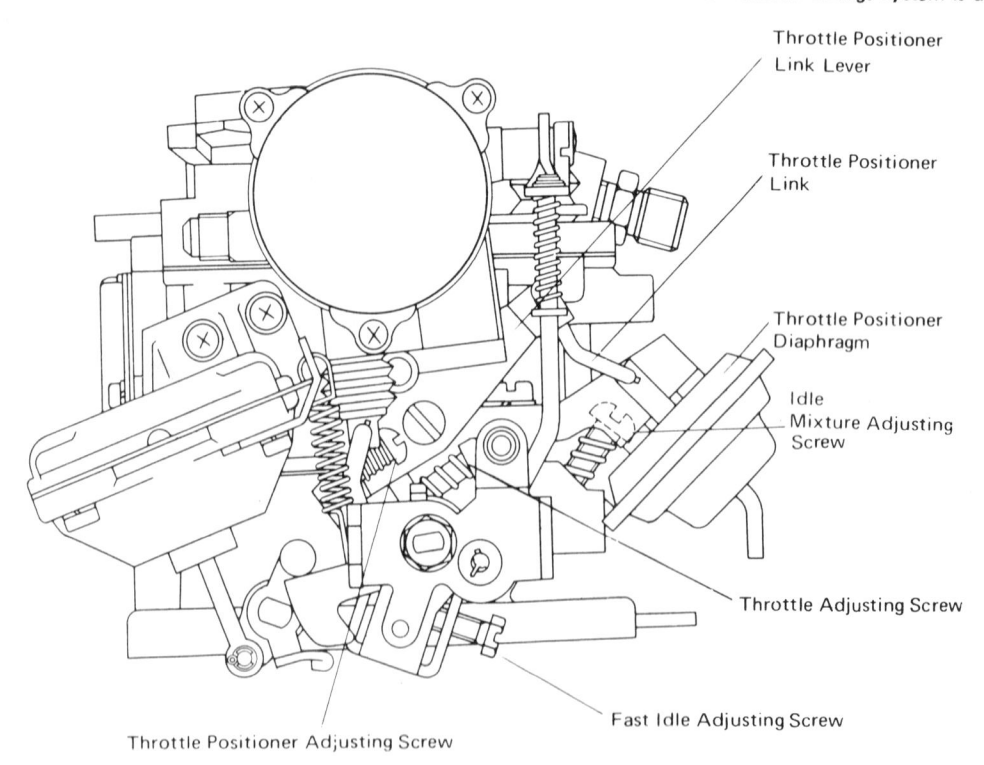

Fig 3.53 Carburettor for 2T-C series engine

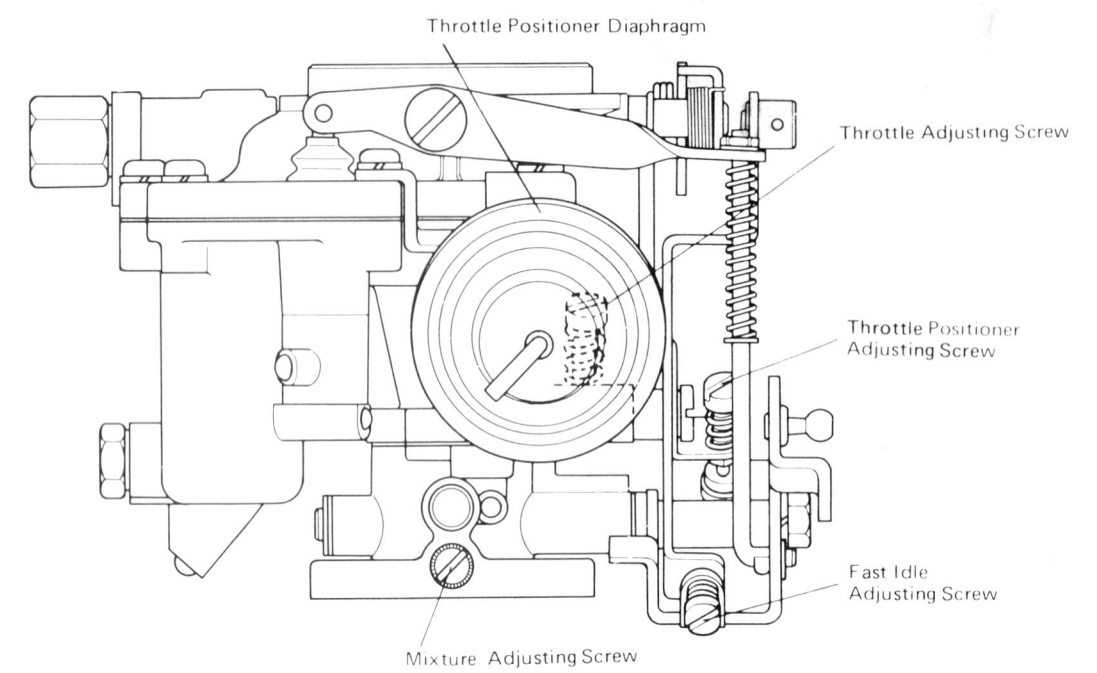

Fig 3.54 Carburettor for 3K-C series engine

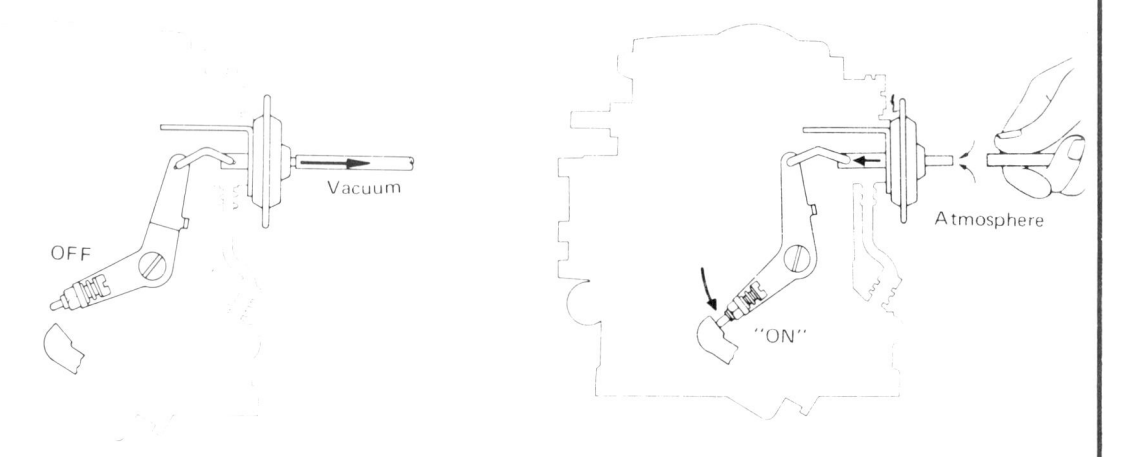

Fig 3.55 Operation of throttle positioner

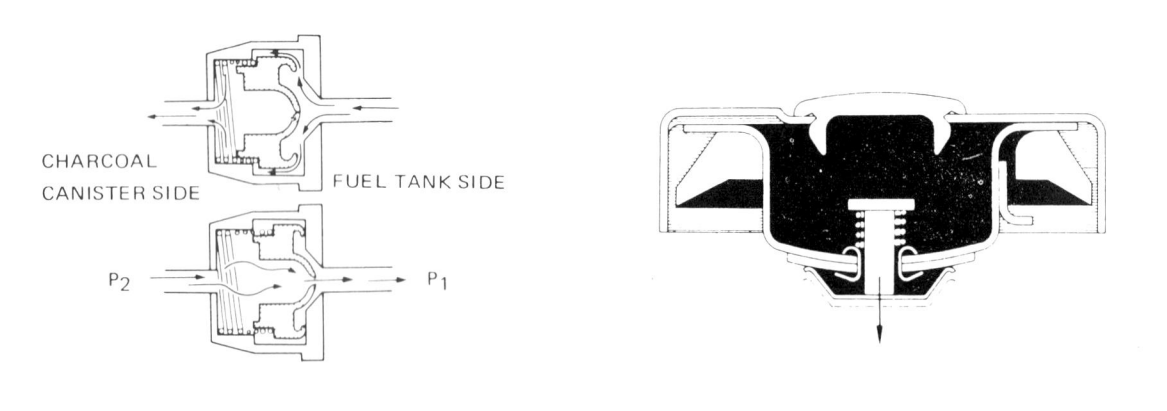

Fig 3.56 Check valve (left) and safety cap (right)

Chapter 3/Fuel system and carburation

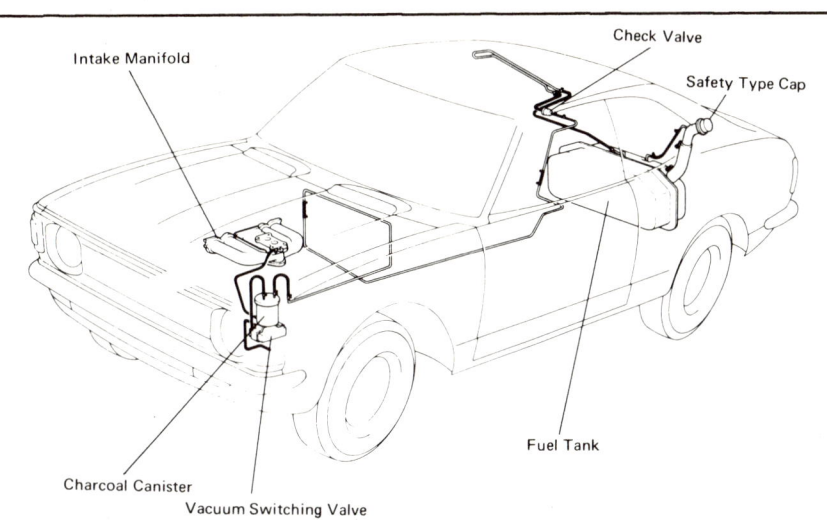

Fig 3.57 Charcoal canister storage system - KE Saloon

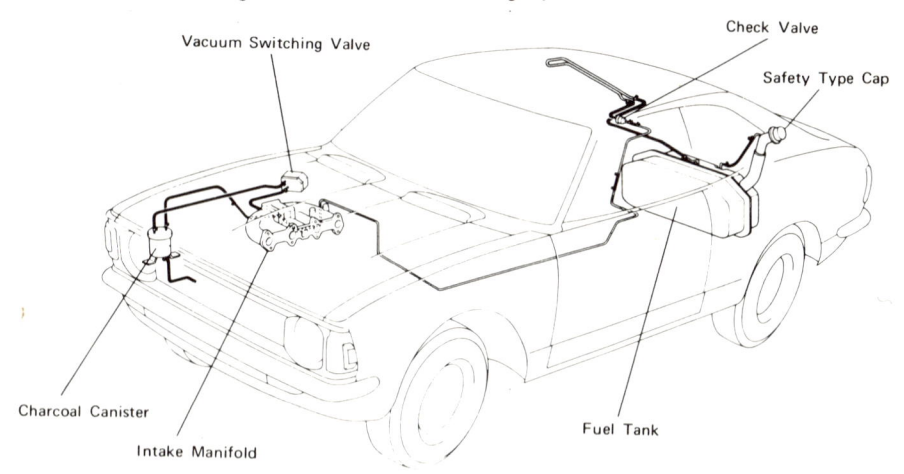

Fig 3.58 Charcoal canister storage system - TE Saloon

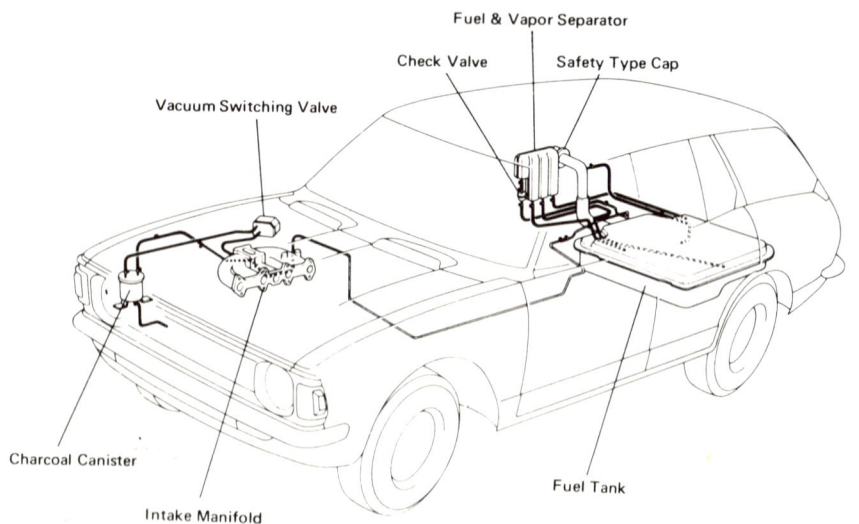

Fig 3.59 Charcoal canister storage system - TE Estate car.

petrol vapours in the fuel system into the inlet manifold and its operation is shown in Fig. 3.56. Its operation is very reliable but there are several points that should be checked during maintenance service.

1 Carefully examine the fuel tank for damage, corrosion or leaks. Rectify any fault found. Check the air tightness of the fuel tank safety cap.

2 Inspect the thermal expansion tank to ensure that it is not cracked or deformed.

3 Disconnect the canister and inspect for signs of blockage. Clean if necessary with an air jet.

4 Check all hoses and clips for security. Renew any hoses that have deteriorated.

26 Fault diagnosis - fuel system and carburation

Unsatisfactory engine performance and excessive fuel consumption are not necessarily the fault of the fuel system or carburettor. In fact they more commonly occur as a result of ignition faults. Before acting on the fuel system it is necessary to check the ignition system first. Even though a fault may lie in the fuel system it will be difficult to trace unless the ignition system is correct. This table may also be read in conjunction with the chart applicable to exhaust emission control models.

Symptom	Cause
Smell of petrol when engine is stopped	Leaking fuel lines or unions. Leaking fuel tank.
Smell of petrol when engine is idling	Leaking fuel line unions between pump and carburettor. Overflow of fuel from float chamber due to wrong level setting or ineffective needle valve or punctured float.
Excessive fuel consumption for reasons not covered by leaks or float chamber faults	Worn needle valve. Sticking needle.
Difficult starting, uneven running, lack of power, cutting out	One or more blockages. Float chamber fuel level too low or needle sticking. Fuel pump not delivering sufficient fuel. Inlet manifold gaskets leaking, or manifold fractured.

Chapter 3/Fuel system and carburation

27 Fault diagnosis - exhaust emission control system

When trouble is being experienced with the fuel system it is recommended that if possible the car be taken to the local Toyota garage. The reason for this is that quite often a fuel system problem does not necessarily originate from the fuel system but from a fault in the ignition or cooling systems or their controls. To find the cause quickly requires the use of test equipment which the average owner driver does not possess. The following chart covers some of the more common symptoms and causes to assist the owner in cases where expert advice is not immediately available.

Symptom	Cause
Engine loss of power	Insufficient engine compression.
	Valve adjustment incorrect.
	Air cleaner blocked.
	Ignition timing incorrect.
	Distributor contact breaker points gap incorrect.
Engine difficult to start (ignition system)	Discharged battery.
	Ignition timing incorrect.
	Distributor contact breaker points gap incorrect.
	Spark plugs gap incorrect or dirty.
(fuel system)	Automatic choke operation incorrect.
	Carburettor adjustment incorrect.
Poor acceleration or misfiring and backfiring on deceleration	
(Ignition system)	Distributor contact breaker points gap incorrect.
	Ignition cable resistance incorrect.
	Ignition timing incorrect.
(Fuel system)	Automatic choke operation incorrect.
	Carburettor adjustment incorrect.
	Blockage in fuel system.
Idling rough	Air cleaner blocked.
	Ignition system malfunction.
	Fuel system malfunction.
	P.C.V. ventilation hoses cracked or connections defective.
	Malfunction in inlet or exhaust system.
	Valve adjustment incorrect.
	Leaks in manifold or valves.
Engine runs on when ignition system is switched off	Wrong spark plugs.
	Idle speed too fast.
	Ignition timing incorrect.
	Engine/cooling system overheating.
	Too low grade of fuel.
Petrol smells	Petrol leak from evaporative emission control system.
	Petrol leak at carburettor
	Petrol leak from tank or lines.
'Blow-by' gas smells	P.C.V. system hose disconnected or cracked
Excessive oil consumption	Oil burning inside cylinder.
	Engine oil leakage.
Excessive fuel consumption	Malfunction in T.C.S. system.
	Malfunction in ignition system.
	Malfunction in fuel system.

Chapter 4 Ignition system

Contents

Condenser - removal, testing and replacement ... 5	Fault diagnosis - engine misfires ... 14
Contact breaker points - adjustment ... 3	Fault diagnosis - ignition system (general) ... 12
Contact breaker points - removal and replacement ... 4	General description ... 1
Distributor - dismantling, overhaul and reassembly ... 8	Ignition system servicing and Federal Regulations (USA only) ... 2
Distributor - lubrication ... 6	Ignition timing ... 10
Distributor - removal ... 7	Spark plugs and HT leads ... 11
Distributor - replacement ... 9	
Fault diagnosis - engine fails to start ... 13	

Specifications

Spark plugs:
- Make and type
  - All except 3K ... Champion N5,
    Bosch W175T2
    AC 45 XL
    Autolite AG3
    NGK B6E
    Denso W17ES
  - 3K ... Denso W20EP
    NGK BP6ES
    Champion N10Y
    Bosch W200T27
- Plug gap ... 0.027 - 0.031 in. (0.70 - 0.80 mm)

Coil:
- Type ... Compound filled
- Primary coil resistance ... 3.6 ohms
- Secondary coil resistance ... 75 ohms
- Insulation resistance ... Over 10 meg - ohms

Ignition timing:
- KE 10, 15, 16 (1100) ... 8° btdc at 600 rpm
- KE 11, 17, 18 (1200) ... 8° btdc at 650 rpm
- KE 20, 25, 26 (1200) ... 5° atdc at 650 rpm
- 3K (1200) ... 8° btdc at 600 rpm
- 2T (1600) ... 10° btdc at 650 rpm
- 2T-C (1600) ... 5° atdc at 650 rpm

- TE (1600):
  - Manual transmission ... 5° btdc at 750 rpm
  - Automatic transmission ... 5° btdc at 650 rpm in 'D'

Distributor:
- Contact breaker points gap ... 0.016 - 0.020 in. (0.4 - 0.5 mm)
- Dwell angle ... 50° - 54°
- Condenser capacity ... 0.20 - 0.24 NF
- Contact breaker points spring tension ... 17.6 - 24.7 oz (500 - 700 gms)
- Spindle bend limit ... 0.002 in. (0.05 mm)
- Spindle thrust clearance ... 0.006 - 0.020 in. (0.15 - 0.50 mm)
- Breaker plate to stationary plate clearance ... 0.008 in. (0.20 mm)
- Breaker plate operating resistance ... 17.6 - 24.7 oz. (500 - 700 gms)
- Octane selector (vernier adjustment) ... One turn approximately 4° crank angle

Firing order: ... 1 3 4 2

Chapter 4/Ignition system

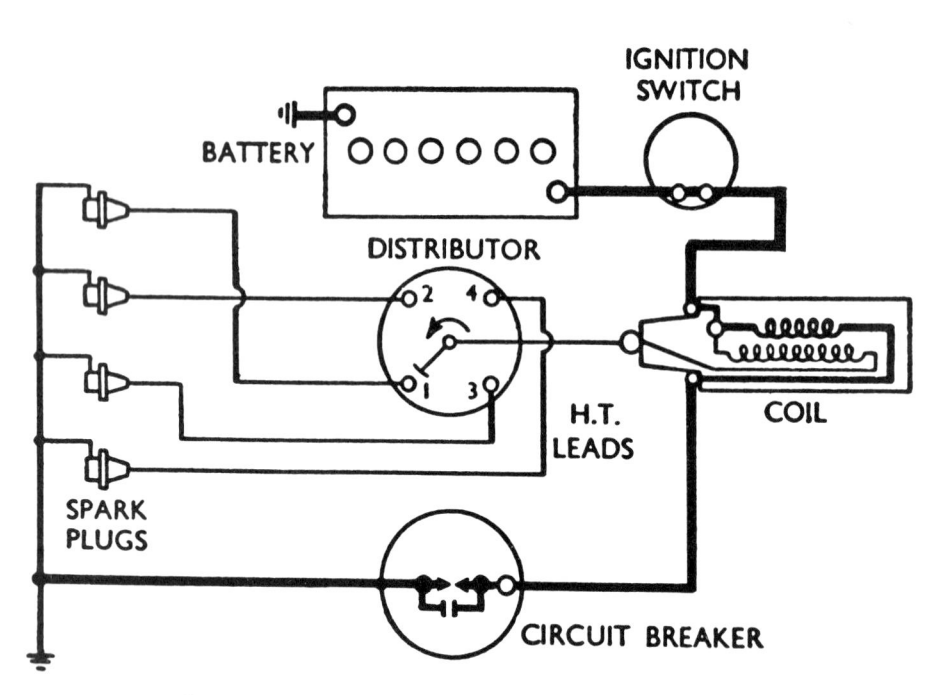

Torque wrench setting:	lb f ft	kg fm
Spark plugs	10.8 - 15.2	1.5 - 2.1

Fig. 4.1. Diagram of the ignition circuit. Primary circuit (low tension) is indicated by heavier lines

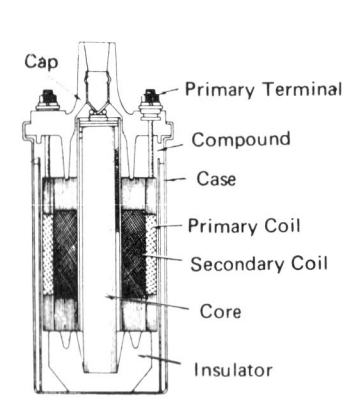

Fig. 4.2. Cross sectional view of ignition coil

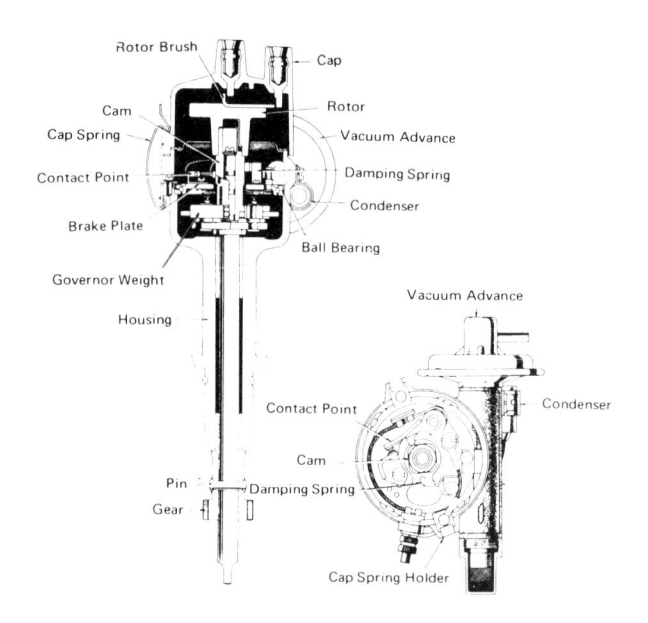

Fig. 4.3. Cross sectional view of distributor

Chapter 4/Ignition system

1 General description

In order that the engine can run correctly it is necessary for an electric spark to ignite the fuel/air mixture in the combustion chamber at exactly the right moment in relation to engine speed and load. The ignition system is based on feeding low tension voltage from the battery to the coil where it is converted into high tension voltage. The high tension voltage is powerful enough to jump the spark plug gap in the cylinders many times a second under high compression, providing that the system is in good condition and that all adjustments are correct. The ignition system is divided into two circuits: low tension and high tension.

The low tension circuit (sometimes known as the primary) consists of the battery, the lead to the ignition switch, the lead from the ignition switch to the low tension on primary coil windings, and the lead from the low tension coil windings to the contact breaker points and condenser in the distributor.

The high tension circuit consists of the high tension or secondary coil windings, the heavy ignition lead from the centre of the coil windings, the heavy ignition lead from the centre of the coil to the centre of the distributor cap, the rotor arm, and the spark plug leads and the spark plugs.

The system functions in the following manner: Low tension voltage is changed in the coil into high tension voltage by the opening and closing of the contact breaker points in the low tension circuit. High tension voltage is then fed, via the carbon bush in the centre of the distributor cap, to the rotor arm of the distributor cap, and each time it comes in line with one of the four metal segments in the cap, which are connected to the spark plug leads, the opening and closing of the contact breaker points causes the high tension voltage to build up, jump the gap from the rotor arm to the appropriate metal segment and so, via the spark plug lead, to the spark plug, where it finally jumps the spark plug gap before going to earth.

The ignition is advanced and retarded automatically, to ensure the spark occurs at just the right instant for the particular load at the prevailing engine speed.

The ignition advance is controlled both mechanically and by a vacuum operated system. The mechanical governor comprises two weights, which move out from the distributor shaft as the engine speed rises due to centrifugal force. As they move outwards they rotate the cam relative to the distributor shaft, and so advance the spark. The weights are held in position by two light springs and it is the tension of these springs which is largely responsible for correct spark advancement.

The vacuum control consists of a diaphragm, one side of which is connected, via a small bore tube, to the carburettor, and the other side to the contact breaker plate. Depression in the inlet manifold and carburettor, which varies with engine speed and throttle opening, causes the diaphragm to move, so moving the contact breaker plate, and advancing or retarding the spark. A fine degree of control is achieved by a spring in the vacuum assembly.

2 Ignition system servicing and Federal regulations (USA only)

In order to conform with the Federal regulations which govern the emission of hydrocarbons and carbon monoxide from car exhaust systems, the engine, carburation and ignition systems have been suitably modified.

It is critically important that the ignition system is kept in good operational order and to achieve this, accurate analytical equipment is needed to check the distributor function. This will be found at the local dealer.

Information contained in this Chapter is supplied to enable the home mechanic to set the ignition system roughly so enabling starting of the engine. Thereafter the car should be taken to the local dealer for final tuning. Failure to do this can result in heavy penalties.

3 Contact breaker points - adjustment

1 To adjust the contact breaker points to the correct gap first release the two clips securing the distributor cap to the distributor body, and lift away the cap. Clean the cap inside, and out, with a dry cloth. It is unlikely that the four segments will be badly burned or scored, but if they are the cap will have to be renewed.

2 Inspect the contact located in the centre of the cap and make sure it is serviceable.

3 Lift off the rotor arm and dust proof cover (photo). Gently prise the contact breaker points open and examine the condition of their faces. If they are rough, pitted or dirty it will be necessary to remove them for refacing or for a replacement set to be fitted (photo).

4 Presuming that the points are satisfactory, or that they have been cleaned and refitted, measure the gap between the points by turning the engine over until the heel of the breaker arm is on the highest point of the cam.

5 A 0.016 - 0.020 inch (0.4 - 0.5 mm) feeler gauge should now just fit between the points.

6 If the gap varies from this amount, slacken the lockscrew and adjust the contact gap by resetting the moving contact position. When the gap is correct, tighten the securing screw and check the gap again. (photo)

7 Refit the dust cover and rotor and replace the distributor cap. Clip the spring blade retainers into position.

4 Contact breaker points - removal and replacement

1 If the contact breaker points are burned, pitted or badly worn they must be removed and renewed.

2 With the distributor cap removed lift off the rotor arm by pulling it straight up from the spindle. Also remove the dust cover.

3.3a Removal of rotor arms and dust-proof cover

3.3b The contact breaker points

3.6 Checking points gap with feeler gauge

3 Detach the contact breaker point wire from the condenser and coil terminal by slackening the through bolt nut and drawing the terminal connection upwards.
4 Undo and remove the two contact breaker points assembly securing screws and washers. Note that the earth wire is retained by one of the screws. Lift away the breaker point.
5 Reassembly is the reverse sequence to removal. The gap must be reset as described in Section 3. **Note:** Should the contact points be badly worn a new assembly must be fitted. As an emergency measure clean the faces with fine emery paper folded over a thin steel rule. It is necessary to remove completely the built up deposits, but not necessary to rub the fitted point right down to the stage where all the pitting has disappeared. When the surfaces are flat a feeler gauge can be used to reset the gap.

5 Condenser - removal, testing and replacement

1 The purpose of the condenser, (sometimes known as a capacitor) is to ensure that when the contact breaker points open there is no sparking across them which would waste voltage and cause wear.
2 The condenser is fitted in parallel with the contact breaker points. If it develops a short circuit, it will cause ignition failure as the points will be prevented from interrupting the low tension circuit.
3 If the engine becomes very difficult to start or begins to misfire after several miles running and the contact breaker points show signs of excessive burning, then the condition of the condenser must be suspect. A further test can be made by separating the points by hand with the ignition switched on. If this is accompanied by a flush it is indicative that the condenser has failed.
4 Without special test equipment the only sure way to diagnose condenser trouble is to replace a suspected unit with a new one and note if there is any improvement.
5 To remove a condenser from the distributor take off the distributor cap to give better access.
6 Detach the condenser lead from the terminal block.
7 Undo and remove the screw and washer securing the condenser to the distributor body. Lift away the condenser and lead.
8 Refitting the condenser is the reverse sequence to removal.

6 Distributor - lubrication

1 It is important that the distributor cam is lubricated with petroleum jelly and the contact breaker arm, centrifugal weights and cam spindle lubricated with engine oil at the specified mileage.
2 Detach the vacuum line from the vacuum advance diaphragm. any excess that finds its way onto the contact breaker points could cause burning and misfiring.
3 To gain access to the cam spindle, lift away the rotor arm and drop no more than two drops of engine oil onto the spindle screw. This will run down the spindle when the engine is hot and lubricate the bearings.
4 To lubricate the automatic timing control allow a few drops of oil to pass through the hole in the contact breaker baseplate through which the four sided cam emerges. Apply not more than one drop of oil to the moving contact pivot post and remove any excess.
5 Refit the rotor arm and distributor cap.

7 Distributor - removal

1 Mark the HT leads and detach from the spark plugs and ignition coil.
2 Detach the vacuum line from the vacuum advance diaphragm.
3 To make refitting simpler rotate the crankshaft until the timing notch on the crankshaft pulley lines up with the scale on the front of the timing cover. (photo) The exact setting will depend on the ignition timing as found in the 'Specifications' Section at the beginning of this Chapter. Ascertain that the number 1 cylinder is on the compression stroke by removing the spark plug and feeling the compression with a thumb as the piston rises in the cylinder. The distributor rotor arm should now point to number 1 cylinder HT lead segment in the cap.
4 Undo and remove the distributor securing bolt, spring and plain washer and withdraw the distributor and clamp (photo).

8 Distributor - dismantling, overhaul and reassembly

It should be noted that the distributor fitted to models covered by this manual can differ slightly in construction. When this becomes apparent refer to the relevant illustration for information. The main difference will be found on distributors fitted to American imports which are modified to help the car comply with the rigid exhaust emission control legislation. A double diaphragm vacuum unit is fitted and information on this is given at the end of this Section commencing at paragraph 36.
1 With the distributor on the bench, release the two spring clips retaining the cap and lift away the cap. (Figs. 4.4/4.5).
2 Pull the rotor arm off the distributor cam spindle.
3 Lift away the dust proof cover.

7.3 Timing marks on front cover and notch in crankshaft pulley

7.4 Distributor clamp

Fig. 4.4. Exploded view of distributor (K and K-B engines)

A Distributor cam
B Governor spring
C Governor weight
D Washer
E Bakelite washer
F Adjusting washer
G Terminal insulator
H Condenser
I Gasket
J Adjuster cap
K Spring clip
L Distributor housing
M 'O' ring
N Gear
O Gear roll pin
P Distributor cap
Q Distributor rotor
R Dust proof cover
S Distributor breaker point
T Contact point plate
U Breaker plate
V Stationary plate
W Vacuum advancer
X Distributor clamp

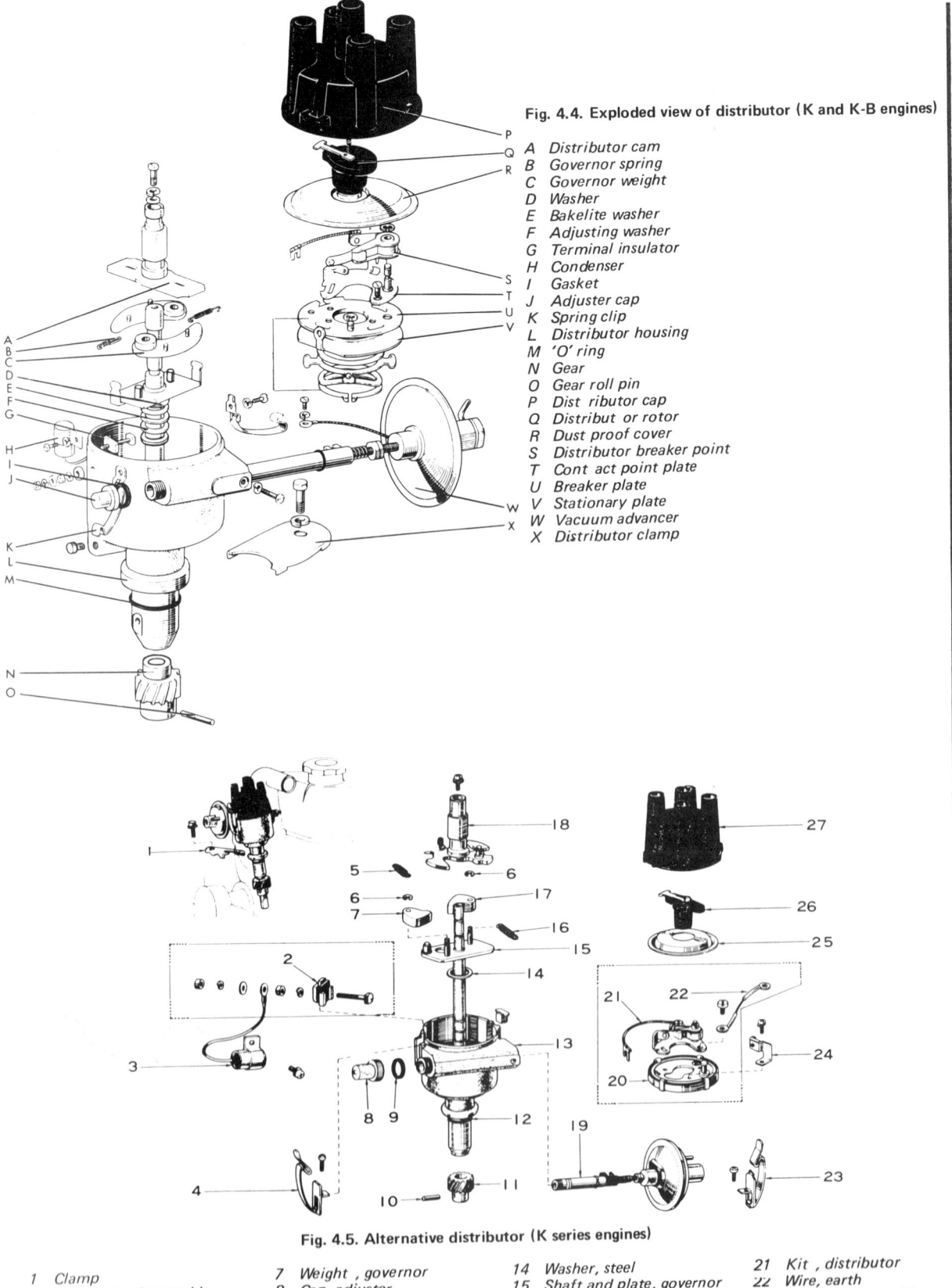

Fig. 4.5. Alternative distributor (K series engines)

1 Clamp
2 Terminal subassembly
3 Condenser
4 Spring subassembly, housing cap, B
5 Spring, governor, B
6 Washer, snap
7 Weight, governor
8 Cap, adjuster
9 Washer, rubber
10 Pin
11 Gear, spiral
12 Ring 'O'
13 Housing subassembly
14 Washer, steel
15 Shaft and plate, governor
16 Spring, governor B
17 Weight, governor
18 Cam subassembly
19 Advancer subassembly
20 Plate subassembly, breaker
21 Kit, distributor
22 Wire, earth
23 Spring subassembly, housing cap A
24 Spring, damping
25 Cover, dust proof
26 Rotor subassembly
27 Cap subassembly

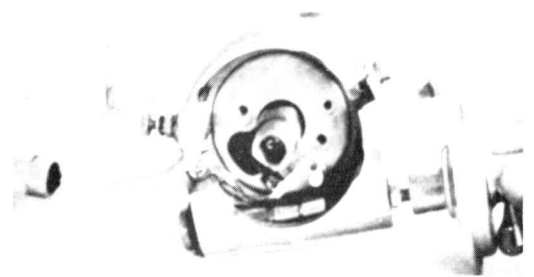

Fig. 4.6. Vacuum advance unit removal

Fig. 4.7. Breaker plate removal

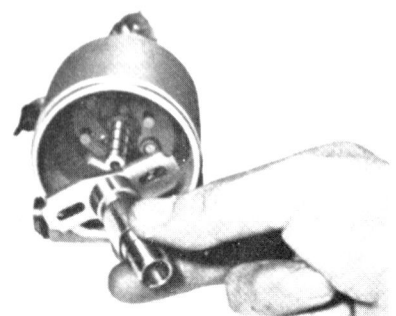

Fig. 4.8. Distributor cam spindle removal

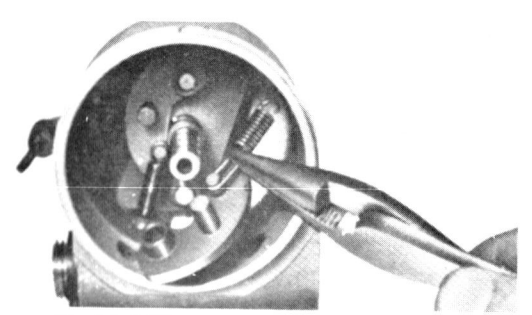

Fig. 4.9. Lifting away centrifugal weight springs

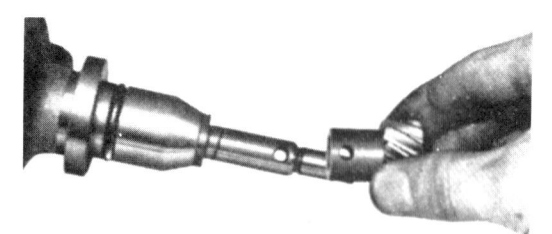

Fig. 4.10. Spiral gear removal

Fig. 4.11. Withdrawing distributor shaft

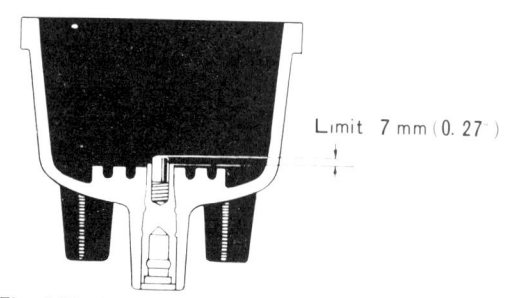

Fig. 4.12. Checking carbon centre electrode protrusion

Limit 7 mm (0.27")

4 Refer to Section 4 and remove the contact breaker points.
5 Unscrew the terminal post through bolt securing nut and disconnect the condenser lead.
6 Undo and remove the screw securing the condenser to the distributor body. Lift the condenser and lead away from the distributor body.
7 Unscrew the vacuum unit adjustment screw (octane selector) and draw the assembly from the distributor body (Fig. 4.6).
8 Undo and remove the two screws securing the distributor cap spring clips to the distributor body. Lift away the two clips noting that the earth wire is retained by one of the clips securing screws.
9 The contact breaker plate assembly may now be lifted from the distributor body. To assist refitting note which way round it is fitted. (Fig. 4.7).
10 Undo and remove the screw located at the top of the cam spindle and lift away the cam. (Fig. 4.8).
11 Using a pair of pliers carefully disconnect and lift away the two centrifugal weight springs (Fig. 4.9).
12 Carefully remove the snap washers and lift away the centrifugal weights.
13 Using a suitable diameter parallel pin punch carefully tap out the pin securing the spiral gear to the spindle. It may be found that the pin ends are peened over. If so it will be necessary to file flat before attempting to drift out the pin. The gear may now be removed from the spindle. (Fig. 4.10).
14 The spindle may now be drawn upwards from the distributor body. Take care to recover the washer(s) fitted between the centrifugal weight plate and distributor body (Fig. 4.11).
15 Wash all parts and wipe dry with a clean non-fluffy rag.
16 Check the contact breaker points for wear. Inspect the distributor cap for signs of tracking (indicated by a thin black line between the segments). Also look at the segments for signs of excessive corrosion. Renew the cap if necessary.
17 If the metal portion of the rotor arm is badly burned or loose renew the arm. If only slightly burned, clean the end with a fine file. Check that the contact in the centre of the distributor cap is in good order. (Fig. 4.12).
18 Examine the centrifugal weights and pivots for wear and the advance springs for slackness. These can best be checked by comparing with new parts. If they are slack they must be renewed.
19 Check the points assembly for fit on the breaker plate, and the cam follower for wear.
20 Examine the fit of the spindle in the distributor body. If

Chapter 4/Ignition system

there is excessive side movement it will be necessary to obtain a new distributor body and spindle.

21 Check the resistance of the breaker plate sliding part. Ideally it should have a resistance of 2.2 lbs (1 kg). If it appears to be tight lubricate with a little engine oil.

22 Check the fit between the cam and spindle. If it is slack new parts will be necessary.

23 To reassemble, first, refit the centrifugal weights to the plate and retain with the snap washers.

24 Lubricate the outer surface of the spindle and slide the cam over the spindle and hook the springs onto the posts.

25 Fit the steel washer onto the shaft and lubricate with a little engine oil. Slide the shaft into the body and locate the spiral gear. Line up the pin holes and insert the pin.

26 Using feeler gauges measure the shaft thrust clearance which should be 0.0006 - 0.020 inch (0.15 - 0.50 mm). If adjustment is necessary select a steel washer of suitable thickness. These are available in a range of thicknesses: 0.098, 0.106 and 0.114 inch (2.5, 2.7 and 2.9 mm).

27 Peen over the ends of the spiral gear retaining pin.

28 Refit the breaker plate assembly to the distributor body and locate the two distributor cap spring clips. Secure the clips with the screws and washers. Do not forget the earth wire is secured by the screw onthe terminal side.

29 Note that the four breaker plate clips must be in position in the distributor body. Also the cap spring without the cap position locator must be on the terminal side of the distributor body.

30 Refit the terminal insulator and through bolt. Position the condenser cable terminal onto the through bolt and retain with the nut. Do not tighten the nut fully.

31 Fit the contact breaker points onto the breaker plate and secure with the two screws and washers. Do not forget the earth wire to be attached to the arm side securing screw.

32 Insert the vacuum advance unit to the housing, engaging it with the breaker plate and screw on the adjustment screw (octane selector) until it is set at the standard position.

33 Secure the condenser to the side of the distributor body with the screw and washer.

34 Refer to Section 3 and adjust the contact breaker points. Connect the wire to the terminal block and tighten the nut.

35 Lubricate the distributor as described in Section 6 and then replace the dustproof cover, rotor arm and distributor cap. The distributor is now ready for refitting.

36 To remove the double diaphragm vacuum unit undo and remove the retaining screw located on the side of the distributor body. Unscrew the vacuum unit. This is the advance unit. (Fig 4.13).

37 **Do** not undo the nuts located at the inner end of the vacuum advance unit.

38 To remove the retard unit, remove the circlip which will free the retard rod from the retard rod retaining pin. The retard vacuum unit may now be removed from the distributor.

39 Reassembly is the reverse sequence to removal but the following additional points should be noted:

Fig. 4.13. Dismantling advance unit (K-C engine)

1 Locknuts

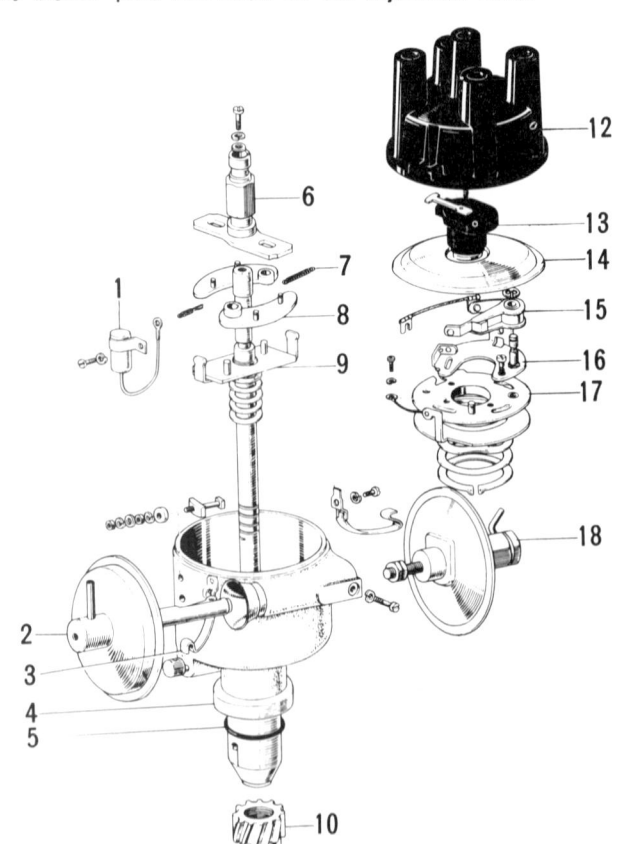

Fig. 4.14. Exploded view of distributor (K-C engine)

1 Condenser
2 Vacuum retarder
3 Cap spring
4 Distributor housing
5 'O' ring
6 Distributor cam
7 Governor spring
8 Governor weight
9 Governor shaft and plate
10 Spiral gear
11 Pin
12 Distributor cap
13 Rotor
14 Dust proof cover
15 Braker point
16 Braker plate
17 Stationary plate
18 Vacuum advancer

9 Distributor - replacement

1 Turn the engine until number 1 cylinder is on the compression stroke and line up the timing notch on the crankshaft pulley and the scale on the front of the timing cover. The exact setting will depend on the ignition timing as found in the 'Sepcification' Section at the beginning of this Chapter. Check that the number 1 cylinder is on the compression stroke by removing the spark plug and feeling the compression with a thumb as the piston rises in the cylinder.
2 Rotate the distributor spindle clockwise until the rotor arm is pointing towards number 1 segment in the distributor cap. The cam should be in such a position that the contact breaker points are just about to open. (Dust proof cover removed)
3 The oil pump driveshaft should now be set so that the slot at its top end will be lined up with the oil pump drive shaft location at the bottom of the distributor spindle. The oil pump driveshaft may be easily turned with a small screwdriver (Fig 4.15).
4 Now turn the rotor arm about 30 degrees (one spiral gear tooth) in a clockwise direction. (Fig. 4.16).
5 Lubricate the distributor spiral gear and oil pump driveshaft end location. Carefully insert the distributor into position.
6 Rotate the distributor housing until the contact breaker points are about to open and secure the distributor with bolt, spring washer and clamp plate.
7 Reconnect the low tension wire and vacuum pipe.
8 Remove the rotor arm and refit the dustproof cover. Refit the rotor arm and distributor cap.
9 Reconnect the HT leads to the spark plugs and ignition coil.
10 Set the distributor octane selector to the standard position.
11 The ignition timing should now be accurately set. Further information will be found in Section 10.

a) When refitting the advance unit screw it fully in and then unscrew it until the retaining screw can be correctly refitted.
b) When locking the distributor cap always take care not to lever against the retard unit.

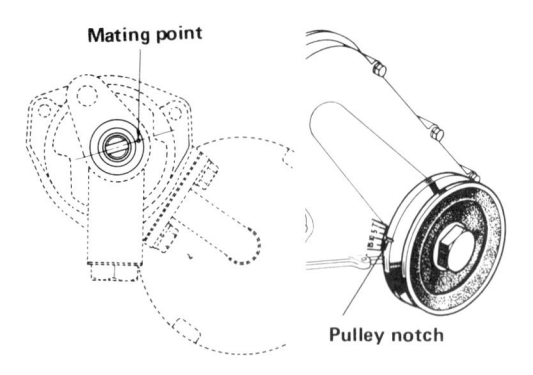

Fig. 4.15. Timing marks and oil pump spindle alignment

10 Ignition timing

1 Refer to Section 3 and check the contact breaker points gap.
2 Refer to Section 9 and follow the instructions given in paragraph 1. Move the octane selector on the side of the distributor to the standard position.
3 Slacken the distributor clamp bolt and rotate the distributor as necessary, until the contact breaker points are *just* opening. Retighten the clamp bolt. The dust proof cover will have to be removed to see the contact breaker points.
4 If it was not found possible to align the rotor arm correctly, one of two things is wrong: Either the distributor spindle has been incorrectly meshed when refitting the distributor in which case it must be removed and refitted as described in Section 9 or the distributor has been incorrectly reassembled after dismantling.
5 Start the engine, allow to warm-up to normal running temperature and then accelerate in top gear from 30 - 50 mph listening for heavy pinking of the engine. If this occurs, the ignition needs to be retarded gradually until only the faintest trace of pinking can be heard under these conditions.
6 Since the ignition advance adjustment enables the firing point to be related correctly to the grade of fuel used, the fullest advantage of any charge of fuel will only be obtained by re-adjustment of the ignition settings.
7 This is done by using the octane selector on the side of the distributor body. (Fig. 4.17).
8 Start the engine and check that the vacuum unit is operating correctly by watching the end opposite the vacuum unit as the engine is speeded up. It should move inwards as the engine speed increases.
9 Difficulty is sometimes experienced in determining exactly

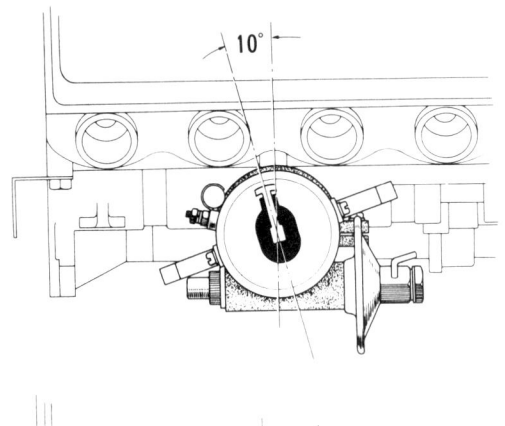

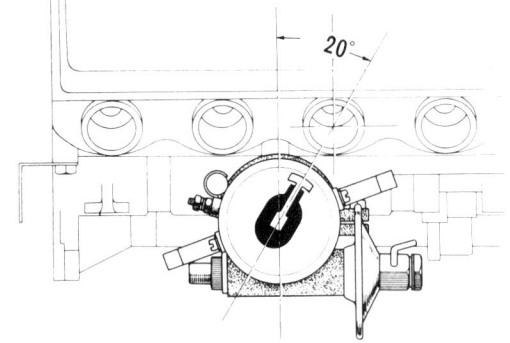

Fig. 4.16. Distributor replacement
(Top) Initial position
(Bottom) Final position with gear in mesh

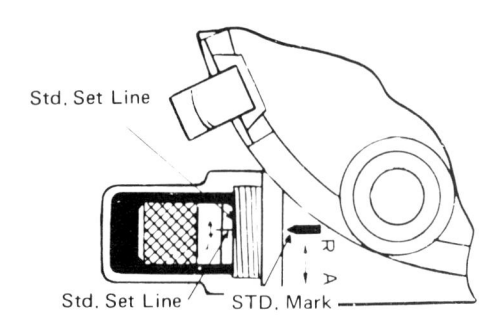

Fig. 4.17. Setting octane selector 'standard position'

when the contact breaker points open. This can be ascertained most accurately by connecting a 12 volt bulb in parallel with the contact breaker points (one lead to earth and the other from the distributor low tension terminal). Switch on the ignition, slacken the distributor clamp bolt and turn the distributor until the bulb lights up indicating that the points have just opened.

11 Spark plugs and HT leads

1 The correct functioning of the spark plugs is vital for the proper running and efficient operation of the engine.
2 At regular intervals the plugs should be removed, examined, cleaned, and if worn excessively, renewed. The condition of the spark plugs can also tell much about the general condition of the engine.
3 If the insulator nose of the spark plug is clean and white, with no deposits, this is indicative of a weak mixture, or too hot a plug (a hot plug transfers heat away from the electrodes slowly - a cold plug transfers heat away quickly).
4 If the insulator nose is covered with hard black looking deposits, then this is indicative that the mixture is too rich. Should the plug be black and oily then it is likely that the engine is worn, as well as the mixture being too rich.
5 If the insulator nose is covered with light tan to greyish brown deposits, then the mixture is correct, and it is likely that the engine is in good condition.
6 If there are any traces of long brown tapering stains on the outside of the white portion of the plug, then the plug will have to be renewed, as this shows that there is a faulty joint between the plug body and the insulator and compression is being allowed to leak away.
7 Plugs should be cleaned by a sand blasting machine, which will free them from carbon completely. The machine will also test the condition of the plugs under compression. Any plug that fails to spark at the recommended pressure should be renewed.
8 The spark plug gap is of considerable importance, as, if it is too large, or too small, the size of spark and its efficiency will be seriously impaired. The spark plug gap should be set as recommended in the 'Specifications' Section at the beginning of this Chapter.
9 To set it, measure the gap with a feeler gauge, and then bend open, or close, the outer plug electorde until the correct gap is obtained. The centre electrode must never be bent as this will crack the insulation and cause plug failure if nothing worse.
10 When replacing the plugs, remember to use new washers and replace the leads from the distributor cap, in the correct firing order which is 1 3 4 2 - number 1 cylinder being the one nearest the fan.
11 The plug leads require no maintaining other than being kept clean and wiped over regularly. At regular intervals, however, pull each lead off the plug in turn and remove them from the distributor cap. Water can seep down there joints giving rise to a white corrosive deposit which must be carefully removed from the end of each cable.

12 Fault diagnosis - ignition system (general)

By far the majority of breakdown and running troubles are caused by faults in the ignition system either in the low tension or high tension circuits.

There are two main symptoms indicating ignition faults. Either the engine will not start or fire, or the engine is difficult to start and misfires. If it is a regular misfire, ie. the engine is running on only two or three cylinders, the fault is almost sure to be in the secondary or high tension circuit. If the misfiring is intermittent, the fault could be in either the high or low tension circuits. If the car stops suddenly, and will not start at all, it is likely that the fault is in the low tension circuit. Loss of power and overheating, apart from faulty combustion settings, are normally due to faults in the distributor or to incorrect ignition timing.

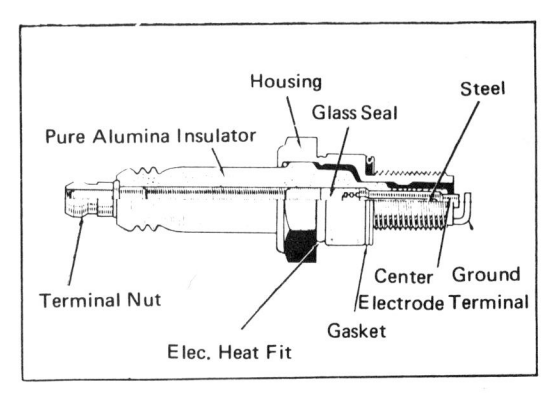

Fig. 4.18. Cross sectional view of spark plug

13 Fault diagnosis - engine fails to start

1 If the engine fails to start and the car was running normally when it was last used, first check there is fuel in the petrol tank. If the engine turns over normally on the starter motor and the battery is evidently well charged, then the fault may be in either the high or low tension ignition circuits. First check the HT circuit. Note: If the battery is known to be fully charged, the ignition light comes on, and the starter motor fails to turn the engine check the tightness of the leads on the battery terminals and also the securing of the earth lead at its connection to the body. It is quite common for the leads to have worked loose, even if they look and feel secure. If one of the battery terminal posts gets very hot when trying to work the starter motor this is a sure indication of a faulty connection to that terminal.
2 One of the commonest reasons for bad starting is wet or damp spark plug leads and/or distributor. Remove the distributor cap and if condensation is visible internally dry the cap with a rag and also wipe over the leads. Replace the cap.
3 If the engine still fails to start, check that current is reaching the plugs, by disconnecting each plug lead in turn at the spark plug end, and holding the end of the cable about 3/16 inch (5 mm) away from the cylinder block. Spin the engine on the starter motor.
4 Sparking between the end of the cable and the block should be fairly strong with a strong regular blue spark.(Hold the lead with rubber to avoid electric shocks). If current is reaching the plugs, then remove them, and clean and regap them. The engine should now start.
5 If there is no spark at the plug leads take off the HT lead from the centre of the distributor cap and hold it to the block as before. Spin the engine on the starter once more. A rapid succession of blue sparks between the end of the lead and the block indicates that the coil is in order and that the distributor cap is cracked, the rotor arm faulty, and the brush in the top of the distributor cap is not making good contact with the rotor arm. Possibly the points are in bad condition. Clean and reset them as described in Sections 3 and 4 of this Chapter.
6 If there are no sparks from the end of the lead from the coil check the connections at the coil end of the lead. If it is in order start checking the low tension circuit.
7 Use a 12v voltmeter or a 12v bulb and two lengths of wire. With the ingition switched on and the points open, test between the low tension wire to the coil (it is marked SW or +) and earth. No reading indicates a break in the supply from the ignition switch. Check the connections at the switch to see if any are loose. Refit them and the engine should run. A reading shows a faulty coil or condenser, or broken lead between the coil and the distributor.
8 Take the condenser wire off the points assembly terminal and with the points open test between the moving point and earth. If there now is a reading then the fault is in the condenser. Fit a new one and the fault is cleared.
9 With no reading from the moving point to earth, take a

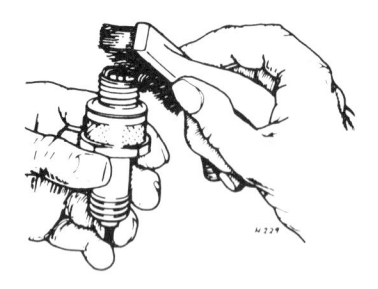

Cleaning deposits from electrodes and surrounding area using a fine wire brush.

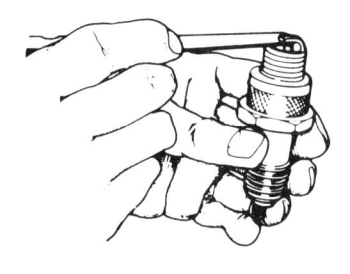

Checking plug gap with feeler gauges

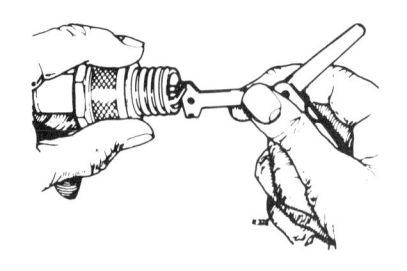

Altering the plug gap. Note use of correct tool.

Fig. 4.19. CORRECT METHOD OF RESETTING SPARK PLUG GAP

White deposits and damaged porcelain insulation indicating overheating

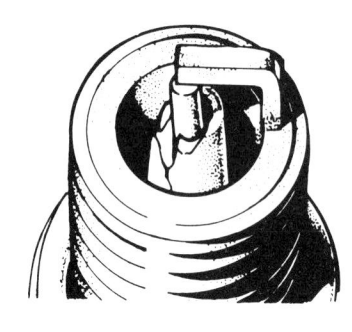

Broken porcelain insulation due to bent central electrode

Electrodes burnt away due to wrong heat value or chronic pre-ignition (pinking)

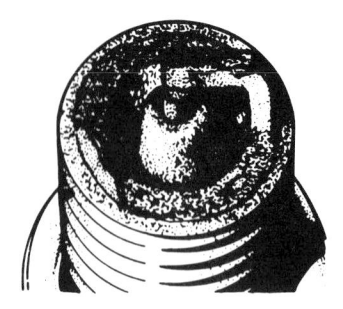

Excessive black deposits caused by over-rich mixture or wrong heat value

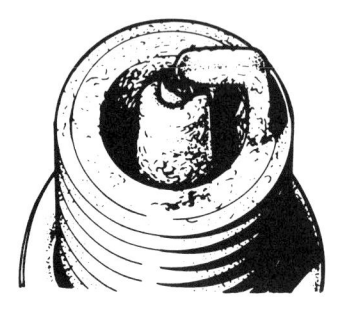

Mild white deposits and electrode burnt indicating too weak a fuel mixture

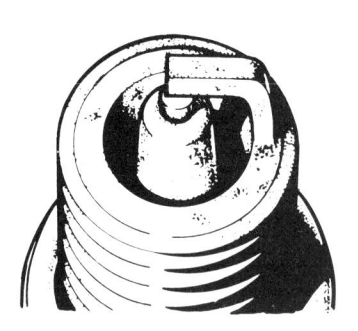

Plug in sound condition with light greyish brown deposits

Sample spark plug electrodes

reading between the earth and CB terminal of the coil (it is marked CB or-). A reading here shows a broken wire which will need to be replaced between the coil and distributor. No reading confirms that the coil has failed and must be replaced, after which the engine will run once more. Remember to refit the condenser wire to the points assembly terminal. For this test it is sufficient to separate the points with a piece of thin, dry, card while testing with the points open.

14 Fault diagnosis - engine misfires

1 If the engine misfires regularly run it at a fast idling speed. Pull off each of the plug caps in turn and listen to the note of the engine. Hold the plug cap in a dry cloth or with a rubber glove as additional protection against a shock from the HT supply.
2 No difference in engine running will be noticed when the lead from the defective circuit is removed. Removing the lead from one of the good cylinders will accentuate the misfire.
3 Remove the plug lead from the end of the defective plug and hold it about 3/16 inch (5 mm) away from the block. Re-start the engine. If the sparking is fairly strong and regular the fault must lie in the spark plug.
4 The plug may be loose, the insulation may be cracked, or the points may have burnt away giving too wide a gap for the spark to jump. Worse still, one of the points may have broken off. Either renew the plug, or clean it, reset the gap and then test it.
5 If there is no spark at the end of the plug lead, or if it is weak and intermittent, check the ignition lead from the distributor to the plug. If the insulation is damaged renew the lead. Check the connections at the distributor cap.
6 If there is still no spark, examine the distributor cap carefully for tracking. This can be recognised by a very thin black line running between two, or more, electrodes; or between an electrode and some other part of the distributor cap. These lines are paths which now conduct electricity across the cap thus letting it run to earth. The only answer is a new distributor cap.
7 Apart from the ignition timing being incorrect, other causes of misfiring have already been dealt with under the section dealing with the failure of the engine to start. To recap, these are:
a) The coil may be faulty giving an intermittent misfire.
b) There may be a damaged wire or loose connection in the low tension circuit.
c) The condenser may be short circuiting.
d) There may be a mechanical fault in the distributor (broken driving spindle or contact breaker spring).
8 If the ignition timing is too far retarded, it should be noted that the engine will tend to overheat, and there will be quite a noticeable drop in power. If the engine is overheating and the power is down, and the ignition timing is correct, then the carburettor should be checked, as it is likely that this is where the fault lies.

Chapter 5 Clutch

Contents

Clutch cable - removal and replacement (KE models) ... 6	Clutch pedal - removal and replacement (TE models) ... 7
Clutch faults ... 15	Clutch release bearing - removal and replacement ... 14
Clutch hydraulic system - bleeding ... 4	Clutch - removal and replacement ... 12
Clutch inspection ... 13	Clutch slave cylinder - dismantling, examination and reassembly ... 11
Clutch judder - diagnosis and cure ... 19	Clutch slave cylinder - removal and replacement ... 10
Clutch master cylinder - dismantling, examination and reassembly ... 9	Clutch slip - diagnosis and cure ... 17
Clutch master cylinder - removal and replacement ... 8	Clutch spin - diagnosis and cure ... 18
Clutch operating system - adjustment (KE models) ... 2	Clutch squeal - diagnosis and cure ... 16
Clutch operating system - adjustment (TE models) ... 3	General description ... 1
Clutch pedal - removal and replacement (KE models) ... 5	

Specifications

Type: ... Single dry plate, diaphragm spring

Actuation:
- KE models (1100, 1200) ... Cable operation
- TE models (1600) ... Hydraulic operation

Clutch disc:
- Lining outer diameter ... 7.087 in. (180.0 mm)
- Inner diameter ... 4.921 in. (125.0 mm)
- Thickness:
  - KE models ... 0.26 in. (6.604 mm)
  - TE models ... 0.14 in. (3.4 mm)
- Maximum runout:
  - KE models ... 0.02 in. (0.508 mm)
  - TE models ... 0.03 in. (0.762 mm)
- Lining wear limit:
  - KE (1100) ... 0.024 in. (0.6096 mm)
  - KE (1200) ... 0.012 in. (0.3048 mm) rivet to face
  - TE (1600) ... 0.012 in. (0.3048 mm) rivet to face

Pressure plate wear limit: ... 0.8 in. (20.32 mm)

Clutch release cable:
- Inner length:
  - Rhd ... 36.8 in. (934 mm)
  - Lhd ... 65.3 in. (1659 mm)
- Inner cable diameter ... 0.15 - 0.16 in. (3.7 - 4.0 mm)
- Outer cable diameter ... 0.19 - 0.20 in. (9.0 - 10.0 mm)
- Adjustable free-play length
  - Rhd ... 6.32 in. (160.5 mm)
  - Lhd ... 34.9 in. (885.5 mm)

Release fork free-play:
- KE (1100) ... 3 grooves ('E' ring)
- KE (1200) ... 4 - 5 grooves ('E' ring)
- TE (1600) ... 0.10 - 0.14 in. (2.54 - 3.4 mm) (slave cylinder)

Pedal height:
- KE models ... 5.5 - 5.9 inch (140 - 150 mm)
- TE models * ... 6.4 - 6.8 inch (160 - 170 mm)
- * Push rod to piston clearance ... 0.02 in (0.508 mm)

Chapter 5/Clutch

Pedal free-play:
- KE models ... 0.8 inch (20.32 mm)
- TE models ... 1.0 - 1.8 inch (25.4 - 45.72 mm)

Torque wrench settings:

	lb f ft	kg f m
KE 1100:		
Fork bolt	14 - 22	1.95 - 3.04
Clutch pedal shaft nut	35 - 40	4.8 - 5.5
Pressure plate to flywheel bolts	7 - 11	1.0 - 1.53
KE 1200:		
Fork bolt	14 - 22	1.94 - 3.04
Clutch pedal shaft nut	36 - 58	4.8 - 7.91
Pressure plate to flywheel bolts	11 - 16	1.53 - 2.21
TE 1600:		
Clutch pedal shaft nut	25 - 33	3.4 - 4.6
Pressure plate to flywheel bolts	11 - 14	1.53 - 1.94
Master cylinder bolts	20	2.77

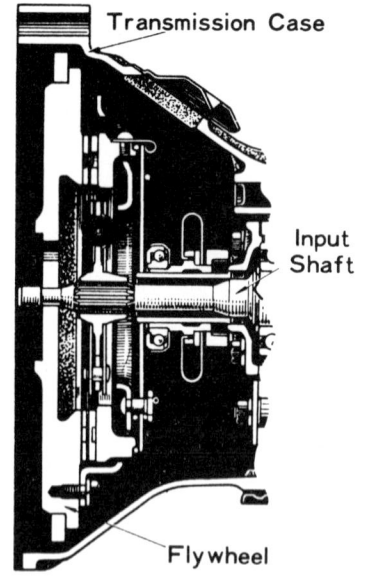

Fig. 5.1. Cross sectional view of clutch assembly

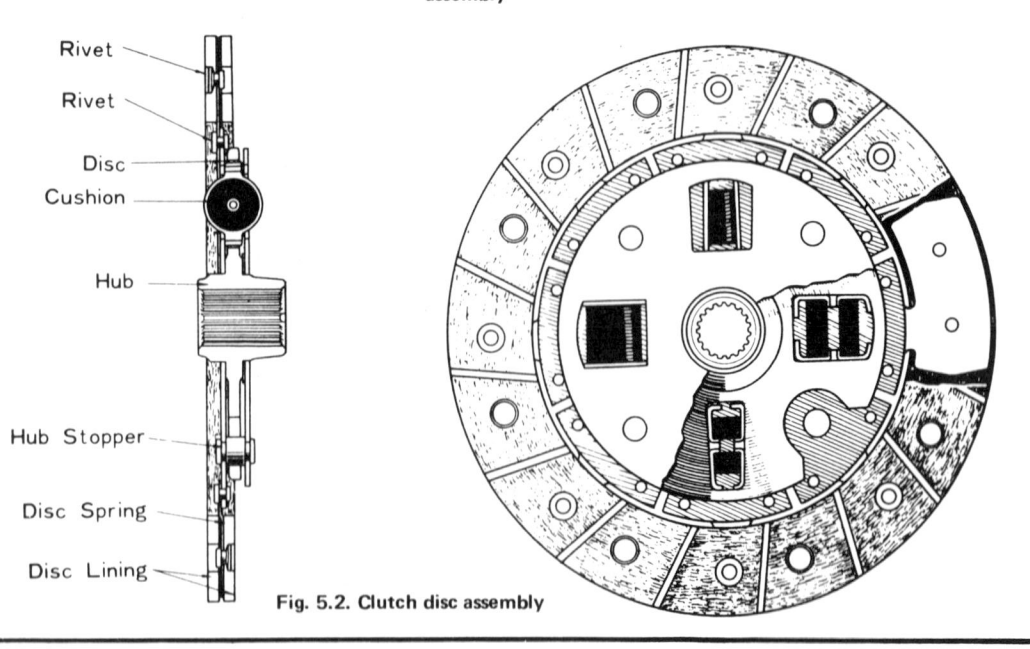

Fig. 5.2. Clutch disc assembly

Chapter 5/Clutch

1 General description

The models covered by this manual are fitted with a diaphragm spring clutch operated mechanically on KE models and hydraulically on TE models.

The clutch comprises a steel cover which is bolted and dowelled to the rear face of the flywheel and contains the pressure plate and clutch disc or driven plate.

The pressure plate and diaphragm spring are attached to the clutch assembly cover.

The clutch disc is free to slide along the splined gearbox input shaft and is held in position between the flywheel and pressure plate by the pressure of the diaphragm spring.

The models covered by this manual are fitted with a diaphragm spring clutch operated mechanically on KE models and hydraulically on TE models.

The clutch comprises a steel cover which is bolted and dowelled to the rear face of the flywheel and contains the pressure plate and clutch disc or driven plate.

The pressure plate and diaphragm spring are attached to the clutch assembly cover.

The clutch disc is free to slide along the splined gearbox input shaft and is held in position between the flywheel and pressure plate by the pressure of the diaphragm spring.

Friction lining material is riveted to the clutch disc which has a cushioned hub to absorb transmission shocks and to help ensure a smooth take off.

The mechanically operated clutch system utilises a pendant pedal which is attached to a heavy duty cable. The other end of the cable is attached to the clutch release arm.

With the hydraulically operated clutch system the pendant clutch pedal is connected to the clutch master cylinder and hydraulic fluid reservoir by a short pushrod. The master cylinder and fluid reservoir are mounted on the engine side of the bulkhead in front of the driver.

Depressing the clutch pedal moves the piston in the master cylinder forwards so forcing hydraulic fluid through to the slave cylinder.

The piston in the slave cylinder moves rearwards on the entry of the fluid and actuates the clutch release arm, via a short pushrod. The opposite end of the release arm is forked and carries the release bearing assembly.

As the pivoted clutch release arm moves rearwards it pushes the release bearing forwards to bear against the diaphragm spring and pushes forwards so moving the pressure plate backwards and disengaging the pressure plate from the clutch disc.

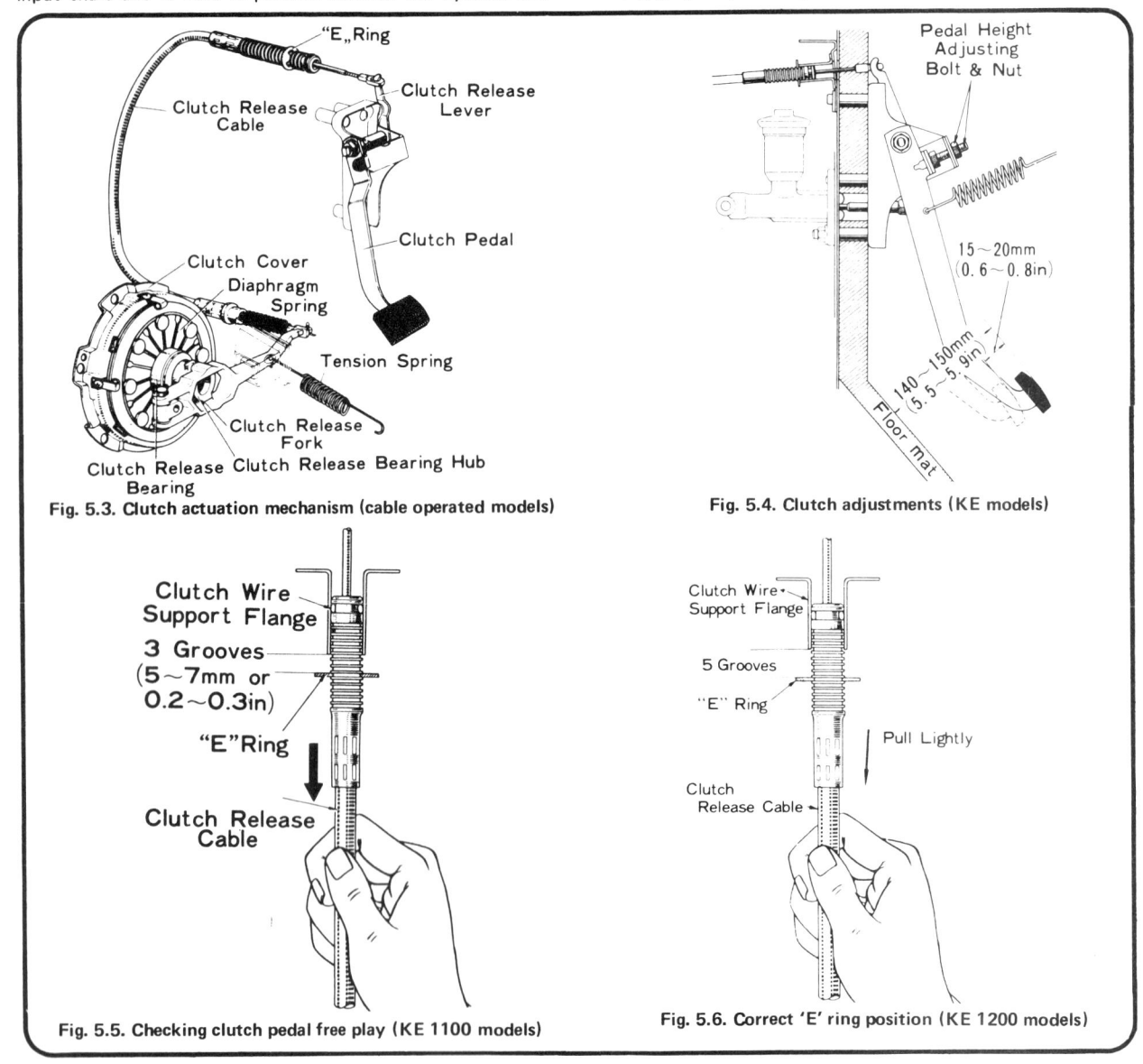

Fig. 5.3. Clutch actuation mechanism (cable operated models)

Fig. 5.4. Clutch adjustments (KE models)

Fig. 5.5. Checking clutch pedal free play (KE 1100 models)

Fig. 5.6. Correct 'E' ring position (KE 1200 models)

When the clutch pedal is released the pressure plate is forced into contact with the high friction bearings on the clutch disc and at the same time pushes the clutch disc a fraction of an inch forwards on its splines so engaging the clutch disc with the flywheel. The clutch disc is now firmly sandwiched between the pressure plate and the flywheel so the drive is taken up.

2 Clutch operating system - adjustment (KE models)

1 There are two clutch adjustments on the KE models which use the cable operated system. These are the pedal height and pedal free-play.
2 Carefully examine the condition of the rubber stopper and renew it if it is cracked or damaged.
3 Slacken the stop bolt lock nut and turn the adjusting bolt until the pedal height is 6.4 - 6.8 inch (160 - 170 mm) from the floorpanel. Retighten the lock nut. (Fig. 5.4).
4 To adjust the pedal free-play, working under the bonnet, grasp the top of the clutch cable housing and pull back until firm resistance is felt.
5 If necessary reposition the "E" ring so that 4-5 grooves appear between it and the end of the support flange. This should produce 0.8 inch (20.32 mm) freeplay at the pedal. (Fig. 5.5/5.6).
6 It may be necessary to remove the "E" ring from the end of the clutch cable to provide sufficient slack for the pedal height adjustment. This is particularly applicable if the rubber stopper has been renewed or if there have been several free-play adjustments over a period of time without making pedal height adjustments.
7 Release cable housing so that the support flange is resting against the "E" ring.
8 Determine the pedal free-play at the pedal pad. Reposition the "E" ring to come as close to 0.8 in (20.32 mm) free-play as possible.

3 Clutch operating system - adjustment (TE models)

1 There are three clutch adjustments on the TE models which use the hydraulically operated system. These are the pedal height, pedal free-play and clutch fork free-play.
2 To reset the pedal height and free-play first disconnect the master cylinder pushrod from the clutch pedal arm by withdrawing the pin.
3 Slacken the adjusting bolt locknut and turn the adjusting bolt until the pedal height is 6.4 - 6.8 inch (160 - 170 mm) from the floorpanel. Retighten the locknut.
4 Slacken the master cylinder pushrod locknut and adjust the length of the pushrod so that there is a clearance of approximately 0.02 in (0.5 mm) between the end of the pushrod and master cylinder piston. Retighten the pushrod locknut.
5 The previous adjustments should give a pedal free-play of 1.0 - 1.8 in (25.4 - 45.72 mm).
6 The clutch fork free-play should be 0.1 - 0.14 in. (2.5 - 3.5 mm) and can be reset by slackening the slave cylinder pushrod locknut and turning the pushrod until the required movement is obtained at the end of the release fork. Retighten the locknut.

4 Clutch hydraulic system - bleeding

1 Gather together a clean glass jar, a length of rubber/plastic tubing which fits tightly over the bleed nipple on the slave cylinder, and a tin of hydraulic brake fluid. You will also need the help of an assistant.
2 Check that the master cylinder reservoir is full. If it is not, fill it and also fill the bottom two inches of the jar with hydraulic fluid.
3 Remove the rubber dust cap from the bleed nipple on the slave cylinder, and with a suitable spanner open the bleed nipple approximately three-quarters of a turn.

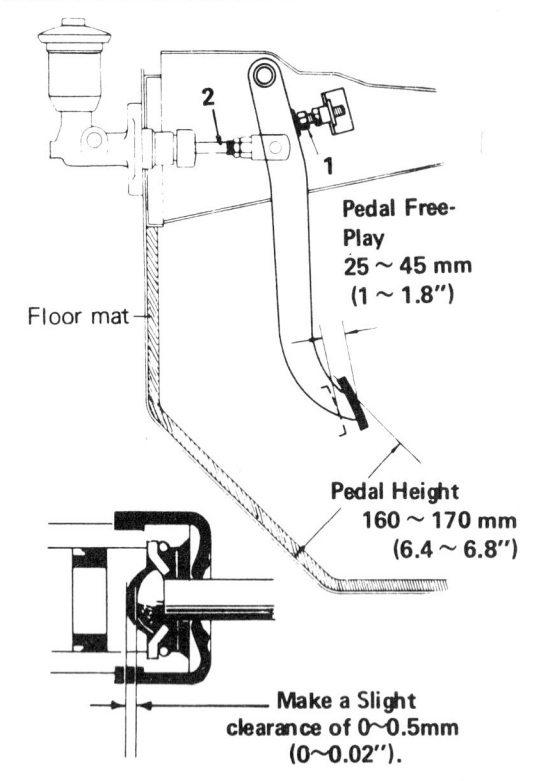

Fig. 5.7. Clutch adjustments (TE models)

4 Place one end of the tube over the nipple and insert the other end in the jar so that the tube orifice is below the level of the fluid.
5 The assistant should now depress the pedal and hold it down at the end of its stroke. Close the bleed screw and allow the pedal to return to its normal position.
6 Continue this series of operations until clean hydraulic fluid without any traces of air bubbles emerges from the end of the tubing. Be sure that the reservoir is checked frequently to ensure that the hydraulic fluid does not drop too far, thus letting air into the system.
7 When no more air bubbles appear tighten the bleed nipple during a downstroke.
8 Replace the rubber dust cap over the bleed nipple.

5 Clutch pedal - removal and replacement (KE models)

1 It should be noted that although the clutch and brake pedal mountings are different on the 1100 (65.7 cu in) and 1200 (71.1 cu in) models the procedure is in fact the same. (Fig. 5.8/5.9).
2 Remove the 'E' ring from the top end of the clutch release outer cable.
3 Disconnect the clutch inner cable from the release lever taking care not to bend the inner cable.
4 Detach the clutch pedal return spring.
5 Undo and remove the pedal shaft nut and withdraw the pedal from the end of the shaft.
6 Remove the shaft and bushes. The pedal support boss can, if necessary, be removed once the two securing bolts are removed.
7 Inspect the clutch pedal pad for wear and damage. Renew if necessary.
8 Check the clutch pedal for signs of damage or distortion. Rectify as necessary.
9 The cushion should be examined for damage and renewed if evident.
10 Check the bushes for wear or damage and the tension spring for weakness. Renew any worn parts.
11 Reassembly is the reverse sequence to removal but the

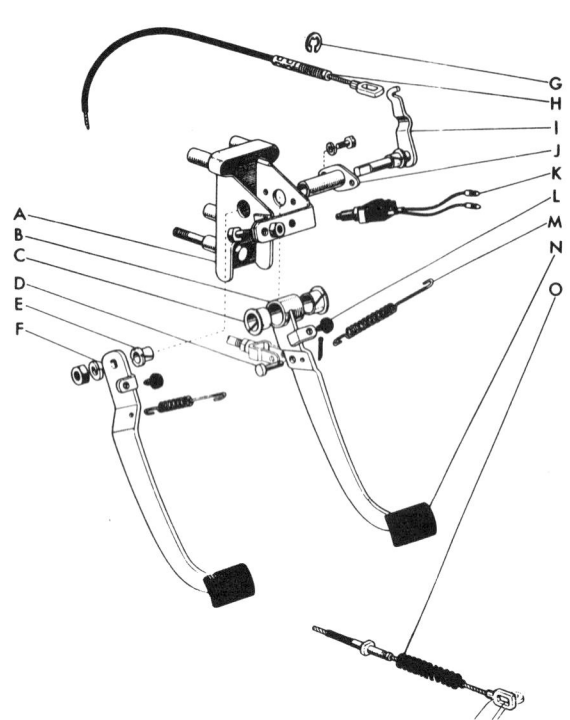

following additional points should be noted:
a) Lubricate the pins and bushes with a little Castrol LM Grease.
b) Tighten the pedal shaft nut to a torque wrench setting of 35 - 50 lb f ft (5 - 7 Kg fm) depending on model - see Specification.
c) Refer to Section 2 and reset the clutch pedal height and free-play.

6 Clutch cable - removal and replacement (KE models)

1 Remove the 'E' ring from the top end of the clutch release outer cable.
2 Remove the split pin located at the top of the clutch release fork and then disconnect the lower end of the inner cable from the clutch release fork (photos).
3 Detach the release cable from the transmission case.
4 Disconnect the top end of the release cable from the clutch pedal release lever and withdraw the release cable assembly.
5 Inspect the hooks at both ends of the inner cable for signs of wear or damage. If evident a new cable assembly will be required.
6 Inspect the outer cable, 'O' ring and rubber boot for damage.
7 Refitting the clutch release cable is the reverse sequence to removal but the following additional points should be noted:
a) Lubricate the ends of the inner cable with a little Castrol LM

Fig. 5.8. Clutch pedal and cable assembly (KE 1100 models)

A Pedal support
B Brake pedal
C Bushing
D W/hole pin
E Bushing
F Clutch pedal
G 'E' ring
H Clutch release cable
I Clutch release lever
J Pedal, support shaft boss
K Stop light switch
L Cushion
M Tension spring
N Pedal pad
O Clutch cable boot

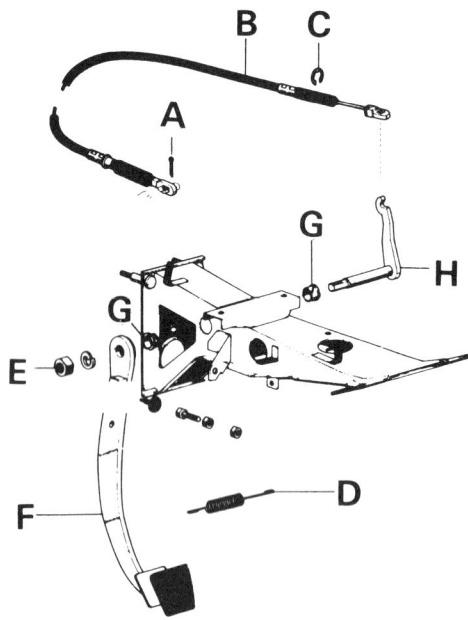

Fig. 5.9. Clutch pedal and cable assembly (KE 1200 models)

A Split pin
B Cable assembly
C 'E' ring
D Spring
E Nut
F Pedal
G Bushes
H Shaft and lever

6.2a Clutch inner cable attached to release fork

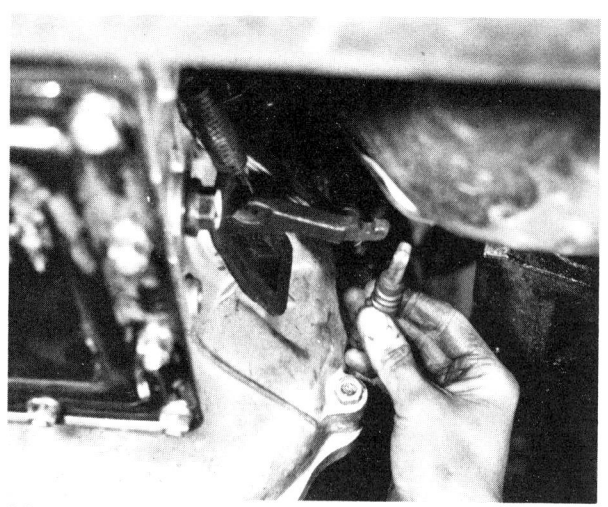

6.2b Detaching inner cable

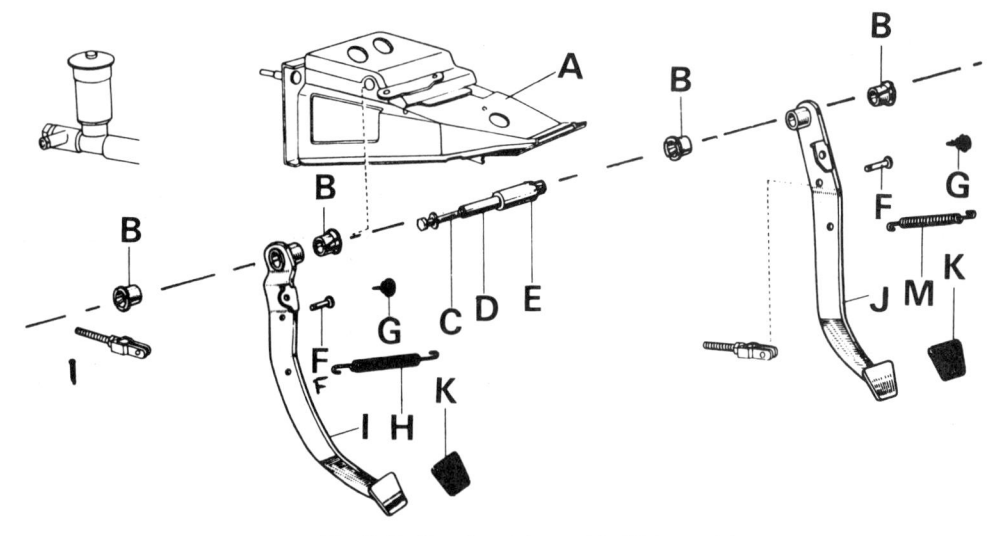

Fig. 5.10. Clutch pedal assembly (TE models)

A Pedal mounting	D Shaft	G Stop pad	J Pedal
B Bush	E Bush	H Spring	K Pedal pad
C Bolt	F Cotter pin	I Pedal	

Fig. 5.11. Exploded view of clutch master cylinder

1 Reservoir filler cap	6 Master cylinder body	11 Compression spring	16 Snap ring (circlip)
2 Reservoir float	7 Inlet valve	12 Spring retainer	17 Rubber dust cover
3 Bolt	8 Conical spring	13 Piston	18 Push rod
4 Washer	9 Inlet valve case	14 Cylinder cup	19 Push rod clevis
5 Master cylinder reservoir	10 Inlet valve connecting rod	15 Piston stop plate	

grease.
b) Refer to Section 2 and reset the clutch pedal free-play.

7 Clutch pedal - removal and replacement (TE models)

The clutch and brake pedals are removed as an assembly. Full information will be found in Chapter 9, Section 19. After replacement it will be necessary to adjust the pedal height and free-play as described in Section 2.

8 Clutch master cylinder - removal and replacement

1 Drain the fluid from the clutch master cylinder reservoir by attaching a rubber or plastic tube to the slave cylinder bleed nipple. Undo the nipple by approximately three-quarters of a turn and then pump the fluid out into a suitable container by operating the clutch pedal. Note that the pedal must be held against the floor at the completion of each stroke and the bleed nipple tightened before the pedal is allowed to return. When the pedal has returned to its normal position loosen the bleed nipple and repeat the process, until the reservoir is empty.

2 Place a rag under the master cylinder to catch any hydraulic fluid that may be spilt. Unscrew the union nut from the end of the metal pipe where it enters the clutch master cylinder and gently pull the pipe clear.

3 Withdraw the split pin that retains the pushrod yoke to the pedal clevis pin and remove the clevis pin.

4 Undo and remove the two nuts and spring washers that

secure the master cylinder to the bulkhead. Lift away the master cylinder taking care not to allow hydraulic fluid to come into contact with the paintwork as it acts as a solvent.

5 Refitting the master cylinder is the reverse sequence to removal. Bleed the system as described in Section 4 and finally adjust the pushrod clearance as described in Section 3.

9 Clutch master cylinder - dismantling, examination and reassembly

If a replacement master cylinder is to be fitted, it will be necessary to lubricate the seals before fitting to the car as they have a protective coating when originally assembled. Remove the blanking plug from the hydraulic pipe union seating. Ease back and remove the pushrod dust cover so that clean hydraulic fluid can be injected at these points. Operate the pushrod several times so that the fluid will spread over all internal surfaces.

If the master cylinder is to be dismantled after removal, proceed as follows:

1 Ease back the pushrod cover and remove the snap ring so that the pushrod and piston stop plate can be withdrawn. They expose the piston with a seal attached and must be removed as a unit. The assembly is separated by lifting the spring retainer leaf over the shouldered end of the plunger. The seal should then be eased off using the fingers only. Note which way round the seal is fitted.

2 Depress the piston retaining spring allowing the valve stem to slide through the keyhole in the retainer thus releasing the tension in the spring.

3 Detach the inlet valve case taking care of the spring dished washer which will be found under the valve head.

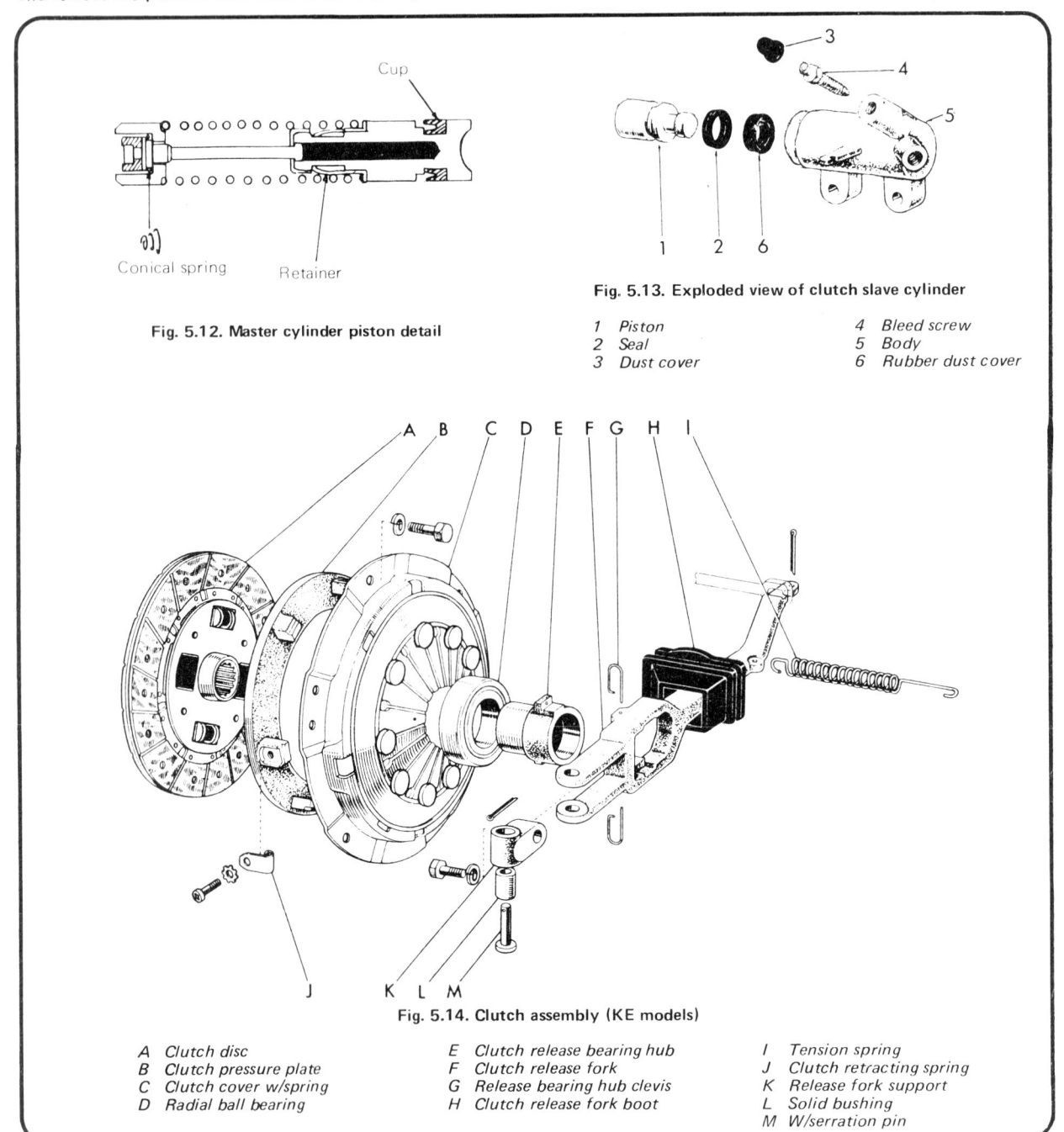

Fig. 5.12. Master cylinder piston detail

Fig. 5.13. Exploded view of clutch slave cylinder

1 Piston
2 Seal
3 Dust cover
4 Bleed screw
5 Body
6 Rubber dust cover

Fig. 5.14. Clutch assembly (KE models)

A Clutch disc
B Clutch pressure plate
C Clutch cover w/spring
D Radial ball bearing
E Clutch release bearing hub
F Clutch release fork
G Release bearing hub clevis
H Clutch release fork boot
I Tension spring
J Clutch retracting spring
K Release fork support
L Solid bushing
M W/serration pin

Chapter 5/Clutch

4 Remove the valve seal from the valve shank.

5 Examine the base of the cylinder carefully for any signs of scores or ridges and, if this is found to be smooth all over, new seals can be fitted. If there is any doubt of the condition of the bore then a new cylinder must be fitted.

6 If examination of the seals show them to be apparently oversize or swollen, or very loose on the piston suspect oil contamination in the system. Ordinary lubricating oil will swell these rubber seals, and if one is found to be swollen it is reasonable to assume that all seals in the clutch hydraulic system will need attention.

7 Thoroughly clean all parts in either fresh hydraulic fluid or Industrial Methylated Spirits. Ensure that the bypass parts are clean.

8 All components should be assembled wetted with clean brake fluid. Fit a new valve seat the correct way round so that the flat side is seating on the valve head.

9 Place the spring dished washer with the dome against the underside of the valve head. Hold it in position with the valve case ensuring that the legs face towards the valve seat.

10 Replace the plunger return spring centrally on the spacer, insert the retainer into the spring and depress until the valve stem engages in the keyhole of the retainer.

11 Ensure that the spring is central on the spacer before fitting a new piston seal onto the piston with the flat face against the face of the piston.

12 Insert the reduced end of the piston into the retainer until the leaf engages under the shoulder of the plunger, and press home the leaf.

13 Check that the master cylinder bore is clean and smear with clean hydraulic fluid. With the piston suitably wetted with hydraulic fluid, carefully insert the assembly into the bore-valve end first. Ease the lips of the piston seal carefully into the bore.

14 Replace the pushrod and refit the snap ring into the groove in the cylinder bore. Smear the sealing areas of the dust cover with a little rubber grease and pack the cover with the rubber grease so as to act as a dust trap. Fit the cover to the master cylinder body. The master cylinder is now ready for refitting to the car.

10 Clutch slave cylinder - removal and replacement

1 Wipe the top of the clutch master cylinder, unscrew the cap and place a piece of polythene sheet over the top to stop hydraulic fluid syphoning out when the slave cylinder is removed. Refit the cap.

2 Wipe the area around the union on the slave cylinder and unscrew the union. Tape the end of the pipe to stop dirt ingress.

3 Detach the return spring between release arm and cylinder body.

4 Slacken the locknut, unscrew the pushrod and lift away from between the release arm and cylinder body.

5 Undo and remove the two cylinder securing bolts and lift away from the side of the clutch housing.

6 Refitting the clutch slave cylinder is the reverse sequence to removal. It will be necessary to bleed the hydraulic system as described in Section 4 and then adjust the pushrod clearance as described in Section 3.

11 Clutch slave cylinder - dismantling, examination and reassembly

1 Clean the exterior of the slave cylinder using a dry non-fluffy rag.

2 Carefully ease back the dust cover from the end of the slave cylinder and lift away.

3 The piston and seal assembly should now be shaken out. If a low pressure air jet is available, the piston and seal may be ejected using this method. Place a rag over the open end so that when the piston is ejected it does not fly out onto the floor.

4 Remove the piston seal using a non-metal pointed rod or the fingers. Do not use a metal screwdriver as this could scratch the piston. Note which way round the seal is fitted.

5 Inspect the inside of the cylinder for score marks caused by impurities in the hydraulic fluid. If there are any found, the cylinder and piston will require renewal.

6 If the cylinder is sound, thoroughly clean it out with clean hydraulic fluid.

7 The old rubber seal will probably be swollen and visibly worn. Smear the new rubber seal with fresh hydraulic fluid and refit it to the stem of the piston ensuring that the smaller periphery, or back of the seal is against the piston.

8 Wet the piston and seal in fresh hydraulic fluid and insert the piston and seal into the bore of the cylinder. Gently ease the edge of the seal into the bore so that it does not roll over.

9 Smear the sealing areas of the dust cover with rubber grease and pack the cover with rubber grease to act as a dust trap. Fit the cover to the slave cylinder body. The slave cylinder is now ready for refitting to the car.

12 Clutch - removal and replacement

1 Remove the gearbox as described in Chapter 6.

2 With a scriber or file mark the relative position of the clutch cover and flywheel to ensure correct refitting if the original parts are to be reused.

3 Remove the clutch assembly by unscrewing the six bolts holding the cover to the rear face of the flywheel. Unscrew the bolts diagonally half a turn at a time to prevent distortion of the cover flange, also to prevent an accident caused by the cover flange binding on the dowels and suddenly flying off. (photo).

4 With the bolts removed, lift the assembly off the locating dowels. The driven plate or clutch disc will fall out at this stage, as it is not attached to either the clutch cover assembly or flywheel. Carefully note which way round it is fitted. (photo)

5 It is important that no oil or grease gets on the clutch disc friction linings, or the pressure plate and flywheel faces. It is advisable to handle the parts with clean hands and to wipe down

12.3 Removal of clutch cover securing bolt

12.4 Lifting away clutch cover and disc from flywheel

12.6 Replacing clutch cover and disc. Note which way round the disc is fitted

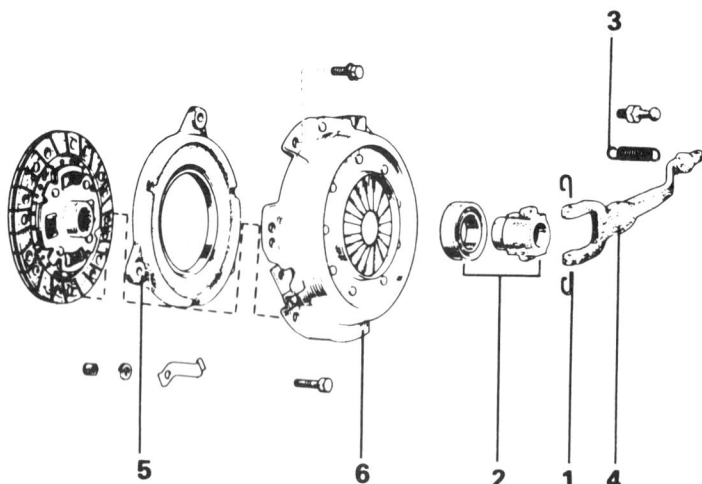

Fig. 5.15. Clutch assembly (TE models)

1. Release bearing hub clips
2. Release bearing hub w/bearing
3. Tension spring
4. Release fork
5. Pressure plate
6. Clutch cover and spring

the pressure plate and flywheel faces with a clean dry rag before inspection or refitting commences.

6 To refit the clutch plate, place the clutch disc against the flywheel with the larger end of the hub away from the flywheel. On no account should the clutch disc be replaced the wrong way round as it will be found impossible to operate the clutch. (photo)

7 Replace the clutch cover assembly loosely on the dowels. Replace the six bolts and tighten them finger tight so that the clutch disc is gripped but can still be moved.

8 The clutch disc must now be centralised so that when the engine and gearbox are mated, the gearbox input shaft splines will pass through the splines in the centre of the hub.

9 Centralisation can be carried out quite easily by inserting a round bar or long screwdriver through the hole in the centre of the clutch, so that the end of the bar rests in the small hole in the crankshaft containing the input shaft bearing bush. Moving the bar sideways or up and down will move the clutch disc in whichever direction is necessary to achieve centralisation.

10 Centralisation is easily judged by removing the bar or screwdriver and viewing the driveplate hub in relation to the hole in the centre of the diaphragm spring. When the hub is exactly in the centre of the release bearing hole, all is correct. Alternatively, if an old input shaft can be borrowed this will eliminate all the guesswork as it will fit the bearing and centre of the clutch hub exactly, obviating the need for visual alignment.

11 Tighten the clutch bolts firmly in a diagonal sequence to ensure that the cover plate is pulled evenly and without distortion of the flange. Tighten the bolts to a torque wrench setting of 7 - 16 lb f ft (1.0 - 2.21 kg fm) depending on model - see 'Specifications' Section (photo).

12 Mate the engine and gearbox, bleed the slave cylinder and check the clutch for correct operation.

13 Clutch inspection

1 In the normal course of events clutch dismantling and reassembly is the term for simply fitting a new clutch pressure plate and friction disc. Under no circumstances should the pressure plate assembly be dismantled. If a fault develops in the assembly an exchange replacement unit must be fitted.

2 If a new clutch disc is being fitted it is false economy not to renew the release bearing at the same time. This will preclude having to replace it at a later time when wear on the clutch linings is very small.

3 Examine the clutch disc friction linings for wear or loose rivets and the disc for rim distortion, cracks and worn splines.

4 It is always best to renew the clutch drive plate as an assembly to preclude further trouble, but, if it is wished to merely renew the linings, the rivets should be drilled out and not knocked out with a centre punch. The manufacturers do not

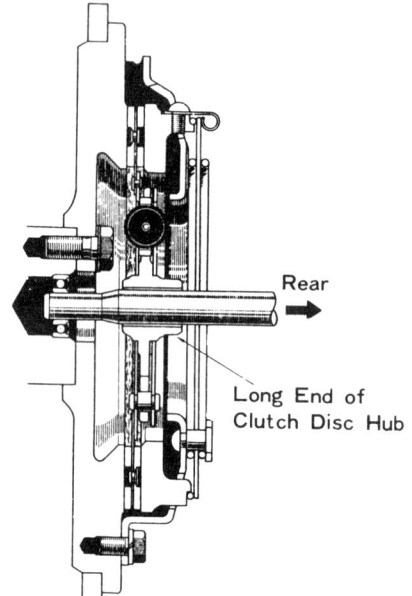

Fig. 5.16. Clutch centralisation

12.11 Clutch cover correctly refitted

Chapter 5/Clutch

advise that the linings only are renewed and personal experience dictates that it is far more satisfactory to renew the driven plate completely than to try to economise by fitting only new friction linings.

5 Check the machined faces of the flywheel and the pressure plate. If either is badly grooved it should be machined until smooth, or replaced with a new item. If the pressure plate is cracked or split it must be renewed.

6 Examine the hub splines for wear and make sure that the centre hub is not loose.

14 Clutch release bearing - removal and replacement

1 To gain access it is necessary to remove the gearbox as described in Chapter 6.

2 Detach the spring clips from the release bearing carrier and release fork. Draw the release bearing carrier from the flat bearing retainer (photos).

3 Check the bearing for signs of overheating, wear or roughness, and, if evident, the old bearing should be drawn off the carrier using a universal two or three leg puller. Note which way round the bearing is fitted.

4 Using a bench vice and suitable packing, press a new bearing onto the carrier. (Fig. 5.17).

5 Apply some high melting point grease to the contact surfaces of the release lever and pivot assembly, and bearing carrier. Pack some grease into the inner recess of the bearing carrier. (photos).

6 Refitting the bearing and carrier is the reverse sequence to removal.

Fig. 5.17. Fitting new bearing to carrier

14.2a Withdrawing spring clip from release bearing carrier

14.2b Removal of bearing carrier

14.5a The release lever assembly

14.5b Release lever assembly mounting

15 Clutch faults

There are four main faults to which the clutch and release mechanism are prone. They may occur by themselves or in conjunction with any of the other faults. They are clutch squeal slip, spin and judder.

16 Clutch squeal - diagnosis and cure

1 If on taking up the drive, or when changing gear, the clutch squeals, this is a sure indication of a badly worn clutch release bearing. As well as regular wear due to normal use, wear of the clutch release bearing is much accentuated if the clutch is ridden, or held down for long periods in gear, with the engine running. To minimise wear of this component the car should always be taken out of gear at traffic lights and for similar hold ups.
2 The clutch release bearing is not an expensive item.

17 Clutch slip - diagnosis and cure

1 Clutch slip is a self evident condition which occurs when the clutch friction plate is badly worn; the release arm free travel is insufficient; oil or grease have got onto the flywheel or pressure plate faces; or the pressure plate itself is faulty.
2 The reason for clutch slip is that, due to one of the faults listed above, there is either insufficient pressure from the pressure plate, or insufficient friction from the friction plate, to ensure solid drive.
3 If small amounts of oil get onto the clutch, they will be burnt off under the heat of clutch engagement, in the process gradually darkening the linings. Excessive oil on the clutch will burn off leaving a carbon deposit which can cause quite bad slip, or fierceness, spin and judder.
4 If clutch slip is suspected, and confirmation of this condition is required, there are several tests which can be made:
a) With the engine in second or third gear and pulling lightly up a moderate incline, sudden depression of the accelerator pedal may cause the engine to increase its speed without any increase in road speed. Easing off on the accelerator will then give a definite drop in engine speed without the car slowing.
b) Drive the car at a steady speed in top gear and, braking with the left leg, try and maintain the same speed by pressing down on the accelerator. Providing the same speed is maintained, a change in the speed of the engine confirms that slip is taking place.
c) In extreme cases of clutch slip the engine will race under normal acceleration conditions.
If slip is due to oil or grease on the linings a temporary cure can sometimes be effected by squirting carbon tetrachloride into the clutch. The permanent cure, of course, is to renew the clutch driven plate, and trace and rectify the oil leak.

18 Clutch spin - diagnosis and cure

1 Clutch spin is a condition which occurs when there is a leak in the clutch hydraulic actuating mechanism; the release arm free travel is excessive; there is an obstruction in the clutch either on the primary gear splines, or in the operating lever itself; or the oil may have partially burnt off the clutch linings and have left a resinous deposit which is causing the clutch disc to stick to the pressure plate or flywheel.
2 The reason for clutch spin is that due to any, or a combination of, the faults just listed, the clutch pressure plate is not completely freeing from the centre plate even with the clutch pedal fully depressed.
3 If clutch spin is suspected, the condition can be confirmed by extreme difficulty in engaging first gear from rest, difficulty in changing gear, and very sudden take-up of the clutch drive at the fully depressed end of the clutch pedal travel as the clutch is released.
4 Check the clutch master and slave cylinders and the connecting hydraulic pipe for leaks. Fluid in one of the rubber boots fitted over the end of either the master or slave cylinders is a sure sign of a leaking piston seal.
5 If these points are checked and found to be in order then the fault lies internally in the clutch, and it will be necessary to remove it for examination.

19 Clutch judder - diagnosis and cure

1 Clutch judder is a self evident condition which occurs when the power unit mountings are loose or too flexible; when there is oil on the faces of the clutch friction plate; or when the clutch has been assembled incorrectly.
2 The reason for clutch judder is that due to one of the faults just listed, the clutch pressure plate is not freeing smoothly from the friction disc, and is snatching.
3 Clutch judder normally occurs when the clutch pedal is released in first or reverse gear, and the whole car shudders, as it moves backwards or forwards.

Chapter 6
Manual gearbox and automatic transmission

Contents

General description ... 1	Gearbox extension housing oil seal - removal and replacement ... 26
KE models: manual gearbox	Gearbox - reassembly ... 25
Countergear - dismantling and reassembly ... 8	Gearbox - removal and replacement ... 14
Fault diagnosis - manual gearbox ... 37	Input shaft - dismantling ... 16
Gearbox components - inspection ... 9	Input shaft - reassembly ... 23
Gearbox - dismantling ... 3	Mainshaft - dismantling ... 17
Gearbox extension housing oil seal - removal and replacement ... 13	Mainshaft - reassembly ... 24
Gearbox - removal and replacement ... 2	Synchro hubs - dismantling and inspection ... 18
Gearbox - reassembly ... 12	Synchro hubs - reassembly ... 19
Input shaft - dismantling ... 4	**All models: automatic transmission**
Input shaft - reassembly ... 10	Automatic transmission - fluid level ... 28
Mainshaft - dismantling ... 5	Automatic transmission - general ... 27
Mainshaft - reassembly ... 11	Automatic transmission - removal and replacement ... 29
Synchro hubs - dismantling and inspection ... 6	Engine idle speed - adjustment (automatic transmission) ... 35
Synchro hubs - reassembly ... 7	Fault diagnosis - automatic transmission ... 36
TE models: manual gearbox	Neutral safety switch - adjustment ... 33
Countershaft - dismantling ... 20	Selector lever - adjustment ... 32
Countershaft - reassembly ... 22	Selector lever - removal, overhaul and replacement (floor mounted) ... 30
Fault diagnosis - manual gearbox ... 37	Selector lever - removal, overhaul and replacement (column mounted) ... 31
Gearbox components - inspection ... 21	Throttle link connecting rod - adjustment ... 34
Gearbox - dismantling ... 15	

Specifications

KE models: manual gearbox

Number of gears:	4 forward, 1 reverse
Type of gears:	Helical, constant mesh
Synchromesh:	All forward gears
Ratios:	
First	3.684 : 1
Second	2.050 (1100/65.7 cu in.) 2.022 : 1 (1200/71.1 cu in.)
Third	1.383 : 1
Fourth	1.000 : 1
Reverse	4.316 : 1
Speedometer gear teeth:	
Drive gear	5
Driven gear:	
Saloon/sedan	19
Estate/Wagon	20
Oil capacity:	3 Imp. pints (1.7 litres, 1.8 US quarts)
Oil grade:	SAE 80

Dimensions and clearances:

	Specified	Limit
Gear backlash:		
Input shaft	0.004 in. (0.1 mm)	0.008 in. (0.2 mm)
First, second and third gears	0.004 in. (0.1 mm)	0.008 in. (0.2 mm)

Gear bore dimensions:
First gear:
    Inner diameter limit ... 1.464 in. (37.15 mm)
    Oil clearance limit ... 0.008 in. (0.2 mm)
    Specified oil clearance ... 0.0024 - 0.0039 in. (0.06 - 0.10 mm)

Second and Third gear:
    Inner diameter limit ... 1.267 in. (32.15 mm)
    Oil clearance limit ... 0.008 in. (0.2 mm)
    Specified oil clearance ... 0.0020 - 0.0039 in. (0.05 - 0.10 mm)

Hub sleeve and reverse gear fork groove width limit ... 0.30 in. (7.5 mm)
Selector fork and reverse selector arms fork to hub clearance limit ... 0.032 in. (0.8 mm)
Clearance between synchroniser ring and gear:
    Limit ... 0.032 in. (0.8 mm)
    Specified ... 0.046 - 0.076 in. (1.18 - 1.94 mm)

Countergear thrust washer thickness limit ... 0.067 in. (1.7 mm)
Reverse idler gear bush inner diameter limit ... 0.71 in. (18.2 mm)
Reverse idler gear shaft diameter limit ... 0.70 in. (17.9 mm)
Input shaft retainer outer diameter limit ... 1.09 in. (27.9 mm)
Selector lever housing lever end cup inner diameter limit ... 0.60 in. (15.2 mm)
    Reverse gear ... 0.006 in. (0.16 mm)   0.012 in. (0.3 mm)
    Reverse idler gear ... 0.007 in. (0.18 mm)   0.012 in. (0.3 mm)
Counter gear thrust clearance:
    Specified ... 0.002 - 0.010 in. (0.05 - 0.25 mm)
    Limit ... 0.012 in. (0.3 mm)
Mainshaft wear limit:
    Gear installation portion diameter ... 1.24 in. (31.8 mm)
    Flange thickness ... 0.14 in. (3.5 mm)
Mainshaft ovality (at centre) ... 0.001 in. (0.03 mm)
Input shaft bearing retaining snapring thickness:
    No. 1 ... 0.091 - 0.095 in. (2.30 - 2.42 mm)
    No. 2 ... 0.097 - 0.101 in. (2.45 - 2.57 mm)

First gear bush:
    Outer diameter limit ... 1.254 in. (31.85 mm)
    Flange thickness ... 0.132 in. (3.35 mm)
Selector lever end and cup clearance ... 0.002 - 0.009 in. (0.05 - 0.22 mm)
Extension housing bush inner diameter limit ... 1.27 in. (32.2 mm)
Extension housing bush inner diameter new ... 1.260 - 1.261 in. (32.00 - 32.03 mm)
Extension housing bush specified oil clearance ... 0.0004 - 0.0024 in. (0.01 - 0.06 mm)
Mainshaft hub spacer clearance ... 0.002 - 0.006 in. (0.05 - 0.15 mm)

Hub spacer thickness:
    No. 1 ... 0.169 - 0.171 in. (4.30 - 4.35 mm)
    No. 2 ... 0.171 - 0.173 in. (4.35 - 4.40 mm)
    No. 3 ... 0.173 - 0.175 in. (4.40 - 4.45 mm)

Mainshaft 3rd/4th speed gear hub minimum thrust clearance ... 0.002 in. (0.05 mm)

Mainshaft snapring thickness:
    No. 1 ... 0.081 - 0.083 in. (2.05 - 2.10 mm)
    No. 2 ... 0.083 - 0.085 in. (2.10 - 2.15 mm)
    No. 3 ... 0.085 - 0.087 in. (2.15 - 2.20 mm)
    No. 4 ... 0.087 - 0.089 in. (2.20 - 2.25 mm)
    No. 5 ... 0.089 - 0.091 in. (2.25 - 2.30 mm)
    No. 6 ... 0.091 - 0.093 in. (2.30 - 2.35 mm)
    No. 7 ... 0.093 - 0.095 in. (2.35 - 2.40 mm)
    No. 8 ... 0.095 - 0.097 in. (2.40 - 2.45 mm)

Gear thrust clearance:
    3rd gear to mainshaft flange ... 0.002 - 0.006 in. (0.05 - 0.15 mm)
    2nd gear to mainshaft flange ... 0.004 - 0.012 in. (0.10 - 0.25 mm)
    1st gear to 1st gear bush flange ... 0.007 - 0.011 in. (0.18 - 0.28 mm)

Input shaft retainer gasket thickness:
    No. 1 ... 0.02 in. (0.5 mm)
    No. 2 ... 0.01 in. (0.3 mm)

Countergear thrust washer thickness:
- No. 0 ... ... 0.051 - 0.053 in. (1.30 - 1.35 mm)
- No. 1 ... ... 0.065 - 0.057 in. (1.40 - 1.45 mm)
- No. 2 ... ... 0.059 - 0.061 in. (1.50 - 1.55 mm)
- No. 3 ... ... 0.063 - 0.065 in. (1.60 - 1.65 mm)

TE models: manual gearbox

Number of gears ... 4 forward, 1 reverse

Type of gears: ... Helical, constant mesh

Synchromesh: ... All forward gears

Ratios:
- First ... 3.587 : 1
- Second ... 2.022 : 1
- Third ... 1.384 : 1
- Fourth ... 1.000 : 1
- Reverse ... 3.484 : 1

Dimensions and clearances:

	Specified - new	maximum
Thrust clearances:		
First gear	0.004 - 0.010 in. (0.10 - 0.25 mm)	0.020 in. (0.5 mm)
Second gear	0.006 - 0.010 in. (0.15 - 0.25 mm)	0.020 in. (0.5 mm)
Third gear	0.006 - 0.012 in. (0.15 - 0.30 mm)	0.024 in. (0.6 mm)
Reverse	0.008 - 0.012 in. (0.20 - 0.30 mm)	0.24 in. (0.6 mm)
Reverse idler	0.002 - 0.020 in. (0.05 - 0.50 mm)	0.031 in. (0.8 mm)

Countergear thrust washers:
- No. 0 ... 0.0882 - 0.0902 in. (2.240 - 2.290 mm)
- No. 1 ... 0.0901 - 0.0925 in. (2.300 - 2.350 mm)
- No. 2 ... 0.0929 - 0.0949 in. (2.360 - 2.410 mm)
- No. 3 ... 0.0953 - 0.0972 in. (2.420 - 2.470 mm)
- No. 4 ... 0.0976 - 0.0996 in. (2.480 - 2.530 mm)
- No. 5 ... 0.100 - 0.1020 in. (2.540 - 2.590 mm)

Reverse idler gear thrust washer:
- A ... 1.120 - 1.122 in. (28.44 - 28.50 mm)
- B ... 1.128 - 1.102 in. (28.64 - 28.70 mm)
- C ... 1.135 - 1.138 in. (28.84 - 28.90 mm)
- D ... 1.143 - 1.146 in. (29.04 - 29.10 mm)

Input shaft circlip:
- No. 1 ... 0.093 - 0.094 in. (2.35 - 2.40 mm)
- No. 2 ... 0.094 - 0.096 in. (2.40 - 2.45 mm)
- No. 3 ... 0.096 - 0.098 in. (2.45 - 2.50 mm)
- No. 4 ... 0.098 - 0.100 in. (2.50 - 2.55 mm)
- No. 5 ... 0.100 - 0.102 in. (2.55 - 2.60 mm)

Countershaft reverse gear:
- No. 1 ... 0.071 - 0.073 in. (1.80 - 1.85 mm)
- No. 2 ... 0.075 - 0.077 in. (1.90 - 1.95 mm)

Mainshaft circlip:
- No. 1 ... 0.077 - 0.079 in. (1.95 - 2.00 mm)
- No. 2 ... 0.079 - 0.081 in. (2.00 - 2.05 mm)
- No. 3 ... 0.081 - 0.083 in. (2.05 - 2.10 mm)
- No. 4 ... 0.083 - 0.084 in. (2.10 - 2.15 mm)
- No. 5 ... 0.084 - 0.086 in. (2.15 - 2.20 mm)

Synchroniser ring and gear clearance limit ... 0.031 in. (0.8 mm)
Shaft fork and hub sleeve clearance limit ... 0.039 in. (1.0 mm)

Gear backlash:	Specified - new	maximum
Input shaft/countergear	0.004 - 0.008 in. (0.10 - 0.20 mm)	0.016 in. (0.40 mm)
Third gear/countergear	0.004 - 0.008 in. (0.10 - 0.20 mm)	0.016 in. (0.40 mm)
Second gear/countergear	0.004 - 0.008 in. (0.10 - 0.20 mm)	0.016 in. (0.40 mm)
First gear/countergear	0.004 - 0.008 in. (0.10 - 0.20 mm)	0.016 in. (0.40 mm)
Reverse gear/countergear	0.004 - 0.008 in. (0.10 - 0.20 mm)	0.016 in. (0.40 mm)

Mainshaft bush O/D max wear limit	1.488 in. (37.8 mm)
Bush flange wear limit	0.157 in. (4.0 mm)
Mainshaft max distortion (at centre)	0.0012 in. (0.03 mm)

Gear inner surface wear limit:
First	1.660 in. (42.15 mm)
Second	1.502 in. (38.15 mm)
Third	1.502 in. (38.15 mm)
Reverse	1.660 in. (42.15 mm)

Synchro hub sleeve and fork groove wear limit	0.355 in. (8.5 mm)
Maximum clearance of fork/groove	0.039 in. (1.0 mm)
Front bearing retainer O/D (maximum)	1.295 in. (32.9 mm)

Gearbox oil capacity: ... ...   2.8 pints (1.54 litres, 3.2 US pints)

Torque wrench settings:

	lb f ft	kg f m
KE models: manual gearbox		
Refill plugs	27 - 31	3.7 - 4.3
Mainshaft nut	32.5 - 55	4.5 - 7.5
Input shaft retainer	7 - 12	1.0 - 1.6
Countergear shaft retainer plate nuts	7 - 12	1.0 - 1.6
Reverse idler shaft dowel bolt	7 - 12	1.0 - 1.6
Side cover nuts	2.9 - 6.5	0.4 - 0.9
Selector lever retainer bolts	10.9 - 15.9	1.5 - 2.2
Extension housing nuts	22 - 33	3.0 - 4.5
Reverse light switch	22 - 36	3.0 - 5.0
Oil pan	2.5 - 2.9	0.55 - 0.70
Drain plug	27 - 31	3.7 - 4.3
Clutch release fork retainer bolt	13.7 - 22.4	1.9 - 3.1
TE models: manual gearbox		
Selector lever shaft housing to main casing	7.2 - 11.6	1.0 - 1.6
Clutch housing to main casing	21.7 - 32.5	3.0 - 4.5
Front bearing retainer to main casing	7.2 - 11.6	1.0 - 1.6
Extension housing to main casing	21.7 - 32.5	3.0 - 4.5
Output shaft bearing nut	32.5 - 54.2	4.5 - 7.5
Reverse idler shaft	9.4 - 13.0	1.3 - 1.8
Drain plug	1.8 - 2.35	0.25 - 0.30
Main casing halves securing bolts	10.9 - 14.5	1.50 - 2.20
Reverse light switch	22 - 36	3.0 - 5.0
Clutch housing to cylinder block	4.8 - 6.8	0.347 - 0.491
All models: automatic transmission		
Drive plate to crankshaft	33 - 39	4.6 - 5.39
Drive plate to torque converter	8 - 11	1.11 - 1.53
Converter housing to engine	37 - 50	5.1 - 6.9
Converter housing to transmission case	14 - 22	1.94 - 3.04

Chapter 6/Manual gearbox and automatic transmission

1 General description

The gearbox fitted may be either a four speed manual gearbox or the two speed Toyoglide automatic transmission unit. Information on the automatic transmission will be found later in this Chapter.

The manual gearbox is fitted with synchromesh on all the forward gears. For quiet operation the gears are helically cut and are in constant mesh with the countergear.

Two types of manual gearbox are fitted. Basically KE models have a gearbox with a one piece casing whereas TE models use a gearbox with a split type casing. Full information is given on both gearboxes.

The input shaft is mounted in the front face of the casing and runs in a single track ball bearing. Needle roller bearings support the countergear assembly on KE models but ball bearings are used on TE models. The mainshaft (output shaft) is located at the rear of the input shaft and extends through the rear of the main casing.

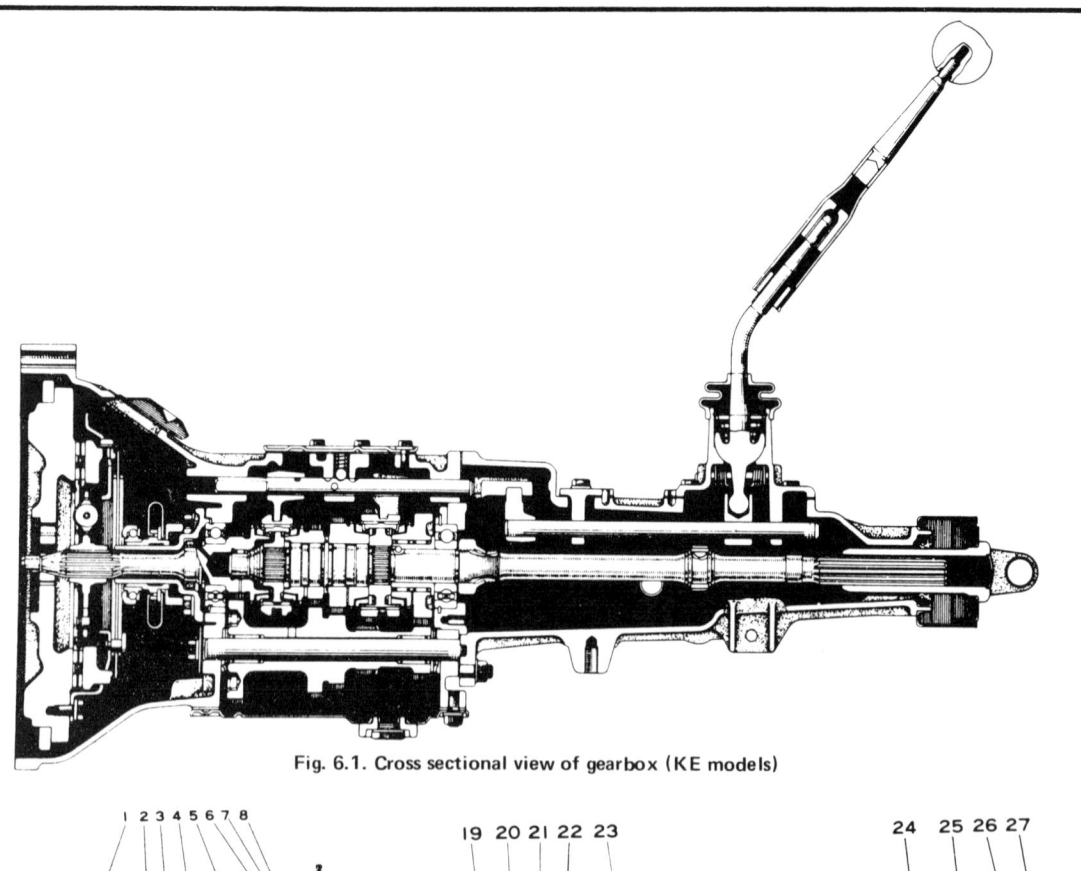

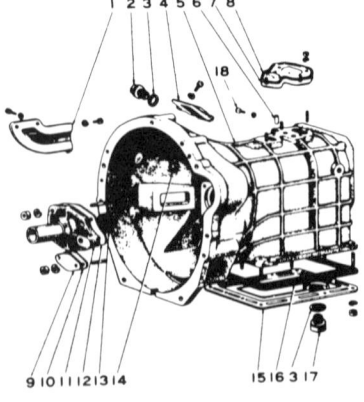

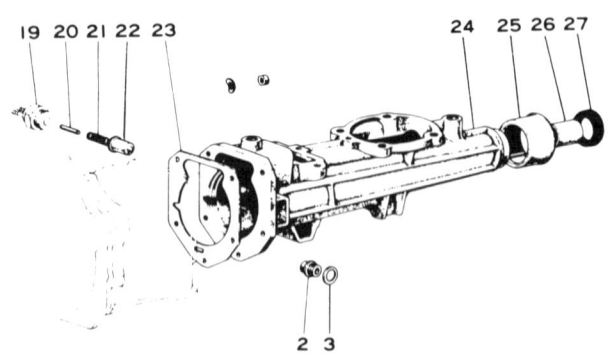

Fig. 6.1. Cross sectional view of gearbox (KE models)

Fig. 6.2. Gearbox external components

1 Stopper plate	7 Gasket	14 Plug	21 Spring
2 Transmission case cover plug	8 Transmission case cover	15 Oil pan	22 Pin
3 Gasket	9 Countershaft cover plate	16 Gasket	23 Gasket
4 Clutch housing cover	10 Gasket	17 Drain plug	24 Extension housing
5 Main casing	11 Front bearing (input shaft retainer)	18 Bolt	25 Dust deflector
6 Shift detent ball spring seat	12 Gasket	19 Reverse light switch	26 Bush
	13 Oil seal	20 Pin	27 Oil seal

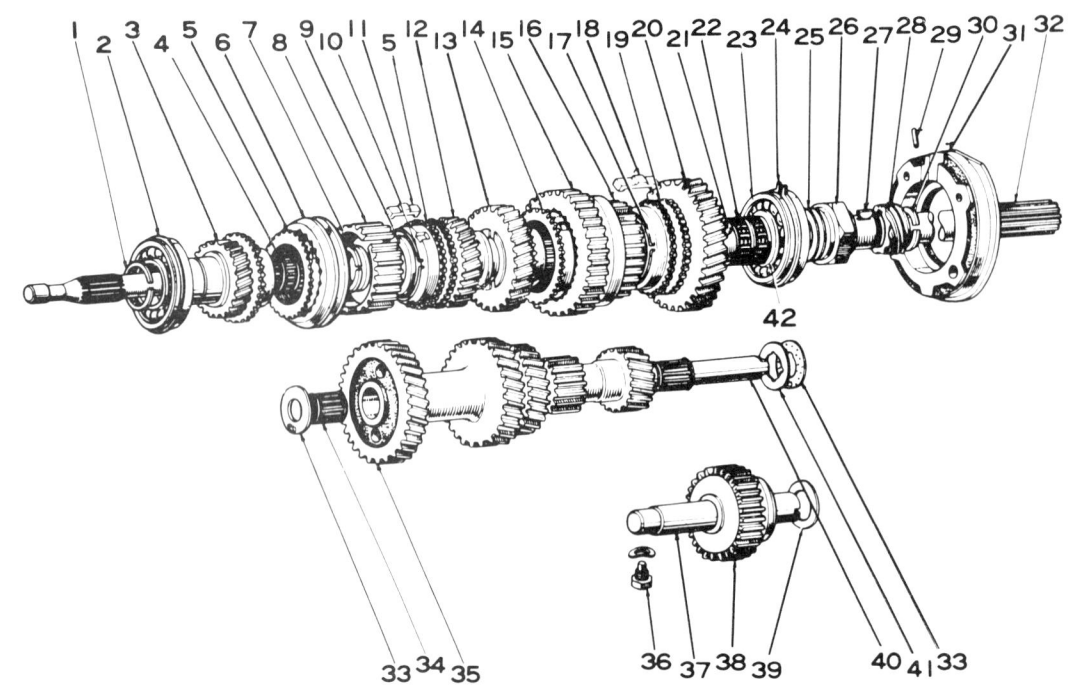

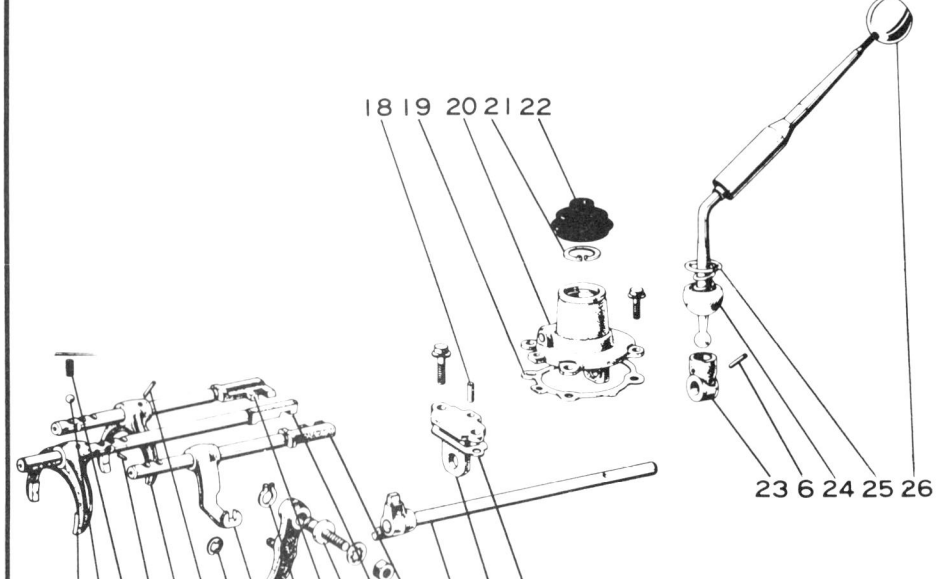

Fig. 6.3. Gearbox internal components

1 Snap ring	11 Key	21 Ball	32 Mainshaft (output shaft)
2 Front bearing	12 Third gear	22 Bush	33 Thrust washer
3 Input shaft	13 Second gear	23 Rear bearing	34 Needle roller bearing
4 Needle roller bearing	14 Synchroniser ring	24 Snap ring	35 Countergear
5 Synchroniser ring	15 Reverse gear	25 Shim	36 Dowel bolt
6 Hub sleeve	16 Hub	26 Nut	37 Idler gear shaft
7 Snap ring	17 Spring	27 Woodruff key	38 Reverse idler
8 Hub	18 Key	28 Speedometer drive gear	39 Spacer (optional fitment)
9 Spacer	19 Synchroniser ring	29 Roll pin	40 Countergear shaft
10 Spring	20 First gear	30 Snap ring	41 Thrust washer
		31 Bearing retainer	42 Needle roller bearing

Fig. 6.4. Gearbox selector mechanism

1 3rd/4th selector fork
2 Ball
3 Spring
4 Pin
5 1st/2nd selector forks
6 Roll pin
7 'E' ring
8 Reverse selector fork
9 Reverse selector arm
10 Snap ring
11 1st/2nd selector fork rod
12 Arm pivot
13 3rd/4th selector fork rod
14 Reverse selector fork rod
15 Selector lever shaft
16 Shaft support
17 Gasket
18 Pin
19 Gasket
20 Retainer
21 Snap ring
22 Boot
23 Housing
24 Selector lever
25 Spring
26 Knob

Chapter 6/Manual gearbox and automatic transmission

At the front of the main casing is the clutch bellhousing and at the rear an extension housing upon which is mounted the gearchange lever and associated linkages.

KE Models: manual gearbox

2 Gearbox (KE models) - removal and replacement.

1 The best method of removing the gearbox is to separate the gearbox bellhousing from the engine and to lever the gearbox away from the underside of the car. It is recommended that during the final stages of removal assistance is obtained because of the weight of the gearbox.
2 Disconnect the battery, raise the car and place on axle stands if a ramp is not available. The higher the car is off the ground the easier it will be to work underneath.
3 Undo and remove the drain plug and drain the oil into a suitably sized container. When all the oil has drained out replace the drain plug.
4 Refer to Chapter 2 and drain the cooling system. Slacken the radiator top hose clips and remove the top hose. (photo)
5 Move the fan until the blades are horizontal.
6 If a console is fitted undo and remove the securing screws and lift away.
7 Remove the front interior carpeting to give access to the base of the gearchange lever. (photo)
8 Undo and remove the screws securing the gearchange lever rubber boot retainer. (photo)
9 Unscrew the gearchange lever knob and remove the rubber boot. (photo)
10 Using a pair of circlip pliers remove the circlip retaining the gearchange lever. (photo)
11 Carefully withdraw the gearchange lever and conical spring. (photo)
12 Disconnect the reverse light switch cable connectors. (photo)
13 Refer to Chapter 7 and remove the propeller shaft. (photos)

2.4 Removal of top hose

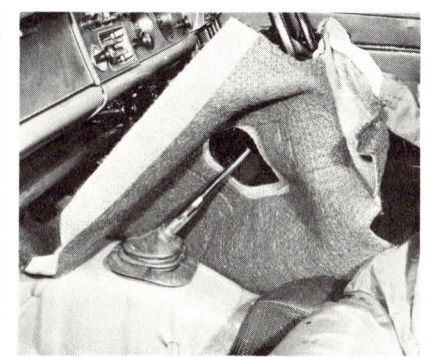

2.7 Lifting away interior carpeting

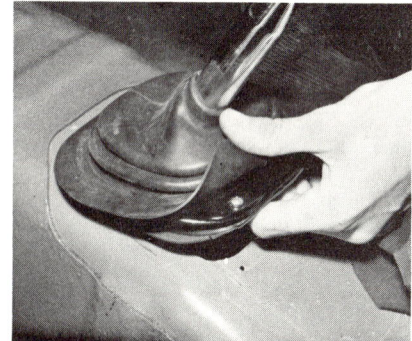

2.8 Gear change lever rubber boot

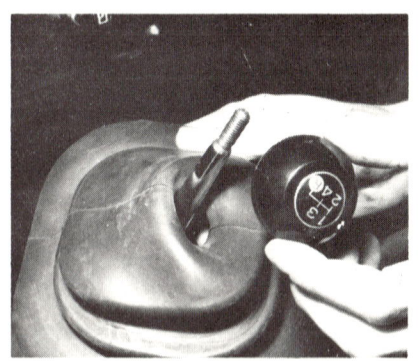

2.9 Removal of lever knob and rubber boot

2.10 Removal of circlip retaining gear change lever

2.11 Lifting away gear change lever

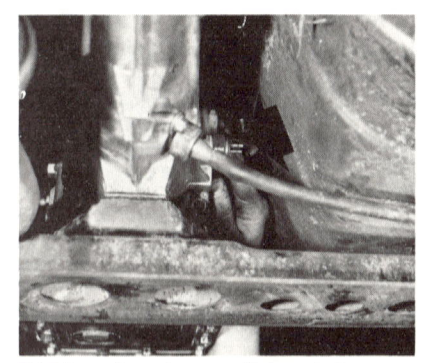

2.12 Location of reverse light switch

2.13a Propeller shaft front end

2.13b Propeller shaft rear end

14 Disconnect the speedometer cable from the right-hand side of the gearbox by unscrewing the knurled nut and withdrawing the cable. Take care not to lose the felt seal (photos).
15 To give better access and allow for engine movement the front half of the exhaust system should be removed.
16 Undo and remove the two nuts and bolts securing the downpipe to silencer pipe clamp halves. (photos)
17 Undo and remove the bolt and washer securing the exhaust pipe support bracket to the left-hand side of the extension housing. Detach the clip and lift away the support bracket. (photo)
18 Undo and remove the nuts securing the exhaust downpipe to manifold clamp and lower the downpipe. Recover the special sealing washer located between the two joint halves (photo).
19 Place a jack under the engine sump to support its weight. (photo)
20 Undo and remove the bolts and washers securing the engine rear mounting to the underside of the body. (photo)
21 Undo and remove the two bolts securing the engine rear mounting to the gearbox extension housing. (photo)
22 The rear mounting may now be lifted away.
23 Make a note of the electrical connections at the rear of the starter motor solenoid. Disconnect the cables. (photo)
24 Undo and remove the nuts and bolts securing the starter motor to the engine backplate. Draw the starter motor forwards and lift away from the side of the engine. (photo) One word of caution: on some models it may be found necessary to completely remove the exhaust manifold assembly to enable the starter motor to be completely withdrawn.
25 Withdraw the split pin securing the clutch release cable to the release arm. Detach the cable end from the release arm.
26 Lower the engine supporting jack to give access to the clutch bellhousing top securing bolts.
27 Undo and remove the remaining bolts, spring washers and nuts securing the clutch bellhousing to the rear of the engine. (photo)
28 Check that all the gearbox attachments have been released and then with the help of a second person take the weight of the gearbox.
29 Lower the engine support jack further until there is sufficient clearance between the top of the bellhousing and the underside of the body.
30 Ease the gearbox rearwards ensuring that the weight of the unit is not supported on the input shaft which is easily bent. (photo)
31 Finally lift the gearbox away from under the car.
32 This photo shows a rear view of the engine with the gearbox removed.
33 Replacement is the reverse sequence to removal. Do not forget to refill the gearbox with the recommended grade of oil. (photo)

3 Gearbox - dismantling

Place the complete unit on a firm bench and ensure that you have the following tools available in addition to a normal range of spanners etc.
a) Good quality circlip pliers. 2 pairs, 1 expanding and 1 contracting.
b) Copper headed mallet: at least 2 lbs.
c) Drifts: steel 3/8 inch and brass 3/8 inch.
d) Small containers.
e) Engineer's vice mounted on a firm bench.

Any attempt to dismantle the gearbox without the foregoing is not necessarily impossible but will certainly be very difficult and inconvenient resulting in possible damage. Read the whole of this Section before starting work.

Take care not to let the synchromesh hub assemblies come apart before you want them to. It accelerates wear if the splines of hub and sleeve are changed in relation to each other. As a precaution it is advisable to make a line or mark with a dab of paint.

Before finally going ahead with dismantling first ascertain the availability of spare parts - particularly shims, which could be difficult to obtain.
1 Refer to Chapter 5 and remove the clutch release drum and bearing assembly.
2 Undo and remove the fan nuts and spring washers securing the front bearing retainer to the inner face of the clutch bellhousing. Slide the retainer from the input shaft. (photo)
3 Undo and remove the five nuts and spring washers securing the side cover and gasket to the side of the main casing. (photo)
4 Located behind the side cover are three springs and ball bearings. Carefully recover these once the cover and gasket have been removed. (photos)
5 Undo and remove the bolts and washers securing the oil pan to the underside of the main casing. Lift away the oil pan and its gaskets.
6 Undo and remove the nuts and spring washers securing the extension housing to the rear face of the main casing.
7 The extension housing may now be lifted up and over the rear of the mainshaft. Recover the gasket. (photos)
8 This photo shows the selector lever shaft in the extension housing.
9 For future reference note the location of the three selector shaft ends. (photo)
10 This photo shows the layout of the gear assemblies which must next be removed.
11 Undo and remove the dowel bolt and washer securing the reverse idler gear shaft to the main casing web. (photo)
12 Withdraw the reverse idler gear shaft and lift away the idler gear. Note which way round it is fitted. (photo)
13 The countergear shaft must next be removed. First undo and remove the two bolts and washers securing the retaining plate to the front face of the main casing. (photo)
14 The countergear shaft may now be withdrawn rearwards. Hold the counter gear cluster. (photo)
15 Lift out the countergear and recover the thrust washers. Note which way round the thrust washers are fitted. (photo)
16 The input shaft is next removed. Using a suitable drift tap the bearing carrier forwards until it is released from the front web of

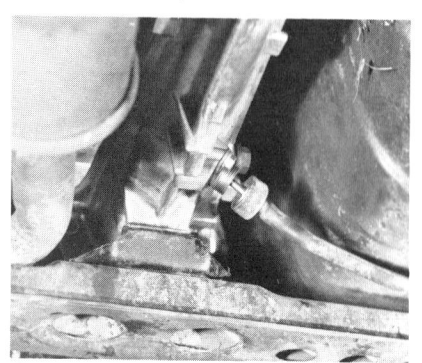

2.14a Removal of speedometer cable

2.14b The felt bush must not be mislaid

2.16a Exhaust downpipe to silencer pipe clamp

2.16b Note the sealing ring

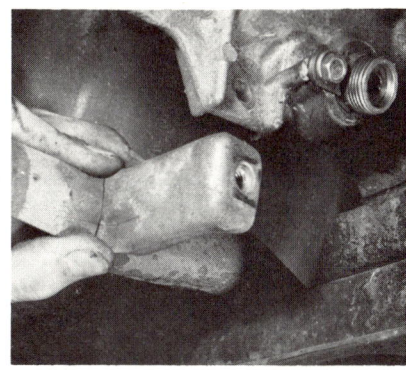

2.17 Exhaust pipe support bracket removal

2.18 Exhaust downpipe with sealing ring

2.19 Jack located under engine sump

2.20 Rear mounting attachment to underside of body

2.21 Rear mounting attachment to gearbox extension housing

2.23 Starter solenoid cable connections

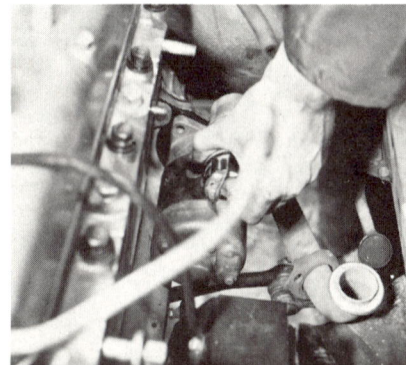

2.24 Removal of starter motor

2.27 Bell housing attaching bolts to engine removal

2.30 Easing gearbox rearwards

2.32 View of engine with gearbox removed

2.33 Topping up gearbox oil level

3.2 Front bearing/input shaft retainer removal

3.3 Side cover removal

3.4a Note the three detent springs

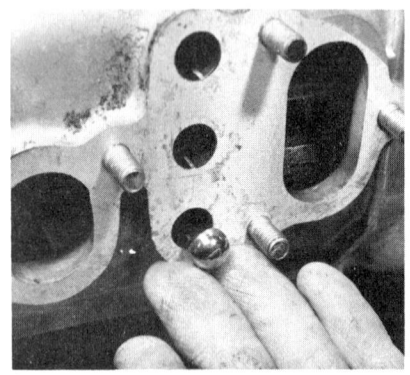

3.4b Do not loose the detent ball bearing

3.7a Lifting away extension housing

3.7b Extension housing gasket

3.8 Selector shaft in extension housing

3.9 Note the location of the three selector shaft ends

3.10 The gear assemblies in the main casing

3.11 Removal of dowel bolt retaining reverse idler shaft

3.12 Withdrawing reverse idler shaft

3.13 Countergear shaft retaining plate

the main casing. (photo)
17 Lift out the input shaft assembly. (photo)
18 The selector (shift) forks are attached to the selector shafts by roll pins and access to these is gained through the side cover aperture. (photo)
19 Using a suitable diameter parallel pin punch drift out the selector fork roll pins. (photo)
20 Withdraw the two outer selector shafts first. Hold the selector forks in position. (photos). Take care to recover the interlock pins.
21 The centre selector shaft is finally removed. (photo)
22 Note the location of the selector forks and remove from the synchromesh sleeves. (photos)
23 The mainshaft may now be withdrawn from the rear of the main casing. If tight use a drift and drive rearwards. (photos)
24 It is not usually necessary to remove the reverse selector arm. (photo)
25 The gearbox may now be considered to be dismantled. It is possible to dismantle the extension housing but is not usually found necessary other than to remove the selector lever retainer for inspection of the speedometer drivegear and selector lever shaft. (photo)
26 Thoroughly flush out the interior of the casing and wipe dry with a non-fluffy rag.

4 Input shaft - dismantling

1 The shaft and bearing are located in the front of the main casing by a large circlip in the outer track of the bearing.
2 To renew the bearing first remove the circlip from the front end of the bearing.
3 Place the outer track of the race on the top of a firm bench vice and drive the input shaft through the bearing. Note that the bearing is fitted with the circlip groove towards the forward end of the input shaft. Lift away the bearing.
4 The spigot bearing needle roller assembly may be slid out of the inner end of the input shaft.

3.14 Withdrawing the countergear shaft

3.15 Countergear thrust washers

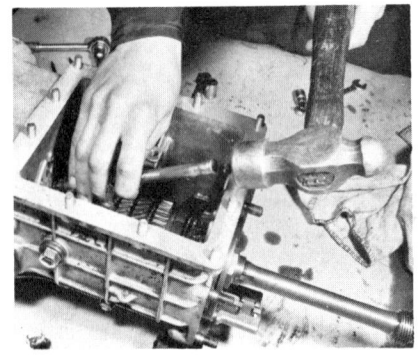

3.16 Tapping out input shaft with drift

3.17 Lifting out input shaft

3.18 Selector fork roll pins

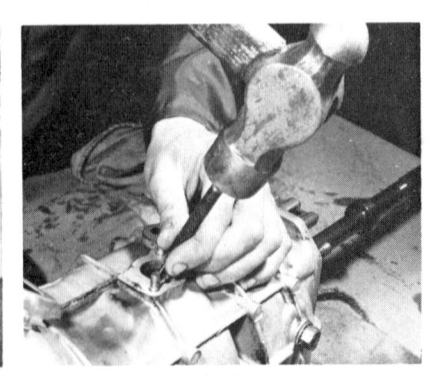

3.19 Tapping out roll pin

3.20a Withdrawing the first selector shaft

3.20b Withdrawing the second selector shaft

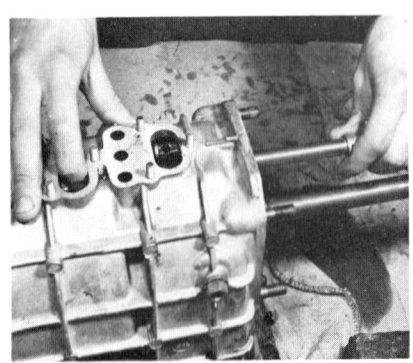

3.21 Withdrawing the third selector shaft

3.22a Removal of the 1st/2nd selector fork

3.22b Removal of the 3rd/4th selector fork

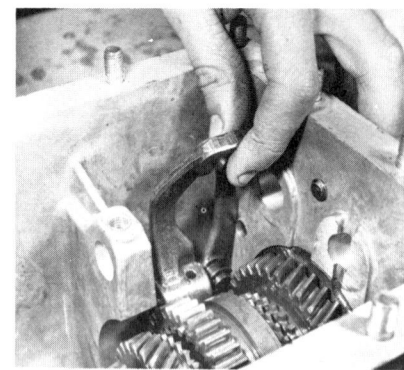

3.22c Lifting out reverse selector

3.23a Withdrawing mainshaft from main casing

3.23b Tap bearing retainer at these points if removal is difficult

3.24 Reverse selector arm

3.25 Extension housing selector lever retainer

5.1 Removal of first circlip from mainshaft

5.2 Speedometer drive gear and woodruff key

5.4 Mainshaft nut removed

5.5 Do not lose the shim(s)

5.6 Sliding off rear bearing retainer

Chapter 6/Manual gearbox and automatic transmission

5 Mainshaft - dismantling.

1 Remove the circlip from the rearmost end of the mainshaft. (photo)
2 Slide off the speedometer drive gear and recover the key. (photo)
3 Remove the second circlip from the rear end of the mainshaft.
4 Hold the mainshaft firmly in the vice, straighten the staking locking the large nut and then remove the nut. (photo)
5 Slide the shim(s) from the end of the mainshaft. (photo)
6 Remove the rear bearing retainer from the end of the mainshaft. (photo)
7 Slide off the first speed gear noting which way round it is fitted. Then remove the synchroniser ring. (photo)
8 The first speed gear bush and needle roller bearing are next removed from the mainshaft. (photo)
9 The first speed gear bush is retained by a ball bearing that should be lifted out from the mainshaft. (photo)
10 The reverse gear and synchroniser assembly may next be removed from the mainshaft. (photo) Then remove the synchroniser ring.
11 Slide off the second speed gear. (photo)
12 Turning to the front end of the mainshaft, remove the shaft snap ring located at the end of the splines. (photo)
13 Slide off the top/third synchromesh unit, noting which way round it is fitted. (photo) Remove the synchroniser ring.
14 Finally slide off the third speed gear and splined thrust washer. (photo)
15 Dismantling of the mainshaft is now complete.

6 Synchro hubs - dismantling and inspection.

1 The synchro hubs are only too easy to dismantle - just push the centre out and the whole assembly flies apart. The point is to prevent this happening, before you are ready. Do not dismantle

5.7 First speed gear removal

5.8 First speed gear, bearing and bush assembly

5.9 Note the ball bearing locking the bush

5.10 Remove the reverse gear and synchronise assembly

5.11 Second speed gear removal

5.12 Mainshaft snap ring on end of splines

5.13 Top/third synchromesh unit removal

5.14 Third gear and splined thrust washer

the hub without reason and do not mix up parts of the hubs.

2 It is most important to check backlash in the splines between the outer sleeve and inner hub. If any is noticeable the whole assembly must be renewed.

3 Mark the hub and sleeve so that you may reassemble them on the same splines. With the hub and sleeve separated, the teeth at the end of the splines which engage with corresponding teeth of the gear wheels, must be checked for damage or wear.

4 Do not confuse the keystone shape at the ends of the teeth. This shape matches the gear teeth shape and it is a design characteristic to minimise jump-out tendencies.

5 If the synchronising cones are being renewed it is sensible also to renew the sliding keys and springs which hold them in position.

7 Synchro hubs - reassembly

1 The hub assemblies are not interchangeable so they must be reassembled with their original or identical new parts.

2 The pipes on the keys are symmetrical so may be refitted either way round into the hub.

3 One slotted key is assembled to each hub for locating the turned out end of the key spring.

4 It should be noted that the keys for each synchromesh unit are of different lengths.

5 The turned out end of each spring must locate in the slotted key and be assembled to the hub in an anticlockwise direction as viewed from either side of the hub.

8 Countergear - dismantling and reassembly.

1 Dismantling of the countergear assembly simply entails the removal of the needle roller bearing assemblies located at either end of the bore. This is a straightforward operation and will present no problems (photo).

2 Refitting the needle roller bearings is the reverse sequence to removal.

9 Gearbox components - inspection.

1 It is assumed that the gearbox has been dismantled for reasons of excessive noise, lack of synchromesh action on certain gears or for failure to stay in gear. If anything more drastic than this (total failure, seizure or main casing cracked) it would be better to leave well alone and look for a replacement, either second hand or an exchange unit.

2 Examine all gears for excessively worn, chipped or damaged teeth. Any such gears should be renewed.

3 Check all synchromesh rings for wear on the bearing surfaces, which normally have clear machined oil reservoir lines in them. If these are smooth or obviously uneven, replacement is essential. Also when the rings are fitted to their gears - as they would be in operation - there should be no rock. This would signify ovality or lack of concentricity. One of the most satisfactory ways of checking is by comparing the fit of a new ring with an old one in the gearwheel cone.

The teeth and cut outs in the synchro rings also wear and for this reason also it is unwise not to fit new ones when the opportunity avails.

4 All ball race bearings should be checked for chatter and roughness after they have been washed out. It is advisable to replace these anyway even though they may not appear too badly worn.

5 Circlips which are all important in locating bearing, gears and hubs should be checked to ensure that they are undamaged and not distorted. In any case a selection of new circlips of varying thicknesses should be obtained to compensate for variations in new components fitted, and wear in old ones. The Specifications indicate what is available.

6 The thrust washers at the end of the countergear should be

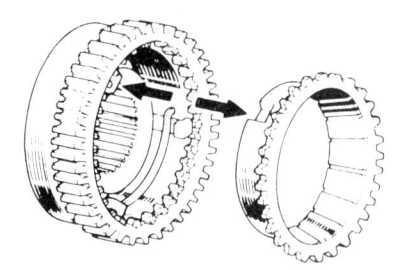

Fig. 6.5. Synchromesh unit reassembly

replaced as they will most certainly have worn if the gearbox is of any age.

7 Needle roller bearings between the input shaft and mainshaft are usually found to be in good order, but if in any doubt replace the needle roller bearing.

8 For details of inspection of the synchro hub assemblies refer to Section 6.

10 Input shaft - reassembly.

1 Using a suitable diameter tubular drift carefully drive the ball race into position. The circlip in the outer track must be towards the front of the input shaft.

2 Retain the bearing in position with a circlip. This is a selective circlip which is in a range of 2 sizes (see Specifications).

3 Work some grease into the needle bearing assembly and insert into the end of the input shaft. (photo)

11 Mainshaft - reassembly

1 Slide the third speed gear and splined thrust washer onto the mainshaft.

2 Fit the third speed gear synchroniser ring onto the synchromesh unit and slide the synchromesh unit onto the end of the mainshaft. Ensure the ring grooves are aligned with the keys.

3 Refit the shaft snap ring located at the end of the mainshaft splines. Measure the thrust clearance between the snap ring and synchromesh unit hub. This should be less than 0.002 in (0.05 mm). A range of 8 snaprings is available to obtain the correct clearance (see Specifications Section).

4 Slide the second speed gear onto the rear end of the mainshaft.

5 Fit the second speed gear synchroniser ring onto the second synchromesh unit and slide the reverse gear and synchromesh unit onto the mainshaft. Ensure the ring grooves are aligned with the keys.

6 Fit the first speed gear synchroniser ring onto the synchromesh unit ensuring the ring grooves are aligned with the keys.

7 Insert the ball bearing onto the mainshaft and assemble the first speed gear bush, needle roller bearing and first speed gear onto the mainshaft.

8 Refit the rear bearing retainer onto the end of the mainshaft and follow this with the shim(s) previously removed. (photo)

9 Hold the mainshaft firmly in the vice and refit the large nut. Do not stake over yet.

10 Using feeler gauges measure the thrust clearance between the 3rd gear and hub. This should be 0.002 - 0.006 inch (0.05 - 0.15 mm) and is adjustable by a range of 3 different thicknesses of hub spacers (see Specification Section) (Fig. 6.6).

11 The following thrust clearances should also be checked using feeler gauges as follows:

a) 2nd gear to output shaft flange: 0.004 - 0.012 in (0.10 - 0.25 mm).

b) 1st gear to 1st gear bush flange: 0.007 - 0.011 in (0.18 - 0.28 mm).

12 When all thrust clearances are correct ensure the mainshaft

Chapter 6/Manual gearbox and automatic transmission

nut is tight and stake the end into the slot in the mainshaft.
13 Fit the first speedometer drivegear circlip to the mainshaft.
14 Replace the woodruff key and slide the speedometer drivegear onto the mainshaft.
16 The mainshaft is now assembled and ready for refitting to the gearbox. (photo)

12 Gearbox - reassembly.

1 With all parts clean reassembly can be begin. (photo)
2 First insert the mainshaft assembly into the gearbox casing. (photo)
3 Make sure that the bearing retainer peg correctly engages in the cut out in the casing. (photo)
4 Place a larger washer and nut onto one of the extension housing securing studs so holding the mainshaft in position. (photo)
5 Replace the 3rd/4th speed selector fork making sure it is the correct way round. (photo)
6 Replace the 1st/2nd speed selector fork making sure it is the correct way round. (photos)
7 Apply a little grease to the interlock pins and insert them into the selector shafts.
8 Insert the 1st/2nd speed selector fork shaft engaging it in the selector fork. (photo)
9 Insert the 3rd/4th speed selector fork shaft engaging it in the selector fork. (photo)
10 Hold the reverse selector fork in position and insert the reverse selector fork shaft. (photos)
11 Line up the selector shafts and insert plunger. (photos and Fig. 6.7).
12 The selector fork securing roll pins should next be refitted. Make sure the hole in the fork and shaft line up and carefully drift the pins into position. (photos)
13 Insert the three selector shaft detent ball bearings and springs into the three holes. (photos)
14 Refit the cover and gasket and secure with the five securing

8.1 Needle roller bearing in countergear

10.3 Bearing in end of input shaft

11.8 Rear bearing retainer replacement

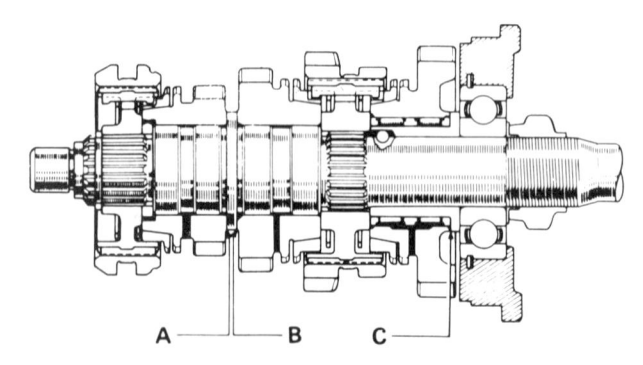

Fig. 6.6. Thrust clearance measurement points (A.B.C.)
Clearance must not exceed 0.012 in. (0.3 mm)

11.16 Mainshaft completely assembled

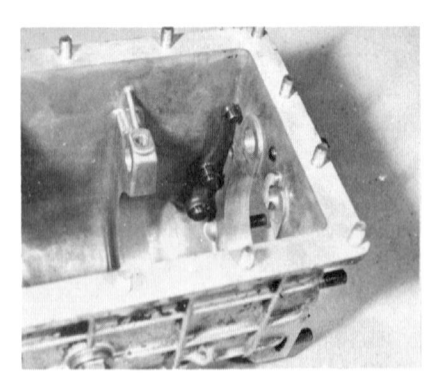

12.1 Gearbox main casing ready for reassembly

12.2 Inserting mainshaft assembly

12.3 Note bearing retainer peg location

12.4 Mainshaft held in position with nut and washer

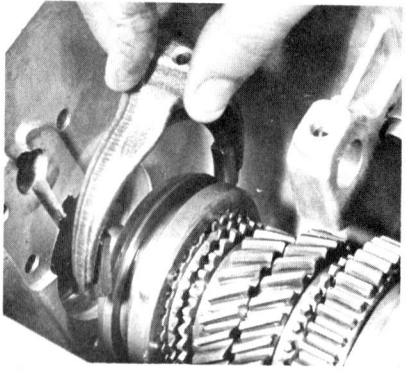

12.5 Refitting 3rd/4th speed selector fork

12.6a Refitting 1st/2nd speed selector fork

12.6b Make sure the selector fork is the correct way round

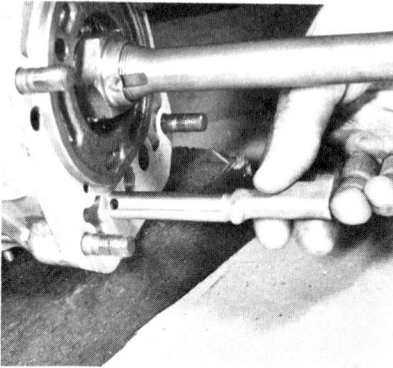

12.8 Inserting 1st/2nd selector fork shaft

12.9 Inserting 3rd/4th speed selector fork shaft

12.10a Holding reverse selector in position

12.10b Inserting reverse selector fork shaft

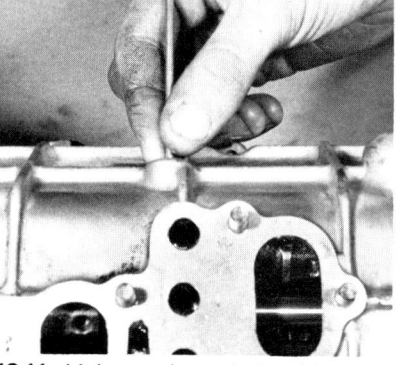

12.11a Lining up plunger holes with piece of wire

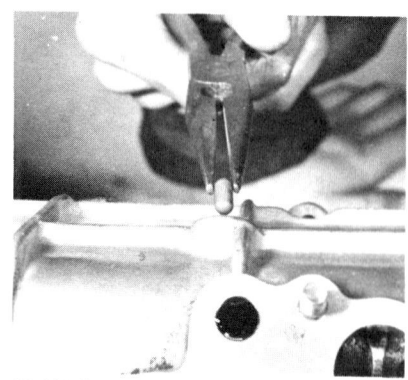

12.11b Inserting plunger

12.12a Drifting in roll pin

12.12b Roll pin correctly fitted (second pin ready for drifting into position)

nuts and washers. (photo)
15 Make sure the fourth speed synchroniser ring is in position and fit the input shaft into the front face of the main casing. (photo)
16 Fit a new gasket and replace the input shaft retainer. Secure with the four nuts and washers. (photo)

17 The reverse idler is next to be refitted. Hold the gear in position (and the correct way round) and slide in the shaft making sure the dowel bolt hole lines up with the hole in the web. (photo)
18 Refit the reverse idler shaft locking dowel bolt and washer. (photo)

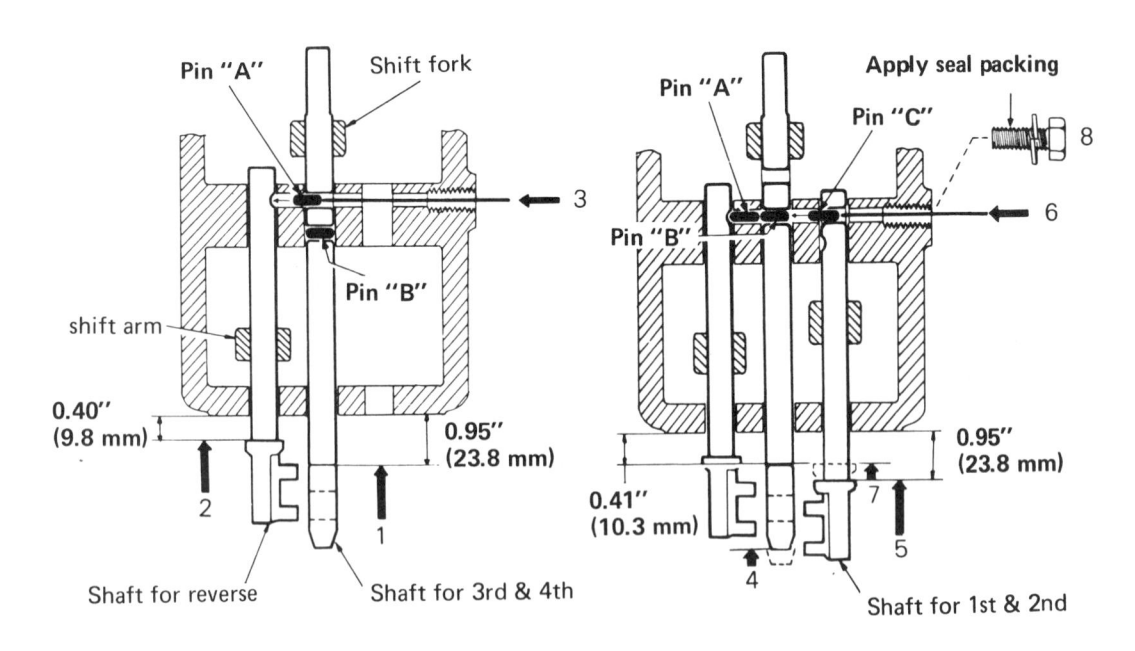

Fig. 6.7. Location of and assembly dimensions for refitting selector fork shaft pins

12.12c Third roll pin ready for refitting

12.13a Selector shaft detent ball bearing and spring

12.13b Selector shaft detent springs

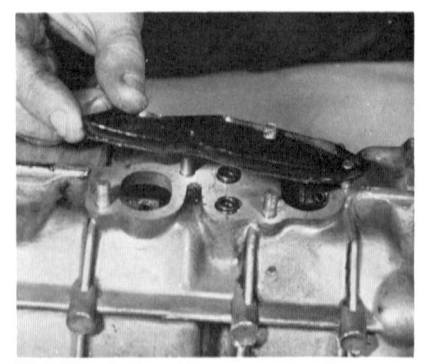

12.14 Replacing side cover and gasket

12.15 Refitting input shaft

12.16 Input shaft retainer replacement

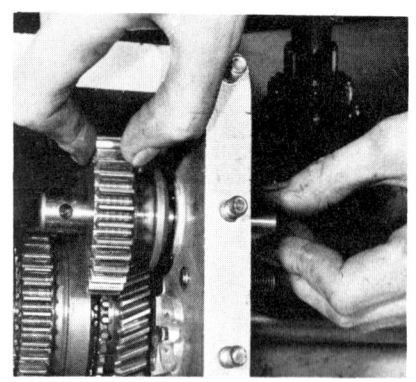

12.17 Reverse idler and shaft replacement

12.18 Refitting dowel bolt and washer

12.19 Countergear thrust washer in position

12.20 Lowering countergear into main casing

12.21 Inserting countergear shaft

12.22a Countergear shaft at rear end of main casing

12.22b Raised portion of shaft correctly positioned

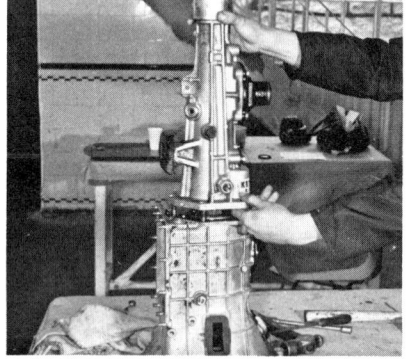

12.24 Lowering extension housing into position

12.26 Refitting oil pan

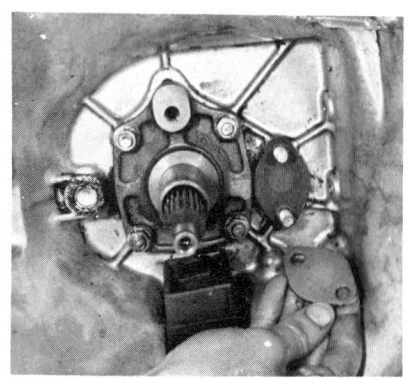

12.27 Refitting countergear shaft retaining plate

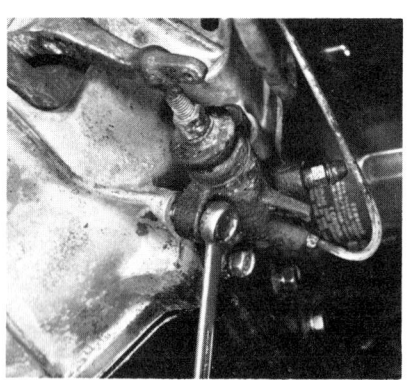

14C Detaching clutch slave cylinder

15.2 Clutch release arm removal

Chapter 6/Manual gearbox and automatic transmission

19 Smear some grease onto the faces of the countergear thrust washers and position them on the inside faces of the main casing. (photo)
20 Carefully lower the countergear into position so as not to dislodge the thrust washers. (photo)
21 Slide the countergear shaft into position from the rear. (photo)
22 The raised position on the end of the countergear shaft must be positioned as shown in these two photos so as to engage in the cut out in the front face of the extension housing.
23 Place the gearbox on end and fit a new gasket to the extension housing mating face. Do not forget to remove the nut and longer washer retaining the mainshaft.
24 Carefully lower the extension housing into position ensuring that the gear selector lever shaft engages with the selector fork shafts. (photo)
25 Secure the extension housing with the nuts and washers.
26 Fit a new oil pan gasket and replace the oil pan. Secure with the twelve nuts and washers, tightening in a progressive and diagonal manner. (photo)
27 Fit a new countergear shaft retaining plate gasket and refit the plate. Secure with the two nuts and washers. (photo)
28 Refit the clutch release drum and bearing assembly as described in Chapter 5.
29 The gearbox is now ready for refitting to the car. Do not forget to refill the gearbox with the recommended grade of oil.

13 Gearbox extension housing oil seal - removal and replacement

1 This oil seal may be removed with the gearbox either in or out of the car.
2 Refer to Chapter 7 and remove the propeller shaft.
3 Wipe the cover around the rear of the extension housing and with a screwdriver or small chisel carefully dismantle the oil seal taking care not to damage the extension housing casting. To get better access, the dust shield may be tapped off the end of the extension housing.
4 The new oil seal may be refitted, lip facing inwards using a suitable diameter tubular drift.

TE Models: manual gearbox

14 Gearbox (TE models) - removal and replacement

The sequence for removal and refitting the manual gearbox is basically identical to that for the earlier KE models. There are a few minor differences but they will not present any problems. These are:
a) The accelerator torque rod must be disconnected
b) Detach the clutch flexable hose support.
c) Undo and remove the bolts securing the clutch slave cylinder to the side of the bellhousing. (photo)

15 Gearbox - dismantling

Place the complete unit on a firm bench and ensure that you have the following tools (in addition to a normal range of spanners etc) available:
a) Good quality circlip pliers: 2 pairs, 1 expanding and 1 contracting
b) Cooper headed mallet at least 2 lbs
c) Drifts: steel 3/8 inch and brass 3/8 inch
d) Small containers
e) Engineer's vice mounted on a firm bench

Any attempt to dismantle the gearbox without the foregoing is not necessarily impossible, but will certainly be very difficult and inconvenient resulting in possible injury or damage. Read the whole of this Section before starting work.

Take care not to let the synchromesh hub assemblies come apart before you want them to. It accelerates wear if the splines of the hub and sleeve are changed in relation to each other. As a precaution it is advisable to make a line up mark with a dab of paint.

Before finally going ahead with dismantling first ascertain the availability of spare parts - particularly shims, which could be difficult.
1 Remove the clutch release bearing carrier to release arm retaining clips. Remove the release bearing assembly.
2 Remove the release arm from inside the clutch bellhousing. (photo)

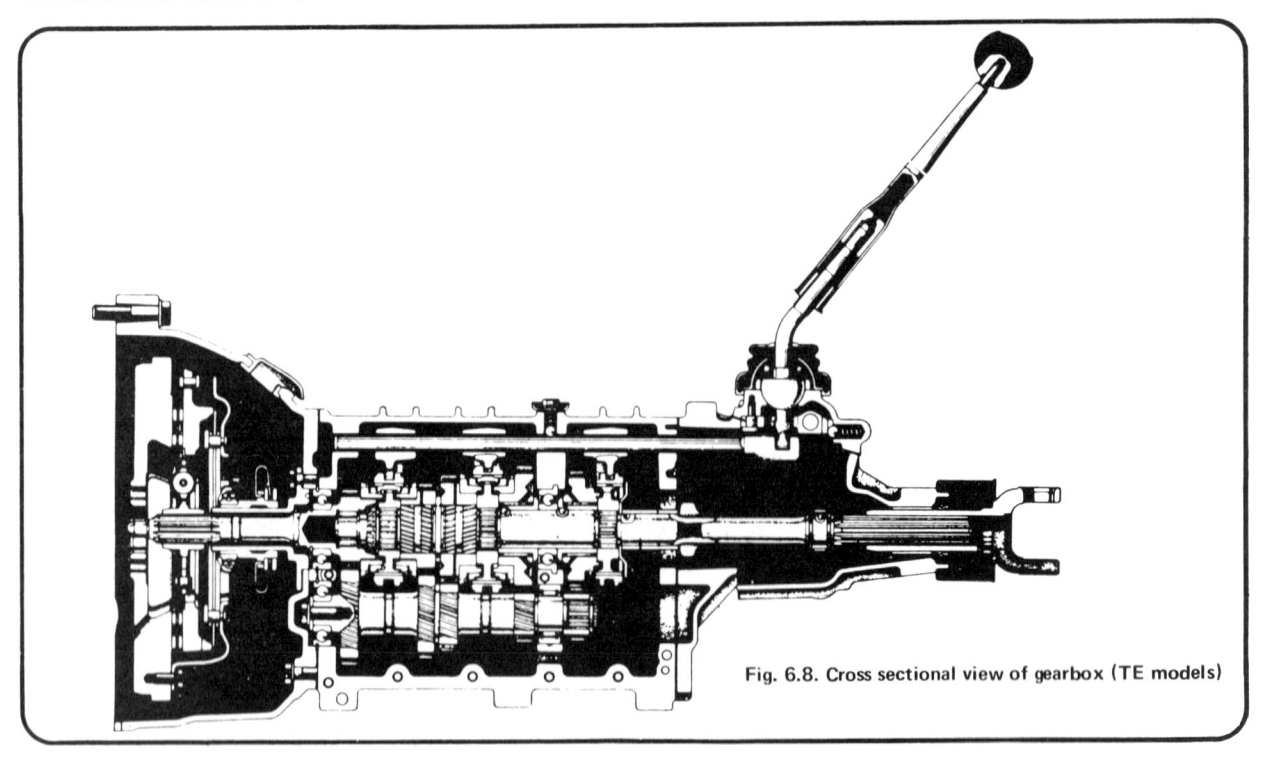

Fig. 6.8. Cross sectional view of gearbox (TE models)

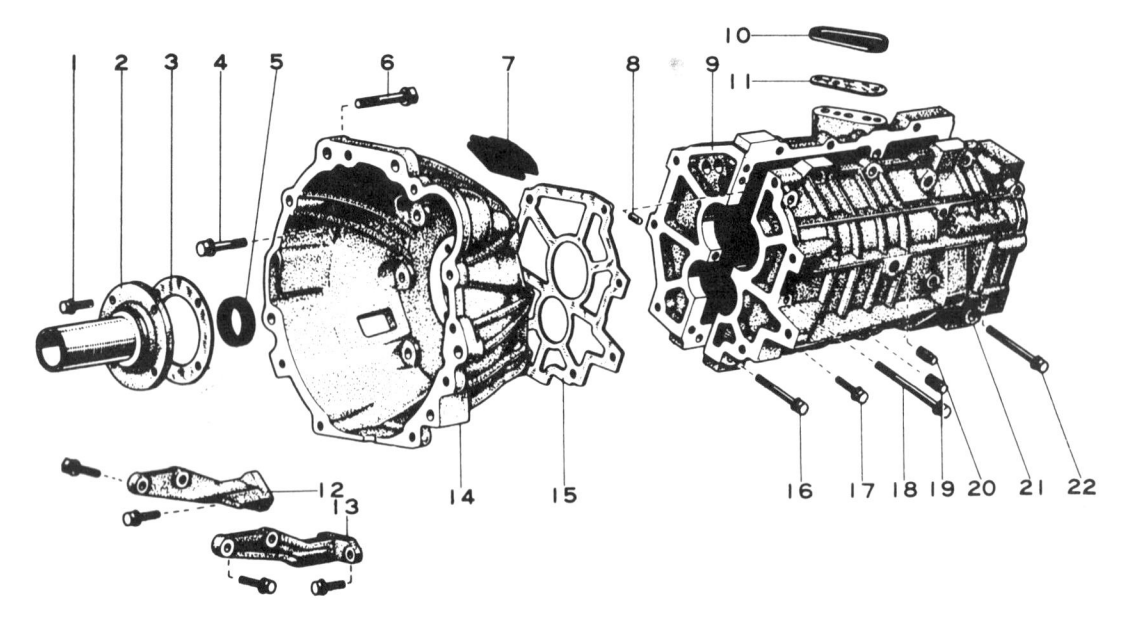

Fig. 6.9. Gearbox external components

1 Bolt and washer	7 Clutch housing cover	13 Stiffener plate (LH)	18 Bolt and washer
2 Front bearing retainer	8 Pin	14 Clutch housing	19 Drain plug
3 Gasket	9 Main casing (RH)	15 Gasket	20 Filler plug
4 Bolt and washer	10 Cover	16 Bolt and washer	21 Main casing (LH)
5 Oil seal	11 Gasket	17 Bolt and washer	22 Bolt and washer
6 Bolt and washer	12 Stiffener plate (RH)		

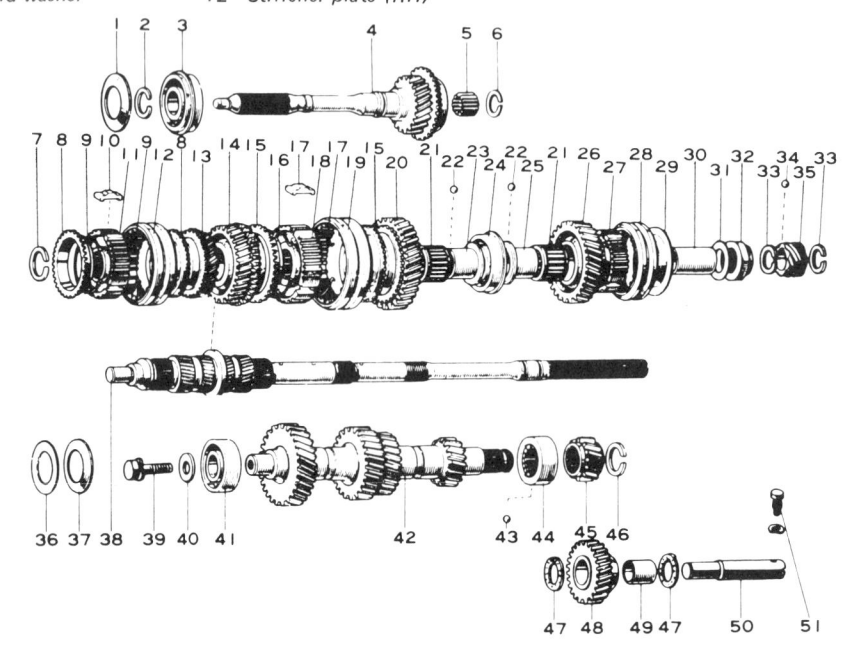

Fig. 6.10. Gearbox internal components

1 Spring, gear thrust cone	14 Second gear assembly	27 Hub	40 Plate washer
2 Ring, snap spring	15 Synchroniser ring No. 2	28 Sleeve	41 Ball bearing race
3 Ball bearing race	16 Spring	29 Spacer	42 Countergear
4 Input shaft	17 Key	30 Spacer	43 Ball
5 Roller	18 Hub	31 Shim	44 Roller bearing
6 Snap ring	19 Sleeve	32 Nut	45 Reverse gear
7 Snap ring	20 First gear assembly	33 Snap ring	46 Snap ring
8 Synchroniser ring No. 1	21 Needle roller bearing	34 Ball	47 Thrust washer
9 Spring	22 Ball	35 Speedometer drive gear	48 Reverse idler gear
10 Key	23 First gear bush	36 Shim	49 Bush
11 Hub	24 Ball bearing	37 Spring	50 Reverse idler gear shaft
12 Sleeve	25 Reverse gear bush	38 Mainshaft	51 Dowel bolt
13 Third gear assembly	26 Reverse gear	39 Bolt and washer	

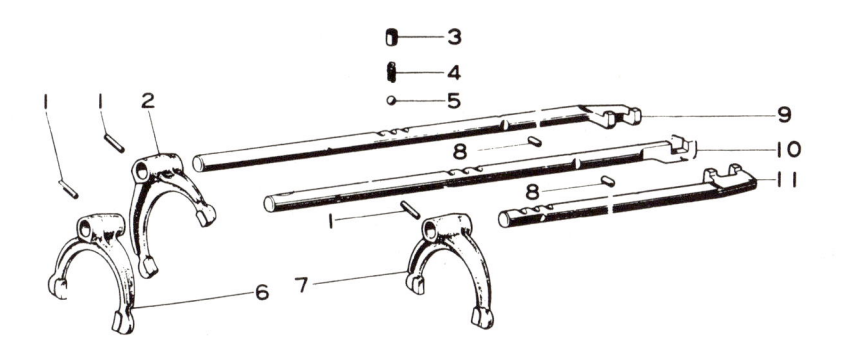

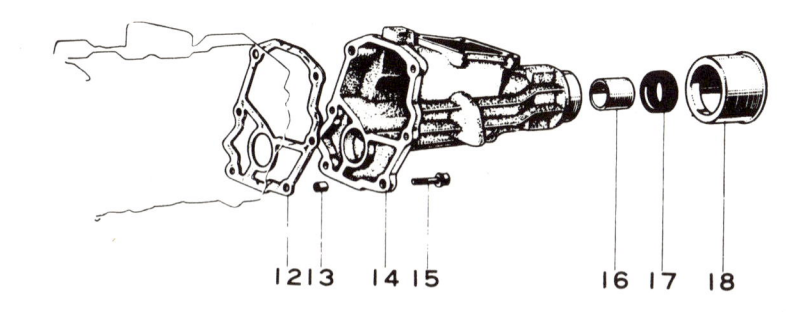

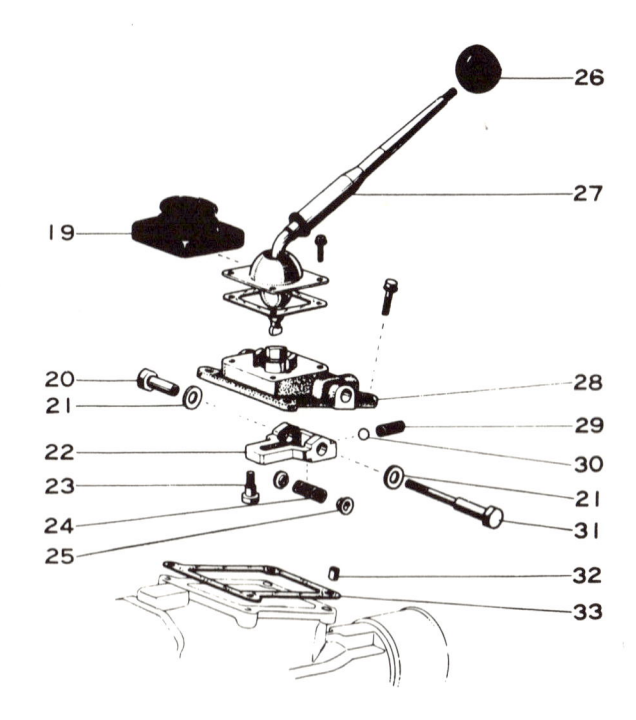

Fig. 6.11. Gearbox extension housing assembly

1 Slotted spring pin	9 Selector rod No. 1	17 Oil seal	25 Spring seat
2 Selector fork No. 1	10 Selector rod No. 2	18 Dust cover	26 Knob
3 Spring seat	11 Selector rod No. 3	19 Boot	27 Gear change lever
4 Spring	12 Gasket	20 Bush	28 Retainer
5 Ball bearing	13 Dowel	21 Gasket	29 Spring
6 Selector fork No. 2	14 Extension housing	22 Selector return plate	30 Ball
7 Selector fork No. 3	15 Bolt and washer	23 Bolt	31 Shaft
8 Pin	16 Bush	24 Spring	32 Bush
			33 Gasket

3 Undo and remove the four bolts and spring washers securing the front bearing retainer to the inner face of the clutch bellhousing. Slide the retainer from the input shaft. (photo)
4 Recover the paper gasket from the retainer or bellhousing face.
5 Undo and remove the bolts and spring washers that secure the clutch bellhousing to the front face of the main casing. Lift away the bellhousing (photo). Recover the gasket.
6 Note the location of the washers which will be exposed when the clutch bellhousing is removed. (photo)
7 Undo and remove the four bolts and spring washes securing the gearchange lever retainer to the upper face of the extension housing. Lift away the retainer and recover the gasket. Note the two locating dowels. (photo)
8 Undo and remove the bolt, spring washer and clip retaining the speedometer driven gear assembly to the extension housing.
9 Using a screwdriver carefully ease the assembly from its location in the extension housing. (photos)
10 Undo and remove the bolts and spring washers securing the extension housing to the main casing. Draw the extension housing rearwards and recover the gasket. (photo)
11 Undo and remove the bolts and spring washers securing the two halves of the gearbox main casing (Fig. 6.12).
12 Tap the joint to release the joint and lift away the upper main casing half. (photo)
13 No gasket is used between these two mating faces.
14 This photo showns the layout of the main casing half with the gear trains, selector rods and forks fitted.
15 Carefully recover the ball bearing located in the central web. (photo)
16 Gently tap the countershaft assembly with a soft faced hammer and lift up from the main casing half.
17 Carefully remove the ball bearing from the countershaft bearing outer track. (photo)
18 Lift away the countershaft assembly. (photo)
19 The mainshaft and input shaft may now be lifted away from the main casing half. (photo)

20 If necessary undo and remove the bolt and spring washer securing the reverse idler gear shaft. (photo)
21 Carefully tap out the idler gear shaft and recover the gear and thrust washers.
22 The gearbox may now be considered to be dismantled. Normally it will not be necessary to remove the selector forks and rods. Should it be desirable to remove these parts mark the relative positions of the selector forks and rods and tap out the fork retaining spring pins using a suitable diameter paralled pin punch. Draw up the selector rods and recover the two pins, ball bearing, spring and spring seat (photo) (Figs. 6.13/6.14).
23 Thoroughly flush out the interior of the casing halves with paraffin and wipe dry with a non-fluffy rag.

16 Input shaft - dismantling

1 Draw the input shaft from the front of the mainshaft. (photo)
2 The shaft and bearing are located in the front of the main casing by a large circlip in the outer track of the bearing.
3 To renew the bearing, first remove the circlip from the front end of the bearing.
4 Place the outer track of the race on the top of a firm bench vice and drive the input shaft through the bearing. Note that the bearing is fitted with the circlip groove towards the forward end of the input shaft. Lift away the bearing.
5 To remove the spigot bearing needle rollers, use a pair of circlip pliers or a small screwdriver and release the circlip.
6 Lift away the needle rollers from the end of the input shaft. (photo)

17 Mainshaft - dismantling

1 Remove the circlip from the front of the mainshaft. (photo)
2 Using a screwdriver, detach the top gear synchroniser

15.3 Front bearing retainer removal

15.5 Clutch bellhousing removal

15.6 These washers must not be misplaced

15.7 Lifting away gear change lever retainer

15.9a Easing out speedometer drive assembly

15.9b Lifting away speedometer drive assembly

15.10 Detaching extension housing

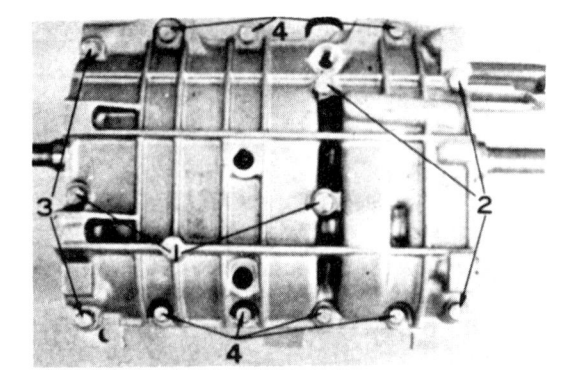

Fig. 6.12. Main casing halves securing bolts
Note differences in length between bolts 1,2,3 and 4

15.12 Parting the two halves of main casing

15.14 Layout of gear trains in main casing half

15.15 Do not loose this ball bearing

15.17 Ball race outer track locking ball

15.18 Lifting away countershaft assembly

15.19 Lifting away input shaft and mainshaft

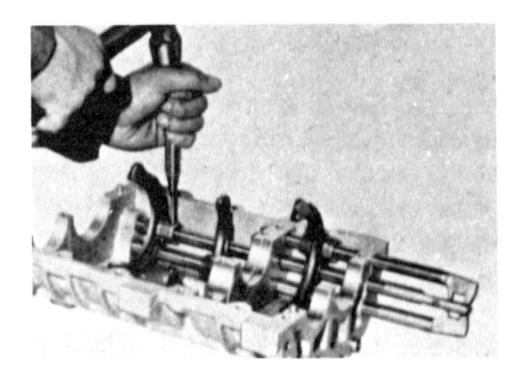

Fig. 6.13. Tapping out slotted spring pin

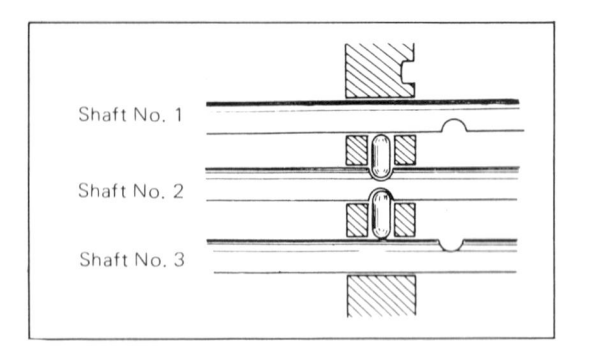

Fig. 6.14. Location of pins between selector shafts

15.20 Reverse idler mounted in main casing half

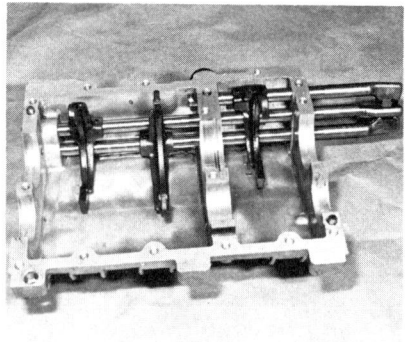

15.22 Main casing half with selector shafts and forks

16.1 Lifting away input shaft

16.6 Needle rollers in end of input shaft

17.1 Circlip removal from front of mainshaft

17.2 Sliding off top gear synchroniser assembly

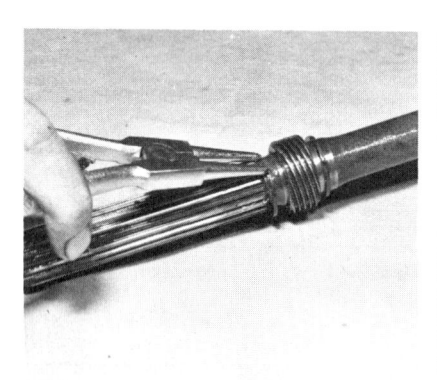

17.3 Removing circlip from rear of speedometer drive gear

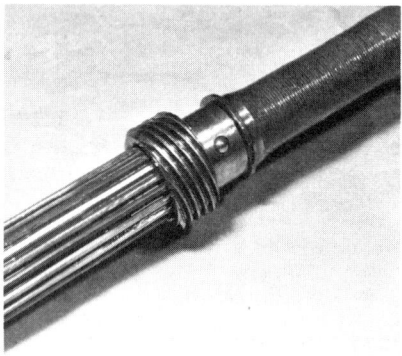

17.4 Removing speedometer drive gear note the ball bearing in the mainshaft

17.7 Removing nut, shim and spacer from mainshaft

17.8 Removal of metal disc

17.9 Removal of reverse gear assembly

17.10 Lifting away reverse gear assembly

17.11 Removal of rear bearing and first gear assembly

17.12 Removal of thrust washer

17.13 Removal of second gear assembly

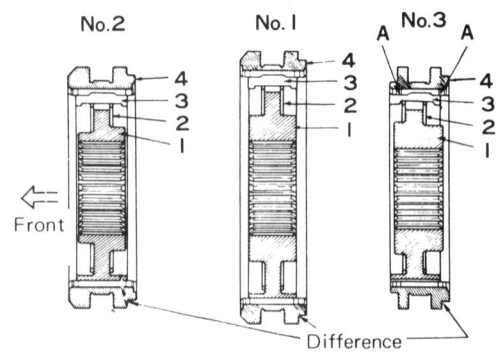

Fig. 6.15. Synchromesh unit identification

1 Hub
2 Spring ring
3 Key
4 Sleeve
A Key offset

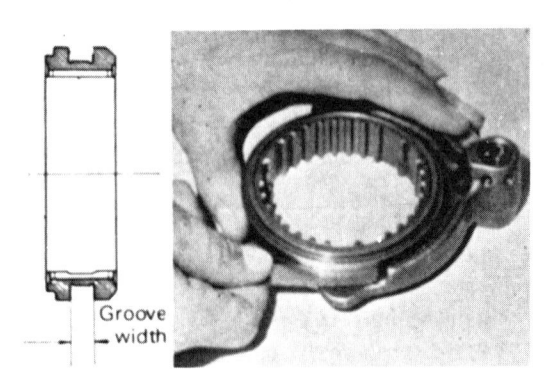

Fig. 6.16. Synchromesh sleeve and fork clearance check

assembly. (photo)
3 Using a pair of circlip pliers remove the circlip from the rear end of the mainshaft. (photo)
4 Carefully tap the speedometer drivegear from the mainshaft. Recover the ball bearing from the hole in the mainshaft.(photo)
5 Remove the second circlip from the rear end of the mainshaft.
6 Hold the mainshaft firmly in the vice and unscrew the large nut.
7 Slide the nut, shim and spacer from the end of the mainshaft. (photo)
8 Slide the metal disc from the mainshaft noting which way round it is fitted. (photo)
9 Hold the mainshaft as shown in this photo and tap the end with a soft faced hammer to release the reverse gear assembly from the mainshaft.
10 Lift away the reverse gear assembly, needle roller race and bush. (photo)
11 Remove the rear bearing ball-race retaining ball bearing and slide off the rear bearing assembly, first gear assembly, needle roller race and bush. (photo)
12 Slide off the thrust washer. (photo)
13 The second gear assembly can now be removed from the mainshaft. (photo)

18 Synchro hubs - dismantling and inspection

1 The synchro hubs are only too easy to dismantle - just push the centre out and the whole assembly flies apart. The point is to prevent this happening, before you are ready. Do not dismantle the hubs without reason and do not mix up the parts of the hubs.
2 It is most important to check backlash in the splines between the outer sleeve and inner hub. If any is noticeable the whole assembly must be renewed.
3 Mark the hub and sleeve so that you may reassemble them on the same splines. With the hub and sleeve separated, the teeth at the end of the splines which engage with corresponding teeth of the gear wheels, must be checked for damage or wear.
4 Do not confuse with wear. the keystone shape at the ends of the teeth. This shape matches the gear teeth shape and it is a design characteristic to minimise jump-out tendencies.
5 If the synchronising cones are being renewed it is sensible also to renew the sliding keys and springs which hold them in position.

19 Synchro hubs - reassembly

1 The hub assemblies are not interchangeable so they must be reassembled with their original or identical new parts.
2 The pips on the sliding keys are symmetrical so may be refitted either way round into the hub.
3 One slotted key is assembled to each hub for locating the turned out end of the key spring.
4 It should be noted that the keys for each synchromesh unit are of different lengths.
5 The turned out end of each spring must locate in the slotted key and be assembled to the hub in an anticlockwise direction as viewed from either side of the hub.

20 Countershaft - dismantling

1 Undo and remove the bolt, spring washer and plain washer holding the ballrace onto the end of the countershaft.
2 Using a universal puller and suitable thrust block draw the bearing from the end of the countershaft. Note which way round the bearing is fitted.
3 Using a pair of circlip pliers remove the circlip retaining the reverse gear on the end of the countershaft.
4 Slide off the reverse gear.
5 Remove the ball bearing and ballrace from the countershaft.

21 Gearbox components - inspection

The sequence is basically identical to that for the earlier type of gearbox. Refer to Section 9 for full details.

22 Countershaft - reassembly

1 Refit the ball bearing and ballrace to the splined end of the countershaft.
2 Slide the reverse gear onto the splines and push fully home.
3 Using feeler gauges measure the circlip groove width and select a new circlip. Two sizes are available:
   0.0709 - 0.0728 in (1.80 - 1.85 mm)
   0.0728 - 0.0748 in (1.85 - 1.90 mm)
4 Fit the new circlip and ensure that there is no gear endfloat.
5 Fit the ballrace to the spigot end of the countershaft and retain in position with the bolt, spring and plain washer. Tighten the bolt to a torque wrench setting of 22-36 lb f ft (3.0-4.5 Kg fm).

23 Input shaft - reassembly

1 Using a suitable diameter tubular drift carefully drive the ball race into position. The circlip in the outer track must be towards the front of the input shaft.
2 Retain the bearing in position with a circlip. This is a selective circlip which is available in a range of 5 different sizes (see Specifications).
3 Smear some grease onto the needle roller bore and insert the needle rollers. The best way to fit the needle rollers is to insert them into the base and push outwards into positions.
4 Retain the needle rollers with the circlip.

24 Mainshaft - reassembly

1 Slide the third speed gear assembly and synchromesh assembly onto the front end of the mainshaft.
2 Refit the circlip and check the endfloat which should be 0.024 inch. If the reading obtained is outside this limit a new circlip will be required. (photo)
3 Slide the second gear assembly onto the mainshaft. (photo)
4 Follow this with the synchromesh unit and needle roller bearing. (photo)
5 Slide on the first gear assembly and bush. A ball bearing must be fitted in the hole in the mainshaft between the synchromesh unit and first gear assembly. (photo)
6 Slide on the ball race and push up to the back of the first gear assembly. (photo)
7 Lock the ball race with a ball bearing in the first exposed hole in the mainshaft.
8 Refit the reverse gear and synchromesh unit together with bush and needler roller bearing. (photo)
9 Slide on the metal disc with the dish located as shown in this photo. Follow this with the spacer, shim and nut.
10 Tighten the nut as tightly as possible. Ideally this should be set to a torque wrench setting of 33 - 54 lb f ft (4.50 - 7.50 Kg f m).
11 Fit the first circlip to the end of the mainshaft. Insert the ball bearing and slide on the speedometer drive gear. (photo)
12 Retain the speedometer drive gear with the second circlip.
13 The mainshaft is now reassembled.
14 Using feeler gauges measure the thrust clearances to ensure that they are within the manufacturer's recommended limits If there is a significant difference the cause must be found and rectified.

New		Maximum
First gear	0.004 - 0.010 in.	0.020 in.
	(0.10 - 0.25 mm)	(0.5 mm)
Second gear	0.006 - 0.010 in.	0.020 in.
	(0.15 - 0.25 mm)	(0.5 mm)
Third gear	0.006 - 0.012 in	0.024 in.
	(0.15 - 0.30 mm)	(0.6 mm)
Reverse gear	0.008 - 0.012 in.	0.024 in.
	(0.20 - 0.30 mm)	(0.6 mm)

25 Gearbox - reassembly

1 If the selector forks and rods have been removed they should be refitted. This is a direct reversal of the renewal procedure.
2 Hold the reverse idle and thrust washers in position in the half casing and slide in the reverse idler shaft. Line up the dowel bolt hole and refit the bolt and spring washer. Tighten the bolt

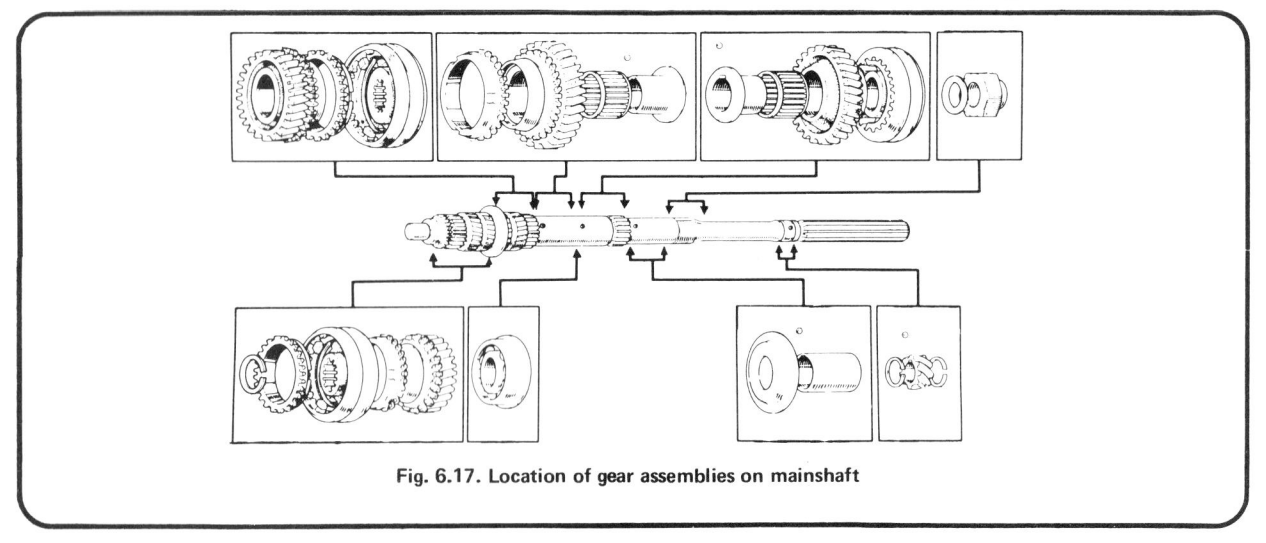

Fig. 6.17. Location of gear assemblies on mainshaft

24.2 Refitting mainshaft front circlip

24.3 Refitting second gear assembly

24.4 Sliding synchromesh unit onto mainshaft

24.5 Refitting first gear assembly

24.6 Sliding rear bearing into position

24.8 Refitting reverse gear assembly

24.9 Refitting metal disc, shim, spacer and nut

24.11 Refitting speedometer drive gear

25.4 Mainshaft and input shaft fitted to main casing half

to a torque wrench setting of 10.0-13.0 lb f ft (1.3-1.8 Kg fm).
3 Check the reverse idler thrust clearance which should be 0.002-0.020 in (0.05-0.50 mm) with a maximum limit of 0.039 in (1.0 mm)
4 With the main casing halves clean, carefully lower the mainshaft into position. (photo)
5 Follow the mainshaft with the countershaft. Do not forget the ball race outer track ball bearing. (photo)
6 Fit the ball bearing to the hole in the central web.
7 Smear a little sealer to the mating face of the main gearbox casing with the exception of an area of 0.5 in (13 mm) around the reverse light switch.
8 Carefully fit the two halves of the main casing and refit the securing bolts and spring washers. Tighten in a progessive and diagonal manner to a final torque wrench setting of 10.9-14.5 lb f ft (1.5-2.0 Kg fm)

Fig. 6.18. Measurement of backlash

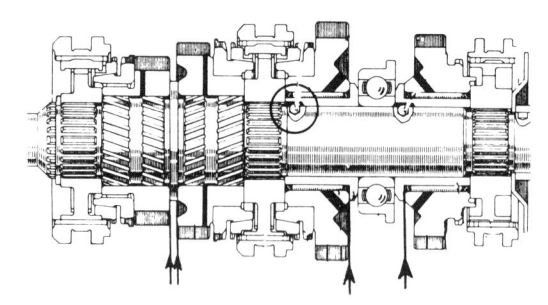

Fig. 6.19. Measurement points for thrust clearances

25.5 Refitting countershaft to main casing half

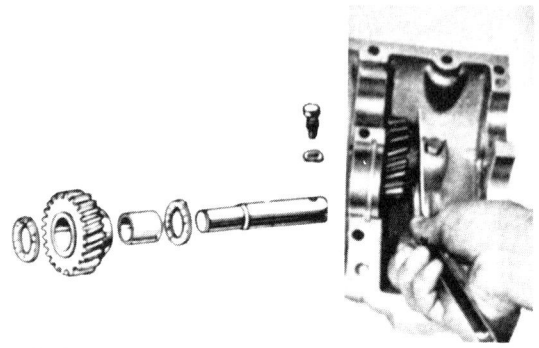

Fig. 6.20. Reverse idler gear assembly and checking endfloat

25.9 Lowering extension housing into position

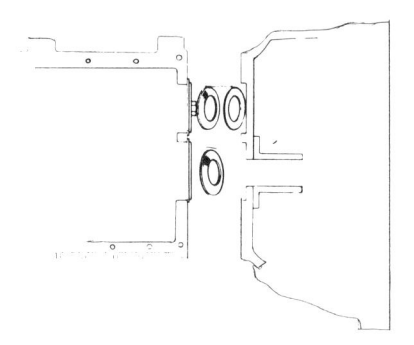

Fig. 6.21 Washer and cone location between clutch housing and main casing

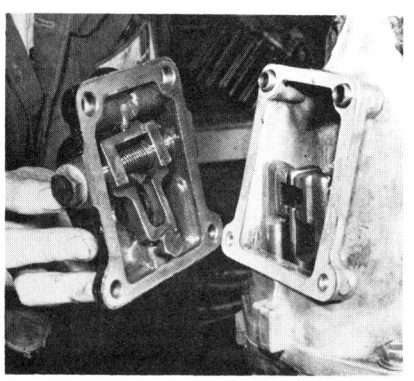

25.11 Refitting gear change lever retainer

25.15 Replacing input shaft bearing retainer

25.17 Refitting clutch release arm.

Chapter 6/Manual gearbox and automatic transmission

9 Fit a new gasket to the extension housing mating face and carefully lower into position. Tighten the securing bolt to a torque wrench setting of 22-33 lb f ft (3.0 - 4.5 Kg fm) (photo).
10 Refit the speedometer driven assembly to the extension housing and retain with the bolt, spring washer and clip. Tighten the bolt to a torque wrench setting of 3.0-5.0 lb f ft (0.4-0.7 Kg fm)
11 Fit a new gasket to the gearchange lever retainer mating face and replace the retainer. Secure with the four bolts and spring washers which should be tightened to a torque wrench setting of 7.2 - 11.6 lb f ft (1.0 - 1.6 kg fm) (photo).
12 Turn the gearbox on end and position the washers and cone onto the end of the countershaft and input shaft.
13 Fit a new gasket and replace the clutch bellhousing. Tighten the securing bolts to a torque wrench setting of 22-33 lb f ft.
14 Inspect the input shaft bearing retainer oil seal and if worn ease out the old seal. Fit a new seal using a drift of suitable diameter.
15 Fit a new gasket to the clutch bellhousing and replace the input shaft bearing retainer. (photo)

16 Replace the four bolts and spring washers. Tighten to a torque wrench setting of 7.2-11.6 lb f ft (1.0-1.6 Kg fm).
17 Refit the clutch release arm and bearing carrier and secure with the two spring clips. (photo)
18 The gearbox is now ready for refitting to the car. Do not forget to refill the gearbox with the recommended grade of oil.

26 Gearbox extension housing oil seal - removal and replacement

1 This oil seal may be removed with the gearbox either in or out of the car.
2 Refer to Chapter 7 and remove the propeller shaft.
3 Wipe the area around the rear of the extension housing and with a screwdriver or small chisel carefully dismantle the oil seal taking care not to damage the extension housing casting. To give better access the dust shield may be tapped off the end of the extension housing.
4 The new oil seal may be refitted, lip facing inwards using a tubular drift of suitable diameter.

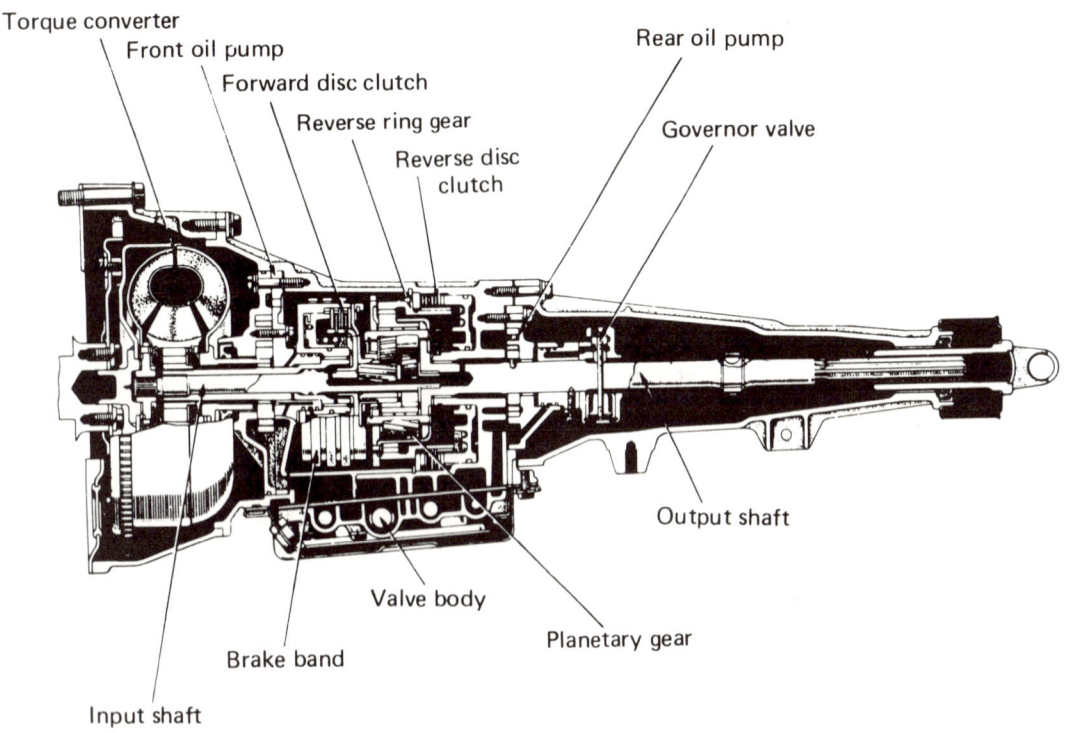

Fig. 6.22. The automatic transmission unit

All Models: automatic transmission

27 Automatic transmission - general

The Toyoglide automatic transmission takes the place of the clutch and gearbox, which are, of course mounted behind the engine.
The system comprises two main components:
1 A three element hydrokinetic torque converter coupling, capable of torque multiplication at an infinitely variable ratio between 2:4:1 and 1:1.
2 A torque / speed responsive and hydraulically operated epicyclic gearbox comprising a planetary gearset providing two forward ratios and one reverse ratio.
Due to the complexity of the automatic transmission unit, if performance is not up to standard, or overhaul is necessary, it is imperative that this be left to the local main agents who will

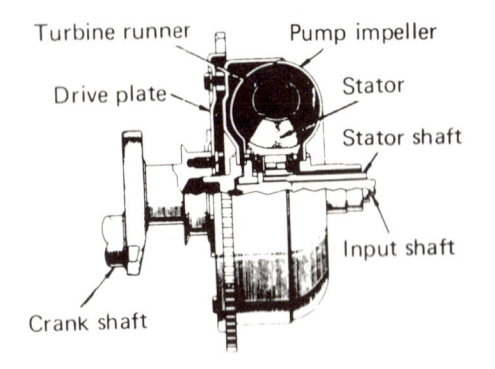

Fig. 6.23. Torque converter components

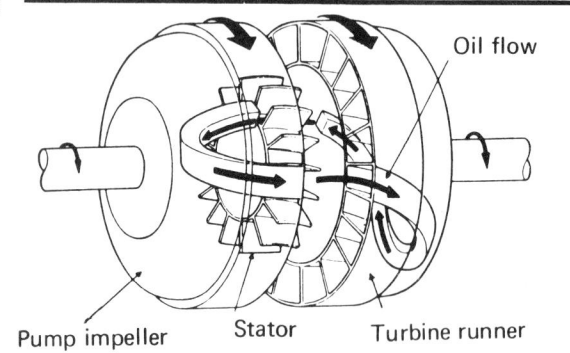

Fig. 6.24. Principle of torque converter operation

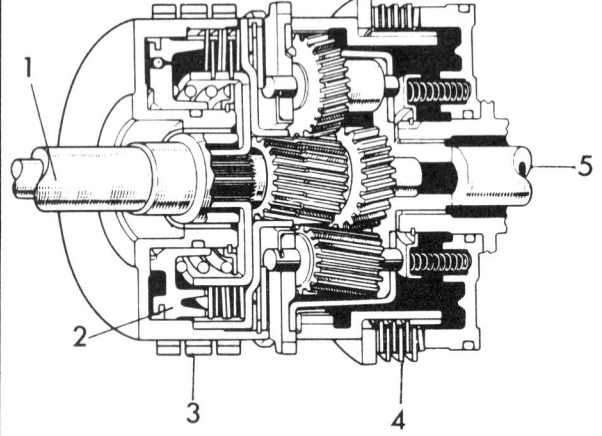

Fig. 6.25. Automatic transmission planetary gear unit

1 Input shaft
2 Forward clutch
3 Low brake band
4 Reverse clutch
5 Output shaft

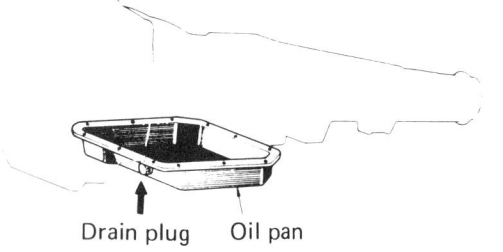

Fig. 6.26. Oil pan and drain plug

Fig. 6.27. Removal of rod end and clamp

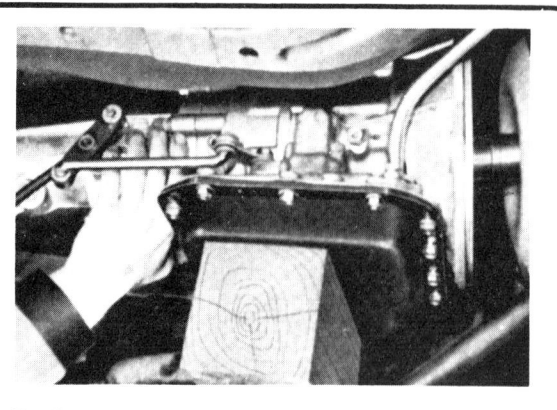

Fig. 6.28. Supporting the weight of the transmission unit

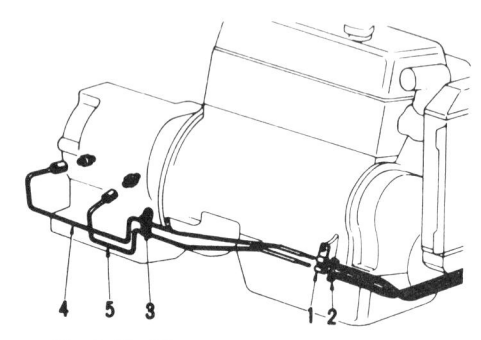

Fig. 6.29. Oil cooler pipes

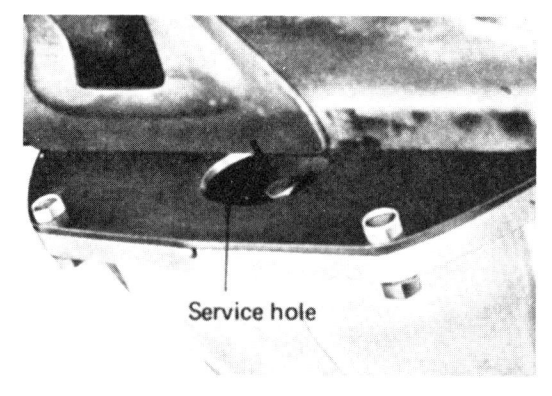

1 Clamp
2 Union nuts
3 Clamp
4 Pipe
5 Pipe

Fig. 6.30. Location of service hole

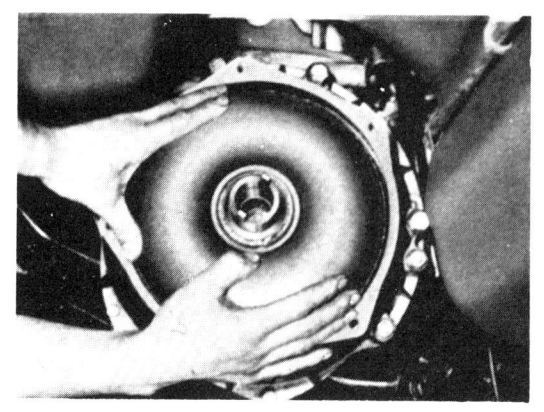

Fig. 6.31. Removal of torque converter

Chapter 6/Manual gearbox and automatic transmission

have the special equipment for fault diagnosis and rectification.

The content of the following Sections is confined to supplying general information and service information and instruction that can be used by the owner.

28 Automatic transmission - fluid level

1 With the engine at its normal operating temperature move the selector lever through all positions from 'P' to 'L' and stop in the 'N' position.
2 With the engine running at idle speed remove the dipstick, wipe clean and replace. Quickly withdraw it again and if necessary top-up with the recommended grade of fluid.
3 If the unit has been drained, it is recommended that only new fluid is used. Fill up to the correct 'HIGH' level by gradually refilling the unit. The exact amount will depend on how much was left in the converter after draining.
4 To ensure adequate cooling the exterior of the converter housing and gearbox is always kept clean of dust or mud.

29 Automatic transmission - removal and replacement

Any suspected faults must be referred to the main agent before unit removal, as with this type of transmission the fault must be confirmed, using specialist equipment, before it has been removed from the car.
1 Open the engine compartment lid and place old blankets over the wings to prevent accidental scratching of the paintwork.
2 For safety reasons disconnect the battery. Raise the car and place on axle stands if a ramp is not available. The higher the car is off the ground the easier it will be to work underneath.
3 Undo and remove the drain plug and drain the oil into a suitable sized container. When all the oil has drained out replace the drain plug. If the car has just been run take extreme care because the oil will be very hot.
4 Refer to Chapter 2 and drain the cooling system. Slacken the radiator top hose clips and remove the top hose.
5 Refer to Chapter 3 and remove the air cleaner.
6 Remove the throttle link connecting rod from the accelerator
7 Detach the heater hose clamp from the engine top cover.
8 Refer to Chapter 7 and remove the propeller shaft.
9 Soak the exhaust manifold to downpipe clamp securing nuts in penetrating oil. Undo and remove the nuts and bolts and separate the joint.
10 Wipe the area around the oil cooler pipe unions on the right-hand side of the automatic transmission unit. Also clean the area around the hose to pipe unions at the front right-hand side of the engine.
11 Unscrew the union nuts at the hose to pipe joint. Release the pipe clamps located at the rear of the hose to pipe joint.
12 Detach the exhaust pipe support bracket from the transmission casing and then disconnect the exhaust downpipe from the centre section.
13 Disconnect the transmission control rod from the central shaft.
14 Disconnect the throttle link connecting rod from the throttle valve outer lever.
15 Disconnect the speedometer cable from the extension housing.
16 Place a jack and suitable packing under the transmission unit and then remove the bolts securing the engine rear support member, and to the underside of the body, and transmission unit. Lift away the support member. (Fig 6.28)
17 Remove the oil cooler pipe clamp located on the side of the torque converter housing and then disconnect the inlet and outlet pipes from the side of the transmission unit. Always use two spanners to do this. Lift away the two pipes.
18 Undo and remove the four bolts securing the transmission case to torque converter housing.

19 Support the weight of the engine and remove the transmission unit jack.
20 Very carefully draw the transmission case rearwards as it is easy to damage the 'T' type oil seal in the front oil pump body. Oil will flow out from the torque converter so be prepared to catch this oil.
21 If it is necessary to remove the torque converter and housing, undo and remove the six torque converter securing bolts. Access to these is through a hole in the rear endplate. Use the crankshaft pulley to turn the torque converter (Fig 6.30).
22 The torque converter may now be lifted away. Be prepared for a further amount of oil to flow from the torque converter.
23 Undo and remove the ten bolts securing the torque converter housing. Lift away the converter housing.
24 To remove the driveplate and ring-gear assembly undo and remove the six securing bolts. Lift the assembly away.
25 Refitting the automatic transmission unit is the reverse sequence to removal, but the following additional points should be noted.
a) When replacing the automatic transmission unit the pump drive keys of the pump impeller must be lined up with the key holes of the pump drive gear.
b) It will be necessary to adjust the throttle link connecting rod and the selector lever as described in Sections 34 and 32 of this Chapter.
c) Refill the transmission unit with the recommended grade of oil before starting the engine and check the oil level as described in Section 28.

30 Selector lever (floor mounted) - removal, overhaul and replacement

1 Chock the front wheels, jack-up the rear of the car and support on firmly based stands.
2 Disconnect the connecting rod swivel pin and also the electric cable terminal connectors.
3 Undo and remove the six securing nuts and bolts and lift away the selector lever assembly. On some models fitted with a centre console this should be removed before access to the securing nuts and bolts can be gained.
4 To dismantle the assembly first detach the selector lever knob cap using a screwdriver.
5 Using a suitable diameter parallel pin punch remove the pin that retains the selector lever knob.
6 Undo and remove the nut located at the end of the selector lever shaft.
7 Undo and remove the screw that secures the indicator plate and upper housing assembly.
8 With all parts clean inspect all moving parts for wear or damage and obtain new as necessary.
9 Reassembly and replacement of the selector lever assembly is the reverse sequence to removal and dismantling. Lubricate all moving parts with a little Castrol LM Grease.

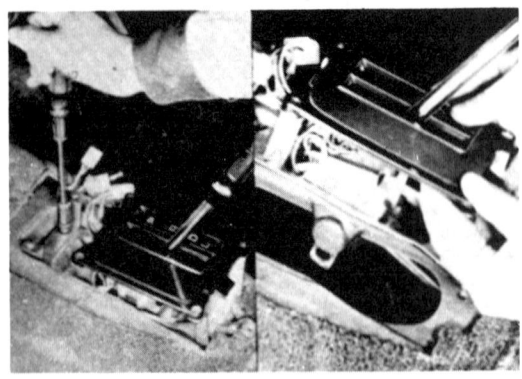

Fig. 6.32. Selector lever removal

Fig. 6.33. Selector lever components

1 Transmission floor shift assembly
2 Selector lever knob cover
3 Selector lever knob
4 Compression spring
5 Slotted spring pin
6 Selector knob button
7 Detent rod
8 Selector lever sub-assembly
9 Safety and reverse switch
10 Selector lever plate sub-assembly
11 Bushing
12 Selector lever boot
13 Control shift sub-assembly
14 Indicator lamp wire sub-assembly
15 Bulb
16 Position indicator lower housing
17 Slide cover
18 Control position indicator plate
19 Position indicator upper housing
20 Connecting rod swivel
21 Bushing

Fig. 6.34. Manual valve lever positions

Fig. 6.35. Adjustment of selector lever

1 Control swivel rod

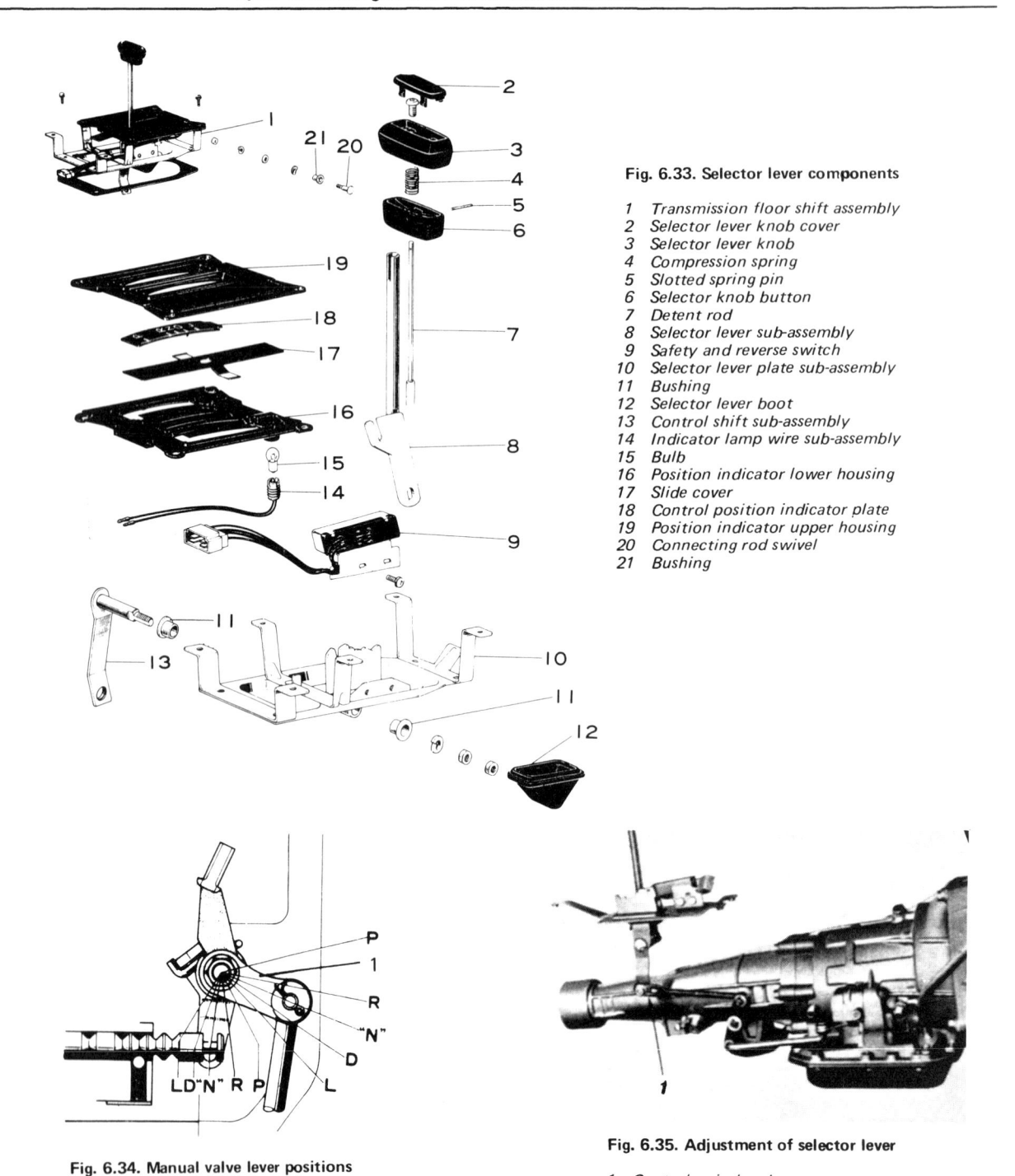

31 Selector lever (column mounted) - removal, overhaul and replacement

The selector lever and linkage is shown in Fig. 6.36 and normally it is not necessary to remove the complete system but rather renewal of an individial part only. In all cases this is a straight forward operation and will present no problems. Do not forget to lubricate any moving parts with a little Castrol LM Grease.

32 Selector lever - adjustment

Floor Mounted

1 Working under the car move the manual valve control outer lever to the 'N' position. This is the third notch from the either end of the lever travel. (Fig. 6.34)

2 Slacken the control rod swivel lock nut and adjust the length of the control-rod until the selector lever pin is in the neutral

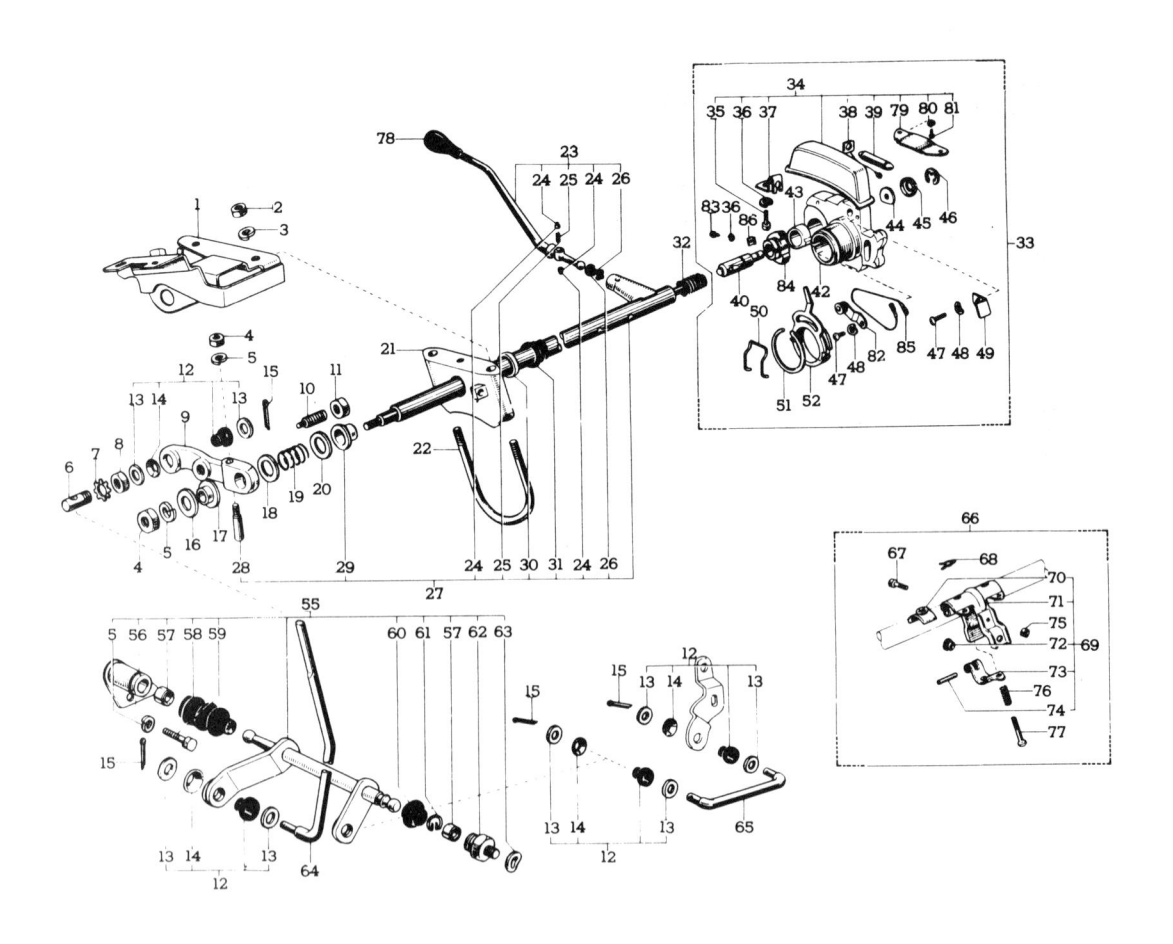

Fig. 6.36. Column selector lever components

1. Control shaft lever retainer
6. Connecting rod swivel
9. Control shaft lever
10. Control shaft lever stopper pin
12. Bushing
17. Bushing
21. Control shaft lower bracket
23. Shift lever
24. Shift lever pin
25. Spring
26. Shift lever housing dust cover
27. Control shaft sub-assembly
28. Lever lock pin
29. Bushing
30. Control shaft dust seal
31. Control shaft hole cover
32. Spring
33. Position indicator retainer assembly
34. Position indicator housing assembly
37. Indicator light ground plate
38. Indicator light wire
39. Bulb
40. Control shaft bracket upper shaft
41. Position indicator drive cord
42. Steering column upper bracket
43. Upper control shaft piece bushing
44. Upper shaft seat
45. Seat retainer
49. Lead wire clamp
50. Retainer
51. Snap ring
52. Position indicator plate
53. Torsion spring
54. Control position indicator
55. Cross shaft assembly
56. Cross shaft support sub-assembly
57. Support bushing
58. Dust cover
60. Dust cover
62. Cross shaft No. 1 support
64. Shifting No. 1 rod
65. Shifting No. 2 rod
66. Control shaft bracket assembly
69. Control shaft brake sub-assembly
70. Control shaft brake lining
71. Control shaft brake plate
72. Control shaft brake slide piece
73. Control shaft brake shoe
74. Control shaft brake shoe pin
78. Shift lever knob

position of the detent plate. Retighten the locknut.

Column Mounted

1 Working under the car move the manual control valve located on the side of the transmission to the neutral position.
2 Slacken the locknut on the side of the connecting rod swivel and adjust the length of the control rod until the selector lever pointer is in the 'N' position. Retighten the locknut. (Fig. 6.37)
3 The relative position between the control shaft lever and lever retainer should now be set so that the clearance between the lever pin and the upper stopper in the neutral range is equal to the clearance between the lever pin and lower stopper in the 'L' range. To carry out this adjustment slacken the locknut on the control shaft lever stopper pin and rotate the stopper pin. Retighten the locknut. (Fig. 6.38)

33 Neutral safety switch - adjustment

Floor Mounted

1 Check that the engine can only be started with the selector lever in the 'N' or 'P' position.
2 To adjust the switch position reposition so that the switch shaft just makes contact with the push plate of the selector lever with the transmission selector lever in the 'D' position.
3 Check that the reverse light only comes on with the selector lever in the 'R' position.

Column Mounted

1 Make a note of the cable connections to the neutral safety switch and disconnect from the switch.
2 Using a test light and battery check that the switch operates correctly in the 'on' and 'off' positions between the 'D' and 'N' selector lever positions.
3 If the switch is not set correctly it may be adjusted by slackening the switch securing bolts and moving the switch slightly one way or the other. This will be a matter of trial and error.

34 Throttle link connecting road - adjustment

1 Remove the air filter as described in Chapter 3 and move the throttle valve to the fully open position. Wedge in this position.
2 Slacken the lock nuts on each end of the turn buckle.
3 Adjust the length of the connecting rod with the turn buckle so that the throttle link indicator lines up with the mark on the side of the transmission. (Fig. 6.39)
4 Retighten the turn buckle locknuts and recheck that the throttle link indicator aligns with the mark on the side of the transmission with the throttle valve in the fully open position.
5 Remove the throttle valve wedge and replace the air cleaner.

35 Engine idle speed - adjustment (automatic transmission)

1 Check the front wheels and firmly apply the handbrake.
2 Start the engine and allow to run until it reaches normal operating temperature.
3 Move the selector lever to the 'D' position and check the idle speed, ideally an electric tachometer should be used for this.

The correct idle speeds are:
Engine model.	Idle speed.
12R	550 ± 50 rpm
3K	600 ± 50 rpm
T. 2T.	650 ± 50 rpm

4 If necessary adjust the slow running setting screw on the carburettor. More information will be found in Chapter 3.

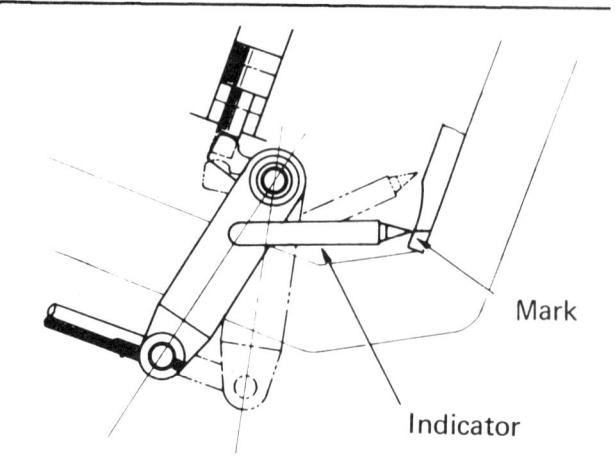

Fig. 6.37. Correct indicator position

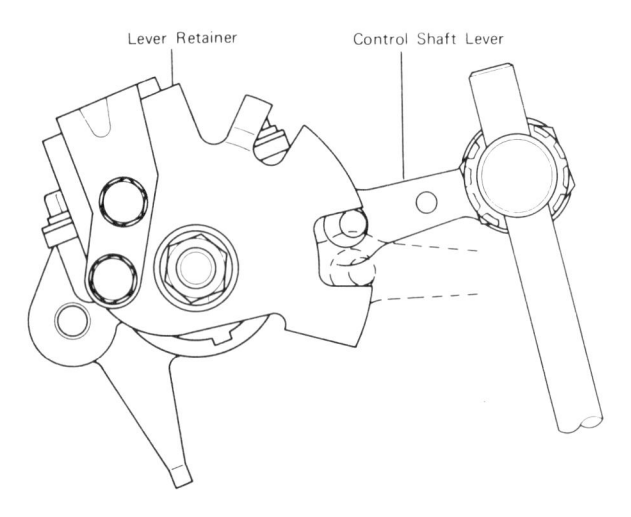

Fig. 6.38. Adjustment of stopper position (column change)

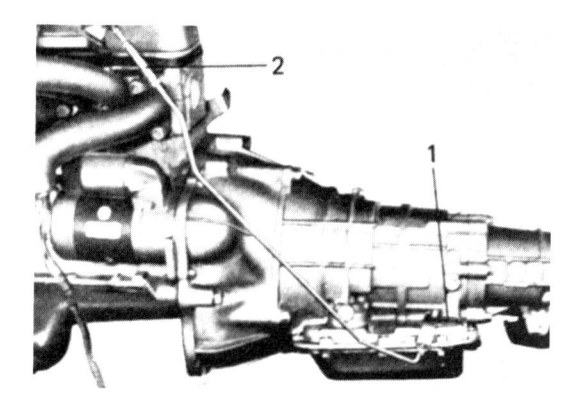

Fig. 6.39. Adjustment of throttle connecting rod

1 Indicator
2 Turn buckle

36 Fault diagnosis - automatic transmission

The object of this Section is to assist the driver in determining whether a fault exists or not. If a fault is confirmed the advice of the local main agent must be sought before any further action is taken.

1 Refer to Section 28 and check the fluid level.
2 Start the engine and allow to reach normal operating temperature.
3 Move the shift lever to the 'D' position and gently accelerate through the transmission range. Make a note of the shift point from low to high gear. Stop the car.
4 With the shift lever in the same position now rapidly accelerate through the transmission range. Again make a note of the shift point. Stop the car.
5 Repeat the tests in paragraphs 3 and 4 at least four times and compare the results.

If the shift points change gradually then the transmission operation is satisfactory. Should the shift points vary check the following:
a) The throttle valve, shift valve and throttle relay valve.
b) The throttle link connecting rod requires adjustment. It is probable that it is too short.

6 Drive the car at a speed of 28-31 mph (45-50 kph) with the shift lever in the 'D' range. Check the kickdown operation by fully depressing the accelerator.

If the downshift does not occur the throttle connecting rod requires adjustment. It is probably too long.

Should the downshift occur before the throttle is fully opened the connecting rod is probably too short.

7 With the car stationary and the selector still in the 'D' position, check if the low gear shift has occurred. To carry this out move the selector lever to the 'L' position. If no evidence is detected at the time of moving the selector lever the system is in the low gear position.

Should the low gear shift fail to occur, the governor valve, shift valve or throttle valve may not be operating correctly.

37 Fault diagnosis - manual gearbox

Symptom	Reason/s	Remedy
Weak or ineffective synchromesh	Synchronising cones worn, split or damaged	Dismantle and overhaul gearbox. Fit new gear wheels and synchronising cones.
	Synchromesh dogs worn, or damaged	Dismantle and overhaul gearbox. Fit new synchromesh unit.
Jumps out of gear	Broken gearchange fork rod spring	Dismantle and replace spring.
	Gearbox coupling dogs badly worn	Dismantle gearbox. Fit new coupling dogs.
	Selector fork rod groove badly worn	Fit new selector fork rod.
Excessive noise	Incorrect grade of oil in gearbox or oil level too low	Drain, refill or top up gearbox with correct grade of oil.
	Bush or needle roller bearings worn or damaged	Dismantle and overhaul gearbox. Renew bearings.
	Gear teeth excessively worn or damaged	Dismantle, overhaul gearbox. Renew gearwheels.
	Countershaft thrust washers worn allowing excessive end play	Dismantle and overhaul gearbox. Renew thrust washers.
Excessive difficulty in engaging gear	Clutch pedal adjustment incorrect	Adjust clutch pedal correctly.

Chapter 7 Propeller shaft and universal joints

Contents

Fault diagnosis - propeller shaft ... 6	Universal joints - dismantling and inspection ... 4
General description ... 1	Universal joints - inspection and repair ... 3
Propeller shaft - removal and replacement ... 2	Universal joints - reassembly ... 5

Specifications

Type: ...	Tubular, one piece
Spider side play (maximum): ...	Less than 0.002 in. (0.05 mm)
Circlip thickness: ...	0.047 in. (1.20 mm) or 0.049 in. (1.25 mm)
Torque wrench setting:	lb f ft kg f m
Propeller shaft securing nuts ...	16 2.2

1 General description

The drive from the gearbox to the rear axle is transmitted by the tubular propeller shaft. Due to the variety of angles caused by the up and down motion of the rear axle in relation to the gearbox, universal joints are fitted to each end of the shaft to convey the drive through the constantly varying angles. As the movement also increases and decreases the distance between the rear axle and the gearbox, the forward end of the propeller shaft is a splined sleeve which is a sliding fit over the rear of the gearbox splined mainshaft.

The splined sleeve runs in an oil seal in the gearbox mainshaft rear cover, and is supported with the mainshaft on the gearbox rear bearing. The splines are lubricated by oil in the rear cover coming from the gearbox.

The universal joints each comprise a four-way trunnion, or spider- each leg of which runs in a needle roller bearing race- preloaded with grease and fitted in the bearing journal yokes of the sliding sleeve and the propeller shaft and flange.

2 Propeller shaft - removal and replacement

1 Jack-up the rear of the car and support on firmly based axle stands.
2 The rear of the propeller shaft is connected to the rear axle pinion by a flange held by four nuts and bolts. Mark the position of both flanges relative to each other, and then undo and remove the nuts and bolts. (Fig. 7.3)
3 Move the propeller shaft forwards to disengage it from the pinion flange and then lower it to the ground.
4 Draw the other end of the propeller shaft, that is the splined sleeve, out of the rear of the gearbox rear cover. The shaft is then clear for removal from the underside of the car.
5 Place a container under the gearbox rear cover opening so as to catch any oil which will certainly come out.
6 Refitting the propeller shaft is the reverse sequence to removal but the following additional points should be noted:
a) Ensure that the mating marks on the propeller shaft and differential pinion flanges are lined up.
b) Don't forget to check the gearbox oil level and top-up if necessary.
c) Tighten the bolts holding the flange to the differential to a torque wrench setting of 16 lb f ft (2.2 kg f m).

3 Universal joints - inspection and repair

1 Wear in the needle roller bearings is characterised by vibration in the transmission, 'clonks' on taking up the drive and in extreme cases of lack of lubrication, metallic squeaking, and ultimately grating and shrieking sounds as the bearings break up.
2 If it easy to check if the needle roller bearings are worn, with the propeller shaft in position, by trying to turn the shaft with one hand, the other hand holding the rear axle flange. Any movement between the propeller shaft and the flange is indicative of considerable wear. If worn, the old bearings and spiders will have to be discarded and a repair kit comprising new universal joint spiders, bearings and oil seals purchased.
3 It is important to note that there could be difficulty in obtaining an overhaul kit in certain areas so ensure that one is to hand before commencing work.
4 The front needle roller bearings should be tested for wear using the same principle as described in paragraph 2.
5 To test the splined coupling for wear, lift the end of the shaft and note any movement in the splines.
6 Check the splined coupling dust cover for signs of damage or looseness on the shaft.

4 Universal joints - dismantling and inspection

1 Clean away all traces of dirt and grease from the universal joint yoke. Using a pair of circlip pliers compress the circlips and lift away. If the circlips are tight in their grooves tap the ends to shock move the bearing cups slightly.
2 Hold the propeller shaft and using a soft faced hammer tap the universal joint yoke so as to remove the bearing cups by 'shock' action.
3 Remove all four bearing cups in the manner described and then free the propeller shaft from the spider.

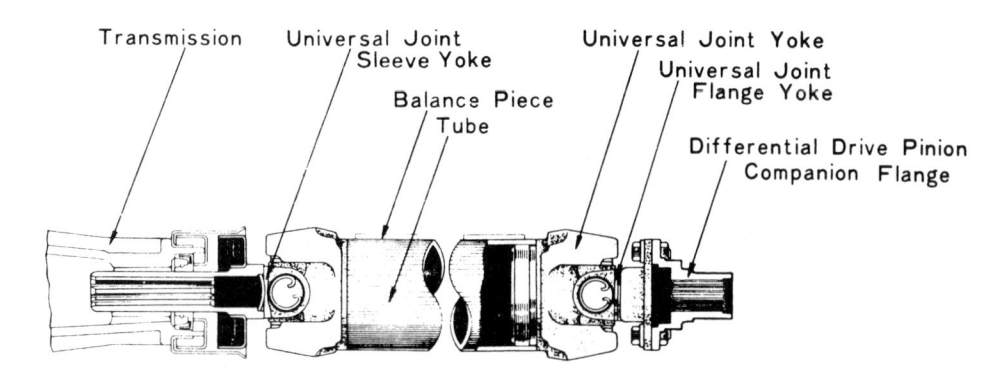

Fig. 7.1. Propeller shaft component parts

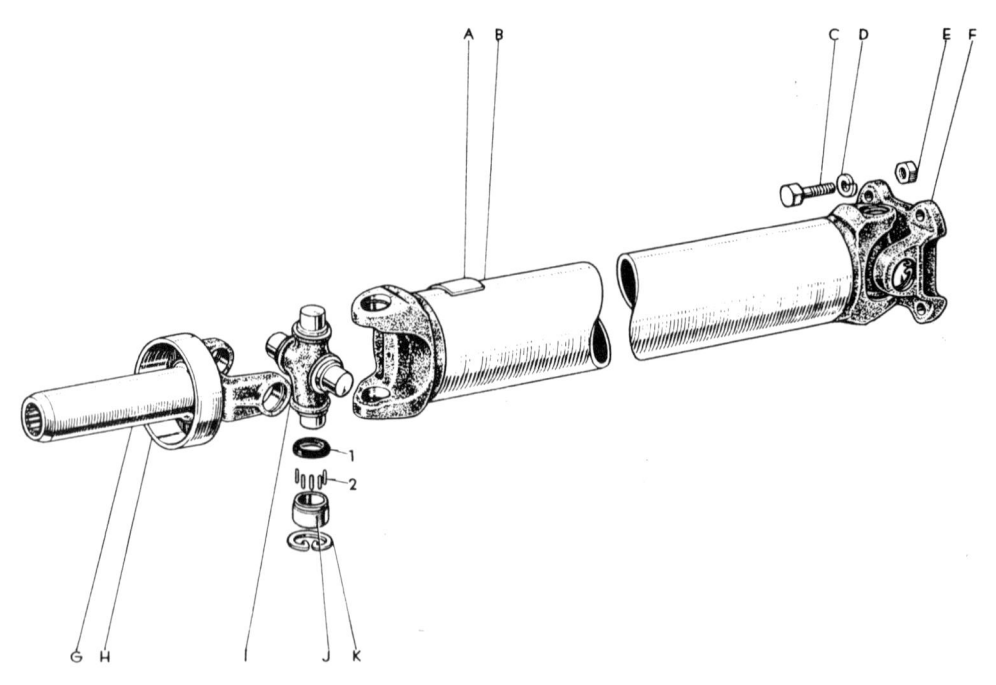

Fig. 7.2. Exploded view of propeller shaft

- A Balance piece
- B Propeller shaft
- C Hexagon bolt
- E Nut
- F Universal joint flange yoke
- G Universal joint sleeve yoke
- H Sliding shaft dust cover
- I Universal joint spider
- J Needle roller cup
- K Hole snap ring
- 1 Spider bearing seal
- 2 Needle roller

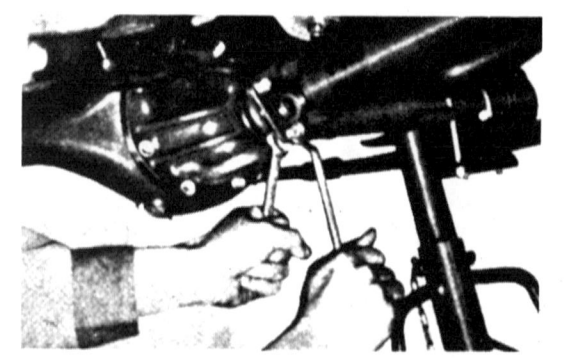

Fig. 7.3. Detaching propeller shaft from rear axle

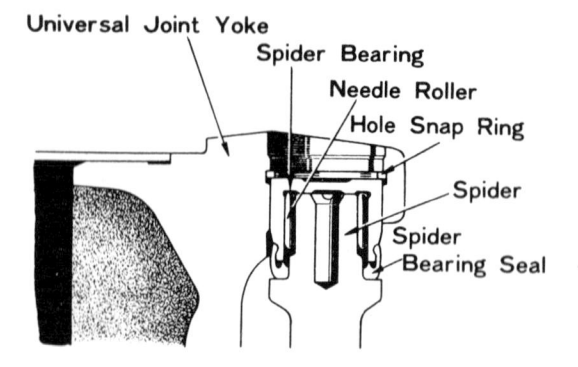

Fig. 7.4. Cross sectional view of universal joint bearing

4 Clean all parts and thoroughly inspect for wear or damage.
5 If possible check the maximum runout at the centre using 'V' blocks and a dial indicator gauge. The runout should not exceed 0.010 in (0.254 mm).
6 Slide the yoke onto the gearbox mainshaft and check for spline wear both radially and vertically. Examine the expansion plug on the end of the yoke for signs of leakage. If leakage is evident, a new plug should be fitted.
7 If the needle bearings are worn it is probable that the spider trunnions are worn also, necessitating renewal.
8 Before obtaining new parts a check must be made to determine which sized parts are required as the trunnion bearings are available in different sizes.

If a 0.236 in (6 mm) diameter drill hole appears on either or both sides of the yoke, oversize bearings are required. These are marked with red paint:

Spider bearing outer diameter: 0.7877 - 0.7882 in
  (20.008 - 20.021 mm). No marks.
                                                 0.7885 - 0.7892 in
  (20.029 - 20.042 mm). Red paint mark.
Yoke Bore diameter: 0.7874 - 0.7882 in
  (20.000 - 20.0021 mm). No marks.
                                                   0.7882 - 0.7892 in
  (20.0021 - 20.0042 mm). Drill marked.

5 Universal joints - reassembly

1 Again clean out the yokes and trunnions and fit new oil seals to the spider journals.

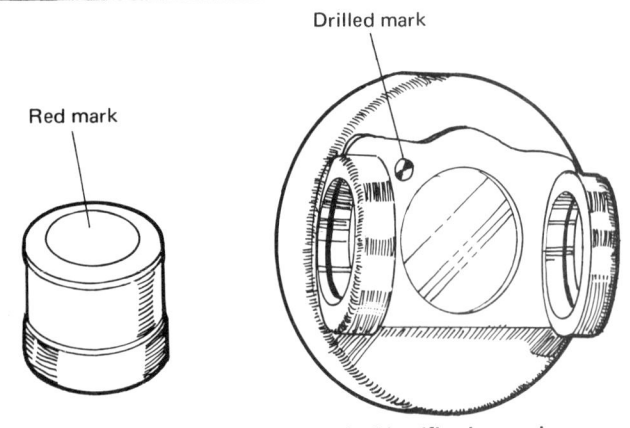

Fig. 7.5. Spider bearing and yoke identification marks

2 Place the spider on the propeller shaft yoke and assemble the needle rollers into the bearing cups retaining them with some thick grease.
3 Fill each bearing cup about ½ full with Castrol LM Grease. Also fill the grease holes on the spider with grease taking care that all air bubbles are eliminated.
4 Refit the bearing cups on the spider and tap the bearings home so that they lie squarely in position.
5 Lock the cups in position with new circlips. Check the spider movement and if it is tight try tapping the yokes with a hammer. If this does not do the trick then something is amiss requiring investigation.

6 Fault diagnosis - propeller shaft and universal joints

Symptom	Reason/s	Remedy
Propeller shaft vibration	Universal joint spider bearing worn or damaged	Replace.
	Incorrect bearing cup circlip thickness	Fit new circlip of greater thickness.
	Bent propeller shaft	Straighten or renew.
	Propeller shaft out of balance	Rebalance or renew.
	Worn gearbox extension housing bush	Replace.
	Universal joint mounting loose	Tighten.
Noisy starting or while coasting	Universal joint spider bearing worn or damaged	Replace.
	Incorrect bearing cup circlip thickness	Fit new circlip of greater thickness.
	Slackness in the spider bearings	Replace.
	Universal joint mounting loose	Tighten.
	No preload of the differential drive pinion bearing	Adjust differential (Chapter 8)
	Worn splines of drive pinion companion flange	Replace.
	Worn splines of universal joint sleeve yoke	Replace.
	Incorrect installation of splined coupling dust cover	Repair or renew.

Chapter 8 Rear axle

Contents

Differential assembly - dismantling, inspection, reassembly and adjustment ... 6	General description ... 1
Differential assembly - removal and replacement ... 5	Halfshaft - removal, overhaul and replacement ... 3
Fault diagnosis - rear axle ... 7	Pinion oil seal - removal and replacement ... 4
	Rear axle - removal and replacement ... 2

Specifications

Type: ... Hypoid, semi-floating with banjo type axle casing

Final drive ratio: ... 4.222 : 1   4.444 : 1
                          3.900 : 1   4.111 : 1

Number of teeth:

Ratio:	Pinion	Crownwheel
3.900 : 1	9	35
4.111 : 1	9	37
4.222 : 1	9	38
4.444 : 1	9	40

Differential gear type: ... Bevel gear

Number of pinion gear teeth: ... 10

Number of side gear teeth: ... 16

Dimensions and clearances:
- Crownwheel runout (max.) ... 0.002 in. (0.04 mm)
- Differential gear backlash ... 0.001 - 0.006 in. (0.02 - 0.15 mm)
- Pinion bearing preload:
  - New bearings ... 2.7 - 4.8 lb f (1.2 - 2.2 kg f)
  - Old bearings ... 0.9 - 2.8 lb f (0.4 - 1.3 kg f)
- Crownwheel/pinion backlash ... 0.004 - 0.006 in. (0.1 - 0.15 mm)
- Pinion gear shaft bore wear limit ... 0.5965 in. (15.1638 mm)
- Side gear thrust washers available:
  - No. 1 ... 0.059 in. (1.4986 mm)
  - No. 2 ... 0.061 in. (1.5494 mm)
  - No. 3 ... 0.063 in. (1.6002 mm)

- Pinion spacer length:
  - No. 1 ... 1.957 in. (49.7 mm)
  - No. 2 ... 1.958 in. (49.74 mm)
  - No. 3 ... 1.960 in. (49.78 mm)
  - No. 4 ... 1.961 in. (49.82 mm)
  - No. 5 ... 1.963 in. (49.86 mm)
  - No. 6 ... 1.965 in. (49.90 mm)

- Rear axle flange runout (max.) ... 0.08 in. (2.032 mm)

Oil capacity: ... 1.8 pints (1.1 litres, 2.25 US pints)

Torque wrench settings:

	lb f ft	kg fm
Breather plug	7 - 9	1.0 - 1.2
'U' bolt nuts	22 - 32	3.04 - 4.4
Shock absorber to spring	26 - 40	3.5 - 5.5
Differential carrier to rear axle housing	16 - 22	2.2 - 3.04

Drive flange to propeller shaft	...	...	...	...	...	...	16.0	2.2
Rear axle bearing outer retainer to rear axle housing			...	...			22.0	3.0
Hub nuts	...	...	...	...	...	...	65 - 85	8.95 - 11.7
Carrier cap bolts	...	...	...	...	...	...	47	6.5
Filler plug	...	...	...	...	...	...	20 - 24	2.77 - 3.3
Pinion flange nut	...	...	...	...	...	...	110.0	15
Crownwheel securing bolts	...	...	...	...	...		55.0	7.5

1 General description

The rear axle is semi-floating and is held in place by semi-elliptic springs. These springs provide the necessary lateral and longitudinal location of the axle. The rear axle incorporates a hypoid crownwheel and pinion and a two pinion differential. All repairs can be carried out to the component parts of the rear axle without removing the axle casing from the car.

The crownwheel and pinion together with the differential gears are mounted in the differential casing which is bolted to the front face of the banjo type axle casing.

Adjustments are provided for the crownwheel and pinion backlash; pinion depth of mesh; pinion shaft bearing preload; and backlash between the differential gears. All these adjustments may be made by varying the thickness of the various shims, of thrust washers and adjustment nuts.

The halfshafts (axleshafts) are easily withdrawn and are splined at their inner ends to fit into the splines in the differential wheels. The inner wheel bearing race is located on the halfshaft and the outer race to the inside of the axle casing.

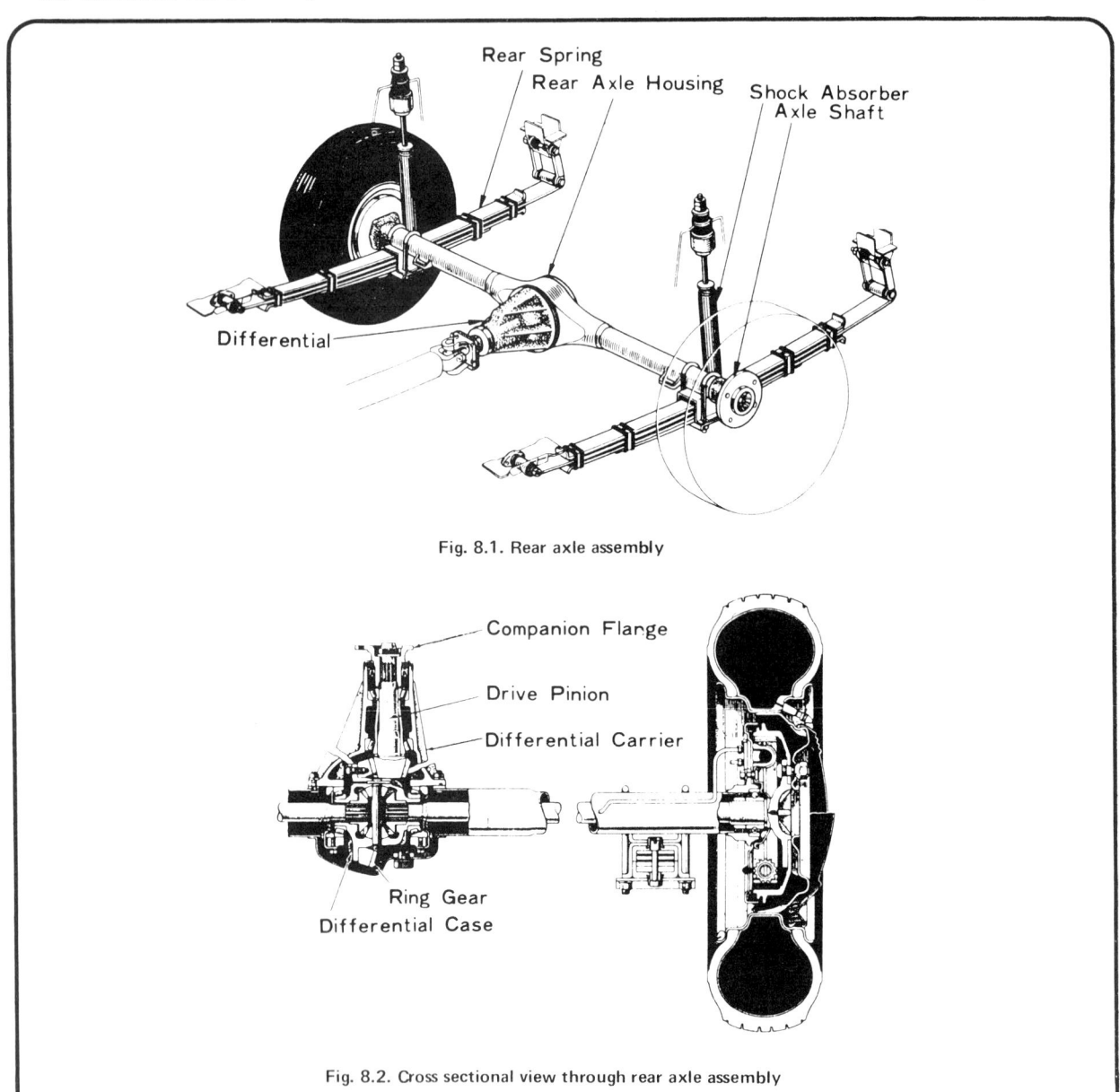

Fig. 8.1. Rear axle assembly

Fig. 8.2. Cross sectional view through rear axle assembly

Chapter 8/Rear Axle

2 Rear axle - removal and replacement

1 Chock the front wheels, jack-up the rear of the car and place on firmly based axle stands located under the body and forward of the rear axle.
2 With a scriber or file mark the pinion and propeller shaft drive flange so that they may be refitted in the same relative position.
3 Undo and remove the four nuts and bolts that secure the rear propeller shaft flange to the pinion flange. Lower the propeller shaft.
4 Remove the rear wheels.
5 Wipe the top of the brake master cylinder reservoir, unscrew the cap and place a piece of thin polythene sheet over the top of the reservoir filler neck. Refit the cap. This will prevent hydraulic fluid syphoning out during subsequent operations.
6 Wipe the area around the union nut on the brake feed pipe to flexible hose and referring to Chapter 9, disconnect the flexible hose. Tape the ends to stop dirt ingress.
7 Disconnect the shock absorber lower mountings.
8 Undo and remove the nuts securing the 'U' bolts to the seats. Remove the seats, 'U' bolts and rear spring bump rubbers.
9 Disconnect the handbrake cable at the equaliser assembly. (see Chapter 9 for further information).
10 If assistance is available it is possible to manoeuvre the axle between the springs and underside of the car. However, if the springs have considerably weakened and flattened there may not be sufficient room for clearance of the brake drums. If this is the case disconnect the rear spring shackles and lower the springs. The axle may then be removed from under the car.
11 Refitting the rear axle assembly is the reverse sequence to removal. It will be necessary to bleed the brake hydraulic system as described in Chapter 9. Do not forget to refill the rear axle if it has been dismantled.

3 Halfshaft - removal, overhaul and replacement

1 Chock the front wheels, jack-up the rear of the car and place on firmly based axle stands. Remove the road wheel.
2 Suitably mark the brake drum and halfshaft to ensure correct replacement. Remove the brake drum.
3 Undo and remove the four nuts securing the bearing retainer and brake backplate to the axle casing.
4 Remove the brake shoe upper return spring and using two suitable length bolts screw them into the tapped holes in the halfshaft flange. Ensure that their ends pass through the holes in the bearing retainer and then tighten them both in a progressive alternating manner until the halfshaft bearing retainer and bearing can be pulled out of the axle casing. Plug the axle casing end to prevent oil getting onto the brake shoes.
5 If the axle oil seal is leaking it should be removed and a new one fitted using a drift of suitable diameter.
6 If it is necessary to fit a new halfshaft bearing obtain a new bearing and retaining ring.

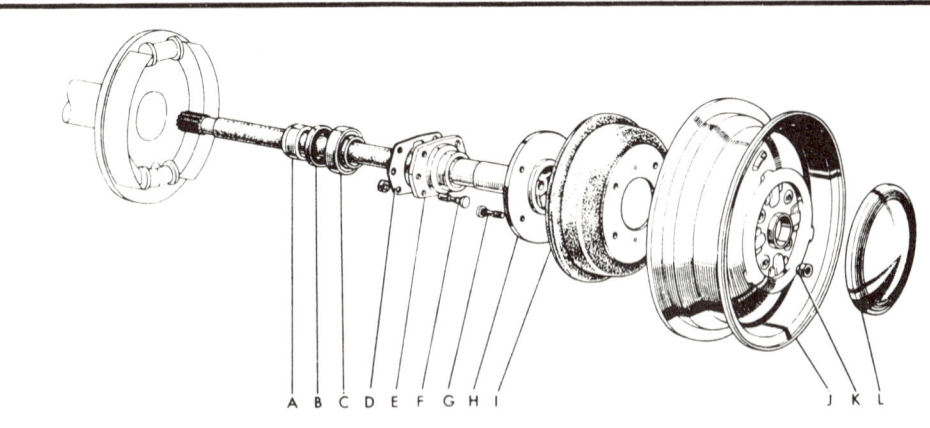

Fig. 8.3. Rear axle shaft components

A Rear axle bearing inner retainer
B 'T' type oil seal
C Bearing
D Rear axle bearing retainer gasket
E Rear axle bearing outer retainer
F Serration bolt
G Hub bolt
H Rear axle shaft
I Brake drum
J Disc wheel
K Hub nut
L Wheel cap

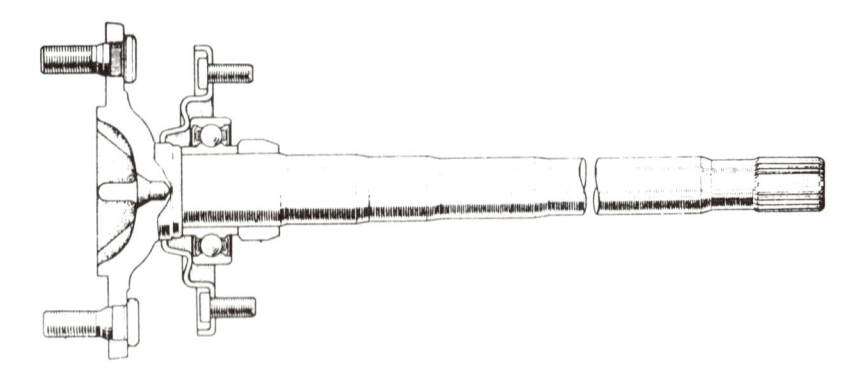

Fig. 8.4. Rear axle shaft with cross section through bearing assembly

7 Fit a nut onto one of the bolts in the bearing retainer and remove the bolt by tapping on the nut. This will prevent damage to the bolt thread.

8 Grind the retaining ring on a grindstone until the point is reached where the halfshaft is just about to be touched by the grinding wheel.

9 Using a chisel break the retaining ring but take extreme care not to mark the halfshaft otherwise it will be severely weakened.

10 With the retaining ring removed, the outer retainer and bearing may be pressed off the shaft.

11 Refit the bolt into the bearing retainer, this being the one removed as described in paragraph 7.

12 Carefully drift or press the new bearing and bearing outer retainer onto the halfshaft up to the shaft flange.

13 The new bearing retaining ring must now be heated in an oven to 150°C (300°F) and quickly pressed onto the shaft and hard up to the bearing. Do **not** use a blowtorch for this as the ring will be severely weakened. Allow the ring to cool naturally.

14 The halfshaft is now ready for refitting into the axle casing: this is a direct reversal of the removal sequence. The following additional points should be noted:
a) As the bearing is a sealed unit it does not require additional lubrication prior to assembling to the axle casing.
b) The surface of the bearing retaining ring on which the oil seal runs should be lightly smeared with axle oil.
c) Tighten the retainer bolts to a torque wrench setting of 22 lb f ft (3 Kg fm).
d) Check the rear axle oil level and top-up if necessary.

4 Pinion oil seal - removal and replacement

1 Chock the front wheels, jack-up the rear of the car and support on firmly based axle stands.

2 With a scriber or file mark the propeller shaft and pinion flanges so that they may be refitted correctly in their original positions.

3 Undo and remove the four nuts and bolts that secure the pinion flange to the propeller shaft flange. Lower the propeller shaft to the floor.

4 Apply the handbrake really firmly.

5 Using a sharp pointed chisel straighten the locked in part of the flange securing nut.

6 With a socket wrench undo the flange nut. Lift away the nut and plain washer.

7 Pull the input flange off the splines of the pinion shaft.

8 The old oil seal may now be pushed out using a screwdriver or thin piece of metal bar with a small hook on one end.

9 Refitting the new oil seal is the reverse sequence to removal. The following additional points should be noted:
a) Soak the new oil seal in Castrol GTX for 1 hour prior to fitting.
b) Fit the new seal with the lip facing inwards using a tubular drift.
c) Tighten the drive flange nut to a torque wrench setting of 110 lb f ft (15 Kg fm) and using a punch lock the nut onto the pinion shaft.

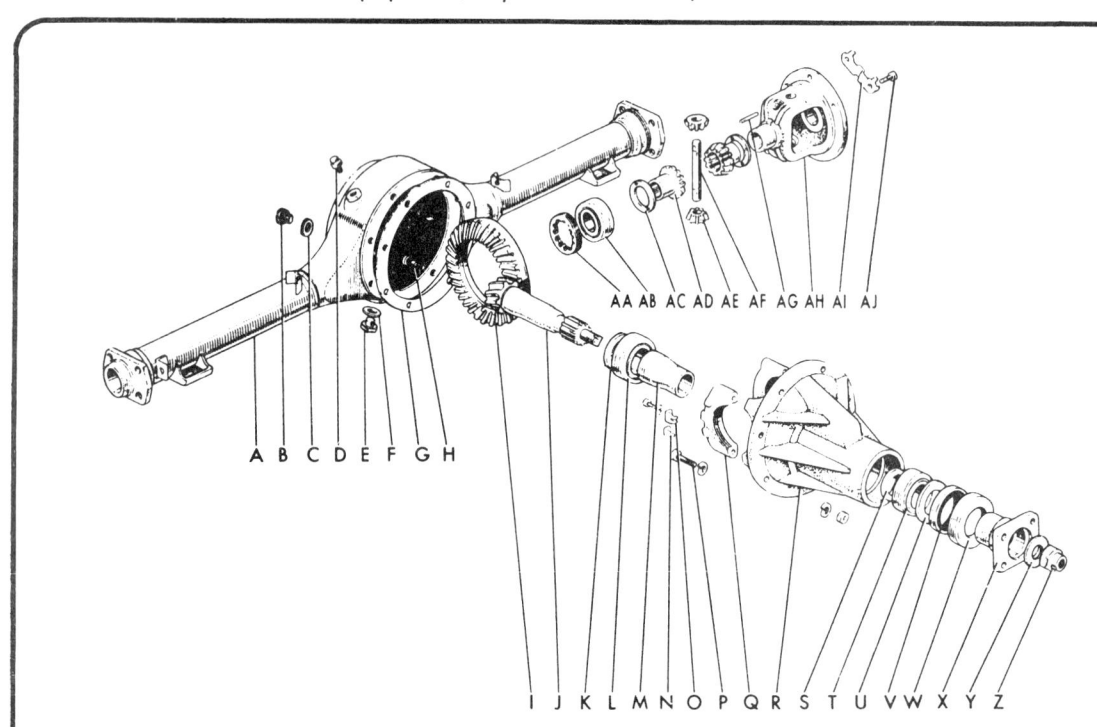

Fig. 8.5. Rear axle components

A	Rear axle housing	L	Tapered roller bearing	T	Tapered roller bearing
B	Filler plug	M	Differential drive pinion bearing spacer	U	Differential drive pinion oil slinger
C	Plug gasket			V	'T' type oil seal
D	Breather plug	N	Differential bearing adjusting nut lock No. 1	W	Dust deflector
E	Drain plug			X	Drive pinion companion flange
F	Plug gasket	O	Differential bearing adjusting nut lock No. 2	Y	Plain washer
G	Differential carrier gasket			Z	Nut
H	Serration bolt	P	Hexagon bolt	AA	Differential bearing adjusting nut
I	Differential ring gear	Q	Differential bearing cap	AB	Tapered roller bearing
J	Differential drive pinion	R	Differential carrier	AC	Differential side gear thrust washer
K	Washer	S	Shim	AD	Differential side gear
				AE	Differential pinion gear
				AF	Differential pinion shaft
				AG	Straight pin
				AH	Differential case
				AI	Differential ring gear attaching bolt lock plate
				AJ	Bolt

5 Differential assembly - removal and replacement

1 If it is wished to overhaul the differential carrier assembly or to exchange it for a reconditioned unit first remove the half-shafts as described in Section 3.
2 Mark the propeller shaft and pinion flanges to ensure their replacement in the same relative position.
3 Undo and remove the four nuts and bolts from the flanges, separate the two parts and lower the propeller shaft to the ground.
4 Undo and remove the nuts and spring washers that secure the differential unit assembly to the axle casing.
6 Draw the assembly forwards from over the studs on the axle casing. Lift away from under the car. Recover the paper joint washer.
7 Refitting the differential assembly is the reverse sequence to removal. The following additional points should be noted:
a) Always use a new joint washer and make sure the mating faces are clean.
b) Do not forget to refill the rear axle. The capacity is 1.875 pints (1.1 litres, 2.25 US pints).

6 Differential assembly - dismantling, inspection, reassembly and adjustment

Most garages will prefer to fit a complete set of gears, bearings, shims and thrust washers rather than renew parts which may have worn. To do the job properly requires the use of special and expensive tools which the majority of garages do not have.

The primary object of these special tools is to enable the mesh of the crownwheel and pinion to be very accurately set, and thus ensure, that noise is kept to a minimum. If any increase in noise cannot be tolerated then it is best to allow a Toyota garage to carry out the repairs.

Differential assemblies have been rebuilt without the use of special tools so if the possibility of a slight increase in noise can be tolerated it is quite possible for any do-it-yourself mechanic to successfully recondition this unit.

1 If the exterior is dirty wash in paraffin or 'Gunk' and dry using an absorbant cloth.
2 Using a chisel straighten the locked part of the nut holding the drive flange. Hold the input flange and unscrew the nut. Lift away the nut and washer and pull off the drive flange from the splines of the pinion shaft.
3 Hold the differential unit vertically in a vice and then using a scriber mark the bearing caps and adjacent side of the differential carrier so that the bearing caps are refitted to their original positions.
4 Remove the adjustment nut locks from the bearing caps and release the bearing cap bolts slightly.
5 Unscrew and remove the adjustment nuts from the bearing housings.
6 Remove the bearing cap bolts and lift away the two caps.
7 The differential case and crownwheel assembly many be lifted out from the housing.
8 Lift off the two bearing outer tracks and ensure that they are not mixed up. They must be refitted in their original position unless, of course the bearings are to be renewed.
9 If the differential gear carrier caps are to be renewed they should next be removed using a universal three legged puller and suitable thrust block.
10 Mark the relative position of the crownwheel and differential carrier to ensure correct refitting.
11 Bend back the lockwasher tabs and remove the bolts securing the crownwheel to the differential carrier.
12 Separate the crownwheel from the differential carrier.
13 Using a sharp chisel clean the peened over area retaining the differential pinion shaft lock-pin and drift out the lock-pin with a suitable diameter parallel pin punch.
14 With a suitable soft metal drift remove the differential pinion shaft.
15 Rotate the differential gearwheels until the differential pinions are opposite the openings in the differential carrier. Remove the differential pinions and their selective thrust

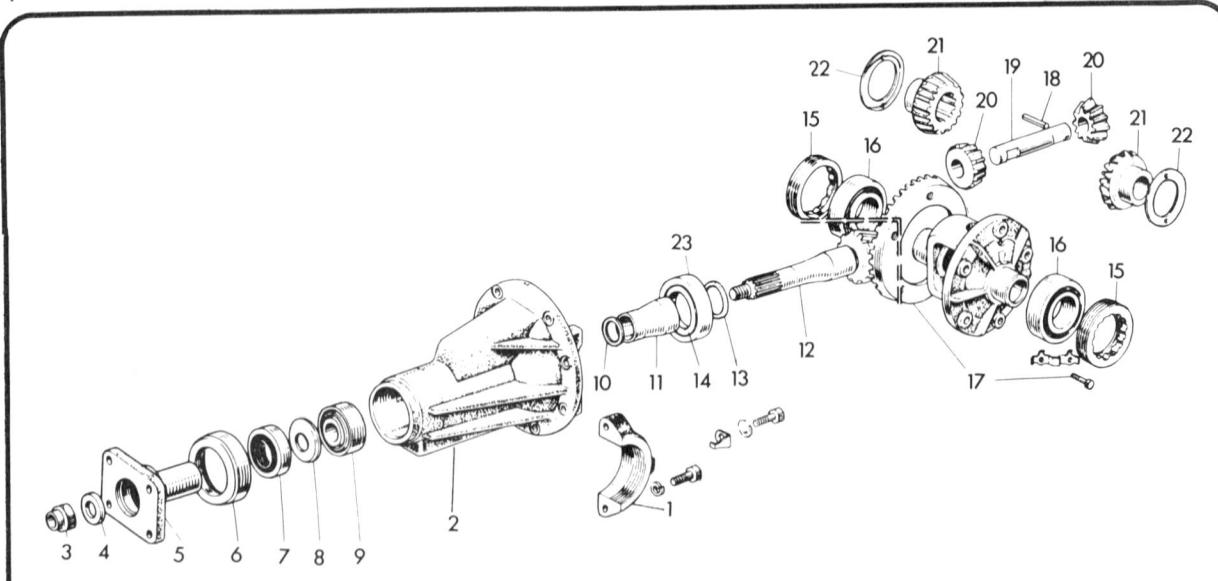

Fig. 8.6. Final drive assembly components

1 Bearing cap
2 Differential case
3 Nut
4 Washer
5 Drive pinion companion flange
6 Dust deflector
7 T-type oil seal
8 Oil slinger
9 Bearing
10 Shim
11 Bearing spacer
12 Drive pinion
13 Washer
14 Bearing
15 Bearing adjusting nut
16 Bearing
17 Ring gear
18 Straight pin
19 Pinion shaft
20 Differential pinion
21 Differential side gear
22 Thrust washer
23 Drive bearing outer race

washers. Keep the pinion and respective thrust washers together.

16 Remove the differential gearwheels and their thrust washers.

17 Drive out the pinion from the differential carrier using a hardwood block and a hammer.

18 Recover the adjustment shims and bearing spacer.

19 If the pinion bearings are to be renewed the inner bearing should be drawn off the pinion using a univeral puller with long legs.

20 Lift off the pinion head washer from behind the pinion head.

21 Using a tapered soft metal drift carefully drive out the pinion outer bearing cap, bearing and oil seal. Also remove the pinion inner bearing cup.

22 Dismantling is now complete. Thoroughly wash all parts in petrol or paraffin and wipe dry using a clean non-fluffy rag.

23 Lightly lubricate the bearings and reassemble. Test for signs of roughness by rotating the inner and outer tracks. Check the rollers for signs of pitting, wear or excessive looseness in their cage. Inspect the thrust washers for signs of excessive wear. Check for signs of wear on the differential pinion shaft and pinion gears. Any parts that shows signs of wear should be renewed.

24 The crownwheel and pinion must only be replaced as a matched pair. The pair number is etched on the outer face of the crownwheel and forward face of the pinion.

25 If it is found that only one of the differential bearings is worn both differential bearings must be renewed. Likewise if one pinion bearing is worn, both pinion bearings must be renewed.

26 To reassemble first fit the differential bearing cones to the gear carrier using a piece of tube of suitable diameter.

27 Place the thrust washers behind the two differential gears and then fit them into their bores in the gear carrier. Make sure the gears rotate easily.

28 Place the two pinion gears in mesh with the two differential gears, slot in the thrust washers and rotate the gear cluster until the pinion pin hole in the carrier is lined up with the pinion. Insert the pinion pin.

29 Press each pinion in turn firmly into mesh with the differential gears. The backlash between the carriers and differential gears should not exceed 0.006 in (0.15 mm). The minimum backlash is 0.001 in (0.02 mm). Adjust if necessary using different thickness thrust washers. Alway fit the same thickness of thrust washer to each differential gear with its oil groove towards the gear.

30 When the backlash is correct align the pinion pin hole with the pin hole in the carrier and fit a new pin. Peen over the end of the pin hole to prevent the pin working out.

31 Carefully clean the crownwheel and gear carrier mating faces and fit the crownwheel. Any burrs can be removed with a fine oil stone. If the original parts are being used line up the previously made marks.

32 Secure the crownwheel with the securing bolts and lockwashers. The bolts should be tightened to a torque wrench setting of 55 lb f ft (7.5 Kg f m). Bend the lockwasher tabs over the bolt heads.

33 Using a tubular drift of suitable diameter drive the taper roller bearings onto the differential carrier ensuring that they are the correct way round.

34 The pinion must next be assembled. Using a suitable diameter tubular drift refit the washer and tapered roller bearing behind the pinion head. Make sure the bearing is fitted the correct way round.

35 Using a suitable diameter drift refit the two pinion bearing outer cups. Again make sure they are fitted the correct way round with the tapers facing outwards.

36 Lubricate the bearing and fit the pinion to the casing. Slide on the bearing spacer, tapered end towards the drive flange followed by the shim that was previously removed.

37 Lubricate the outer bearing and then fit to the end of the pinion.

38 Fit the drive flange and nut. Tighten the nut to a torque wrench setting of 110 lb f ft (15 Kg fm). Rotate the pinion several times before the nut is fully tightened so that the bearings settle to their running positions.

39 If available use a pull scale and determine the bearing preload by wrapping string around the pinion flange and tying the other end onto the pull scale. The reading should be 0.9 - 2.8 lb f (0.4 - 1.3 Kg f) for old bearings or 2.7 - 4.8 lb f (1.2 - 2.2 Kg f) for new bearings. Should the reading be in excess of this amount the shim thickness should be increased and conversely if the reading is too low decrease the shim thickness.

40 Remove the pinion nut pinion and outer bearing and fit the required thickness shim to the pinion. The shim thickness available is 0.01 in (0.25 mm) and for larger adjustments a range of 6 different length spacers are available.

No. 1   1.957 in (49.70 mm)
No. 2   1.958 in (49.74 mm)
No. 3   1.960 in (49.78 mm)
No. 4   1.961 in (49.82 mm)
No. 5   1.963 in (49.86 mm)
No. 6   1.965 in (49.90 mm)

For assistance 0.001 in (0.25 mm) thickness shim equals approximately 4 lb f in (0.046 Kg fm) preload.

41 Soak a new oil seal in Castrol GTX for 1 hour and then fit to the differential case. Replace the drive flange, washer and nut and tighten the nut to a torque wrench setting of 110 lb f ft (15 Kg fm).

42 Do not lock the nut yet as it may be necessary to dismantle it again.

43 Place the bearing cups on the differential bearings and fit the differential carrier into the case. Push the crownwheel fully into

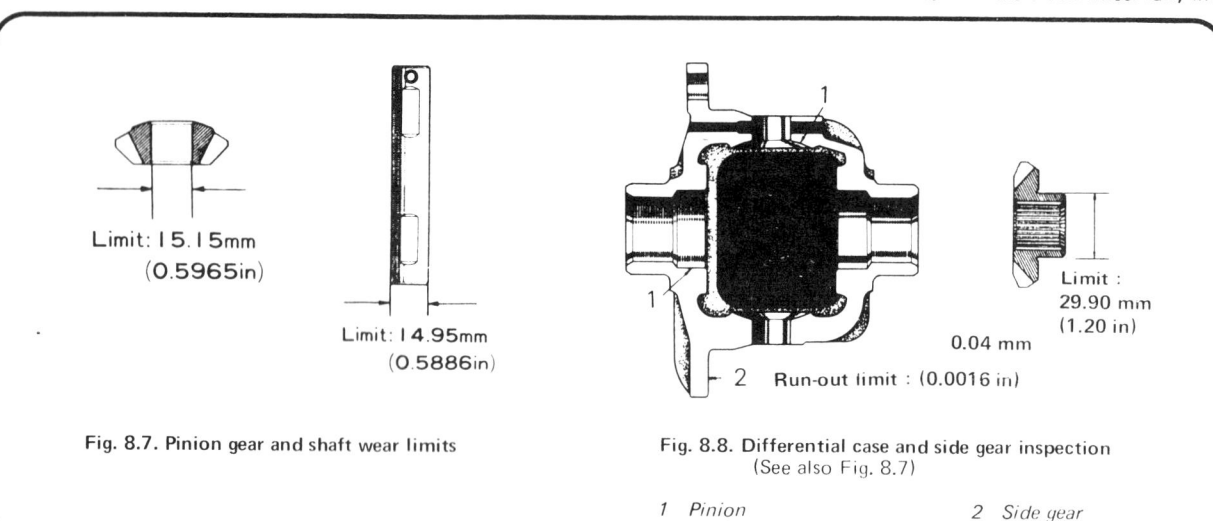

Fig. 8.7. Pinion gear and shaft wear limits

Fig. 8.8. Differential case and side gear inspection (See also Fig. 8.7)

1 Pinion   2 Side gear

Chapter 8/Rear Axle

mesh with the pinion.

44 Replace the adjustment nuts on either side of the bearings and refit the bearing caps taking extreme care that the adjusting nuts are seating properly in the threads of the caps and the housings before lightly tightening the cap bolts. They must not be so tight that the adjusting nuts cannot be turned in the housings and caps.

45 Slacken the adjustment nut on the pinion side of the crownwheel and tighten the opposite nut gently until the crownwheel is fully in mesh with the pinion with no backlash whatsoever.

46 Now back off this nut as near to four notches as possible to align a notch with the locking tongue.

47 Tighten the pinion side nut hard against the bearing to move the whole assembly against the crownwheel side adjustment nut. Now back off the pinion nut until it is free of the bearing and screw it in again until it just makes good contact with the bearing. Tighten from one to one and a half notches until it aligns with the locking tongue.

48 Tighten the bearing cap bolts to a torque wrench setting of 47 lb f ft (6.5 Kg fm) and lock the nuts.

49 Using a dial indicator gauge or feeler gauges determine the total backlash which should be between 0.004 - 0.006 in (0.10 -0.15 mm).

50 Should adjustment be necessary slightly reset the position of the adjustment nuts not forgetting to slacken the cap bolts first.

51 The best check the do-it-yourself enthusiast can make to ascertain the correct meshing of the crownwheel and pinion is to smear a little engineer's blue onto the crownwheel and then rotate the pinion. The contact mark should appear right in the middle of the crownwheel teeth. Refer to Fig 8.11 where the correct tooth pattern is shown. Also shown are incorrect tooth patterns and the method of obtaining the correct pattern. Obviously this will take time and further dismantling, but will be worth it.

52 Check the tightness of the bearing cap bolts and lock the pinion flange nut.

53 Finally test the crownwheel runout using a dial indicator gauge. The runout should not exceed 0.002 in (0.04 mm) at the outer circumference. If it exceeds this there is probaby dirt on the differential carrier or crownwheel mating faces.

54 The differential assembly is now ready for refitting to the rear axle.

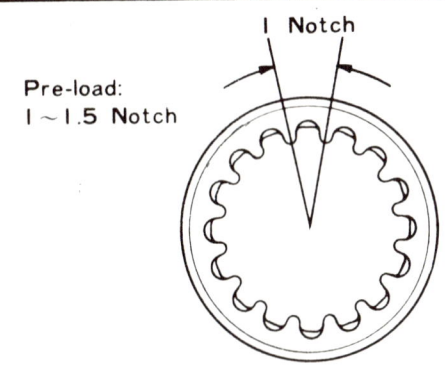

Fig. 8.9. Side bearing pre-load adjustment

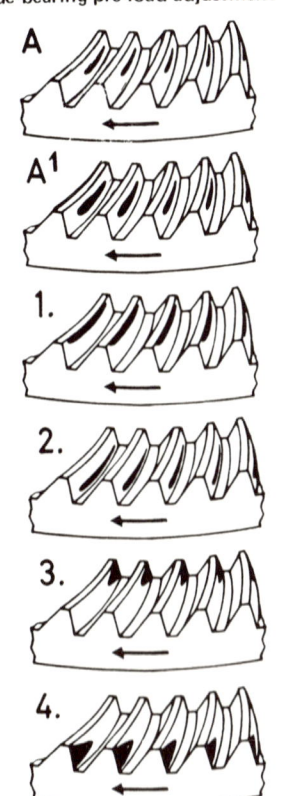

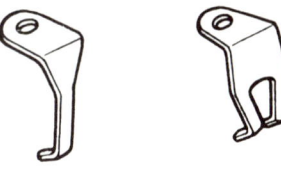

Fig. 8.10. Alternative adjusting nut locks

Fig. 8.11. Contact marking on crownwheel

A Correct contact marking picture without load.
A1 When subjected to load the contact picture is displaced somewhat towards the outside.
Displacement of the crownwheel changes primarily the backlash, in addition the contact picture is displaced in the axial direction of the teeth.
Displacement of the pinion primarily moves the contact marking in the direction of the tooth height, while the backlash changes only marginally.
In addition the four fundamentally **false** contact markings, which usually occur in conjunction with each other, but knowledge of which simplifies the actual adjustment work.
1 High, narrow contact marking (tip contact) on crownwheel.
Correction: displace the pinion toward the crownwheel axis and, if necessary, correct backlash by moving the crownwheel away from the pinion.
2 Deep, narrow contact marking (roof contact) on crownwheel.
Correction: move the pinion away from the crownwheel axis and, if necessary, correct backlash by pushing the crownwheel toward the pinion.
3 Short contact marking on smallest tooth end (toe contact) of the crownwheel. **Correction: move the crownwheel away from the pinion** and, if necessary, move the pinion closer toward the crownwheel axis.
4 Short contact marking on large tooth end (heel contact) of the crownwheel. **Correction: move the crownwheel toward the pinion** and, it necessary, move the pinion away from the crownwheel axis.

7 Fault diagnosis - rear axle

Symptom	Reason/s	Remedy
Rear wheel noise	Loose rear wheel nuts	Check condition of axle and wheel and tighten. Renew nut or stud/bolt.
	Faulty brake components	Renew faulty components (Chapter 9).
	Worn or defective axle shaft bearing or lack of lubrication	Renew faulty components.
	Bent rear axle housing or halfshaft	Renew axle housing and/or shaft.
	Wheel out of balance or buckled	Balance wheel. If buckled renew.
Final drive gear noise	Faulty pinion bearings	Renew pinion bearings and adjust gears.
	Faulty differential carrier bearings	Renew carrier bearings and adjust gears.
	Lack of lubrication	Generally check condition of assembly. Refill with fresh oil.
	Incorrect crownwheel and pinion mesh	Check gears, renew if necessary and adjust.
	Incorrect bearing preload (pinion or carrier bearings)	Check bearings, renew if necessary and adjust.
	Excessive noise or grinding noise under load	Overhaul assembly and renew faulty components.
	Excessive noise or grinding noise when coasting	Faulty gears or incorrect mesh. Renew parts and re-adjust.
Excessive differential backlash	Looseness between halfshaft and side gear splines	Check and renew halfshaft and/or side gears.
	Worn differential side gear thrust washers	Check and renew differential side gear thrust washers.
	Worn differential pinion thrust washers	Check and renew differential pinion thrust washers.
	Excessive backlash between differential side gears and pinions	Check condition of gear and pinion teeth and renew gear and/or pinion thrust washers.
	Excessive wear between differential shaft and pinions and/or shaft bore in carrier housing	Check and renew faulty parts.
Pinion shaft will rotate but will not drive car	Broken half shaft	Check and fit new half shaft.
	Sheared axle shaft splines	Check and renew faulty parts.
Continual halfshaft failure	Bent axle housing	Check and renew housing.
	Repeated overloading	Do not carry so much.
	Incorrect clutch operation	Check clutch (Chapter 5). Driving method?
	Incorrectly tightened axle shaft bearing retainer plate nuts	Check and retighten nuts to correct torque wrench setting.
Continual loss of rear axle oil	Faulty final drive pinion or halfshaft oil seals	Check and renew oil seal/s.
	Blocked axle housing breather	Remove breather, wash out and refit.
	Leaking gasket between differential carrier and axle housing	Renew gasket.
	Incorrect grade lubricant used	Drain, flush and refill with correct grade oil.

Chapter 9 Braking system

Contents

Bleeding the hydraulic system	2
Brake master cylinder (single) - dismantling, examination and reassembly	21
Brake master cylinder (single) - removal and replacement	20
Brake master cylinder (tandem) - dismantling, examination and reassembly	23
Brake master cylinder (tandem) - removal and replacement	22
Brake pedal - removal and replacement	19
Brake pedal travel - adjustment	18
Fault diagnosis - braking system	28
Flexible hose - inspection, removal and replacement	3
Front brake disc and hub - removal and replacement	6
Front brake pads - removal, inspection and refitting	4
Front disc brake caliper - removal, overhaul and replacement	5
Front drum brake - adjustment	10
Front drum brake backplate - removal and replacement	9
Front drum brake shoes - inspection, removal and refitting	7
Front drum brake wheel cylinder - removal, inspection and overhaul	8
General description	1
Handbrake - adjustment	16
Handbrake lever and cable assembly - removal, overhaul and replacement	17
Hydraulic pipes and hoses	26
Pressure control valve	27
Rear drum brake adjuster - removal, overhaul and replacement	14
Rear drum brake - adjustment	15
Rear drum brake backplate - removal and replacement	13
Rear drum brake shoes - inspection, removal and refitting	11
Rear drum brake wheel cylinder - removal, inspection and overhaul	12
Vacuum servo unit - description	24
Vacuum servo unit - removal and replacement	25

Specifications

Brake system type:
- Early models ... Front and rear drum brakes. Hydraulically operated on all four wheels
- Later models ... Front disc and rear drum brakes. Hydraulically operated on all four wheels. Servo assisted on some models
- Handbrake ... Mechanical, on rear wheels only

Front drum brakes:
- Drum diameter ... 7.87 in. (200 mm)
- Lining:
  - Width ... 1.4 in. (35 mm)
  - Thickness ... 0.16 in. (4 mm)
  - Length ... 7.0 in. (192 mm)
  - Area ... 2 x 20.83 sq in. (134.4 sq cm)
- Wheel cylinder diameter ... 0.75 in. (19.05 mm)

Front disc brakes:
- Disc:
  - Outer diameter ... 7.87 in. (200 mm)
  - Thickness ... 0.39 in. (10 mm)
  - Minimum thickness ... 0.35 in. (9 mm)
  - Maximum runout ... 0.006 in. (0.15 mm)
- Pads:
  - Braking area ... 4.73 sq in. (30.5 sq cm)
  - Thickness ... 0.55 in. (14 mm)
  - Minimum thickness ... 0.236 in. (0.6 mm)
- Caliper cylinder diameter ... 1.75 in. (44.45 mm)

Rear drum brakes:
- Drum diameter ... 7.87 in. (200 mm)
- Lining:
  - Width ... 1.2 in. (30 mm)
  - Thickness ... 0.16 in. (4 mm)
  - Length ... 7.0 in. (192 mm)
  - Area ... 2 x 17.86 sq in. (115.2 sq cm)
- Wheel cylinder diameter ... 0.6868 in. (17.45 mm)

Master cylinder diameter*
    Drum brakes ... 0.6258 in. (15.87 mm)
    Disc/drum brakes ... 0.626 in. (15.869 mm)

Subject to modifications. Confirm with Toyota dealer.

Brake fluid pressure: ... 1541 lb/in^2 (108.5 kg/cm^2)

Brake pedal:
    Ratio ... 4.3 : 1
    Stroke ... 4.7 - 5.1 in. (120 - 130 mm)

Torque wrench settings:

	lb f ft	kg f m
Master cylinder union bolt	20 - 25	2.7 - 3.5
Flexible hose union	9 - 13	1.3 - 1.8
Wheel cylinder to backplate (Front brakes)	7 - 12	1.0 - 1.6
Handbrake - front cable attachment	11 - 16	1.5 - 2.2
Wheel nuts	65 - 85	9.0 - 12.0
Bleed screw	6 - 9	0.8 - 1.3
Clutch pedal nut	36 - 50	5.0 - 7.0
Master cylinder reservoir bolt	10 - 13	1.4 - 1.8
Master cylinder nuts	11 - 16	1.5 - 2.2
Backplate to mounting	11 - 16	1.5 - 2.2
Pipe union nut	6 - 9	0.8 - 1.3
Adjuster bolts (Rear brakes)	7 - 12	1.0 - 1.6
Wheel cylinder to backplate (Rear brakes)	3 - 5	0.4 - 0.7
Propeller shaft nuts	11 - 16	1.5 - 2.2

1 General description

On earlier KE 1200 models drum brakes were fitted at front and rear, but on all later models disc brakes were fitted to the front and drum brakes to the rear.

The pedal operated master cylinder is located behind the brake pedal. On all drum brake models the reservoir is attached to the top of the master cylinder whilst on some of the later models a separate reservoir is used. With the latter system a dual-line braking system is used ensuring that should a leak occur in the hydraulic system it does not automatically make all brakes useless.

On later models hydraulic pressure to all wheels is boosted by a vacuum servo unit which is mounted between the brake pedal and the master cylinder.

The parking or emergency brakes are mechanically operated, activating the rear brakes only via a hand operated lever mounted on the floor between the front seats. The lever is connected to the rear wheel brake shoes by stranded cables and operating links in the rear wheel brake assemblies.

The front brake disc is secured to the front wheel hub and the caliper mounted on the steering swivel. From Fig. 9.3 it will be seen that on the inner disc face side of the caliper is a single hydraulic cylinder in which is placed a piston which is in contact with one pad. When hydraulic pressure is applied to the piston the adjacent pad is pushed into contact with the disc face. Further pressure will cause the second pad to contact the second disc face by reaction through the cylinder operating two shoes. When hydraulic pressure is applied to the cylinder, the pistons - in contact with the ends of the shoes - move outwards and force the linings into contact with the drum inner circumference. The brakes are thus applied. When the brake pedal is released the shoes are drawn off the drums by springs which link the pairs of shoes together inside each wheel drum. The shoe to drum clearance is adjusted by a serrated adjustment nut on the adjustment link.

On early produced models with front drum brakes two wheel cylinders are fitted to each brake unit.

An adjuster is attached to each wheel cylinder.

The vacuum servo unit, when fitted, uses the vacuum of the inlet manifold of the engine to operate what is, in effect, another pump to apply pressure to the hydraulic system. This reduces the pressure required on the conventional brake pedal when operating the brakes.

A pressure control valve is fitted in the rear brake hydraulic pipe line to prevent rear wheel locking during sudden stops.

2 Bleeding the hydraulic system

1 Removal of all the air from the hydraulic system is essential to the correct operation of the hydraulic system, and therefore before undertaking this, examine the fluid reservoir cap(s) to ensure that the vent hole is clear. Check the level of fluid in the reservoir(s) and top-up as required.

2 Check all brake line unions and connections for possible seepage, and at the same time check the condition of the rubber hoses.

3 If the condition of the caliper or wheel cylinders is in doubt, check for possible signs of fluid leakage.

4 If there is any possibility that incorrect fluid has been used in the system, drain all the fluid out and flush through with methylated spirits. Renew all piston seals and cups since they will be affected and could possibly fail under pressure.

5 On advantage of a dual line braking system is that if work is done to either the front or rear part of the system it will only be necessary to bleed half the system provided that the level of fluid in the reservoir has not fallen below half full.

6 Gather together a clean jam jar, a 12 inch (307 mm) length of tubing which fits tightly over the bleed screws and a tin of the correct brake fluid.

7 To bleed the system, clean the area around the rear right-hand wheel bleed screw furthermost from the master cylinder and remove the dust cap.

8 Place the end of the tube in the clean jar which should contain sufficient fluid to keep the end of the tube underneath during operation.

9 Open the bleed screw ¼ turn with a spanner and have an assistant depress the brake pedal. When the brake pedal reaches the floor close the bleed screw and slowly return the pedal.

10 Open the bleed screw and continue the sequence in paragraph 9 until air ceases to flow from the end of the pipe. At intervals make certain that the reservoir is kept topped-up, otherwise air will enter at this point.

11 Finally press the pedal down fully and hold it there whilst the bleed screw is tightened. To ensure correct seating it should be tightened to a torque wrench setting of 5-7 lb f ft (0.70 - 1.0 Kg fm).

12 Repeat this operation on the left-hand rear brake, and then

the right and left front wheels.

13 When completed check the level of the fluid in the reservoir and then check the feel of the brake pedal, which should be firm and free from any 'spongy' action - which is normally associated with air in the system.

14 When a servo unit is fitted it will be noticed that during the bleeding operation the effort required to depress the pedal the full stroke will increase because of the loss of vacuum assistance as it is destroyed by repeated operation of the servo unit. Although the servo unit will be inoperative as far as assistance is concerned it does not affect the brake bleed operation.

3 Flexible hose - inspection, removal and replacement

1 Inspect the condition of the flexible hydraulic hoses leading

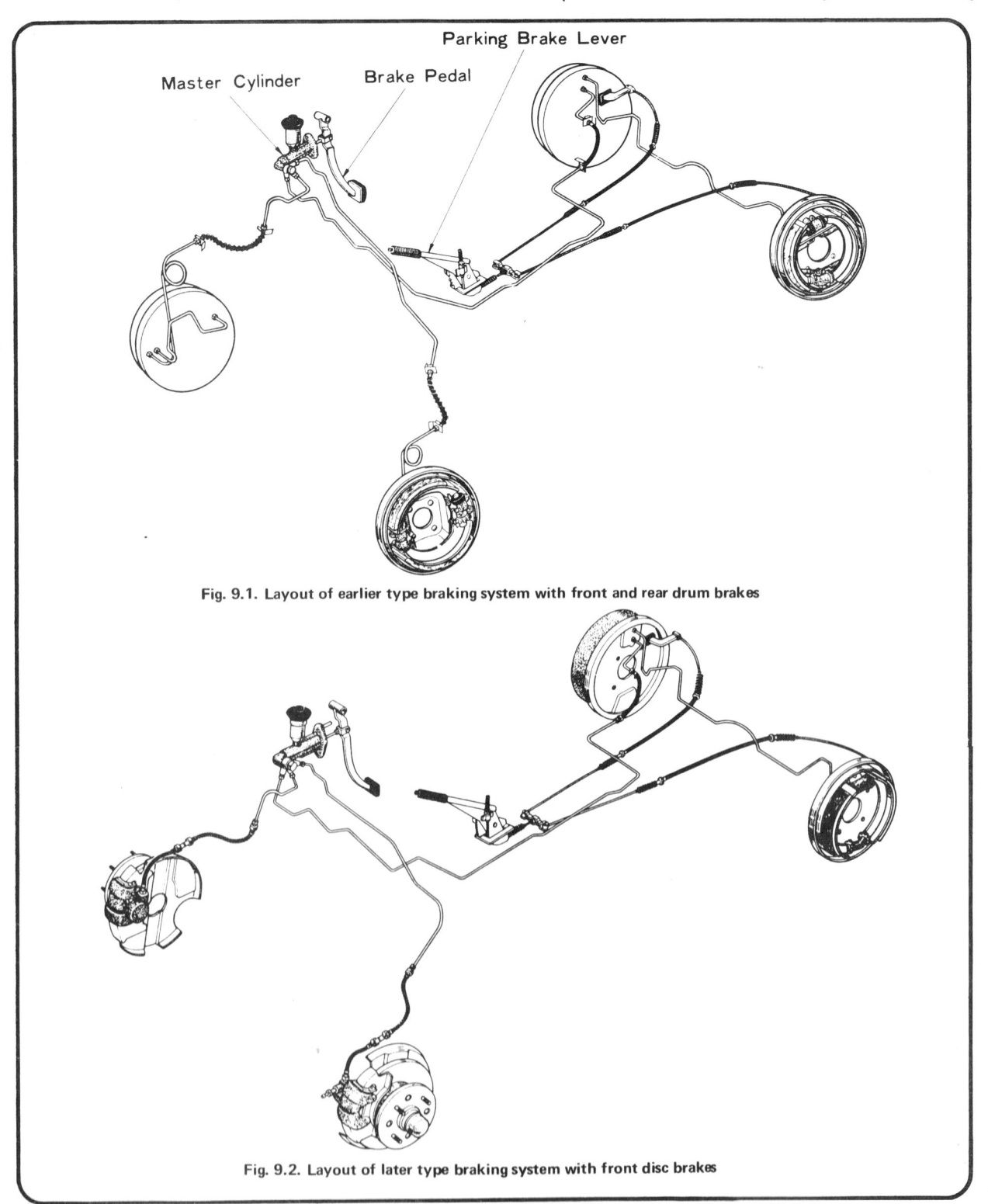

Fig. 9.1. Layout of earlier type braking system with front and rear drum brakes

Fig. 9.2. Layout of later type braking system with front disc brakes

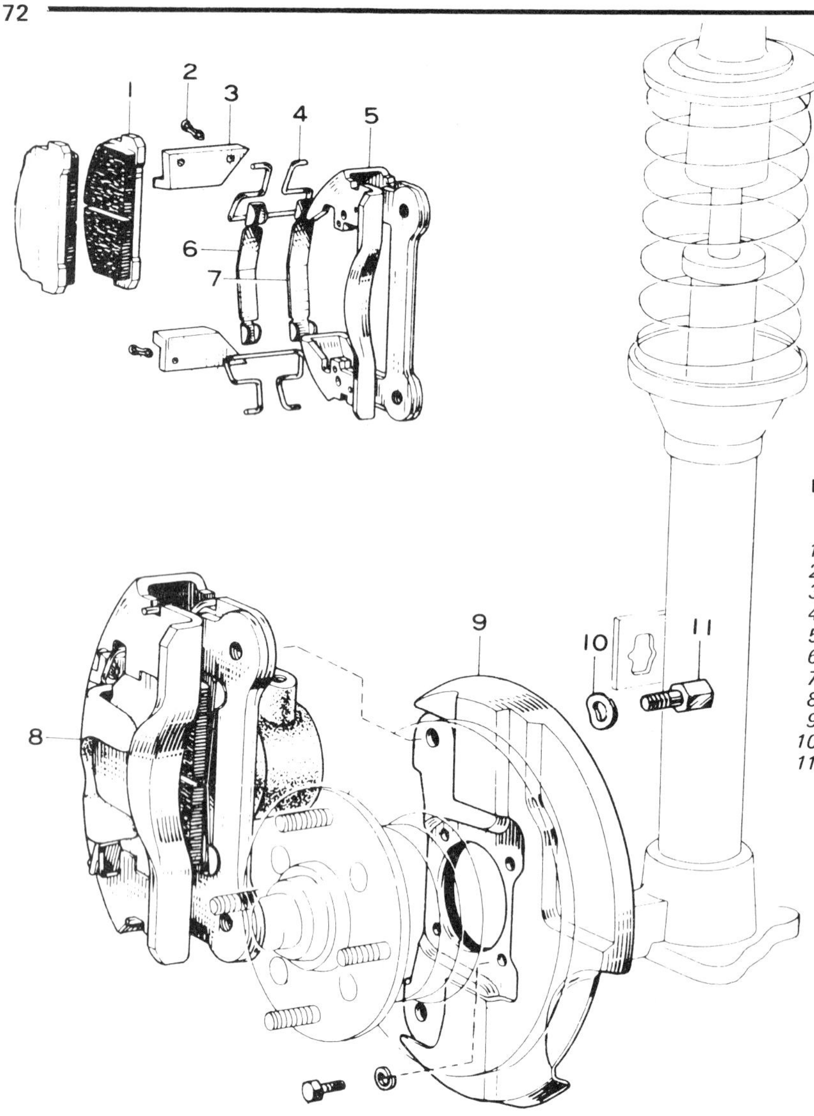

Fig. 9.3. Component parts of disc brake assembly

1 Disc brake pad
2 Clip
3 Disc brake guide
4 Cylinder support spring
5 Disc brake cylinder mounting
6 Pad support No. 2 plate
7 Pad support No. 1 plate
8 Disc brake left cylinder
9 Disc brake dust cover
10 Spring washer
11 Bolt

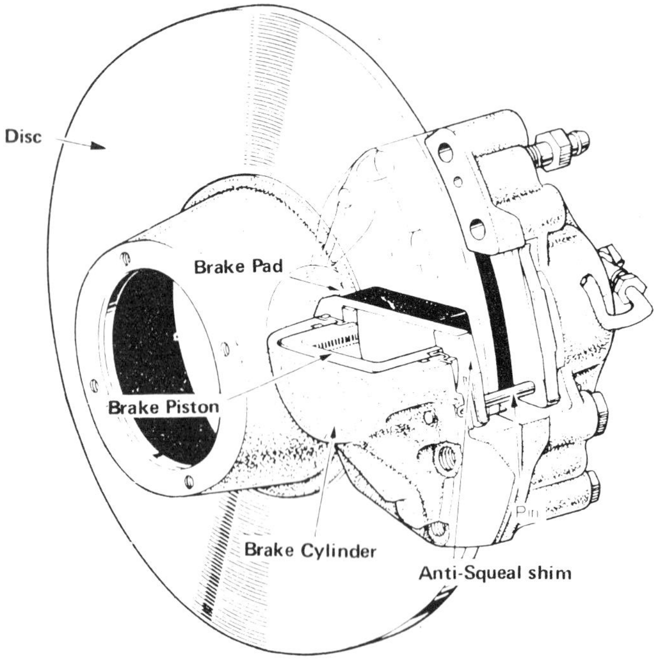

Fig. 9.4. Cross sectional view of disc brake assembly

Chapter 9/Braking system

to the front and rear brakes. If they are swollen, damaged or chafed, they must be renewed.

2 Wipe the top of the brake master cylinder reservoir(s) and unscrew the cap(s). Place a piece of polythene sheet over the top of the reservoir(s) and refit the cap(s). This is to stop hydraulic fluid syphoning out during subsequent operations.

3 Wipe the area around the unions and brackets free of dust and undo the union nuts from the metal pipe ends.

4 Undo and remove the locknuts and plain washers securing each flexible hose end to the bracket and lift away the hose end.

5 Unscrew the hose from the rear of the wheel cylinder or caliper and remove the hose.

6 Refitting a flexible hose is the reverse sequence to removal. It will be necessary to bleed the brake hydraulic system as described in Section 2. If one hose has been removed it is only necessary to bleed either the front or rear brake hydraulic system.

4 Front brake pads - removal, inspection and refitting

1 Apply the handbrake, remove the front wheel trim, slacken the wheel nuts, jack-up the front of the car and support on firmly based axle stands. Remove the front wheel.

2 Withdraw the spring clips from the end of the caliper cylinder guide using a pair of pliers. (photo)

3 Carefully ease out the two caliper cylinder guides (photo).

4 The caliper cylinder may now be lifted away from the mounting. (photo)

5 The pads may now be lifted from each side of the disc. (photo)

6 Pull off the complete hub and disc assembly from the stub axle.

7 Inspect the pad surface for excessive grooving which, if evident, the pad assembly should be renewed. It will also be necessary to inspect the disc surface and take the necessary action, (see Section 6 for further information). (photo)

8 Wipe down the caliper assembly and retract the piston into the cylinder. If this is difficult open the bleed screw so as to displace a little hydraulic fluid. Tighten the bleed screw again.

9 Refit the pads into their location in the cylinder mounting assembly and then replace the caliper.

10 Refit the caliper guides and retain with the clips.

11 If the bleed screw was opened it will be necessary to bleed the hydraulic system as described in Section 2.

12 Refit the road wheel and lower the car. Tighten the wheel nuts securely and replace the wheel trim.

13 To correctly seat the piston, pump the brake pedal several times and finally top-up the hydraulic fluid level in the master cylinder reservoir as necessary.

5 Front disc brake caliper - removal, overhaul and replacement

1 Refer to Section 3 and disconnect the flexible hose from the disc brake cylinder.

2 Withdraw the spring clips from the end of the guides using a pair of pliers.

3 Carefully ease out the two caliper cylinder guides.

4 The caliper cylinder may now be lifted away from the mounting.

5 Wipe the exterior of the cylinder to remove any dust and dirt with a non-fluffy rag.

6 Carefully remove the cylinder boot taking care not to damage it.

7 It is now necessary to eject the piston. This is easily done by using a compressed air jet in the bleed screw hole. Be careful not to damage the piston as it moves out.

8 The ring may now be removed from the piston.

9 Carefully inspect the cylinder bore and piston for signs of scoring, pitting or corrosion and, if evident, a new assembly will be required.

10 It is preferable for a new cylinder boot and piston ring to be fitted on reassembly.

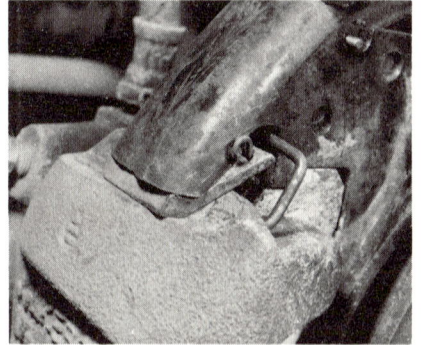

4.2 The spring clips must first be removed

4.3 Removal of caliper cylinder guide

4.4 Caliper cylinder removal

4.5 Lifting away the pads

4.7 The disc surface must be inspected before fitting new pads

11 Thoroughly wash all parts in clean hydraulic fluid and wipe dry with a clean non-fluffy rag.
12 Smear a little hydraulic fluid onto the piston and ring and fit the ring to the piston.
13 Smear a little clean hydraulic fluid or rubber grease onto the cylinder bore and carefully insert the piston into the bore.
14 Finally refit the rubber boot.
15 Refit the pads into their location in the cylinder mounting assembly and then replace the caliper cylinder.
16 Refit the cylinder guides and retain with the clips.
17 It will now be necessary to bleed the brake hydraulic system as described in Section 2.
18 Refit the roadwheel and lower the car. Tighten the wheel nuts securely and replace the wheel trim.
19 To correctly seat the piston, pump the brake pedal several times and finally top-up the hydraulic fluid level in the master cylinder as necessary.

6 Front brake disc and hub - removal and replacement

1 After jacking-up the car and removing the front wheel, remove the pads as described in Section 4. (photo)
2 Undo and remove the bolts and spring washers that secure the disc brake cylinder mounting assembly and lift away the complete assembly.
3 By judicious tapping and levering remove the dust cap from the centre of the hub.
4 Remove the split pin from the castellated nut and then remove the nut.
5 Lift away the thrust washer and outer bearing.
6 Pull off the complete hub and disc assembly from the stub axle.
7 From the back of the hub assembly carefully push out the grease seal and lift away the inner bearing.
8 Carefully clean out the hub and wash the bearings with petrol making sure that no grease or oil is allowed to get onto the brake disc.
9 Should it be necessary to separate the disc from the hub for renewal or regrinding, first bend back the locking tabs and undo the four securing bolts. With a scriber mark the relative positions of the hub and disc to ensure refitting in their original positions and separate the disc from the hub.
10 Thoroughly clean the disc and inspect for signs of deep scoring or excessive corrosion. If these are evident, the disc may be reground but no more than to give a total thickness of not less than 0.354 inch (9.0 mm). It is, however, more desirable to fit a new disc if possible.
11 To reassemble make quite sure that the mating faces of the disc and hub are very clean and place the disc on the hub, lining up any previously made marks.
12 Fit the four securing bolts and tabwashers (if fitted) and tighten the bolts in a progressive and diagonal manner. Bend up the locking tabs.
13 Work some grease well into the bearing, fully pack the bearing cages and rollers. Note: Leave the hub and grease seal empty to allow for subsequent expansion of the grease.
14 To reassemble the hub, first fit the inner bearing and then gently tap the grease seal back into the hub. A new seal must always be fitted, as during removal, it was probably damaged. The lip must face inwards to the hub.
15 Replace the hub and disc assembly onto the stub axle and slide on the outer bearing and thrust washer.
16 Fit the castellated nut and tighten to a torque wrench setting of 23 lb f ft (3.2 Kg fm). Now turn the disc several times to ensure the bearings have seated correctly.
17 Slacken the nut until it can be turned using the fingers and then retighten finger tight. This should give the required preload of between 5.5 and 13 oz.
18 Lock the castellated nut with a new split pin but do not bend over the ears yet.
19 If a dial indicator gauge is available, it is advisable to check the disc for run-out. The measurement should be taken as near to the edge of the worn yet smooth part of the disc, and must not exceed 0.006 inch (0.15 mm). If the figure obtained is found to be excessive, check the mating surfaces of the disc and hub for dirt or damage and also check the bearings and cups for excessive wear or damage.
20 If a dial indicator is not available the run-out can be checked by means of a feeler gauge placed between the cylinder mounting and the disc. Establish a reasonably tight fit with the feeler gauge between the top of the mounting and the disc and rotate the disc and hub. Any high or low spots will immediately become obvious by extra tightness or looseness of the fit of the feeler gauges. The amount of runout can be checked by adding or subtracting feeler gauges as necessary. It is only fair to point out that this method is not as accurate as when using a dial indicator gauge.
21 Once the disc runout has been checked and found to be correct bend the ends of the split pin back and replace the dust cap.

7 Front drum brake shoes - inspection, removal and refitting

After high mileages, it will be necessary to fit replacement shoes with new linings. Refitting new brake linings to shoes is not considered economic, or possible, without the use of special equipment. However, if the services of a local garage or workshop having brake relining equipment are available then there is no reason why the original shoes should not be successfully relined. Ensure that the correct specification linings are fitted to the shoes.
1 Check the rear wheels, jack-up the front of the car and place on firmly based axle stands. Remove the roadwheel.
2 Carefully ease off the hub dust cap.
3 Remove the split pin and castellated nut from the steering knuckle end and draw off the drum and hub assembly. If the drum is tight, back off the brake adjusters and using a soft faced hammer tap on the outer circumferences of the drum.
4 The brake linings should be renewed if they are so worn that the rivet heads are flush with the surface of the lining. If bonded linings are fitted, they must be renewed when the lining material has worn down to 0.6 inch (1.52 mm) at its thinnest part.
5 To remove the shoes remove the tension spring located on the cylinder piston side using a pair of pliers or a hook shaped tool as shown in Fig. 9.7.
6 Remove the hold down spring pin and spring using a pair of pliers to push and rotate through 90°.
7 Remove the brake shoe from the groove in the wheel cylinder piston and remove the brake shoe with the tension spring.
8 If the shoes are to be left off for a while, place a warning on the steering wheel as accidental depression of the brake pedal will eject the piston from the wheel cylinders.
9 Thoroughly clean all traces of dust from the shoes, backplate and drum using a stiff brush. It is recommended that compressed air is **not** used as it creates dust clouds. Brake shoe dust must not be inhaled. Excessive amounts of brake dust within the drum can cause judder or squeal. It is therefore, important to clean out as described.
10 Check that the piston is free in each cylinder, that the rubber dust covers are undamaged and in position and that there are no hydraulic fluid leaks.
11 Check the drum for signs of excessive wear, ovality or deep grooving. If any of these conditions exist the drum should either be renewed or skimmed on a lathe. If the latter course of action is taken the hub must be left attached.
12 The inner diameter must not exceed 7.95 inch (202 mm).
13 To separate the hub from the drum undo and remove the two securing screws and separate the two parts.
14 Refitting the drum to the hub is the reverse sequence to removal. Tighten the securing screws to a torque wrench setting of 7-12 lb f ft (1.0 - 1.6 Kg fm).
15 Inspect the tension spring for signs of weakness or distortion. The spring free length limit is 2.74 inch (69.6 mm) for the piston side and 2.68 inch (68.1 mm) for the adjuster side.

Chapter 9/Braking system

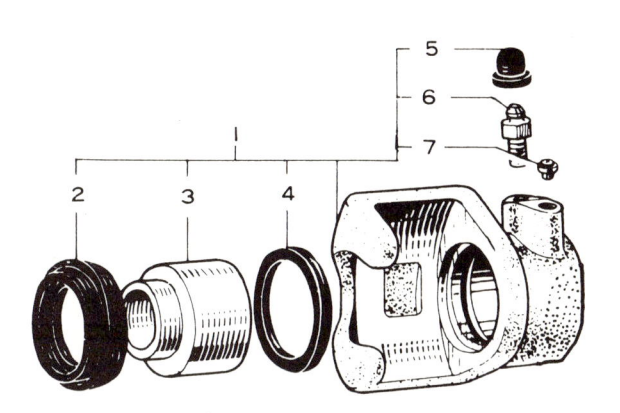

Fig. 9.5. Component parts of caliper cylinder assembly

1 Disc brake left cylinder assembly
2 Cylinder boot
3 Disc brake piston
4 Piston seal ring
5 Bleeder plug cap
6 Bleeder plug
7 Union seat

6.1 Disc and hub assembly with pads and caliper cylinder detached

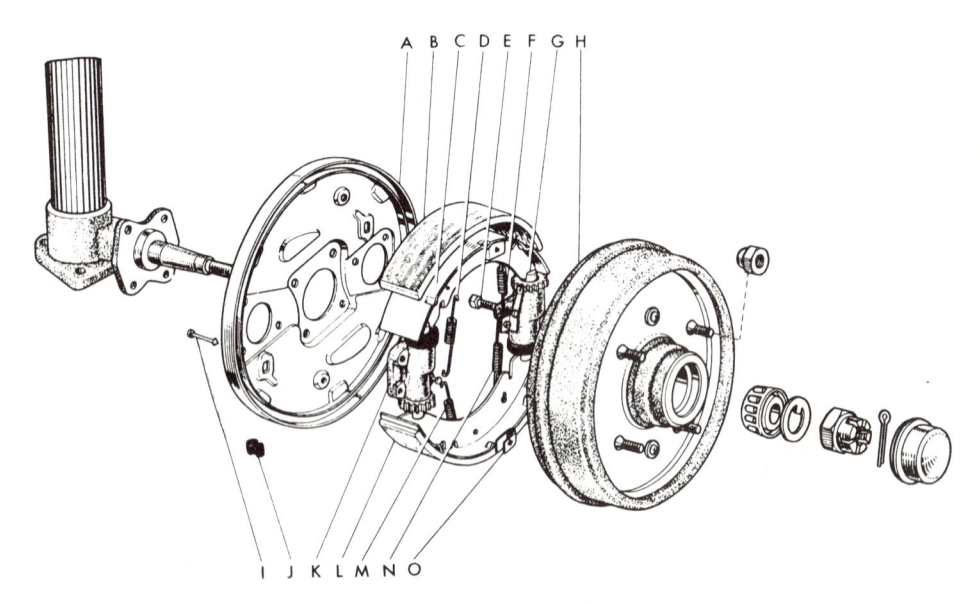

Fig. 9.6. Front drum brake assembly components

A Front brake backing plate
B Brake shoe lining
C Brake shoe
D Tension spring (dia. 1.4 mm)
E Shoe retracting spring hanger
F Tension spring (dia. 2.0 mm)
G Front No. 1 wheel brake cylinder (Front side)
H Front axle hub and brake drum
I Shoe hold-down spring pin
J Shoe adjusting hole plug
K Front No. 2 wheel brake cylinder (Rear side) (with bleeder plug)
L Brake shoe assembly No. 1
M Tension spring (dia. 2.0 mm)
N Tension spring (dia. 1.4 mm)
O Shoe hold-down spring

Fig. 9.7. Hook shaped tool for removal and refitment of brake shoe springs

16 To reassemble first apply a light coating of high melting point grease on the places where the brake shoes contact the backplate.
17 Hook the tension spring onto the spring hanger and the hole on the shoe located at the shoe adjuster side.
18 Next, fit the adjuster side end of the shoe into the groove of the shoe adjusting bolt. Expand and fit the second shoe end into the groove located in the wheel brake cylinder piston end.
19 Fit the shoe hold down spring and pin to the brake shoe web.
20 Follow this with the tension spring of the piston side using a pair of pliers.
21 Fit the second brake shoe in a similar manner to the first shoe.
22 Apply a light coating of chassis grease onto the lip of the 'V'

type oil seal located in the axle hub.
23 Refit the drum and hub assembly onto the steering knuckle.
24 Refit the thrust washer and castellated nut and tighten to a torque wrench setting of 19-23 lb f ft (2.6 - 3.2 Kg fm).
25 Rotate the hub and drum assembly in both directions to seat the bearings and check the hub for play in an axial direction.
26 Slacken the castellated nut until it can be turned freely with the fingers and then retighten the nut using a box spanner or socket, minus tommy bar handle.
27 Lock the castellated nut using a new split pin. If the split pin hole does not line up, slightly tighten the nut until the holes are in line. This should give the required bearing preload of 5.6-13.2 ounces (135 - 160 grms).
28 Adjust the front brakes as described in Section 10 and refit the roadwheel. Tighten the wheel nuts to a torque wrench setting of 65 - 85 lb f ft (9.0 - 12.0 Kg fm).
29 Lower the car and road test to ensure correct operation of the rear brakes.

8 Front drum brake wheel cylinder - removal, inspection and overhaul

If hydraulic fluid is leaking from the brake wheel cylinder, it will be necessary to dismantle it and replace the seals. Should brake fluid be found running down the side of the wheel, or if it is noticed that a pool of fluid forms alongside one wheel or the level in the master cylinder drops it is indicative of seal failure.
1 Refer to Section 7, and remove the brake drum and hub assembly and shoes. Clean down the rear of the backplate using a stiff brush. Place a quantity of rag under the backplate to catch any hydraulic fluid that may issue from the open pipe or wheel cylinder.
2 Wipe the top of the brake master reservoir and unscrew the cap. Place a piece of polythene sheet over the top of the reservoir and replace the cap. This is to stop hydraulic fluid syphoning out.

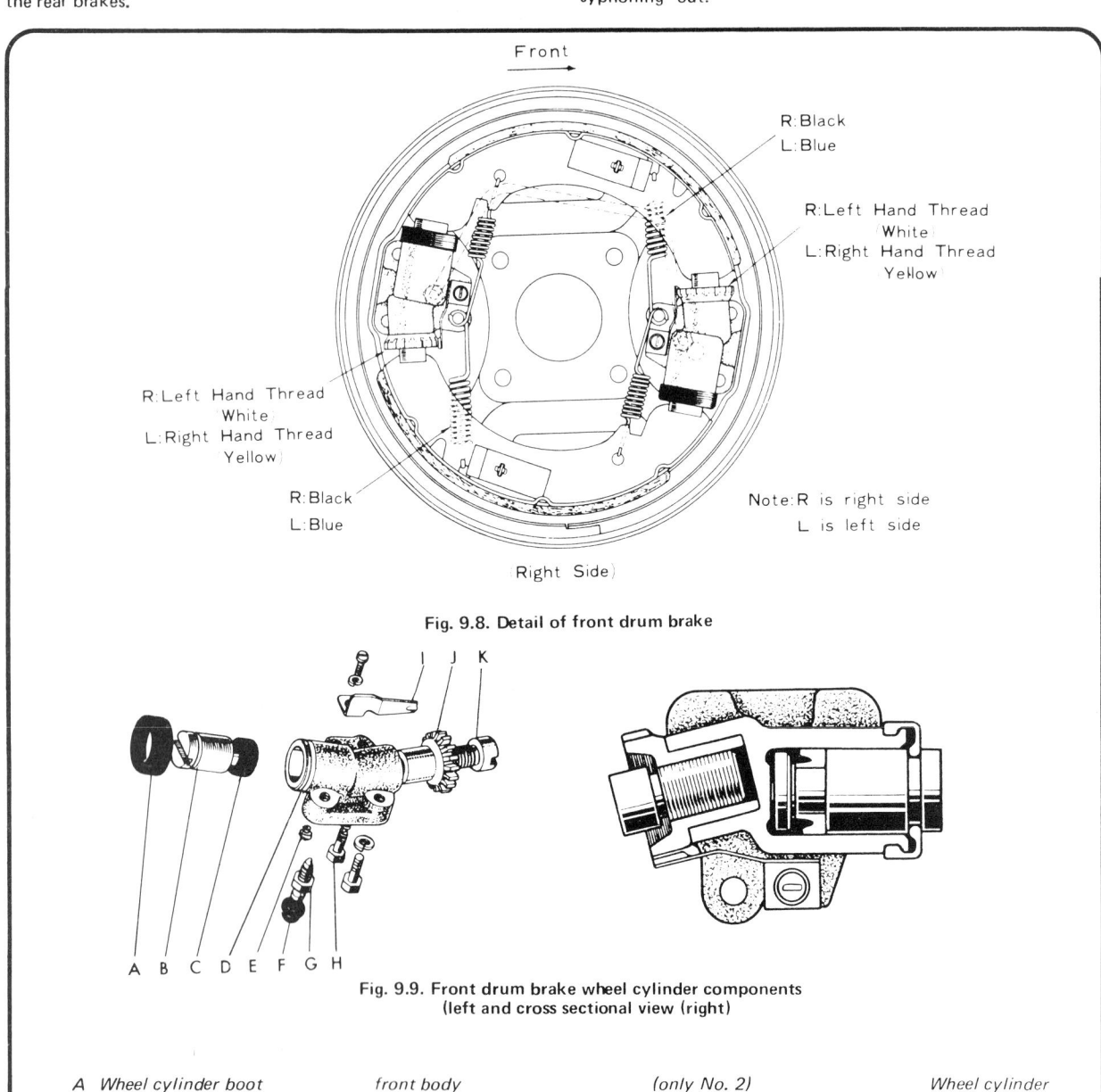

Fig. 9.8. Detail of front drum brake

Fig. 9.9. Front drum brake wheel cylinder components (left and cross sectional view (right)

A Wheel cylinder boot
B Wheel brake cylinder piston
C Cylinder cup
D Wheel brake cylinder front body
E Union seat
F Bleeder plug cap (only No. 2)
G Bleeder plug
H Shoe retracting spring hanger (only No. 2)
I Adjusting lock spring
J Adjusting nut
K Wheel cylinder adjusting bolt

Wheel cylinder

3 Using an open ended spanner remove the brake tube from the wheel cylinder by unscrewing the union nut.
4 Undo and remove the wheel cylinder to backplate securing screws and lift away the wheel cylinder.
5 To dismantle the wheel cylinder first ease off the rubber boot and adjuster lock spring from the cylinder body.
6 Pull out the adjusting nut from the cylinder body and detach the adjusting nut from the adjusting bolt.
7 Remove the piston and cylinder cap from the cylinder body.
8 Inspect the inside of the cylinder for score marks caused by impurities in the hydraulic fluid. If any are found, the cylinder and piston will require renewal. **Note:** If the wheel cylinder requires renewal always ensure that the replacement is exactly similar to the one removed.
9 If the cylinder is sound, throughly clean it out with fresh hydraulic fluid.
10 Inspect the piston for signs of score marks, damage or corrosion - if these maladies are evident the piston and cylinder must be renewed in a similar manner to that described in paragraph 8.
11 The inner diameter of the wheel cylinder must not exceed 0.758 inch (19.15 mm) and the diameter of the piston must not be less than 0.747 inch (18.98 mm). The clearance between the two parts must not exceed 0.006 inch (0.15 mm).
12 The old rubber seal will probably be swollen and visibly worn and should be renewed whenever the wheel cylinder is dismantled.
13 Wet all parts with fresh hydraulic fluid and fit the cap onto the piston. Make sure it is the correct way round.
14 Carefully insert the piston with cap attached into the cylinder bore ensuring that the edge of the cap does not roll when inserting into the bore.
15 Apply a little high melting point grease on the adjusting nut and bolt and screw the adjusting bolt into the nut.
16 **Note.** There are two types of adjusting bolt. They have left--hand and right-hand threads. The right-hand thread adjusting nut is coloured yellow and used for the left wheel. The left-hand thread adjusting nut is coloured white and used for the right wheel.
17 Fit the adjusting nut and bolt to the cylinder body.
18 Refit the adjusting lock spring onto the cylinder body and secure with the lock spring screw.
19 Refit the wheelcylinder to the backplate and secure with the two bolts and spring washers.
20 Reconnect the brake pipe to the rear of the wheel cylinder taking care not to cross-thread the union nut.
21 Refit the brake shoes and drum as described in Section 7.
22 Refer to Section 2, and bleed the brake hydraulic system.

9 Front drum brake backplate - removal and replacement

1 Refer to Section 7, and remove the drum and hub assembly.
2 Wipe the top of the brake master cylinder reservoir and unscrew the cap. Place a piece of polythene sheet over the top of the reservoir and replace the cap. This is to stop hydraulic fluid syphoning out.
3 Refer to Section 3, and detach the brake flexible hose. To prevent dirt ingress tape over the pipe end.
4 Undo and remove the four bolts and spring washers securing the backplate to the swivel hub assembly.
5 The brake backplate may now be lifted away.
6 Refitting is the reverse sequence to removal. It will be necessary to bleed the brake hydraulic system as described in Section 2.

10 Front drum brake - adjustment

1 Chock the rear wheels, apply the handbrake, jack-up the front of the car and support in firmly based axle stands.
2 Clean down the rear of the backplate and remove the shoe adjusting hole plugs from the backplate.

3 Expand one brake shoe by turning the wheel cylinder adjusting nut with a screwdriver until the wheel locks.
4 Depress the brake pedal several times to ensure the shoes contact the drum on the entire lining surface. If the wheel turns after this operation turn the adjusting nut further until the wheel locks firmly.
5 Back off the adjusting nut about 4 notches so that the drum rotates freely without signs of dragging.
6 Depress the brake pedal several times and ensure the wheel rotates freely.
7 Repeat the sequence described in paragraphs 3 to 6 inclusive for the second brake shoe.
8 Adjust the second front brake assembly shoes in a similar manner to that described earlier in this Section.

11 Rear drum brake shoes - inspection, removal and refitting

Earlier models

1 Refer to the introduction to Section 7.
2 Check the front wheels, jack-up the rear of the car and place on firmly based axle stands. Remove the roadwheel.
3 Release the handbrake and suitably mark the brake drum and axle shaft to ensure correct refitment.
4 Using a soft faced hammer on the outer circumference of the brake drum remove it from over the wheel studs. If it is tight release the brake shoe adjustment.
5 Refer to Section 7, and inspect the linings as described in paragraph 4.
6 To remove the brake shoes first release the tension spring which is located on the upper side of the brake shoes. Next release the tension spring located on the lower side of the brake shoes. For this a hook shaped tool will make the job far easier. (Fig. 9.7)
7 Release the shoe hold down spring from the brake shoe web using a pair of pliers to depress and turn through 90° so detaching it from the pin.
8 The brake shoes may now be lifted away.
9 If the shoes are to be left off for a while, place a warning on the steering wheel, as accidental depression of the brake pedal will eject the pistons from the wheel cylinder.
10 Whilst the shoes have been detached the handbrake bellcrank and strut should be examined for wear. If wear is evident, the linkage should be dismantled and overhauled.
11 Disconnect the handbrake cable from the bellcrank by removing the pin and tension spring connection to the bellcrank and bellcrank support plate.
12 Remove the bellcrank with the handbrake shoe strut from the brake backplate.
13 Remove the bellcrank boot and retainer located at the rear of the backplate.
14 Loosen and remove the 'C' washer which is located on the bellcrank pin. Detach the shoe strut from the bellcrank.
15 Thoroughly clean all traces of dust from the shoes, backplate and drum using a stiff brush. It is recommended that compressed air is **not** used as it creates dust clouds. Brake dust must not be inhaled. Excessive amounts of brake dust within the drums can cause judder or squeal - it is, therefore, important to clean out as described.
16 Check that the pistons are free in the cylinder, that the rubber dust covers are undamaged and in position, and that there are no hydraulic fluid leaks.
17 Check the operation of the adjuster to ensure that the adjusting nuts and bolts are free.
18 Inspect the tension springs for weakness. The free length of the wheel cylinder side spring should be less than 1.63 inch (41.4 mm). The free length of the adjuster cylinder side spring should be less than 2.68 inch (68.1 mm).
19 To reassemble first apply a light coating of high melting point grease on the places where the bellcrank contacts the shoe strut and assemble the shoe strut onto the bellcrank with the wave washer and 'C' type washer. Crimp the ears of the 'C' washer to

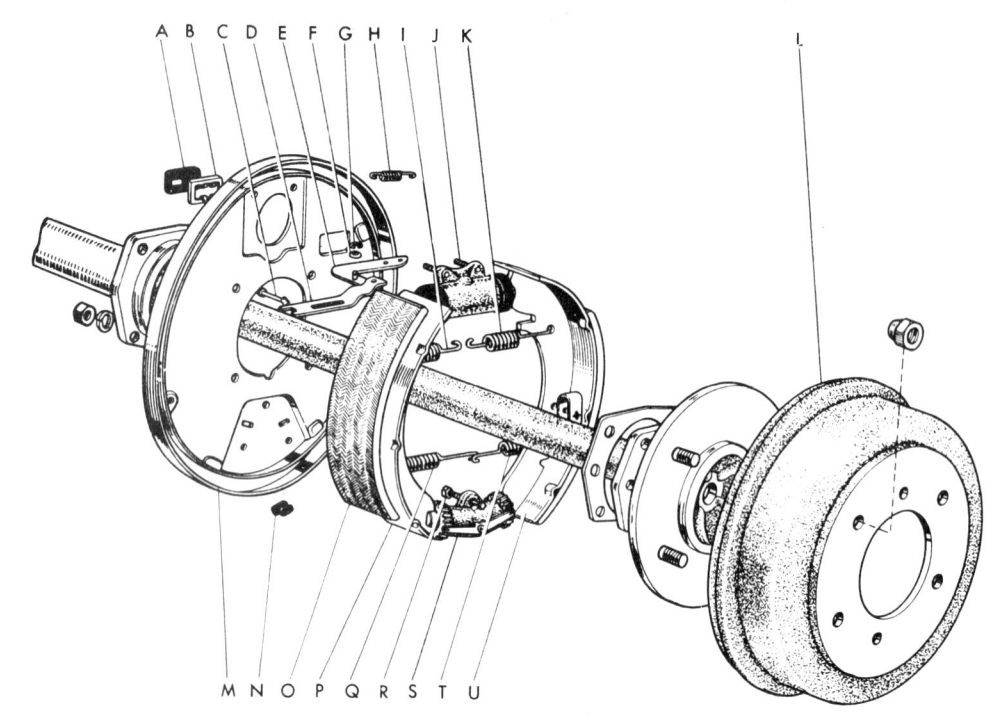

Fig. 9.10. Rear drum brake components (earlier type)

- A Bell crank boot
- B Bell crank boot retainer
- C Shoe hold-down spring pin
- D Parking brake shoe strut
- E Parking brake bell crank
- F Wave washer
- G 'C' type washer
- H Tension spring
- I Tension spring (dia. 1.4 mm)
- J Rear wheel brake cylinder
- K Tension spring (dia. 1.4 mm)
- L Brake drum
- M Rear backing plate
- N Shoe adjusting hole plug
- O Brake shoe lining
- P Brake shoe
- Q Tension spring (dia. 2.0 mm)
- R Shoe retracting spring hanger
- S Adjusting cylinder
- T Tension spring (dia. 2.0 mm)
- U Brake shoe assembly

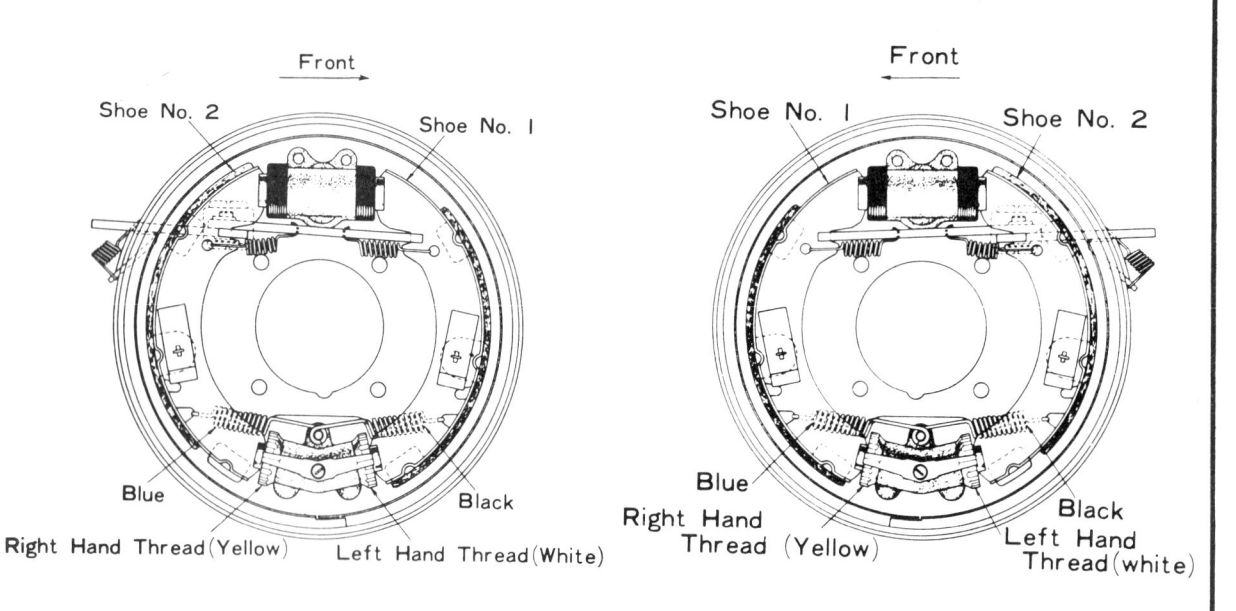

Fig. 9.11. Rear drum brake detail (earlier type)

Chapter 9/Braking system

prevent it dropping out.
20 Fit the bellcrank boot retainer and boot onto the backing plate, and install the bellcrank with the shoe strut onto the backing plate.
21 Hook the end of the tension spring onto the bellcrank and hook the other end of the spring onto the bellcrank support located on the backplate.
22 Connect the handbrake cable onto the bellcrank, insert the pin and lock it with a new split pin.
23 Smear a trace of brake grease on the shoe support pads, brake shoe pivots and on the adjuster nut and bolt threads.
24 Check which is the correct way round the tension spring is to be fitted and hook the end of the adjuster side tension spring into the hole located on the brake shoe. Hook the other end of the spring onto the shoe retracting spring hanger with a suitable hook shaped tool or a screwdriver. (photo)
25 Fit the shoe hold down spring and pin onto the brake shoe web.
26 Fit the piston side tension spring onto the brake shoe.
27 The second brake shoe is fitted in the same manner as the first spring.
28 Align the previously made marks and fit the brake drum onto the axle shaft. Replace the roadwheel and nuts and lower the car to the ground. Tighten the wheel nuts to a torque wrench setting of 65-85 lb f ft (9.0-12.0 Kg fm).
29 The shoes must next be centralised by the brake pedal being depressed firmly several times and then adjusted as described in Section 15.

Later Models.

The sequence for dismantling the rear brake assembly is slightly different and the following sequence should be followed.
30 Refer to paragraphs 1 to 5 inclusive. (photos)
31 Using a pair of pliers rotate each shoe holding down spring clip through 90° to disengage it from the pin attached to the backplate. Lift away the spring clip. (photo)
32 Ease one shoe from the wheel cylinder so as to release the upper spring tension. (photo)
33 Using a pair of pliers detach the upper spring from the shoe web. Make a note of the spring location and which way round it is fitted.
34 Detach the shoe from the lower tension spring beneath the anchor plate.
35 Pivot the second shoe and handbrake lever assembly downwards to give access to the handbrake cable. (photos)
36 Detach the handbrake cable from the handbrake lever and lift away the second shoe assembly.
37 To remove the relay lever assembly, using a screwdriver push open the 'U' clip on the rear brake shoe and lift away the relay lever assembly. The 'U' clip must be discarded and a new one obtained ready for reassembly.
38 Inspection and cleaning of the brake assembly is similar to that described earlier in this Section. (photo)
39 Prior to reassembly smear a trace of brake grease on the shoe support pads, brake shoe pivots and on the adjuster threads.
40 To reassemble first fit the relay lever assembly to the rear

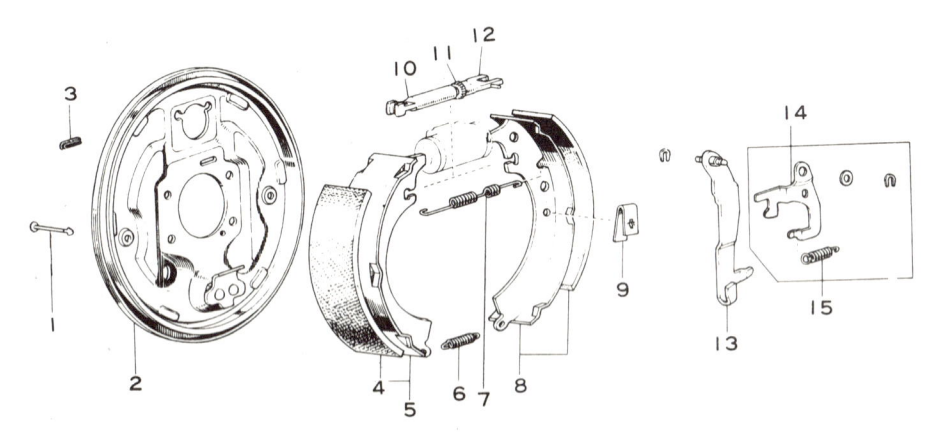

Fig. 9.12. Rear drum brake components (later type)

1 Pin, shoe hold down spring
2 Plate, brake backing
3 Plug, shoe adjusting hole
4 Lining, brake shoe
5 Shoe assembly, brake No. 2
6 Spring, tensioner (for anchor)
7 Spring, tension
8 Shoe assembly, brake No. 3
9 Spring, shoe hold down
10 Strut, parking brake shoe No. 2
11 Bolt, with strut, left
12 Piece, shoe support
13 Lever, parking brake shoe No. 2
14 Lever, adjuster
15 Spring, tension

11.30a Removal of brake drum

11.30b Lining inspection

11.31 Brake shoe hold down spring

11.32 Detail of shoe attachment at wheel cylinder end

11.35a Removal of brake shoe

11.35b Rear shoe and handbrake cable link (later type)

11.38 Backplate assembly cleaned

11.43a Correct fitment of brake shoes

11.43b Latest type shoe and adjuster layout

brake shoe and retain in position using a new 'U' clip. Using a pair of pliers close up the ends of the clip.

41 Fit the retracting springs to the rear shoe web in the same position as was noted during removal. Replace the adjusting strut.

42 Position the rear brake shoe on the anchor plate and attach the handbrake cable to the lever.

43 Fit the second shoe to the anchor plate with the top end adjacent to the wheel cylinder and attach the two springs. (photos)

44 Carefully lever the second shoe into position on the wheel cylinder.

45 Place each shoe holding down clip on its pin. Compress with a pair of pliers and rotate through 90° to lock in position. Make sure each shoe is firmly seated on the backplate.

46 Rotate the strut until all shake in the strut is removed.

47 Refit the brake drum and push it up the studs as far as it will go. Replace the road wheel and adjust the brakes as described in Section 15.

12 Rear drum brake wheel cylinder - removal, inspection and overhaul.

1 Refer to the introduction to Section 8.

2 Refer to Section 11, and remove the brake drum and shoes. Clean down the rear of the backplate using a stiff brush. Place a quantity of rag under the backplate to catch any hydraulic fluid that may issue from the open pipe or wheel cylinder.

3 Wipe the top of the brake master cylinder reservoir and unscrew the cap. Place a piece of polythene sheet over the top of the reservoir and replace the cap. This is to stop hydraulic fluid syphoning out.

4 Using an open ended spanner carefully unscrew the hydraulic pipe connection union to the rear of the wheel cylinder. To

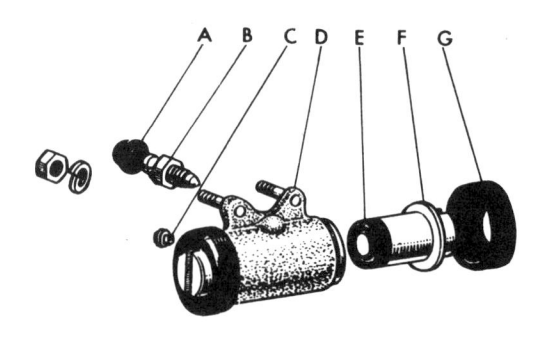

Fig. 9.13. Rear drum brake wheel cylinder components

A Bleeder plug cap (only for left side wheel)
B Bleeder plug (only for left side wheel)
C Union seat
D Rear wheel brake cylinder body
E Cylinder cup
F Rear wheel brake cylinder piston
G Wheel brake cylinder boot

prevent dirt ingress tape over the pipe end.

5 Undo and remove the two nuts and spring washers that secure the wheel cylinder to the brake backplate.

6 Withdraw the wheel cylinder from the front of the brake backplate.

7 To dismantle the wheel cylinder first ease off the rubber boots from the ends of the wheel cylinder.

8 The cylinder caps and piston assemblies may now be withdrawn from the wheel cylinder body.

9 Inspect the inside of the cylinder for score marks caused by impurities in the hydraulic fluid. If any are found, the cylinder

Chapter 9/Braking system

and pistons will require renewal. **Note:** If the wheel cylinder requires renewal always ensure that the replacement is exactly similar to the one removed.

10 If the cylinder is sound, thoroughly clean it out using fresh hydraulic fluid.

11 Inspect the pistons for signs of score marks, corrosion or other damage. If any of these maladies are evident the pistons and cylinder must be renewed in a similar manner to that described in paragraph 9.

12 The inner diameter of the cylinder body should be less than 0.691 inch (17.55 mm) and the diameter of the piston should be more than 0.685 inch (17.40 mm).

13 The clearance between the piston and cylinder bore should not exceed 0.06 inch (0.15 mm).

14 The old rubber seals will probably be swollen and visibly worn and ideally should be renewed whenever the wheel cylinder is dismantled.

15 Wet all parts with fresh hydraulic fluid and fit the seals to the pistons. Make sure they are the correct way round.

16 Carefully insert the piston and seal assemblies into the cylinder bore ensuring that the edges of the seals are not damaged as they are inserted into the bore.

17 Position the rubber boots on each end of the wheel cylinder.

18 Refit the wheel cylinder to the backplate and secure with the two bolts and spring washers.

19 Reconnect the brake pipe to the rear of the wheel cylinder taking care not to cross-thread the union nut.

20 Refit the brake shoes and drum as described in Section 11.

21 Refer to Section 2, and bleed the brake hydraulic system.

13 Rear drum brake backplate - removal and replacement

1 To remove the backplate first refer to Chapter 8 and remove the axle shaft.

2 Detach the handbrake cable from the handbrake lever at the rear of the backplate.

3 Wipe the top of the master cylinder reservoir and unscrew the cap. Place a piece of polythene sheet over the top of the reservoir and replace the cap. This is to stop hydraulic fluid syphoning out.

4 Using an open ended spanner carefully unscrew the hydraulic pipe connection union to the rear of the wheel cylinder. To prevent dirt ingress tape over the pipe end.

5 The brake backplate may now be lifted away.

6 Refitting is the reverse sequence to removal. It will be necessary to bleed the brake hydraulic system as described in Section 2.

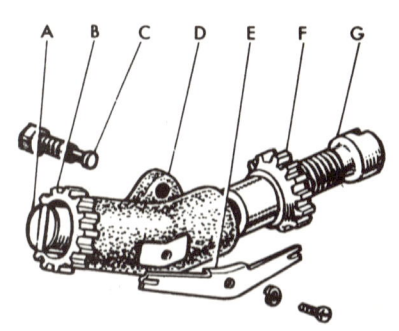

14 Rear drum brake adjuster - removal, overhaul and replacement

This Section is only applicable to early models with backplate mounted adjuster.

1 Refer to Section 11, and remove the brake drums and shoes.

2 Undo and remove the bolt and washer securing the adjuster to the brake backplate. Lift away the adjuster.

3 Remove the adjuster lock spring from the adjuster cylinder body by removing the securing screw and washer.

4 Remove the adjusting nut and bolt assembly from each end of the adjuster body. Unscrew the bolt from the adjuster nut.

5 Inspect the adjuster cylinder, adjusting nut and bolt for signs of scouring, rust, seizure or other damage. If evident a new adjuster assembly should be obtained.

6 To reassemble the adjuster is the reverse sequence to removal. Lubricate the cylinder bore with a little high melting point grease. Note the adjusting bolt has a left or right-hand thread. The right-hand threaded nut is coloured yellow and is used for the rear side of the right wheel and the front side of the left wheel. The left-hand threaded nut is coloured white and is used for the front side of the right wheel and the rear side of the left wheel.

15 Rear drum brake adjustment.

1 Chock the front wheels, jack-up the rear of the car and support on firmly based axle stands. Release the handbrake.

2 Remove the adjuster hole plug and with a screwdriver rotate each adjuster nut so as to expand the brake shoes. (photo)

3 Depress the brake pedal several times and check that the shoes are hard against the drums by trying to rotate the roadwheel.

4 Back off the adjuster nuts by four notches and check that the roadwheel is free to rotate.

5 Check the travel of the handbrake lever. When correctly adjusted it should have a ratchet movement of between 5 and 9 notches. Usually by adjusting the rear brakes the handbrake is automatically adjusted but when the cables have stretched it will be necessary to adjust the handbrake independently of the rear brakes. Further information will be found in Section 16.

16 Handbrake - adjustment

1 Check the front wheels and release the handbrake. Slowly apply the handbrake and count the number of notches on the

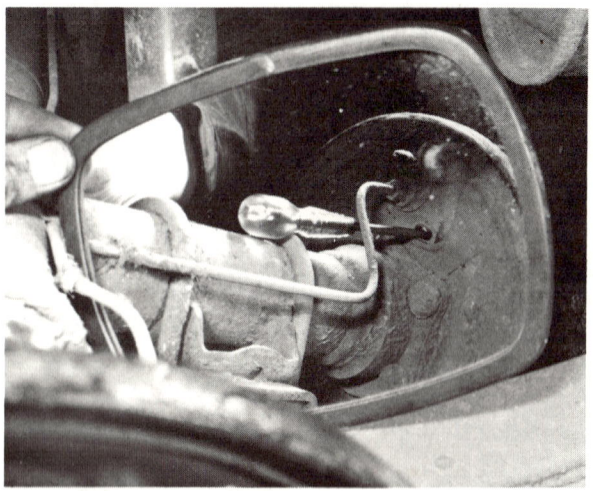

Fig. 9.14. Rear drum brake adjuster assembly components

A Left wheel cylinder adjusting bolt (LH thread)
B Left wheel cylinder adjusting nut (LH thread)
C Shoe retracting spring hanger
D Shoe adjuster body
E Adjuster lock spring
F Right wheel cylinder adjusting bolt (RH thread)
G Right wheel cylinder adjusting bolt (RH thread)

15.2 Adjustment of rear brakes

ratchet before it is fully applied. When correctly adjusted this should be between 5 and 9.
2 Refer to Section 15, and adjust the rear brakes.
3 Adjustment of the cable is carried out inside the car. Remove any excess carpeting from the base of the handbrake lever.
4 Slacken the cable locknut and screw in the adjusting cap nut until the correct ratchet travel is obtained. Retighten the locknut.
5 Release the handbrake and with the rear of the car suitably supported check that the rear wheels can be rotated without signs of binding.

17 Handbrake lever and cable assembly - removal and replacement.

1 Chock the front wheels, jack-up the rear of the car and support on firmly based axle stands. To give better access remove the rear wheels.
2 Release the handbrake and detach the No 2 cable from the bellcrank by removing the split pin and clevis pin (early models). Later models - remove the brake drum and detach the cable from the bellcrank lever.

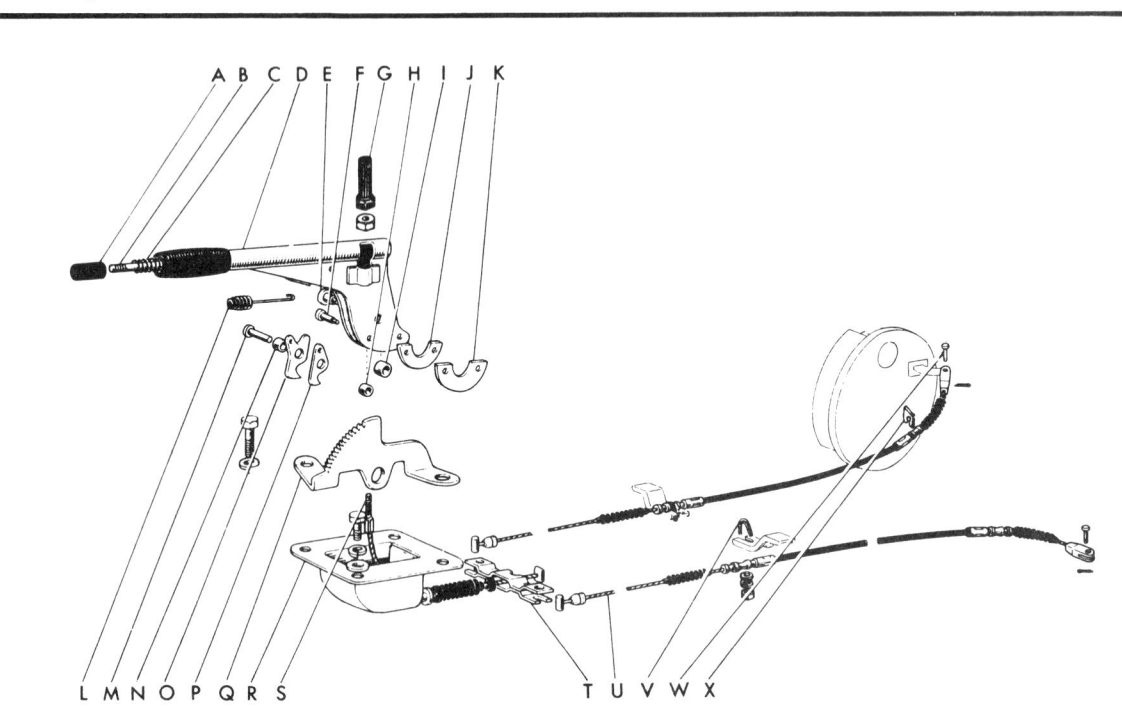

Fig. 9.15. Handbrake lever and cable assembly components

A   Hand brake release rod knob
B   Hand brake pawl release rod
C   Compression spring
D   Hand brake lever
E   Lever pivot pin
F   Pin
G   Wire adjusting cap
H   Spacer
I   Spacer
J   Hand brake cable guide
K   Hand brake cable guide support
L   Tension spring
M   Pin
N   Spacer
O   Hand brake pawl No. 2
P   Hand brake pawl No. 1
Q   Hand brake lever sector
R   Hand brake lever boot
S   Hand brake cable No. 1
T   Hand brake equalizer
U   Hand brake cable No. 2
V   Cable clamp
W   Pin
X   Cable clip

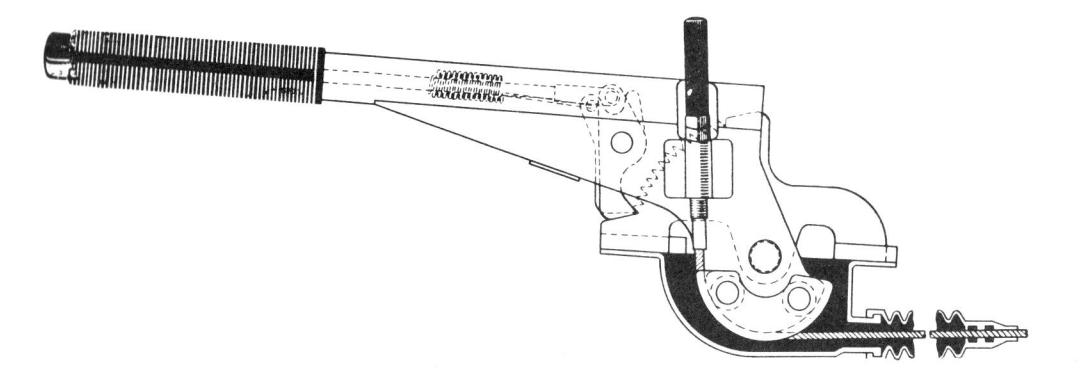

Fig. 9.16. Cross sectional view of handbrake lever assembly

Chapter 9/Braking system

3 Remove the cable clip which is located on the rear axle housing.
4 Refer to Chapter 7, and remove the propeller shaft.
5 Remove the cable clamp by slackening or removing the clamp attaching nut located under the centre of the floor panel.
6 Remove the grommet from the cable guide located under the centre of the floor panel.
7 Disconnect the front end of the No 2 cable from the handbrake cable equalizer.
8 Remove the interior floor matting from the handbrake area.
9 Remove the handbrake lever assembly lever boot, No. 1 cable and equalizer by undoing and removing the four securing bolts and spring washers.
10 Remove the cable adjusting cap and lock nut located on the end of the No 1 cable. Now remove the No 1 cable with the lever boot from the handbrake lever.
11 Remove the No 1 cable from the lever boot.
12 Remove the end cover which is located on the rear end of the No 1 cable and then detach the equalizer from the No 1 cable.
13 It is possible to dismantle the handbrake lever to renew the ratchet and pawl but first ensure that spare parts are available.
14 Using a 0.24 inch (6 mm) drill remove the three pawl pin leads and drive out the pins using a suitable diameter punch.
15 Grind or file the lever pivot pin head and drive out the lever pivot pin using a suitable diameter punch.
16 Remove the release rod from the handbrake lever and lift out the handbrake lever components.
17 Inspect the two cables for signs of wear, rust and ease of movement of the inner cable in the outer cable.
18 Inspect the handbrake equaliser and boot for signs of damage or wear.
19 If the lever assembly has been dismantled check the ratchet (sector), pawls, spacer and release rod for wear and damage. Finally check the tension and compression springs for weakness, damage or deformation.
20 To reassemble the handbrake lever first assemble pawl No 1 and No 2, the spacer and tension spring onto the pawl release rod. Insert these parts in the handbrake lever.
21 Carefully align the spacer located on the centre of the pawl with the hole located on the centre of the lever and fit the pin into the hole using a centre punch.
22 Using a hammer peen the pin to stop it working out.
23 Assemble the sector and spacer onto the rear end of the lever and fit the lever pivot pin and spacer onto the rear end of the lever. Peen the pivot pin using a hammer.
24 Assemble the cable guides, cable guide support and the two spacers onto the lever and retain with the two pins. Peen the pins using a centre punch.
25 Insert the compression spring into the lever and fit the release rod knob into the lever until the protruding length of the knob is 0.36 -0.4 inch (9.10 mm).
26 The assembly is now ready for refitting to the car. First fit the equaliser onto the No 1 cable.
27 Smear a little grease at the moving point on the No 1 cable and fit the lever boot and No 1 cable onto the lever, aligning the No 1 cable with the cable guide.
28 Fit the nut and cable adjustment cap nut onto the end of the No 1 cable.
29 Replace the handbrake lever assembly and secure with the four bolts and washers which should be tightened to a torque wrench setting of 7-12 lb f ft (1.0-1.6 Kg fm).
30 Connect each front end of the No 2 cable onto both ends of the equaliser.
31 Fit the grommet located at the front end of the No 2 cable to the cable guide which is located under the floor centre panel.
32 Fit the rear of the No 2 cable onto the handbrake bellcrank, insert the clevis pin and lock it with a new split pin.
33 Fit the rear end of the No 2 outer cable onto the bracket located on the rear axle housing by installing the clip.
34 Fit the front end of the No 2 outer cable onto the bracket located under the centre of the floor panel and lock with the cable clamp nuts which should be tightened to a torque wrench setting of 11-16 lb f ft (1.5-2.2 Kg fm). **Important**: When fitting the cable clamp it should be fitted to the 'A' groove located on the front end of the No 2 outer cable. However if easier the 'B' groove may be used instead. (Fig 9.17)
35 Refit the propeller shaft as described in Chapter 7 and then the brake drum (later models) and road wheel.
36 Refer to Section 16 and adjust the handbrake cable.

18 Brake pedal travel - adjustment

1 For safety reasons disconnect the battery and then the stop light switch terminal connectors.
2 Slacken the stop light switch locknut and adjust the pedal height to 5.5 - 6.0 inch (140 - 150 mm) between the pedal and the floor mat by rotating the stop light switch.
3 Tighten the stop light switch locknut.
4 Slacken the master cylinder pushrod locknut and adjust the length of the pushrod to give a clearance of 0.02-0.12 inch (0.5-3.0 mm) between the pushrod and piston. Retighten the pushroad locknut. Reconnect the stop light switch wire terminals and battery.

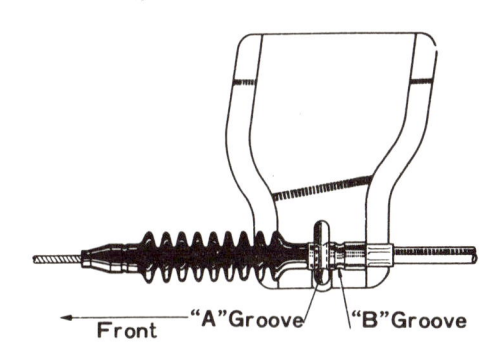

Fig. 9.17. Installation of No. 2 outer cable

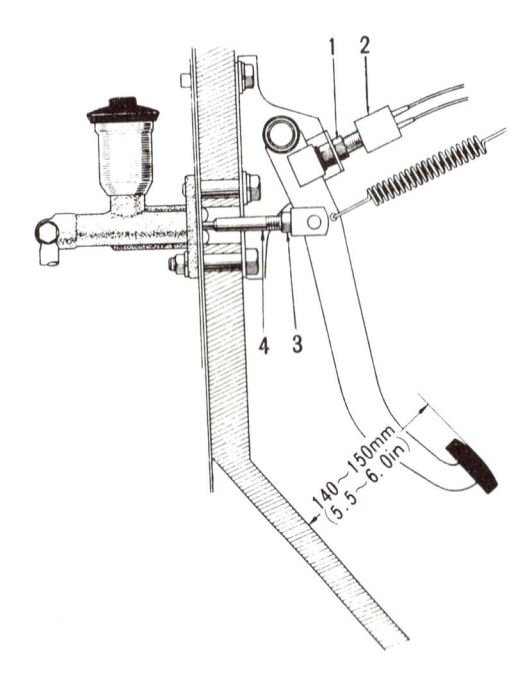

Fig. 9.18. Brake pedal adjustment

1 Locknut
2 Stop light switch
3 Locknut
4 Pushrod

19 Brake pedal - removal and replacement

1 Refer to Chapter 5, and remove the clutch pedal and clutch release lever.
2 Detach the brake pedal return spring.
3 Remove the split pin and cotter pin from the pushrod clevis.
4 Undo and remove the two bolts and washers and remove the pedal support shaft base from the pedal support.
5 Lift away the brake pedal and master cylinder pushrod.
6 Inspect the pedal rubber pad for wear or damage and renew if necessary.
7 Carefully inspect the brake pedal for signs of damage or distortion.
8 Check that the pedal support shaft boss is not damaged or the bushing worn.
9 Inspect the pedal return spring for weakness or deformation and obtain new if evident.
10 Check the master cylinder pushrod clevis and pin for damage or wear.
11 To reassemble first apply a little grease onto the bushes and brake pedal boss. Fit the bushes into the brake pedal base.
12 Replace the master cylinder pushrod and fit the brake pedal to the pedal support. Insert the pedal support shaft boss into the support.
13 Connect the master cylinder pushrod to the brake pedal, line up the clevis and insert the pin. Lock with a new split pin.
14 Refit the clutch release lever with bushes onto the pedal support shaft boss and fit the clutch pedal, lock washer and nut onto the clutch release lever shaft. Tighten the nut to a torque wrench setting of 36-50 lb f ft (5-7 Kg f m).
15 Refer to Section 18, and adjust the brake pedal travel.

20 Brake master cylinder (single) - removal and replacement

1 Apply the handbrake, and check the front wheels. Drain the fluid from the master cylinder reservoir and master cylinder by attaching a plastic bleed tube to one of the brake bleed screws. Unscrew the screw one turn and then pump the fluid out into a clean glass jar by means of the brake pedal. Hold the brake pedal against the floor at the end of each stroke and tighten the bleed screw. When the pedal has returned to its normal position loosen the bleed screw and repeat the process until the reservoir is empty.
2 Wipe the area around the three-way connection on the master cylinder body and unscrew the union bolt and washers. Tape over the end of the three-way connection to prevent dirt ingress.
3 Undo and remove the two master cylinder securing nuts and lift away the master cylinder.
4 Be careful not to allow hydraulic fluid to contact the paintwork as it acts as a solvent.
5 Refitting the master cylinder is the reverse sequence to removal. It will be necessary to bleed the hydraulic system: full details will be found in Section 2.

21 Brake master cylinder (single) - dismantling, examination and reassembly

If a replacement master cylinder is to be fitted, it will be necessary to lubricate the seals before fitting to the car as they have a protective coating when originally assembled. Remove the blanking plug from the end of the master cylinder. Inject clean hydraulic fluid into the master cylinder and push in the piston several times so that fluid spreads over all the internal working surfaces.
To dismantle the master cylinder after removal proceed as follows:
1 Drain any fluid from the reservoir or master cylinder body.
2 Remove the rubber boot from the end of the master cylinder body.
3 Using a pair of circlip pliers remove the snapring (circlip)

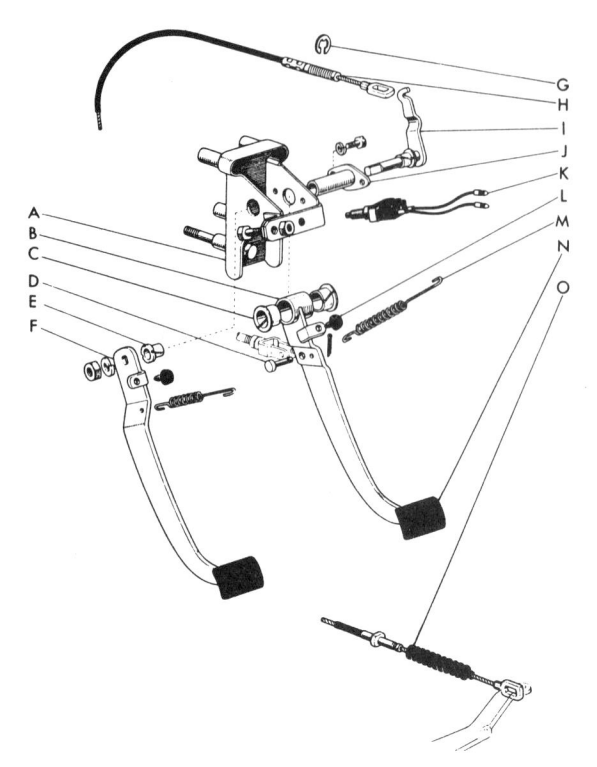

Fig. 9.19. Brake and clutch pedal assembly components

A Pedal support	I Clutch release lever
B Brake pedal	J Pedal support shaft
C Bushing	boss
D W/hole pin	K Stop light switch
E Bushing	L Cushion
F Clutch pedal	M Tension spring
G 'E' ring	N Pedal pad
H Clutch release cable	O Clutch cable boot

from the end of the cylinder bore.
4 Remove the piston assembly from the cylinder bore and then the primary cup, spring and outlet check valve using a compressed air jet.
5 Using a suitable screwdriver remove the reservoir securing bolt and washer and lift away the reservoir.
6 Make a careful note of the location of the seal on the piston and remove the seal.
7 Examine the bore of the cylinder carefully for any signs of scores or ridges. If this is found to be smooth all over new seals can be fitted. If however, there is any doubt about the condition of the bore then a new cylinder must be fitted.
8 If examination of the seals shows them to be apparently over size or swollen, or very loose on the piston, suspect oil contamination in the system. Oil will swell these rubber seals, and if one is found to be swollen, it is reasonable to assume that all seals in the braking system will need renewal.
9 Thoroughly clean all parts in clean hydraulic fluid or methylated spirits. Ensure that all drillings are clean.
10 If possible measure the cylinder bore diameter - it must not exceed 0.6272 inch (15.93 mm). Also measure the piston diameter; this must not be less than 0.6213 inch (15.78 mm). The cylinder to piston clearance must not be more than 0.006 inch (0.15 mm).
11 Inspect the piston return spring for signs of weakness. The free-length must not exceed 2.4 inch (60 mm).
12 Check that the air hole in the cap is not blocked.
13 All components should be assembled wet by dipping in clean brake fluid. Handle the cup seals with fingers only.
14 Fit the reservoir onto the master cylinder body and secure with the bolt which should be tightened to a torque wrench

Chapter 9/Braking system

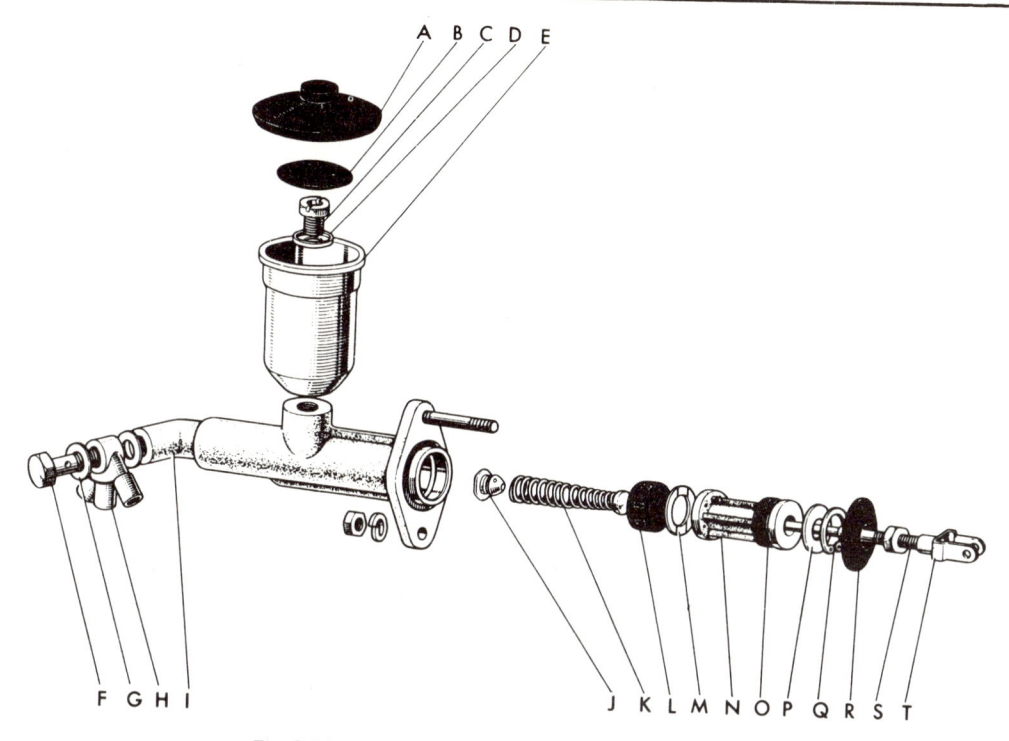

Fig. 9.20. Master cylinder components (single)

- A Reservoir filler cap
- B Reservoir float
- C Reservoir attaching bolt
- D Reservoir attaching bolt washer
- E Reservoir
- F Union bolt
- G Gasket
- H Three-way connection
- I Master cylinder body
- J Outlet check valve
- K Piston return spring
- L Cylinder cup (primary cup)
- M Piston cup spacer
- N Master cylinder piston
- O Cylinder cup (secondary cup)
- P Plain washer
- Q Hole snap ring
- R Master cylinder boot
- S Master cylinder push rod
- T Push rod clevis

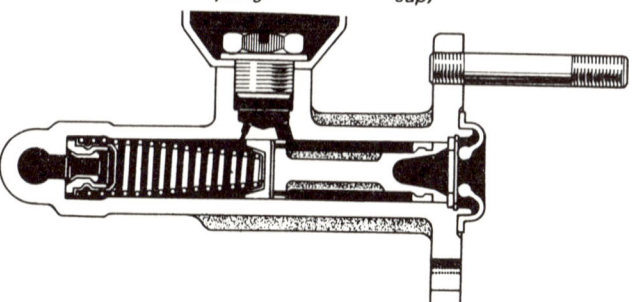

Fig. 9.21. Cross sectional view of single master cylinder

setting of 10-13 lb f ft (1.4-1.8 Kg f m).

15 Carefully refit the secondary cup onto the piston ensuring that it is the correct way round.

16 Insert the outlet check valve - the correct way round - followed by the piston return spring, primary cup, and piston cup spacer into the cylinder bore. The groove in the piston cup spacer must be towards the rear.

17 Insert the piston and plain washer and retain in position with the snapring.

18 To assist bleeding the hydraulic system pour a little fresh hydraulic fluid into the reservoir and push the piston slowly down the bore. Close the outlet with a finger and allow the piston to return slowly. Repeat this sequence several times.

19 Finally refit the rubber boot to the end of the master cylinder.

22 Brake master cylinder (tandem) - removal and replacement

1 Apply the handbrake and chock the front wheels. Drain the fluid from the master cylinder reservoir and master cylinder by attaching a plastic bleed tube to one of the brake bleed screws. Unscrew the screw one turn and then pump the fluid out into a clean glass jar by means of the brake pedal. Hold the brake pedal against the floor at the end of each stroke and tighten the bleed screw. When the pedal has returned to its normal position loosen the bleed screw and repeat the process until the reservoir is empty.

2 Wipe the area around the pipe union nuts on the master cylinder body and disconnect the brake lines. Where an independent reservoir is fitted also detach the two hoses.

3 Disconnect the leads to the master cylinder pressure switches.

4 *Models without servo unit only.* Remove the split pin and clevis pin securing the master cylinder pushrod to the brake pedal.

5 Undo and remove the bolts (or nuts) and washers securing the master cylinder to the bulkhead (or rear of servo unit) and lift away the master cylinder being careful not to allow hydraulic fluid to contact paintwork as it acts as a solvent.

6 Refitting is the reverse sequence to removal. Always start the

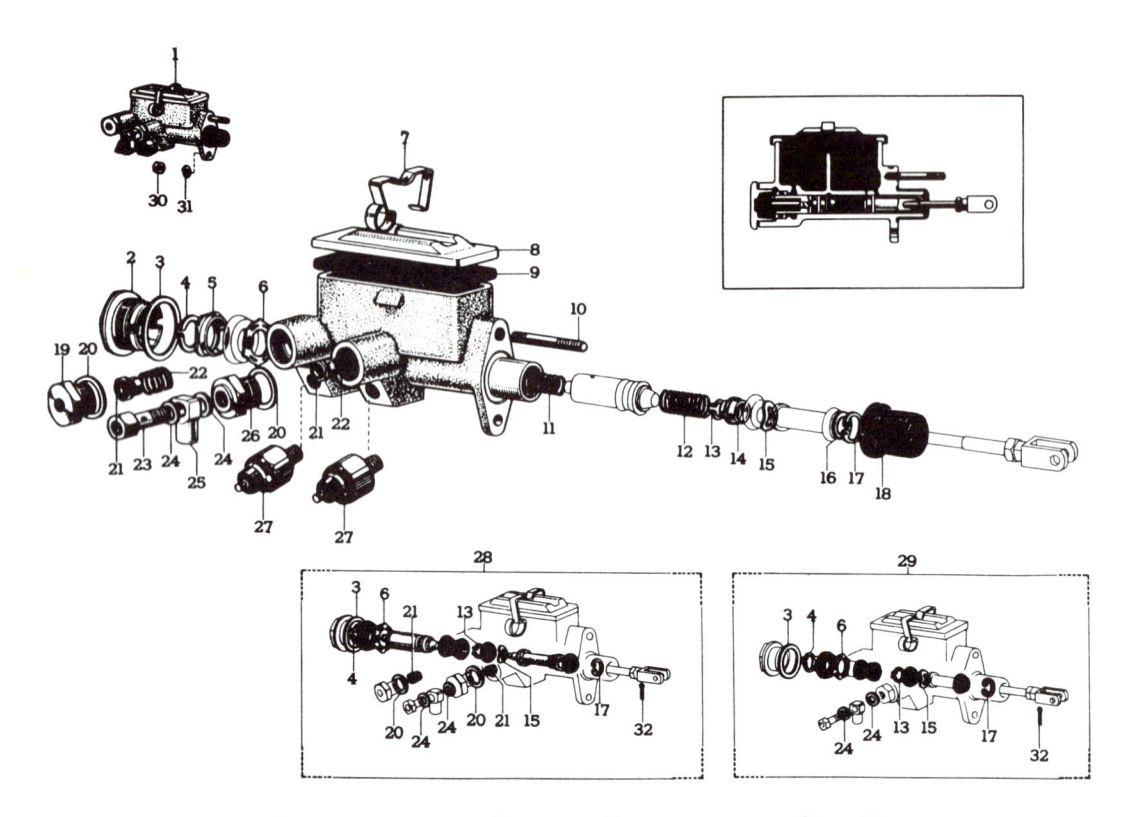

Fig. 9.22. Tandem master cylinder assembly component parts (Type 1)

1 Tandem master cylinder assembly
2 Master cylinder plug
3 Gasket
4 Snap ring
5 Master cylinder piston cup retainer
6 Master cylinder piston cup spacer
7 Filler cap set plate
8 Reservoir filler cap
9 Filler cap fluid deflector
10 Stud bolt
11 Compression spring
12 Compression spring
13 Shaft snap ring
14 Piston return spring retainer
15 Master cylinder piston cup spacer
16 Plate washer
17 Hole snap ring
18 Master cylinder boot
19 Master cylinder fluid outlet plug
20 Gasket
21 Master cylinder outlet check valve
22 Compression spring
23 Bolt union
24 Gasket
25 Union
26 Master cylinder fluid outlet plug
27 Brake pressure switch
28 Brake master cylinder kit
29 Brake master cylinder cup kit
30 Nut
31 Spring washer
32 Cotter pin

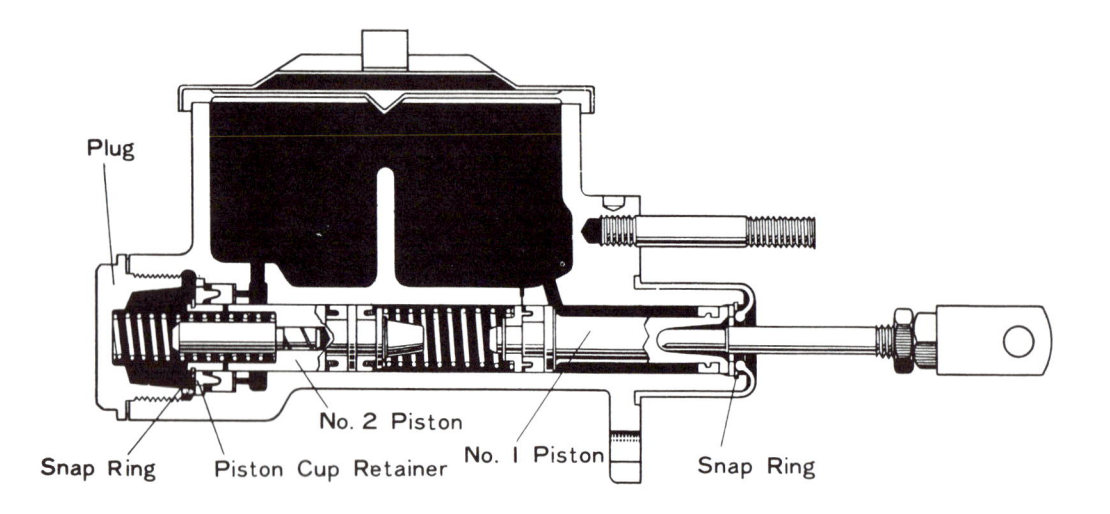

Fig. 9.23. Cross sectional view of tandem master cylinder (Type 1)

Chapter 9/Braking system

union nuts before finally tightening the master cylinder bolts (or nuts). It will be necessary to bleed the hydraulic system; full details will be found in Section 2.

23 Brake master cylinder (tandem) - dismantling, examination and reassembly

Corolla models produced since 1968 have been fitted with tandem master cylinders and although externally they look different, internally they are basically similar.

The main differences are that on one model the reservoir is mounted independently of the cylinder; another model has a single partitioned reservoir which is an integral part of the master cylinder casting; and a further version, usually used for servo unit application, has independent reservoirs mounted on the top of the master cylinder body.

1 Refer to Section 21, if a new master cylinder is to be fitted.
2 When applicable undo and remove the reservoir union securing bolts from the master cylinder body.
3 Lift away the reservoir and two pipes taking care to recover the washers positioned on each side of the unions.
4 Unscrew the two oil pressure switches located at the bottom of the master cylinder body.
5 Using a pair of circlip pliers remove the circlip (snap ring) holding the pistons into the bore.
6 The primary (No1) piston assembly and spring may now be removed from the open end of the cylinder bore.
7 Undo and remove the peg bolt and washer located at the side of the master cylinder body. This will release the secondary (No 2) piston assembly which may be removed by shaking.
8 Also remove the inlet valve seat.
9 Undo and remove the outlet plugs and washers and recover the check valves.
10 Make a careful note of how the pistons, springs and seals are assembled and then dismantle the No 1 piston assembly. It will be necessary to remove the snap ring before the piston return spring retainer, cup seal and piston stop plate can be removed.
11 Use ones fingers to remove the seals: do not use a screwdriver.
12 To dismantle the No 2 piston assembly first compress the compression spring and pry up the lips of the return spring retainer. Use a small screwdriver for this operation.
13 Finally remove the cylinder cup from the inlet valve seat.
14 Examine the bore of the cylinder carefully for any signs of scores or ridges. If the cylinder bore is found to be smooth all over new cup seals can be fitted. If however, there is any doubt about the condition of the bore then a new cylinder must be fitted.
15 If examination of the seals shows them to be apparently oversize or swollen, or very loose on the pistons, suspect oil contamination in the hydraulic system. Oil will swell these rubber seals, and if one is found to be swollen, it is reasonable to assume that all seals in the braking system will need renewal.
16 Thoroughly clean all components in clean hydraulic fluid or methylated spirits.
17 Check the clearance between the pistons and cylinder bores - this must not exceed 0.006 inch (0.15 mm). If this tolerance is exceeded a new master cylinder will have to be fitted.
18 All components should be assembled wet after dipping in clean brake fluid. Handle the cup seals with fingers only.
19 Assembly of the pistons and valve is the reverse sequence to dismantling. Lay all parts out in order taking care that the cup seals are the correct way round. Assemble the inlet valve first and follow this with the No 2 and No 1 piston.
20 Fit the outlet check valves into the body and screw on the outlet plugs and washers. Tighten the plugs to a torque wrench setting of 80-94 lb f ft (11.00-13.0 Kg f m).
21 Insert the inlet valve seat and follow this with No 2 piston assembly. Refit the dowl bolt and washer to the side of the master cylinder body. It will be necessary to push the piston assembly. Refit the dowel bolt and washer to the side of the screwed in.
22 Insert the No 1 piston assembly and spring into the bore and retain in position with the snap ring.
23 Refit the oil pressure switches to the underside of the master cylinder body.
24 Refit the master cylinder unions with a washer on each side and secure with the union bolts.
25 The master cylinder is now refitted to the car.

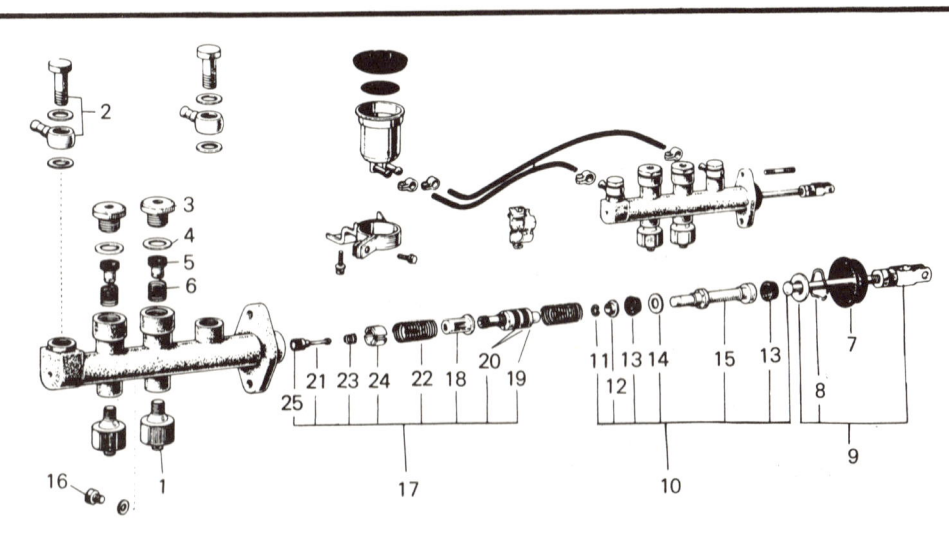

Fig. 9.24 Tandem master cylinder assembly component parts (Type 2)

1 Oil pressure switches
2 Union and union bolts
3 Outlet plugs
4 Gaskets
5 Outlet check valves
6 Compression springs
7 Master cylinder boot
8 Hole snap ring
9 Push rod with piston stop plate and clevis
10 Piston assembly No. 1
11 Snap ring
12 Piston return spring retainer
13 Cylinder cups
14 Spacer
15 Piston No. 1
16 Stopper bolt
17 Piston assembly No. 2
18 Piston return spring retainer
19 Piston
20 Cylinder cups
21 Connecting rod
22 Compression spring
23 Conical spring
24 Valve case
25 Inlet valve

Fig. 9.25 Major components of servo unit

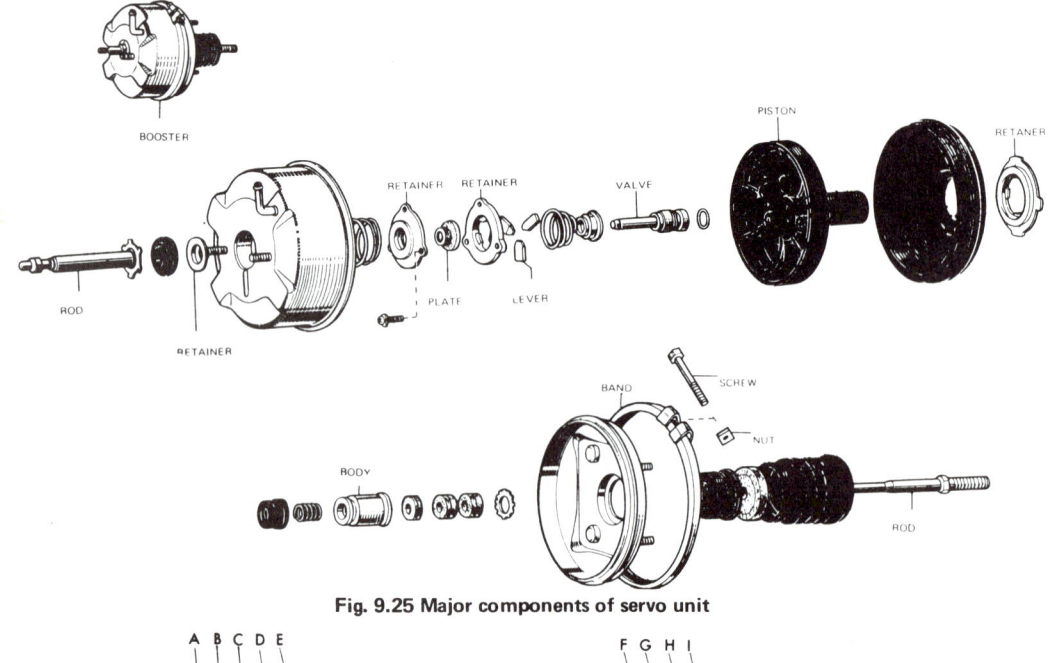

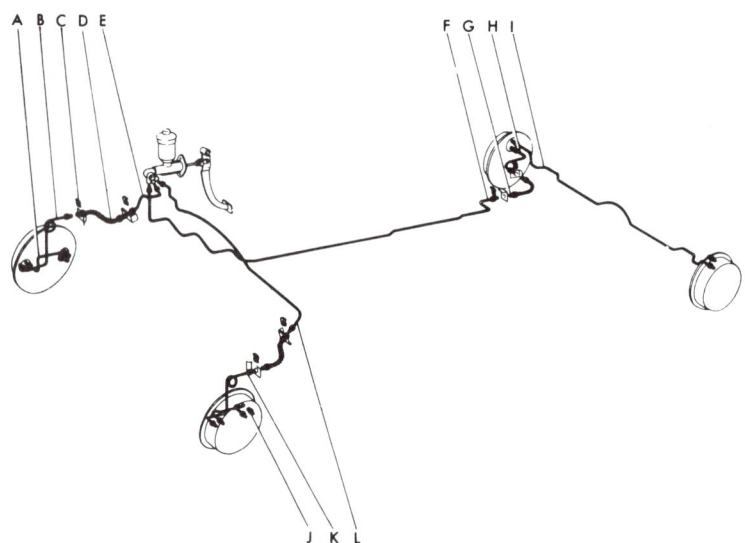

Fig. 9.26 Hydraulic pipe and hose layout (Drum brake models)

A Cylinder front bridge tube
B Wheel cylinder front right tube
C Clip
D Flexible hose
E Master cylinder to front right flexible hose tube
F Master cylinder to rear flexible tube
G Flexible hose
H Flexible hose to rear right brake tube
I Rear right brake to rear left brake tube
J Bleeder plug
K Wheel cylinder front left tube
L Master cylinder to front left flexible hose tube

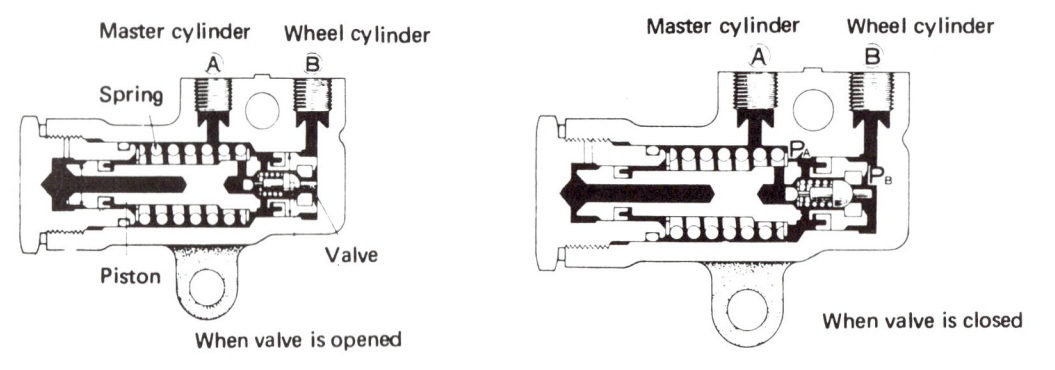

Fig. 9.27 Operation of pressure control valve

24 Vacuum servo unit - description

A vacuum servo unit is fitted into the brake system to provide assistance to the driver when the brake pedal is depressed. This reduces the effort required by the driver to operate the brakes under all braking conditions. It is mounted in series with the brake master cylinder.

The unit operates by vacuum obtained from the induction manifold and comprises basically a booster diaphragm and control valve assembly.

The servo unit and hydraulic master cylinder are connected together so that the servo unit piston rod (valve rod) acts as the master cylinder pushrod. The driver's braking effort is transmitted through another pushrod to the servo unit piston and its built in control system. The servo unit piston does not fit tightly into the cylinder, but has a strong diaphragm to keep its edges in constant contact with the cylinder wall, so ensuring an air tight seal between the two parts. The forward chamber is held under vacuum conditions created in the inlet manifold of the engine and, during periods when the brake pedal is not in use, the controls open a passage to the rear chambers so placing it under vacuum conditions as well. When the brake pedal is depressed, the vacuum passage to the rear chamber is cut off and the chamber opened to atmospheric pressure. The consequent rush of air pushes the servo piston forwards in the vacuum chamber and operates the main pushrod to the master cylinder.

The controls are designed so that assistance is given under all conditions. When the brakes are not required, vacuum is established in the rear chamber when the brake pedal is released.

Under normal operating conditions the vacuum servo unit is very reliable and does not require overhaul except at very high mileage. In this case it is far better to obtain a servo exchange or new unit, rather than repair the original unit.

25 Vacuum servo unit - removal and replacement

1 Slacken the clip securing the vacuum hose to the servo unit. Carefully draw the hose from its union.
2 Refer to Section 22, and remove the brake master cylinder.
3 Using a pair of pliers, extract the split pin in the end of the brake pedal to pushrod yoke clevis pin. Withdraw the clevis pin. To assist this it may be necessary to release the pedal return spring - note into which holes it is fitted.
4 Undo and remove the four nuts and spring washers that secure the unit to the bulkhead. Lift the unit away from the engine bulkhead.
5 Refitting the servo unit is the reverse sequence to removal. Check the brake pedal movement and adjust as necessary as described in Section 18.

26 Hydraulic pipes and hoses

1 Periodically all brake pipe, pipe connections and unions should be carefully examined.
2 First examine for signs of leakage where the pipe unions occur. Then examine the flexible hoses for signs of chafing and fraying and, of course, leakage. This is only a preliminary part of the flexible hose inspection, as exterior condition does not necessarily indicate the interior condition, which will be considered later.
3 The steel pipes must be examined carefully and methodically. They must be cleaned off and examined for any signs of dents, or other damage, and rust and corrosion. Rust and corrosion should be scraped off and, if the depth of pitting in the pipes is significant, they will need replacement. This is particularly likely in those areas underneath the car body and along the rear axle where the pipes are exposed to full force of road and weather conditions.
4 If any section of the pipe is to be taken off, first wipe clean and then remove the fluid reservoir cap. Place a piece of polythene sheet over the reservoir and refit the cap. This will stop syphoning during subsequent operations.
5 Rigid pipe removal is usually quite straightforward. The unions at each end are undone, the pipe and union pulled out, and the centre sections of the pipe removed from the body clips. Where the pipes are exposed to full force of road and weather they will sometimes be very tight. As one can only use an open ended spanner and the unions are not large, burring of the flats is not uncommon when attempting to undo them. For this reason a self-locking grip wrench (mole) is often the only way to unscrew a stubborn union.
6 Removal of flexible hoses is described in Section 3.
7 With the flexible hose removed, examine the internal bore. If it is blown through first, it should be possible to see through it. Any specks of rubber which come out or signs of restriction in the bore, means that the rubber lining is breaking up and the pipe must be replaced.
8 Rigid pipes which need replacement can usually be purchased at any garage where they have the pipe unions and special tools to make up the pipe flares. All they need to know is the total length of the pipe, the type of flare used at each end with the union, and the length and thread of the union.
9 Replacement of the pipe is a straightforward reversal of the removal procedure. If the rigid pipes have been made up it is best to get all the sets (bends) in them before trying to install them. Also if there are any acute bends, ask your supplier to put these in for you on a special tube bender. Otherwise you may kink the pipe and thereby decrease the bore area and fluid flow.
10 With the pipes replaced, remove the polythene from the reservoir cap and bleed the system as described in Section 1.

27a Pressure control valve

27 Pressure control valve

Models equipped with disc brakes use a special pressure control valve to ensure that the rear wheels do not lock during sudden braking conditions. (photo)

The valve is located in the hydraulic line between the master cylinder and the rear wheel cylinder. It is usually mounted on the right-hand side of the engine compartment.

For 'Fault diagnosis' see next page.

28 Fault diagnosis - braking system

Symptom	Reason/s	Remedy
Pedal travels almost to the floor before brakes operate	Brake fluid level too low	Top up master cylinder reservoir. Check for leaks.
	Wheel cylinder or caliper leaking	Dismantle wheel cylinder or caliper, clean, fit new rubbers and bleed brakes.
	Master cylinder leaking (Bubbles in master cylinder fluid)	Dismantle master cylinder, clean, and fit new rubbers. Bleed brakes.
	Brake flexible hose leaking	Examine and fit new hose if old hose leaking. Bleed brakes.
	Brake line fractured	Replace with new brake pipe. Bleed brakes.
	Brake system unions loose	Check all unions in brake system and tighten as necessary. Bleed brakes.
	Linings over 75% worn	Fit replacement shoes and brake linings.
	Drum brakes badly out of adjustment	Jack up car and adjust rear brakes.
	Master cylinder push rod out of adjustment causing too much pedal free movement	Reset to manufacturer's specifications.
Brake pedal action feels springy	New linings not yet bedded-in	Use brakes gently until springy pedal feeling leaves.
	Brake drums or discs badly worn and weak or cracked	Fit new brake drums or discs.
	Master cylinder securing nuts loose	Tighten master cylinder securing nuts. Ensure spring washers are fitted.
Brake pedal action feels 'spongy' and soggy	Wheel cylinder or caliper leaking	Dismantle wheel cylinder or caliper, clean, fit new rubbers, and bleed brakes.
	Master cylinder leaking (Bubbles in master cylinder reservoir)	Dismantle master cylinder, clean, and fit new rubbers and bleed brakes. Replace cylinder if internal walls scored.
	Brake pipe line or flexible hose leaking	Fit new pipeline or hose.
	Unions in brake system loose	Examine for leaks, tighten as necessary.
Brakes pull to one side	Linings and brake drums or discs contaminated with oil, grease, or hydraulic fluid	Ascertain and rectify source of leak, clean brake drums, fit new linings.
	Tyre pressures unequal	Check and inflate as necessary.
	Radial ply tyres fitted at one end of car only	Fit radial ply tyres of the same make to all four wheels.
	Brake backplate caliper or disc loose	Tighten backplate caliper or disc securing nuts and bolts.
	Brake shoes or pads fitted incorrectly	Remove and fit shoes or pads correct way round.
	Different type of linings fitted at each wheel	Fit the linings specified by the manufacturer's all round.
	Anchorages for front or rear suspension loose	Tighten front and rear suspension pick-up points including spring locations.
	Brake drums or discs badly worn, cracked or distorted	Fit new brake drums or discs.
Brakes bind, drag or lock-on	Brake shoes adjusted too tightly	Slacken off rear brake shoe adjusters two clicks.
	Handbrake cable over-tightened	Slacken off handbrake cable adjustment.
	Master cylinder push rod out of adjustment giving too little brake pedal free movement	Reset to manufacturer's specifications.
	Reservoir vent hole in cap blocked with dirt	Clean and blow through hole.
	Master cylinder by-pass port restricted - brakes seize in 'on' position	Dismantle, clean, and overhaul master cylinder. Bleed brakes.
	Wheel cylinder seizes in 'on' position	Dismantle, clean and overhaul wheel cylinder. Bleed brakes.
	Rear brake shoe pull off springs broken, stretched or loose	Examine springs and replace if worn or loose.
	Rear brake shoe pull off springs fitted wrong way round, omitted or wrong type used	Examine and rectify as appropriate.
	Handbrake system rusted or seized in the 'on' position	Apply 'Plus Gas' to free, clean and lubricate.

Chapter 10 Electrical system

Contents

Alternator - fault diagnosis and repair	10
Alternator - general description	6
Alternator - maintenance	7
Alternator regulator - general description	11
Alternator - removal and replacement	9
Alternator - special procedures	8
Battery - charging	5
Battery - electrolyte replenishment	4
Battery - maintenance and inspection	3
Battery - removal and replacement	2
Cigarette lighter - adjustment, removal and replacement	43
Combination meter (Type 1) - dismantling and reassembly	30
Combination meter (Type 2) - dismantling and reassembly	34
Combination meter (Type 3) - dismantling and reassembly	40
Combination meter (Type 1) - removal and replacement	29
Combination meter (Type 2) - removal and replacement	33
Combination meter (Type 3) - removal and replacement	39
Fault diagnosis - electrical system	46
Flasher unit and relay - general	42
Fuses and fusible link - general description	28
General description	1
Glove compartment (Type 1) - removal and replacement	32
Headlight sealed beam unit - removal and replacement	16
Heater unit and controls - removal and replacement	44
Heater unit - dismantling and reassembly	45
Horn - fault diagnosis and rectification	22
Horn - servicing and adjustment	23
Ignition switch (Type 3) - removal and replacement	41
Interior light bulb - removal and replacement	21
Instrument panel safety pad (Type 1) - removal and replacement	31
Instrument panel safety pad (Type 2) - removal and replacement	35
Rear direction indicator, stop and tail light bulbs - removal and replacement	18
Rear number plate light bulb - removal and replacement	20
Side flasher light bulb - removal and replacement	19
Side light and direction indicator bulb - removal and replacement	17
Starter motor - dismantling, overhaul and reassembly	15
Starter motor - general description	12
Starter motor - removal and replacement	14
Starter motor - testing on engine	13
Switches (Type 1) - removal and replacement	36
Switches (Type 2) - removal and replacement	38
Windscreen wasner - general	37
Windscreen wiper arm and blade - removal and replacement	24
Windscreen wiper linkage - removal and replacement	26
Windscreen wiper mechanism - fault diagnosis and rectification	25
Windscreen wiper motor - removal and replacement	27

Specifications

Battery
Type	Lead/Acid 12 volt
Polarity	Negative earth
Capacity	35 amp/hours at 20 hour rate

Alternator
1100 models:

Voltage	12
Maximum output (amps)	25
Maximum output power (watts)	300
No load (rpm)	850 ± 100
No load voltage	13.5
Output (amps)	19-27
Output voltage	13.5 - 14.5
Output (rpm)	1,800
Minimum brush length	0.35 in. (8.89 mm)
Maximum brush protrusion (fitted)	0.51 in. (12.954 mm)
Performance test speed at 14 volts	650 - 950
Performance test speed at 14 volts and 25 amps	1,800
Rotor coil continuity (ohms)	4.1 - 4.3 ohms

1200 models:

Voltage	12
Maximum output (amps)	25
No load (rpm)	900 ± 100
No load voltage	14
Output (amps)	25

Output voltage	14
Output (rpm)	3,000
Minimum brush length	0.22 in. (5.59 mm)
Maximum brush protrusion (fitted)	0.49 in. (12.45 mm)
Performance test speed at 14 volts	800 - 1,000
Performance test speed at 14 volts and 25 amps	3,000

1600 models:

Voltage	12
Maximum output (amps)	40
No load (rpm)	800 ± 150
Output (amps)	30
Output voltage	14
Output (rpm)	3,500
Performance test speed at 14 volts	650 - 950
Performance test speed at 14 volts and 30 amps	3,500

Regulator (all models):

Relay:

Spring distortion	0.008 - 0.018 in. (0.2032 - 0.4572 mm)
Point resistance	100 ohms
Point gap	0.016 - 0.047 in. (0.4064 - 1.194 mm)
Arm gap	0.008 - 0.018 in. (0.2032 - 0.4572 mm)
Shaft runout	0.002 in. (0.0508 mm)
Shaft endplay	0.006 - 0.020 in. (0.1524 - 0.508 mm)
Coil resistance	23 ohms
Breaker plate tension	17.5 oz
Condenser capacity	0.20 - 0.24 uf

Regulator:

Arm gap: 1100	0.024 - 0.032 in. (0.6096 - 0.8128 mm)
1200, 1600	0.012 in. (0.3048 mm)
Arm resistance	12 ohms
Point gap	0.010 - 0.018 in. (0.254 - 0.4572 mm)
Distortion	0.008 in. (0.2032 mm)
Angle gap	0.008 in. (0.2032 mm)
Relay operating voltage	4.5 - 5.8
Regulator operating voltage	13.8 - 14.8

Starter motor:

1100 models:

Rating voltage	12
Output	0.59 kw
Armature bush internal diameter	0.494 in. (12.548 mm)
Shaft/bush clearance	0.004 in. (0.1016 mm)
Shaft/bush clearance (maximum)	0.008 in. (0.2032 mm)
Commutator outside diameter (minimum)	1.46 in. (26.568 mm)
Commutator mica depth	0.02 - 0.03 in. (0.508 - 0.762 mm)
Commutator mica depth limit	0.008 in. (0.2032 mm)
Commutator ovality limit	0.012 in. (0.3048 mm)
Brush length (minimum)	0.51 in. (12.954 mm)
Brush spring tension	36 - 48.7 oz
Brush spring tension (minimum)	21 oz
Pinion gap	0.04 - 0.12 in. (1.016 - 3.048 mm)
Thrust clearance	0.002 - 0.013 in. (0.0508 - 0.3302 mm)
Thrust clearance (minimum)	0.03 in. (0.762 mm)

No load characteristics:

Voltage	11
Current	55
Rpm	3,500

Lock characteristics:

Voltage	8.5
Current	100
Torque	5.78 lb f ft
Drive pinion shift lever link protrusion from solenoid housing	1.344 in. (34.138 mm)

1200 models:

Rating voltage	12
Output power	0.81 or 1.12 kw
Armature shaft outside diameter	0.492 in. (12.497 mm)
Armature bush internal diameter	0.494 in. (12.548 mm)
Shaft/bush clearance	0.004 in. (0.1016 mm)
Shaft/bush clearance (maximum)	0.008 in. (0.2032 mm)

Chapter 10/Electrical system

Commutator outside diameter	1.528 in. (38.608 mm)
Commutator outside diameter (minimum)	1.449 in. (36.825 mm)
Commutator mica depth	0.020 - 0.031 in. (0.508 - 0.7874 mm)
Commutator mica depth limit	0.008 in. (0.2032 mm)
Commutator ovality limit	0.012 in. (0.3048 mm)
Brush length	0.748 in. (18.999 mm)
Brush length (minimum)	0.511 in. (12.954 mm)
Brush spring tension	37 - 48 oz
Brush spring tension (minimum)	21 oz
Pinion gap	0.039 - 0.157 in. (0.9906 - 3.9878 mm)
No load characteristics:	
Voltage	11
Current	55
Rpm	3,500
Load characteristics:	
Voltage	8.5
Current	450
Torque	8.0 lb f ft
Drive pinion shift lever link protrusion from solenoid housing	1.344 in. (34.138 mm)

1600 models:

Rating voltage	12
Output power	0.8 kw
Armature shaft outside diameter	0.489 - 0.490 in. (12.42 - 12.446 mm)
Armature internal diameter	0.494 - 0.495 in. (12.548 - 12.573 mm)
Shaft/bush clearance	0.004 - 0.006 in. (0.1016 - 0.1524 mm)
Shaft/bush clearance (maximum)	0.008 in. (0.2032 mm)
Commutator outside diameter	1.221 in. (31.013 mm)
Commutator mica depth	0.020 - 0.032 in. (0.508 - 0.7875 mm)
Commutator mica depth limit	0.008 in. (0.2032 mm)
Commutator ovality limit	0.012 in. (0.3048 mm)
Brush length	0.748 in. (18.999 mm)
Brush length (minimum)	0.472 in. (11.9888 mm)
Brush spring tension	37 - 47 oz
Brush spring tension (minimum)	21 oz
Pinion gap	0.04 - 0.16 in. (1.016 - 4.064 mm)
Thrust clearance (maximum)	0.032 in. (0.8128 mm)
No load characteristics:	
Voltage	11
Current	50
Rpm	5,000
Load characteristics:	
Voltage	7.7
Current	470
Torque	9.4 lb f ft
Drive pinion shift lever link protrusion from solenoid housing	1.344 in. (34.138 mm)

Windscreen wiper motor (early models):

Rated voltage	14 volts
Wiping angle - right	90 - 95°
left	97 - 103°
Blade movement	Parallel
Arm connection	Spline
No load current	Less than 4.5 amps
With load operating current	Less than 13.0 amps
Commutator outside diameter (maximum)	0.886 in. (22.5044 mm)
Brush length (minimum)	0.310 in. (7.874 mm)
Contact point height	0.335 - 0.354 in. (8.509 - 8.9916 mm)
Armature shaft to bush clearance (maximum)	0.004 in. (0.1016 mm)
Shaft endplay adjustment	0.002 in. (0.0508 mm)
Two speed type speeds:	
Low	40 - 48 rpm
High	55 - 69 rpm

Windscreen wiper motor (later models):

Wiping method	Parallel linkage type
Wiping angle:	
Right	88.5° ± 3°
Left	103° ± 3°
Motor type	Ferrite magnet
Rated voltage	12V

Unloaded operating current	Less than 2.5 amps
Current at high speed	Less than 14 amps
Wiring speed:	
Low	40 - 50 rpm
High	58 - 72 rpm
Brush length	0.49 in. (12.5 mm)
Brush length (minimum)	0.31 in. (8.0 mm)
Commutator diameter	0.905 in. (23.0 mm)
Commutator diameter (minimum)	0.886 in. (22.5 mm)
Shaft thrust gap	Less than 0.004 in. (0.1 mm)
Contact point height	0.335 - 0.354 in. (8.5 - 9.0 mm)

Heater:

Type 1:

Type	Hot water
An inlet	Fresh air and recirculating
Adjustment devices:	Two stage blower - Water control valve
Heating capacity	2,000 K cal/hr
Motor voltage	12 volts
Motor capacity	30 watts
Motor speed	3,600 rpm
Blower capacity	150 cu metres/hr
Brush wear limit	0.28 in. (7 mm)
Brush specified length	0.43 in. (11 mm)
Commutator wear limit	0.69 in. (17.5 mm)
Commutator specified diameter	0.73 in. (18.5 mm)

Type 2:

Type	Hot water
Air inlet	Fresh air and recirculating
Adjustment devices	Two stage blower. Water control valve
Heating capacity	2,600 or 2,800 K cal/hr
Blower capacity	220 cu metres/hr
Operating current	50 watts
Rated voltage	12 volts
Motor speed	3,000 rpm
Brush wear limit	0.275 in. (7 mm)
Brush specified length	0.394 in. (10 mm)
Commutator wear limit	0.738 in. (18.75 mm)
Commutator specified diameter	0.747 in. (19.15 mm)

Windscreen washer:

Type 1:

Motor	Magnetic type
Pump	Gear pump
Rated voltage	12 volts
Operating current	Less than 3 amps
Time rating	20 seconds
Delivery pressure	5.7 lb/sq in. (0.4 kg/sq cm)
Delivery capacity	More than 100 cc per 10 secs.
Tank capacity	1.1 Imp qt (1.2 litres, 1.3 US Qt)

Type 2:

Motor	Ferrite magnet
Pump	Centrifugal
Rated voltage	12 volts
Operating current	Less than 3 amps
Time rating	20 seconds
Delivery pressure	7.11 lb/sq in. (0.5 kg/sq cm)
Delivery capacity	More than 100 cc per 10 secs.
Tank capacity	1.3 Imp qt. (1.5 litres, 1.8 US Qt)

Horn:

Type 1 (Denso)

Rated voltage	12
Current	1.5 - 2.5 amps
Decibel	100 - 110
Frequency:	
High	405 - 435 cycles
Low	325 - 355 cycles
Usable voltage range	9 - 15 volts

Chapter 10/Electrical system

Type 2 (Maruko)
Rated voltage	12
Current	1.5 - 2.5 amps
Decibel	100 - 110
Frequency:	
High	415 - 445 cycles
Low	343 - 373 cycles
Usable voltage range	10 - 14 volts

Type 3 (Denso Trumpet)
Rated voltage	13
Current	1.5 - 2.5
Decibel	100 - 110
Frequency:	
High	410 - 440 cycles
Low	325 - 355 cycles
Usable voltage range	9 - 14.5

Type 4 (Maruko Trumpet)
Rated voltage	13
Current	2.5 (maximum)
Decibel	100 - 110
Frequency:	
High	415 - 445 cycles
Low	343 - 373 cycles
Usable voltage range	10 - 14

Type 5 (Denso Vibrator)
Rated voltage	13
Current	1.5 - 3
Decibel	103 - 113
Frequency:	
High	375 - 405 cycles
Low	310 - 340 cycles
Usable voltage range	9.0 - 14.5

Type 6 (Maruko Vibrator)
Rated voltage	13
Current	2.5 (maximum)
Decibel	105 - 110
Frequency:	
High	365 - 395 cycles
Low	285 - 315 cycles
Usable voltage range	10 - 14

Flasher unit:

Up to 1971:
Voltage	12
Type	Condenser relay
Capacity	25 + 25 + 6 + 3 watts
Cycle	50 - 120 per minute

KE 20, 25 series and TE 21, 25 and 27 series:

	Direction indicator	Hazard
Rated voltage	12V	12V
Applied load	23W x 3 + 75 + 3.4W	23 max. 7
Flashing cycle	60 - 120 per minute	60 - 120 per minute
Operating voltage range	10 - 15V	10 - 15V

KE 26V series and TE 28 series:

	Direction indicator	Hazard
Rated voltage	12V	12V
Applied load	23W x 2 + 7.5W + 3.4W	23W max. 5
Flashing cycle	60 - 120 per minute	60 - 120 per minute
Operating voltage range	10 - 15V	10 - 15V

Bulbs*

	Standard	Optional
Front side and direction indicator	23/8W	21/5W
Front direction indicator (optional)	23W	21W
Parking (optional)	8W	5W
Side marker	8W	5W
Tail, stop and rear direction indicator	23/8W	21/5W
Tail and stop (optional)	23/8W	21/5W

Chapter 10/Electrical system

Rear direction indicator (optional)	23W	21W
Reverse	23W	21W
Number plate	7.5W	5W
Interior	5W	5W
Heater control	3W	3W
Headlight (sealed beam)	50/40W	

Always check with handbook as these recommendations can vary.

1 General description

The electrical system is of the 12 volt negative earth type and the major components comprise a 12 volt battery of which the negative terminal is earthed, an alternator which is driven from the crankshaft pulley and a starter motor.

The battery supplies a steady amount of current for the ignition, lighting, and other electrical circuits and provides a reserve of electricity when the current consumed by the electrical equipment exceeds that being produced by the alternator.

The alternator has its own regulator which ensures a high output if the battery is in a low state of charge or the demand from the electrical equipment is high, and a low output if the battery is fully charged and there is little demand from the electrical equipment.

When fitting electrical accessories to cars with a negative earth system it is important (if they contain silicon diodes or transistors), that they are connected correctly, otherwise serious damage may result to the components concerned. Items such as radios, tape players, electronic ignition systems, automatic headlight dipping etc, should all be checked for correct polarity.

It is important that if the battery is to be boost charged the positive lead is always disconnected first. Also if body repairs are to be carried out using electric arc welding equipment, the alternator must be disconnected otherwise serious damage can be caused to the more delicate instruments. Whenever the battery has to be disconnected it must always be reconnected with the negative terminal earthed.

2 Battery - removal and replacement

1 The battery should be removed once every three months for cleaning and testing. Disconnect the positive and negative leads from the battery terminals by slackening the clamp bolts and lifting away the clamps.

2 Undo and remove the nut and washer securing the battery clamp and lift away the clamp. Carefully lift the battery from its carrier and hold it vertically to ensure that none of the electrolyte is spilled.

3 Replacement is a direct reversal of the removal procedure.

Smear the terminals and clamps with vaseline to prevent corrosion. **Never** use ordinary grease.

3 Battery - maintenance and inspection

1 Normal weekly battery maintenance consists of checking the electrolyte level of each cell to ensure that the separators are covered by ¼ inch of electrolyte. If the level has fallen, top-up the battery using distilled water only. Do not overfill. If a battery is overfilled or any electrolyte spilled, immediately wipe away the excess as electrolyte attacks and corrodes any metal it comes into contact with very rapidly.

2 As well as keeping the terminals clean and covered with petroleum jelly, the top of the battery, and especially the top of the cells, should be kept clean and dry. This helps prevent corrosion and ensures that the battery does not become partially discharged by leakage through dampness and dirt.

3 Once every three months remove the battery and inspect the battery securing bolts, the battery clamp plate, tray and battery leads for corrosion (white fluffy deposits on the metal which are brittle to touch). If any corrosion is found, clean off the deposit with ammonia and paint over the clean metal with an anti-rust anti-acid paint.

4 At the same time inspect the battery case for cracks. If a crack is found, clean and plug it with one of the proprietary compounds marketed by firms such as Holts for this purpose. If leakage through the cracks has been excessive then it will be necessary to refill the appropriate cell with fresh electrolyte as detailed later. Cracks are frequently caused to the top of the battery cases by pouring in distilled water in the middle of winter *after* instead of *before* a run. This gives the water no chance to mix with the electrolyte and so the former freezes and splits the battery case.

5 If topping-up the battery becomes excessive and the case has been inspected for cracks that could cause leakage, but none are found, the battery is being overcharged and the voltage regulator will have to be checked and reset.

6 With the battery on the bench at the three monthly interval check, measure the specific gravity with a hydrometer to determine the state of charge and condition of the electrolyte. There should be very little variation between the different cells and if a variation in excess of 0.025 is present it will be due to either:

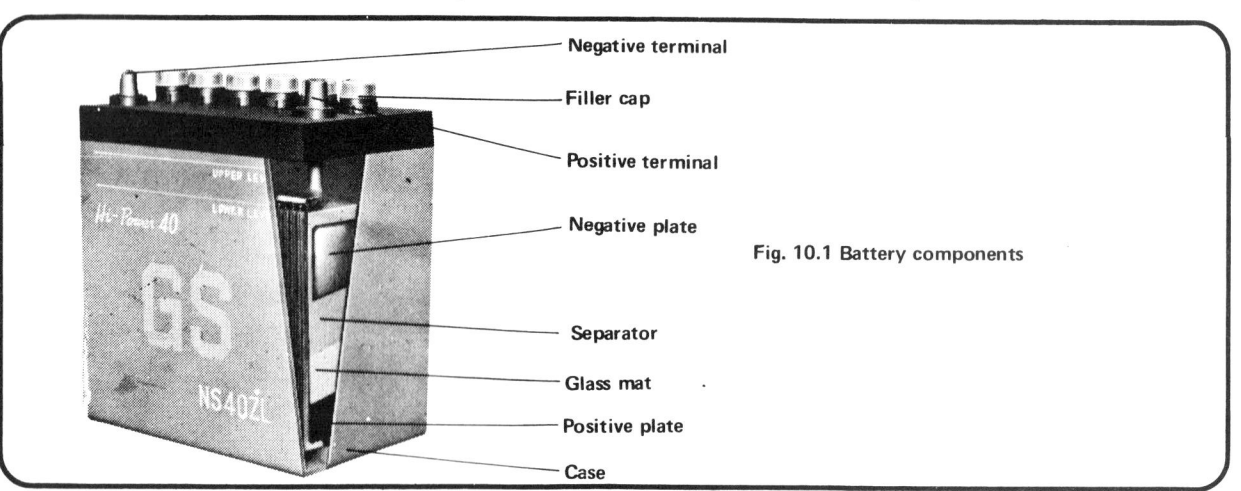

Fig. 10.1 Battery components

Chapter 10/Electrical system

(a) loss of electrolyte from the battery at some time caused by spillage or a leak, resulting in a drop in the specific gravity of the electrolyte when the deficiency was replaced with distilled water instead of fresh electrolyte.
(b) an internal short circuit caused by buckling of the plates or a similar malady pointing to the likelihood of total battery failure in the near future.

7 The specific gravity of the electrolyte for fully charged conditions at the electrolyte temperature indicated, is listed in Table A. The specific gravity of a fully discharged battery at different temperatures of the electrolyte is given in Table B.

Table A

Specific gravity - battery fully charged
1.268 at 100°F or 38°C electrolyte temperature
1.272 at 90°F or 32°C   "   "
1.276 at 80°F or 27°C   "   "
1.280 at 70°F or 21°C   "   "
1.284 at 60°F or 16°C   "   "
1.288 at 50°F or 10°C   "   "
1.292 at 40°F or 4°C   "   "
1.296 at 30°F or -1.5°C   "   "

Table B

Specific gravity - battery fully discharged
1.098 at 100°F or 38°C electrolyte temperature
1.102 at 90°F or 32°C   "   "
1.106 at 80°F or 27°C   "   "
1.110 at 70°F or 21°C   "   "
1.114 at 60°F or 16°C   "   "
1.118 at 50°F or 10°C   "   "
1.122 at 40°F or 4°C   "   "
1.126 at 30°F or -1.5°C   "   "

4 Battery - electrolyte replenishment

1 If the battery is in a fully charged state and one of the cells maintains a specific gravity reading which is .025 or more lower than the others, and a check of each cell has been made with a voltage meter to check for short circuits (a four to seven second test should give a steady reading of between 1.2 and 1.8 volts), then it is likely that electrolyte has been lost from the cell with the low reading at some time.
2 Top-up the cell with a solution of 1 part sulphuric acid to 2.5 parts of water. If the cell is already fully topped-up draw some electrolyte out of it with a pipette.
3 When mixing the sulphuric acid and water **never add water to sulphuric acid** - always pour the acid slowly onto the water in a glass container. **If water is added to sulphuric acid it will explode.**
4 Continue to top-up the cell with the freshly made electrolyte and then recharge the battery and check the hydrometer readings.

5 Battery - charging

1 In winter time when heavy demand is placed upon the battery such as when starting from cold, and much electrical equipment is continually in use, it is a good idea to occasionally have the battery fully charged from an external source at the rate of 3.5 to 4 amps.
2 Continue to charge the battery at this rate until no further rise in specific gravity is noted over a four hour period.
3 Alternatively, a trickle charger, charging at the rate of 1.5 amps can be safely used overnight.
4 Specially rapid 'boost' charges which are claimed to restore the power of the battery in 1 to 2 hours are most dangerous as they can cause serious damage to the battery plates through overheating.

Fig. 10.2 Testing battery specific gravity

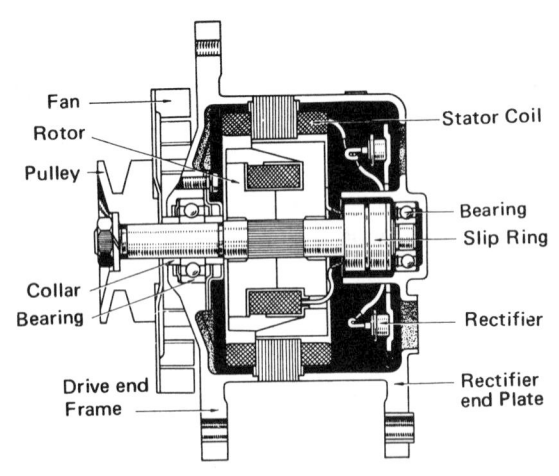

Fig. 10.3 Cross sectional view through alternator

5 While charging the battery note that the temperature of the electrolyte should never exceed 100°F (37.8°C).

6 Alternator - general description

The main advantage of the alternator over a dynamo lies in its ability to provide a high charge at low revolutions.
An important feature of the alternator system is its output control, this being based on thick film hybrid integrated minor circuit techniques.
The alternator is of the rotating field, ventilated design. It comprises principally, a laminated stator on which is wound a star connected 3 phase output; and an 8 pole rotor carrying the field winding. The front and rear ends of the rotor shaft run in ball races each of which is lubricated for life, and natural finish die cast end brackets incorporating the mounting lugs.
The rotor is belt driven from the engine through a pulley keyed to the rotor shaft and a pressed steel fan adjacent to the pulley draws cooling air through the machine. This fan forms an integral part of the alternator specifications. It has been designed to provide adequate air flow with a minimum of noise and to withstand the high stress associated with maximum speed.
The brush gear of the field system is mounted in the slip ring end-brackets. Two carbon brushes bear against a pair of concentric brass slip rings carried on a moulded disc attached to the end of the rotor. Also attached to the slip ring end-bracket are six silicone diodes connected in a three phase bridge to rectify the generated alternating current for use in charging the battery and supplying power to the electrical system.
The alternator output is controlled by an electric voltage regulator unit and warning light control unit to indicate to the driver when all is not well.

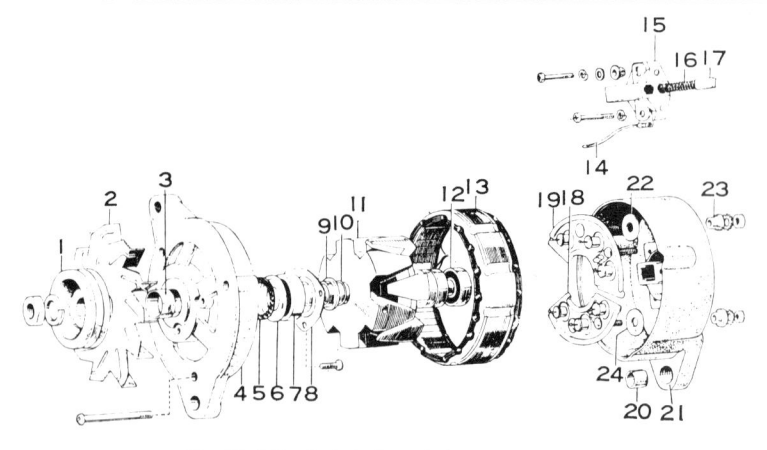

Fig. 10.4 Exploded view of alternator

1 Alternator pulley
2 Alternator fan
3 Collar
4 Drive end frame
5 Felt
6 Felt cover
7 Bearing
8 Bearing retainer
9 Spacer ring
10 Snap ring
11 **Alternator rotor**
12 Bearing
13 Alternator stator
14 Lead wire
15 Alternator holder
16 Brush spring
17 Alternator brush
18 With rectifier minus holder
19 With rectifier plus holder
20 Bushing
21 Rectifier end frame
22 Insulator washer
23 "B" insulator terminal
24 Insulator washer

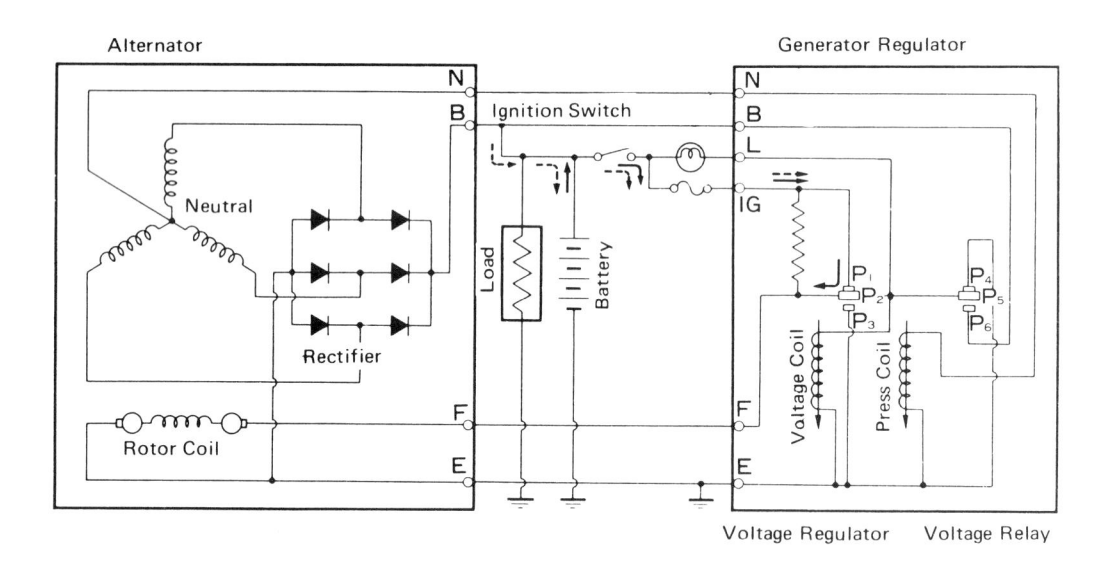

Fig. 10.5 Alternator charging circuit

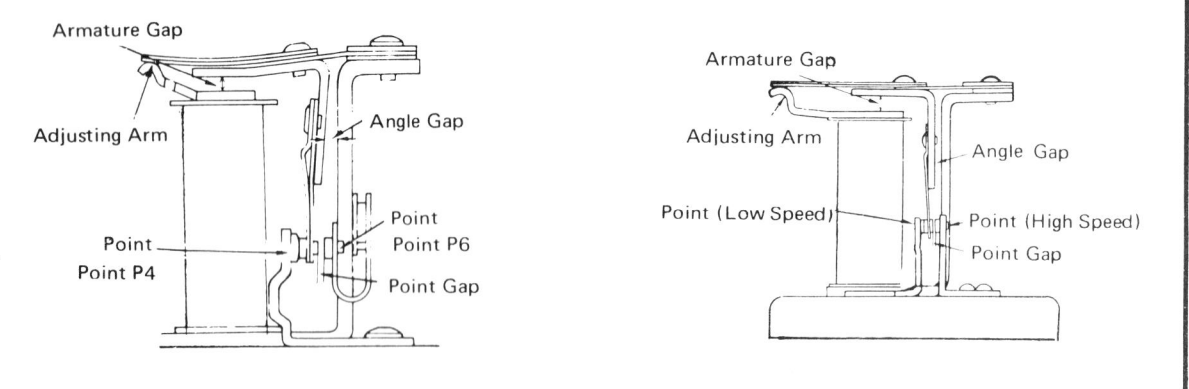

Fig. 10.6 Alternator regulator part names

Relay *Regulator*

Chapter 10/Electrical system

7 Alternator - maintenance

1 The equipment has been designed for the minimum amount of maintenance in service, the only items being subject to wear are the brushes and bearings.
2 Brushes should be examined after about 75,000 miles (120,000 Km) and renewed if necessary. The bearings are pre-packed with grease and should not require further attention for life.
3 Check the drive belt regularly for correct adjustment. Depress with the finger and thumb between the alternator and water pump and check that it is within the limits as described in Chapter 2.

8 Alternator - special procedures

Whenever the electrical system of the car is being worked on, or an external means of starting the engine is used, there are certain precautions that must be taken otherwise serious and expensive damage to the alternator can result.
1 Always make sure that the negative terminal of the battery is earthed. If the terminal connections are accidentally reversed or if the battery has been reverse charged the alternator will burn-out.
2 The output terminal of the alternator must never be earthed but should always be connected directly to the positive terminal of the battery.
3 Whenever the alternator is to be removed, or when disconnecting the terminals of the alternator circuit, always disconnect the battery first.
4 The alternator must never be operated without the battery to alternator cable connected.
5 If the battery is to be charged by external means always disconnect both battery cables before the external charger is connected.
6 Should it be necessary to use a booster charge or booster battery to start the engine always double check that the negative cables are connected to negative terminals and positive cables to positive terminals.

9 Alternator - removal and replacement

1 Disconnect both the battery leads.
2 Make a note of the terminal connections at the rear of the alternator and disconnect the cables and terminal connector.
3 Undo and remove the alternator adjustment arm bolt, slacken the alternator mounting bolt and remove the drivebelt from the pulley.
4 Remove the mounting bolt and lift the alternator away from the car.
5 Take care not to knock or drop the alternator; this can cause irreparable damage.
6 Refitting the alternator is the reverse sequence to removal. Adjust the fan belt as described in Chapter 2.

10 Alternator - fault diagnosis and repair

Due to the specialist knowledge and equipment required to test and service an alternator it is recommended that if its performance is suspect, it be taken to an automobile electrician who will have the facilities for such work. Because of this recommendation no further detailed information is given.

11 Alternator regulator - general description

The regulator basically comprises, a voltage regulator and a charge relay. The voltage regulator has two sets of contact points to control the alternator voltage. An armature plate placed between the two sets of contacts, moves to the left or right or vibrates. When closed the points either complete the field circuit direct to earth or alternatively complete the field circuit to earth through a field coil resistance and thereby produce the alternator output.
The charge relay is basically similar to that of the voltage regulator. When the points are closed the ignition warning light goes out. If the regulator performance is suspect refer to the recommendations given in Section 10.

12 Starter motor - general description

The starter motor comprises a solenoid, a lever, starter drive gear and the motor. The solenoid is fitted to the top of the motor. The plunger inside the solenoid is connected to a centre pivoting lever the other end of which is in contact with the drive sleeve and drive gear.
When the ignition switch is operated, current from the battery flows through the series and shunt solenoid coils thereby magnetizing the solenoid. The plunger is drawn into the solenoid so that it operates the lever and moves the drive pinion into the starter ring gear. The solenoid switch contacts close after the drive pinion is partially engaged with the ring gear.
When the solenoid switch contacts are closed the starter motor rotates the engine while at the same time cutting current flow to the series coil in the solenoid. The shunt coil's magnetic pull is now sufficient to hold the pinion in mesh with the ring-gear.
When the engine is running and the driver releases the ignition switch so breaking the solenoid contact, a reverse current will flow through the series coil and a magnetic field will build up this time in the same direction in which the plunger moves back, out of the solenoid. When this happens the resultant force of the magnetic field is in the shunt coil and the series coil will be nil.
A return spring then actuates the lever causing it to draw the plunger out which will allow the solenoid switch contact to open. The starter motor stops.
An over running clutch is fitted to give a more positive mesh engagement and disengagement of the pinion and ring gear. It uses a lever to slide the pinion along the armature shaft in or out of mesh with the ring gear. The over-run clutch is designed to transmit driving torque from the motor armature to the ring gear but also permits the pinion to over-run the armature after the engine has started.

13 Starter motor - testing on engine

1 If the starter motor fails to operate then check the condition of the battery by turning on the headlights. If they glow brightly for several seconds and then gradually dim, the battery is in an undercharged condition.
2 If the headlights continue to glow brightly it is obvious that the battery is in good condition, then check the tightness of the earth lead from the battery terminal to its connection on the body frame. Check also the other battery lead connections. Check the tightness of the connections at the rear of the solenoid. Do not forget to check that the engine earth leads on either side of the engine are also in good condition. If available check the wiring with a voltmeter or test lights for breaks or short circuits.
3 If the wiring is in good order check the starter motor for continuity using a voltmeter.
4 If the battery is fully charged, the wiring is in order and the motor electrical circuit continuity correct and it still fails to operate, then it will have to be removed from the engine for examination.
5 Before this is done, however, make sure that the pinion gear has not jammed in mesh with the ring gear due either to a broken solenoid spring or dirty pinion gear splines. To release the pinion, engage a low gear (not automatics) and with the

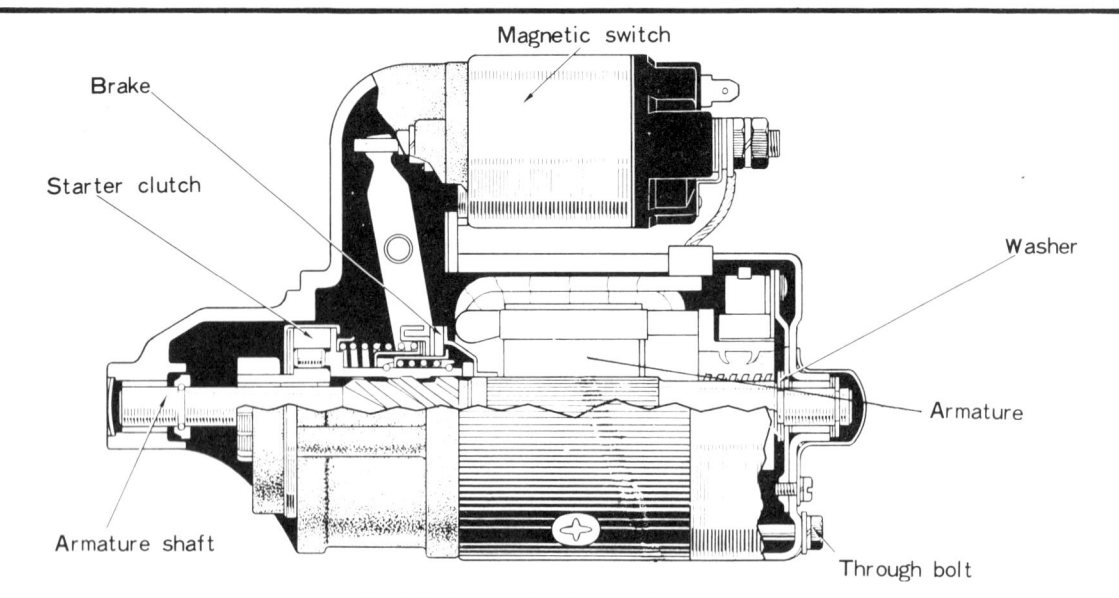

Fig. 10.7 Cross sectional view of starter motor

Labels: Magnetic switch, Brake, Starter clutch, Armature shaft, Through bolt, Armature, Washer

Fig. 10.8 Removal of manifold assembly

Fig. 10.9 Removal of starter motor

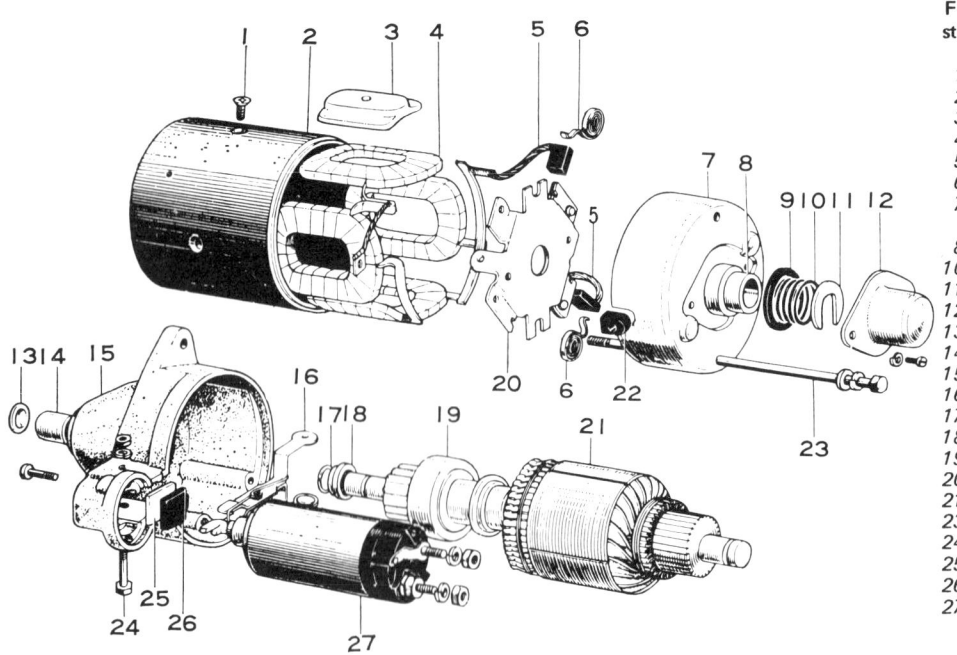

Fig. 10.10 Exploded view of starter motor (Earlier Type)

1. Screw
2. Starter yoke
3. Pole core
4. Starter field coil
5. Starter brush
6. Starter brush spring
7. Commutator end frame
8. Bushing
9. Starter plate
10. Starter plate
11. Lock plate
12. Bearing cover
13. Bushing cover
14. Bushing
15. Starter housing
16. Pinion drive lever
17. Snap ring
18. Pinion stop nut
19. Starter clutch
20. Starter brush holder
21. Starter armature
22. Bolt
23. Bolt
24. Drive pinion set pin
25. Plate
26. Rubber
27. Magnetic switch

ignition switch off, rock the car backwards and forwards which should release the pinion from mesh with the ring gear. If the pinion still remains jammed the starter motor must be removed.

14 Starter motor - removal and replacement

1 Disconnect the battery terminals.
2 Make a note of the electrical connections at the rear of the solenoid and disconnect the heavy duty cable. Also release the low tension cables. There is no need to undo the heavy duty cable that passes from the rear of the solenoid into the motor body.
3 Undo and remove the starter motor securing bolts. It should now be possible to remove the starter motor from the side of the engine but it may be found that the exhaust manifold is in the way in which case it will have to be removed. This is a straightforward operation and will present no difficulties. (Figs. 10.8/10.9)
4 Generally replacement is a straightforward reversal of the removal sequence. Check that the electrical cable connections are clean and firmly attached to their respective terminals.

15 Starter motor - dismantling, overhaul and reassembly

1 Disconnect the field coil lead from the solenoid main terminal.
2 Undo and remove the two screws securing the solenoid to the starter housing and then withdraw the solenoid far enough for it to be unhooked from the drive engagement lever fork.
3 Undo and remove the two screws and spring washer securing the bearing cover to the commutater end frame. Lift away the bearing cover.
4 Remove the lockplate, spring and seal washer from the end of the armature.
5 Undo and remove the two through bolts, spring and plain washers securing the starter yoke and commutator endframe to the starter housing. Withdraw the commutator endframe and brush-holder followed by the yoke from the starter housing.
6 Undo and remove the engagement lever pivot bolt from the side of the starter housing and then detach the rubber buffer and its backing plate. Remove the armature assembly complete with drive engagement lever from the starter housing.
7 Using a tubular drift, drive the pinion stop collar up the armature shaft far enough to enable the circlip to be removed. Pull the stop collar from the shaft and slide off the clutch assembly.
8 Check for wear in the armature shaft bearings. The specified clearance between shaft and bearing is between 0.037 and 0.053 in (0.095 and 0.135 mm) with a maximum of 0.008 in (0.2 mm). Normally the bearings will require renewal by pressing out the old ones from the starter housing and commutator endframe and pressing in the new ones. Before doing this check the diameter of the armature shaft which should be 0.492 in (12.5 mm). If this is worn then a new armature will be required and it will be more economical to exchange the starter motor complete for a reconditioned unit.
9 Armature shaft bearings are available in standard and undersizes as follows:

Standard		0.4935-0.4945 in	(12.535-12.560 mm)
Undersize	(1)	0.4817-0.4827 in	(12.235-12.260 mm)
	(2)	0.4738-0.4748 in	(12.035-12.060 mm)

If copper lined shell bearings are fitted to the starter motor as

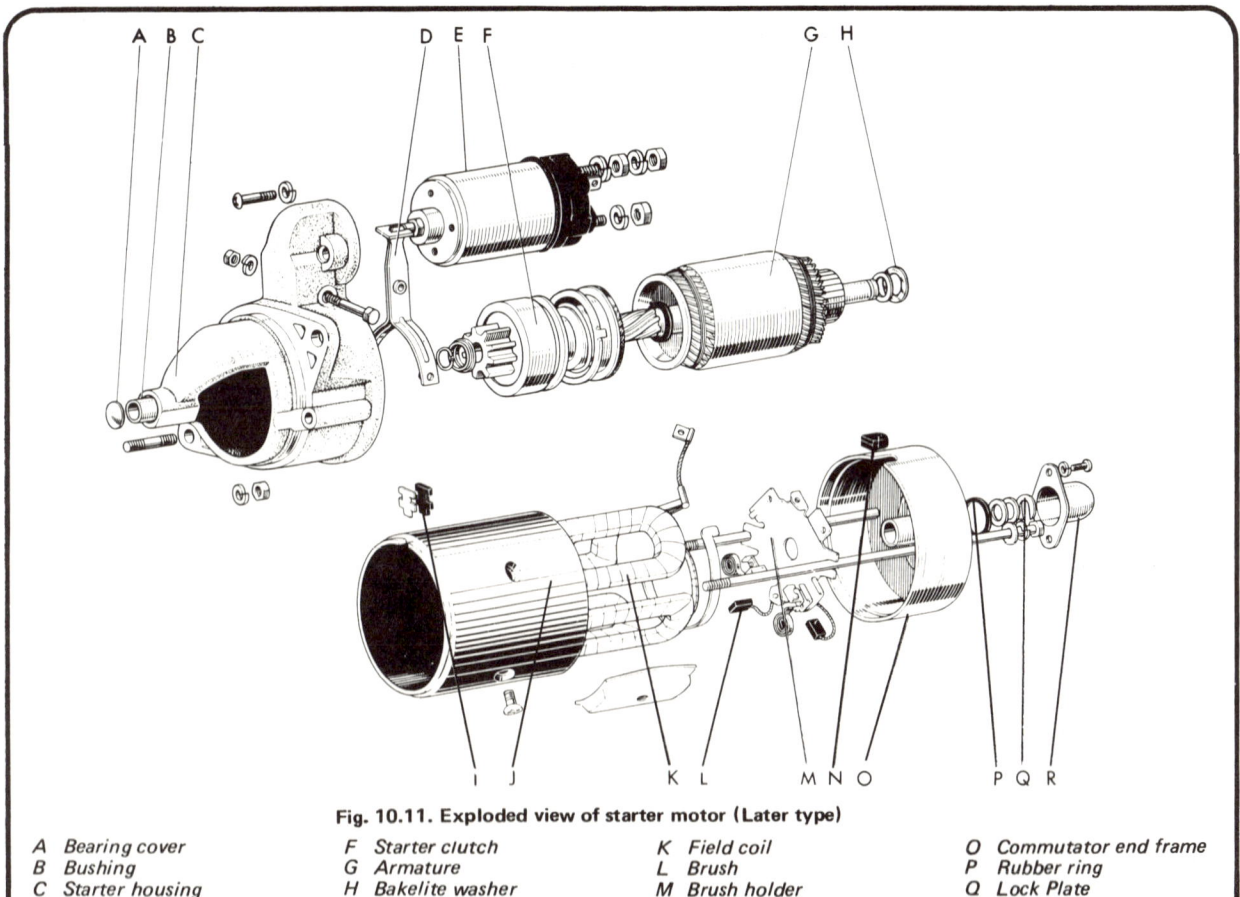

Fig. 10.11. Exploded view of starter motor (Later type)

A Bearing cover
B Bushing
C Starter housing
D Pinion drive lever
E Magnetic switch
F Starter clutch
G Armature
H Bakelite washer
I Rubber
J Starter yoke
K Field coil
L Brush
M Brush holder
N Rubber insulator
O Commutator end frame
P Rubber ring
Q Lock Plate
R End frame cover

original equipment, then after renewal they must be reamed to conform with the armature shaft fitting diameter and the specified running clearance.

10 Check the armature shaft for distortion or ovality and renew if evident.

11 Check the commutator segments and undercut the mica insulators using a hacksaw blade ground to the correct thickness. If the commutator is burned or discoloured, clean it with a piece of fine glass paper (not emery or carborundum) and finally wipe with a petrol moistened cloth.

12 With the starter motor dismantled, test the four field coils for an open circuit. Connect a 12 volt battery with a 12 volt bulb in one of the leads between the field terminal post and the tapping points of the field coils to which the brushes are connected. An open circuit is proved by the bulb not lighting.

13 If the bulb lights, it does not necessarily mean that the field coils are in order, as there is a possibility that one of the coils will be earthed to the starter yoke or pole shoes. To check this, remove the lead from the brush connector and place it against a clean position of the starter yoke. If the bulb lights the field coils are earthing. Replacement of the field coils calls for the use of a wheel operated screwdriver, a soldering iron, caulking and riveting operations and is beyond the scope of the majority of owners. The starter yoke should be taken to a reputable electrical engineering works for new field coils to be fitted. Alternatively, purchase an exchange starter motor.

14 If the armature is damaged this will be evident after visual inspection. Look for signs of burning or discolouration of the wires.

15 Check the insulation of the brush holders and the length of the brushes. If these have worn to below 0.47 in (12 mm), renew them. Before fitting them to their holders, dress them to the correct contour by wrapping a piece of emery cloth round the commutator and rotating the commutator back and forth.

16 Check the starter clutch assembly for wear or sticky action, or chipped pinion teeth and renew the assembly if necessary.

17 Locate the centre bearing and brake components on the armature shaft. Grease them and see that the brake spring ends are engaged in the holes in the centre bearing support plate and the brake spring holder. Fit the clutch assembly to the armature shaft followed by a new pinion stop collar and circlip. Pull the stop collar forward and stake the collar rim over the circlip. Grease all sliding surfaces.

18 Locate the drive engagement lever to the armature shaft with

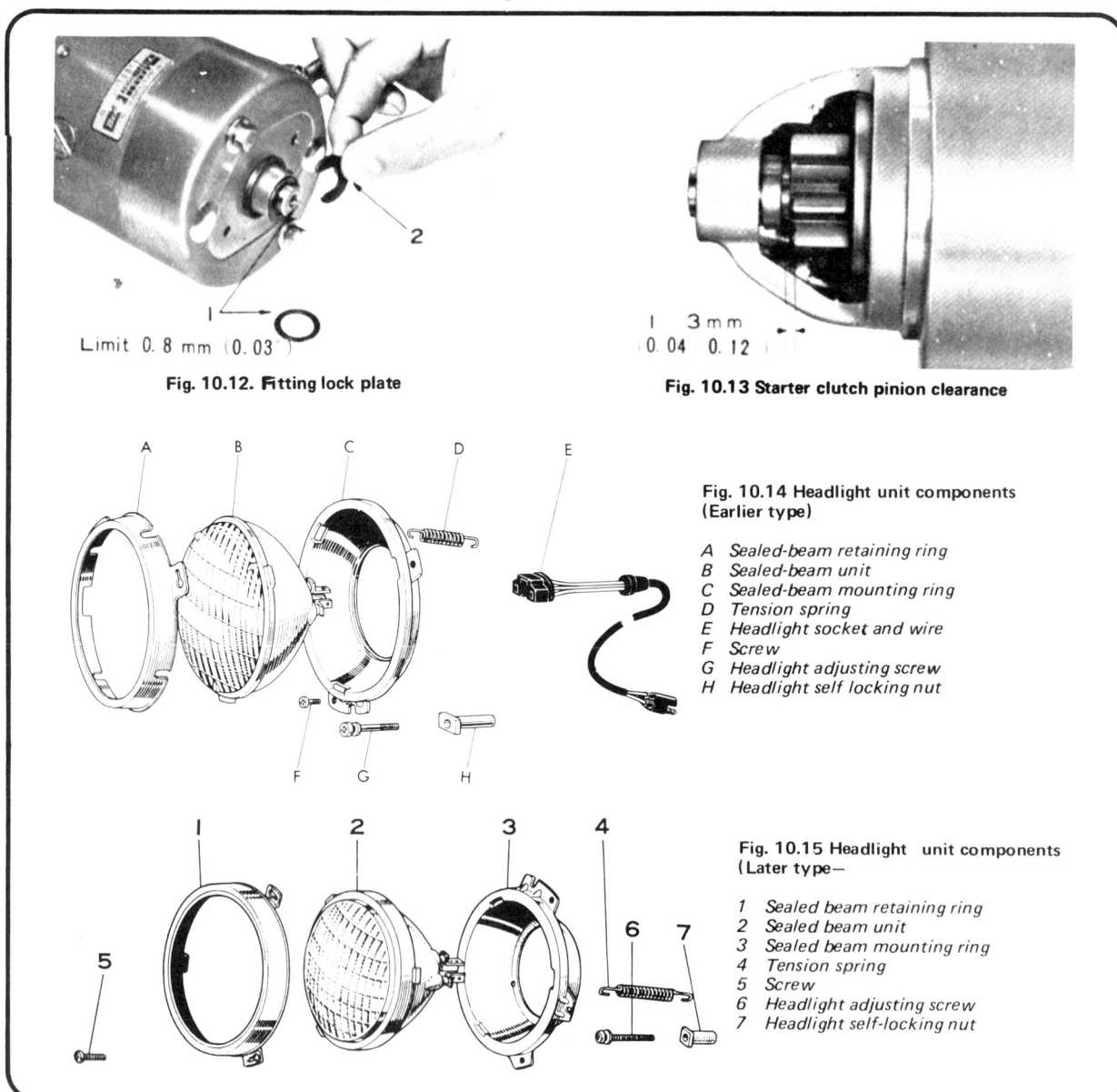

Fig. 10.12. Fitting lock plate

Fig. 10.13 Starter clutch pinion clearance

Fig. 10.14 Headlight unit components (Earlier type)

A Sealed-beam retaining ring
B Sealed-beam unit
C Sealed-beam mounting ring
D Tension spring
E Headlight socket and wire
F Screw
G Headlight adjusting screw
H Headlight self locking nut

Fig. 10.15 Headlight unit components (Later type—

1 Sealed beam retaining ring
2 Sealed beam unit
3 Sealed beam mounting ring
4 Tension spring
5 Screw
6 Headlight adjusting screw
7 Headlight self-locking nut

Chapter 10/Electrical system

the spring towards the armature and the steel washer up against the clutch.
19 Apply grease to all sliding surfaces and locate the armature assembly in the starter housing. Refit the drive engagement lever pivot bolt, well greased.
20 Fit the rubber buffer together with its backing plate and then align and offer into position the yoke to the starter housing.
21 Fit the brush holder to the armature and then insert the brushes.
22 Grease the commutator endframe bearing and then fit the end frame into position. Insert and tighten the two through bolts, spring and plain washers.
23 Fit the seal, washer and endcover (half-packed with multi purpose grease). Check the armature endfloat, if this exceeds 0.03 in (0.8 mm) remove the endcover and fit an additonal thrust-washer. If a spring was found on dismantling, this is used instead of thrust-washers. Retain in position with the lockplate. (Fig. 10.12)
24 Install the solenoid switch making sure that its hook engages *under* the spring of the engagement lever fork.
25 Connect up a 12 volt battery to the solenoid so that it is energised and insert a feeler gauge between the endface of the clutch pinion and the pinion stop collar. There should be a clearance of between 0.04 and 0.16 in (1.0 and 4.0 mm). If the clearance is incorrect, remove the solenoid switch and adjust the length of the adjustable stud by loosening its locknut. (Fig.10.13)
26 The starter motor is now ready for refitting to the car.

16 Headlight sealed beam unit - removal and replacement

1 For safety reasons, disconnect the battery.
2 Undo and remove the two screws securing the trim cover and lift away the trim cover. (photos)
3 Unscrew but do not remove the three retaining ring securing screws. (photo)
4 Turn the retainer ring anticlockwise and carefully pul forwards.
5 Take care not to disturb the headlight beam adjustmen screws.
6 Unplug the sealed beam unit from its terminal connector and lift away the unit. (photos)
7 Refitting the sealed beam unit is the reverse sequence to removal. It is recommended that the headlight unit alignment be checked by the local Toyota garage who will have the necessary optical equipment.

17 Sidelight and direction indicator bulbs - removal and replacement

1 For safety reasons, disconnect the battery.
2 Undo and remove the two screws securing the lens to the light unit.
3 Lift away the lens taking care not to damage the seal. (photo)
4 To detach the bulb press in and turn in an anticlockwise direction to release the bayonet fixing. Lift away the bulb.
5 Refitting the bulb and lens is the reverse sequence to removal.

18 Rear direction indicator, stop and tail light bulbs - removal and replacement

Saloon models

1 For safety reasons, disconnect the battery.
2 Open the boot lid and detach the relevant bulb socket by turning anticlockwise and drawing out rearwards. (photos)
3 To detach the bulb press in and turn in an anticlockwise direction to release the bayonet fixing. Lift away the bulb.
4 Refitting the bulb and socket is the reverse sequence to removal.

16.2a Detaching terminal block

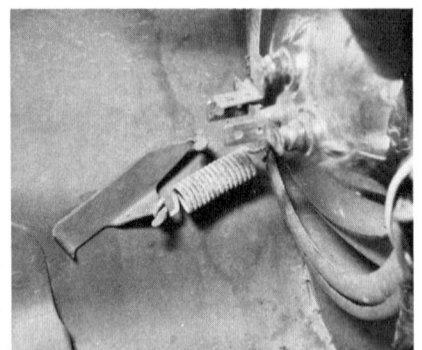

16.2b Rear view of light unit

16.3 Unscrewing light unit retaining screws

16.6a Lifting away the light unit

16.6b Separating the light unit

Fig. 10.16 Headlight unit removal (later type)

Chapter 10/Electrical system

17.3 Lifting away the lens

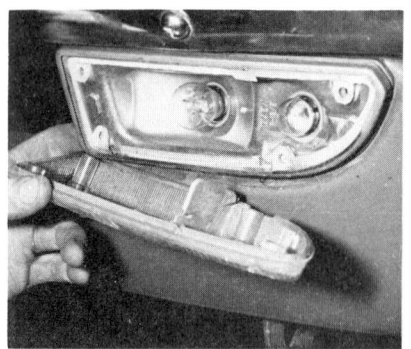

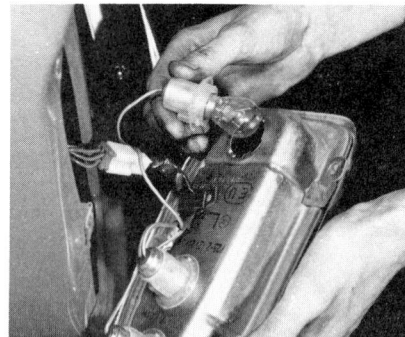

18a Removing bulb and holder

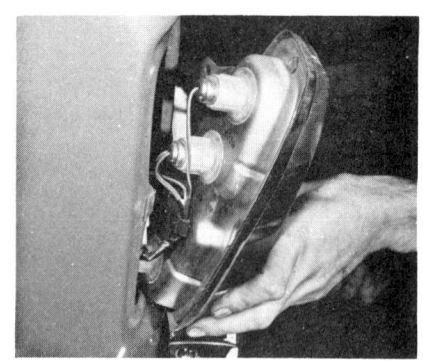

18b Lifting away complete light unit

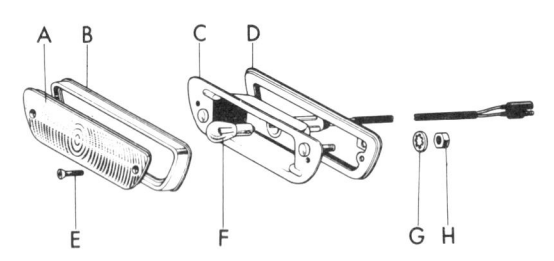

Fig 10.17 Front side and direction indicator light components (early models)

A Lens
B Rim
C Light body
D Gasket
E Screw
F Bulb
G Toothed washer
H Nut

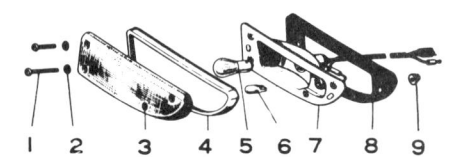

Fig 10.18 Front direction indicator light components (later models)

1 Screw
2 Nylon washer
3 Lens
4 Light rim
5 Bulb
6 Bulb
7 Light body
8 Light body gasket
9 Nut

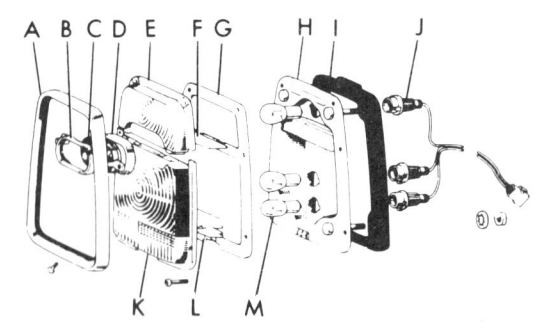

Fig. 10.19 Rear combination light assembly (early models)

A Rim
B Moulding
C Reflex reflector
D Seat
E Lens
F Shade
G Gasket
H Body
I Gasket
J Socket and wire
K Lens
L Shade
M Bulb

Estate cars

1 For safety reasons, disconnect the battery.
2 Undo and remove the six screws securing the lens to the light unit.
3 Lift away the lens taking care not to damage the seal.
4 To detach the bulb press in and turn in an anticlockwise direction to release the bayonet fixing. Lift away the bulb.
5 Refitting the bulb and lens is the reverse sequence to removal.

19 Side flasher light bulb - removal and replacement

1 For safety reasons, disconnect the battery.
2 Undo and remove the two screws securing the rim, lens and gasket to the light unit body. Lift away the rim and lens. (photo)
3 To detach the bulb press in and turn in an anticlockwise direction to release the bayonet fixing. Lift away the bulb.
4 Refitting the bulb and lens is the reverse sequence to removal.

20 Rear number plate light bulb - removal and replacement

Saloon models

1 For safety reasons, disconnect the battery.
2 Undo and remove the two screws securing the lens cover, and lens to the light body. Lift away the cover and lens taking care not to damage the gasket.
3 To detach the bulb press in and turn in an anticlockwise direction to release the bayonet fixing. Lift away the bulb.
4 Refitting the bulb and lens is the reverse sequence to removal.

Estate cars

1 For safety reasons, disconnect the battery.
2 Undo and remove the two screws securing the lens to the light unit body. Lift away the lens taking care not to damage the gasket.
3 To detach the bulb press in, and turn in an anticlockwise direction to release the bayonet fixing. Lift away the bulb.

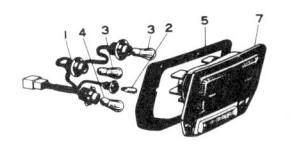

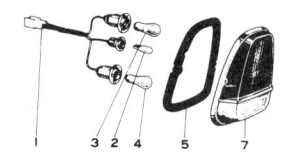

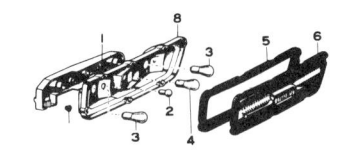

Fig. 10.20 Rear combination light components (later models)

1 Socket and wire
2 Bulb
3 Bulb
4 Bulb
5 Gasket
6 Lens
7 Lens and body
8 Light body

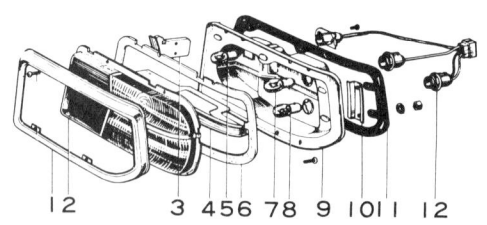

Fig. 10.21 Rear combination light components (KE 15 and 17 models)

1 Rim
2 Lens
3 Shade
4 Shade
5 Bulb
6 Gasket
7 Bulb
8 Bulb
9 Light body
10 Bracket
11 Gasket
12 Socket and wire

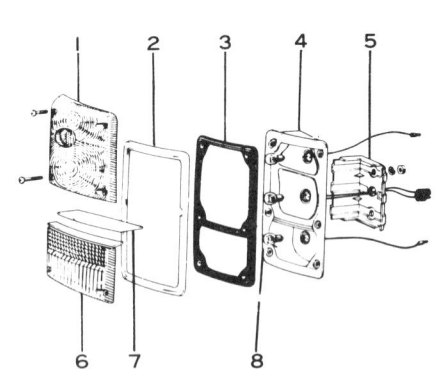

Fig 10.22 Rear combination light components (KE 16V models)

1 Lens
2 Rim
3 Gasket
4 Body
5 Retainer
6 Lens
7 Shade
8 Bulb

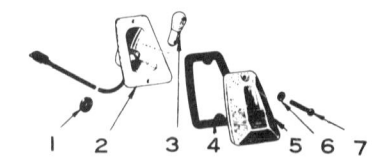

Fig 10.23 Side repeater light assembly (later models)

1 Grommet
2 Body
3 Bulb
4 Gasket
5 Lens
6 Nylon washer
7 Screw

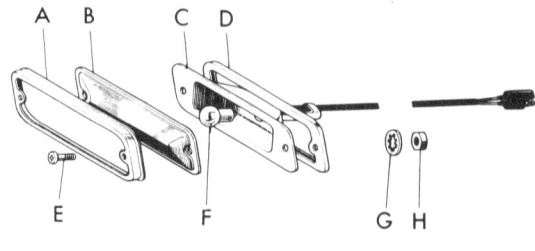

Fig 10.24 Side repeater light assembly (earlier models)

A Rim
B Lens
C Body
D Gasket
E Screw
F Bulb
G Toothed washer
H Nut

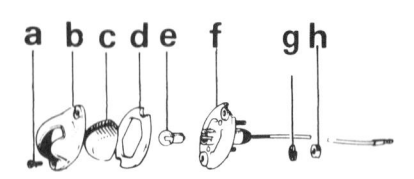

Fig. 10.25 Rear number plate light (earlier models)

A Screw
B Cover
C Lens
D Gasket
E Bulb
F Body
G Lock washer
H Nut

19.2 Removal of repeater light lens

Fig. 10.26 Rear number plate light components (later models)

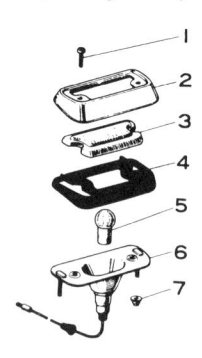

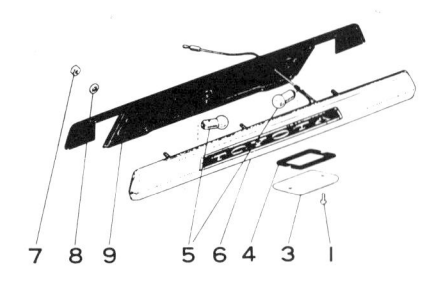

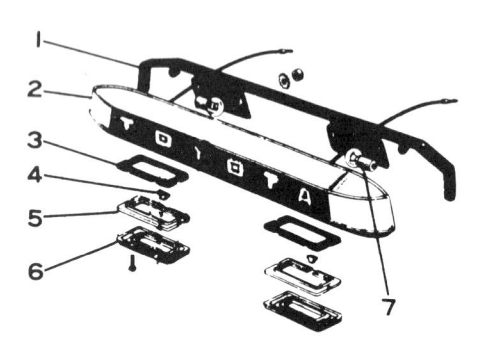

1. Screw
2. Rim
3. Lens
4. Gasket
5. Bulb
6. Body
7. Nut
8. Tooth washer
9. Gasket

Fig.10.27 Rear number plate light (KE 16V models)

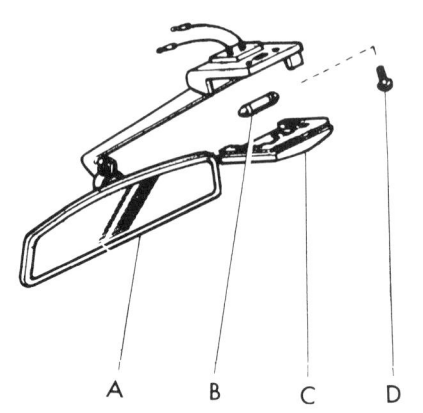

1. Gasket
2. Body
3. Gasket
4. Filter
5. Lens
6. Rim
7. Bulb

Fig. 10.28 Interior light assembly

A Mirror and light assembly
B Bulb
C Lens
D Screw

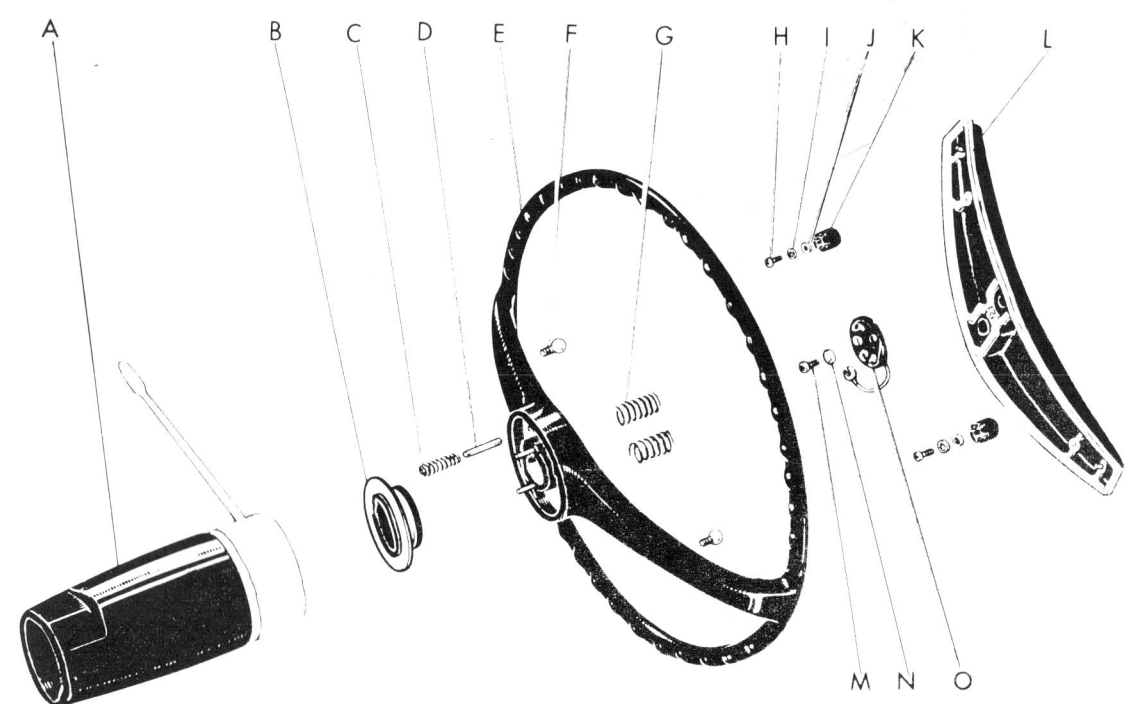

Fig. 10.29 Horn button/push bar assembly

A Steering housing
B Contact plate
C Compression spring
D Straight pin
E Steering wheel
F Balljoint
G Compression spring
H Screw
I Toothed washer
J Plate washer
K Joint socket
L Horn button
M Screw
N Toothed washer
O Contact ring

Chapter 10/Electrical system

4 Refitting the bulb and lens is the reverse sequence to removal.

21 Interior light bulb - removal and replacement

1 To renew the interior light bulb carefully release the light cover. This is a snap fit.
2 The festoon bulb may now be withdrawn from the spring blade contacts.
3 Refitting the bulb and cover is the reverse sequence to removal.

22 Horn - fault diagnosis and rectification

1 If a horn works badly or fails completely first check the wiring leading to it for short circuits, blown fuse or loose connections. Also check that the horn is firmly secured and there is nothing lying on the horn body.
2 If a horn loses its adjustment it will not alter the pitch as the tone of a horn depends on the vibration of an air column. It will however give a softer or more harsh sound. Also excessive current will be required which can cause fuses to blow.
3 Further information on servicing is given in Section 23.

23 Horn - servicing and adjustment

The horn should never be completely dismantled but it is possible to adjust it. This adjustment is to compensate for wear only and will not affect the tone. Two types of horns can be fitting to models covered by this manual:

Vibrator type horn

1 Disconnect the wires from each horn that lead to the horn button.
2 Slacken the adjustment screw locknut.
3 Connect an ammeter to the earth terminal as shown in Fig 10.33 and make any adjustments necessary.
4 As the adjusting screw is turned anticlockwise the pitch and current will increase. Too great a current (over 2.5 amps) will burn the contact points so do not exceed this figure.

Trumpet type horn

1 Adjustment for this type of horn is basically identical to that for the vibrator type horn.
2 Remove the cover to gain access to the adjustment nut.
3 Connect an ammeter as shown in Fig 10.34 and make any

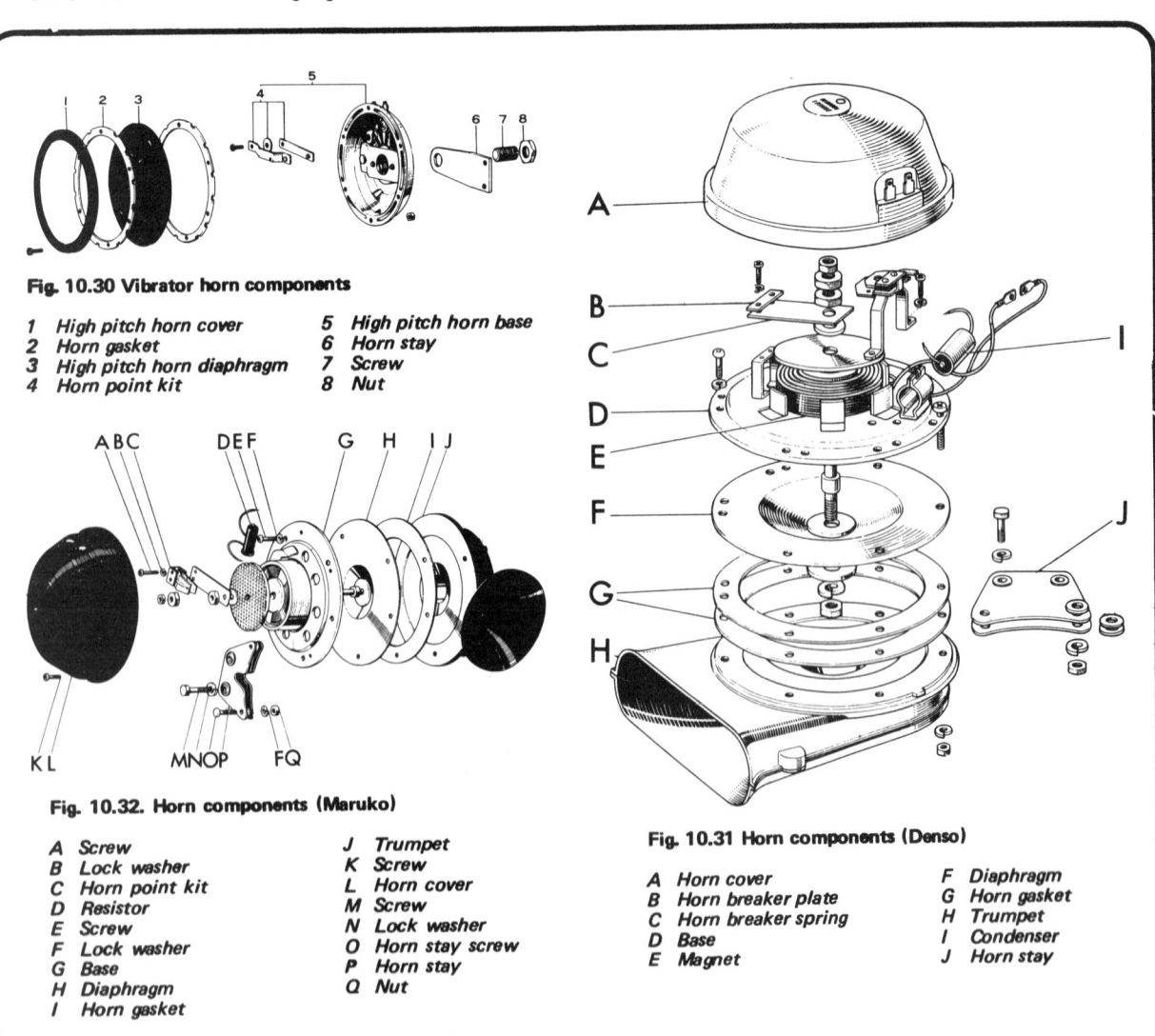

Fig. 10.30 Vibrator horn components

1 High pitch horn cover
2 Horn gasket
3 High pitch horn diaphragm
4 Horn point kit
5 High pitch horn base
6 Horn stay
7 Screw
8 Nut

Fig. 10.32. Horn components (Maruko)

A Screw
B Lock washer
C Horn point kit
D Resistor
E Screw
F Lock washer
G Base
H Diaphragm
I Horn gasket
J Trumpet
K Screw
L Horn cover
M Screw
N Lock washer
O Horn stay screw
P Horn stay
Q Nut

Fig. 10.31 Horn components (Denso)

A Horn cover
B Horn breaker plate
C Horn breaker spring
D Base
E Magnet
F Diaphragm
G Horn gasket
H Trumpet
I Condenser
J Horn stay

24a Some models have arm securing screws

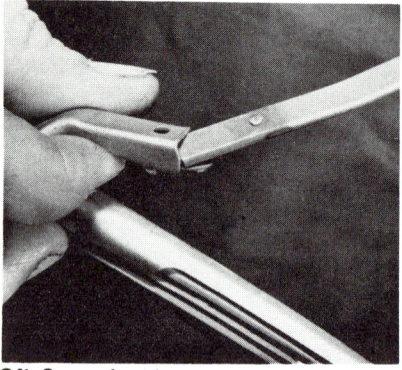

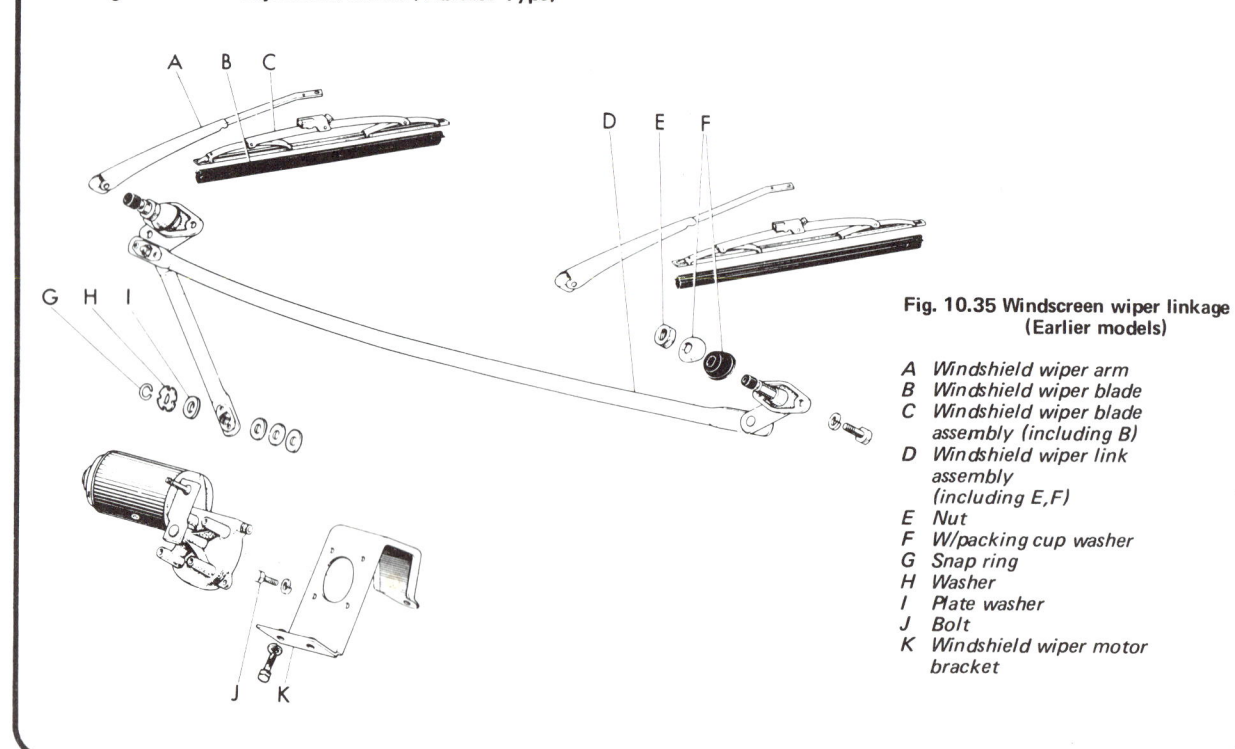

24b Separating blade for arm

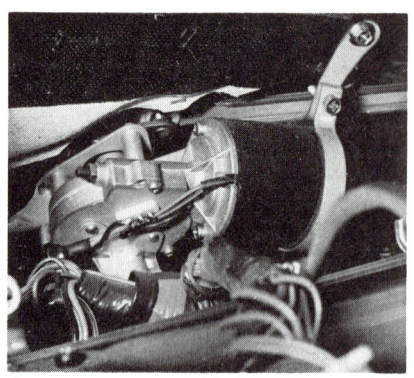

27.2 Windscreen wiper motor (later models)

Fig. 10.33 Horn adjustment circuit (Vibrator Type)

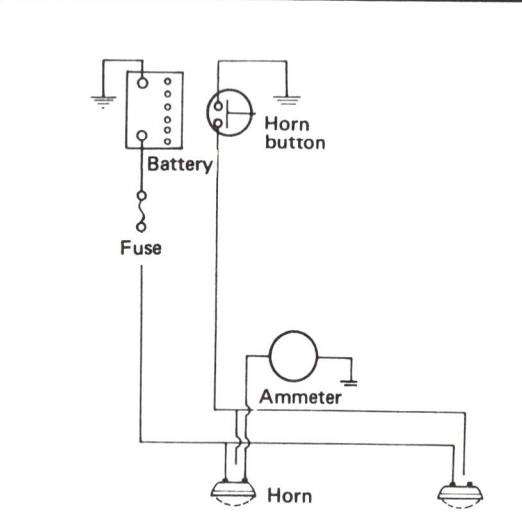

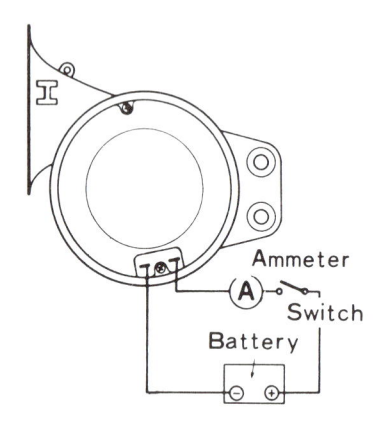

Fig. 10.34 Horn adjustment circuit (Trumpet Type)

Fig. 10.35 Windscreen wiper linkage (Earlier models)

- A Windshield wiper arm
- B Windshield wiper blade
- C Windshield wiper blade assembly (including B)
- D Windshield wiper link assembly (including E, F)
- E Nut
- F W/packing cup washer
- G Snap ring
- H Washer
- I Plate washer
- J Bolt
- K Windshield wiper motor bracket

Chapter 10/Electrical system

Fig. 10.36. Windscreen wiper motor assembly (early models)

A Screw
B End frame
C Brush holder
D Ball
E Armature
F Stator
G Gear housing
H Screw
I Nut
J Crank housing cover packing
K Crank housing cover plate
L Screw
M Crank arm
N Shaft supporter
O Gear
P Cam plate

adjustments necessary.
4 A second adjustment is available on this type of horn. Adjust the air gap so that the horn will operate at 9 volts but the plate will not contact the core at 15 volts.
5 Refit the cover.

24 Windscreen wiper arm and blade - removal and replacement

1 Before removing a wiper arm, turn the windscreen wiper switch on and off to ensure the arms are in their normal parked position parallel with the bottom of the windscreen.
2 To remove an arm carefully ease back the spring clip and pull the arm from the spindle splines. (photos)
3 When replacing an arm, place it so it is in the correct relative parked position and push it onto the splindle splines.

25 Windscreen wiper mechanism - fault diagnosis and rectification

Should the windscreen wipers fail, or work very slowly then check the terminals for loose connections, and make sure the insulation of the external wiring is not damaged or broken. If this is in order then check the current the motor is taking by connecting a 0-20 ammeter in the circuit and turning on the wiper switch. Consumption should be approximately 2-3 amps.

If no current is flowing check that the fuse has not failed. If it has, check the wiring of the motor and other electrical circuits serviced by this fuse for short circuits. If the fuse is in good order check the wiper switch.

Should the motor take a very low current ensure that the battery is fully charged. If the motor takes a high current then it is an indication that there is an internal fault or partially seized linkage.

It is possible for the motor to be stripped and overhauled but the availability of spare parts could present a problem. Either take a faulty unit to the local automobile electricians or obtain a replacement unit.

26 Windscreen wiper linkage - removal and replacement

1 For safety reasons, disconnect the battery.
2 Disconnect the windscreen wiper arms as described in Section 25.
3 Remove the left-hand defroster nozzle and hose. For this it may be necessary to remove the combination meter on some models.

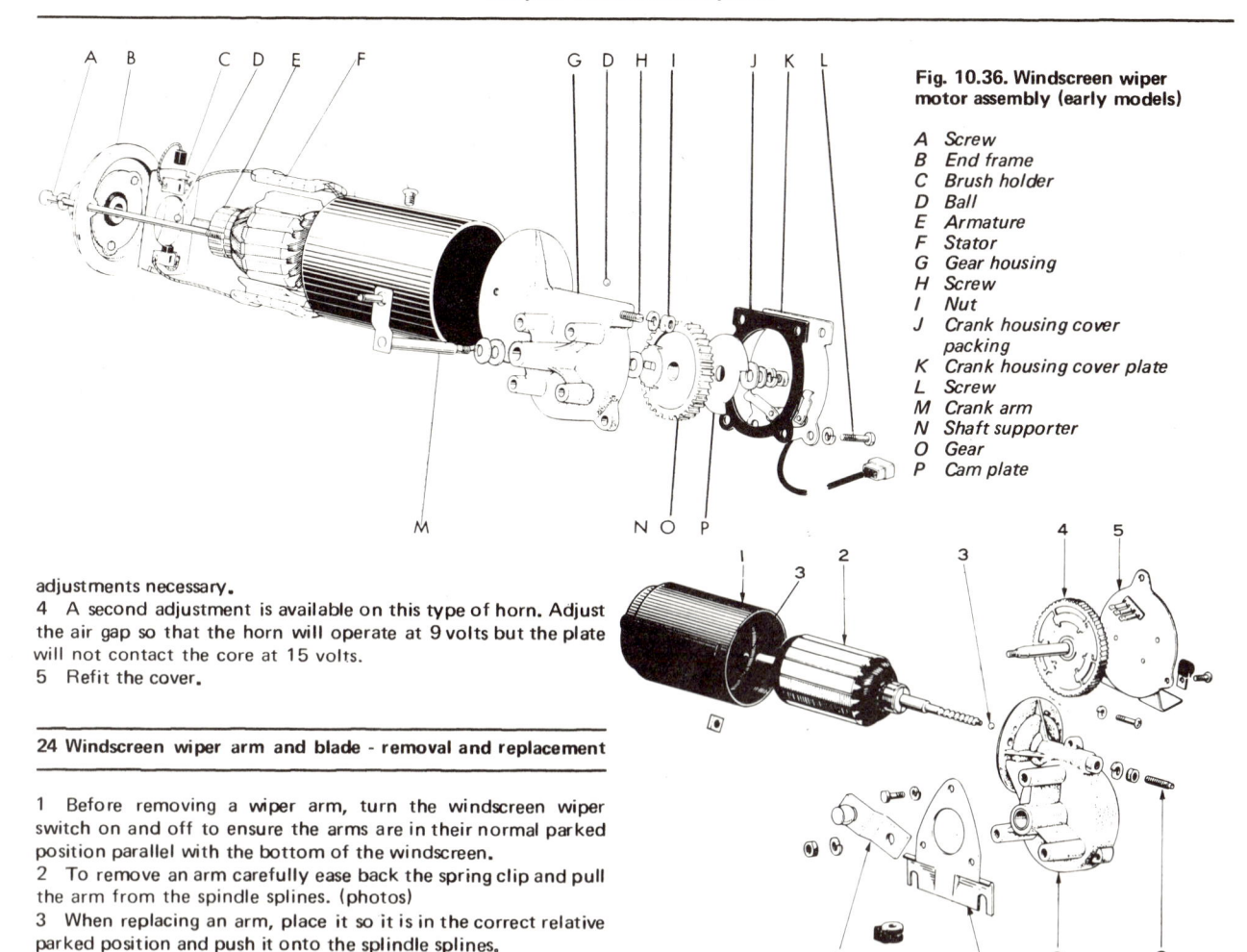

Fig. 10.37. Exploded view of windscreen wiper motor (later models)

1 Body
2 Armature
3 Ball
4 Gear
5 Cover plate
6 Crank
7 Bracket
8 Gear housing
9 Adjustment screw

4 On later models disconnect the wiper motor and link-joint using a screwdriver.
5 On early models the bracket and link are removed together with the motor.
6 Unscrew the spindle retaining nuts and washers. The assembly may now be removed from the car.
7 Refitting the windscreen wiper linkage is the reverse sequence to removal. Do not overtighten the spindle retaining nuts. Lubricate all moving parts with a little grease.

27 Windscreen wiper motor - removal and replacement

1 For safety reasons, disconnect the battery.
2 Disconnect the electric cable terminal connectors to the wiper motor. (photo)
3 Carefully disconnect the linkage from the wiper motor by easing apart with a screwdriver. On earlier models it will be necessary to remove the spindle and wiper motor securing bolts. The motor is then removed together with the bracket and link. Once the motor has been freed detach the link from the crank arm and the bracket from the motor.
4 One some late models it may be found beneficial to remove the parcel tray.

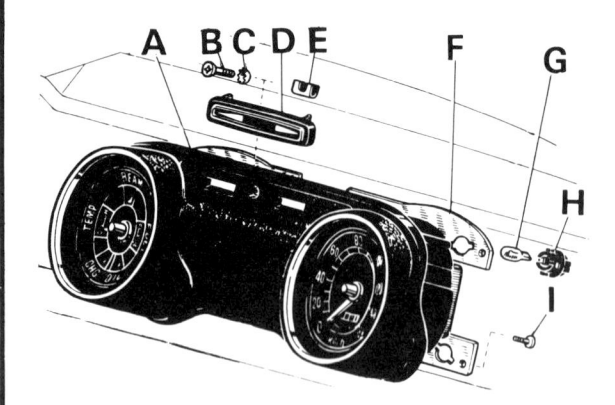

Fig. 10.38. Combination meter attachments (Type 1)

- A Combination meter
- B Screw
- C Washer
- D Emblem
- E Spring nut
- F Meter circuit plate
- G Bulb
- H Bulb socket
- I Screw

Fig. 10.39. Combination meter removal (Type 1)

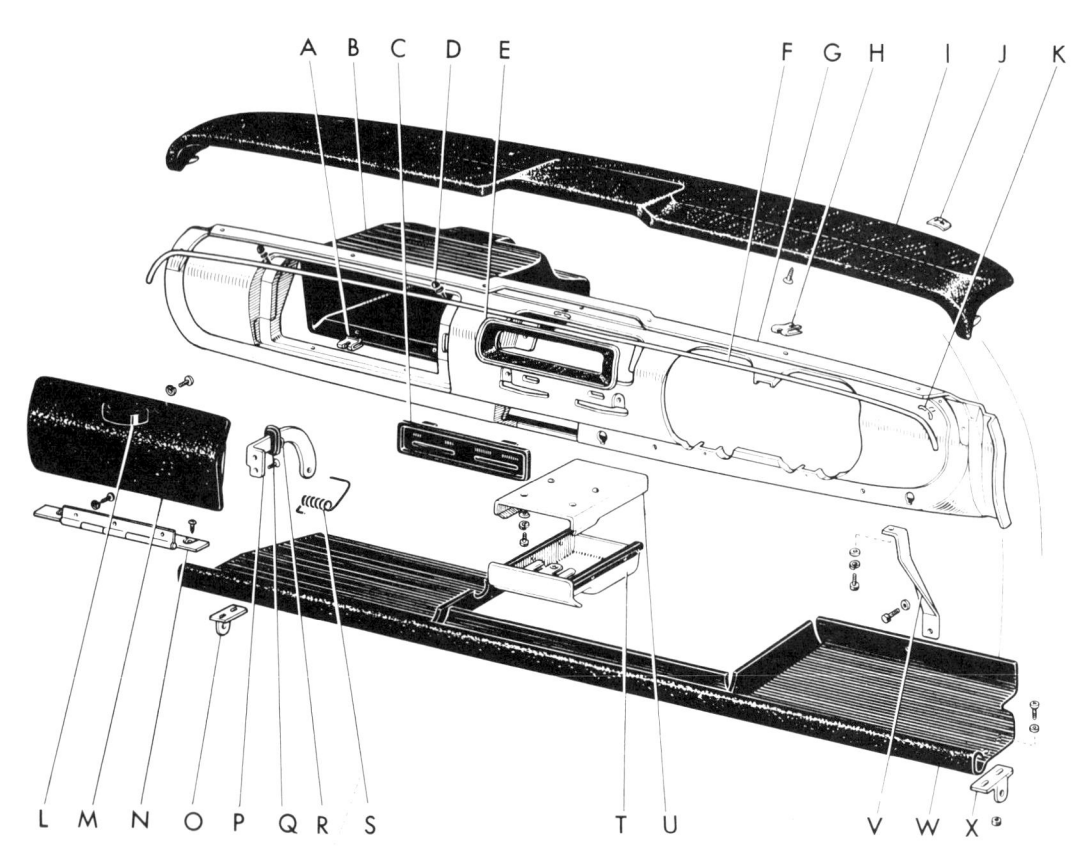

Fig. 10.40. Instrument panel assembly (Type 1)

- A Glove compartment attaching nut
- B Glove compartment
- C Heater control hole cover
- D Cushion
- E Radio control hole cover
- F Instrument panel moulding
- G Instrument lower panel
- H Spring nut
- I Instrument panel safety pad
- J Spring nut
- K Clip
- L Glove compartment door knob
- M Glove compartment door
- N Glove compartment door hinge
- O Under tray left retainer
- P Glove compartment door check arm
- Q Door check arm hole guide
- R Glove compartment door arm stopper
- S Torsion spring
- T Front ash receptacle
- U Ash receptacle retainer
- V Instrument panel under tray bracket
- W Instrument panel under tray
- X Under tray right retainer

Chapter 10/Electrical system

28 Fuses and fusible link - general description

Commencing with the later produced KE models the ignition and lighting circuits are protected by a special fusible link in each wiring harness instead of individual fuses. These links are located near to the battery and comprise a low current capacity copper wire that melts if a high current is produced in a circuit by direct earthing.

Should one of these links burn, the short circuit should be traced and rectified before a new link in fitted.

The fuse box location depends on the model but is usually found on the driver's side of the parcel shelf end panel on later models.

As each new model has been introduced so the number of fuses has been increased. For instance on early KE models there are 6 fuses whereas on the latest models there are 10 fuses.

Each fuse application is printed on the transparent fuse box cover.

When renewing a fuse always find the cause of the trouble before fitting the new fuse. Always replace with the same rated fuse.

29 Combination meter (Type 1) - removal and replacement

1 For safety reasons, disconnect the battery.
2 Disconnect the speedometer drive cable from the rear of the speedometer head.
3 Make a note of and then detach the terminal connections to the rear of the combination meter assembly.
4 Remove the direction indicator light emblem and then the three securing screws.
5 The combination meter may now be drawn forwards and away from the instrument panel. (Fig. 10.39)
6 Replacement of the combination meter is the reverse sequence to removal.

30 Combination meter (Type 1) - dismantling and reassembly

1 Turn the combination meter bulb socket anticlockwise and remove it.
2 Next pull out the bulb.
3 Undo and remove the meter sub-assembly securing screws and lift away the meter and gauges.
4 Remove the fuel gauge, speedometer, water temperature gauge and light cover.
5 Finally the meter circuit plate can be removed once the securing screws have been removed.
6 Reassembly the combination meter assembly is the reverse sequence to dismantling. Take great care not to damage the circuit plate.

31 Instrument panel safety pad (Type 1) - removal and replacement

1 Refer to Section 30, and remove the combination meter.
2 Refer to Section 32, and remove the glove compartment.
3 Undo and remove the six screws and eight spring nuts securing the safety pad assembly to the instrument panel and body. (Fig. 10.41)
4 Carefully lift away the safety pad assembly.
5 Refitting the safety pad assembly is the reverse sequence to removal.

32 Glove compartment (Type 1) - removal and replacement

1 Undo and remove the screws securing the glove compartment lid and lift away the lid.
2 Undo and remove the three glove compartment securing screws and carefully remove the glove compartment.
3 Refitting the glove compartment and lid is the reverse sequence to removal.

33 Combination meter (Type 2) - removal and replacement

1 For safety reasons, disconnect the battery.
2 Disconnect the speedometer drive cable from the rear of the speedometer head.
3 Make a note of and then detach the terminal connections to the rear of the combination meter assembly.
4 Undo and remove the four screws that secure the combination meter to the instrument panel.
5 The combination meter may now be drawn forwards and away from the instrument panel. (Fig 10.42)
6 Replacement of the combination meter is the reverse sequence to removal.

34 Combination meter (Type 2) - dismantling and reassembly

1 Turn the combination meter bulb socket anticlockwise and remove.
2 Next pull out the bulbs.
3 Carefully nip the trip meter resetting shaft with a pair of long nose pliers and turn the resetting knob anticlockwise to remove it.
4 Undo and remove the self-tapping screws securing the meter cover.
5 Undo and remove the screws that secure the window case.
6 Remove from the meter case the fuel gauge, water temperature gauge and speedometer.
7 Undo and remove the meter circuit plate securing screws and

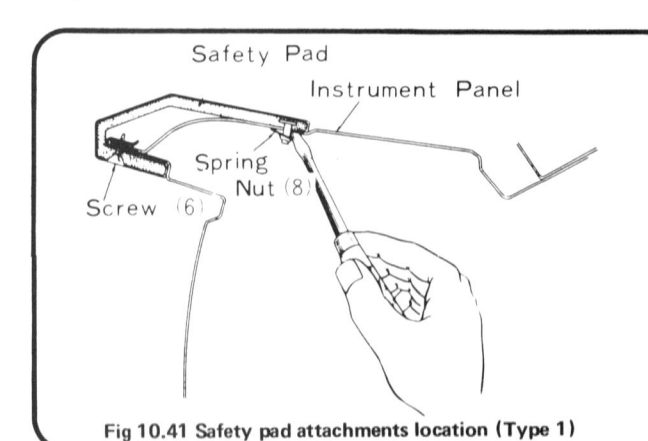

Fig 10.41 Safety pad attachments location (Type 1)

Fig 10.42 Combination meter removal (Type 2)

Fig 10.43 Combination meter components (Type 2)

1. Combination meter
2. Speedometer
3. Water temperature receiver gauge
4. Fuel receiver gauge
5. Meter circuit plate
6. Bulb
7. Bulb socket

Fig 10.44 Instrument panel assembly (Type 2)

1. Instrument panel name plate
2. Instrument panel moulding
3. Instrument panel safety pad
4. Choke control ornament
5. Radio tuner hole cover
6. Instrument lower panel
7. Ignition switch hood
8. Glove compartment
9. Glove compartment door check arm
10. Golve compartment door hinge
11. Under tray
12. Glove compartment door
13. Ash receptacle

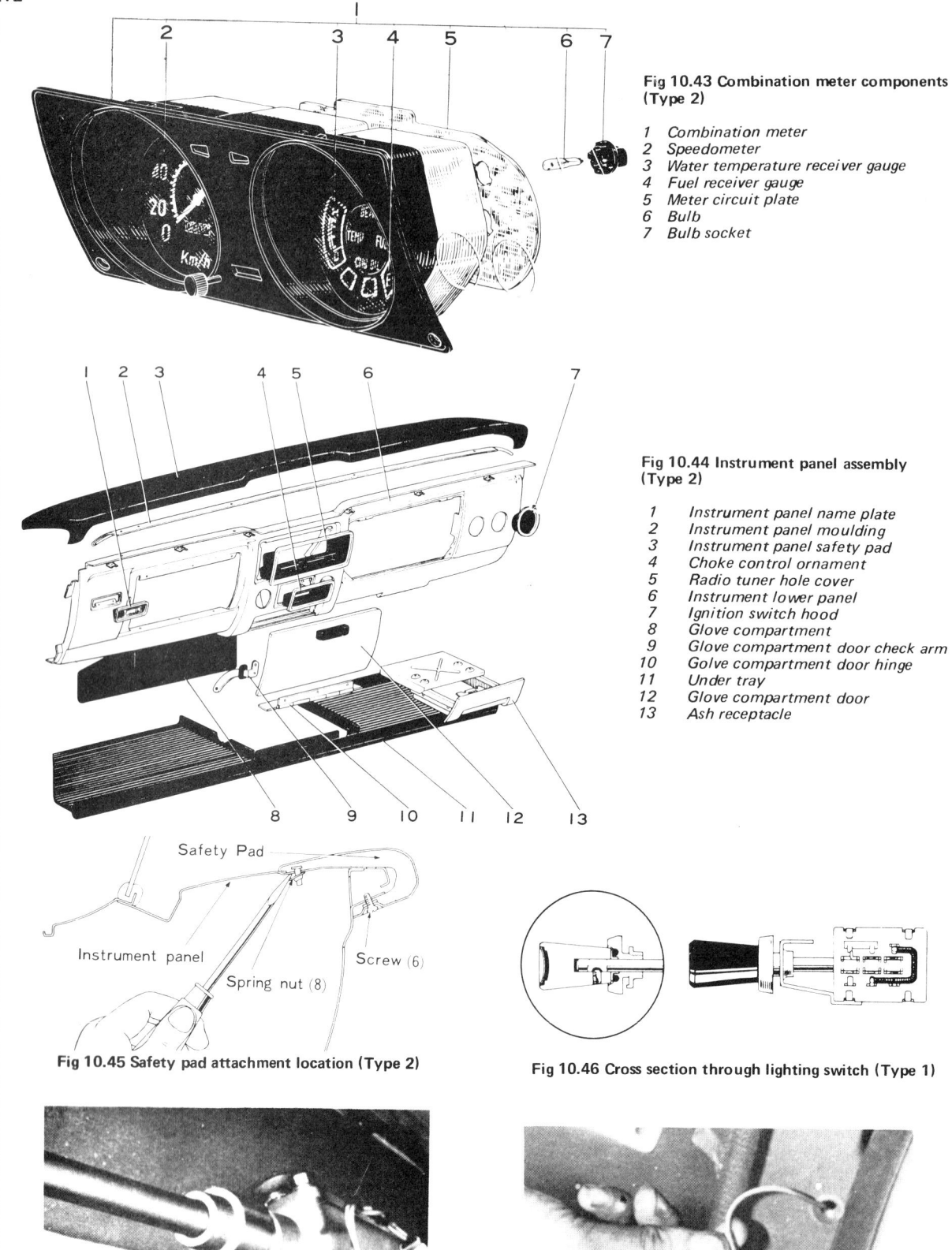

Fig 10.45 Safety pad attachment location (Type 2)

Fig 10.46 Cross section through lighting switch (Type 1)

Fig 10.47 Reverse light switch (manual transmission)

Fig 10.48 Courtesy light switch removal

Chapter 10/Electrical system

lift away the circuit plate.
8 Reassembling the combination meter assembly is the reverse sequence to dismantling. Take great care not to damage the circuit plate.

35 Instrument panel safety pad (Type 2) - removal and replacement

For full information, see Section 31.

36 Switches (Type 1) - removal and replacement

For safety reasons, always disconnect the battery before commencing work.

Ignition switch

1 Disconnect the wiring connector, at the rear of the switch.
2 Using a small 'C' spanner unscrew the ring nut and lift the ignition switch from the rear of the instrument panel.
3 Refitting the ignition switch is the reverse sequence to removal.

Lighting and wiper switches

1 Unscrew and remove the lockscrew and remove the knob. (Fig. 10.46)
2 Unscrew the switch by grasping the switch spindle and turning, so unscrewing it. Lift the switch from the rear of the instrument panel. Detach the cable connector.
3 Refitting the lighting or wiper switch is the reverse sequence to removal.

Reverse light switch. (manual gearbox)

Removal of the reverse light switch on earlier models entails detaching the gearbox rear mounting and tilting downwards. Follow the instructions given in Chapter 6 for gearbox removal as far as detaching the gearbox from the engine. To summarise the work entailed:
a) Remove floor carpeting.
b) Remove gearchange lever.
c) Disconnect reverse light switch terminal connector at rear right-hand side of engine.
d) Disconnect battery.
e) Drain cooling system and remove radiator inlet hose.
f) Move radiator fan to horizontal position.
g) Detach exhaust downpipe from manifold.
h) Remove propeller shaft.
i) Remove exhaust pipe support bracket.
j) Disconnect speedometer drive cable.
k) Detach gearbox rear mounting from body.
l) Lower rear of gearbox to gain access to switch.

Courtesy light switch

The switch is screwed in the door pillar. Using a socket or ring spanner carefully unscrew from the pillar and disconnect the wiring connector. (Fig. 10.48)
Refitting the switch is the reverse sequence to removal.

Direction indicator switch

1 Remove the steering wheel as described in Chapter 11.
2 Disconnect the wiring connector from the switch and horn.
3 Position the direction indicator switch lever to the right position.
4 Slacken and push down the switch securing screw and remove the switch assembly from the steering column tube.
5 Undo the steering housing securing screws and lift the housing halves from the column tube.

6 Finally pull out the switch wiring connector from the housing.
7 Should the switch develop a fault it must be renewed as it is a sealed unit and cannot be repaired.
8 Refitting the direction indicator switch is the reverse sequence to removal.

Stop light switch

1 Detach the brake pedal tension spring.
2 Disconnect the wiring connector.
3 Slacken the locknut and remove the switch.
4 Refitting the switch is the reverse sequence to removal. It will be necessary to check and reset the pedal height as described in Chapter 9.

Oil pressure switch

1 Disconnect the wiring connector and unscrew the oil pressure switch.
2 Refitting the oil pressure switch is the reverse sequence to removal.

37 Windscreen washer - general

The windscreen washer switch is integral with the wiper switch and operates when the switch is turned clockwise. The pump must not be operated without any fluid in the reservoir. Also do not allow the motor to run continuously for more than 20 seconds.

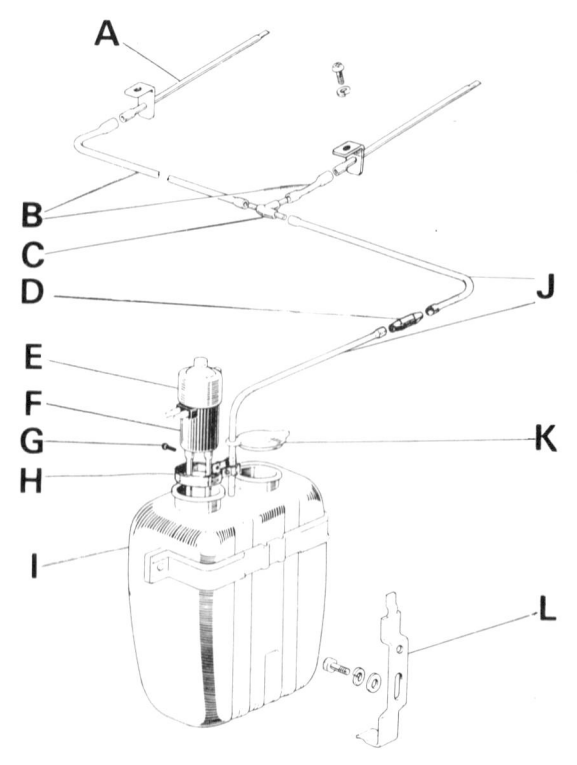

Fig 10.49 Windscreen washer assembly (earlier models)

A Nozzle
B Hose
C Joint "T"
D Joint
E Cap
F Motor and pump assembly
G Screw
H Motor supporter
I Tank assembly
J Hose
K Cap
L Bracket

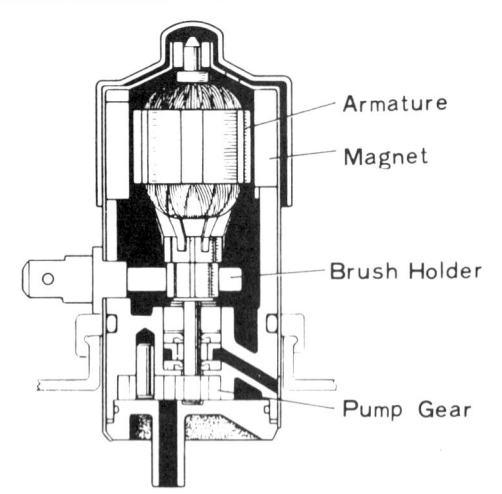

Fig 10.50 Windscreen washer motor and pump (earlier models)

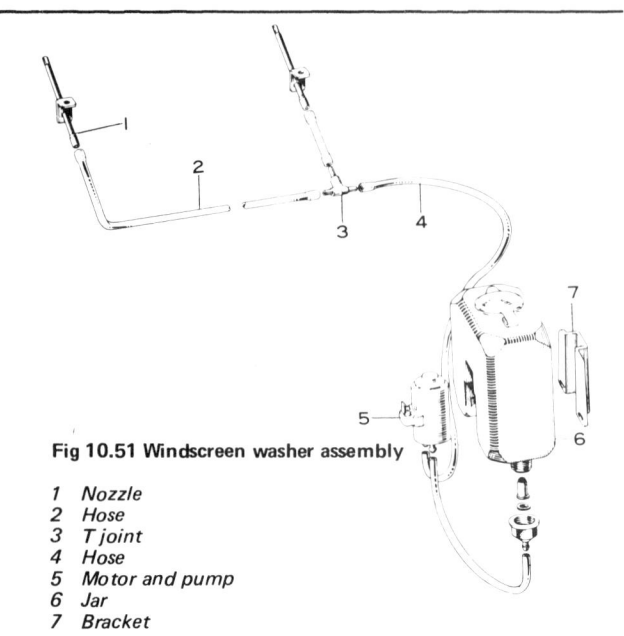

Fig 10.51 Windscreen washer assembly

1. Nozzle
2. Hose
3. T joint
4. Hose
5. Motor and pump
6. Jar
7. Bracket

Fig 10.52 Handbrake warning light switch removal

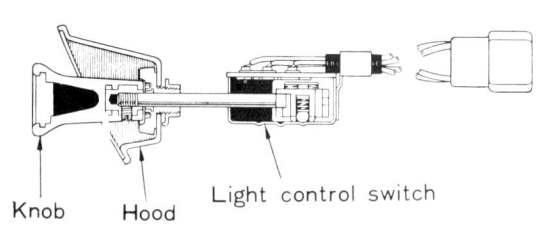

Fig 10.53 Light control switch cross section (Type 2)

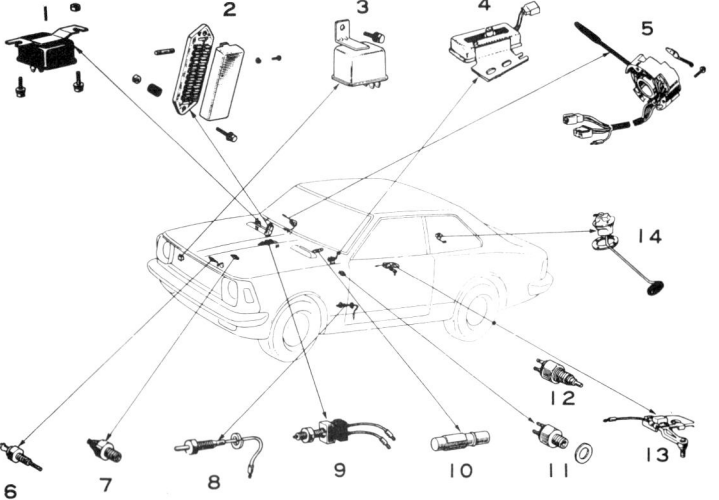

Fig 10.54 Location of various switches (later models)

1. Turn signal flasher
2. Fuse block assembly with fuses
3. Side turn signal relay
4. Neutral safety switch
5. Turn signal switch
6. Water temperature sender gauge
7. Oil pressure switch
8. Courtesy light switch
9. Stoplight switch
10. Fuse with retainer
11. Back-up light switch (on floor-shift car)
12. Back-up light switch (on remote control car)
13. Parking brake light switch
14. Fuel sender gauge

38 Switches (Type 2) - removal and replacement

As for Type 1 with the following exceptions:

Handbrake light switch

1 Undo and remove the bolt that secures the switch at the handbrake lever. Detach to terminal connector and lift away the switch. Fig. 10.52)
2 Refitting the switch is the reverse sequence to removal. After refitting adjust the switch so that the warning light goes out when the lever is fully released.

Direction indicator switch

Follow the instructions as for Type 1 but note that on 'H' models the control shaft upper bracket, brush and 'E' ring must be removed before the switch securing screws are unscrewed.

Lighting switch and ignition switch

When refitting the switch note that the projections on the switch body and switch hood must be mated with the slot in the instrument panel.

39 Combination meter (Type 3) - removal and replacement

1 For safety reasons, disconnect the battery.
2 Disconnect the speedometer cable from the rear of the instrument.
3 Carefully remove the instrument panel centre and right-hand mouldings. (photo)
4 Undo and remove the screw that secures the combination meter and instrument panel moulding retainer. (photo)
5 Undo and remove the two nuts that secure the combination meter from behind the instrument panel.
6 Ease the combination meter out slightly, and disconnect the various cables. (photos)
7 The combination meter may now be completely removed but in doing so take extreme care not to scratch the meter or steering upper housing.
8 Refitting the combination meter is the reverse sequence to removal but the following additional points should be noted:
a) Make sure the wire harness clamp is firmly secure behind the combination meter.
b) Do not pinch the wire harness between the combination meter and instrument panel.
c) Ensure the speedometer cable is not forced or unduly bent when replacing the combination meter.

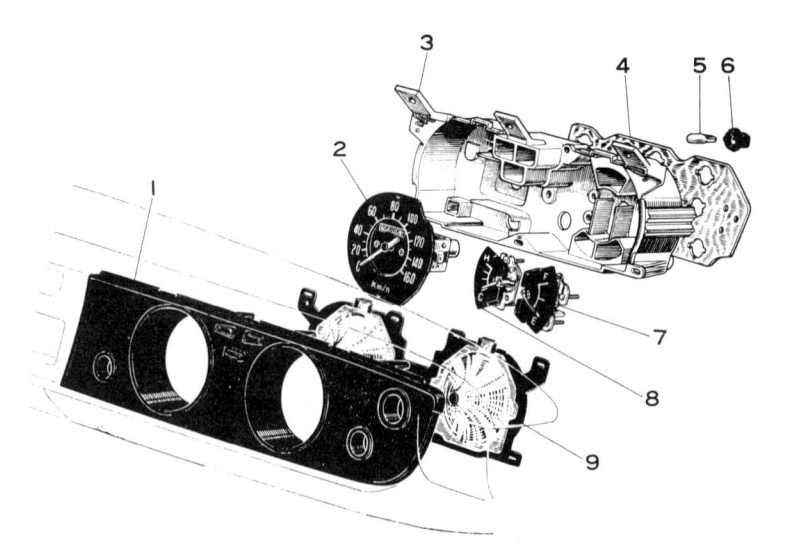

Fig 10.55 Combination meter components (Type 3)

1. Meter panel
2. Speedometer assembly
3. Meter case
4. Meter circuit plate sub-assy.
5. Bulb (3.5W)
6. Meter bulb socket sub-assy.
7. Fuel receiver gauge assy.
8. Water temperature receiver gauge assembly
9. Meter lens body

39.3 Lifting away centre moulding

39.4 Combination meter assembly securing screw removal

39.6a Easing combination meter assembly for instrument panel

39.6b Rear view of combination meter

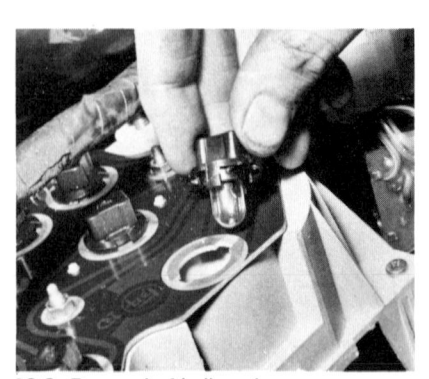

39.6c Removal of bulb and socket

40 Combination meter (Type 3) - dismantling and reassembly

1 Turn the meter bulb sockets anticlockwise and remove.
2 Next pull out the capless bulbs.
3 Turn the trip meter cancelling knob anticlockwise and remove. The trip meter cancelling knob shaft should be held with a pair of long nose pliers.
4 Undo and remove the self tapping screw that secures the meter body. Separate the body and meter hood.
5 If necessary remove the fuel gauge, water temperature gauge and speedometer from the meter body.
6 *'D' models only:* Disconnect the tachometer cables and remove the tachometer from the meter body.
7 Undo and remove the meter circuit plate securing screw and lift away the meter circuit plate.

8 Reassembly of the combination meter is the reverse sequence to dismantling.

41 Ignition switch (Type 3) - removal and replacement

1 Disconnect the battery for safety reasons.
2 Undo and remove the steering column upper cover securing screws and lift away the upper cover.
3 Move the ignition key to the 'ACC' position and insert a needle into the hole at the side of the key cylinder.
4 Pull out the key cylinder whilst pushing in the pin.
5 Disconnect the ignition switch connector wires.
6 Undo and remove the screw that retains the ignition switch and withdraw the switch (photos). Note on models fitted with collapsible steering column this last operation is not necessary.

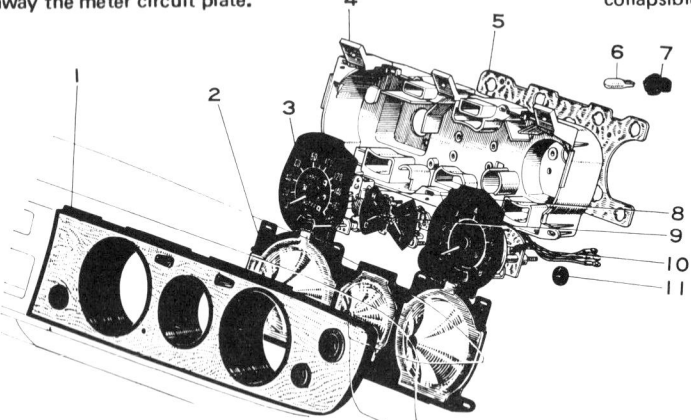

Fig 10.56 Combination meter components (Type 3 - 'S' models)

1 Meter panel
2 Meter lens body
3 Speedometer assembly
4 Meter case
5 Meter circuit plate sub-assy.
6 Bulb
7 Meter bulb socket sub-assy.
8 Water temperature receiver gauge assy.
9 Fuel receiver gauge assy.
10 Engine tachometer assy.

41.6a Ignition switch mounted on cover

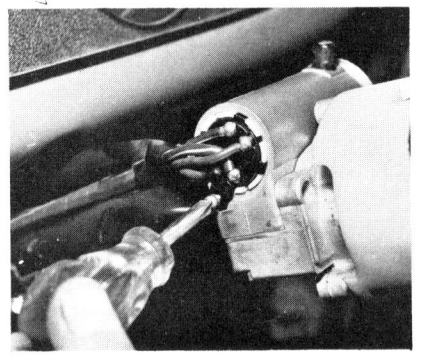

41.6b Removal of switch securing screw

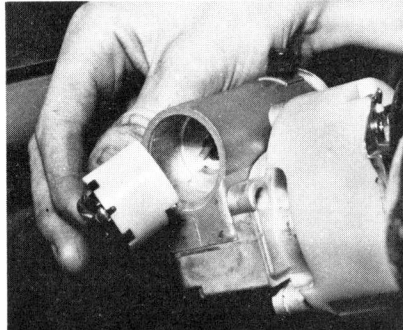

41.6c Lifting away switch

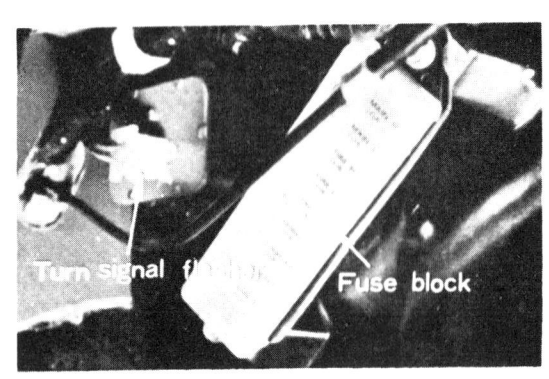

Fig 10.57 Direction indicator flasher unit location

Fig 10.58 Direction indicator relay

Chapter 10/Electrical system

7 Slacken the two bolts that secure the steering column clamp and pull out the connector from the clamp opening whilst pushing down on the column tube.
8 Refitting the ignition switch assembly is the reverse sequence to removal.

42 Flasher unit and relay - general

Should the direction indicators fail on one bulb only it is reasonable to assume that the bulb has blown, or poor connection or broken cable. However if all the bulbs do not operate or do not flash then it is possible that the flasher unit has failed and the easiest way to check this is by substitution. It is located adjacent to the fuse box.

Should an ohmmeter be available the internal resistances may be tested. If all is well the following results should be obtained:

Terminals	Value
B - L1	1 ohm (approx)
B - L2	70 ohms (approx)

If the direction indicators operate intermittently, or not at all, then the relay should be checked by an automobile electrician or by substitution. It is located on the right-hand inner wing panel. Should an ohmmeter be available the internal resistance may be tested. If all is well the following results should be obtained:

Terminals	Value
1 - 2	0.7 ohm (approx)
3 - 4	0.7 ohm (approx)
5 - 6	0 ohm.

43 Cigarette lighter - adjustment, removal and replacement

1 The cigarette lighter is considered to be in good order when it ejects after 7 to 17 seconds from the time of being pushed in. The element should also be red hot.
2 If it ejects too early and is not hot enough, disconnect the battery and bend the bimetallic strip inwards slightly.
3 To remove the unit first disconnect the battery and detach the terminal connector from the rear.
4 Unscrew the retainer in an anticlockwise direction and lift away the socket.
5 Refitting the cigarette lighter assembly is the reverse sequence to removal.

44 Heater unit and controls - removal and replacement

Water valve

1 Refer to Chapter 2, and drain the cooling system.
2 Disconnect the heater control cable from the water control valve.
3 Disconnect the water hose from the water valve and remove the water valve.

Heater unit

4 If an instrument panel undertray is fitted it must next be removed.
5 Remove the defroster hose and nozzles.
6 Disconnect the water inlet hose and outlet hose from the heater.

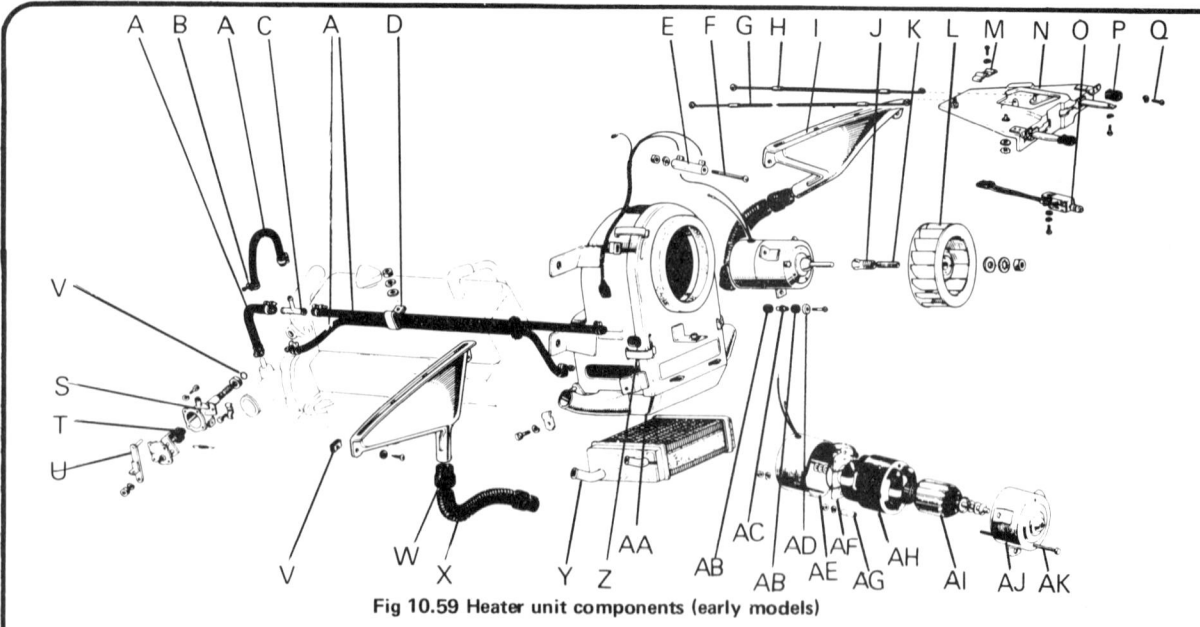

Fig 10.59 Heater unit components (early models)

A	Hose	N	Heater control box		spring	
B	Hose clamp	O	Heater blower switch	AA	Heater case	
C	Water hose connector	P	Heater control lever	AB	Bushing	
D	Water hose retainer		knob	AC	Collar	
E	Resistance	Q	Screw	AD	Washer	
F	Through bolt	R	"O" ring	AE	Blower motor housing	
G	Heater control cable	S	Water valve body	AF	Blower motor brush holder	
H	Defroster control cable	T	Water valve controller	AG	Bushing	
I	Defroster nozzle	U	Water valve lever	AH	Blower motor stator	
J	Adaptor	V	Anchor nut	AI	Blower motor armature	
K	Pipe	W	Defroster hose adaptor	AJ	Blower motor housing	
L	Blower fan	X	Defroster hose	AK	Bolt	
M	Heater control wire	Y	Radiator			
	clamp	Z	Heater case fastening			

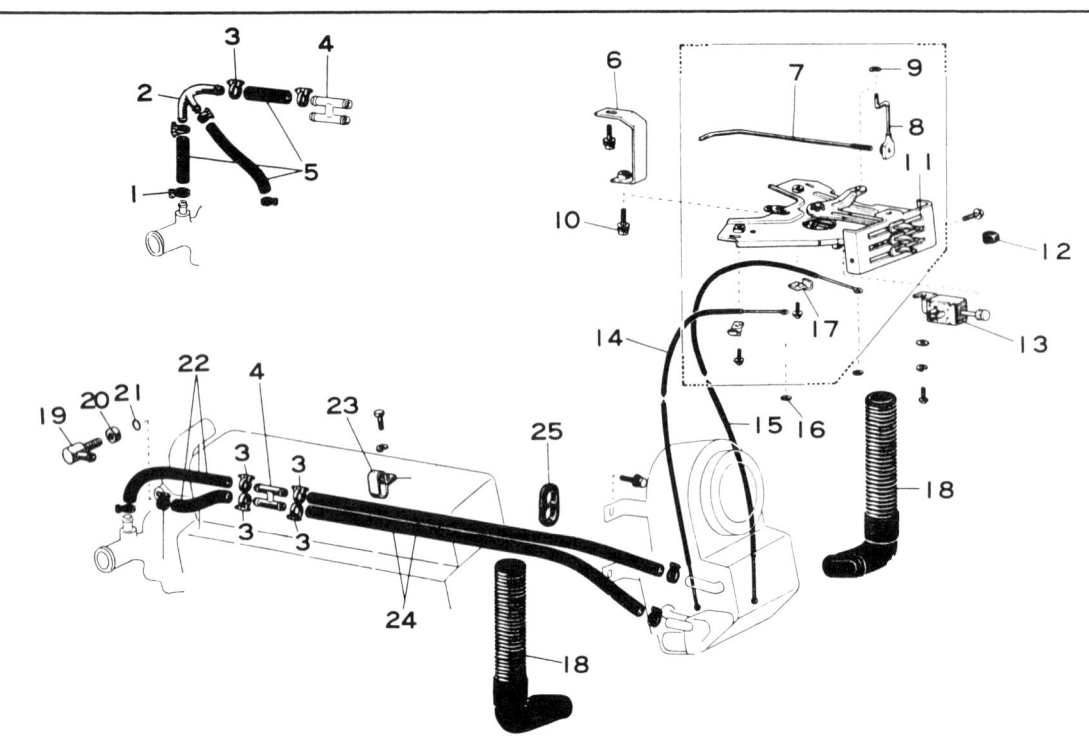

Fig. 10.60 Heater unit controls (later models)

1	Hose clamp	8	Link	15	Defroster control cable	22 Hose
2	Water hose connector	9	"E" ring	16	Retainer	23 Water hose retainer
3	Hose clamp	10	Bolt w/washer	17	Heater control clamp	24 Hose
4	Water pipe	11	Heater control	18	Defroster hose	25 Grommet
5	Hose	12	Heater control lever	19	Water hose through joint	
6	Heater control bracket	13	Heater block switch	20	Hexagon nut	
7	Link	14	Heater control cable	21	"O" ring	

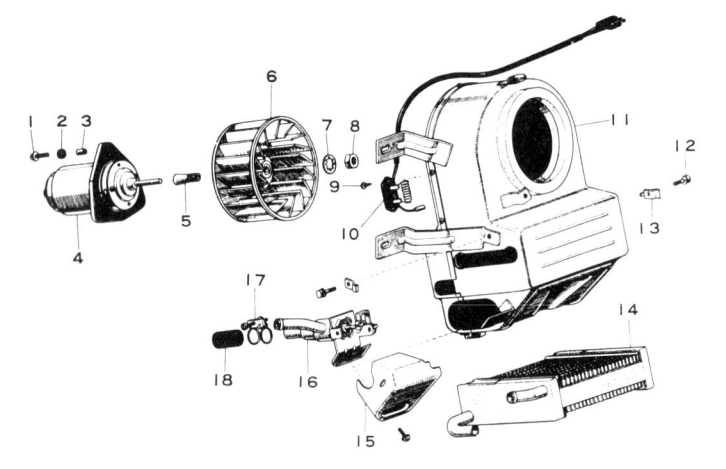

Fig. 10.61 Heater unit components (later models)

1 Screw w/washer
2 Bushing
3 Bushing
4 Blower motor
5 Adaptor
6 Blower fan
7 Tooth washer
8 Nut
9 Screw w/washer
10 Resistor
11 Blower casing complete
12 Bolt w/washer
13 Clamp
14 Radiator unit
15 Cover (for water cover)
16 Water valve
17 Clamp
18 Hose

7 Disconnect the defroster control cable.
8 Disconnect the wiring connector to the heater motor.
9 Undo and remove the nuts and bolts securing the heater unit and lift away the heater assembly. Take care not to spill any water on the carpeting or upholstery.

Heater controls

10 Disconnect the control cables from the heater and water valve.
11 Remove the control lever knobs and moulding.
12 Remove the ashtray and ash receptacle retainer.
13 Remove the heater control assembly securing screws and retainer. Lift away the heater control assembly.
14 Reassembly or replacement is the reverse sequence to dismantling or removal.

45 Heater unit - dismantling and assembly

1 Remove the heater case endplate.
2 Slide out the radiator matrix.
3 Undo and remove the fan securing nuts and lift away the fan.
4 Remove the motor resistor and finally the motor and cables.
5 Reassembly of the heater is the reverse sequence to dismantling.

Chapter 10/Electrical system

46 Fault diagnosis - electrical system

Symptom	Reason/s	Remedy
Starter motor fails to turn engine	Battery discharged	Charge battery.
	Battery defective internally	Fit new battery.
	Battery terminal leads loose or earth lead not securely attached to body	Check and tighten leads.
	Loose or broken connections in starter motor circuit	Check all connections and check any that are loose.
	Starter motor switch or solenoid faulty	Test and replace faulty components with new.
	Starter motor pinion jammed in mesh with ring gear	Disengage pinion by turning squared end of armature shaft.
	Starter brushes badly worn, sticking or brush wires loose	Examine brushes, replace as necessary, tighten down brush wires.
	Commutator dirty, worn, or burnt	Clean commutator, recut if badly burnt.
	Starter motor armature faulty	Overhaul starter motor, fit new armature.
	Field coils earthed	Overhaul starter motor.
Starter turns engine very slowly	Battery in discharged condition	Charge battery.
	Starter brushes badly worn, sticking, or brush wires loose	Examine brushes, replace as necessary, tighten down brush wires.
	Loose wires in starter motor circuit	Check wiring and tighten as necessary.
Starter motor operates without turning engine	Starter motor pinion sticking on the screwed sleeve	Remove starter motor, clean starter motor drive.
	Pinion or ring gear teeth broken or worn	Fit new gear ring and new pinion to starter motor drive.
Starter noisy or excessively rough engagement	Pinion or ring gear teeth broken or worn	Fit new ring gear, or new pinion to starter motor drive.
	Starter drive main spring broken	Dismantle and fit new main spring.
	Starter motor retaining bolts loose	Tighten starter motor securing bolts. Fit new spring washer if necessary.
Battery only holds charge for a short period	Battery defective internally	Remove and fit new battery.
	Electrolyte level too low or electrolyte too weak due to leakage	Top up electrolyte level to just above plates.
	Plate separators no longer fully effective	Remove and fit new battery.
	Battery plates severely sulphated	Remove and fit new battery.
	Fan belt slipping	Check belt for wear, replace if necessary, and tighten.
	Battery terminal connections loose or corroded	Check terminals for tightness, and remove all corrosion.
	Alternator not charging properly	Remove and overhaul alternator.
	Short in lighting circuit causing continual battery drain	Trace and rectify.
Ignition light fails to go out, battery runs flat	Fan belt loose and slipping, or broken	Check, replace, and tighten as necessary.
	Alternator not charging correctly	Seek specialist advice if all electrical connections are satisfactory.

Failure of individual electrical equipment to function correctly is dealt with alphabetically, item-by-item, under the headings listed below:

Fuel gauge

Fuel gauge gives no reading	Fuel tank empty!	Fill fuel tank.
	Electric cable between tank sender unit and gauge earthed or loose	Check cable for earthing and joints for tightness.
	Fuel gauge case not earthed	Ensure case is well earthed.
	Fuel gauge supply cable interrupted	Check and replace cable if necessary.
	Fuel gauge unit broken	Replace fuel gauge.
Fuel gauge registers full all the time	Electric cable between tank unit and gauge broken or disconnected	Check over cable and repair as necessary.

Horn

Horn operates all the time	Horn-push either earthed or stuck down	Disconnect battery earth. Check and rectify source of trouble.
	Horn cable to horn push earthed	Disconnect battery earth. Check and rectify source of trouble.
Horn fails to operate	Blown fuse	Check and renew if broken. Ascertain cause.
	Cable or cable connection loose, broken or disconnected	Check all connections for tightness and cables for breaks.

Chapter 10/Electrical system

Horn emits intermittent or unsatisfactory noise	Horn has an internal fault	Remove and overhaul horn.
	Cable connections loose	Check and tighten all connections.
	Horn incorrectly adjusted	Adjust horn until best note obtained.

Lights

Lights do not come on	If engine not running, battery discharged	Push-start car, charge battery.
	Light bulb filament burnt out or bulbs broken	Test bulbs in live bulb holder.
	Wire connections loose, disconnected or broken	Check all connections for tightness and wire cable for breaks.
	Light switch shorting or otherwise faulty	By-pass light switch to ascertain if fault is in switch and fit new switch as appropriate.
Lights come on but fade out	If engine not running battery discharged	Push-start car, and charge battery.
Lights give very poor illumination	Lamp glasses dirty	Clean glasses.
	Reflector tarnished or dirty	Fit new reflectors.
	Lamps badly out of adjustment	Adjust lamps correctly.
	Incorrect bulb with too low wattage fitted	Remove bulb and replace with correct grade.
	Existing bulbs old and badly discoloured	Renew bulb units.
	Electrical wiring too thin not allowing full current to pass	Rewire lighting system.
Lights work erratically - flashing on and off, especially over bumps	Battery terminals or earth connection loose	Tighten battery terminals and earth connection.
	Lights not earthing properly	Examine and rectify.
	Contacts in light switch faulty	By-pass light switch to ascertain if fault is in switch and fit new switch as appropriate.

Windscreen wipers

Wiper motor fails to work	Blown fuse	Check and replace fuse if necessary.
	Wire connections loose, disconnected or broken	Check wiper wiring. Tighten loose connections.
	Brushes badly worn	Remove and fit new brushes.
	Armature worn or faulty	If electricity at wiper motor remove and overhaul and fit replacement armature.
	Field coils faulty	Purchase reconditioned wiper motor.
Wiper motor works very slowly and takes excessive current	Commutator dirty, greasy or burnt	Clean commutator thoroughly.
	Drive to wheelboxes, too bent or unlubricated	Examine drive and straighten out severe curvature. Lubricate.
	Wheelbox spindle binding or damaged	Remove, overhaul, or fit replacement.
	Armature bearings dry or unaligned	Replace with new bearings correctly aligned.
	Armature badly worn or faulty	Remove, overhaul, or fit replacement armature.
Wiper motor works slowly and takes little current.	Brushes badly worn	Remove and fit new brushes.
	Commutator dirty, greasy, or burnt	Clean commutator thoroughly.
	Armature badly worn or faulty	Remove and overhaul armature or fit replacement.
Wiper motor works but wiper blades remain static	Driving cable rack disengaged or faulty	Examine and if faulty, replace.
	Wheelbox gear and spindle damaged or worn	Examine and if faulty, replace.
	Wiper motor gearbox parts badly worn	Overhaul or fit new gearbox.

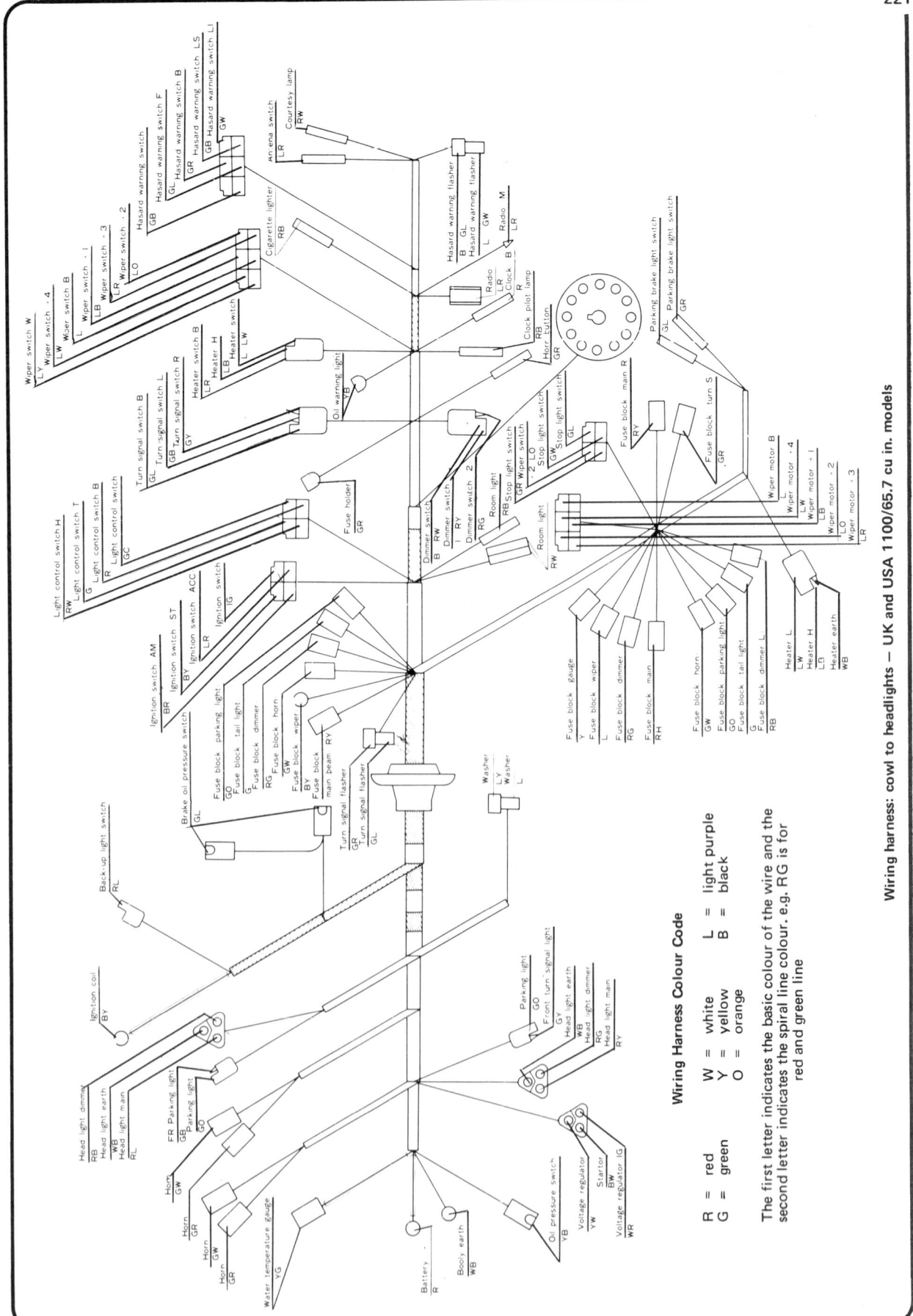

Wiring harness: cowl to headlights – UK and USA 1100/65.7 cu in. models

222

Wiring harness: cowl to headlights — UK and USA 1200/71.1 cu in. models

Wiring Harness Colour Code

R = red
G = green
W = white
Y = yellow
O = orange
L = light purple
B = black

The first letter indicates the basic colour of the wire and the second letter indicates the spiral line colour. e.g. RG is for red and green line

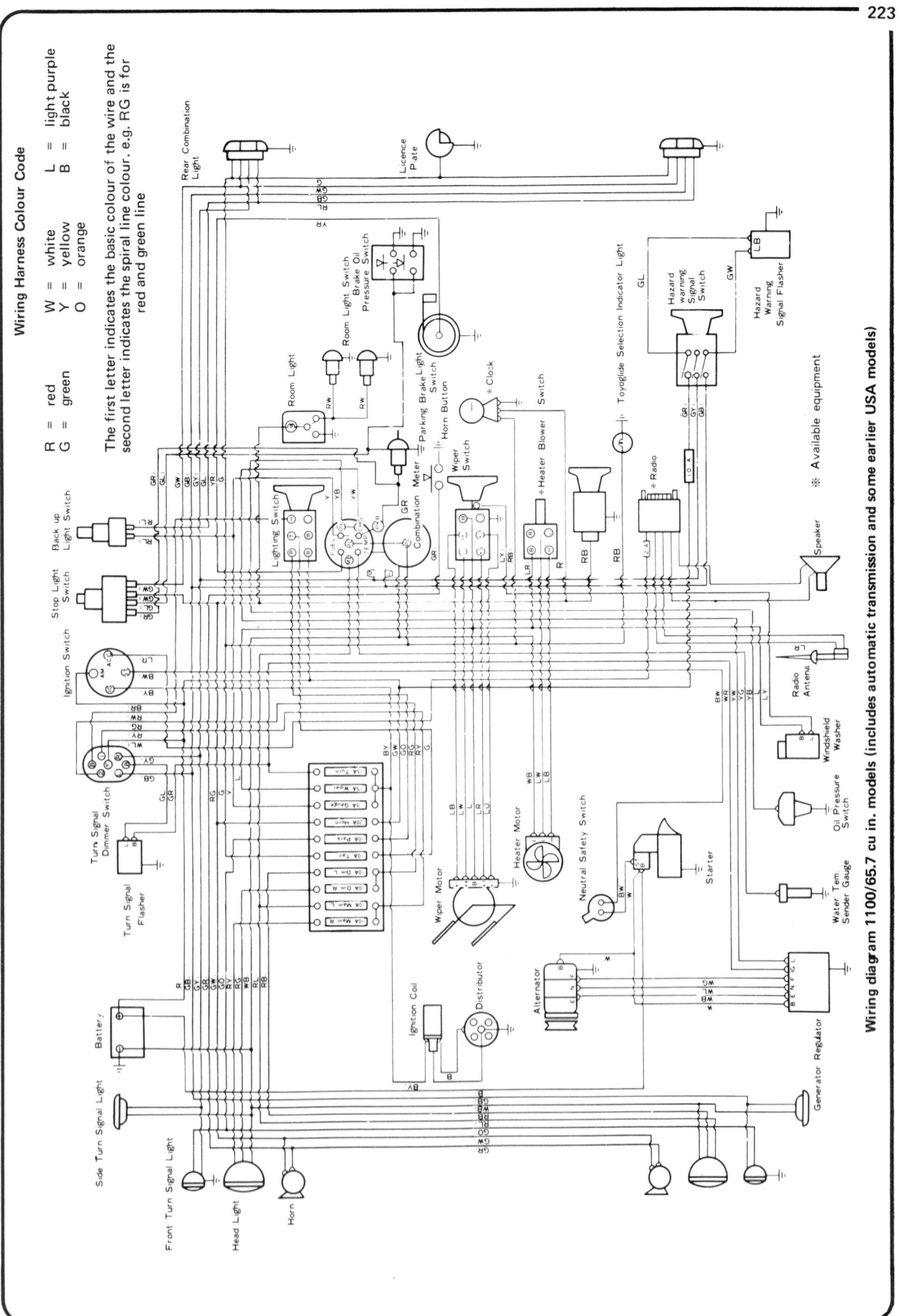

Wiring diagram 1100/65.7 cu in. models (includes automatic transmission and some earlier USA models)

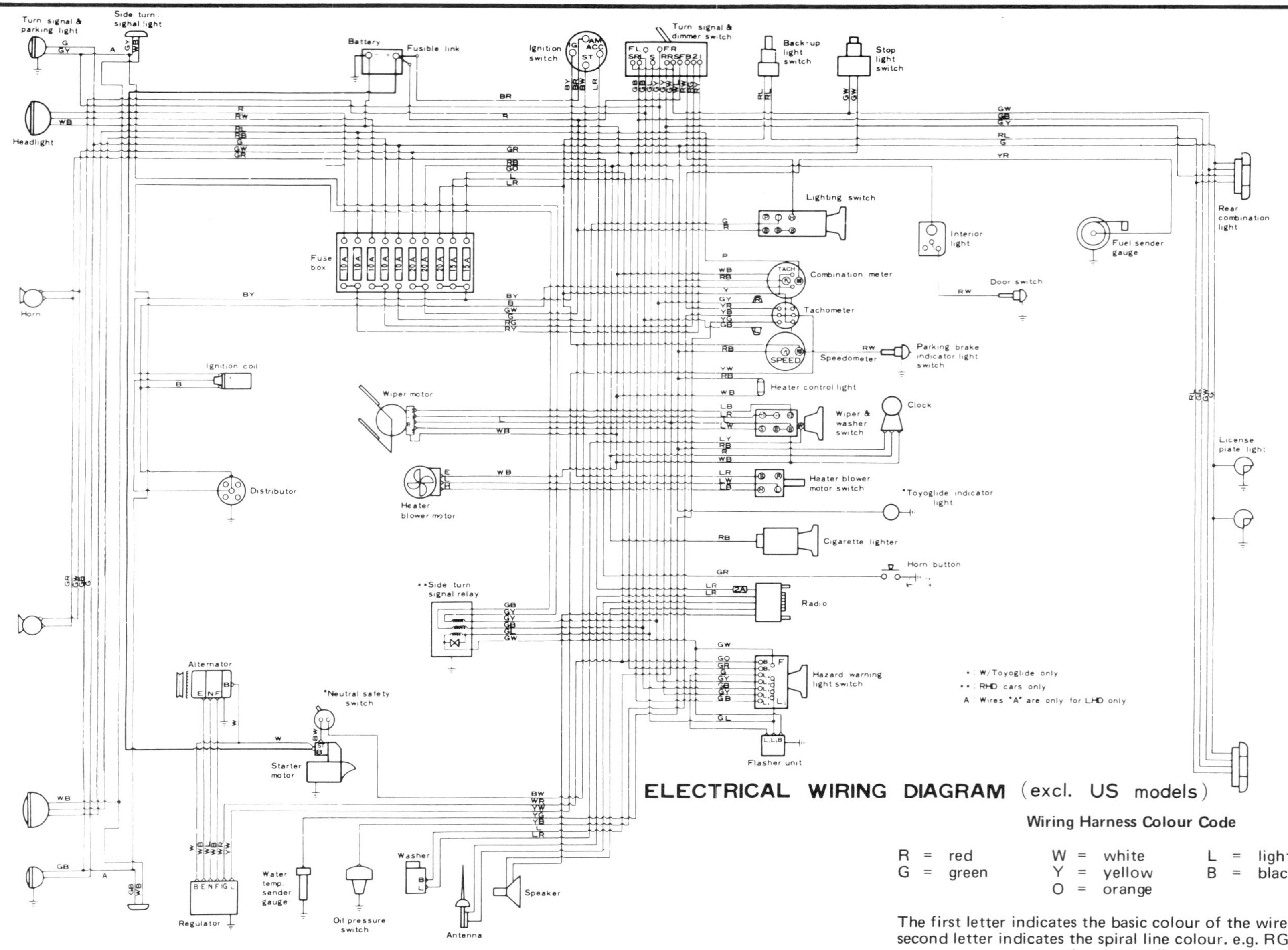

ELECTRICAL WIRING DIAGRAM (excl. US models)

Wiring Harness Colour Code

R = red	W = white	L = light purple
G = green	Y = yellow	B = black
	O = orange	

The first letter indicates the basic colour of the wire and the second letter indicates the spiral line colour. e.g. RG is for red and green line

Wiring diagram – all UK/USA early 1200/71.1 cu in. models, including automatic transmission

225

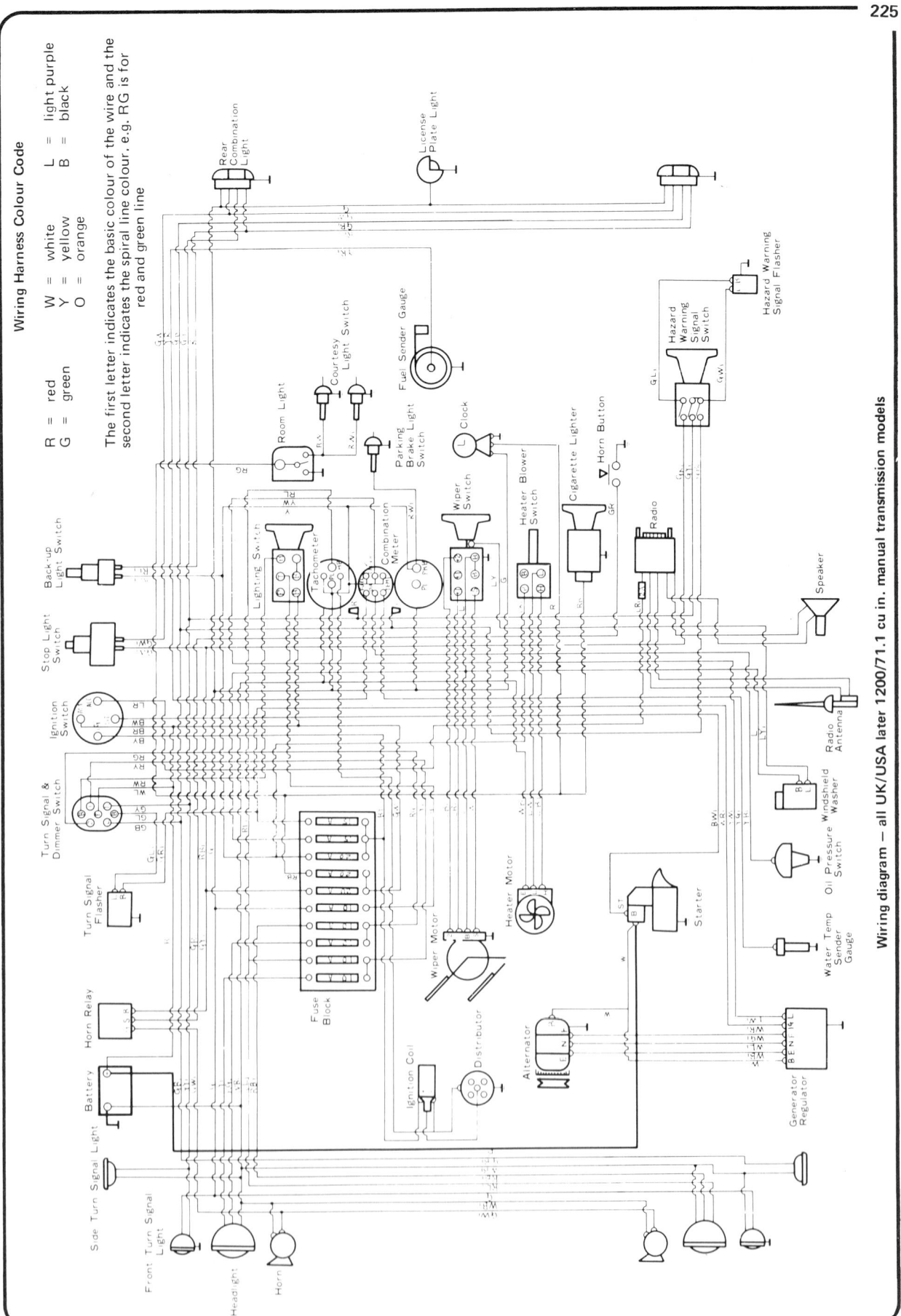

Wiring diagram — all UK/USA later 1200/71.1 cu in. manual transmission models

Wiring diagram – all UK/USA later 1200/71.1 cu in. automatic transmission models

Wiring diagram – USA KE and TE models

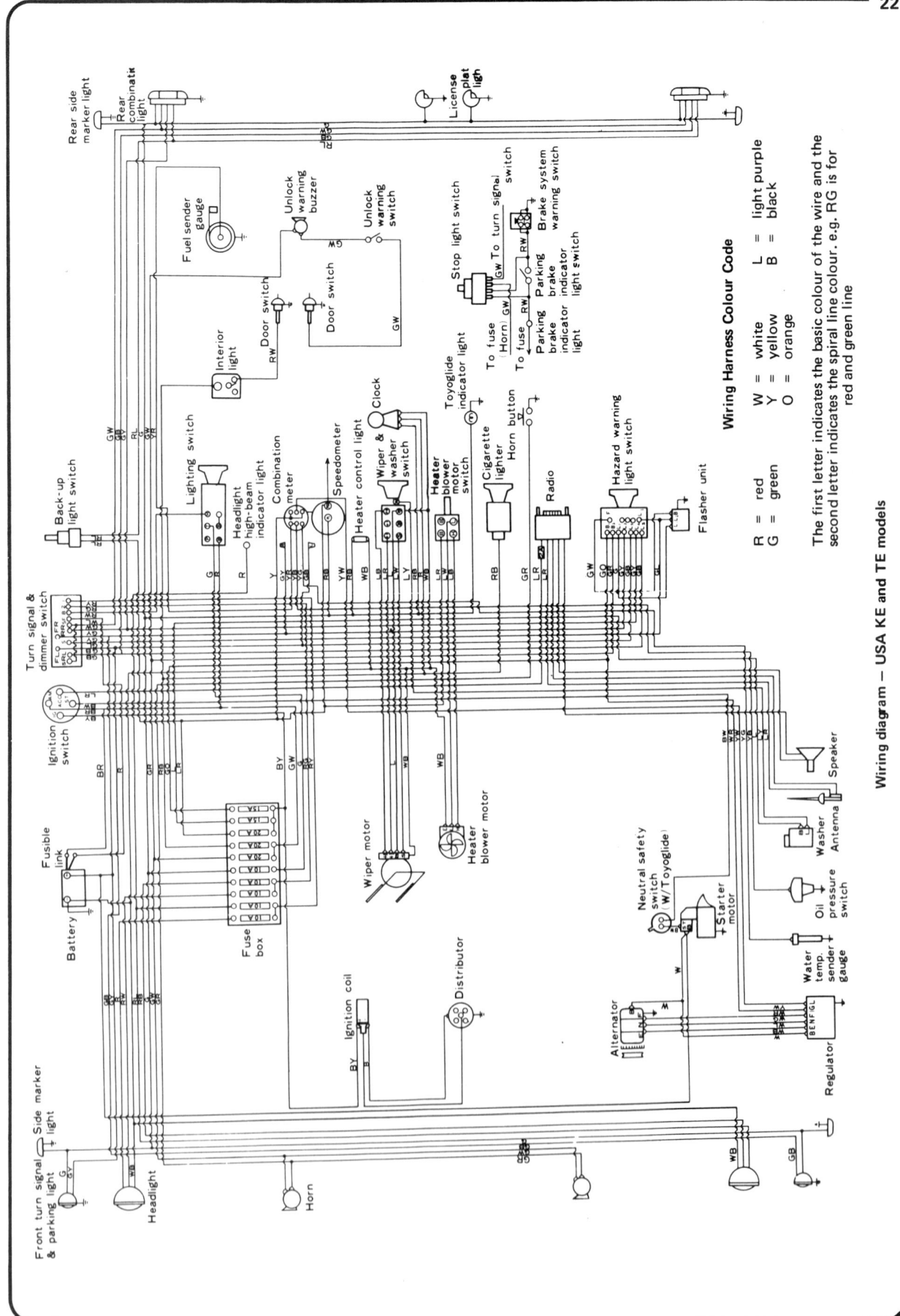

Chapter 11 Suspension and steering

Contents

Fault diagnosis - suspension and steering	17
Front brake disc - removal and replacement	3
Front suspension arm and balljoints (TE models) - removal and replacement	7
Front suspension arm, balljoints and leaf springs (early KE models) - removal and replacement	6
Front suspension unit strut - removal and replacement	4
Front suspension unit strut - dismantling, overhaul and reassembly	5
Front wheel hub - removal and replacement	2
General description	1
Rear shock absorbers - removal and replacement	8
Rear spring - removal and replacement	9
Steering gearbox - adjustment	15
Steering gear assembly - removal and replacement	11
Steering gearbox (worm & sector) - dismantling, overhaul and reassembly	13
Steering gearbox (recirculating ball) - dismantling - overhaul and reassembly	14
Steering geometry - checking and adjustment	16
Steering linkage - removal and replacement	12
Steering wheel - removal and replacement	10

Specifications

Front suspension

Type ... Independent coil spring and Mac Pherson strut with lower control arm and stabilizer. Early KE models fitted with transverse leaf spring

Front coil springs (prior to April 1968):

Free-length:	
KE10 - B	12.0 in. (305 mm)
KE10L - B/rhd	11.6 in. (295 mm)
KE10L - B/lhd	12.5 in. (318 mm)
Fitted length:	5.71 in. (145 mm)
Fitted load	155 lb f (72 kg f)
Coil wire diameter	0.3 in. (8 mm)
Number of coils	4
Deflection rate	33 lb f in. (0.59 kg f mm)

Front coil spring - driver's side (April 1968 on):

Free-length	15.7 in. (399 mm)
Wire diameter	0.34 in. (8.5 mm)
Coil diameter	4.8 in. (120 mm)
Number of coils	7
Number of effective coils	5.5
Fitted length	5.71 in. (145 mm)
Fitted load	296 lb f (134 kg f)
Deflection rate	30.9 lb f in. (0.55 kg f mm)
Colour identification	Green

Front coil spring - passenger's side (April 1968 on):

Free-length	14.4 in. (365 mm)
Wire diameter	0.32 in. (8.2 mm)
Coil diameter	4.8 in. (120 mm)
Number of coils	6.4
Number of effective coils	4.8
Fitted length	5.71 in. (145 mm)
Fitted load	251 lb f (114 kg f)
Deflection rate	30.9 lb f in. (0.55 kg f mm)
Colour identification	Orange

Front leaf spring:

Length (loaded)	40.25 in. (1022 mm)
Camber (loaded):	
Before April 1968	1.30 in. (33.0 mm)
After April 1968	1.29 in. (32.8 mm)

Width:
- Before April 1968 ... 2.36 in. (60 mm)
- After April 1968 ... 2.75 in. (70 mm)

Thickness:
- Before April 1968 ... 0.24 in. (6.0 mm)
- After April 1968 ... 0.275 in. (7.0 mm)

Number of leaves:
- Before April 1968 ... 2
- After April 1968 ... 1

Deflection rate:
- Before April 1968 ... 92 lb f in. (1.65 kg f mm)
- After April 1968 ... 78.5 lb f in. (1.40 kg f mm)

Shock absorbers (strut):
Type ... Double acting, hydraulic telescopic
Length:
- Maximum ... 25.37 in. (644 mm)
- Minimum ... 17.95 in. (453 mm)

Stroke ... 5.53 in. (191 mm)

Damping force (in compression):
- Before April 1968 ... 60 - 95 lb at 24 in./sec. (27 - 43 kg at 0.6 m/sec.)
- After April 1968 ... 148 lb at 24 in./sec. (67 kg at 0.6 m/sec.)

Damping force (in rebound):
- Before April 1968 ... 110 - 150 lb f (50 - 70 kg at 0.6 m/sec.)
- After April 1968 ... 110 lb at 24 in./sec. (50 kg at 0.6 m/sec.)

Fluid type ... Automatic transmission fluid Type A - Suffix A

Fluid capacity:
- KE1100 ... 16.5 cu in. (272 cc)
- KE1200 ... 17.1 cu in. (281 cc)
- TE1600 ... 16.7 - 17.4 cu in. (274 - 285 cc)

Rear suspension

Type ... Semi elliptic spring, double acting telescopic shock absorbers

Rear leaf springs (early KE models):

Number of leaves:
- Saloon/Sedan ... 4
- Estate/Wagon ... 4

Length:
- Saloon/Sedan ... 45.3 in. (1150.62 mm)
- Estate/Wagon ... 45.3 in. (1150.62 mm)

Width ... 1.97 in. (50.038 mm)

Thickness:
- Leaf 1:
  - Saloon/Sedan ... 6 mm
  - Estate/Wagon ... 7 mm
- Leaf 2:
  - Saloon/Sedan ... 6 mm
  - Estate/Wagon ... 7 mm
- Leaf 3:
  - Saloon/Sedan ... 7 mm
  - Estate/Wagon ... 6 mm
- Leaf 4: (Aux)
  - Saloon/Sedan ... 4 mm
  - Estate/Wagon ... 13 mm

Camber:
- Saloon/Sedan ... 4.45 in. (113.03 mm)
- Estate/Wagon ... 5.47 in. (138.938 mm)

Rear leaf springs (late KE models and all TE models):

Number of leaves:
- Saloon/Sedan ... 4
- Estate/Wagon ... 5

Length:
- Saloon/Sedan ... 43.3 in. (1099.82 mm)
- Estate/Wagon ... 43.3 in. (1099.82 mm)

Width ... 1.97 in. (50.038 mm)

Thickness:
- Leaf 1:
  - Saloon/Sedan ... 7 mm
  - Estate/Wagon ... 6 mm

Leaf 2:
    Saloon/Sedan ... ... 6 mm
    Estate/Wagon ... ... 6 mm
Leaf 3:
    Saloon/Sedan ... ... 6 mm
    Estate/Wagon ... ... 6 mm
Leaf 4: (Aux)
    Saloon/Sedan ... ... 4 mm
    Estate/Wagon ... ... 13 mm
Leaf 5:
    Estate/Wagon only ... ... 5 mm

Suspension and steering geometry

Front wheel alignment (KE 1100 models):
- Caster ... ... 1°
- Camber ... ... 1.5°
- King pin inclination ... ... 7°
- Toe-in ... ... 0.14 in. (3.5 mm)
- Turning angle:
  - Inner ... ... 37 - 38°
  - Outer ... ... 32 - 33°

Front wheel alignment (KE 1200 models):
- Caster ... ... 2°
- Camber ... ... 0.33°
- King pin inclination ... ... 8.42°
- Toe-in ... ... 0.0 in. (0.0 mm)
- Turning angle:
  - Inner ... ... 38.5 - 41.5°
  - Outer ... ... 30 - 36°

Front wheel alignment (TE 1600 models):
- Caster ... ... 2°
- Camber ... ... 0.5°
- King pin inclination ... ... 8.42°
- Toe-in ... ... 0.0 in. (0.0 mm)
- Turning angle:
  - Inner ... ... 38.5 - 41.5°
  - Outer ... ... 30 - 36°

Steering

Type:
- KE1100 ... ... Worm and sector roller
- KE1200 and TE1600 ... ... Recirculating ball

Ratio:
- KE1100 ... ... 18 : 1
- KE1200 and TE1600 ... ... 18.1 : 1

Dimensions, clearances and settings (KE 1100 models):
- Total length (gear and housing) ... ... 31.02 in. (787.9 mm)
- Sector shaft outer diameter (not less than) ... ... 0.98 in. (24.9 mm)
- Sector shaft bush inner diameter (not to exceed) ... 0.989 in. (25.1 mm)
- Oil clearance ... ... 0.004 in. (0.1 mm)
- Worm bearing preload ... ... 2.6 - 2.7 lb f (1.2 - 1.7 kg f)
- Sector shaft arm backlash ... ... 0.006 - 0.007 in. (0.16 - 0.19 mm)
- Steering housing/direction indicator switch clearance ... 0.016 in. (0.4064 mm)
- Steering wheel/direction indicator switch clearance ... 0.12 in. (3.048 mm)
- Steering wheel to column clearance ... ... 0.10 in. (2.54 mm)
- Gear housing capacity ... ... 9.8 cu in. (161 cc)

Chapter 11/Suspension and steering

Dimensions, clearances and settings (KE 1200 and TE 1600 models):

Total steering gear pre-load	14 - 22 lb (6.3 - 9.9 kg)
Sector shaft outer diameter (not less than)	1.1024 in. (28.016 mm)
Sector shaft bush inner diameter (not to exceed)	1.1032 in. (28.02 mm)
Oil clearance	0.0003 in. (0.0076 mm)
Worm bearing preload	5.5 - 14.0 lb f (2.5 - 6.35 kg f)
Sector shaft arm backlash	0
Gear housing capacity	12.8 cu in. (209 cc)

Wheels and Tyres

For wheel and tyre sizes and tyre pressures, consult the operator's handbook supplied with the car.

Torque wrench settings:	lb f ft	kg f m
Front suspension		
Hub adjustment torque	19 - 23	2.6 - 3.2
Piston rod nut	36 - 43	5.0 - 6.0
Ring nut	75 - 110	10 - 15
Piston rod to support	30 - 50	4.0 - 5.5
Support to front wing	11 - 16	1.5 - 2.2
Steering arm	15 - 22	2.0 - 3.0
Brake hose to pipe	9 - 13	1.3 - 1.8
Wheel nuts	65 - 85	9.0 - 12.0
Balljoint grease plug	3 - 5	0.4 - 0.7
Steering lever to balljoint	36 - 53	5 - 7
Crossmember to body	30 - 40	4.0 - 5.5
Crossmember to engine mounting	25 - 40	3.5 - 5.5
Fulcrum shaft to crossmember	50 - 60	7.0 - 8.5
Front spring bush to arm	11 - 16	1.5 - 2.2
Steering lever to damper	15 - 22	2.0 - 3.0
Trackrod-ends	22 - 32	3.0 - 4.5
Steering angle locks	11 - 16	1.5 - 2.2
Models produced after April 1968 - as above with exceptions:		
Wheel nuts	58 - 80	8 - 11
Fulcrum shaft to crossmember	68 - 87	9 - 12
Steering lever to damper	16 - 26	2.0 - 3.5
Rear suspension		
Spring 'U' bolts	22 - 32	3.0 - 4.5
Shock absorber:		
Bottom	25 - 40	3.5 - 5.5
Top	14 - 22	1.9 - 3.1
Wheel nuts	65 - 85	9.0 - 12.0
Steering		
Adjustment screw locknut	60 - 70	8 - 10
Steering cover	11 - 16	1.5 - 2.2
Steering cover locknut	18 - 29	2.5 - 4.0
Steering box bolts	16	1.5 - 2.2
Sector shaft arm	50 - 80	7.0 - 11.0
Column clamp to instrument panel:		
Before April 1968	15 - 22	2.0 - 3.0
After April 1968	29 - 36	4.0 - 5.0
Steering wheel nut	15 - 22	2.0 - 3.0
Idler arm nut	36 - 50	5.0 - 7.0
Sector shaft arm to centre-rod	36 - 50	5.0 - 7.0
Idler arm to centre-rod	36 - 50	5.0 - 7.0
Trackrods to centre-rod	22 - 32	2 - 3
Trackrods to steering arm	22 - 32	2 - 3
Idler arm to sidemember	7 - 10	1.0 - 1.4
Trackrod locknuts	25 - 40	3.5 - 5.5

Chapter 11/Suspension and steering

1 General description

The front suspension system fitted to models covered by this manual comprises a single strut with the shock absorber forming the spindle around which the front wheels are able to pivot. It is surrounded at its upper end by a coil spring, the top mounting of which is secured to the underside of the front wheel housing.

The shock absorber piston rod is secured to the upper centre of the spring upper mounting by a thrust assembly in the form of a moulded rubber bush and seating.

At the lower end, the suspension unit strut is attached to the suspension foot which also carries the wheel hub stub axle. Also attached to the lower end, is the steering arm bracket which turns on a sealed balljoint on the transverse arm hinged to the front suspension crossmember.

Two tension rods which are secured to the ends of the link arms are at one end, and to the crossmember rubber mounting at the other, control lateral movement of the suspension unit.

A stabiliser bar is attached to the body forwards of the suspension unit lower arm by a rubber bush. This ensures parallel vertical movement between the two arms and restricts forward movement of the body relative to the suspension.

The balljoints at the foot of the struts are sealed for life and the upper parts of the shock absorbers are protected by a collapsible rubber boot located within the coil spring.

Any excessive vertical movement is prevented by bump rubbers.

On very early KE models a transverse leaf spring was fitted but on later KE and TE models it was eliminated.

Steering geometry angles - caster, camber and kingpin inclination - are set during production and cannot be adjusted in service. Should a deviation from these settings exist it is an indication of worn parts or accident damage.

The front wheels are mounted on the stub axles and run on tapered roller bearings which are packed with grease for a life of 24,000 miles (40,000 Km).

The rear suspension comprises semi-elliptic leaf springs, mounted on rubber bushed shackle pins and double acting telescopic hydraulic shock absorbers - which are fitted to absorb road shocks and dampen spring oscillations.

The steering gear is of the recirculating ball type, with the exception of very early KE models which have worm and sector roller type steering gear fitted. Later KE and all TE models are fitted with a steering lock and collapsible steering column.

The steering shaft rotates in two balltype thrust bearings and at the steering column end in a bearing. The sector shaft moves in bushes and has a seal at the lower end. The upper end of the sector shaft engages a rack which is integral with the ball nut.

Steering shaft bearing adjustment is controlled by a large adjustment screw at the column end of the steering gear housing and an adjustment screw on the sector shaft endcover.

The steering gear linkage consists of a steering connecting rod, located by a ball joint at one end to the steering gear pitman arm, and at the other end the steering idler arm. The idler arm pivots on a support mounted on the bodyframe. On each side of the steering linkage is an adjustable tie-rod which is attached by ball joints to the steering arms on the front suspension units. These tie-rods provide a means of setting the front wheel toe-in.

2 Front wheel hub - removal and replacement

1 Apply the handbrake, chock the rear wheels, jack-up the front of the car and support on firmly based axle stands. Remove the roadwheel.
2 Using a screwdriver carefully prise off the dust cover from the centre of the hub.
3 Straighten the ears of the split pin and withdraw the split pin. Remove the castellated nut, washer and outer bearing.
4 On later KE models, and all TE models with disc brakes, undo and remove the two caliper securing bolts.
5 Lift off the caliper assembly from the stub axle flange and suspend it on wire or string to prevent straining the hose.
6 With drum brake models withdraw the drum and hub assembly. If it proves difficult back off the adjusters as described in Chapter 9 and tap the circumference with a soft faced hammer.
7 To dismantle the hub place the assembly in a vice and with a suitable drift remove the grease seal.
8 Lift away the inner bearing cone and then using a drift remove the inner and outer bearing outer tracks from the

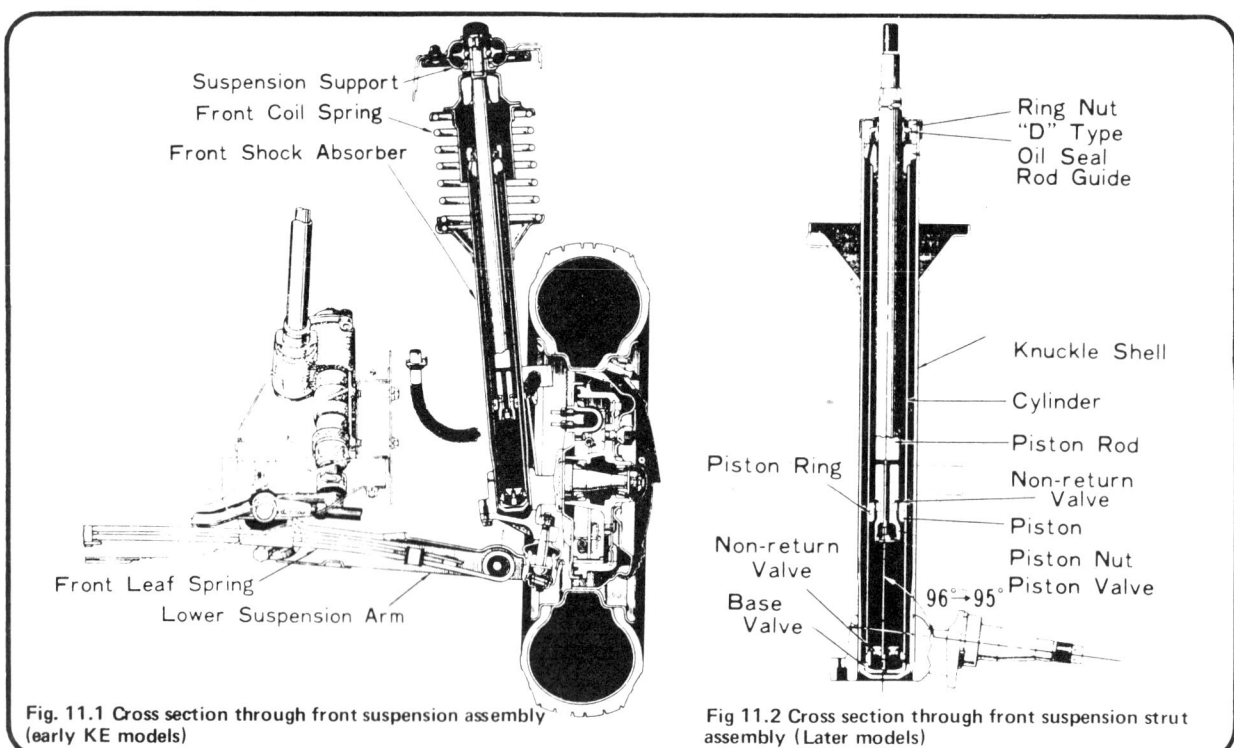

Fig. 11.1 Cross section through front suspension assembly (early KE models)

Fig 11.2 Cross section through front suspension strut assembly (Later models)

Chapter 11/Suspension and steering

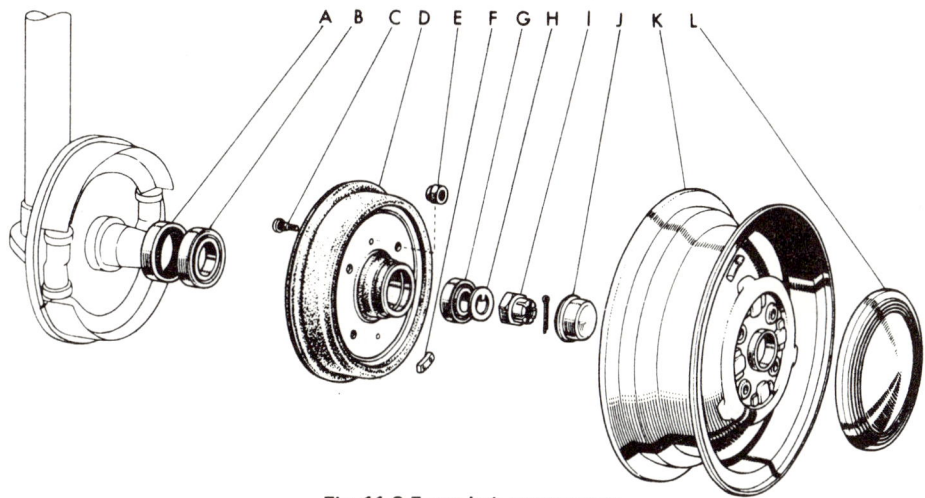

Fig. 11.3 Front hub components

A "V" type oil seal
B Inner tapered roller bearing
C Hub bolt
D Front axle hub and brake drum
E Hub nut
F Balance weight
G Outer tapered roller bearing
H Claw washer
I Castle nut
J Front hub grease cap
K Disc wheel
L Wheel cap

Fig. 11.4 Removal of hub and brake drum assembly

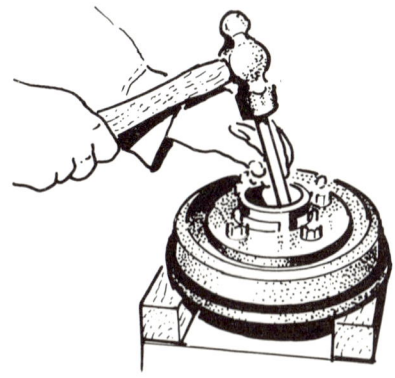

Fig. 11.5 Removal of inner bearing cone

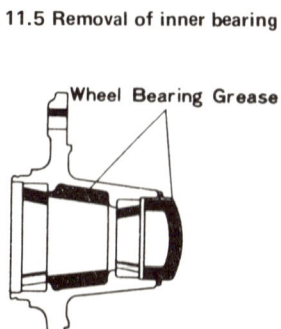

Fig. 11.6 Correct packing of wheel hub with grease

interior of the hub assembly. Note which way round the tapers face. (Fig. 11.5)
9 Wash the bearings, cups and hub assembly in paraffin and wipe dry with a non-fluffy rag.
10 Look at the bearing outer tracks and cones for signs of overheating, scoring, corrosion or damage. Reassemble each race and check for roughness of movement. If any of these faults are evident new races must be fitted.
11 Inspect the drum or disc as described in Chapter 9.
12 To reassemble the hub first fit the bearing outer tracks making sure that the tapers face outwards. Use a suitable diameter tubular drift and drive fully home.
13 Pack the two bearing cone assemblies with a recommended grease.
14 Insert the inner bearing cone assembly and then refit the seal (lip innermost) using a tubular drift. Take care that the seal is not distorted as it is being driven home.
15 Smear a little grease on the seal lip to provide initial lubrication.
16 Pack the hub with grease and refit to the stub axle. (Fig 11.6)
17 Insert the outer bearing cone assembly and refit the washer and nut. Tighten the nut to a torque wrench setting of 19-23 lb f ft (2.6-3.2 Kg fm).
18 Rotate the hub assembly in both directions to seat the bearings.
19 Slacken the nut until it can be turned with the fingers and then retighten finger tight. Check there is no endfloat between the nut and bearing.
20 Lock the nut with a new split pin. Replace the dust cap.
21 Refit the caliper and secure with the two bolts.
22 Adjust the front drum brakes and refit the roadwheel.

3 Front brake disc - removal and replacement

1 Refer to Section 2, and remove the hub and disc assembly.
2 Mark the relative positions of the hub and disc so that they may be refitted in their original positions, unless new parts are to be fitted.
3 Undo and remove the bolts that secure the disc to the hub, and separate the two parts.
4 Clean the disc and inspect for deep scoring, chipping, or cracking and, if evident, a new disc should be obtained.
5 To refit the disc check that the two mating faces are really clean and assemble the two parts. Replace the securing bolts and tighten in a diagonal and progressive manner.
6 Reassemble the hub to the stub axle as described in Section 2.
7 If a dial indicator gauge is available check for disc run-out which should not exceed 0.006 inch (0.15 mm) at the outer circumference. Should this figure be exceeded check that the mating faces are clean and refit to the hub 180° from its first position. If the run-out is still excessive a new disc and / or hub will be necessary.

4.6 Suspension strut top mounting

4 Front suspension unit strut - removal and replacement

1 Chock the rear wheels, jack-up the front of the car and support on firmly based axle stands. Remove the roadwheel.
2 Refer to Section 2, and remove the front hub assembly.
3 *Drum brake models.* Refer to Chapter 9 and detach the front brake backplate and suspend it on wire or string to prevent damage to the hose.
4 On early KE models with a transverse leaf spring, place a jack under the lower control arm.
5 Undo and remove the bolts located at the bottom of the strut. Note that there are three bolts on KE models.
6 Undo and remove the three nuts that secure the suspension support to the underside of the wing panel. (photo)
7 The strut assembly may now be lifted away from the underside of the wing. Note that on some models the brake hose to metal pipe junction is retained by a bracket mounted on the strut outer casing. If this is the case disconnect the flexible hose as described in Chapter 9.
8 To remove the coil spring a special tool is required to compress the spring. Without the use of this tool the job can be dangerous so take the assembly along to the local Toyota garage who will be able to do the job for you.
9 Clean the outside of the strut and check for leaks or weak operation. If evident the strut will have to be either overhauled or renewed.
10 Check the shell for damage or deformation, the bump rubber for weakness and the spring seat for deformation or cracks. Also check the dust seal for deterioration and the bearing stud cover for damage.
11 Inspect the front suspension support bearing for wear, the cushion for deterioration and the serrated bolts for damage. Rectify any worn parts as necessary.
12 Refitting the strut is the reverse sequence to removal but the following additional points should be noted:

   a) If one strut or coil spring is to be renewed the second one must also be renewed to compensate for any settlement or wear.
   b) Always use a new self lock nut when refitting the suspension support to the piston rod.
   c) Apply a little universal grease to the suspension support bearing and when fitted pack the space at the top part of the support.
   d) If the front brake assembly has been removed the wheel bearing pre-load must be reset as described in Section 2.
   e) Refer to Chapter 9 and reconnect the flexible hose. It will also be necessary to bleed the hydraulic system.

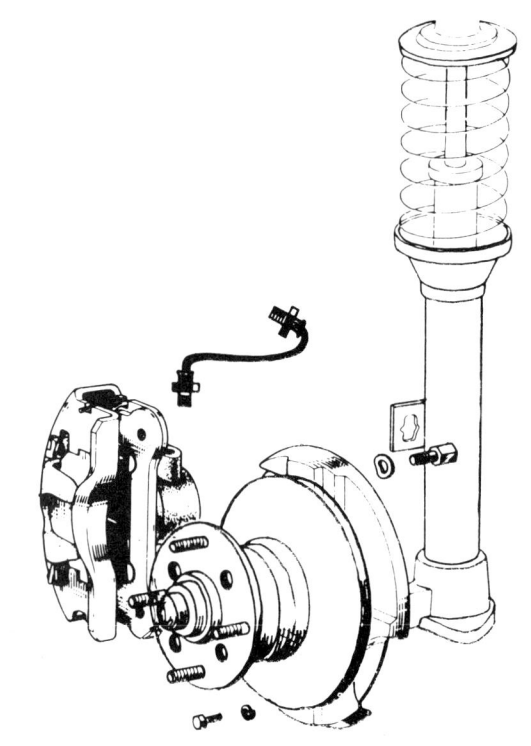

Fig. 11.7 Front suspension strut assembly with disc brake (later models)

5 Front suspension unit strut - dismantling, overhaul and reassembly

1 Before dismantling check that spare parts are available as some difficulty could be experienced in some areas.
2 Before commencing work it will be necessary to obtain some special tools from the local Toyota garage. Without these the job is virtually impossible:
   a) Ring nut oil seal replacer.
   b) Oil seal remover.
   c) Ring nut oil seal remover.
   d) Front spring seat holding tool.

Chapter 11/Suspension and steering   235

e) Ring nut wrench.
f) Oil seal guide.
g) Piston valve wrench.

3 Wipe down the exterior of the strut and then mount vertically in a firm bench vice. Do not hold the tube itself but at the lowermost end.

4 Dismantling can now begin. First remove the strut cushion and the bearing dust cover.

5 Detach the lower end of the coil spring lower seat and remove the coil spring by rotating in a clockwise direction.

6 Hold the bump-rubber front seating to prevent rotation and unscrew the nut that secures the piston rod to the suspension support.

7 The suspension support, suspension support dust seal, bump-rubber front seat, dust cover, front spring seat upper and bump-rubber may now be removed from the strut.

8 Refer to Section 2, and remove the front hub assembly if it is still in position.

9 Undo and remove the four bolts that secure the brake back-plate (or dust deflector - disc brakes) to the steering knuckle and lift away.

10 Remove the upper cap from the strut and straighten the staking on the upper end of the shell.

11 Undo the ring nut using the correct special tool ('e' in paragraph 2) and remove it taking care not to damage the 'D' type oil seal in the ring nut.

12 Using a knitting needle or similar carefully ease out the gasket between the rod guide and shell.

13 Remove the cylinder from the shell and pour out the hydraulic fluid into a clean glass jar.

14 Using a long metal drift remove the base valve from the cylinder.

15 Remove the shell from the vice and pour out the remaining hydraulic fluid.

16 Carefully pry out and separate the base valve sub-assembly from the base valve case.

17 Now hold the top end of the piston rod in a firm vice with soft faces on the jaws. Undo and remove the piston valve in the piston nut using the correct special tool ('g' in paragraph 2).

18 Using a socket wrench of suitable size undo and remove the piston nut. Remove the piston, non-return valve, spring and non-return valve stopper from the piston rod.

19 Remove the piston rod from the vice and carefully ease the piston ring from the piston.

20 The unit is now dismantled. Clean all components and wipe dry with a clean non-fluffy rag. For cleaning purposes it is best to use some automatic transmission fluid.

21 Carefully inspect the coil spring for signs of distortion, damage or excessive corrosion. Also check its free-length which

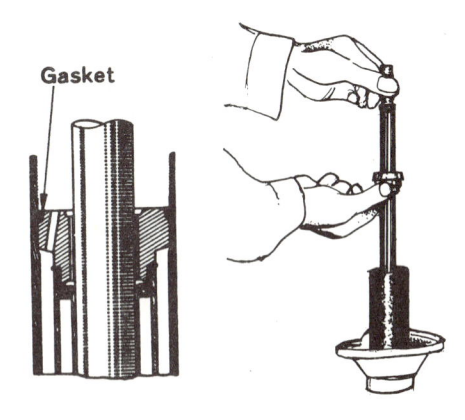

Fig. 11.8 Removal of strut piston rod

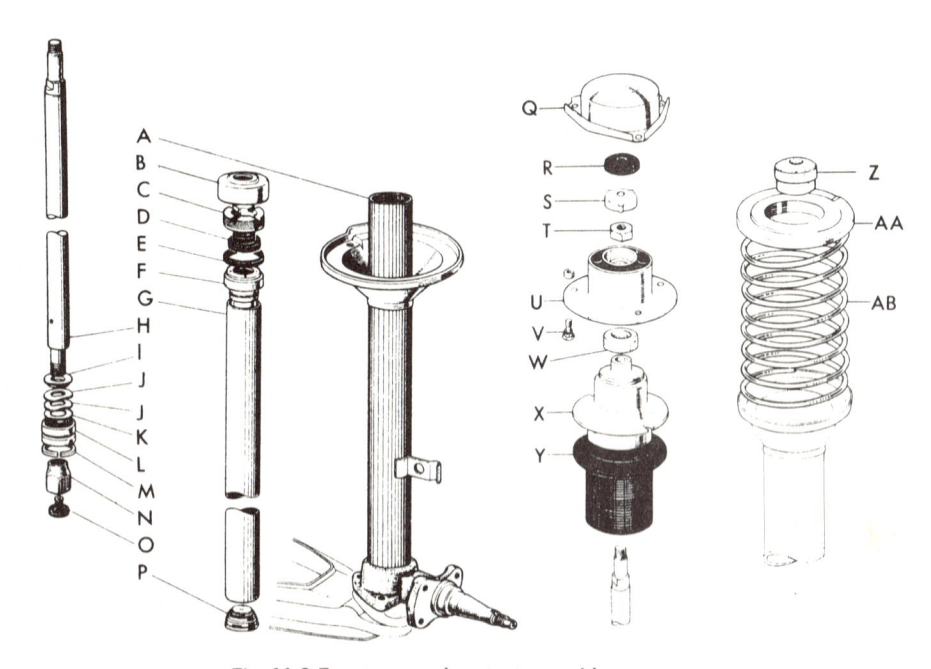

Fig. 11.9 Front suspension strut assembly

A W/Steering knuckle shell
B Shock absorber upper cap
C Shock absorber ring nut
D "D" type oil seal
E Gasket
F Rod guide
G Cylinder
H Piston rod
I Non-return valve stopper No. 1
J Non-return valve spring
K Non-return valve
L Piston
M Piston ring
N Piston nut
O Piston valve
P Base valve
Q Suspension support cover
R Cushion
S Bearing dust cover
T Nut
U Front suspension support
V Serration bolt
W Suspension support dust seal
X Bumper front seat
Y Dust cover
Z Front spring bumper
AA Front spring upper seat
BB Front coil spring

will give an indication of whether it has weakened.
22 Inspect the shell for signs of leaking or damage.
23 Carefully inspect the steering knuckle for signs of cracks.
24 Check the front spring bump-rubber and dust cover for signs of cracks.
25 Inspect the suspension support for signs of weakness at the cushion, roughness at the bearing and damage to the serration bolts.
26 Inspect the piston rod for signs of wear, scoring or distortion at the piston rod surface and contacting plate with the piston valve.
27 Measure the piston rod diameter and check for wear or ovality.
28 Measure the piston diameter and check for wear or ovality.
29 Check the contact surfaces of the piston with the non-return valve for wear or damage.
30 Inspect the threads on the piston valve and valve thread. Also check the non-return valve and spring.
31 Inspect the base valve and the riveted section for wear and the casing for damage.
32 Check the cylinder inner diameter for wear or ovality and the cylinder for distortion. Inspect the bush and oil lock tube of the rod guide for wear or damage. Measure the bushing inner diameter for ovality or wear.
33 Check the ring nut for thread wear and the lip of the 'D' type oil seal for wear or damage. If the oil seal is suspect, renew. For this special tools ('a','b' and 'c' in paragraph 2) will be required.
34 With all parts clean, reassembly can begin. Mount the top end of the piston rod in a bench vice with soft faces over the jaws and refit the non-return valve stopper, two non-return valve springs, non-return valve, and the piston nut onto the piston rod lower end.
35 Tighten the piston nut to a torque wrench setting of 36-43 lb f ft (5-6 Kg fm).
36 Using a centre punch stake the threads between the piston nut and piston rod at two joints 180° apart.
37 Start and screw the piston valve onto the piston nut using tool ('g' see paragraph 2) until the centre shaft of the piston valve contacts the piston rod through the main valve. When a slight resistance is felt unscrew the piston valve two complete turns (Fig 11.11)
38 Using a centre punch stake the threads between the piston nut and the piston valve at two joints 180° apart.
39 Fit the base valve case onto the base valve sub-assembly in a vice and then fit the whole assembly into the cylinder. For this a soft faced hammer will be required. (Fig 11.12)
40 Fit the piston rod into the cylinder ensuring that the piston ring is not damaged. Fit the cylinder into the shell.
41 Fill the strut shell with exactly 16.5 cu in (270 cc) of automatic transmission fluid.
42 Fit the rod guide into the shell and follow with a new gasket between the rod guide and shell.
43 Smear a little grease onto the lip of the 'D' type oil seal and fit the oil seal guide using tool ('f' see paragraph 2) onto the top of the piston rod.
44 Refit the ring nut onto the piston rod taking care not to damage the oil seal. Remove the seal guide and tighten the ring nut to a torque wrench setting of 75-110 lb f ft (10-15 Kg fm).
45 Stake the top end of the shell with a centre punch to prevent the ring nut working loose.
46 Fit the upper cap onto the top end of the shell.
47 The unit is now ready for having the coil spring refitted.

6 Front suspension arm, balljoints and leaf spring (early KE models) - removal and replacement

1 Apply the handbrake, chock the rear wheels, jack-up the front of the car and support on firmly based axle stands. Remove the roadwheel.
2 Remove the tie-rod end securing nut and using a universal balljoint separator part the tie-rod end from the steering knuckle arm.

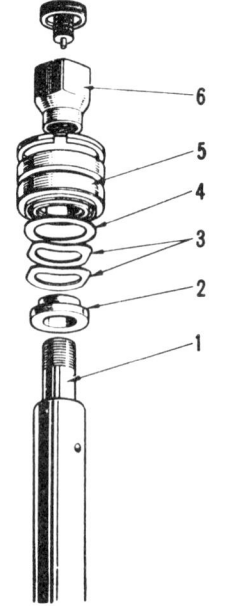

Fig. 11.10 Piston assembly components

1 Piston rod
2 Non-return valve stopper No 1
3 Non-return valve spring
4 Non-return valve
5 Piston
6 Piston nut

3 Using a small jack raise the suspension arm.
4 Undo and remove the three bolts that secure the steering knuckle arm.
5 Lower the jack slowly whilst supporting the end of the front leaf spring. Remove the jack completely.
6 Undo and remove the bolt that secures the suspension arm to the front leaf spring eye.
7 Undo and remove the two bolts that secure the lower arm shaft to the front suspension crossmember.
8 Remove the suspension arm with front leaf spring seat from the front suspension crossmember.
9 If it is desired to removed the front leaf spring remove the second suspension arm and withdraw the leaf spring.
10 Wash all parts and wipe dry ready for inspection.
11 Check the suspension arm for signs of cracks, distortion or other damage.
12 Inspect the leaf spring for wear or damage at the clip and rubber pad.
13 Check the spring bushings and leaf spring seat for wear, distortion or other damage.
14 Inspect the crossmember for signs of distortion or fractures.
15 Check the lower arm shaft for damage.
16 Check the suspension arm bushes for wear, damage or deterioration. The bushes can be renewed if necessary as described in the following paragraphs.
17 Undo and remove the two bolts at both ends of the lower arm shaft. The lower arm bushes can now be removed using a suitable puller.
18 Fit the thrust bushing onto the lower arm shaft and then install the lower arm shaft onto the suspension arm. Make sure that the lower arm shaft is fitted in the correct direction. The thrust washer attaching the lower arm shaft must be to the front side of the car and the centre protruded mark must face towards the lower side.
19 Fit the bush onto the front end of the suspension arm using the bench vice and suitable diameter socket.
20 Fit the bush onto the rear end of the suspension arm using the bench vice and suitable diameter socket.
21 Refit the plate washer, lock washer and bolts onto both ends of the lower arm shaft and temporarily tighten to a torque wrench setting of 3.6 lb f ft (0.5 Kg fm). The final setting is made with the car on the ground.
22 Check the ball joint for wear or slackness at the stud. If the revolving torque of the balljoint stud is less than 2.6 lb f in (3.0 Kg f cm) without the dust cover the balljoint must be renewed.
23 Remove the split pin and castellated nut from the balljoint stud and detach the knuckle arm from the balljoint using a

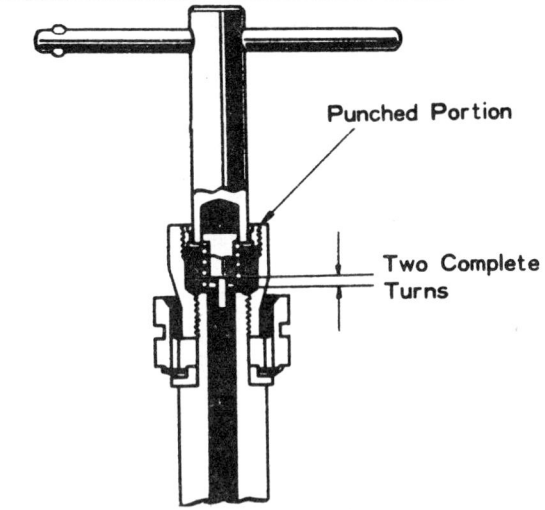

Fig. 11.11 Fitting piston valve into front suspension strut

Fig. 11.12 Front suspension strut sub valve assembly (later models)

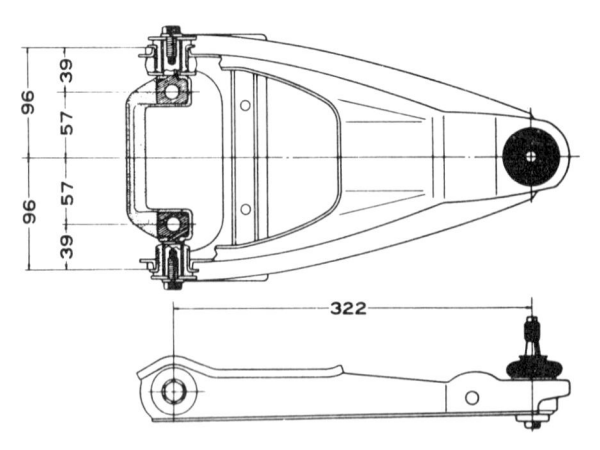

Fig. 11.13 Suspension arm checking dimensions (All measurements in millimetres)

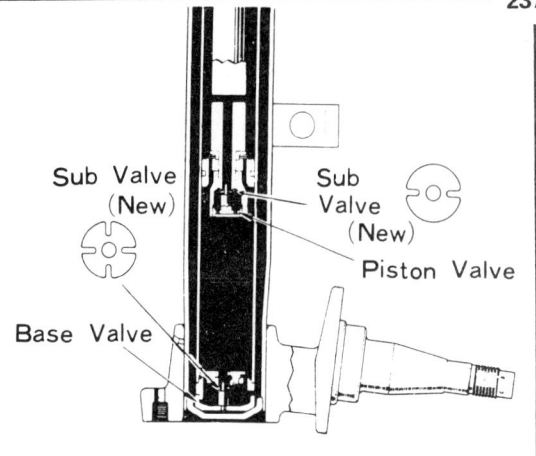

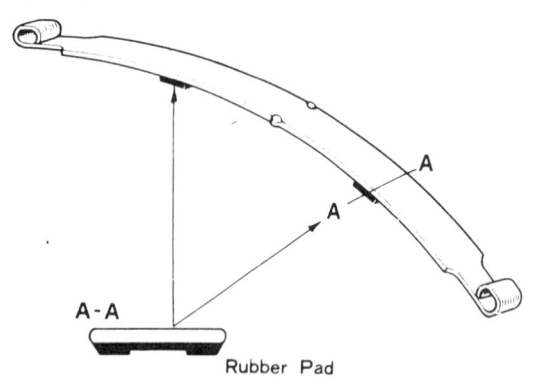

Fig. 11.14 Front suspension leaf spring (early KE models)

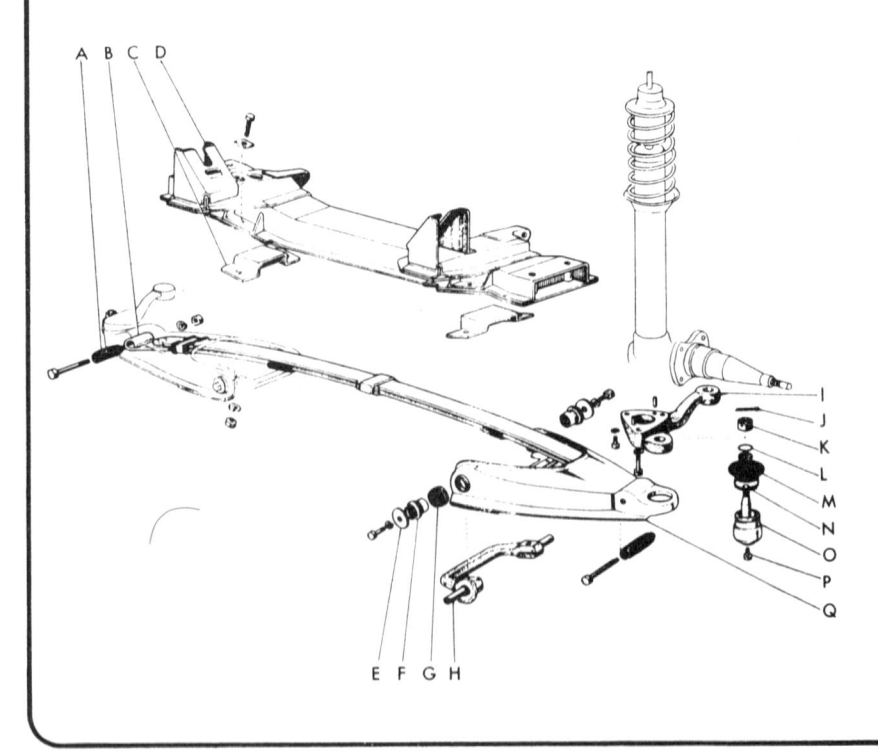

Fig. 11.15 Front suspension assembly (early KE models)

A Front spring bushing
B Front spring leaf
C Front spring seat
D Front suspension cross-member
E Plate washer
F Lower arm bushing
G Lower arm strut bushing
H Lower arm shaft
I Steering knuckle arm
J Cotter pin
K Castle nut
L Ring
M Lower ball joint dust cover
N Set ring
O Lower ball joint
P W/Head tapered screw plug
Q Suspension lower arm

universal balljoint separator.

24 Remove the dust cover and then detach the balljoint from the suspension arm using a bench vice and suitable packing.

25 Fit the new balljoint onto the suspension arm using the bench vice and suitable packing. This being the reverse procedure to removal.

26 Place a 0.008 in (2.0 mm) diameter wire in parallel with the balljoint stud to allow the air to escape during greasing and then fit the balljoint dust cover onto the balljoint. Replace the set ring and rubber ring onto the dust cover.

27 Remove the plug from the balljoint, fit a grease nipple and refill the balljoint with a recommended grease until the dust cover is three quarters full. **Always use a molybdenum disulphide lithium base grease.**

28 Remove the 0.008 in (2.0 mm) diameter wire and grease nipple and replace the plug which should be tightened to a torque wrench setting of 3-5 lb f ft (0.4-0.7 Kg fm).

29 Fit the knuckle arm onto the balljoint and tighten the castellated nut to a torque wrench setting of 36-53 lb f ft (5-7 Kg fm).

30 Reassembly of all other parts is the reverse sequence to removal. The lower arm shaft to crossmember nuts should be tightened to a torque wrench setting of 30-40 lb f ft (4.15-5.5 Kg fm).

7 Front suspension arm and balljoints (TE models) - removal and replacement

1 Apply the handbrake, chock the rear wheels, jack-up the front of the car and support on firmly based axle stands. Remove the roadwheel.

2 Undo and remove the steering knuckle securing bolts.

3 Remove the tie-rod end securing nut and using a universal balljoint separator part the tie-rod end from the steering knuckle arm.

4 Undo and remove the stabilizer bolt and the strut bolt.

5 Undo and remove the suspension arm bolt and lift away the suspension arm.

6 Remove the balljoint dust cover. Inspect the balljoint and if it is worn the suspension arm and balljoint can only be renewed as an assembly. Lubricate the balljoint with a molybdenum disulphide lithuim based grease.

7 The suspension arm bushes can be renewed using a bench vice and suitable diameter sockets. Take care to ensure that the new bushes are fitted with the shoulder facing in the right direction.

8 Reassembly is the reverse sequence to removal. Any information required and not mentioned in this Section, may be found in Section 6.

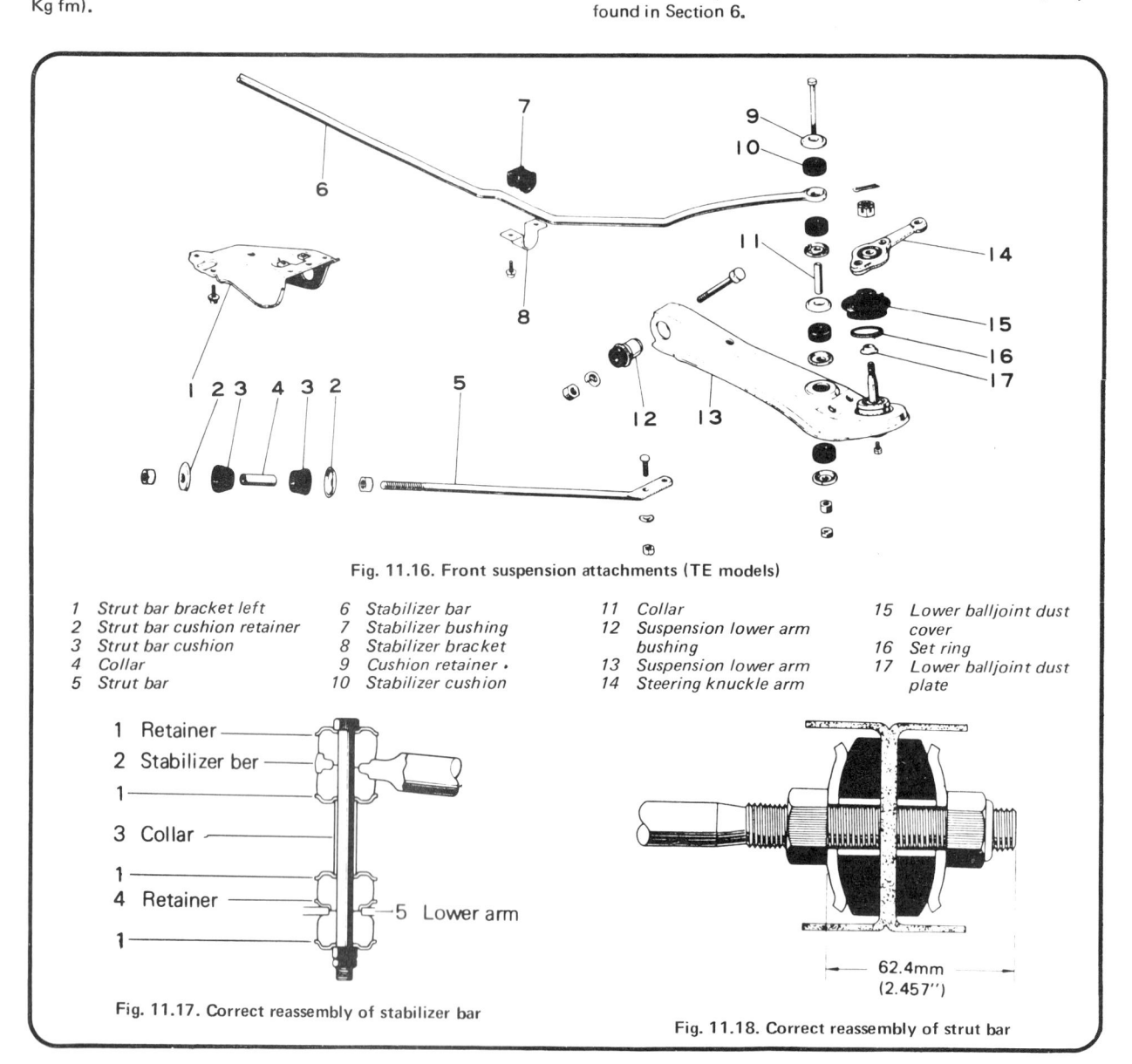

Fig. 11.16. Front suspension attachments (TE models)

1 Strut bar bracket left
2 Strut bar cushion retainer
3 Strut bar cushion
4 Collar
5 Strut bar
6 Stabilizer bar
7 Stabilizer bushing
8 Stabilizer bracket
9 Cushion retainer
10 Stabilizer cushion
11 Collar
12 Suspension lower arm bushing
13 Suspension lower arm
14 Steering knuckle arm
15 Lower balljoint dust cover
16 Set ring
17 Lower balljoint dust plate

Fig. 11.17. Correct reassembly of stabilizer bar

Fig. 11.18. Correct reassembly of strut bar

Chapter 11/Suspension and steering

8 Rear shock absorbers - removal and replacement

1 Chock the front wheels, jack-up the rear of the car and support on firmly based axle stands. Remove the roadwheel.
2 Using a jack support the rear axle housing.
3 Open the luggage compartment lid and remove the nuts, cushion retainer and cushion at the top shock absorber mounting which is located by the wheelarch.
4 Working under the car undo and remove the bolt that secures the lower end of the shock absorber to the axle housing. Lift away the shock absorber from the underside of the car.
5 Inspect the shock absorber for signs of hydraulic fluid leakage which, if evident, indicates that the unit must be renewed.
6 Clean the exterior and wipe dry with a non-fluffy rag.
7 Inspect the shaft for signs of corrosion or distortion and the body for damage.
8 Check the action by expanding and contracting to ascertain if equal resistance is felt on both strokes. If the resistance is very uneven the unit should be fully expanded and contracted at least eight times. It this does not cure the problem the unit must be renewed.
9 Check the rubber bushes and washers for signs of deterioration and obtain new if evident.
10 To refit first install the rear spring bump, bump cover, cushion retainer and cushion onto the shock absorber rod.
11 Fit the rod of the shock absorber onto the body bracket.
12 Working inside the luggage compartment refit the cushion retainer, cushion, and nut.
13 Tighten the nut until the rod protrudes 0.47-0.51 inch (12-13 mm) and then lock it with the locknut. Tighten the nut to a torque wrench setting of 14-22 lb f ft (1.9-3.1 Kg fm) (Fig 11.19)
14 Fit the lower end of the shock absorber onto the rear axle housing and tighten the securing nut to a torque wrench setting of 25-40 lb f ft (3.5-5.5 Kg fm). (Fig 11.20)
15 Refit the wheel and lower the car to the ground.

9 Rear spring - removal and replacement

1 Chock the front wheels, jack-up the rear of the car and support on firmly based axle stands. Remove the roadwheel.
2 Support the weight of the rear axle.
3 Undo and remove the bolt that secures the lower end of the shock absorber to the rear axle housing.
4 Undo and remove the 'U' bolt nuts and washers. Lift away the 'U' bolt seat and under spring pad.
5 Undo and remove the nuts and washers securing the shackle and remove the shackle plate from the rear end of the spring.
6 Using a suitable pry bar ease out the shackle and recover the four bushes.
7 Undo and remove the two nuts, bolts and washers that secure the spring bracket pin to the bracket at the front end of the rear spring.
8 Ease a screwdriver between the spring bracket pin and bracket. Part them and remove the rear spring and bracket pin.
9 Clean all parts ready for inspection.
10 Check the bushes and spring pads for wear, deterioration or other damage.
11 Inspect the shackle, bracket pin and 'U' bolts for wear or damage.
12 Carefully inspect the spring leaves for signs of wear, cracking, breakage or weakness.
13 To refit the rear spring, first fit the rubber bushes into the front end of the spring and connect the front end of the spring to the front bracket on the body by inserting the bracket pin.

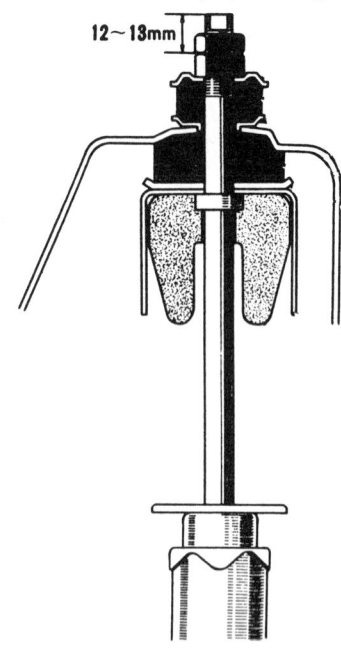

Fig. 11.19. Shock absorber upper attachment

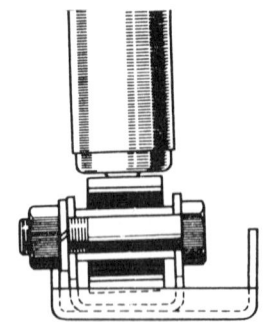

Fig. 11.20. Shock absorber lower attachment

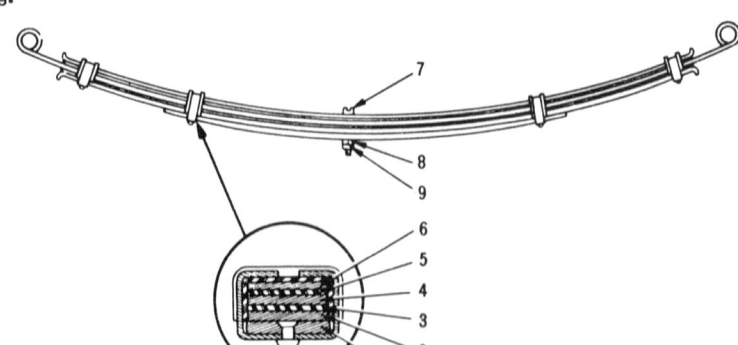

Fig. 11.21. Rear spring detail

1 Leaf
2 Leaf
3 Inter-leaf
4 Leaf
5 Inter-leaf
6 Leaf tensioner
7 Centre bolt
8 Distance piece
9 Nut

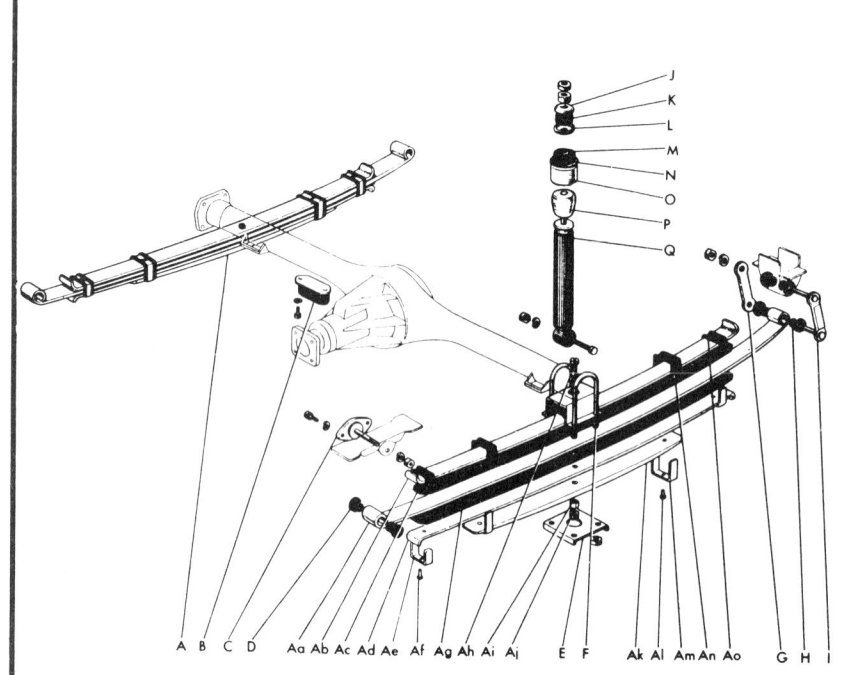

Fig. 11.22. Rear suspension assembly (earlier models)

A	Rear spring assembly
B	Differential carrier bumper
C	Spring bracket pin
D	Bushing
E	Rear spring U-bolt seat
F	U-bolt
G	Spring shackle outer plate
H	Bushing
I	Spring shackle No. 2
J	Shock absorber cushion retainer
K	Shock absorber cushion
L	Shock absorber cushion retainer
M	Shock absorber cushion
N	Cushion retainer
O	Rear bumper cover
P	Rear spring bumper
Q	Rear shock absorber
AA	Rear leaf spring No. 1
AB	Rear leaf spring tension
AC	Rear spring inter-leaf No. 2
AD	Rear leaf spring with clip No. 1
AE	Rear spring clip No. 1
AF	Round head rivet
AG	Rear spring inter-leaf No. 1
AH	Rear spring centre bolt
AI	Distance piece
AJ	Nut
AK	Rear leaf spring with clip No. 2
AL	Round head rivet
AM	Rear spring clip No. 2
AN	Rear spring clip spacer No. 2
AO	Rear spring clip spacer No. 1

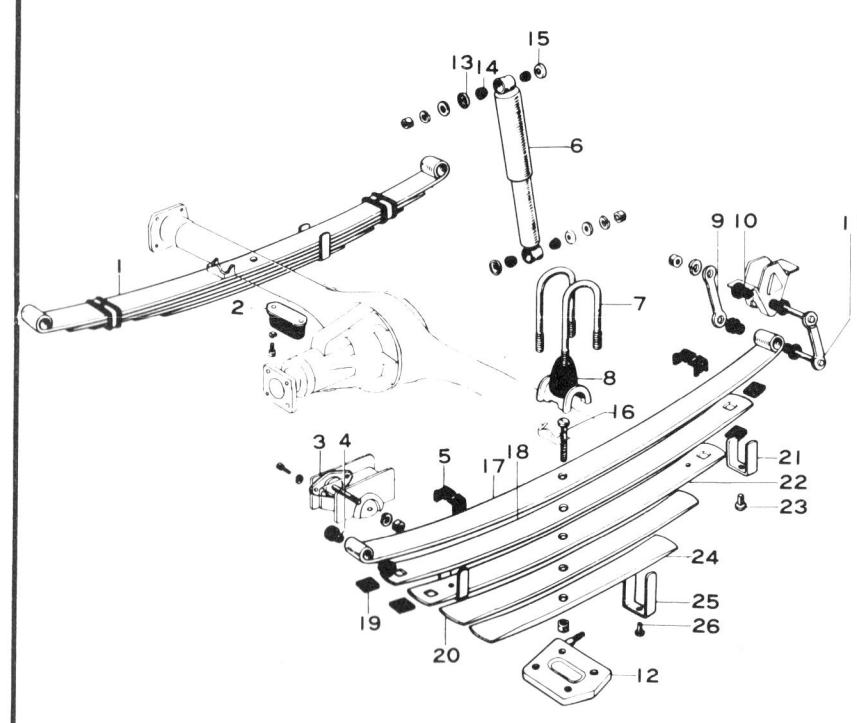

Fig. 11.23. Rear suspension assembly (later models)

1	Rear spring
2	Differential carrier bumper
3	Spring bracket pin
4	Bushing
5	Rear spring clip seat
6	Shock absorber
7	'U' bolt
8	Rear spring bumper
9	Spring shackle outer plate
10	Bushing
11	Spring No. 2 shackle
12	Spring 'U' bolt seat
13	Shock absorber cushion washer
14	Bushing
15	Shock absorber cushion washer
16	Rear spring centre bolt
17	Rear spring No. 1 leaf
18	Rear spring No. 2 leaf
19	Rear spring silencer
20	Rear spring No. 4 leaf
21	Rear spring No. 1 clip
22	Rear spring No. 3 leaf
23	Rivet
24	Rear spring No. 5 leaf
25	Rear spring No. 2 clip
26	Rivet

Chapter 11/Suspension and steering 241

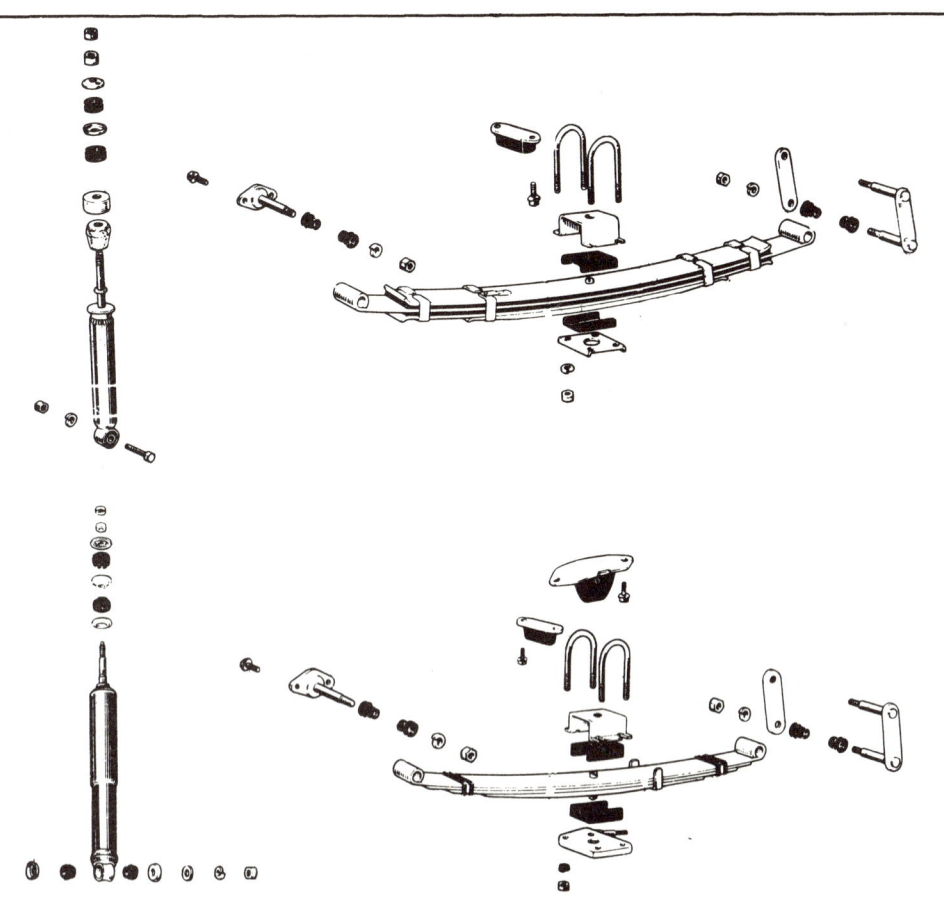

Fig. 11.24. Alternative rear suspension components
(Top) Saloon and Coupe (Bottom) Estate
(For component names refer to Fig. 11.23.)

14 Tighten the two bolts and one nut onto the bracket pin finger tight only.
15 Fit the rubber bushes into the rear end of the spring and rear bracket of the body and connect the rear end of the spring onto the rear bracket of the body by installing the shackle.
16 Refit the shackle plate, washers and nuts which should be tightened finger tight only.
17 Refit the upper pad and pad retainer between the rear spring and rear axle housing seat.
18 Refit the 'U' bolts, lower pad and 'U' bolts seat and secure with the four 'U' bolt nuts which should be tightened to a torque wrench setting of 22-32 lb f ft (3.0-4.5 Kg fm).
19 Change the supporting positions from the body to the rear axle housing.
20 Tighten the two bolts attaching the bracket pin to a torque wrench setting of 7-12 lb f ft (1.0-1.6 Kg fm) and the nut to a torque wrench setting of 15-22 lb f ft (2.0-3.0 Kg fm).
21 Tighten the shackle securing nuts to a torque wrench setting of 15-22 lb f ft (2.0-3.0 Kg fm).

10 Steering wheel - removal and replacment

1 For safety reasons, disconnect the battery.
2 Turn the steering wheel until it is in the 'straight-ahead' position and note the position of the spokes.
3 Disconnect the wiring at the harness connector to the horn and twist the horn button anticlockwise to remove. When a horn button push bar is fitted it may be detached by removing the screws located at the rear of the spokes. (photo)
4 Using a suitably sized socket undo and remove the nut securing the steering wheel to the shaft.
5 With a pencil or scriber mark the relative positions of the steering wheel hub and shaft to assist replacement.
6 Using the palms of the hand on the rear of the steering wheel spokes thump the steering wheel so releasing it from the splines on the shaft. If it is very tight a puller will have to be used.
7 Refitting the steering wheel is the reverse sequence to

10.3 Removal of horn button push bar

Chapter 11/Suspension and steering

removal. Should new parts be fitted or the initial alignment marks lost, jack-up the front of the car and turn the wheels to the straight-ahead position. Lower the car again. Fit the steering wheel so that the spokes are parallel with the ground.
8 Refit the securing nut and tighten to a torque wrench setting of 15-22 lb f ft (2.0-3.0 Kg fm)
9 Finally refit the horn button or push pad as applicable. This being the reverse sequence to removal.

11 Steering gear assembly - removal and replacement

1 Refer to Section 10 and remove the steering wheel.
2 Disconnect the direction indicator harness at the multi pin connector located under the instrument panel.
3 Remove the upper column clamp securing bolt(s).
4 Refer to Chapter 12, and remove the parcel shelf.
5 On some models it will be necessary to remove the clutch pedal as described in Chapter 5 so that access can be gained to the toe pan cover which must next be removed.
6 Undo and remove the sector arm securing nut and using a suitable puller withdraw the sector shaft.
7 Remove the steering column cover which will then expose the lock mechanism and direction indicator switch. (photos)
8 The steering lock mechanism is retained by shear-bolts and can be removed once the bolts have been removed. For this a special screw extractor is necessary. Drill a 0.20 in (5.08 mm) hole 0.75 inch (19.05 mm) deep and screw in the extractor. Undo and remove the screws and lift away the switch. (Fig 11.24)
9 Move the direction indicator switch lever to the right turn position. Undo and remove the switch securing screw and lift away the switch.
10 Undo and remove the three bolts securing the steering gearbox to the body front sidemember.
11 Disconnect the speedometer drive cable from the steering

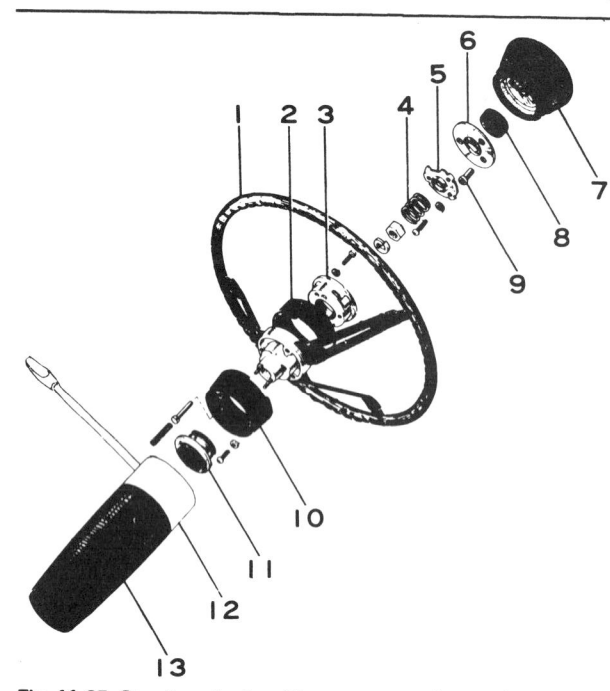

Fig. 11.25. Steering wheel and horn assembly (Type 1)

1 Steering wheel
2 Steering wheel boss upper cover
3 Horn button contact seat
4 Compression spring
5 Horn button stop plate
6 Horn button stop plate
7 Horn button
8 Horn button cushion
9 Horn button setting washer
10 Steering wheel boss lower cover
11 Insulator
12 Turn signal switch
13 Steering housing

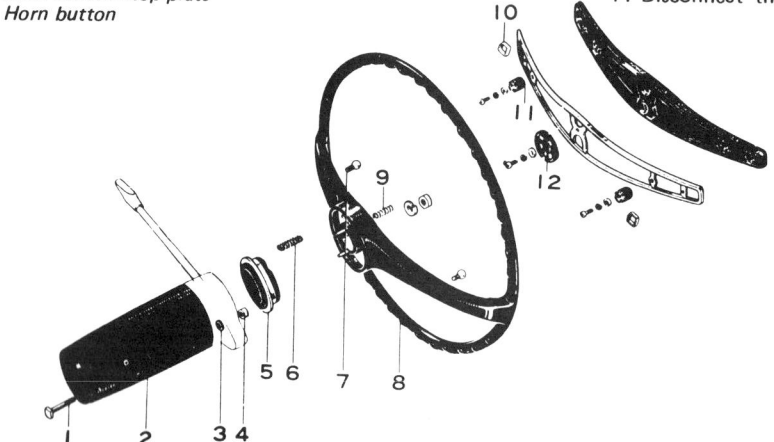

Fig. 11.26. Steering wheel and horn assembly (Type 2)

1 Square bolt
2 Steering housing
3 Toothed washer
4 Nut
5 Insulator
6 Compression spring
7 Horn button ball joint
8 Steering wheel
9 Compression spring
10 Horn button joint socket clip
11 Horn button joint socket
12 Horn button contact ring

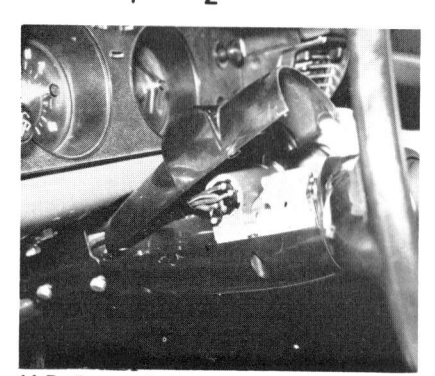

11.7a Removal of top half of steering column cover....

11.7b ....and the bottom half

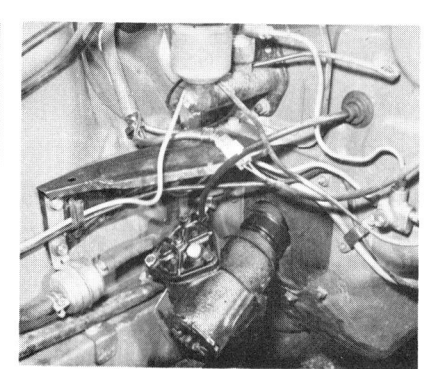

11.11 The steering gearbox. Note clip securing speedometer drive cable

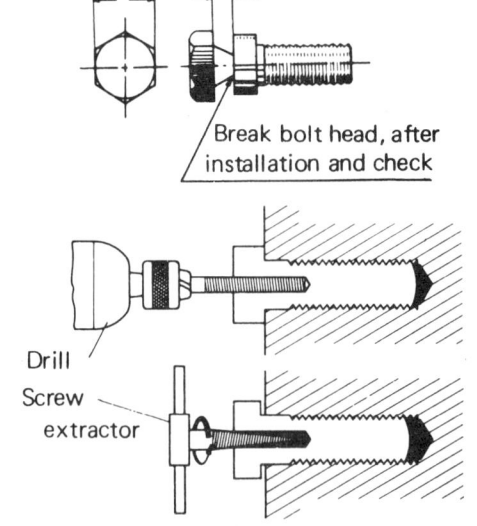

Fig. 11.27. Removal of steering lock sheer bolts

gear housing. (photo)

12 Disconnect the wiring from the oil pressure sender unit and the water temperature sender unit.

13 Remove the securing screw and remove the steering housing from the steering column.

14 Jack-up the front of the car and support on firmly based axle stands. Turn the wheels to the left.

15 When an engine undercover is fitted this must next be removed.

16 The steering gear housing assembly and column may now be drawn out from the underside of the car.

17 Refitting the steering column and housing is the reverse sequence to removal but the following additional points should be noted:
a) Before fitting the gear housing to the front sidemember install the column tube temporarily onto the instrument panel to obtain the correct gear housing position.
b) Line up the mating marks on the sector shaft and arm.
c) Check the clearance between the steering housing and direction indicator switch and the clearance between the switch and steering wheel. These clearances should be 0.016 in (0.4064 mm) and 0.12 in (3.048 mm), respectively.

Adjustment is effected by moving the steering housing slightly from the column tube.

9 If the steering gearbox has been dismantled do not forget to refill with the correct amount of recommended lubricant.

12 Steering linkage - removal and replacement

1 Chock the rear wheels, apply the handbrake, jack-up the front of the car and support on firmly based axle stands. Remove the roadwheels.

2 Detach the idler arm from the front sidemember.

3 Undo and remove the sector arm securing nut and using a universal puller draw off the sector arm.

4 Remove the split pins and castellated nuts and then using a universal balljoint separator detach the tie-rod ends from the steering knuckles.

5 The steering linkage may now be removed from the underside of the car.

6 Remove the split pins and castellated nuts and using a universal balljoint separater detach the tie-rod ends from the relay rod.

7 Slacken the locknuts at the inner end of each tie-rod balljoint and unscrew the tie-rod ends.

8 Remove the split pins and castellated nuts and using a universal balljoint separator detach the sector arm and idler arm from the relay rod.

9 Remove the split pin and castellated nut from the idler arm and remove the idler arm support.

10 Finally remove the dust seals from the tie-rods, sector arm and idler arm.

11 The dismantled parts should be cleaned and inspected for signs of wear, distortion or damage and new parts obtained as necessary.

12 To reassemble first fit the idler arm onto the idler arm support with the idler arm parallel to the installing surface of the idler arm support on the body.

13 Fit the castellated nut onto the idler arm support. Tighten the nut to a torque wrench setting of 36-50 lb f ft (4.8-6.9 Kg fm). Lock with a new split pin.

14 Clean the dust seals and then pack with a little lithium base grease and fit them onto the tie-rod and other joints.

15 Fit the clips and rings onto the respective dust seals.

16 Grease the threads of the tie-rod ends and fit them onto the tie-rods. It should be noted that the inner ends of each tie-rod and tie-rod end are righ-hand threaded and the outer ends left-hand threaded to facilitate adjustment.

17 Screw in the tie-rod ends on each tie-rod by an equal amount until the distance between the centres of the tie-rod end studs is

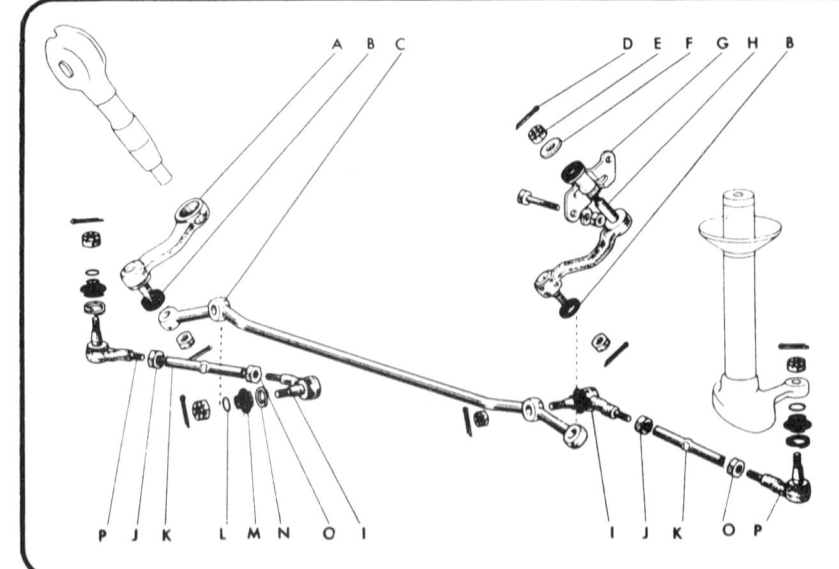

Fig. 11.28. Steering linkage components (Rhd)

A Pitman arm
B Idler arm dust seal
C Relay rod
D Cotter pin
E Castle nut
F Plate washer
G Idler arm support
H Idler arm
I Tie-rod end No. 1 (RH thread)
J Nut (RH thread)
K Tie-rod
L Ring
M Link joint dust seal
N Clip
O Nut (LH thread)
P Tie-rod end No. 2 (LH thread)

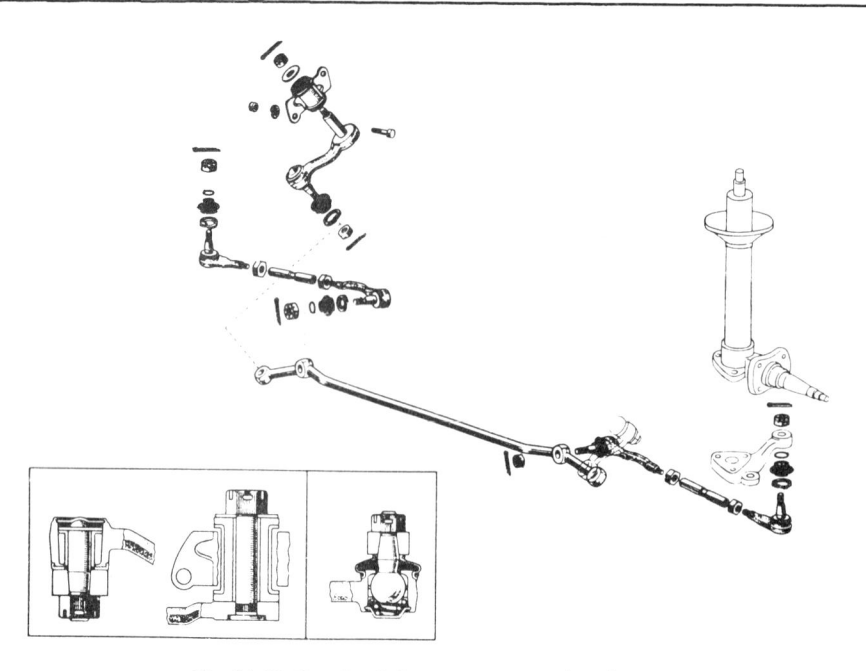

Fig. 11.29. Steering linkage components (Lhd)

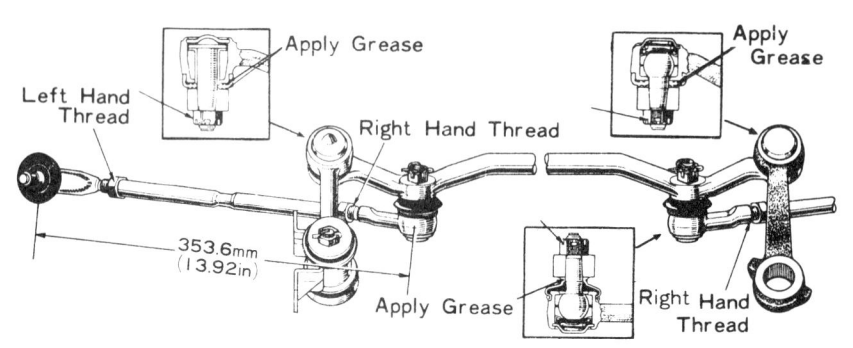

Fig. 11.30. Correct reassembly of steering linkage

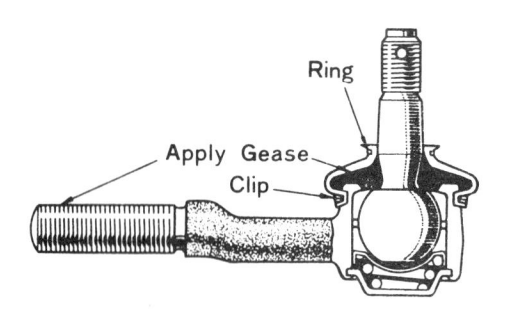

Fig. 11.31. Correct reassembly of tie-rod end

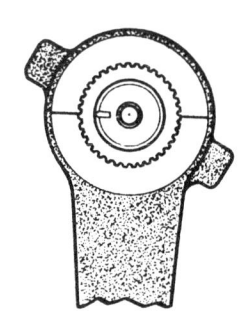

Fig. 11.32. Alignment marks on sector shaft arm and shaft

13.92 inch (353.57 mm). Temporarily tighten the locknuts.
18 Fit the sector arm and idler arm onto the relay rod and tighten the securing nuts to a torque wrench setting of 36-50 lb f ft (4.8-6.9 Kg fm). Fit new split pins to lock the nuts.
19 Lightly coat the dust seals of each tie-rod end with grease and fit the tie-rod ends onto the end of the knuckle arms. Tighten the securing nuts to a torque wrench setting of 22-32 lb f ft (3.04-4.4 Kg fm). Lock with new split pins.
20 Align the mating marks on the sector shaft and sector arm and slide on the sector arm followed by the plate washer, lock washer and nut. Tighten the nut to a torque wrench setting of 50-80 lb f ft (6.9-11.06 Kg fm). Lock with a new split pin.
21 Fit the idler arm to the front body sidemember and tighten the nuts to a torque wrench setting of 7.0-10 lb f ft (1.0-1.38 Kg fm).
22 Refit the front wheels and lower the car to the ground.
23 It will be necessary to check and reset the front wheel toe-in. Further information will be found in Section 16.

13 Steering gearbox (worm and sector) - dismantling, overhaul and reassembly

1 Suitably mount the steering gearbox in a firm bench vice and undo and remove the three bolts and spring washers that secure the endcover to the housing.
2 Slacken the sector shaft adjustment screw locknut and withdraw the endcover by screwing in the adjusting screw.
3 Drain out as much oil from the steering gearbox as possible.
4 Using a 'C' wrench of suitable size unscrew the worm bearing adjustment screw locknut.
5 Using a suitable wrench remove the worm bearing adjusting screw.
6 Carefully remove the 'O' ring located between the adjusting screw and the outer race of the ball bearing.
7 Temporarily fit a nut at the steering wheel end of the steering mainshaft and tap it with a soft faced hammer.
8 Remove the mainshaft, worm assembly and bearings from the gearhousing.
9 Be sure not to mix up the inner races, ball cages and outer races as they must not be interchanged on reassembly.
10 Carefully remove the bush and collar from the top end of the steering column tube.
11 Clean all parts ready for inspection. First examine the steering wheel for cracks or damage.
12 Check the steering shaft bearings for wear or pitting and renew if necessary.
13 Check the mainshaft and worm gear for wear or damage.
14 Carefully examine the surfaces of the sector shaft which contact the bushes and 'S' type oil seal for wear or damage. The diameter should not be less than 0.98 inch (24.9 mm).
15 Check the sector shaft for signs of wear at the gear contact surface or roughness at the bearing. If the sector roller is worn it is possible to renew it as follows:
  a) Carefully grind the welded position of the sector roller shaft and unscrew the nut.

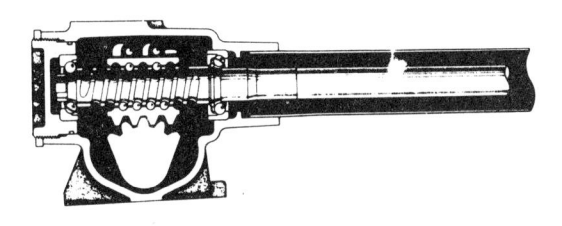

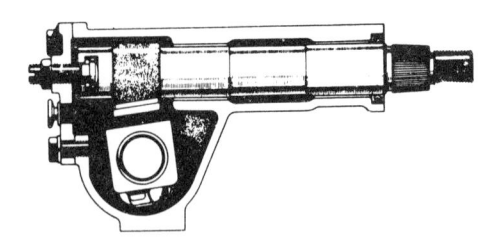

Fig. 11.33. Cross sectional view through steering gearboxes (Top) Worm and sector (Bottom) Recirculating ball, sector roller and shims

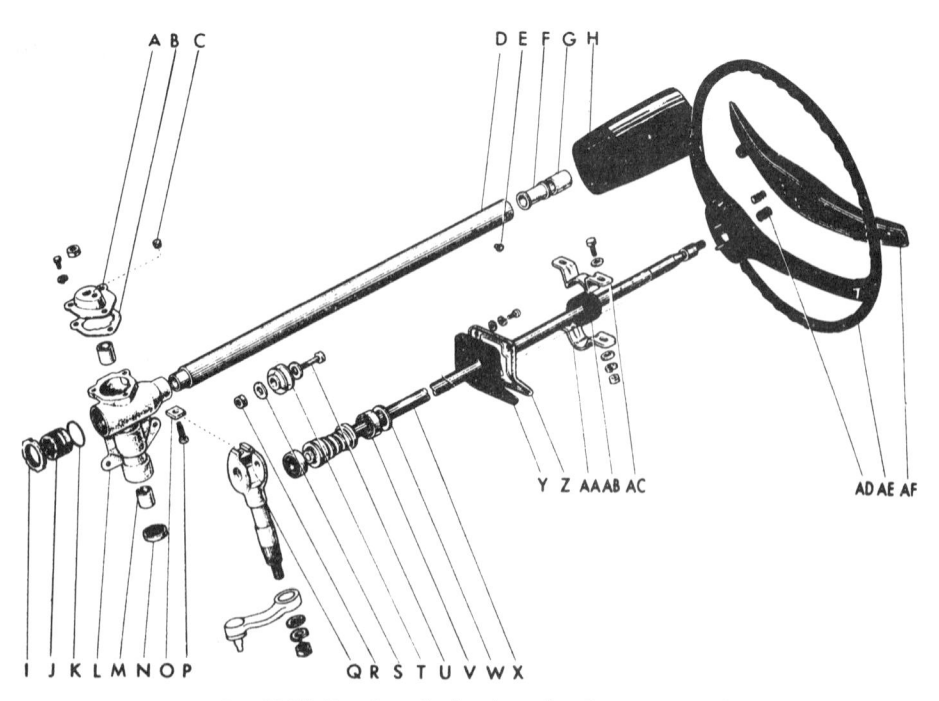

Fig. 11.34. Steering wheel and gear housing components

A Sector shaft end cover	L Steering gear housing	W Shim
B Sector shaft end cover gasket	M Bi-metal formed bushing	X Steering main shaft
C Steering gear housing oil plug	N 'A' type oil seal	Y Steering column weather seal
D Steering column tube	O Sector shaft thrust washer	Z Steering column opening cover plate
E Steering housing clamp	P Sector shaft adjusting screw	AA Steering column lower clamp
F Bushing	Q Steering sector shaft	AB Grommet
G Collar	R Hexagon nut	AC Steering column upper clamp
H Steering housing	S Shim	AD Compression spring
I Worm bearing adjusting lock nut	T Steering sector roller	AE Steering wheel
J Worm bearing adjusting screw	U Steering sector roller shaft	AF Horn button
K 'O' ring	V Radial ball bearing	

b) Remove the sector roller shaft from the sector shaft.
c) Fit a new roller to the shaft and tighten the nut to a torque wrench setting of 11-14 lb f ft (1.5-2.0 Kg fm).
d) Adjust the shim(s) until there is no sector shaft clearance and the roller rotates freely; then retighten the nut. (Fig 11.35)
e) Ideally the retaining nut should be welded so locking it. The local garage will be able to do this.

16 Check the sector shaft bushes in the housing for wear and renew if necessary. The inner diameter of the bushes should not exceed 0.989 in (25.1 mm) and the running clearance between bush and sector shaft should be less than 0.004 in (0.1 mm).

17 Check the 'S' type oil seal located at the end of the sector shaft bore in the housing. Renew if necessary.

18 Check the steering column tube for wear, cracks or damage.

19 Finally check the bushes and collar at the upper end of the column for wear or damage. Renew if necessary.

20 With all parts clean reassembly can begin. First assemble the bearings onto both sides of the worm gear. Lubricate the shaft and bearings and insert into the gear housing.

21 Smear a new 'O' ring oil seal with gease and fit. Follow this with the worm bearing adjustment screw and locknut onto the gear housing.

22 The steering worm preload must now be adjusted. Wrap a piece of cord onto the top end of the mainshaft and attach a pull spring balance scale to the free end of the cord.

23 Pull the scale evenly so as to rotate the shaft and note the reading which should be 2.6-2.7 lb f (1.2-1.7 Kg f)

24 If the desired reading is not obtained adjust the preload with the adjustment screw. For this the 'C' spanner will be required.

25 Tighten the adjustment screw locknut to a torque wrench setting of 60-70 lb f ft (8-10 Kg fm) taking care not to disturb the preload. Recheck the preload as described in paragraphs 22 and 23.

26 Select and fit a sector shaft thrust washer which gives a minimum clearance between the shaft and thrust washer. Thrust washers are available in the following sizes:

1) 0.079 in (2.01 mm)
2) 0.082 in (2.07 mm)
3) 0.083 in (2.11 mm)
4) 0.085 in (2.15 mm)

27 Apply a little gear oil onto the sector shaft and the 'S' type oil seal. Fit the sector shaft with the sector shaft adjusting bolt and thrust-washer into the gear housing.

28 Fit the endcover and gasket onto the gear housing whilst screwing the adjusting bolt anticlockwise into the endcover.

29 Fit the three securing bolts and the speedometer drive cable clamb onto the endcover and tighten the three bolts to a torque wrench setting of 11-16 lb f ft (1.5-2.2 Kg fm).

30 It is now necessary to adjust the backlash between the sector roller and worm as follows:
a) Temporarily refit the sector shaft arm and nut onto the sector shaft.
b) Hold the assembly in the bench vice and mount a dial indicator gauge so that the probe rests on the end of the sector shaft arm.
c) Adjust the backlash with the sector shaft adjusting screw until a backlash of 0.006-0.007 in (0.16-0.19 mm) is obtained at the end of the arm.
d) Tighten the adjustment screw locknut to a torque wrench setting of 18-29 lb f ft (2.5-4.0 Kg fm). Take care not to upset the backlash setting.

31 Check the relative position of the sector shaft and worm as follows:
a) Rotate the mainshaft fully clockwise and then turn it back anticlockwise by exactly 180°
b) Check the backlash as described in paragraph 30. This time the backlash should be 0.04-0.06 in (0.9-1.6 mm).
c) Now rotate the mainshaft fully anticlockwise and then turn it back clockwise through exactly 180°. Again, the backlash should be 0.04-0.06 in (0.9-1.6 mm).
d) Should there be a difference between the right side backlash

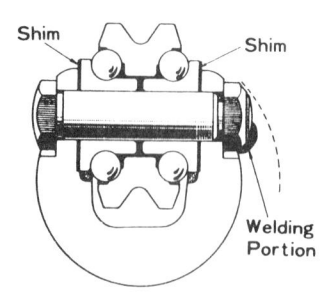

Fig. 11.35 Sector roller and shims

and the left side backlash exceeding 0.03 in (0.7 mm) it will be necessary to adjust the position of the worm by changing the adjustment shims. These are available in the following sizes:

1) 0.004 in (0.1 mm)
2) 0.008 in (0.2 mm)
3) 0.012 in (0.3 mm)
4) 0.016 in (0.4 mm)

e) If the backlash on the clockwise side is more than on the anticlockwise side, increase the thickness of the adjustment shims. Conversely if less, decrease the thickness of the adjustment shims.
f) It should be noted that replacement of this shim means removal of the upper bearing outer race. It will then be necessary to adjust the steering worm preload as described earlier in this Section.

32 Apply a little grease and then fit the bush and collar onto the top end of the steering column tube.

33 Remove the sector shaft arm and nut.

34 The steering gearbox is now ready for refitting to the car. Do not forget to refill with the recommended grade of oil.

14 Steering gearbox (recirculating ball) - dismantling, overhaul and reassembly

The overhaul sequence is basically identical to that as described in Section 13. The differences in design will be seen in Fig 3.33. The only point to watch is with the sector shaft thrust washer, and below is given the range available:
available.

1 0.078-0.079 in (1.98-2.01 mm)
2 0.080-0.081 in (2.04-2.07 mm)
3 0.082-0.083 in (2.08-2.11 mm)
4 0.083-0.084 in (2.12-2.15 mm)
5 0.085-0.086 in (2.16-2.19 mm)
6 0.087-0.088 in (2.21-2.24 mm)

15 Steering gearbox - adjustment

1 Jack-up the front of the car until the weight of the car is just off the tyre treads.

2 Turn the steering wheel until the wheels are in the 'straight-ahead' position.

3 Lower the jack and check the amount of free travel at the circumference of the steering wheel. The amount of free-travel should not exceed 1.25 in (30 mm).

4 If this is exceeded slacken the locknut and turn the adjustment screw until the correct degree of steering wheel free-movement is obtained. Tighten the locknut to a torque wrench setting of 18-29 lb f ft (2.5-4.0 Kg fm). Take care not to upset the backlash setting.

5 Raise the jack and turn the steering wheel from lock-to-lock to check for tight spots. If these are evident it is possible that the steering gearbox requires overhaul.

Chapter 11/Suspension and steering 247

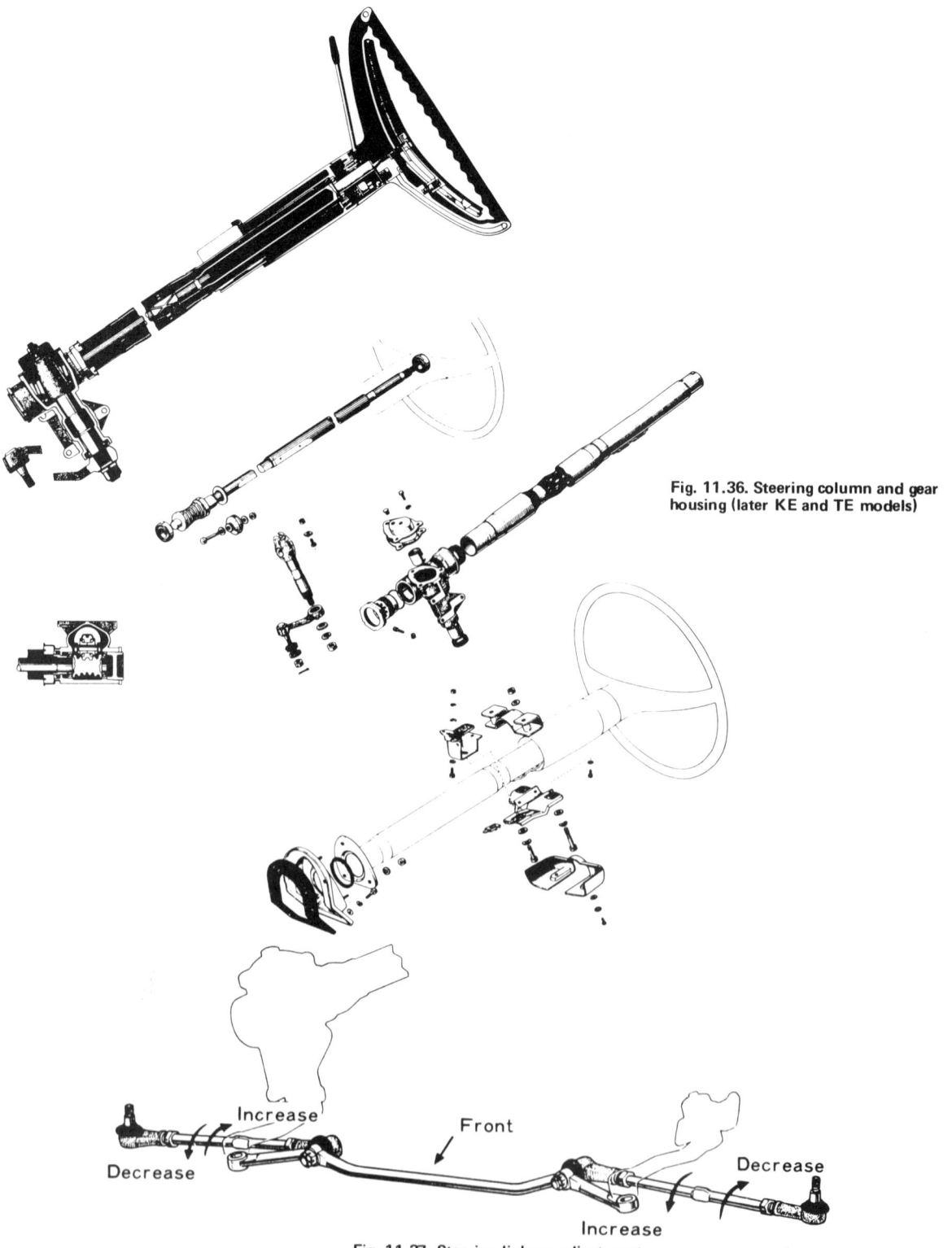

Fig. 11.36. Steering column and gear housing (later KE and TE models)

Fig. 11.37. Steering linkage adjustment

16 Steering geometry - checking and adjustment

1 Unless the front suspension has been damaged, the castor angle, camber angle and king pin inclination angles will not alter, provided of course, that the suspension balljoints are not worn excessively.
2 The toe-in of the front wheels is a setting which may be reset if new components are fitted - for example, after fitting new tie-rod balljoints it will be necessary to reset the toe-in.
3 Indications of incorrect wheel alignment (toe-in) are uneven tyre wear on the front wheels and erratic steering particularly when turning. To check toe-in accurately needs optical alignment equipment, so this is one job that must be left to the local Toyota garage. Ensure that they examine the linkage to ascertain the cause of any deviation from the original setting.

17 Fault diagnosis - suspension and steering

Before diagnosing faults from the following chart check the irregularities are not caused by:
1. *Binding brakes*
2. *Incorrect 'mix' of radial and crossply tyres*
3. *Incorrect tyre pressures*
4. *Misalignment of the body frame*

Symptom	Reason/s	Remedy
Steering wheel can be moved considerably before any sign of movement is apparent at the road wheels	Wear in steering linkage, gear and column coupling	Check all joints and gears. Renew as necessary.
Vehicle difficult to steer in a straight line - 'wanders'	As above Wheel alignment incorrect (shown by uneven front tyre wear) Front wheel bearings loose Worn suspension unit swivel joints	As above. Check wheel alignment. Adjust or renew. Renew as necessary.
Steering stiff and heavy	Incorrect wheel alignment (uneven or excessive tyre wear) Wear or seizure in steering linkage joints Wear or seizure in suspension linkage joints Excessive wear in steering gear unit	Check and adjust. Grease or renew. Grease or renew. Adjust or renew.
Wheel wobble and vibration	Road wheels out of balance Road wheels buckled Wheel alignment incorrect Wear in steering and suspension linkages Broken front spring	Balance wheels. Check for damage. Check. Check or renew. Renew.
Excessive pitching and rolling on corners and during braking	Defective damper and/or broken spring	Renew.

Chapter 12 Bodywork and fittings

Contents

Door alignment - hinge adjustment	8
Door latch striker - alignment	9
Doors - tracing of rattles and rectification	7
General description	1
Maintenance - bodywork exterior	2
Maintenance - bodywork interior	3
Maintenance - hinges, door catches and locks	6
Major body damage - repair	5
Minor body damage - repair	4

2 Door Saloon/Sedan (1968 - 1970)

Bonnet and lock - removal and replacement	15
Boot lid and lock - removal and replacement	16
Cowl side trim panel - removal and replacement	21
Cowl ventilator - removal and replacement	25
Dash panel trim board - removal and replacement	22
Door glass - removal and replacement	13
Door lock assembly - removal and replacement	14
Door trim and interior handles - removal and replacement	11
Door window regulator - removal and replacement	12
Front and rear bumper - removal and replacement	17
Front door - removal and replacement	10
Front seat - removal and replacement	26
Front wing - removal and replacement	28
Lower shroud panel - removal and replacement	29
Rear parcel tray trim panel - removal and replacement	24
Rear quarter trim panel - removal and replacement	23
Rear quarter window - removal and replacement	20
Rear screen - removal and replacement	19
Rear seat - removal and replacement	27
Windscreen - removal and replacement	18

Estate/Wagon (1968 - 1970)

Back door glass - removal and replacement	36
Back door lock - removal and replacement	35
Back door - removal, replacement and adjustment	33
Back door side stopper - adjustment	34
Front quarter glass - removal and replacement	37
Rear door glass - removal and replacement	31
Rear door lock and remote control - removal and replacement	32
Rear door window regulator - removal and replacement	30
Rear quarter glass - removal and replacement	38
Rear seat backrest - removal and replacement	39

All models (after 1970)

Front door lock and regulator - removal and replacement	40

2 Door Saloon/Sedan (1971 on. KE20 and 21 series)

Bonnet and lock - removal and replacement	45
Boot lid and lock - removal and replacement	46
Cowl side trim board - removal and replacement	54
Door lock assembly - removal and replacement	44
Door trim and interior handles - removal and replacement	42
Door window glass and regulator - removal and replacement	43
Front and rear bumper - removal and replacement	58
Front door - removal and replacement	41
Front seat - removal and replacement	59
Front wing - removal and replacement	61
Glove compartment - removal and replacement	52
Instrument panel knee pad - removal and replacement	51
Instrument panel safety pad - removal and replacement	50
Lower shroud panel - removal and replacement	62
Quarter trim panel - removal and replacement	55
Radiator grille - removal and replacement	63
Rear pillar garnish and parcel tray trim - removal and replacement	56
Rear quarter window - removal and replacement	49
Rear screen - removal and replacement	48
Rear seat - removal and replacement	60
Roof side vent louvre and duct - removal and replacement	57
Ventilators - removal and replacement	53
Windscreen - removal and replacement	47

4 Door Saloon/Sedan (1971 on. KE 20F series)

Rear door glass - removal and replacement	65
Rear door lock - removal and replacement	66
Rear door window regulator - removal and replacement	64

2 Door Saloon/Sedan (1971 on. KE 25, TE 25 and 27 series)

Front wing garnish - removal and replacement	68
Roof side vent and inner duct - removal and replacement	67

Estate/Wagon (1971 on. KE 26V and TE 28V series)

Back door glass - removal and replacement	72
Back door lock - removal and replacement	71
Back door - removal, replacement and adjustment	69
Back door side stopper - adjustment	70
Front quarter glass - removal and replacement	73
Rear quarter glass - removal and replacement	74
Rear seat backrest - removal and replacement	75
Roof side vent, side louvre and duct - removal and replacement	76

1 General description

The body used on the Corolla models is of the combined body and underframe integral construction type where all panels are welded. Openings in it provide for the engine compartment, luggage compartment, doors and windows. The rear suspension is bolted directly to it at the sidemembers. The front of the body under the engine compartment is braced by a crossmember which also acts as a location for the bottom half of the front suspension. Reinforced panels in the inner wing panels support the upper ends of the front suspension units.

The engine and gearbox assembly is supported at three points - forward by flexible mountings attached to the front suspension crossmember and at the rear by a detachable crossmember underneath the gearbox bolted to the floor panel.

The interior is fully equipped as standard with many items which are normally only offered as optional extras.

2 Maintenance - bodywork exterior

1 The general condition of a car's bodywork is the one thing that significantly affects its value. Maintenance is easy but needs to be regular and particular. Neglect - particularly after minor damage - can quickly lead to futher deterioration and costly repair bills. It is important also to keep watch on those parts of the bodywork not immediately visible, for example the underside, inside all the wheelarches and the lower part of the engine compartment.
2 The basic maintenance routine for the bodywork is washing - preferably with a lot of water from a hose. This will remove all the loose solids which may have stuck to the car. It is important to flush these off in such a way as to prevent grit from scratching the finish. The wheel arches and underbody need washing in the same way, to remove any accumulated mud which will retain moisture and tend to encourage rust. Paradoxically enough, the best time to clean the underbody and wheelarches is in wet weather when the mud is thoroughly wet and soft. In very wet weather the underbody is usually cleared of large accumulations automatically and this is a good time for inspection.
3 Periodically, it is a good idea to have the whole of the underside of the car steam cleaned, engine compartment included, so that a thorough inspection can be carried out to see what minor repairs and renovations are necessary. Steam cleaning is available at many garages and is necessary for removal of accumulation of oily grime which sometimes collects thickly in areas on and near the engine, gearbox and back axle. If steam cleaning facilities are not available there are several excellent grease solvents available which can be brush applied. The dirt can then be simply hosed off.
4 After washing the paintwork wipe it off with a chamois leather to give a clean unspotted finish. A coat of clear wax polish will give added protection against chemical pollutants in the air and will survive several subsequent washings. If the paintwork sheen has dulled or oxidised use a cleaner/polish combination to restore the brilliance of the shine. This requires a little more effort but is usually caused because regular washing has been neglected! Always check that door and ventilator drain holes and pipes are completely clear so that water can drain out. Brightwork should be treated in the same way as the paintwork. Windscreens and windows can be kept clear of the smeary film which often appears, if a little ammonia is added to the water. If glass work is scratched a good rub with a proprietary metal polish will often clean it. Never use any form of wax or other paint/chromium polish on glass.

3 Maintenance - bodywork interior

Mats and carpets should be brushed or vacuum cleaned regularly to keep them free of grit. If they are badly stained, remove them from the car for scrubbing or sponging and make quite sure that they are dry before replacement. Seat and interior trim panels can be kept clean with a wipe over with a damp cloth. If they do become stained, (which can be more apparent on light coloured upholstery) use a little liquid detergent and a soft nailbrush to scour the grime out of the grain of the material. Do not forget to keep the headlining clean in the same way as the upholstery. When using liquid cleaners inside the car do not over-wet the surfaces being cleaned. Excessive damp could get into the upholstery seams and padded interior, causing stains, offensive odours or even rot. If the inside of the car gets wet accidentally it is worthwhile taking some trouble to dry it out properly, particularly where carpets are involved. **Do not** leave oil or electric heaters inside the car for this purpose.

4 Minor body damage - repair

See also the photo sequences on pages 251, 252 and 253.

Repair of minor scratches in the car's bodywork

If the scratch is very superficial, and does not penetrate to the metal of the bodywork - repair is very simple. Lightly rub the area of the scratch with a paintwork renovator (eg; T-Cut), or a very fine cutting paste, to remove loose paint from the scratch and to clear the surrounding bodywork of wax polish. Rinse the area with clean water.

Apply touch-up paint to the scratch using a thin paint brush; continue to apply thin layers of paint until the surface of the paint in the scratch is level with the surrounding paintwork. Allow the new paint at least two weeks to harden; then, blend it into the surrounding paintwork by rubbing the paintwork in the scratch area with a paintwork renovator (eg; T-Cut), or a very fine cutting paste. Finally apply wax polish.

An alternative to painting over the scratch is to use Holts 'Scratch-Patch'. Use the same preparation for the affected area; then simply, pick a patch of a suitable size to cover the scratch completely. Hold the patch against the scratch and burnish its backing paper; the patch will adhere to the paintwork, freeing itself from the backing paper at the same time. Polish the affected area to blend the patch into the surrounding paintwork.

Where a scratch has penetrated right through to the metal of the bodywork, causing the metal to rust, a different repair technique is required. Remove any loose rust from the bottom of the scratch with a penknife; then apply rust inhibiting paint (eg; Kurust) to prevent the formation of rust in the future. Using a rubber or nylon applicator fill the scratch with body-stopper paste. If required this paste can be mixed with cellulose thinners to provide a very thin paste which is ideal for filling narrow scratches. Before the stopper-paste in the scratch hardens, wrap a piece of smooth cotton rag around the tip of a finger. Dip the finger in cellulose thinners and then quickly sweep it across the surface of the stopper-paste in the scratch; this will ensure that the surface of the stopper-paste is slightly hollowed. The scratch can now be painted over as described in this Section.

Repair of dents in the car's bodywork

When deep denting of the car's bodywork has taken place, the first task is to pull the dent out, until the affected bodywork almost attains its original shape. There is little point in trying to restore the original shape completely, as the metal in the damaged area will have stretched on impact and cannot be reshaped fully to its original contour. It is better to bring the level of the dent up to a point which is about 1/8 inch (3 mm) below the level of the surrounding bodywork. In cases where the dent is very shallow anyway, it is not worth trying to pull it out at all.

If the underside of the dent is accessible, it can be hammered out gently from behind, using a mallet with a wooden or plastic head. Whilst doing this, hold a suitable block of wood firmly against the outside of the dent. This block will absorb the impact from the hammer blows and thus prevent a large area of bodywork from being 'belled-out'.

Should the dent be in a section of the bodywork which has a double skin or some other factor making it inaccessible from behind, a different technique is called for. Drill several small holes through the metal inside the dent area - particularly in the deeper sections. Then screw long self-tapping screws into the holes just sufficiently for them to gain a good purchase in the metal. Now the dent can be pulled out by pulling on the protruding heads of the screws with a pair of pliers.

The next stage of the repair is the removal of the paint from the damaged area, and from an inch or so of the surrounding 'sound' bodywork. This is accomplished most easily by using a wire brush or abrasive pad on a power drill, although it can be done just as effectively by hand using sheets of abrasive paper. To complete the preparations for filling, score the surface of the bare metal with a screwdriver or tang of a file, or alternatively, drill small holes in the affected area. This will provide a really good key for the filler paste.

To complete the repair see the Section on filling and respraying.

Preparation for filling
Typical example of rust damage to a body panel. Before starting ensure that you have all of the materials required to hand. The first task is to ...

... remove body fittings from the affected area, except those which can act as a guide to the original shape of the damaged bodywork - the headlamp shell in this case.

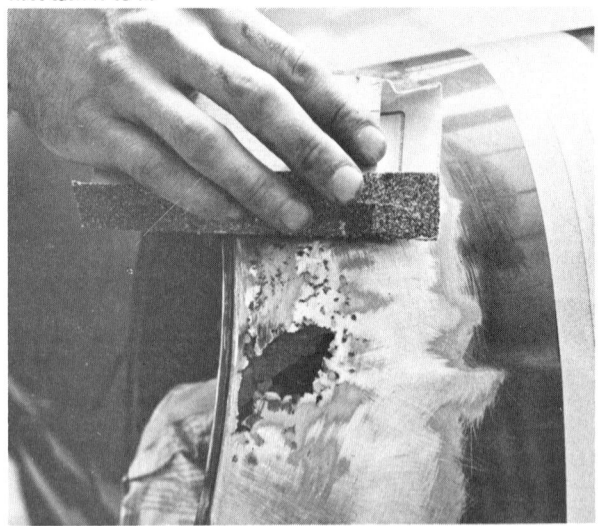

Remove all paint from the rusted area and from an inch or so of the adjoining 'sound' bodywork - use coarse abrasive paper or a power drill fitted with a wire brush or abrasive pad. Gently hammer in the edges of the hole to provide a hollow for the filler.

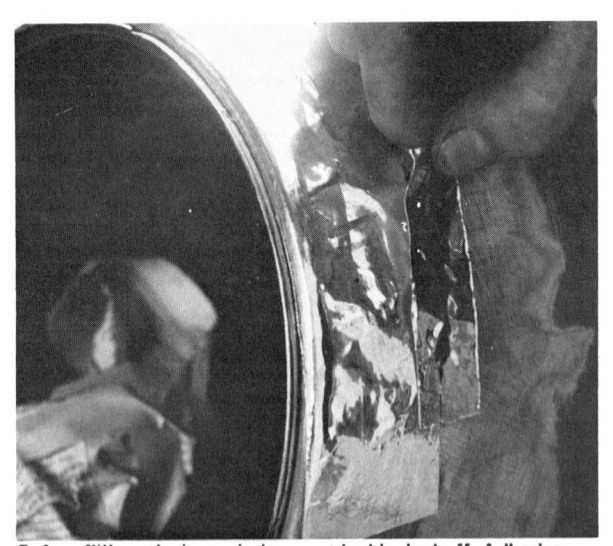

Before filling, the larger holes must be blocked off. Adhesive aluminium tape is one method; cut the tape to the required shape and size, peel off the backing strip (where used), position the tape over the hole and burnish to ensure adhesion.

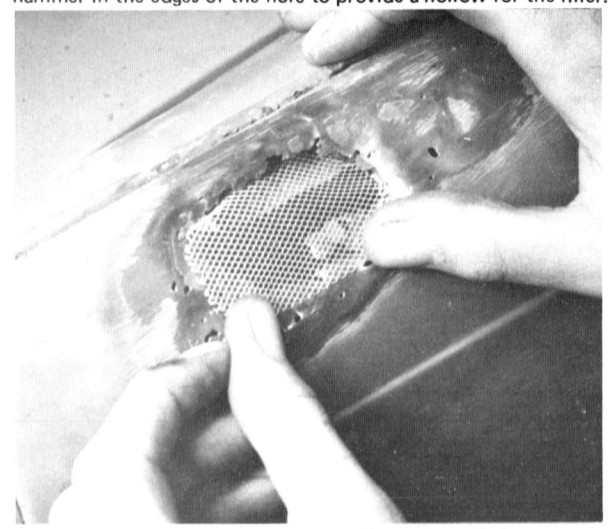

Alternatively, zinc gauze can be used. Cut a piece of the gauze to the required shape and size; position it in the hole below the level of the surrounding bodywork; then ...

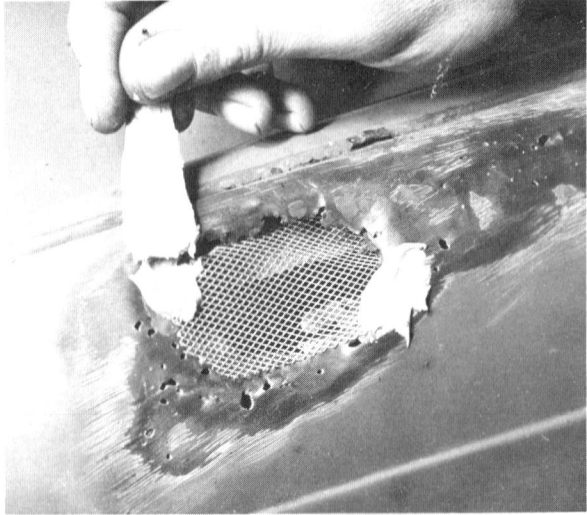

... secure in position by placing a few blobs of filler paste around its periphery. Alternatively, pop rivets or self-tapping screws can be used. Preparation for filling is now complete.

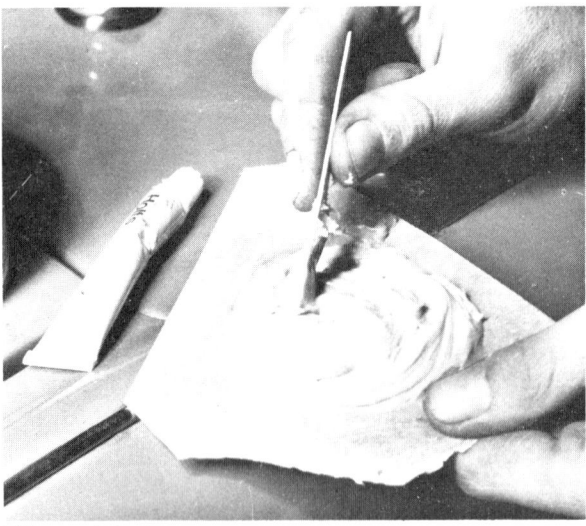

Filling and shaping
Mix filler and hardener according to manufacturer's instructions - avoid using too much hardener otherwise the filler will harden before you have a chance to work it.

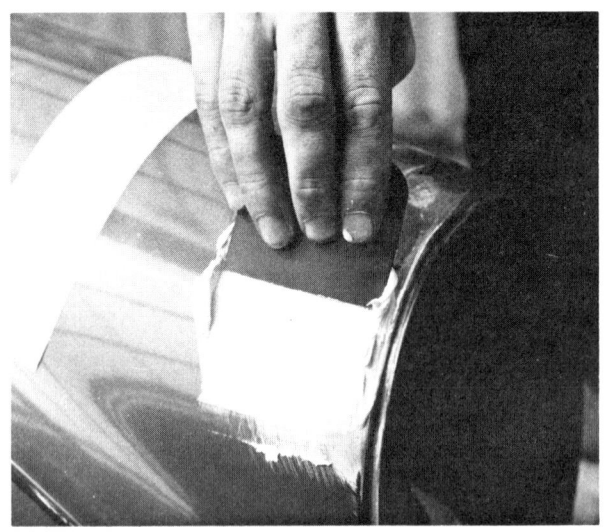

Apply the filler to the affected area with a flexible applicator - this will ensure a smooth finish. Apply thin layers of filler at 20 minute intervals, until the surface of the filler is just 'proud' of the surrounding bodywork. Then ...

... remove excess filler and start shaping with a Surform plane or a dreadnought file. Once an approximate contour has been obtained and the surface is relatively smooth, start using ...

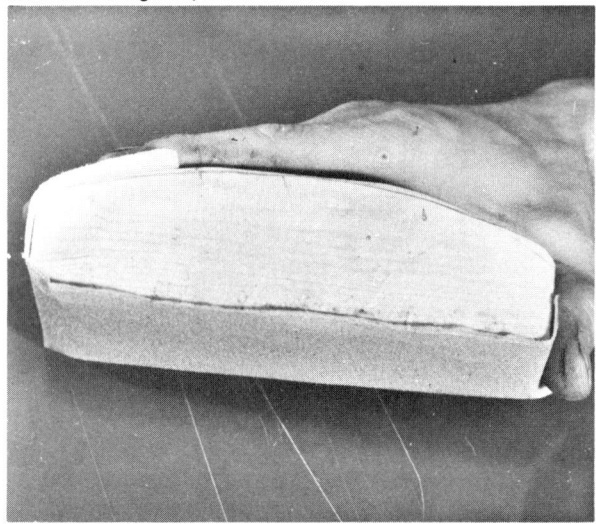

... abrasive paper. The paper should be wrapped around a flat wood, cork or rubber block - this will ensure that it imparts a smooth surface to the filler.

40 grit production paper is best to start with, then use progressively finer abrasive paper, finishing with 400 grade 'wet-and-dry'. When using 'wet-and-dry' paper, periodically rinse it in water ensuring also, that the work area is kept wet continuously.

Rubbing-down is complete when the surface of the filler is really smooth and flat, and the edges of the surrounding paintwork are finely 'feathered'. Wash the area thoroughly with clean water and allow to dry before commencing re-spray.

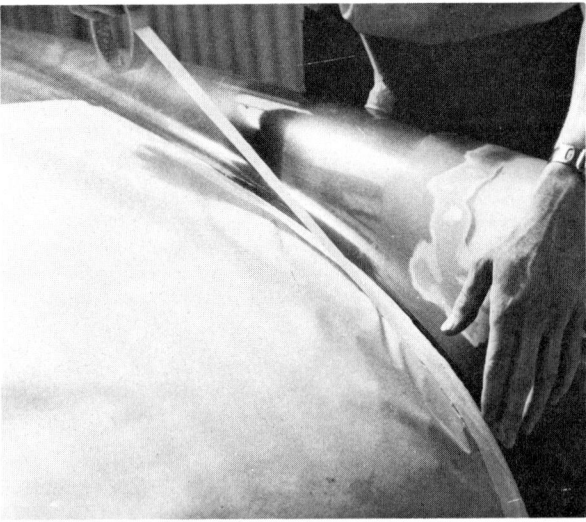

Masking and spraying
Firstly, mask off all adjoining panels and the fittings in the spray area. Ensure that the area to be sprayed is completely free of dust. Practice using an aerosol on a piece of waste metal sheet until the technique is mastered.

Spray the affected area with primer - apply several thin coats rather than one thick one. Start spraying in the centre of the repair area and then work outwards using a circular motion - in this way the paint will be evenly distributed.

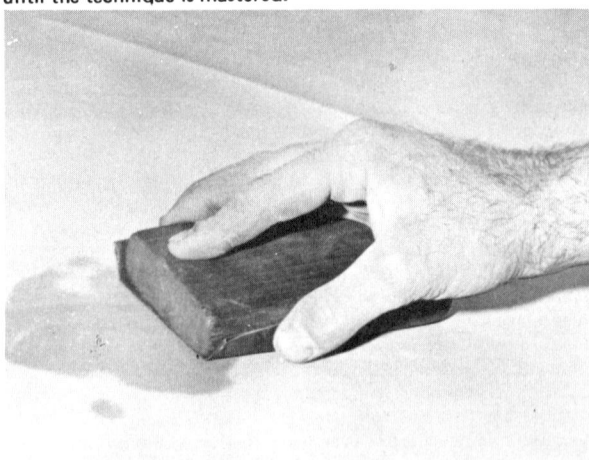

When the primer has dried inspect its surface for imperfections. Holes can be filled with filler paste or body-stopper, and lumps can be sanded smooth. Apply a further coat of primer, then 'flat' its surface with 400 grade 'wet-and-dry' paper.

Spray on the top coat, again building up the thickness with several thin coats of paint. Overspray onto the surrounding original paintwork to a depth of about five inches, applying a very thin coat at the outer edges.

Allow the new paint two weeks, at least, to harden fully, then blend it into the surrounding original paintwork with a paint restorative compound or very fine cutting paste. Use wax polish to finish off.

The finished job should look like this. Remember, the quality of the completed work is directly proportional to the amount of time and effort expended at each stage of the preparation.

Repair of rustholes or gashes in the car's bodywork

Remove all paint from the affected area and from an inch or so of the surrounding 'sound' bodywork, using an abrasive pad or a wire brush on a power drill. If these are not available a few sheets of abrasive paper will do the job just as effectively. With the paint removed you will be able to gauge the severity of the corrosion and therefore decide whether to replace the whole panel (if this is possible) or to repair the affected area. Replacement body panels are not as expensive as most people think and it is often quicker and more satisfactory to fit a new panel than to attempt to repair large areas of corrosion.

Remove all fittings from the affected area, except those which will act as a guide to the original shape of the damaged bodywork (eg; headlamp shells etc.,). Then, using tin snips or a hacksaw blade, remove all loose metal and any other metal badly affected by corrosion. Hammer the edges of the hole inwards in order to create a sligh depression for the filler paste.

Wire brush the affected area to remove the powdery rust from the surface of the remaining metal. Paint the affected area with rust inhibiting paint (eg; Kurust); if the back of the rusted area is accessible treat this also.

Before filling can take place it will be necessary to block the hole in some way. This can be achieved by the use of one of the following materials: Zinc gauze, Aluminium tape or Polyurethane foam.

Zinc gauze is probably the best material to use for a large hole. Cut a piece of the approximate size and shape of the hole to be filled, then position it in the hole so that its edges are below the level of the surrounding bodywork. It can be retained in position by several blobs of filler paste round its periphery. Aluminium tape should be used for small or very narrow holes. Pull a piece off the roll and trim it to the approximate size and shape required, then pull off the backing paper (if used) and stick the tape over the hole; it can be overlapped if the thickness of one piece is insufficient. Burnish down the edges of the tape with the handle of a screwdriver or similar, to ensure that the tape is securely attached to the metal underneath.

Polyurethane foam is best used where the hole is situated in a section of bodywork of complex shape, backed by a small box section (eg; where the sill panel meets the rear wheel arch - most cars). The usual mixing procedure for this foam is as follows: Put equal amounts of fluid from each of the two cans provided in the kit, into one container. Stir until the mixture begins to thicken, then quickly pour this mixture into the hole, and hold a piece of cardboard over the larger apertures. Almost immediately the polyurethane will begin to expand, gushing frantically out of any small holes left unblocked. When the foam hardens it can be cut back to just below the level of the surrounding bodywork with a hacksaw blade.

Having blocked off the hole the affected area must now be filled and sprayed - see Section on bodywork filling and re-spraying.

Bodywork repairs - filling and re-spraying

Before using this Section, see the Sections on dent, deep scratch, rust hole and gash repairs.

Many types of bodyfiller are available, but generally speaking those proprietary kits which contain a tin of filler paste and a tube of resin hardener (eg; Holts Cataloy) are best for this type of repair. A wide, flexible plastic or nylon applicator will be found invaluable for imparting a smooth and well contoured finish to the surface of the filler.

Mix up a little filler on a clean piece of card or board - use the hardener sparingly (follow the maker's instructions on the packet), otherwise the filler will set very rapidly.

Using the applicator apply the filler paste to the prepared area; draw the applicator across the surface of the filler to achieve the correct contour and to level the filler surface. As soon as a contour that approximates the correct one is achieved, stop working the paste - if you carry on too long the paste will become sticky and being to 'pick-up' on the applicator. Continue to add thin layers of filler paste at twenty-minute intervals until the level of the filler is just 'proud' of the surrounding body-work.

Once the filler has hardened, excess can be removed using a Surform plane or Dreadnought file. From then on, progressively finer grades of abrasive paper should be used, starting with a 40 grade production paper and finishing with 400 grade 'wet-and-dry' paper. Always wrap the abrasive paper around a flat rubber, cork, or wooden block - otherwise the surface of the filler will not be completely flat. During the smoothing of the filler surface the 'wet-and-dry' paper should be periodically rinsed in water - this will ensure that a very smooth finish is imparted to the filler at the final stage.

At this stage the 'dent' should be surrounded by a ring of bare metal, which in turn should be encircled by the finely 'feathered' edge of the good paintwork. Rinse the repair area with clean water, until all of the dust produced by the rubbing-down operation is gone.

Spray the whole repair area with a light coat of grey primer - this will show up any imperfections in the surface of the filler. Repair these imperfections with fresh filler paste or bodystopper, and once more smooth the surface with abrasive paper. If bodystopper is used, it can be mixed with cellulose thinners to form a really thin paste which is ideal for filling small holes. Repeat this spray and repair procedure until you are satisfied that the surface of the filler, and the feathered edge of the paintwork are perfect. Clean the repair area with clean water and allow to dry fully.

The repair area is now ready for spraying. Paint spraying must be carried out in a warm, dry, windless and dust free atmosphere. This condition can be created artificially if you have access to a large indoor working area, but if you are forced to work in the open, you will have to pick your day very carefully. If you are working indoors, dousing the floor in the work area with water will 'lay' the dust which would otherwise be in the atmosphere. If the repair area is confined to one body panel, mask off the surrounding panels; this will help to minimise the effects of a slight mis-match in paint colours. Bodywork fittings (eg; chrome strips, door handles etc.,) will also need to be masked off. Use genuine masking tape and several thicknesses of newspaper for the masking operation.

Before commencing to spray, agitate the aerosol can thoroughly, then spray a test area (an old tin, or similar) until the technique is mastered. Cover the repair area with a thick coat of primer; the thickness should be built up using several thin layers of paint rather than one thick one. Using 400 grade 'wet-and-dry' paper, rub down the surface of the primer until it is really smooth. While doing this, the work area should be thoroughly doused with water, and the wet-and-dry paper periodically rinsed in water. Allow to dry before spraying on more paint.

Spray on the top coat, again building up the thickness by using several thin layers of paint. Start spraying in the centre of the repair area and then, using a circular motion, work outwards until the whole repair area and about 2 inches of the surrounding original paintwork is covered. Remove all masking material 10 to 15 minutes after spraying on the final coat of paint.

Allow the new paint at least 2 weeks to harden fully; then, using a paintwork renovator (eg., T-Cut) or a very fine cutting paste, blend the edges of the new paint into the existing paintwork. Finally, apply wax polish.

5 Major body damage - repair

Where serious damage has occurred or large areas of the body need renewal due to rusting it means certainly that complete new sections or panels will need welding in and this is best left to the professionals. If the damage is due to impact it will also be necessary to completely check the alignment of the body shell structure. Due to the principle of construction the strength and shape of the whole car can be affected by damage to a relatively small area. In such instances the services of a Toyota garage with specialist jigs are essential. If a body is left misaligned it is first of all dangerous as the car will not handle properly and secondly

Chapter 12/Bodywork and fittings

uneven stresses will be imposed on the steering, engine and transmission, causing abnormal wear or complete failure. Tyre wear may also be excessive.

6 Maintenance - hinges, door catches and locks

1 Oil the hinges of the bonnet, boot and doors with a drop or two of light oil periodically. A good time is after the car has been washed.
2 Oil the bonnet safety catch thrust pin periodically.
3 Do not over-lubricate door latches and strikers. Normally one or two drops regularly applied is better than a lot at one go.

7 Door - tracing of rattles and rectification

1 Check first that the door is not loose at the hinges and that the latch is holding the door firmly in position. Check also that the door lines up with the aperture in the body.
2 If the hinges are loose or the door is out of aligment it will be necessary to reset the hinge position as described in Section 8.
3 If the latch is holding the door properly it should hold the door tightly when fully latched and the door should line up with the body. If it is out of alignment it needs adjustment as described in Section 9. If loose some part of the lock mechanism must be worn out and requiring renewal.
4 Other rattles from the door would be caused by wear or loosenesss in the window winder, the glass channels and sill strips or the door buttons and interior latch release mechanism. All these are dealt with in subsequent Sections.

8 Door alignment - hinge adjustment

The hinges are adjustable both on the door and pillar mountings. Access to some of the bolts will require removal of trim and the use of a bent spanner.

2 When re-aligning is necessary first slacken the bolts holding the hinge to the door and reposition the door as required and make sure the bolts are thoroughly tightened up again. If the amount of movement on the door half of the hinge is insufficient it may be adjusted at the door pillar.
3 If the hinges themselves are worn at the hinge pin the door should be detached from the hinges, the hinges removed and new ones fitted.

9 Door latch striker - alignment

1 Assuming that the door hinges are correctly aligned but the trailing edge of the door is not flush with the body when the door is fully latched, then the striker plate needs adjusting.
2 Slacken the two crosshead screws holding the striker plate to the door pillar just enough to hold the striker plate in position and then push the plate to the inner limit of its position. Try and shut the door, moving the striker plate outwards until the latch is able to engage fully. (photo)
3 Without pulling on the release handle but working inside the car push the door outwards until it is flush with the bodywork. This will move the striker plate along with the latch.
4 Release the latch very carefully so as not to disturb the striker plate and open the door. Tighten down the striker plate securing screws.

2 Door Saloon/Sedan (1968 - 1970)

10 Front door - removal and replacement

1 The help of an assistant should be obtained to support the weight of the door.
2 Undo and remove the bolts securing the upper and lower hinges to the body. Lift away the door assembly with care as it is heavy.
3 Refitting the door assembly is the reverse sequence to removal. It will be necessary to adjust the door position as described in Section 8.

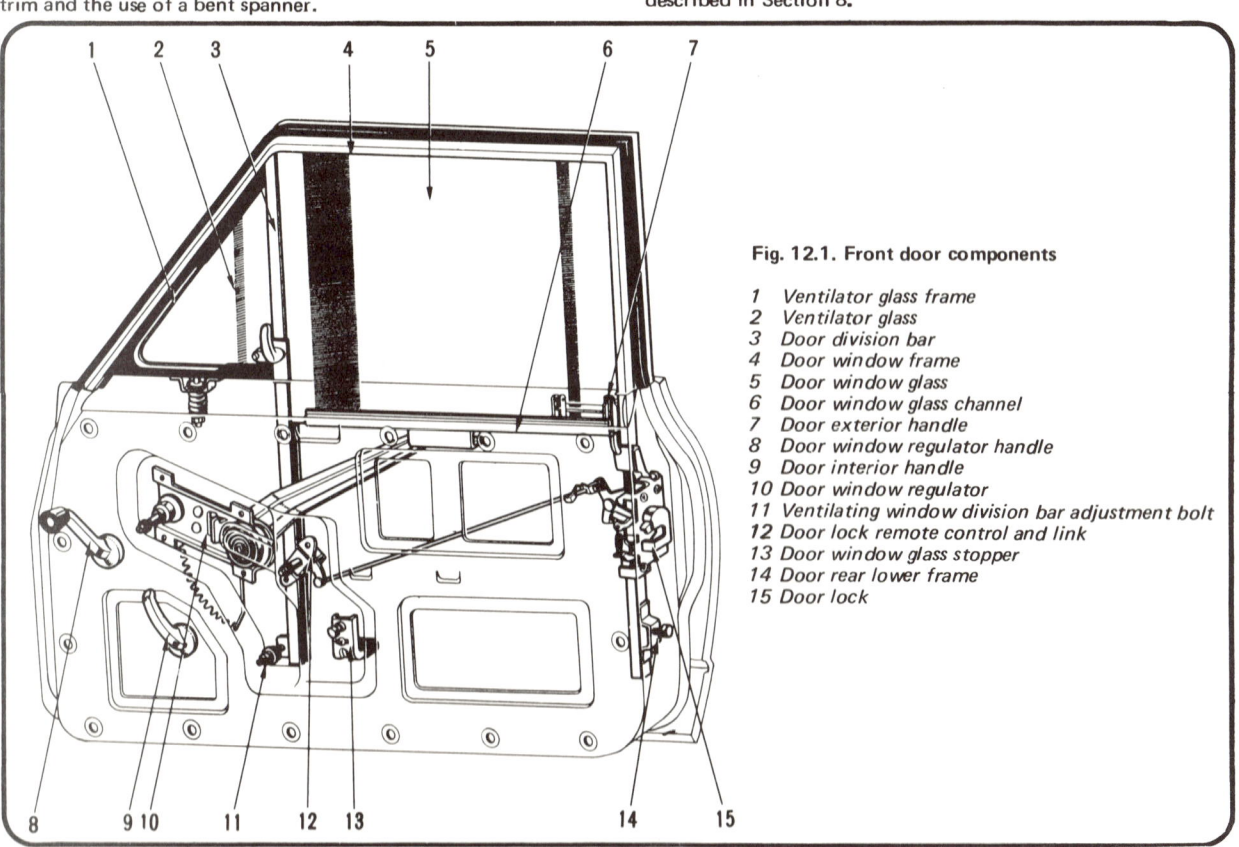

Fig. 12.1. Front door components

1 Ventilator glass frame
2 Ventilator glass
3 Door division bar
4 Door window frame
5 Door window glass
6 Door window glass channel
7 Door exterior handle
8 Door window regulator handle
9 Door interior handle
10 Door window regulator
11 Ventilating window division bar adjustment bolt
12 Door lock remote control and link
13 Door window glass stopper
14 Door rear lower frame
15 Door lock

9.2 Later type door latch striker

11 Door trim and interior handles - removal and replacement

1 Using a 'V' shaped blade or two thin screwdrivers inserted between the handle flange and escutcheon release the horseshoe shaped retaining clip and lift away the handle and escutcheon.
2 When an arm rest is fitted undo and remove the two securing screws and lift away the arm rest.
3 Using a knife or hacksaw blade (with teeth ground down) inserted between the door trim panel, carefully ease each clip from its hole in the door inner panel. (Fig 12.3)
4 Inspect the dust and splash shields to ensure that they are correctly fitted and also not damaged.
5 Inspect the trim panel retaining clips and inserts for excessive corrosion or damage. Obtain new as necessary.
6 Refitting the door trim panel is the reverse sequence to removal.

12 Door window regulator - removal and replacement

1 Refer to Section 11, and remove the door trim and interior handles.
2 Remove the service hole cover.
3 Remove the glass travel stop.

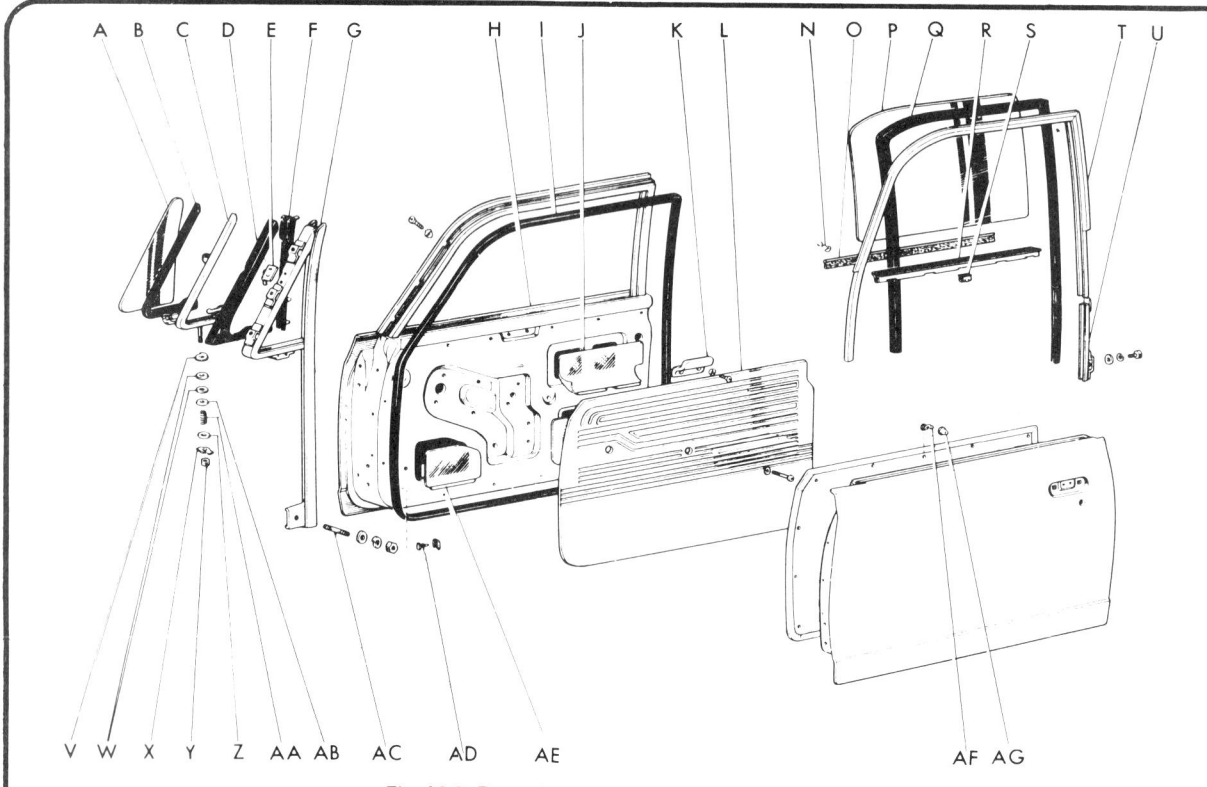

Fig. 12.2. Front door panel and glass assemblies

A	Ventilating window glass	L	Door trim panel	
B	Ventilating window frame strip	M	Clip	
C	Ventilating window glass frame	N	Door window glass inner weatherstrip	
D	Ventilating window weatherstrip No. 1	O	Door window glass	
E	Ventilating window upper pivot bracket	P	Door window glass run	
F	Ventilating window weatherstrip No. 2	Q	Door window glass outer weatherstrip	
G	Division bar	R	Door window glass weatherstrip clip	
H	Door panel	S	Door window frame	
I	Door weatherstrip	T	Door rear lower frame	
J	Door lock hole cover	U	Door ventilating window	
K	Door inside pull handle		opening stopper	
		V	Plate washer	
		W	Lock washer	
		X	Nut	
		Y	Plate washer	
		Z	Compression spring	
		AA	Door ventilating window lower pivot revolving washer	
		AB	Division bar adjusting bolt	
		AC	Door weatherstrip clip	
		AD	Service hole cover	
		AE	Door trim retainer	
		AF	Door trim retainer cap	

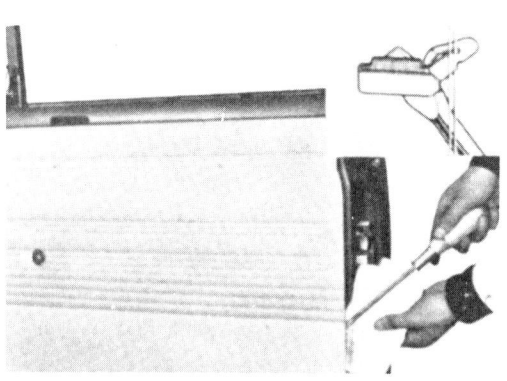

Fig. 12.3. Door trim panel removal

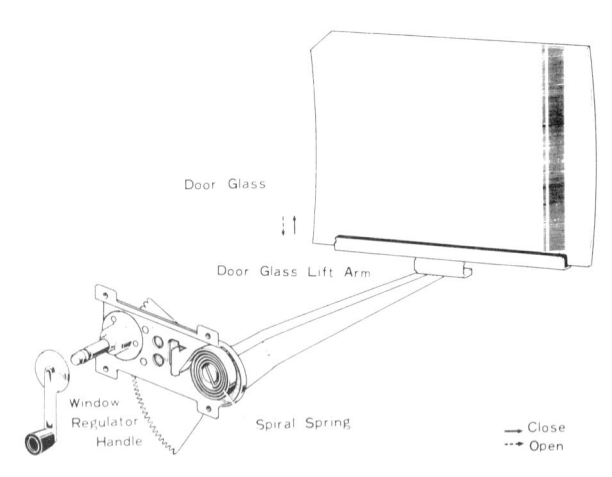

Fig. 12.4. Window regulator assembly

4 Raise the door glass and support in this position.
5 Undo and remove the regulator securing bolts and lower the regulator so as to disconnect the regulator roller from the glass channel.
6 Lift away the regulator assembly.
7 Refitting the regulator assembly is the reverse sequence to removal. Lubricate all moving parts with a little Castrol LM Grease.

13 Door glass - removal and replacement

1 Refer to Section 12, and remove the door window regulator.
2 Lower the glass fully and then using a screwdriver carefully ease out the door window glass inner weatherstrip.
3 Remove the door window glass outer weatherstrip using a wood chisel or wide bladed screwdriver. Be careful not to chip the paintwork.
4 Remove the division bar adjustment bolts and then remove the door window glass run from the division bar.
5 Undo and remove the three screws that secure the division bar to the door and move the division bar rearwards, whilst tilting the top of the ventilator assembly rearwards. Lift away the assembly.
6 The door window glass can now be removed from the door.
7 It is possible to detach the channel from the bottom of the glass using a soft faced hammer.
8 To refit the channel onto the glass, position the glass channel with weatherstrip on the glass so that it is central and tap the channel base with a soft faced hammer. If it is tight lubricate with a concentrated soap and water solution or washing up liquid.
9 If necessary the ventilator window glass can be removed from the frame. First remove the upper pivot bracket securing nut.
10 The glass can now be removed from the frame.
11 To refit the glass apply a little adhesive to the glass frame and install the frame strip.
12 Apply a little adhesive to the frame strip and fit the glass to the glass frame.
13 The glass frame may now be fitted to the division frame. Adjust the ventilator window tension by resetting the com-

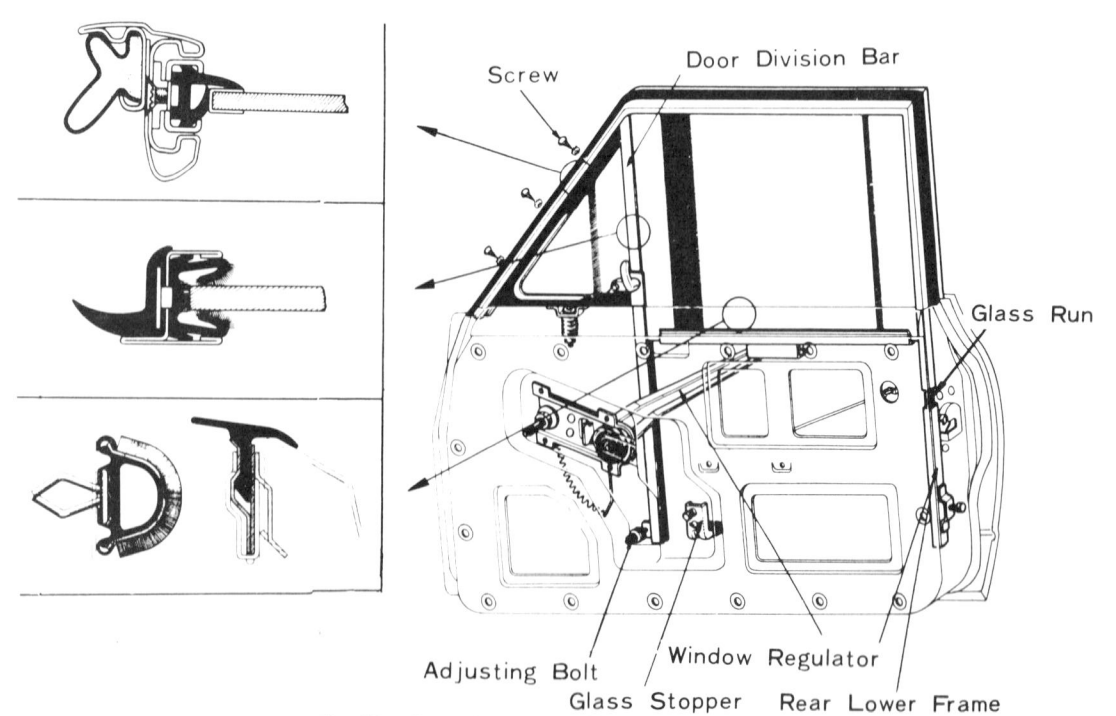

Fig. 12.5. Door glass and ventilator details

pression spring nut and then lock the nut with a lockplate.
14 To reassemble first insert the door glass into the door.
15 Fit the door window glass run to the door division bar.
16 Insert the door division bar assembly into the door and locate the division bar on the glass. Fit the three securing screws.
17 Fit the door window glass inner weatherstrip and then the outer weatherstrip.
18 Raise the glass and support in this position.
19 Position the window regulator in the door and insert the regulator roller into the glass channel. Apply a little grease onto the glass channel.
20 Secure the regulator to the door.
21 Fit the door window glass stopper.
22 Fit the division bar adjustment bolt and adjust the location of the division bar to give a smooth, even movement without rattling. (Fig 12.6)
23 Replace the service hole cover and then the door trim panel and handles.

14 Door lock assembly - removal and replacement

Lock assembly

1 Refer to Section 11 and remove the door trim panel and service hole cover.
2 Raise the glass fully and detach the remote control link and rod from the door lock.
3 Undo and remove the door rear lower frame securing bolt and door lock securing screws. The door lock may now be lifted away from inside the door.
4 Refitting the door lock assembly is the reverse sequence to removal. The following additional points should be noted:
a) If the door lock cushion is worn or damaged it should be renewed.
b) Lubricate all moving parts with a little Castrol LM Grease.

Lock striker

1 To remove the door lock striker undo and remove the two securing bolts. Lift away the striker.
2 Refitting the door lock striker assembly is the reverse sequence to removal. Lightly tighten the striker securing bolts and align the door before finally tightening.
3 If the rear of the door has dropped do not adjust the striker but reset the door hinge positions.

Exterior handle

1 Refer to Section 11, and remove the door trim panel and service hole cover.
2 Raise the glass fully and working inside the door undo and remove the two nuts and washers securing the exterior handle to the outer door panel.
3 Push the door lock open lever under finger pressure and disengage the release lever from the lock arm. Lift away the exterior handle.
4 Refitting the exterior handle is the reverse sequence to removal.

Lock cylinder

1 Refer to Section 11, and remove the door trim panel and service hole cover.
2 Detach the retaining clip from the control rod and then ease off the cylinder retaining clip. Withdraw the lock cylinder. (Fig 12.8)
3 Refitting the lock cylinder is the reverse sequence to removal. Lubricate the operating surfaces of the lock cylinder with a little Castrol LM Grease.

Remote control

1 Refer to Section 11, and remove the door trim panel and service hole cover.
2 Disconnect the remote control link and then undo and remove the two securing bolts. Lift away the remote control assembly.
3 Refitting the remote control is the reverse sequence to removal. Ensure that the small end of the conical spring is located towards the door panel.

15 Bonnet and lock - removal and replacement

1 With the bonnet open, use a soft pencil and mark the outline position of both hinges at the bonnet to act as a datum for refitment.
2 With the help of an assistant to support the front of the bonnet undo and remove the support securing bolts.
3 Undo and remove the two bolts and washers securing the bonnet to each hinge. Lift away the bonnet from over the front of the car.
4 To remove the hinges first remove the cowl ventilator louvre grill located beneath the windscreen.
5 Undo and remove the two bolts that secure each hinge to the body. Lift away the hinge.
6 Removal of the bonnet lock and release lever is a straightforward operation and will not present any problems. The battery should be disconnected to prevent accidental short circuiting.
7 Reassembly and replacement as applicable is the reverse sequence to removal. Several adjustments are necessary and should be carried out as follows:

Bonnet

a) Adjustment of the bonnet in the aperture is effected by slackening the bonnet to hinge securing bolts and repositioning the bonnet in the aperture.
b) To lift the rear edge of the bonnet, the hinge can be raised once the securing bolts to the body have been slackened.
c) To lift the front edge of the bonnet slacken the bonnet lock dowel securing nut and screw out the dowel by the required amount. Tighten the locknut. (Fig 12.9)

Bonnet lock

a) Before adjusting the bonnet lock ensure that the bonnet is correctly seated in the aperture.
b) If the lock does not engage properly when the bonnet is closed slacken the bonnet lock dowel securing nut and turn anticlockwise to lengthen or clockwise to shorten the dowel. When correctly adjusted there should be just a little play when the bonnet is closed and hard pressure is applied.
c) If the bonnet lock dowel does not engage in the bonnet lock, slacken the lock securing bolts or the dowel retaining bolts and reposition the lock or dowel as necessary. Retighten the securing bolts.

Safety catch

The bonnet safety catch may be adjusted by slackening the securing bolts and moving its position as necessary. Tighten the securing bolts.

16 Boot lid and lock - removal and replacement

1 With the boot lid open mark the fitted position of the hinge relative to the boot lid.
2 An assistant should now support the weight of the boot lid and then undo and remove the four bolts and washers securing the boot lid to the hinges.

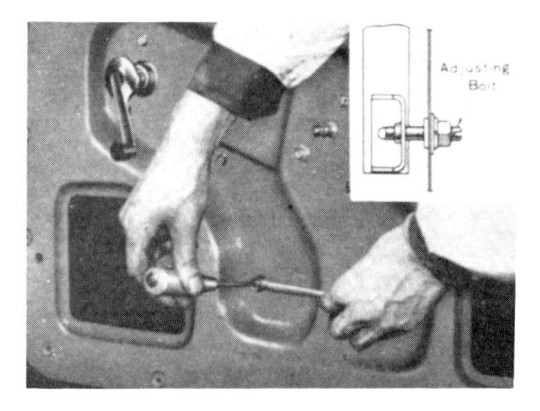

Fig. 12.6. Division bar adjustment

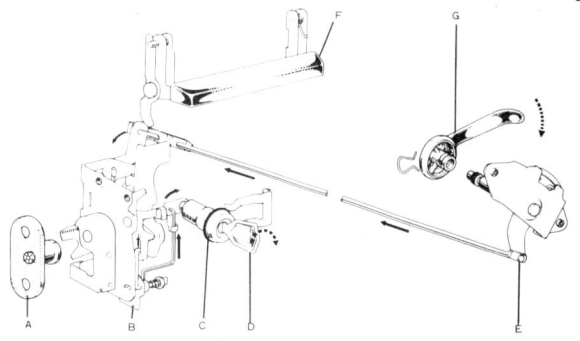

Fig. 12.7. Door lock components

A Striker
B Lock
C Cylinder and sleeve
D Key
E Remote control
F Outside handle
G Inside handle

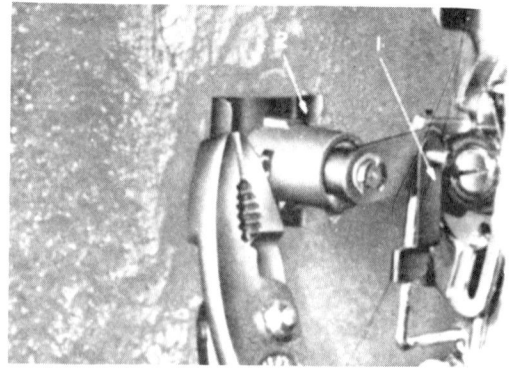

Fig. 12.8. Door lock cylinder removal

1 Retainer   2 Clip

Fig. 12.9. Bonnet lock dowel and safety catch adjustments

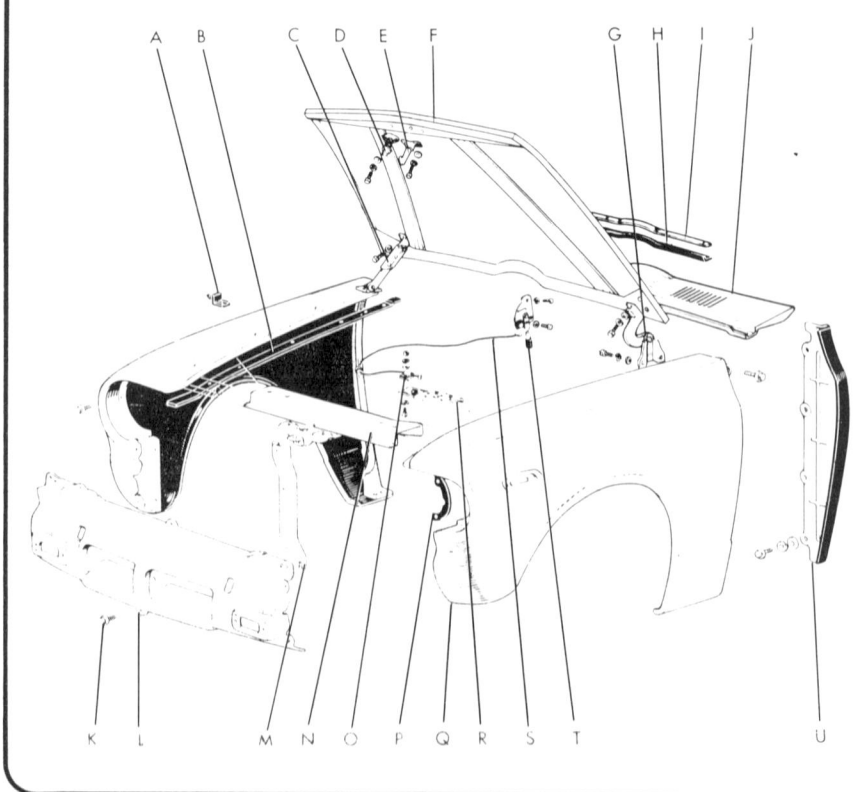

Fig. 12.10. Front body components

A Bonnet bumper
B Front wing main packing
C Bonnet support
D Bonnet hook
E Bonnet auxiliary catch hook
F Bonnet
G Bonnet hinge
H Bonnet to cowl top weatherstrip
I Bonnet to cowl top weatherstrip retainer
J Cowl ventilator louver
K Washer based head hexagon bolt
L Lower shroud panel
M Bonnet lock base with T nut brace
N Bonnet lock base
O Bonnet lock control wire A clamp
P Front wing front packing
Q Front wing
R Bonnet lock
S Bonnet lock control cable
T Bonnet lock release lever
U Front wing splash shield

3 Lift away the boot lid and recover the hinge spacers.
4 If necessary the torsion bar may be removed by detaching at one end to release the tension and then lifting away.
5 To remove the lock cylinder release the spring retainer with a pair of pliers, detach the pull rod and lift away the lock cylinder.
6 To remove the lock from the boot lid undo and remove the three securing bolts and washers.
7 Reassembly and replacement of the boot lid, lock and hinges is the reverse sequence to removal. Several adjustments are necessary and should be carried out as follows:

Boot lid

a) Adjustment of the boot lid in the aperature is effected by slackening the boot lid to hinge securing bolts and re-positioning the boot lid in the aperture.
b) To lift or lower the hinge end of the boot lid fit or remove hinge spacers as necessary. Each spacer is 0.063 in (1.6 mm).

Boot lid lock

To adjust the lock slacken the lock striker securing bolts and move the striker as necessary. Tighten the securing bolts.

17 Front and rear bumper - removal and replacement

Front

1 Undo and remove the four bumper stay securing nuts, bolts and washers.
2 Undo and remove the two side retainer securing bolts and washers. Lift away the front bumper assembly.
3 Refitting the front bumper assembly is the reverse sequence to removal.

Rear

The sequence is basically identical to that for the front bumper. Do not forget to detach the rear number plate light cable.

18 Windscreen - removal and replacement

1 Windscreen replacement is no light task. Leave this to the specialist if possible. Instructions are given below for the more ambitious.
2 Remove the windscreen wiper arms and blades and also the interior mirror.
3 Carefully ease out the windscreen mouldings from the weatherstrip.
4 The assistance of a second person should now be enlisted, ready to catch the glass when it is released from its aperture.
5 Using a screwdriver break the seal between the weatherstrip and the aperture taking care not to scratch the paintwork.
6 Working from inside the car, commencing at one top corner, press the glass and ease it and the rubber weatherstrip from the aperture lip.
7 Remove the rubber weatherstrip from the glass.
8 Now is the time to remove all pieces of glass if the screen has shattered. Use a vacuum cleaner to extract as much as possible. Switch on the heater boost motor and adjust the controls to 'Screen Defrost' but watch out for flying pieces of glass which might be blown out of the ducting.
9 Carefully inspect the rubber weatherstrip for signs of splitting or other deterioration. Clean all traces of sealing compound from the weatherstrip and windscreen aperture flange.
10 To refit the glass first place the rubber weatherstrip onto the glass edge.
11 Place a piece of cord onto the body flange groove of the weatherstrip and cross the ends at the top centre of the

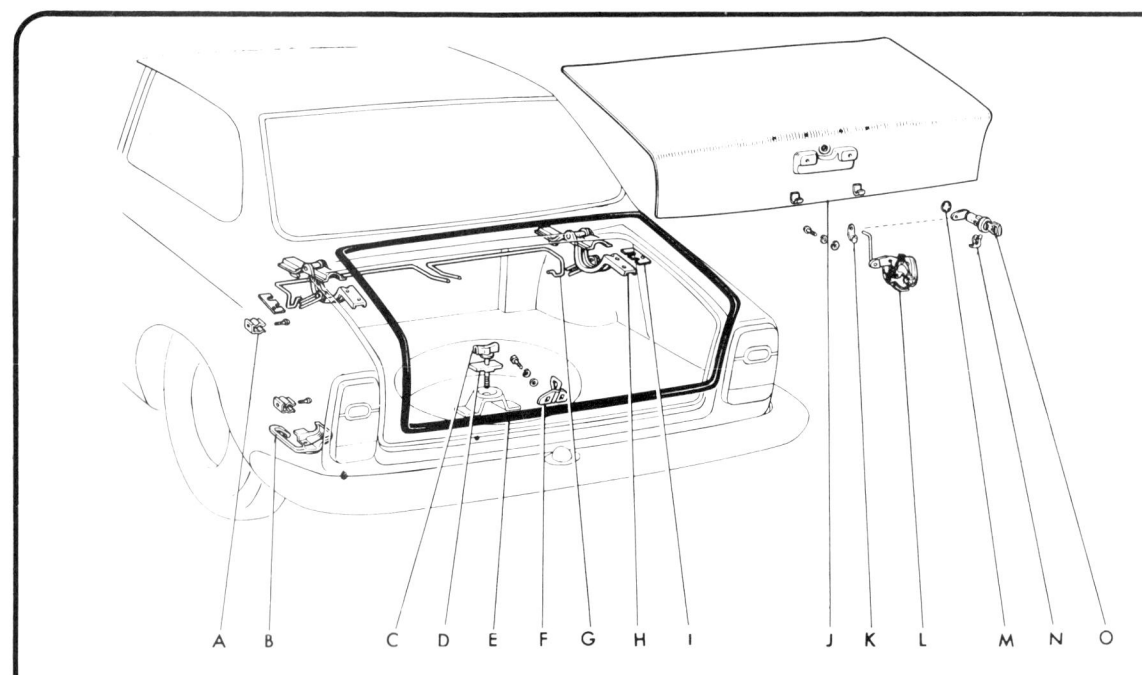

Fig. 12.11. Rear body components

A   Jack handle clamp
B   Jack carrier
C   Spare wheel clamp screw
D   Spare wheel clamp plate
E   Weatherstrip
F   Door lock striker
G   Torsion bar
H   Hinge
I   Hinge spacer
J   Boot lid
K   Rod snap clip
L   Lock
M   Cylinder pad lock
N   Cylinder retainer
O   Cylinder lock

Chapter 12/Bodywork and fittings

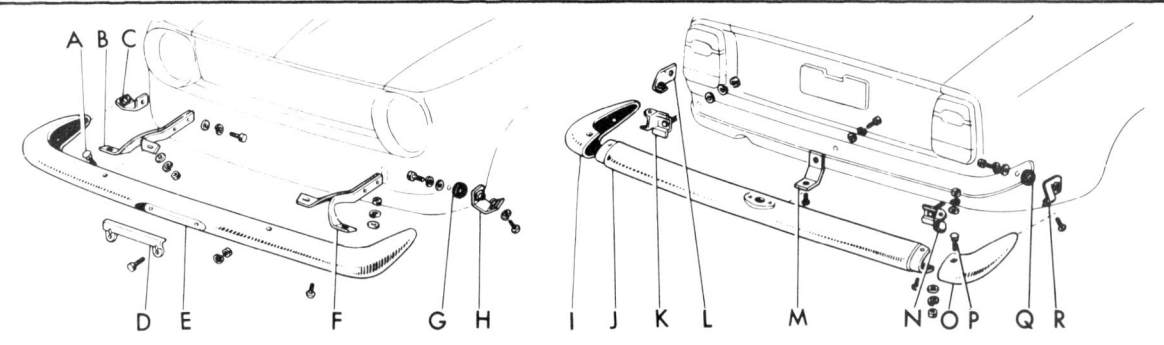

Fig. 12.12. Front and rear bumpers

- A Round head square neck bolt
- B Stay RH
- C Side retainer RH
- D License plate bracket
- E Bumper bar
- F Stay LH
- G Cushion
- H Side retainer LH
- I Side bar LH
- J Centre bar
- K Stay LH
- L Side retainer LH
- M Centre bracket
- N Stay RH
- O Side bar RH
- P Round head square neck bolt
- Q Cushion
- R Side retainer RH

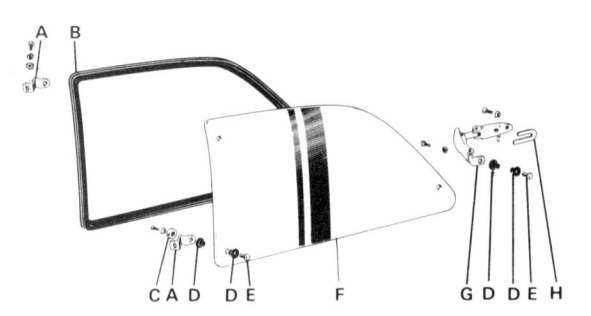

Fig. 12.13. Quarter window components

- A Hinge plate
- B Weatherstrip
- C Hinge finish plate
- D Hinge packing
- E Hinge retainer
- F Glass
- G Lock
- H Lock support spacer

Fig. 12.14. Instrument panel under-tray removal

Fig. 12.15. Cowl side trim panel removal

weatherstrip.

12 Offer up the glass and weatherstrip to the aperture and using the cord pull the rubber lip over the body flange. Whilst this is being done a person outside the car must apply firm pressure to the glass to ensure that the weatherstrip seats correctly onto the body flange.

13 If the weatherstrip is new, or stiff, lubricate the aperture and weatherstrip flanges with a little concentrated soap and water solution or washing-up liquid.

14 Apply some adhesive cement between the weatherstrip and the body and also between the weatherstrip and the glass.

15 Carefully refit the weatherstrip moulding using a screwdriver and finally replace the interior mirror and the wiper arms.

19 Rear screen - removal and replacement

The sequence for removal and replacement of the rear screen is the same as that for the windscreen. Disregard the instruction given in paragraph 2 of Section 18.

20 Rear quarter window - removal and replacement

1 To remove the glass assembly undo and remove the screws that secure the hinges and lock assembly to the window aperture.
2 Lift away the glass assembly.
3 To remove the hinges and lock from the glass undo and remove the securing bolts. Take care not to lose or damage the rubber packing pieces.

4 Reassembly and replacement is the reverse sequence to removal. To adjust the glass location slacken the hinge and lock securing bolts and reposition the glass. Retighten the securing bolts.
5 To adjust the quarter window for correct contact with the weatherstrip add or subtract the number of shims at the window lock.

21 Cowl side trim panel - removal and replacement

1 If an instrument panel under-tray is fitted this must first be removed. (Fig 12.14)
2 Remove the bonnet lock release lever and cowl side trim board securing screws. Lift away the cowl side trim panel. (Fig 12.15)

Chapter 12/Bodywork and fittings

3 Refitting the cowl side trim panel is the reverse sequence to removal.

22 Dash panel trim board - removal and replacement

1 If an instrument panel under-tray is fitted this must first be removed.
2 Remove the heater installation as described in Chapter 10.
3 Chock the rear wheels jack-up the front of the car and support on firmly based stands.
4 Remove the steering gearbox and column assembly as described in Chapter 11.
5 Remove the brake, clutch and accelerator pedals. Further information will be found in Chapters 3, 5 and 9.
6 Disconnect the cable attachments to the fuse box and combination meter. Do not forget to make a note of all conections.
7 Disconnect the bonnet lock control cable and also the choke control cable.
8 Finally remove the dash panel trim board clamp and lift away the trim board. (Fig 12.16)
9 Refitting the dash panel trim board is the reverse sequence to removal.

23 Rear quarter trim panel - removal and replacement

1 Carefully remove the rear seat cushion and wheel arch moulding.
2 Remove the door opening trim and quarter trim retainer.
3 Ease the cemented surface of the quarter trim panel from the body and lift away the rear quarter trim panel.
4 Refitting the rear quarter trim panel is the reverse sequence to removal.

24 Rear parcel tray trim panel - removal and replacement

1 Remove the rear seat backrest from the interior of the car.
2 Undo and remove the six parcel tray trim retainers and lift away the trim panel.
3 Refitting the rear parcel tray trim panel is the reverse sequence to removal.

25 Cowl ventilator - removal and replacement

1 Detach the cowl ventilator rod bracket which is mounted on the body.
2 Undo and remove the rear seat securing nuts from the inside duct to the body and lift away the duct.
3 Refitting the cowl ventilator duct is the reverse sequence to removal.

26 Front seat - removal and replacement

Standard fitment

1 To remove a front seat undo and remove the four securing bolts and lift away the front seat.
2 To remove the track undo and remove the two securing bolts and lift away the seat track.
3 Refitting the track and seat is the reverse sequence to removal. Apply a little Castrol LM Grease to the seat track to ensure easy movement.

Fully reclining

The removal and replacement sequence for the seat and track is identical to that for standard fitment seats.

27 Rear seat - removal and replacement

1 Remove the rear seat right and left-hand back stay split pins and washers. Detach the stay.
2 Undo and remove the rear seat securing nuts from the inside of the luggage compartment. Lift away the rear seat.
3 Refitting the rear seat is the reverse sequence to removal.

28 Front wing - removal and replacement

1 For safety reasons, disconnect the battery.
2 Remove the windscreen wiper arm assemblies and then the cowl ventilator louvre located at the base of the windscreen.
3 Remove the rocker panel moulding.
4 Remove the wing splash shield.
5 Refer to Chapter 10, and remove the headlight assembly and then the radiator grille.
6 Refer to Section 17, and remove the front bumper.
7 Undo and remove the 13 nuts, bolts and screws securing the front wing to the body (Fig 12.19). Lift away the front wing panel. When removing the left-hand wing do not forget to disconnect the radio aerial.
8 Refitting the front wing is the reverse sequence to removal. Do not tighten the wing securing nuts, bolts and screws until its final fitted position has been adjusted at the bonnet aperture and leading edge of the front door. Then tighten the attachments.

29 Lower shroud panel - removal and replacement

1 The lower shroud panel is located beneath the radiator grille.
2 Refer to Chapter 10, and remove the headlight assemblies and then the radiator grille.
3 Refer to Section 17, and remove the front bumper.

Fig. 12.16. Dash panel trim board removal

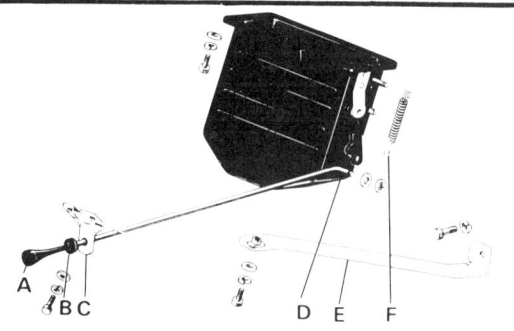

Fig. 12.17. Cowl ventilator components

A Control rod
B Grommet
C Rod bracket
D Duct
E Bracket
F Tension spring

Chapter 12/Bodywork and fittings

4 Disconnect the side and direction indicator light unit terminal connector.

5 Undo and remove the nine nuts, bolts and screws securing the lower shroud panel to the front body and wings. (Fig 20). Lift away the lower shroud panel.

6 Refitting the lower shroud panel is the reverse sequence to removal. Do not tighten the securing nuts, bolts and screws until its final fitted position has been adjusted to line with the front wings.

Estate/Wagon (1968 - 1970)

30 Rear door window regulator - removal and replacement

1 Refer to Section 11, and remove the door trim and interior handles.

2 Remove the service hole cover.

3 Raise the door glass and support in this position.

4 Undo and remove the regulator securing bolts. Lower the regulator with the regulator securing bracket facing the bottom

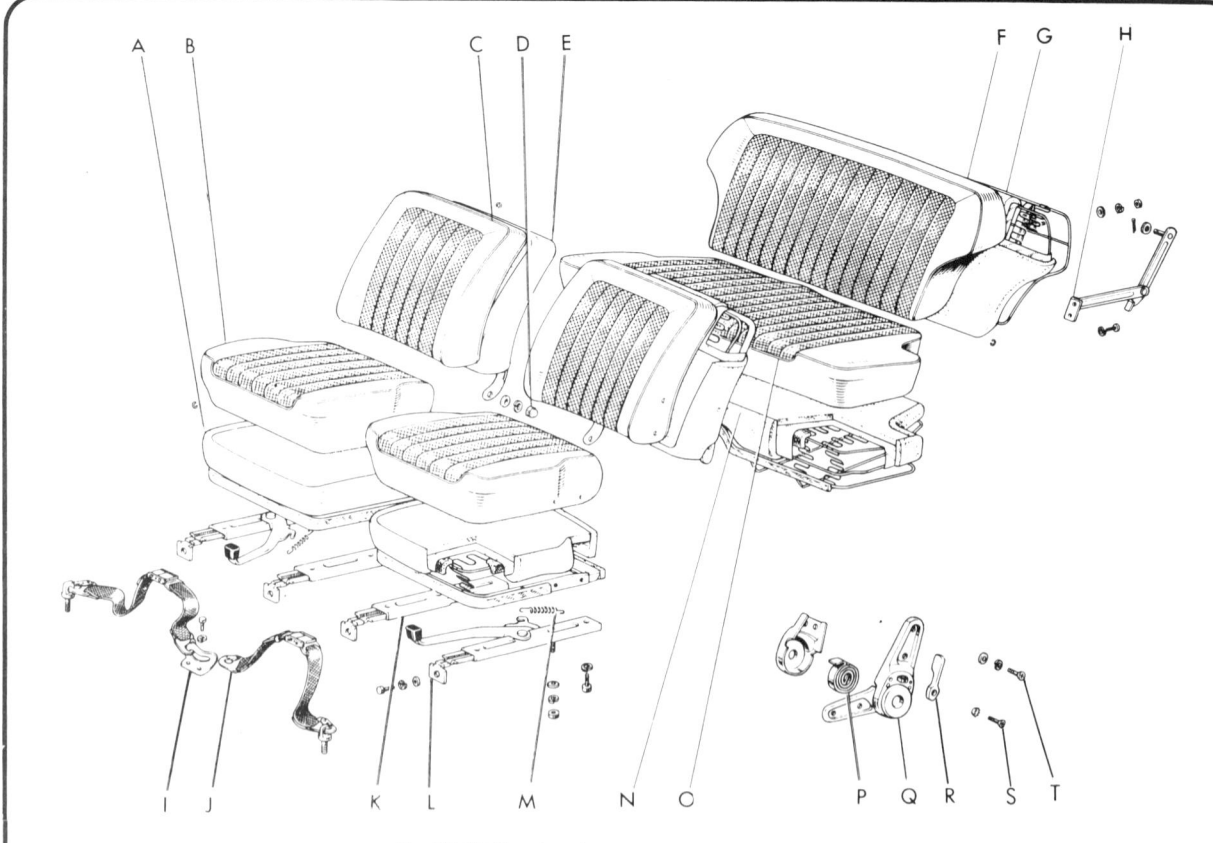

Fig. 12.18 Front and rear seat components
(Front reclining seat shown)

A Cushion
B Cushion cover
C Back cover
D Cap nut
E Back
F Back cover
G Back
H Back stay
I Lap type harness RH
J Lap type harness LH
K Seat inner track
L Seat outer track
M Tension spring
N Cushion
O Cushion cover
P Spiral spring
Q Reclining seat back adjuster
R Reclining adjusting handle
S Screw
T Screw

Fig. 12.19. Front wing attachment points

Fig. 12.20. Lower shroud panel attachment points

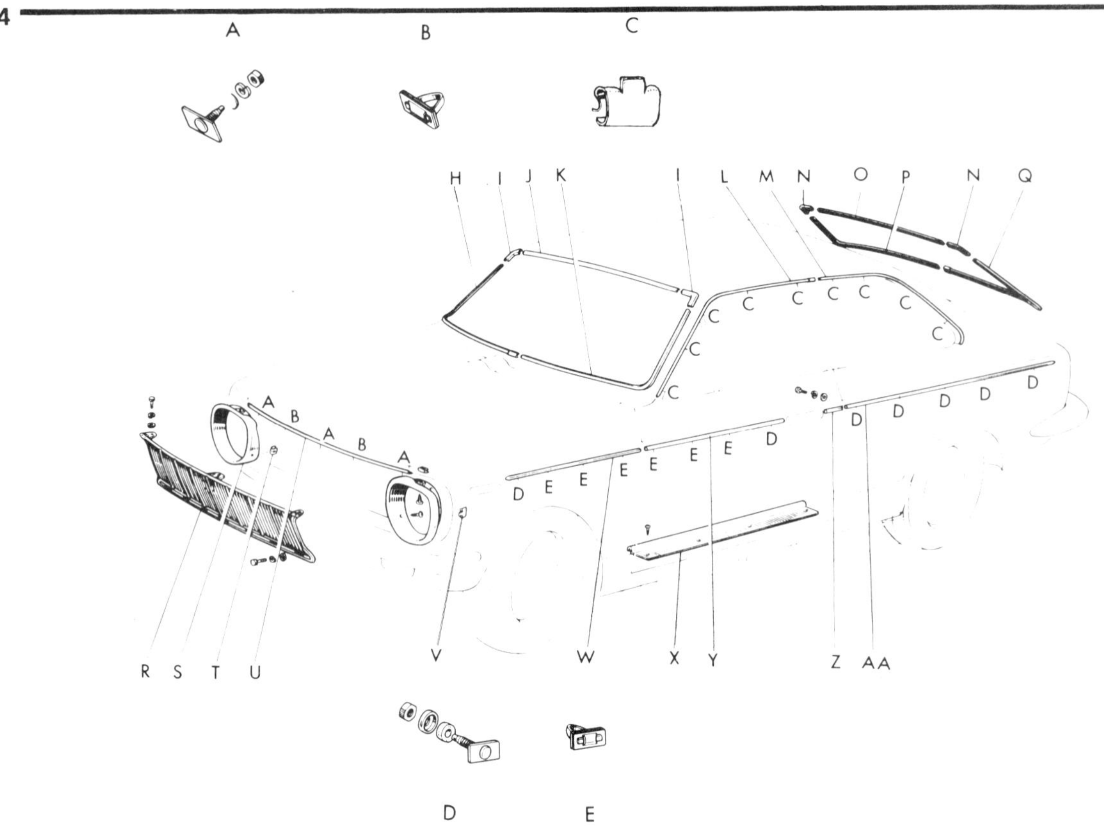

Fig. 12.21. Body exterior trim

A	Front moulding retainer	
B	Outside moulding retainer	
C	Roof drip side finish moulding retainer	
D	Outside moulding retainer	
E	Outside moulding retainer	
F	Rocker panel moulding retainer No. 1	
G	Rocker panel moulding retainer No. 2	
H	Windshield outside moulding RH	
I	Windshield outside moulding joint upper cover	
J	Windshield outside upper moulding	
K	Windshield outside moulding LH	
L	Roof drip side finish front moulding	
M	Roof drip side finish rear moulding	
N	Back window outside moulding joint upper cover	
O	Back window outside upper moulding	
P	Back window outside moulding RH	
Q	Back window outside moulding LH	
R	Radiator grille	
S	Headlight trim	
T	Lock nut	
U	Radiator grille opening upper moulding	
V	Headlight spring	
W	Front wing side moulding	
X	Step plate	
Y	Door outside moulding No. 1	
Z	Door outside moulding No. 2	
AA	Quarter panel outside moulding	

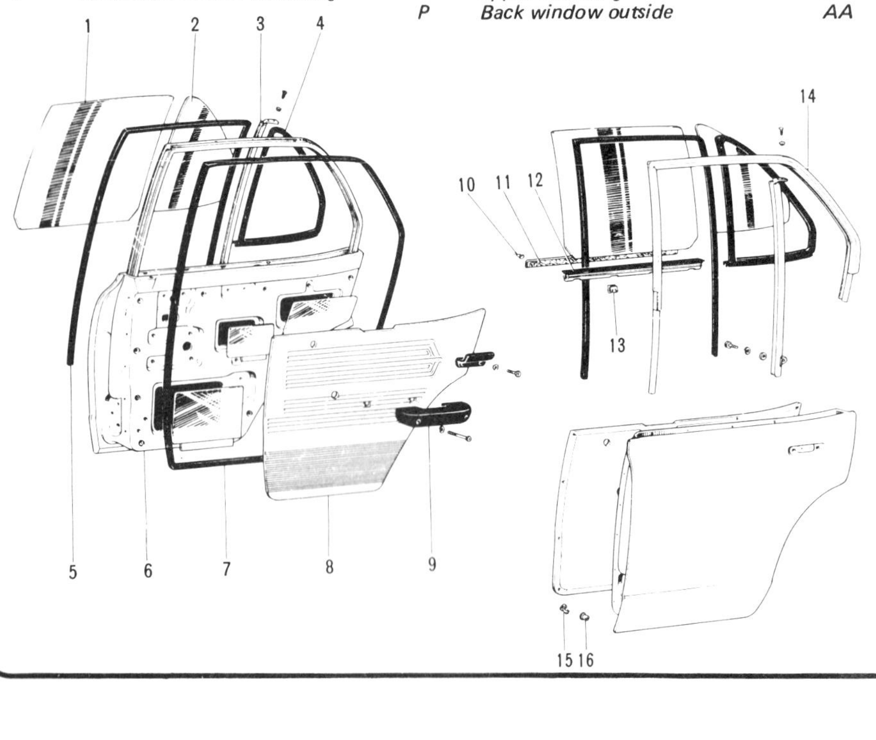

Fig. 12.22. Rear door components

1. Glass
2. Quarter window glass
3. Window division bar
4. Quarter window weatherstrip
5. Glass run
6. Panel
7. Weatherstrip
8. Trim panel
9. Arm rest
10. Clip
11. Glass inner weatherstrip
12. Glass outer weatherstrip
13. Glass weatherstrip clip
14. Window frame
15. Trim retainer
16. Trim retainer cap

edge of the door.
5 Disconnect the regulator roller from the door glass channel and lift away the regulator.
6 Refitting the door glass regulator is the reverse sequence to removal. Lubricate all moving parts with a little Castrol LM Grease.

31 Rear door glass - removal and replacement

1 Refer to Section 30 and remove the regulator assembly.
2 Remove the glass stopper.
3 Undo and remove the division bar securing bolt and screws.
4 Carefully, partially pull out the division bar whilst moving the top edge forwards. It will be necessary to draw out the door glass run at the same time.
5 Lower the door glass fully and remove the door glass inner weatherstrip using a screwdriver.
6 Remove the door glass outer weatherstrip using a wood chisel or wide bladed screwdriver. Take care not to chip the paintwork.
7 Completely remove the division bar.
8 Remove the door glass and the quarter window glass. If the latter proves difficult to remove lubricate the weatherstrip with a little concentrated soap and water solution or washing-up liquid.
9 To reassemble first lubricate the quarter window weatherstrip with a little concentrated soap and water solution or washing-up liquid.
10 Fit the quarter window glass assembly into the door frame.
11 Insert the door glass into the door.
12 Fit the glass run into the division bar.
13 Fit the division bar into the door, fitting the division bar to the glass. Tilt the division bar forwards to facilitate fitting the door glass inner weatherstrip.
14 Completely lower the door glass and fit the door glass inner weatherstrip. Fit the clips onto the attaching holes and push the door glass inner weatherstrip using the palm of the hand.
15 Fit the quarter window weatherstrip onto the door division bar. Secure the division bar with the two attaching screws.
16 Fit the door glass outer weatherstrip and then raise the door glass halfway up its travel. Support in this position.
17 Fit the hole seal onto the window regulator and insert the door and locate the regulator roller in the glass channel.
18 Secure the regulator to the door and then refit the door glass stopper.
19 Refit the division bar securing bolt.
20 The trim panel and interior handles should now be refitted, this being the reverse sequence to removal. Note that this larger diameter of the conical spring should be positioned adjacent to the trim panel.

32 Rear door lock and remote control - removal and replacement

Lock

1 Refer to Section 11 and remove the interior trim and handles.
2 Remove the hole cover.
3 Raise the door glass and disconnect the remote control link from the door lock.
4 Undo and remove the three screws securing the lock to the door and lift away the lock assembly.

Remote control

1 Unscrew the remote control push button.
2 Undo and remove the two remote control securing bolts. Lift

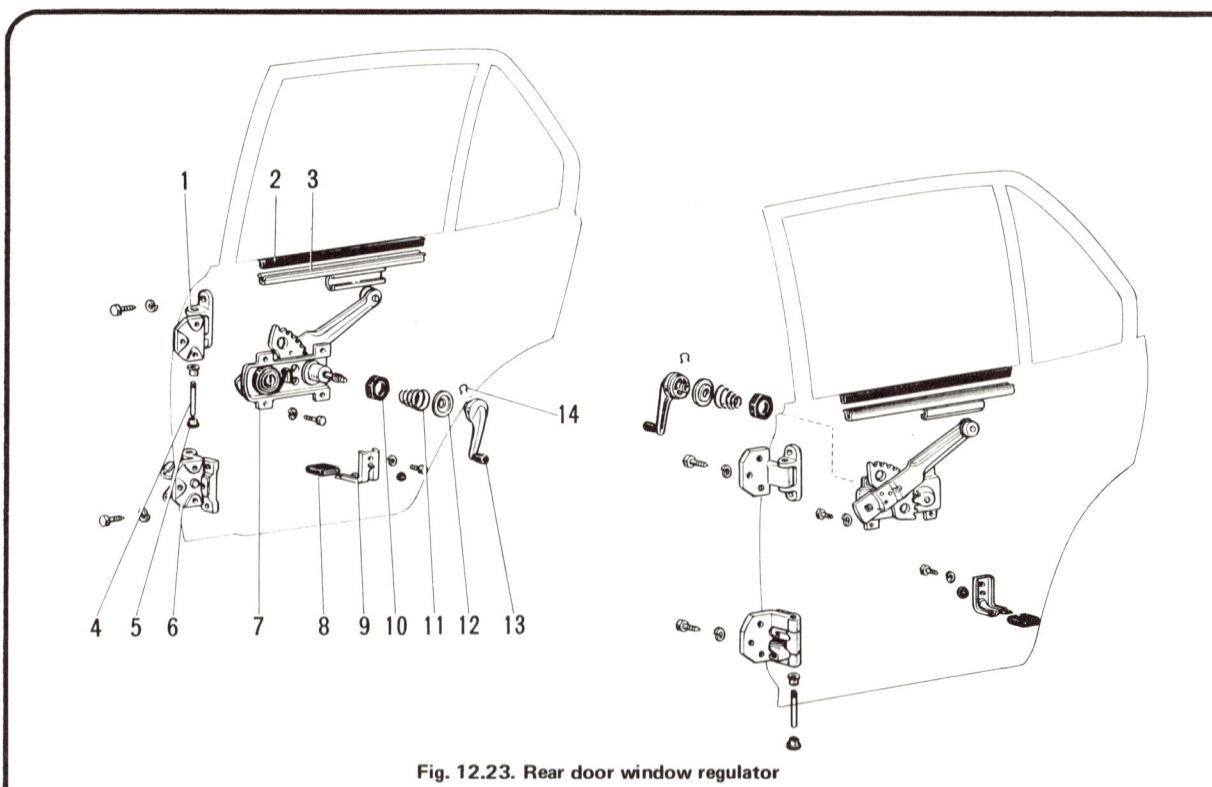

Fig. 12.23. Rear door window regulator

1	Upper hinge	4	W/serration pin	8	Ring	12	Window regulator and inside handle plate
2	Glass channel weatherstrip	5	Bushing	9	Door glass stopper	13	Window regulator handle
3	Glass channel	6	Lower hinge	10	Window regulator hole seal	14	Shaft snap ring
		7	Window regulator	11	Conical spring		

Fig. 12.24. Rear door lock components

1. Locking remote control push button
2. Grommet
3. Outside handle
4. Locking remote control and link
5. Gasket
6. Inside handle caution plate
7. Window regulator and inside handle plate
8. Inside handle
9. Lock
10. Lock cushion
11. Lock striker plate

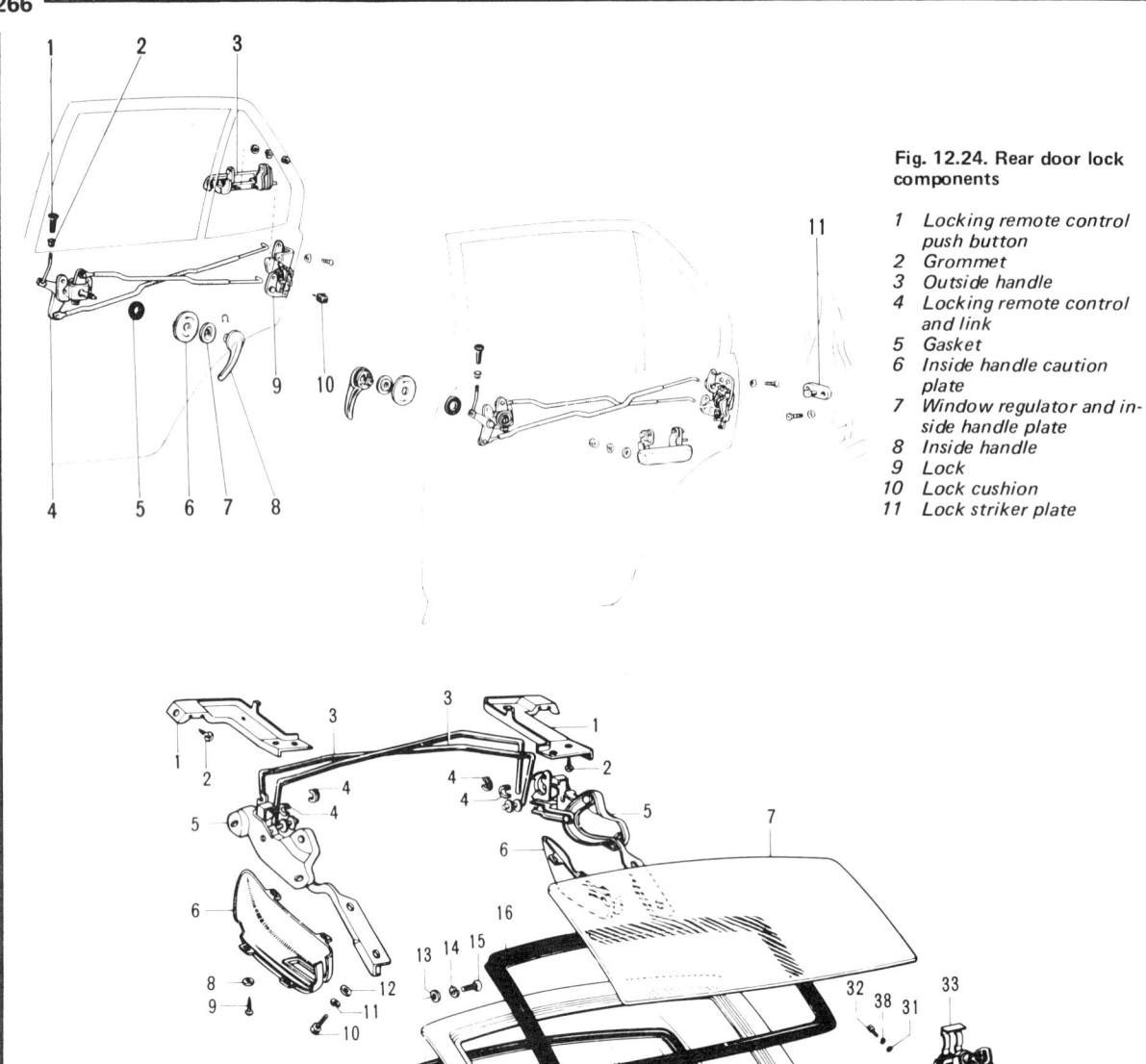

Fig. 12.25. Back door components

1 Hinge cover retainer	11 Washer	21 Trim board	31 Washer
2 Screw	12 Washer	22 Screw	32 Screw
3 Torsion bar	13 Washer	23 Washer	33 Lock cylinder retainer
4 Torsion bar support collar	14 Washer	24 Side female lower stopper	34 Lock control link
5 Hinge	15 Screw	25 Bolt	35 Lock cylinder and key set
6 Hinge cover	16 Glass weatherstrip	26 Side male lower stopper	36 Bolt
7 Glass	17 Weatherstrip	27 Lock striker shim	37 Washer
8 Washer	18 Side male stopper	28 Lock striker	38 Washer
9 Screw	19 Screw	29 Panel	39 Lock control link snap
10 Bolt	20 Nut	30 Bolt	40 Lock

away the remote control and link.

Exterior handle

1 With the interior trim removed (Section 11) and the service hole cover removed, raise the door glass.
2 Disconnect the remote control link.
3 Undo and remove the two exterior handle securing nuts and washers and lift away the handle.

Reassembly

Reassembly in all cases is the reverse sequenece to reassembly.

33 Back door - removal, replacement and adjustment

1 Open the back door and disconnect the number plate light terminal connector.
2 An assistant should now take the weight of the door. Undo and remove the hinge securing bolts and carefully lift away the back door.
3 To remove a hinge, undo and remove the hinge cover securing screws and lift away the hinge cover.
4 Carefully detach the interior headlining from the rear of the upper panel and then remove the rear door hinge cover retainer.
5 Using a suitable pry bar detach the torsion spring.
6 Undo and remove the rear door hinge bracket securing bolts and lift away the hinge.
7 Reassembly and refitting is the reverse sequence to removal. However, the following additional points should be noted:
a) To adjust the back door position in the aperture slacken the bolts securing the hinge to the body and move the back door forwards or backwards as necessary. Tighten the bolts.
b) To adjust the vertical position of the back door slacken the bolts securing the hinge to the door and move the back door upwards or downwards as necessary. Tighten the bolts.
c) Check that the back door closes correctly. Adjust the position of the door lock stricker by adding or subtracting shims.

34 Back door side stopper - adjustment

Lower side

1 Slacken the female lower stopper adjustment screws.
2 Close the back door and position the female lower stopper against the male lower stopper from the inside of the car. Mark the position of the female lower stopper.
3 Open the back door and move the female lower stopper rearwards by 0.04 in (1 mm) from the marked position. Retighten the securing screws.

Upper side

1 Mark the position in the same manner as described for the lower side.
2 Open the back door and move it rearwards by 0.14 in (3.5 mm) from the marked position. Retighten the securing screws.

35 Back door lock - removal and replacement

1 Remove the back door trim board.
2 Disconnect the back door lock control link.
3 Remove the back door lock securing clip and lift away the lock assembly.
4 Undo and remove the two bolts securing the lock control link assembly to the back door. Lift away the lock and control link assembly.
5 Refitting the back door lock assembly is the reverse sequence

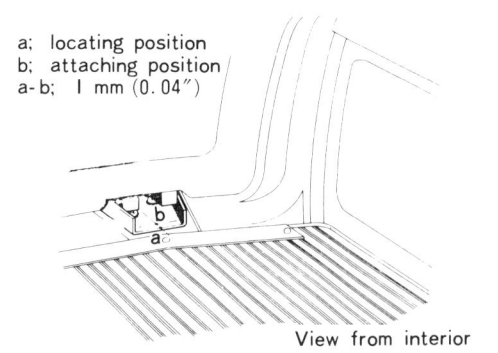

a; locating position
b; attaching position
a-b; 1 mm (0.04")

Fig. 12.26 Back door side stopper adjustment

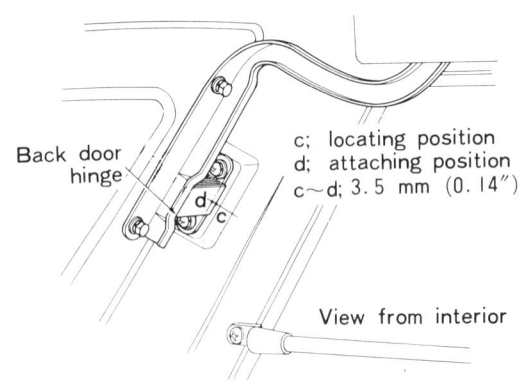

c; locating position
d; attaching position
c~d; 3.5 mm (0.14")

Fig. 12.27 Back door hinge adjustment

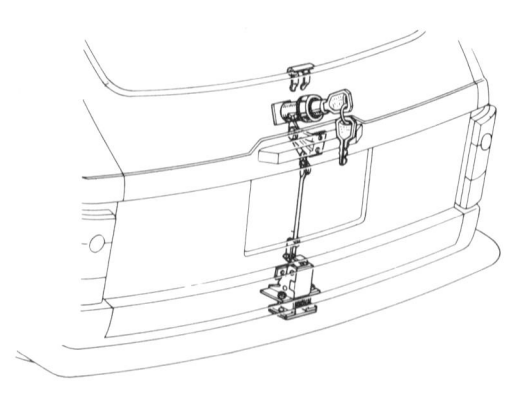

Fig. 12.28 Back door lock

to removal.

36 Back door glass - removal and replacement

1 Like the windscreen the back door glass should be removed and refitted by a specialist but can be carried out by the more ambitious owner.
2 Carefully remove the back door window moulding.
3 Using a screwdriver release the weatherstrip from the body. Take care not to scratch the paintwork.
4 The assistance of a second person should now be enlisted ready to catch the glass when it is released from its aperture.
5 Working inside the car, commencing at one top corner, press the glass and ease it and the rubber weatherstrip from the aperture lip.
6 Remove the rubber weatherstrip from the glass.
7 Carefully inspect the rubber weatherstrip for signs of splitting or other deterioration. Clean all traces of sealing compound from

the weatherstrip and glass aperture flange.

8 To refit the glass first place the rubber weatherstrip onto the glass edge.

9 Place a piece of cord into the aperture flange groove of the weatherstrip, and cross the ends at the top centre of the weatherstrip.

10 Offer up the glass and weatherstrip to the aperture and, using the cord, pull the rubber lip over the body flange. Whilst this is being done, a person outside the car must apply pressure to the glass to ensure the weatherstrip seats correctly onto the flange. flange.

11 If the weatherstrip is new or stiff lubricate the aperture and weatherstrip flanges with a little concentrated soap and water solution or washing-up liquid.

12 Apply some adhesive cement between the weatherstrip and the body and also between the weatherstrip and the glass.

13 Carefully refit the weatherstrip moulding using a screwdriver.

37 Front quarter glass - removal and replacement

The sequence is basically identical to that for two door saloon models as described in Section 20.

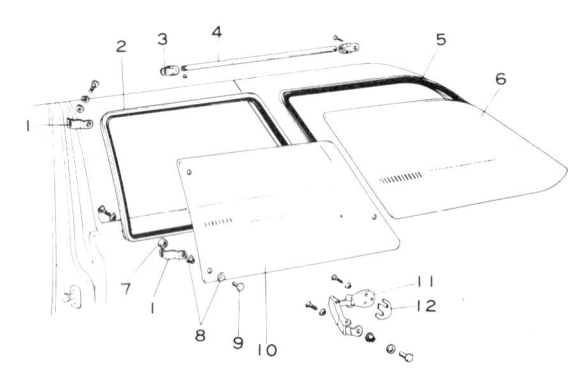

Fig. 12.29. Quarter window components

1 Hinge plate
2 Front weatherstrip
3 Guard bracket
4 Guard horizontal tube
5 Rear weatherstrip
6 Rear glass
7 Hinge finish plate
8 Hinge packing
9 Hinge retainer
10 Front glass
11 Lock
12 Lock support spacer

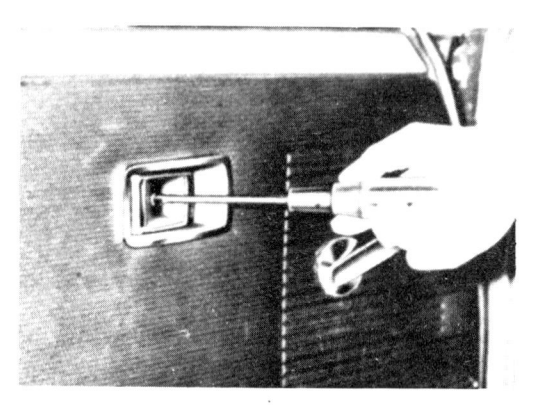

Fig. 12.30. Interior handle removal

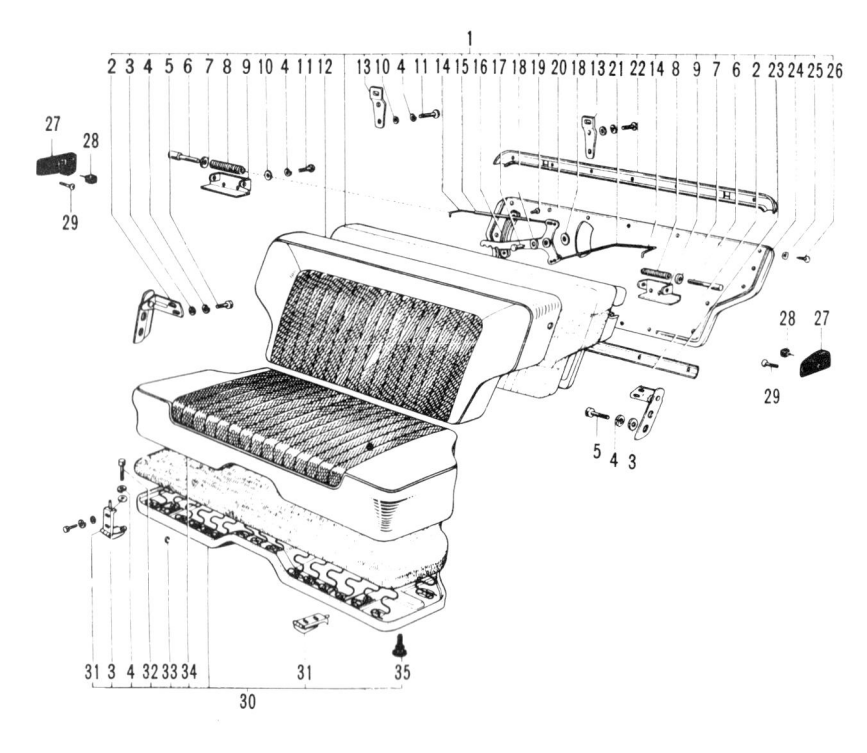

Fig. 12.31. Rear seat components

1 Rear seat back
2 Back hinge
3 Washer
4 Washer
5 Bolt
6 Back locking rod
7 Washer
8 Spring
9 Back stop bracket
10 Washer
11 Screw
12 Back cover
13 Back holder
14 Back control wire
15 Hose
16 Control lever guide
17 Back control lever pin
18 Washer
19 Rivet
20 Back rod control lever
21 Hose
22 Back mat support upper plate
23 Back mat support lower plate
24 Back panel mat
25 Washer
26 Screw
27 Back stop
28 Cushion
29 Screw
30 Cushion
31 Cushion hinge
32 Bolt
33 Small hog ring
34 Cushion cover
35 Cushion

38 Rear quarter glass - removal and replacement

The sequence is basically identical to that as described in Section 36, which covered removal and replacement of the back door glass.

39 Rear seat backrest - removal and replacement

1 Fold the rear seat backrest forwards.
2 Undo and remove the rear seat backrest hinge securing bolts. Lift away the backrest assembly.
3 Refitting the backrest is the reverse sequence to removal.

All models (after 1970)

40 Front door lock and regulator - removal and replacement

This Section is applicable to earlier KE models fitted with the safety type door handles that are recessed into the door. The information given in this Section gives the operational differences to the modified parts only.

Door lock remote control

1 Refer to Section 11, and remove the door trim panel. Lift away the service hole cover. The lock handle surround is retained by one screw which must be removed before releasing the trim panel. (Fig 12.30)
2 Undo and remove the interior handle securing bolts and lift away the interior handle and remote control link which must be detached from the lock.
3 Refitting is the reverse sequence to removal.

Door window regulator

1 Refer to Section 11, and remove the door trim panel. Lift away the service hole cover. The lock handle surround is retained by one screw which must be removed before releasing the trim panel.
2 Remove the door lock remote control as described earlier in this Section.
3 Remove the glass stopper and then raise the glass to the fully closed position. Support in this position.
4 Undo and remove the regulator securing bolts and lower the regulator at the same time disconnecting the regulator roller from the glass channel.
5 Lift away the regulator assembly.
6 Refitting the regulator assembly is the reverse sequence to removal.

2 Door Saloon/Sedan (1971 on KE20 and 21 series)

41 Front door - removal and replacement

Removal of the doors is similar to that as described in Section 10. (photo)

42 Door trim and interior handles - removal and replacement

1 Using a 'V' shaped blade or two thin screwdrivers inserted between the handle flange and escutcheon release the horse shoe shaped retaining clip and lift away the handle and escutcheon. See also photo sequence for alternative panel layout.
2 When an arm rest or door pull is fitted undo and remove the two securing screws and lift away the arm rest.
3 To disengage the door lock remote control finisher apply an even pressure over the whole finisher and push the two sides inwards slightly. Move the interior to the open position and slide the entire finisher rearwards whilst disengaging the finisher from

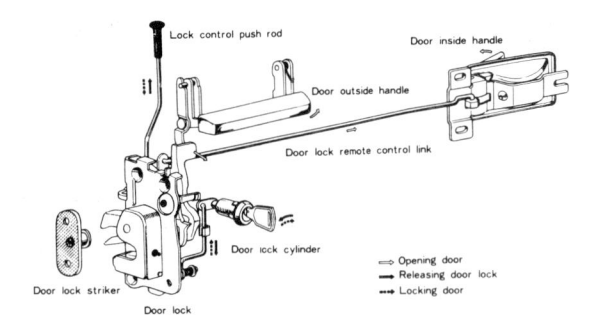

Fig. 12.32. Front door lock components

41.a Front door lower hinge (later type)

the handle which should be in the open position.
4 Using a knife or hacksaw blade (with teeth ground down) inserted between the door trim panel carefully ease each clip from its hole in the door inner panel.
5 Inspect the trim panel retaining clip and insert it from the front, feeding through the lock handle. The lock should be in the open position.

43 Door window glass and regulator - removal and replacement

1 Refer to Section 42, and remove the door trim and interior handles.
2 Completely lower the glass and remove the service hole cover.
3 Undo and remove the two glass holder plates securing bolts. (photos)
4 Pull out the glass from the top whilst turning the glass through 90°.
5 Undo and remove the 6 bolts securing the window regulator to the door inner panel.
6 The regulator may now be removed from the door inner panel.
7 To refit the regulator first replace the regulator inside the door and temporarily secure with the bolts.
8 Carefully insert the glass and with the regulator in the fully lowered position secure the glass with the glass holder plates without disengaging from the rubber seats.
9 Temporarily refit the regulator handle and tighten the bolts so that the equaliser arm bracket is horizontal when the door glass is lowered 1.2-1.4 in (30-60 mm) from the fully raised position.
10 Reassembly is now the reverse sequence to removal.

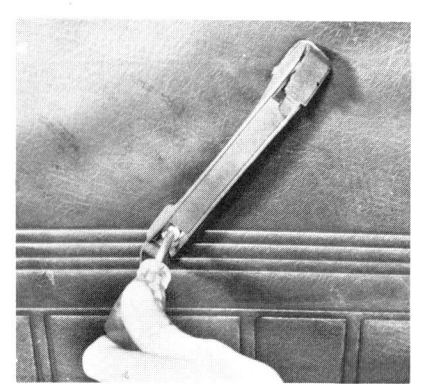

42a Removal of door pull

42b Removal of remote control moulding I

42c Removal of remote control moulding II

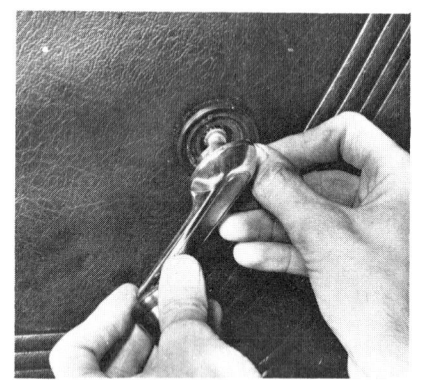

42d Removal of window regulator handle

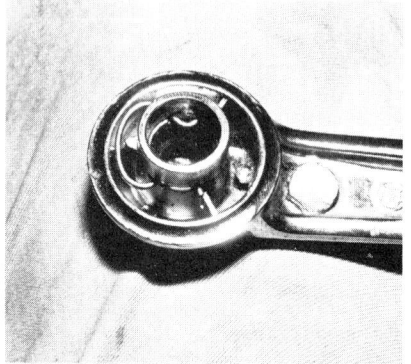

42e Horseshoe shaped clip located in handle

42f Lifting away door trim panel

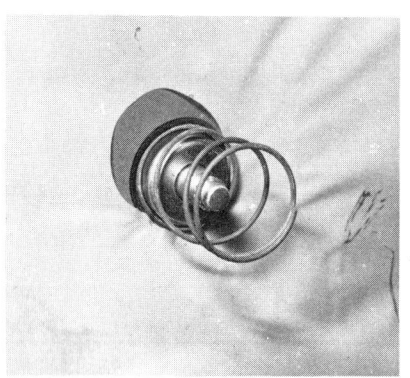

42g Note which way round this spring is fitted

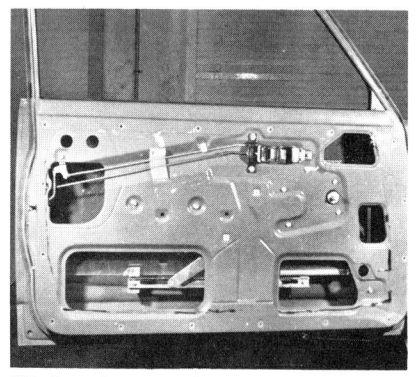

42h Door inner panel with service hole cover removed

43.3a Window regulator channel (rear)

43.3b Window regulator channel (Front)

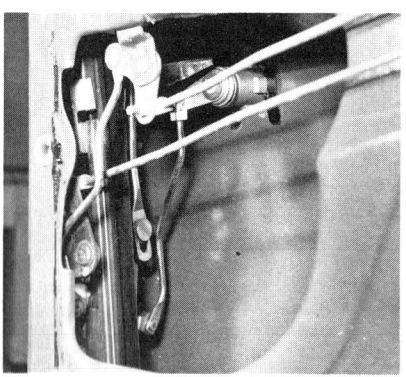

44a Door lock control attachments

44b Door lock remote control

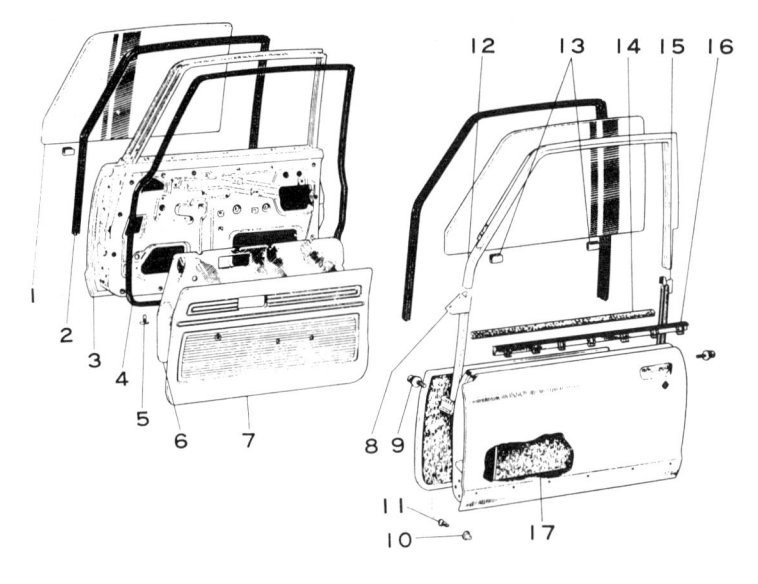

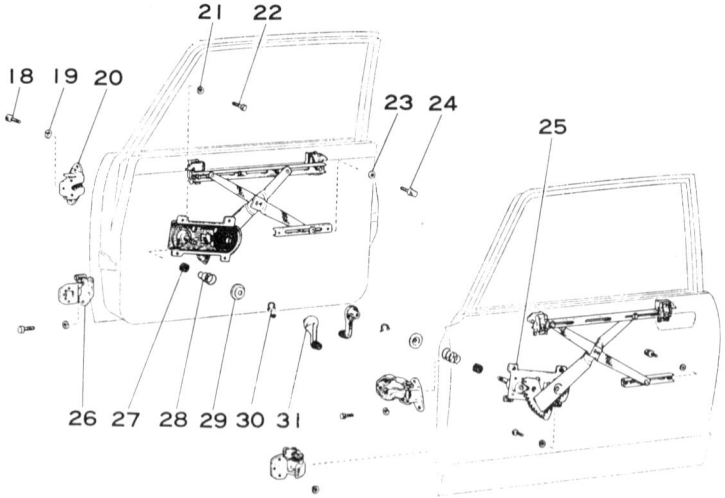

Fig. 12.33. Front door components

1. Glass
2. Glass run
3. Panel
4. Weatherstrip
5. Weatherstrip clip
6. Service hole cover
7. Trim panel
8. Front lower frame
9. Bolt w/washer
10. Trim retainer cap
11. Trim retainer
12. Window frame
13. Glass seat
14. Glass inner weatherstrip
15. Rear lower frame
16. Glass outer weatherstrip
17. Silencer pad
18. Bolt
19. Lockwasher
20. Upper hinge
21. Lock washer
22. Bolt
23. Lock washer
24. Bolt w/washer
25. Window regulator
26. Lower hinge
27. Window regulator hole seal
28. Conical spring
29. Window regulator and inner handle plate
30. Shaft snap ring
31. Window regulator handle

44 Door lock assembly - removal and replacement

Lock assembly

1 Refer to Section 42, and remove the door trim and interior handles.
2 Raise the door glass fully and then disconnect the remote control link and rod from the door lock. (photos)
3 Undo and remove the bolt that secures the door rear lower frame and also the bolt that secures the lock bellcrank.
4 Undo and remove the four screws that secure the door lock to the door panel. The lock may now be lifted away.
5 Refitting the door lock assembly is the reverse sequence to removal. Lubricate all moving parts with a little Castrol LM Grease.

Lock striker

1 To remove the door lock striker undo and remove the two securing screws. Lift away the striker.
2 Refitting the striker assembly is the reverse sequence to removal. Lightly tighten the striker securing screws and align the door before finally tightening.
3 If the rear of the door has dropped do not adjust the striker but reset the door hinge positions.

Exterior handle

1 Refer to Section 42, and remove the door trim panel and service hole cover.
2 Raise the glass fully and working inside the door undo and remove the two nuts and washers securing the exterior handle to the outer door panel.
3 Disconnect the exterior handle and control link. Lift away the exterior handle.
4 Refitting the exterior handle is the reverse sequence to removal, but it will be necessary to reset the link adjustment as follows:
a) The opening control should be set when the exterior handle is raised by 0.02-0.04 in (0.5-1.0 mm) from its rest position.
b) Set the adjuster at the top of the link so that the exterior handle rod and clip can be refitted.
c) If the exterior handle does not operate check for excessive play between the opening lever and the door lock ratchet pawl.
d) It should be noted that when the opening control link is in its lowermost position the required play will not exist. Always set the linkage with the handle raised.

Lock cylinder

1 Refer to Section 42, and remove the door trim panel and

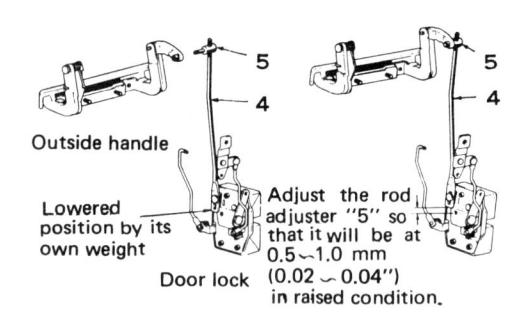

Fig. 12.34. Door lock control link adjustment

Outside handle — Lowered position by its own weight
Door lock — Adjust the rod adjuster "5" so that it will be at 0.5~1.0 mm (0.02~0.04") in raised condition.

service hole cover.
2 Detach the control rod spring clip and carefully remove the lock cylinder clamp.
3 Refitting the lock cylinder is the reverse sequence to removal. Lubricate the operating surfaces of the lock cylinder with a little Castrol LM Grease.

Interior handle and control link

1 Refer to Section 42 and remove the door trim panel and service hole cover.
2 Detach the control link spring clip and carefully disconnect the control link.
3 Undo and remove the interior handle securing screws and lift away the interior handle assembly.
4 Refitting the interior handle is the reverse sequence to removal. It will be necessary to adjust the control link as follows:

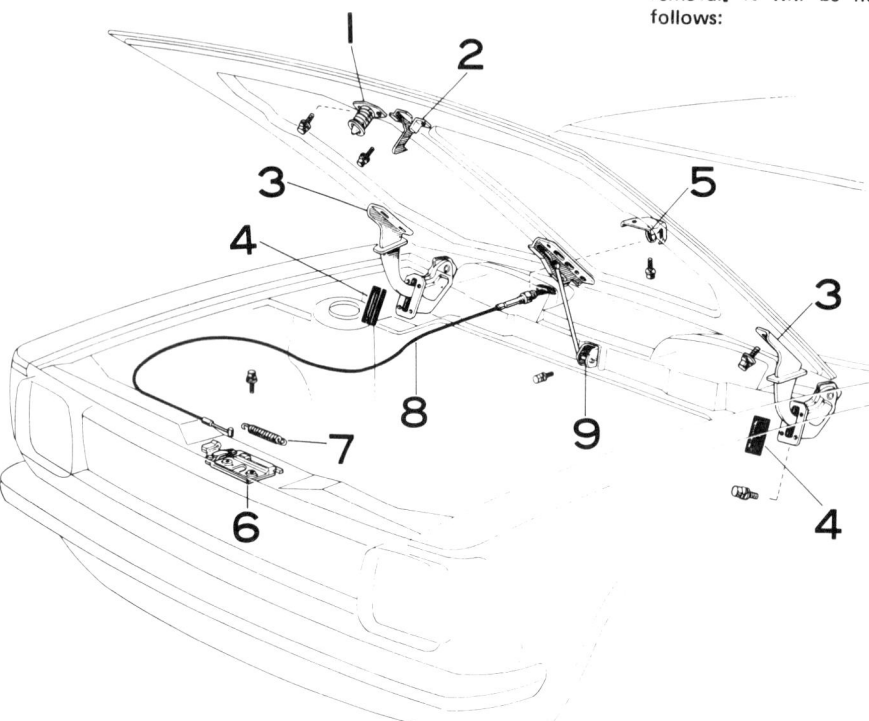

Fig. 12.35. Bonnet hinge and lock assemblies

1 Hook assembly
2 Opening catch hook assembly
3 Hinge assembly
4 Hinge seal
5 Lock control cable bracket
6 Lock assembly
7 Tension spring
8 Lock control cable assembly
9 Support assembly

45.1 Windscreen washer hose attached to bonnet

45.5 Bonnet lock assembly

Chapter 12/Bodywork and fittings

a) Temporarily tighten the locking control bellcrank which is attached to the lock assembly.
b) Move the interior handle assembly forwards and then rearwards by 0.02-0.04 in (0.5-1.0 mm) from the fully forwards position. Tighten the interior handle securing screws.
c) Move the interior handle locking button to the locked position and tighten the bellcrank whilst holding the locking button.

45 Bonnet and lock - removal and replacement

1 With the bonnet open, use a soft pencil and mark the outline position of the bolt hinges at the bonnet to act as a datum for refitment. Detach the windscreen washer hose from the bonnet. (photo)
2 With the help of an assistant support the front of the bonnet and then release the bonnet support.
3 Undo and remove the two bolts and washers securing the bonnet to each hinge. Lift away the bonnet from over the front of the car.
4 To remove the hinges undo and remove the four bolts and washers securing each hinge to the bulkhead. Lift away the hinges.
5 To remove the bonnet lock is a straightforward operation and will not present any problems. Do not forget to disconnect the lock control cable from the lock. For safety reasons, disconnect the battery to prevent accidental short circuiting. (photo)
6 Reassembly and replacment as applicable is the reverse sequence to removal. Several adjustments are necessary and should be carried out once the bonnet is correctly aligned in the aperture as follows:
a) If the bonnet does not lock on closing, the bonnet lock dowel should be lengthened by slackening the locknut and screwing out by turning anticlockwise. Retighten the locknut.
b) If the bonnet lock dowel does not engage in the bonnet lock, slacken the lock securing bolts or the dowel retainer bolts, and reposition the lock or dowel as necessary. Retighten the securing bolts.
c) Check that the bonnet safety catch engages correctly. It may be adjusted by slackening the securing bolts and moving its position as necessary. Tighten the securing bolts.

46 Boot lid and lock - removal and replacement

1 With the boot lid open mark the fitted position of the hinge relative to the boot lid.
2 An assistant should now support the weight of the boot lid and then undo and remove the four bolts and washers securing the boot lid to the hinges.
3 Lift away the boot lid and recover the hinge spacers.
4 If necessary the torsion bar may be removed by detaching at one end to release the tension and then lifting away.
5 To remove the lock cylinder release the spring retainer with a pair of pliers, detach the pullrod and lift away the lock cylinder.
6 To remove the lock from the boot lid undo and remove the three securing bolts and washers.
7 Reassembly and replacement of the boot lock and lid is the reverse sequence to removal. Several adjustments are necessary and should be carried out as follows:

Boot lid

a) Adjustment of the boot lid in the aperture is effected by slackening the boot lid to hinge securing bolts and repositioning the boot lid in the aperture.
b) To lift or lower the hinge end of the boot lid fit or remove hinge spacers as necessary. Each spacer is 0.063 in (1.6 mm).

Boot lid lock

To adjust the lock slacken the lock striker securing bolts and

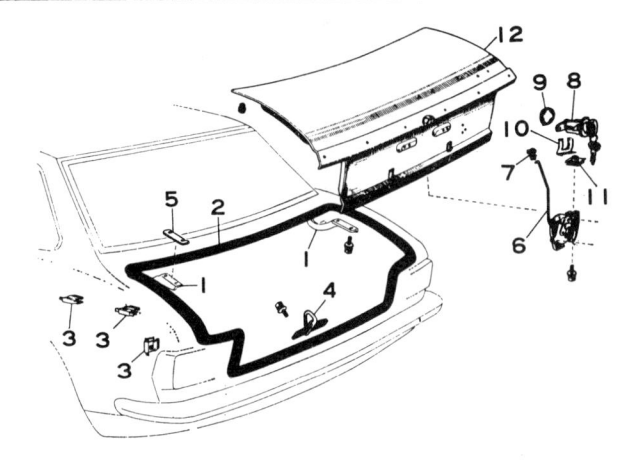

Fig. 12.36. Rear body components

1 Hinge assembly
2 Weatherstrip
3 Jack handle clamps
4 Lock striker
5 Hinge support
6 Lock assembly
7 Rod, snap
8 Lock cylinder and key
9 Lock, cylinder pad
10 Lock, cylinder retainer
11 Nut
12 Panel sub-assembly

move the striker as necessary. Tighten the securing bolts.

47 Windscreen - removal and replacement

The sequence is basically identical to that as described in Section 18.

48 Rear screen - removal and replacement

The sequence is basically identical to that as described in Sections 18 and 19.

49 Rear quarter window - removal and replacement

The sequence is basically identical to that as described in Section 20.

50 Instrument panel safety pad - removal and replacement

1 For safety reasons, disconnect the battery.
2 Carefully detach the instrument panel mouldings starting at the centre one and following by the two outer ones.
3 Refer to Chapter 10, and remove the combination meter.
4 Remove the glove compartment as described in Section 52.
5 Remove the instrument panel centre section. For this the radio set control knobs will have to be detached.
6 Refer to Section 53 and remove the side ventilator louvres.
7 Undo and remove the five nuts and washers that secure the instrument panel upper garnish.
8 The instrument panel safety pad may now be removed.
9 Refitting the instrument panel safety pad is the reverse sequence to removal.

51 Instrument panel knee pad - removal and replacement

1 Locate the retaining screw/s and then undo and remove them.
2 Carefully pull out the knee pad together with the five retainers.

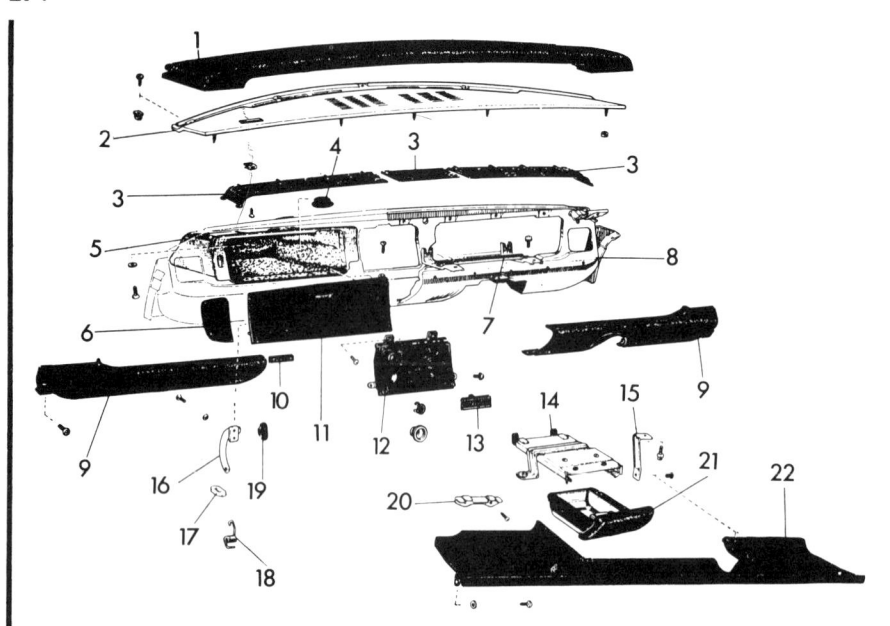

Fig. 12.37. Instrument panel components

1. Safety pad
2. Upper garnish
3. Moulding
4. Hole plug
5. Glove compartment
6. Glove compartment side garnish
7. Meter bracket
8. Instrument lower panel
9. Knee pad and garnish
10. Emblem
11. Glove compartment door
12. Centre ornament
13. Radio tuner hole cover
14. Ash receptacle retainer
15. Under-tray bracket
16. Glove compartment door check arm
17. Glove compartment door arm stopper
18. Torsion spring
19. Cushion
20. Under-tray front retainer
21. Ash receptacle
22. Under-tray

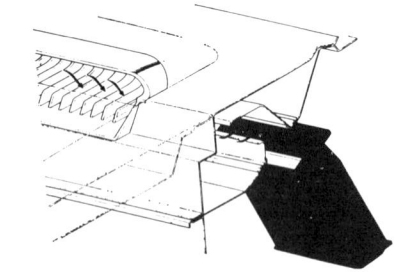

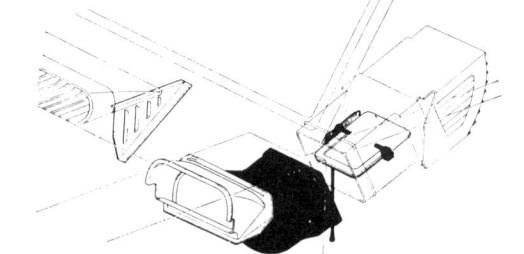

Fig. 12.38. Cowl ventilator (left) and side ventilator (right)

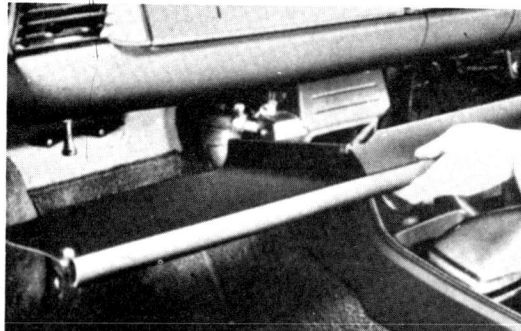

Fig. 12.39. Under-tray removal

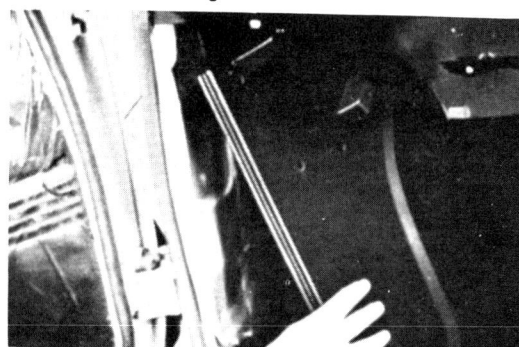

Fig. 12.40. Cowl side trim board removal

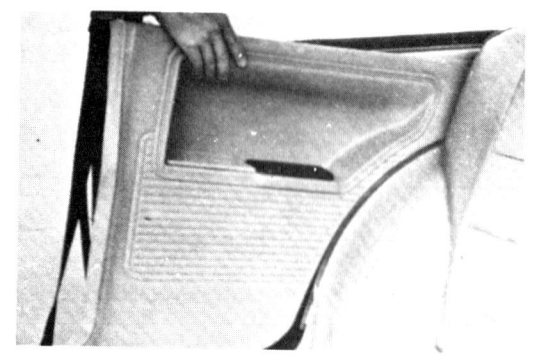

Fig. 12.41. Quarter trim panel removal

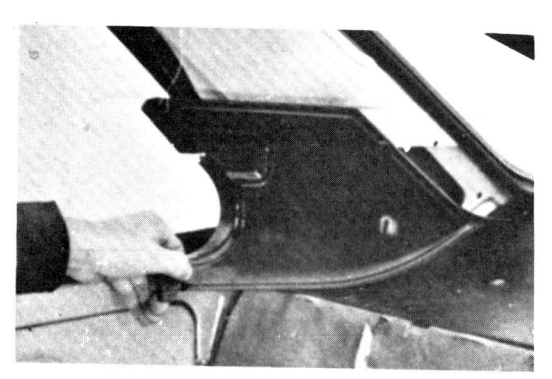

Fig. 12.42. Rear pillar garnish removal

Chapter 12/Bodywork and fittings

3 Refitting the instrument panel knee pad is the reverse sequence to removal.

52 Glove compartment - removal and replacement

1 Disconnect the glove compartment lid hinges and the check arm. Lift away the glove compartment lid.
2 Using a screwdriver carefully remove the glove compartment side garnish.
3 Undo and remove the three screws that secure the glove compartment to the instrument panel. The glove compartment may now be pulled out from its location.
4 Refitting the glove compartment and lid is the reverse sequence to removal.

53 Ventilators - removal and replacement

Cowl ventilator

1 Disconnect the cowl ventilator control rod from the ventilator.
2 Undo and remove the two cowl ventilator securing bolts.
3 When a heater is fitted undo and remove the bolt that secures the heater and duct.
4 The cowl ventilator may now be removed from under the instrument panel.
5 Refitting the cowl ventilator is the reverse sequence to removal.

Side ventilator (Instrument panel)

1 Undo but do not remove the two side ventilator louvre securing screws and pull out the louvre.
2 Detach the side ventilator hose.
3 Undo and remove the screw that secures the side ventilator duct and pull out the duct assembly.
4 Refitting the side ventilator is the reverse sequence to removal.

54 Cowl side trim board - removal and replacement

1 Remove the instrument panel under-tray (Fig 12.39)
2 Undo and remove the three bolts that secure the cowl side trim board.
3 When removing the right-hand side trim board it will be necessary to remove the fuse block and direction indicator flasher unit.
4 Using a screwdriver carefully detach the two retainers.
5 Finally remove the relevant section of the door aperture trim and lift away the cowl side trim board. (Fig. 12.40)
6 Refitting the cowl side trim board is the reverse sequence to removal.

55 Quarter trim panel - removal and replacement

1 Remove the rear seat cushion.
2 Remove the rear wheel housing trim moulding.
3 Remove the relevant section of the door opening trim.
4 Release the adhesive securing the quarter trim panel to the door aperture and lift away the quarter trim panel. (Fig 12.41)
5 Refitting the quarter trim panel is the reverse sequence to removal.

56 Rear pillar garnish and parcel tray trim - removal and replacement

1 Remove the rear seat backrest.
2 Detach the quarter window lock from the rear pillar.

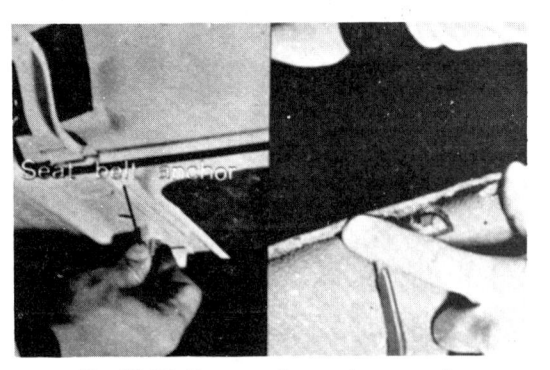

Fig. 12.43. Rear parcel tray trim removal

3 Remove the relevant section of the quarter window inside trim.
4 Carefully pull out the three retainers securing the rear pillar garnish using a screwdriver. Lift away the garnish. (Fig 12.42)
5 Remove the one parcel tray trim retainer and the two seat belt anchor bolts (or hole plugs) from the inside of the luggage compartment.
6 Hold the centre of the parcel tray trim and release the three retainers. Lift away the parcel tray trim.
7 Refitting the parcel tray trim and rear pillar garnish is the reverse sequence to removal.

57 Roof side vent louvre and duct - removal and replacement

1 Detach the quarter window lock from the rear pillar.
2 Carefully remove the quarter inside trim.
3 Refer to the previous Section and remove the rear pillar garnish.
4 Remove the relevant section of the quarter window weatherstrip from the pillar side and the rear pillar hole corner trim.
5 Carefully ease back the interior headlining. Do not stretch or tear the headlining.
6 Undo and remove the four nuts that secure the roof side vent louvre and then pull out the roof side vent louvre towards the exterior of the car.
7 Remove the ventilator plate and roof side vent duct assembly from inside the car.
8 Refitting the roof side vent louvre and duct is the reverse sequence to removal.

58 Front and rear bumper - removal and replacment

The sequence is basically identical to that as described in Section 17.

59 Front seat - removal and replacement

1 Move the seat fully to the rear and then undo and remove the two front securing bolts.
2 Move the seat fully forwards and then undo and remove the two nuts located at the rear. Lift away the front seat assembly.
3 Refitting the seat is the reverse sequence to removal. Apply a little Castrol LM Grease to the seat track to ensure easy movement.

60 Rear seat - removal and replacement

1 Remove the rear seat cushion.
2 Undo and remove the two bolts that secure the lower edge of the backrest. Note that when seat belts are fitted these bolts are also used as anchorages for the seat belts.
3 Lift the backrest and remove from inside the car.

61 Front wing - removal and replacement

1 For safety reasons, disconnect the battery.
2 Refer to Chapter 10, and remove the headlight assembly finisher and the side direction indicator light assembly.
3 Carefully remove the front wing garnish.
4 Refer to Sections 17 and 58 and remove the front bumper.
5 Undo and remove the 11 bolts and 3 screws that secure the front wing to the body. (Fig 12.45). Lift away the front wing panel. When removing the left-hand wing do not forget to disconnect the radio aerial.
6 There is a rubber splash shield between the inner and outer wing panels. This is retained by 3 screws and 2 bolts and should be renewed if damaged or deteriorated.
7 Refitting the front wing is the reverse sequence to removal. Do not tighten the wing securing bolts and screws until its final fitted position has been adjusted at the bonnet aperture and leading edge of the front door. Then tighten the attachments.

62 Lower shroud panel - removal and replacement

1 Refer to Section 63 and remove the radiator grille.
2 Remove the headlight assembly finisher as described in Chapter 10.
3 Remove the radiator grille lower moulding lower centre bolt and the three underside nuts and bolts.
4 Refer to Sections 17 and 58 and remove the front bumper.
5 Disconnect the front direction indicator and side light harness clamp and terminal connectors.
6 Undo and remove the 6 bolts and 6 screws that secure the lower shroud panel to the front body and wings. Lift away the lower shroud panel. (Fig 12.46)
7 Refitting the lower shroud panel is the reverse sequence to removal. Do not tighten the attachments until its final fitted position has been adjusted to line with the front wings.

63 Radiator grille - removal and replacement

1 Remove the headlight assembly finisher as described in Chapter 10.
2 Undo and remove the five screws that secure the radiator grille to the body. Lift away the radiator grille.
3 Refitting the radiator grille is the reverse sequence to removal. Do not tighten any screws until all have been started and partially tightened.

4 Door Saloon/Sedan (1971 on KE20F series)

64 Rear door window regulator - removal and replacement

1 Refer to Section 42 and remove the door trim and interior

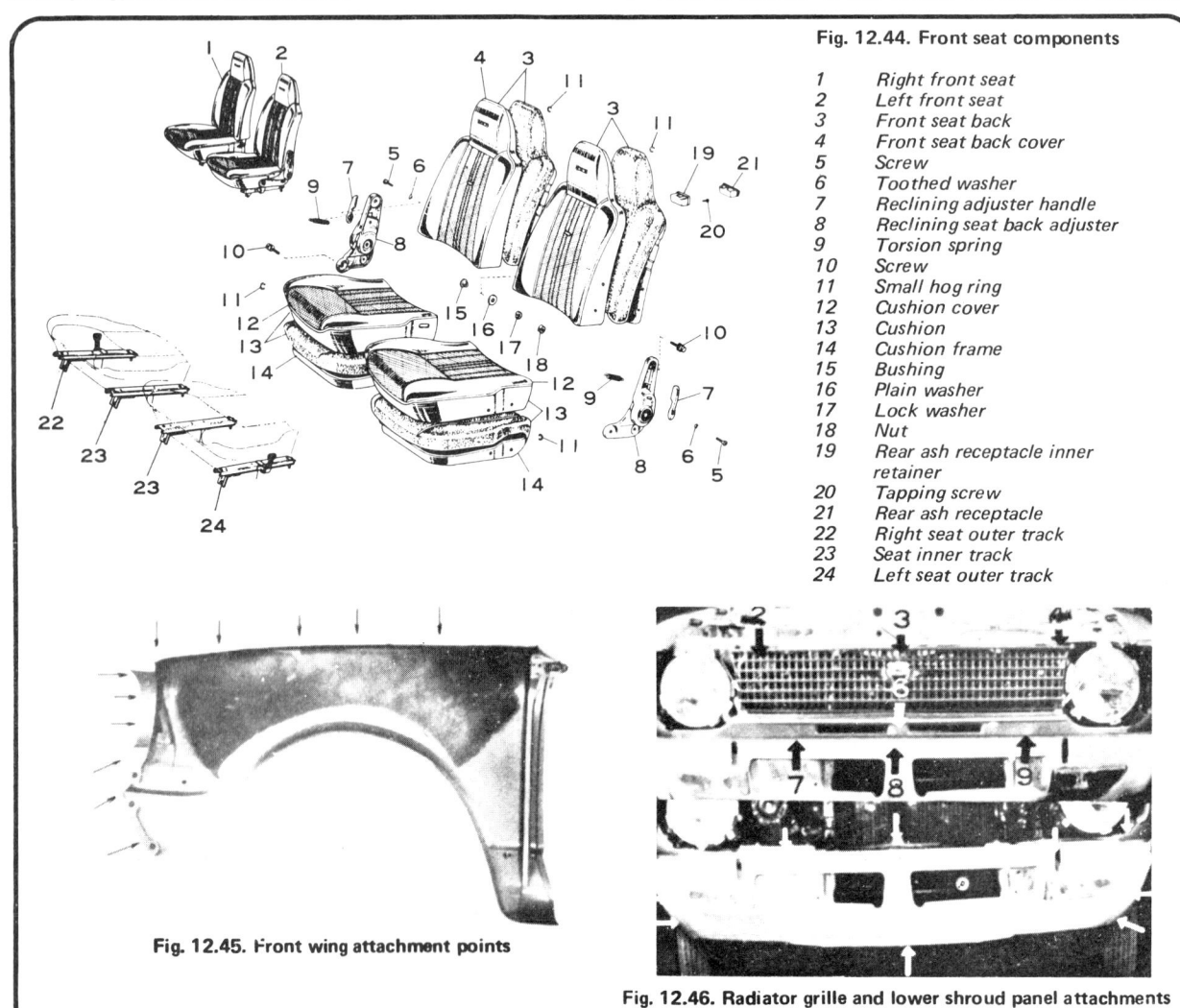

Fig. 12.44. Front seat components

1 Right front seat
2 Left front seat
3 Front seat back
4 Front seat back cover
5 Screw
6 Toothed washer
7 Reclining adjuster handle
8 Reclining seat back adjuster
9 Torsion spring
10 Screw
11 Small hog ring
12 Cushion cover
13 Cushion
14 Cushion frame
15 Bushing
16 Plain washer
17 Lock washer
18 Nut
19 Rear ash receptacle inner retainer
20 Tapping screw
21 Rear ash receptacle
22 Right seat outer track
23 Seat inner track
24 Left seat outer track

Fig. 12.45. Front wing attachment points

Fig. 12.46. Radiator grille and lower shroud panel attachments

Chapter 12/Bodywork and fittings

handles.
2 Remove the service hole cover.
3 Lower the door glass fully and then undo and remove the bolts that secure the glass to the regulator assembly.
4 Raise the door glass and support in this position.
5 Undo and remove the bolts that secure the window regulator to the door inner panel.
6 Lift away the door window regulator assembly.

7 Refitting the door window regulator assembly is the reverse sequence to removal. Lubricate all moving parts with a little Castrol LM Grease.

65 Rear door glass - removal and replacement

1 Refer to Section 64, and remove the window regulator

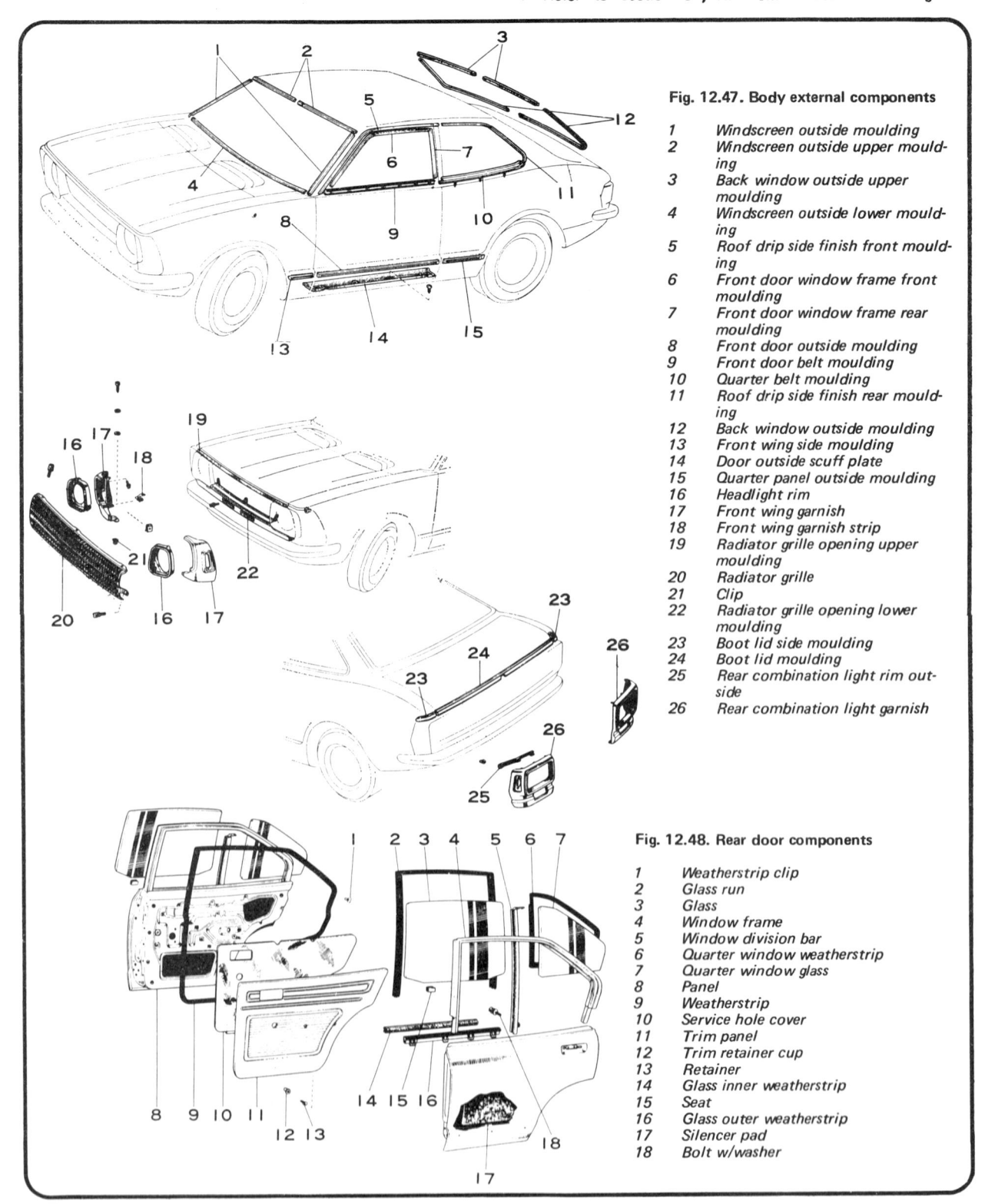

Fig. 12.47. Body external components

1 Windscreen outside moulding
2 Windscreen outside upper moulding
3 Back window outside upper moulding
4 Windscreen outside lower moulding
5 Roof drip side finish front moulding
6 Front door window frame front moulding
7 Front door window frame rear moulding
8 Front door outside moulding
9 Front door belt moulding
10 Quarter belt moulding
11 Roof drip side finish rear moulding
12 Back window outside moulding
13 Front wing side moulding
14 Door outside scuff plate
15 Quarter panel outside moulding
16 Headlight rim
17 Front wing garnish
18 Front wing garnish strip
19 Radiator grille opening upper moulding
20 Radiator grille
21 Clip
22 Radiator grille opening lower moulding
23 Boot lid side moulding
24 Boot lid moulding
25 Rear combination light rim outside
26 Rear combination light garnish

Fig. 12.48. Rear door components

1 Weatherstrip clip
2 Glass run
3 Glass
4 Window frame
5 Window division bar
6 Quarter window weatherstrip
7 Quarter window glass
8 Panel
9 Weatherstrip
10 Service hole cover
11 Trim panel
12 Trim retainer cup
13 Retainer
14 Glass inner weatherstrip
15 Seat
16 Glass outer weatherstrip
17 Silencer pad
18 Bolt w/washer

assembly.

2 Remove one side of the glass holder plate and lower the glass fully.
3 Remove the glass outer weatherstrip but ensure that the belt moulding and clips remain in position.
4 Remove the glass inner weatherstrip.
5 Remove the bolt securing the division bar and window frame screw. Pull out the division bar whilst easing it towards the front. It will be necessary to partially detach the door glass run.
6 Remove the glass from the door.
7 Pull the quarter window glass towards the front bringing with it the weatherstrip and remove from the door. If the latter proves difficult to remove lubricate the weatherstrip with a little concentrated soap and water solution or washing-up liquid.
8 To reassemble first fit the quarter window glass to the door frame. If necessary lubricate as described in paragraph 7.
9 Fit the door glass into the door ensuring that the front of the glass engages with the glass run.
10 Insert the glass run into the division bar and fit the division bar into the door. Temporarily secure with the two screws and lower securing bolt.
11 Check and if necessary adjust the glass run.
12 Refit the glass inner weatherstrip. For this the door glass must be fully lowered.
13 Refit the glass outer weatherstrip by aligning with the clips and pushing into position.
14 Raise and lower the door glass and when the glass moves easily without excessive looseness fully tighten the division bar.
15 Secure the door glass to the window regulator. The holder plates must not be detached from the rubber seats stuck to the glass.
16 Reassembly is now the reverse sequence to removal.

66 Rear door lock - removal and replacement

Lock

1 Refer to Section 42 and remove the door trim and interior handles.
2 Remove the service hole cover.
3 Fully raise the door glass and disconnect the remote control link from the door lock.
4 Undo and remove the three screws securing the lock to the door and lift away the lock assembly.
5 Refitting the lock to the door is the reverse sequence to removal. Lubricate all moving parts with a little Castrol LM Grease.

Remote control

1 Refer to Section 42, and remove the door trim and interior handles.
2 Remove the service hole cover.
3 Disconnect the control link from the door lock.
4 Undo and remove the screw that retains the remote control and lift away.
5 Refitting the remote control is the reverse sequence to removal. It will however be necessary to adjust the linkage as follows:
a) Temporarily secure the remote control and connect the control link to the door lock.
b) Move the locking button to the locked position.
c) Move the remote control fully forwards and then back by 0.02-0.04 in (0.5-1.0 mm) from the fully forwards position. Fully tighten the remote control attachments.

Exterior handle

1 Refer to Section 42 and remove the door trim and interior handles.
2 Remove the service hole cover.
3 Undo and remove the two nuts and washers securing the exterior handle to the door outer panel.
4 Turn the exterior handle release lever 180° and lift away the exterior handle.
5 Refitting the exterior handle is the reverse sequence to removal.

2 Door Saloon/Sedan (1971 on KE25, TE25 and 27 series)

67 Roof side vent and inner duct - removal and replacement

1 Remove the roof side vent louvre from the luggage compartment interior. Remove the duct.
2 Remove the rear seat backrest and remove the rear pillar garnish.
3 Remove the roof side vent inner duct.
4 Refitting the roof side vent and inner duct is the reverse sequence to removal. To facilitate refitting replace the duct and inner duct from the interior before replacing the pillar garnish.

68 Front wing garnish - removal and replacement

1 Refer to Chapter 10 and remove the headlight assembly.
2 Disconnect the front direction indicator light terminal connector and then remove the light unit.
3 Undo and remove the securing screws and lift away the front wing garnish.
4 Refitting the front wing garnish is the reverse sequence to removal.

Estate/Wagon (1971 on KE26V and TE28V series)

69 Back door - removal, replacement and adjustment

1 With the back door open remove the hinge cover securing screw. Lift away the hinge cover. (photo)
2 Disconnect the number plate light terminal connector.
3 The assistance of a second person will now be required to take the weight of the door.
4 Undo and remove the bolts that secure the door to the hinge. Lift away the back door assembly.
5 To remove a hinge carefully detach the interior headlining from the rear of the upper panel. Do not stretch or tear the headlining.
6 Using a suitable pry bar detach the torsion spring.

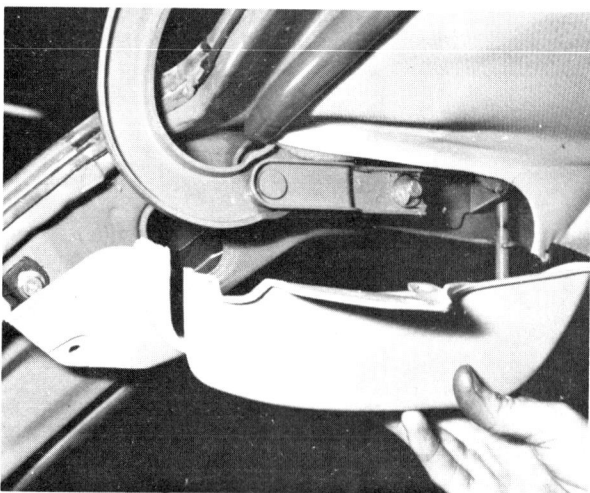

69.1 Removal of hinge cover

Chapter 12/Bodywork and fittings

7 Undo and remove the bolts that secure the back door hinge bracket. Lift off the hinge.
8 Reassembly and refitting is the reverse sequence to removal. The following additional points should however be noted:
a) To adjust the back door position in the aperture slacken the bolts securing the hinge to the body and move the back door forwards or backwards as necessary. Tighten the bolts.
b) To adjust the vertical position of the back door slacken the bolts securing the hinge to the door and move the back door upwards or downwards as necessary. Tighten the bolts.
c) Check that the back door closes correctly. Adjust the position of the door lock striker by adding or subtracting shims.

70 Back door side stopper - adjustment

The principle of adjustment is similar to that as described in Section 34.

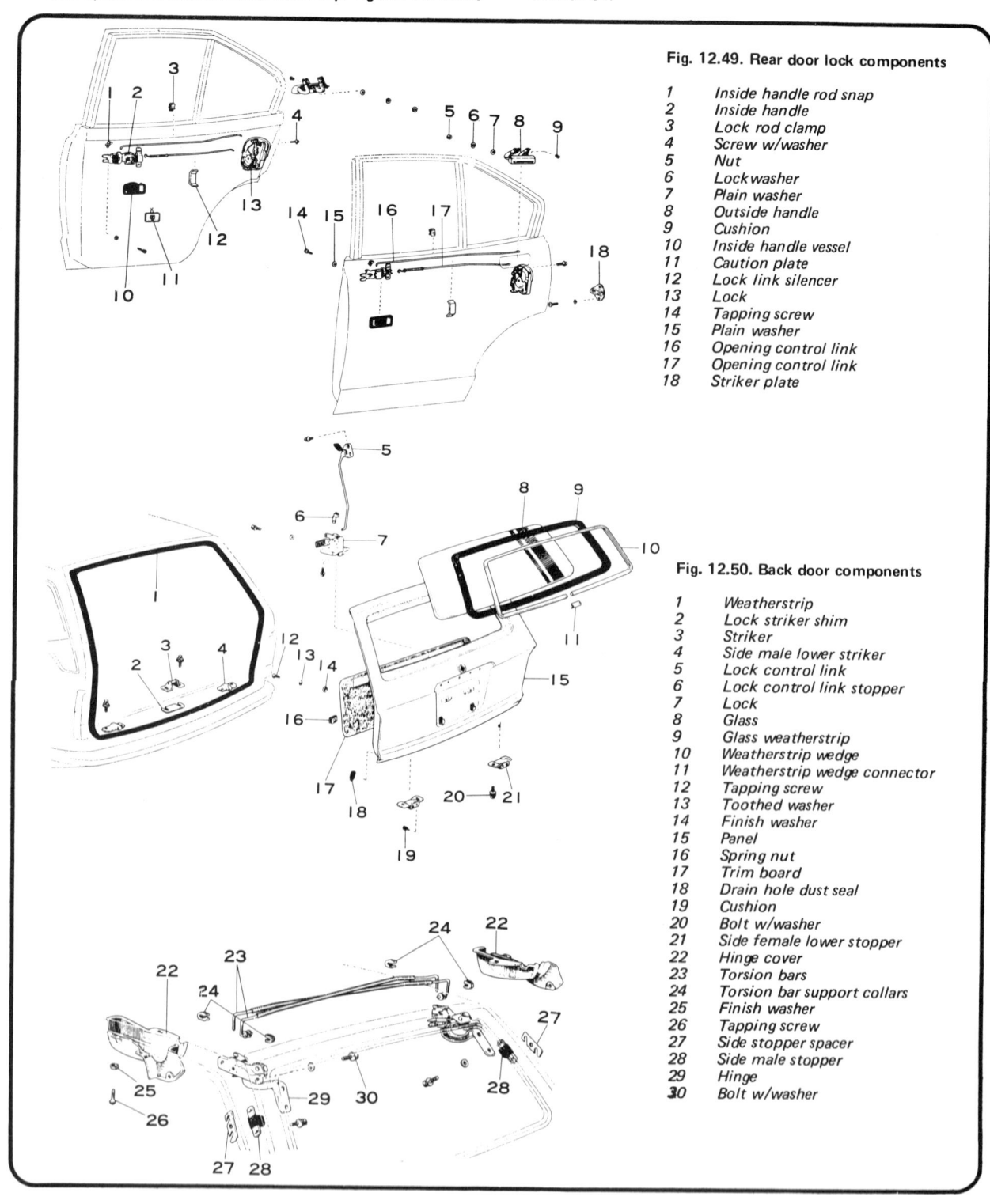

Fig. 12.49. Rear door lock components

1 Inside handle rod snap
2 Inside handle
3 Lock rod clamp
4 Screw w/washer
5 Nut
6 Lockwasher
7 Plain washer
8 Outside handle
9 Cushion
10 Inside handle vessel
11 Caution plate
12 Lock link silencer
13 Lock
14 Tapping screw
15 Plain washer
16 Opening control link
17 Opening control link
18 Striker plate

Fig. 12.50. Back door components

1 Weatherstrip
2 Lock striker shim
3 Striker
4 Side male lower striker
5 Lock control link
6 Lock control link stopper
7 Lock
8 Glass
9 Glass weatherstrip
10 Weatherstrip wedge
11 Weatherstrip wedge connector
12 Tapping screw
13 Toothed washer
14 Finish washer
15 Panel
16 Spring nut
17 Trim board
18 Drain hole dust seal
19 Cushion
20 Bolt w/washer
21 Side female lower stopper
22 Hinge cover
23 Torsion bars
24 Torsion bar support collars
25 Finish washer
26 Tapping screw
27 Side stopper spacer
28 Side male stopper
29 Hinge
30 Bolt w/washer

71 Back door lock - removal and replacement

The sequence is basically identical to that as described in Section 35.

72 Back door glass - removal and replacement

The sequence is basically identical to that as described in Section 36.

73 Front quarter glass - removal and replacement

The sequence is basically identical to that for earlier two door saloon models as described in Section 20.

74 Rear quarter glass - removal and replacement

The sequence is basically identical to that as described in Section 36, which describes removal and replacement of the back door glass.

75 Rear seat backrest - removal and replacement

The sequence is basically identical to that described in Section 39.

76 Roof side vent, side louvre and duct - removal and replacement

1 Undo and remove the three screws that secure the roof side vent louvre to the body outer panel.
2 Lift away the louvre.
3 Pull out the roof side vent duct.
4 Replacement of all parts is the reverse sequence to removal.

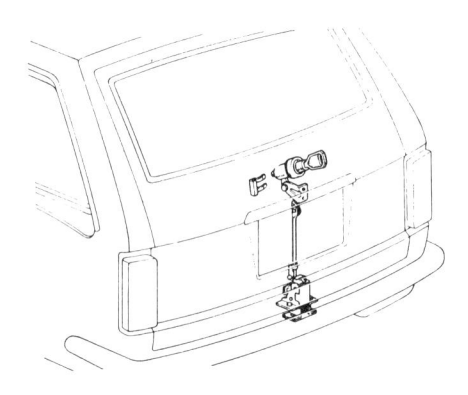

Fig. 12.51 Back door lock assembly

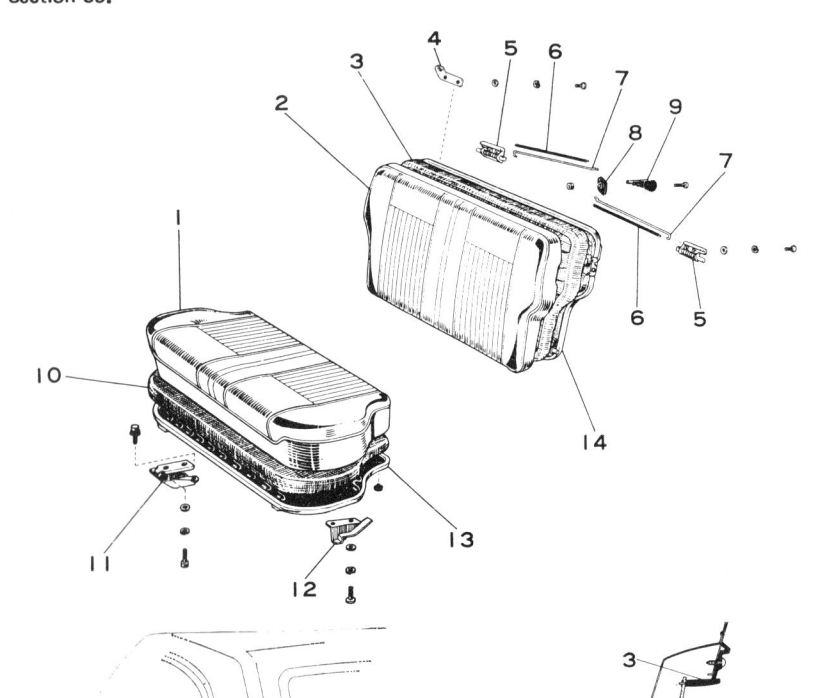

Fig. 12.52 Rear seat components

1 Cushion cover
2 Back cover
3 Back pad
4 Back holder
5 Cushion stopper
6 Hose
7 Back control wire
8 Back rod control outer lever
9 Back rod control outer lever
10 Cushion pad
11 Cushion hinge
12 Cushion holder bracket
13 Cushion spring
14 Back spring

Fig 12.53 Roof side vent components

1 Roof side vent louvre
2 Roof side vent duct
3 Room ventilator grille
4 Butterfly valve

List of illustrations

Chapter 1/Part A: Engine KE models

	Page
Cross sectional view of KE engine	18
Longitudinal cross sectional view of KE engine	19
Correct sequence for slackening cylinder head bolts	25
Valve components	25
Removal of piston rings with feeler gauge	29
Engine lubrication system	29
Measurement of piston ring groove clearance	31
Piston ring identification	31
Measurement of piston ring end gap	31
Valve head angles	33
Valve seat angles	33
Valve rocker assembly	33
Oil pump and strainer components	33
Relief valve located in filter bracket	33
Correct reassembly of oil pump rotors	34
Piston and connecting rod reassembly marks	35
Timing chain identification and alignment (crankshaft gearwheel)	37
Timing chain identification and alignment (camshaft gearwheel)	37
Valve rocker assembly pedestal and rocker arm identification	41
Cylinder head gasket top side identification	41
Correct sequence for tightening cylinder head bolts	41
Oil pump shaft alignment	43
Position of rotor arm before refitting distributor	43
Position of rotor arm after refitting distributor	43
Correct fan belt tension	43

Chapter 1/Part B: Engine TE models

Cross sectional view of TE engine	46
Longitudinal cross sectional view of TE engine	50
Cross sectional view of oil filter	52
Flywheel and backplate assembly	52
Cylinder head removal - engine in car	53
Cylinder head component parts	53
Cylinder head securing bolt removal sequence	54
Valve and spring assembly	54
Rocker and rocker shaft components	54
Camshaft and camshaft drive assembly	54
Piston, connecting rod and crankshaft assemblies	55
Engine lubrication system	57

List of Illustrations

Engine cylinder block and crankshaft	57
Oil filter circuit	58
Oil pump component parts	58
Piston and cylinder identification marks	58
Standard piston rings	58
Oil pump rotor mating marks	58
Valve seat correction angles	58
Measurement of crankshaft endfloat	60
Piston and connecting rod mating marks	60
Valve and attachments removed from cylinder head	62
Timing chain and sprocket alignment marks	62
Measurement of timing chain deflection	62
Assembling timing chain tensioner	62
Areas to which liquid sealer must be applied	63
Cylinder head bolt tightening sequence	64
Valve adjustment sequence	64

Chapter 2 - Cooling system

Cross sectional view of cooling system	68
Operation of radiator cap	68
Operation of thermostat	69
Thermostat removal	71
Exploded view of water pump	71
Correct fitment of water pump bearing assembly	71
Correct location of water pump shaft flange	71

Chapter 3 - Fuel system and carburation

Layout of fuel system	75
Air cleaner component parts	76
Fuel pump component parts (Type 1)	77
Cross sectional view of fuel pump	77
Fuel pump component parts (Type 2)	77
Separating upper and lower bodies of fuel pump	79
Removal of fuel pump rocker arm pin	79
Removal of fuel pump rocker arm link	79
Fuel pump valves	79
Cross sectional view of carburettor (1100, 1200 models)	79
Carburettor air horn and main body components (1100, 1200 models)	80
Cross sectional view of auxiliary slow system (some 1100, 1200 models)	80
Auxiliary slow system components	81
Carburettor main body components (1600 models)	81
Carburettor air horn components (1600 models)	82
Carburettor air horn removal	82
Removal of carburettor float from air horn	82
Automatic choke removal	83
Choke shaft removal	83
Ball and flange removal	83
Jet and venturi removal	83
Valve and petrol level gauge removal	83
Diaphragm removal	83
Throttle valve shaft removal	84
Float top level adjustment	84
Float adjustment parts	84
Float bottom level adjustment	85
Throttle valve opening adjustment	85
Second throttle lever contact adjustment	85
Kick-up adjustment	85
Fast idle adjustment	85
Unloader adjustment	85
Automatic choke adjustment	85
Idle adjustment screw	85
Cross sectional view of fuel filter (disposable type)	86
Exploded view of fuel filter	86
Fuel tank and attachments (Saloon models)	87
Later type fuel tank installation fitted to Estate cars	87
Inlet manifold components (1100, 1200 models)	88
Exhaust system components (1600 models)	88
Exhaust system components (1100, 1200 models)	88
Operation of PCV system	89
Engine connections - Full emission Control system (Part 1)	89
Engine connections - Full emission Control system (Part 2)	90

List of Illustrations

Mixture control system - Idling or low speed operation	91
Mixture control system - Intermediate and high speed operation	91
Mixture control system - Sudden deceleration	91
Testing of operation of mixture control system	91
Transmission controlled spark system	91
Movement of distributor octane selector	92
Checking speed sensor	93
Throttle positioner system	93
Carburettor for 2 T-C series engine	93
Carburettor for 3 K-C series engine	94
Operation of throttle positioner	94
Check valve and safety cap	94
Charcoal canister storage system - KE saloon	95
Charcoal canister storage system - TE saloon	95
Charcoal canister storage system - TE estate car	95

Chapter 4 - Ignition system

Diagram of the ignition circuit	100
Cross sectional view of ignition coil	100
Cross sectional view of distributor	100
Exploded view of distributor (K and K-B engines)	103
Alternative distributor (K series engines)	103
Vacuum advance unit removal	104
Breaker plate removal	104
Distributuro cam spindle removal	104
Lifting away centrifugal weight springs	104
Spiral gear removal	104
Withdrawing distribtuor shaft	104
Checking carbon centre electrode protrusion	104
Dismantling advance unit (K-C engine)	105
Exploded view of distributor (K-C engine)	105
Timing marks and oil pump spindle alignment	106
Distributor replacement	106
Setting octane selector 'standard position'	106
Cross sectional view of spark plug	107
Some sample spark plugs	108

Chapter 5 - Clutch

Cross sectional view of clutch assembly	111
Clutch disc assembly	111
Clutch actuation mechanism (cable operated models)	112
Clutch adjustments (KE models)	112
Checking clutch pedal free play (KE 1100 models)	112
Correct 'E' ring position (KE 1200 models)	112
Clutch adjustments (TE models)	113
Clutch pedal and cable assembly (KE 1100 models)	114
Clutch pedal and cable assembly (KE 1200 models)	114
Clutch pedal assembly (TE models)	115
Exploded view of clutch master cylinder	115
Master cylinder piston detail	116
Exploded view of clutch slave cylinder	116
Clutch assembly (KE models)	116
Clutch assembly (TE models)	118
Clutch centralisation	118
Fitting new bearing to carrier	119

Chapter 6 - Manual gearbox and automatic transmission

Manual gearbox : KE models

Cross sectional view of gearbox	127
Gearbox external components	127
Gearbox internal components	128
Gearbox selector mechanism	128
Synchromesh unit reassembly	136
Thrust clearance measurement points	137
Location of and assembly dimensions for refitting selector fork shaft pins	139

Manual gearbox : TE models

Cross sectional view of gearbox	141

Gearbox external components	142
Gearbox internal components	142
Gearbox extension housing assembly	143
Main casing halves securing bolts	145
Tapping out slotted spring pin	145
Location of pins between selector shafts	145
Synchromesh unit identification	147
Synchromesh sleeve and fork clearance check	147
Location of gear assemblies on mainshaft	148
Measurement of backlash	149
Measurement points for thrust clearances	150
Reverse idler gear assembly and checking endfloat	150
Washer and cone location between clutch housing and main casing	150

Automatic transmission : all models

The automatic transmission unit	151
Torque converter components	151
Principle of torque converter operation	152
Automatic transmission planetary gear unit	152
Oil pan and drain plug	152
Removal of rod end and clamp	152
Supporting the weight of the transmission unit	152
Oil cooler pipes	152
Location of service hole	152
Removal of torque converter	152
Selector lever removal	153
Selector lever components	154
Manual valve lever positions	154
Adjustment of selector lever	154
Column selector lever components	155
Correct indicator position	156
Adjustment of stopper position (column change)	156
Adjustment of throttle connecting rod	156

Chapter 7 - Propeller shaft

Propeller shaft component parts	159
Exploded view of propeller shaft	159
Detaching propeller shaft from rear axle	159
Cross sectional view of universal joint bearing	159
Spider bearing and yoke identification marks	160

Chapter 8 - Rear axle

Rear axle assembly	162
Cross sectional view through rear axle assembly	162
Rear axle shaft components	163
Rear axle shaft with cross section through bearing assembly	163
Rear axle components	164
Final drive assembly components	165
Pinion gear and shaft wear limits	166
Differential case and side gear inspection	166
Side bearing pre-load adjustment	167
Alternative adjusting nut locks	167
Contact marking on crown wheel	167

Chapter 9 - Braking system

Layout of earlier type braking system with front and rear drum brakes	171
Layout of later type braking system with front disc brakes	171
Component parts of disc brake assembly	172
Cross sectional view of disc brake assembly	172
Component parts of caliper cylinder assembly	175
Front drum brake assembly components	175
Hook shaped tool for removal and refitment of brake shoe springs	175
Detail of front drum brake	176
Front drum brake wheel cylinder components and cross sectional view	176
Rear drum brake components (earlier type)	178
Rear drum brake detail (earlier type)	178
Rear drum brake components (later type)	179
Rear drum brake wheel cylinder components	180
Rear drum brake adjuster assembly components	181

List of Illustrations

Handbrake lever and cable assembly components	182
Cross sectional view of handbrake lever assembly	182
Installation of No. 2 outer cable	183
Brake pedal adjustment	183
Brake and clutch pedal assembly components	184
Master cylinder components (single)	185
Cross sectional view of single master cylinder	185
Tandem master cylinder assembly component parts (Type 1)	186
Cross sectional view of tandem master cylinder (Type 1)	186
Tandem master cylinder assembly component parts (Type 2)	187
Major components of servo unit	188
Hydraulic pipe and hose layout (drum brake models)	188
Operation of pressure control valve	188

Chapter 10 - Electrical system

Battery components	196
Testing battery specific gravity	197
Cross sectional view through alternator	197
Exploded view of alternator	198
Alternator charging circuit	198
Alternator regulator part names	198
Cross sectional view of starter motor	200
Removal of manifold assembly	200
Removal of starter motor	200
Exploded view of starter motor (earlier type)	200
Exploded view of starter motor (later type)	201
Fitting lock plate	202
Starter clutch pinion clearance	202
Headlight unit components (earlier type)	202
Headlight unit components (later type)	202
Headlight unit removal (later type)	203
Front side and direction indicator light components (early models)	204
Front direction indicator light components (later models)	204
Rear combination light assembly (early models)	204
Rear combination light components (later models)	205
Rear combination light components (KE15 and 17 models)	205
Rear combination light components (KE16V model)	205
Side repeater light assembly (later models)	205
Side repeater light assembly (earlier models)	205
Rear number plate light (earlier models)	205
Rear number plate light components (later models)	206
Rear number plate light (KE16V models)	206
Interior light assembly	206
Horn button/push bar assembly	206
Vibrator horn components	207
Horn components (Denso)	207
Horn components (Marako)	207
Horn adjustment circuit (Vibrator type)	208
Horn adjustment circuit (Trumpet type)	208
Windscreen wiper linkage (earlier models)	208
Windscreen wiper motor assembly (early models)	209
Exploded view of windscreen wiper motor (later models)	209
Combination meter attachments (Type 1)	210
Combination meter removal (Type 1)	210
Instrument panel assembly (Type 1)	210
Safety pad attachments location (Type 1)	211
Combination meter removal (Type 2)	211
Combination meter components (Type 2)	212
Instrument panel assembly (Type 2)	212
Safety pad attachment location (Type 2)	212
Cross section through lighting switch (Type 1)	212
Reverse light switch (manual transmission)	212
Courtesy light switch removal	212
Windscreen washer assembly (earlier models)	213
Windscreen washer motor and pump (earlier models)	214
Windscreen washer assembly (later types)	214
Handbrake warning light switch removal	214
Light control switch cross section (Type 2)	214
Location of various switches (later models)	214
Combination meter components (Type 3)	215
Combination meter components (Type 3 - 'S' models)	216

Direction indicator flasher unit location — 216
Direction indicator relay — 216
Heater unit components (early models) — 217
Heater unit controls (later models) — 218
Heater unit components (later models) — 218

Chapter 11 - Suspension and steering

Cross section through front suspension assembly (early KE models) — 232
Cross section through front suspension strut assembly (later models) — 232
Front hub components — 233
Removal of hub and brake drum assembly — 233
Removal of inner bearing cone — 233
Correct packing of wheel hub with grease — 233
Front suspension strut assembly with disc brake (later models) — 234
Removal of strut piston rod — 235
Front suspension strut assembly — 235
Piston assembly components — 236
Fitting piston valve into front suspension strut — 237
Front suspension strut sub-valve assembly (later models) — 237
Front suspension leaf spring (early KE models) — 237
Front suspension assembly (early KE models) — 237
Front suspension attachments (TE models) — 238
Correct reassembly of stabilizer bar — 238
Correct reassembly of strut bar — 238
Shock absorber upper attachment — 239
Shock absorber lower attachment — 239
Rear spring detail — 239
Rear suspension assembly (earlier models) — 240
Rear suspension assembly (later models) — 240
Alternative rear suspension components — 241
Steering wheel and horn assembly (Type 1) — 242
Steering wheel and horn assembly (Type 2) — 242
Removal of steering lock sheer bolts — 243
Steering linkage components (Rhd) — 243
Steering linkage components (Lhd) — 244
Correct reassembly of steering linkage — 244
Correct reassembly of tie-rod end — 244
Alignment marks on sector shaft arm and shaft — 244
Cross sectional view through steering gearboxes — 245
Steering wheel and gear housing components — 245
Sector roller and shims — 246
Steering column and gear housing (later KE and TE models) — 247
Steering linkage adjustment — 247

Chapter 12 - Bodywork

2 - Door Saloon/Sedan (1968 - 1970)

Front door components — 255
Front door panel and glass assemblies — 256
Door trim panel removal — 257
Window regulator assembly — 257
Door glass and ventilator details — 257
Division bar adjustment — 259
Door lock components — 259
Door lock cylinder removal — 259
Bonnet lock dowel and safety catch adjustments — 259
Front body components — 259
Rear body components — 260
Front and rear bumpers — 261
Quarter window components — 261
Instrument panel under-tray removal — 261
Cowl side trim panel removal — 261
Dash panel trim board removal — 262
Cowl ventilator components — 262
Front and rear seat components — 263
Front wing attachment points — 263
Lower shroud panel attachment points — 263
Body exterior trim — 264

List of illustrations

Estate/Wagon (1968 - 1970)

Rear door components	264
Rear door window light regulator	265
Rear door lock components	266
Back door components	266
Back door side stopper adjustment	267
Back door hinge adjustment	267
Back door lock	267
Quarter window components	268
Rear seat components	268

All models (after 1970)

Interior handle removal	268

2-Door Saloon/Sedan (1971 on: KE20 and 21 series)

Front door lock components	269
Front door components	271
Door lock control link adjustment	272
Bonnet hinge and lock assemblies	272
Rear body components	273
Instrument panel components	274
Cowl ventilator and side ventilator	274
Under-tray removal	274
Cowl side trim board removal	274
Quarter trim panel removal	274
Rear pillar garnish removal	274
Rear parcel tray trim removal	275
Front seat components	276
Front wing attachment points	276
Radiator grille and lower shroud panel attachments	276
Body external components	277

4-Door Saloon/Sedan (1971 on: KE20F series)

Rear door components	277
Rear door lock components	279

Estate/Wagon (1971 on: KE26V and TE28V series)

Back door components	279
Back door lock assembly	280
Rear seat components	280
Roof side vent components	280

Index

A

Air cleaner - 76
Alternator - description - 197
    fault diagnosis - 199
    maintenance - 199
    regulator - 199
    removal and replacement - 199
    special procedures - 199
Antifreeze coolant solution - 71
Automatic transmission - description - 151
    engine idle speed adjustment - 156
    fault diagnosis - 157
    fluid level - 153
    neutral safety switch adjustment - 156
    removal and replacement - 153
    selector lever (column mounted) - adjustment - 156
    selector lever (column mounted) - overhaul - 154
    selector lever (floor mounted) - adjustment - 154
    selector lever (floor mounted) - overhaul - 153
    throttle link connecting rod adjustment - 156
    torque wrench settings - 126

B

Battery - charging - 197
    electrolyte replenishment - 197
    maintenance - 196
    removal and replacement - 196
Bodywork - description - 249
    door alignment - 255
    door latch striker alignment - 255
    door rattles - 255
    maintenance - 250, 255
    major repairs - 254
    minor repairs - 250
Bodywork (all models after 1970) - front door lock and regulator - 269
Bodywork (Estate/Wagon 1968 - 1970) - back door - 267
    back door glass - 267
    back door lock - 267
    back door side stopper - 267
    front quarter glass - 268
    rear door glass - 265
    rear door lock and remote control - 265
Bodywork (Estate/Wagon 1968 - 1970) - rear door window regulator - 263
    rear quarter glass - 269
    rear seat backrest - 269
Bodywork (Estate/Wagon 1971 on: KE26V and TE28V series) - back door - 278
    back door glass - 280
    back door lock - 280
    back door side stopper - 279
    front quarter glass - 280
    rear quarter glass - 280
    rear seat backrest - 280
    roof side vent, side louvre and duct - 280
Bodywork (4 door Saloon/sedan 1971 on KE20F series) - rear door glass - 277
    rear door lock - 278
    rear door window regulator - 276
Bodywork (2 door saloon/sedan 1968 - 1970) - bonnet and lock - 258
    boot lid and lock - 258
    bumpers - 260
    cowl side trim panel - 261
    cowl ventilator - 262
    dash panel trim board - 262
    door glass - 257
    door lock assembly - 258
    door trim and interior handles - 256
    door window regulator - 256
Bodywork (2 door saloon/sedan 1968 - 1970) - front door - 255
    front seat - 262
    front wing - 262
    lower shroud panel - 262
    rear parcel tray trim panel - 262
    rear quarter trim panel - 262
    rear quarter window - 261
    rear seat - 262

Index

rear screen - 261
windscreen - 260
Bodywork (2 door saloon/sedan 1971 on: KE20 and 21 series - bonnet and lock - 273
    boot lid and lock - 273
    bumpers - 275
    cowl side trim board - 275
    door lock assembly - 271
    door trim and interior handles - 269
    door window glass and regulator - 269
Bodywork (2 door Saloon/sedan 1971 on: KE20 and 21 series) - front door - 269
    front seat - 275
    front wing - 276
    glove compartment - 275
    instrument panel knee pad - 273
    instrument panel safety pad - 273
    lower shroud panel - 276
    quarter trim panel - 275
    radiator grille - 276
    rear pillar garnish and parcel tray trim - 275
    rear quarter window - 273
    rear screen - 273
    rear seat - 275
    roof side vent louvre and duct - 275
    ventilators - 275
    windscreen - 273
Bodywork (2 door saloon/sedan 1971 on: KE25, TE25 and 27 series) - front wing garnish - 278
    roof side vent and inner duct - 278
Braking system - bleeding - 170
    brake pedal removal and replacement - 184
    brake pedal travel adjustment - 183
    description - 170
    fault diagnosis - 190
    flexible hose - 171
    front brake disc and hub - 174, 234
    front brake pads - 173
    front disc brake caliper - 173
    front drum brake adjustment - 177
    front drum brake backplate - 177
    front drum brake shoes - 174
    front drum brake wheel cylinder - 176
    handbrake adjustment - 181
    handbrake lever and cable assembly - 182
    hydraulic pipes and hoses - 189
    master cylinder (single) - 184
    master cylinder (tandem) - 185, 187
    pressure control valve - 189
    rear drum brake adjuster - 181
    rear drum brake adjustment - 181
    rear drum brake backplate - 181
    rear drum brake shoes - 177
    rear drum brake wheel cylinder - 180
    specifications - 169
    torque wrench settings - 170
    vacuum servo unit - 189

C

Carburettor - adjustment - 86
    automatic choke adjustment - 84
    description - 78
    dismantling and reassembly - 78
    float level adjustment - 84
    idle speed adjustment - 84
    removal and replacement - 78
    throttle valve opening adjustment - 84
Clutch - adjustment (KE models) - 113
    adjustment (TE models) - 113
    bleeding - 113
    cable (KE models) - 114
    description - 112
    faults - 120
    inspection - 118
    judder - 120
    master cylinder dismantling and reassembly - 116
    master cylinder removal and replacement - 115
    pedal (KE models) - 113
    pedal (TE models) - 115
    release bearing - 119
    removal and replacement - 117
    slave cylinder dismantling and reassembly - 117
    slave cylinder removal and replacement - 117
    specifications - 110
    slip - 120
    spin - 120
    squeal - 120
    torque wrench settings - 111
Condenser - 102
Contact breaker points - adjustment - 101
    removal and replacement - 101
Cooling system - description - 68
    draining - 69
    fault diagnosis - 72
    filling - 69
    flushing - 69
    specifications - 67

D

Distributor - lubrication - 102
    overhaul - 102
    removal - 102
    replacement - 106

E

Electrical system - cigarette lighter - 217
    combination meter (Type 1) - 211
    combination meter (Type 2) - 211
    combination meter (Type 3) - 215, 216
    description - 196
    fault diagnosis - 219
    flasher unit - 217
    glove compartment (Type 1) - 211
    ignition switch (Type 3) - 216
    instrument panel safety pad (Type 1) - 211
    instrument panel safety pad (Type 2) - 213
    lights - 203
    specifications - 191
    switches (Type 1) - 213
    switches (Type 2) - 214
Engine - fails to start - 107
    misfires - 109
Engine (KE models) - ancillaries removal - 24
    backplate replacement - 39
    big-end bearing removal - 26
    big-end bearings renovation - 30
    camshaft reassembly - 37
    camshaft removal - 26
    camshaft renovation - 32
    clutch replacement - 39
    components examination for wear - 30
    connecting rod reassembly - 35
    connecting rod removal - 26
    connecting rod renovation - 32
    connecting rod to crankshaft reassembly - 37
    crankshaft front oil seal removal - 26
    crankshaft rear oil seal removal - 26
    crankshaft rear oil seal replacement - 39
    crankshaft removal - 28
    crankshaft renovation - 30
    crankshaft replacement - 35
    cylinder bores renovation - 30
    cylinder head decarbonisation - 33
    cylinder head removal - 24
    cylinder head replacement - 39
    description - 18

Index

dismantling - 23
distributor replacement - 41
fault diagnosis - 44
final assembly - 42
flywheel and engine backplate removal - 26
flywheel replacement - 39
front plate replacement - 37
gudgeon pin removal - 28
gudgeon pin renovation - 32
initial start-up after overhaul - 43
main bearing removal - 28
main bearing renovation - 30
oil pump overhaul - 33
oil pump replacement - 39
operations possible with engine in place - 18
operations requiring engine removal - 19
piston reassembly - 35
piston removal - 26
piston renovation - 30
piston replacement - 37
piston ring removal - 28
piston ring renovation - 30
piston ring replacement - 35
reassembly - 35
removal less gearbox - 23
removal methods - 19
removal with gearbox - 19
replacement - 43
rocker arm/valve adjustment - 41
rocker shaft reassembly - 39
rocker shaft replacement - 41
rockers renovation - 32
Engine (KE models) - specifications - 13
   sump removal - 26
   sump replacement - 39
   tappets renovation - 32
   tappets replacement - 41
   tuning gears reassembly - 37
   timing gears removal - 24
   timing gears renovation - 32
   torque wrench settings - 17
   valve reassembly - 39
   valve removal - 24
   valve renovation - 32
Engine (TE models) - ancillaries removal - 51
   backplate replacement - 64
   big-end bearing removal - 56
   camshaft removal - 55
   camshaft replacement - 63
   components renovation - 59
   connecting rod reassembly - 61
   connecting rod removal - 56
   connecting rod to crankshaft refitting - 61
   crankshaft pulley replacement - 64
   crankshaft rear oil seal removal - 56
   crankshaft rear oil seal replacement - 63
   crankshaft removal - 56
   crankshaft replacement - 59
   cylinder head removal - 53, 54
   cylinder head replacement - 64
   description - 50
   dismantling - 51
   fault diagnosis - 66
   final assembly - 64
   flywheel refitting - 64
   flywheel renovation - 52
   front cover replacement - 63
   gudgeon pin removal - 56
   initial start-up after overhaul - 66
   lubrication and crankshaft ventilation system - 56
   main bearings removal - 56
   methods of removal - 51
   mountings removal and replacement - 51
   oil filter removal and replacement - 52
   oil pump removal - 55
   oil pump replacement - 63
   operations requiring engine removal - 51
   operations with engine in place - 50
   piston reassembly - 61
   piston removal - 56
   piston replacement - 61
   piston ring removal - 56
   piston ring replacement - 61
   reassembly - 59
   refitting - 66
   removal less gearbox - 51
   removal with gearbox - 51
   rocker arms reassembly - 64
   rocker assembly dismantling - 55
Engine (TE models) - specifications - 47
   sump removal - 55
   sump replacement - 63
   tappets removal - 56
   timing chain tensioner removal - 56
   timing gears removal - 55
   timing gears replacement - 63
   torque wrench settings - 50
   valve clearance adjustment - 64
   valve reassembly - 61
   valve removal - 54
Exhaust emission Control - charcoal canister storage system - 93
   ventilation valve - 57
   description - 89
   fault diagnosis - 97
   mixture control system - 91
   throttle positioner system - 92
   transmission controlled spark system - 91

F

Fan belt - 72
Fault diagnosis - automatic transmission - 157
   braking system - 190
   clutch - 120
   cooling system - 72
   electrical system - 219
   engine - 44
   exhaust emission control system - 97
   fuel system - 96
   ignition - 107
   manual gearbox - 157
   propeller shaft - 160
   rear axle - 168
   steering - 248
   suspension - 248
   universal joints - 160
Front suspension - arm and balljoints (TE) - 238
   arm, balljoints and leafspring (early KE) - 236
   description - 232
   fault diagnosis - 248
   specifications - 228
   strut - 234
   torque wrench settings - 231
Fuel filter - 86
Fuel gauge sender unit - 87
Fuel pipes and lines - 87
Fuel pump - description - 76
   dismantling and reassembly - 76
   removal and replacement - 76
   testing - 76
Fuel system - description - 76
   fault diagnosis - 96
   Federal regulations (USA) - 76
   specifications - 73
Fuel tank - cleaning and repair - 87
   removal and replacement - 86

Index

Fuses and fasible link - 211

G

Gearbox (manual) (KE models) - components inspection - 136
    countergear - 136
    description - 127
    dismantling - 130
    extension housing oil seal - 141
    fault diagnosis - 157
    input shaft dismantling - 133
    input shaft reassembly - 136
    mainshaft dismantling - 135
    mainshaft reassembly - 136
    reassembly - 137
    removal and replacement - 129
    specifications - 122
    synchro hubs dismantling - 135
    synchro hubs reassembly - 136
    torque wrench settings - 126
Gearbox (manual) (TE models) - components inspection - 148
    countershaft dismantling - 148
    countershaft reassembly - 148
    description - 127
    dismantling - 141
    extension housing oil seal - 151
    fault diagnosis - 157
    input shaft dismantling - 144
    input shaft reassembly - 148
    mainshaft dismantling - 144
    mainshaft reassembly - 148
    reassembly - 148
    removal and replacement - 141
    specifications - 124
    synchro hubs dismantling - 147
    synchro hubs reassembly - 147
    torque wrench settings - 126

H

Heater - 217, 218
Horn - fault diagnosis - 207
    servicing and adjustment - 207
Hub (front) - 232

I

Ignition system - description - 101
    fault diagnosis - 107
    Federal regulations (USA) - 101
    specifications - 99
    timing - 106

L

Lights - 203

P

Propeller shaft - description - 158
    fault diagnosis - 160
    removal and replacement - 158
    specifications - 158

Radiator - 69
Rear axle - description - 162
    differential assembly - 165
    fault diagnosis - 168
    halfshaft - 163
    pinion oil seal - 164
    removal and replacement - 163
    specifications - 161
    torque wrench settings - 161
Rear suspension - description - 232
    fault diagnosis - 248
    shock absorbers - 239
    specifications - 229
    spring - 239

S

Spare parts - buying - 9
Spark plugs - 107
Starter motor - description - 199
    overhaul - 201
    removal and replacement - 201
    testing - 199
Steering - description - 232
    fault diagnosis - 248
    gear - 242
    gearbox adjustment - 246
    gearbox (recirculating ball) - 246
    gearbox (worm and sector) - 245
    geometry - 247
    linkage - 243
    specifications - 230
    torque wrench settings - 231
    wheel - 241
Suspension (front) - see Front Suspension
Suspension (rear) - see Rear Suspension

T

Thermostat - 70
Tyre pressures - 231
Tyres - 231

V

Universal joints - description - 158
    dismantling - 158
    fault diagnosis - 160
    reassembly - 160
    repair - 158
    specifications - 158

W

Water pump - overhaul - 71
    removal and replacement - 71
Wheels - 231
Windscreen washer - 213
Windscreen wiper - arm and blade - 209
    linkage - 209
    mechanism - 209
    motor - 209
Wiring diagrams - 221 - 227

Printed by
J. H. HAYNES & Co. Ltd
Sparkford Yeovil Somerset
ENGLAND